BIG LEAGUES

BIG LEAGUES

Professional Baseball, Football, and Basketball in National Memory

Stephen Fox

William Morrow and Company, Inc. • *New York*

Library of Congress Cataloging-in-Publication Data

Fox, Stephen R.
Big leagues : professional baseball, football, and basketball in
national memory / Stephen Fox.
p.   cm.
Includes index.
ISBN 0-688-09300-0
1. Baseball—United States—History. 2. Football—United States—
History.   3. Basketball—United States—History.
4. Professionalism in sports.   I. Title.
GV863.A1F69   1994
796.357'0973—dc20
94-6155
CIP

Printed in the United States of America

First Edition

1 2 3 4 5 6 7 8 9 10

BOOK DESIGN BY LINEY LI

For Alexandra

Contents

Contents

Sports Time
and Historical Time

This book is a work of history written without the usual linear
structure of historical time. Normally a historian like me stands
across a timeline, looks backward and forward, and so feels comfortably oriented by the familiar benchmarks of dates and sequence. But not in this case. This book's chapters may be read in
any order (though perhaps most intelligibly in the arrangement
here presented). Some chapters are topical, some chronological.
The story may run straight downfield, or veer across to the sidelines; time freezes, zips forward, or doubles back on itself. The
book's organization suggests an essential feature of what the big
leagues mean. Calendars don't matter so much in sports history
because our games offer a literal *time out,* off the clock: a self-
bounded, internally coherent universe carved from time out of a
given day, or out of an earlier phase of one's life, or out of the
historical past. External time stops when the ball goes in play and
the internal game clock starts. As a balance to the rushing, time-
driven world of modernity, sports slow down—may even entic-
ingly halt or reverse—the on-stretching chunks of chronology by
which we measure out our lives.

In any of these chapters, then, the reader is dropped into

quite stable, familiar games amid quite variable historical circumstances. Many "serious" sports books wander far from the ballgames themselves. Though this book has reasonably serious aspirations, I have tried to stay near the field, close to the sweating, grunting action, to convey a sense of how these sports have been played in different places and moments. In their most significant aspects—the sports themselves, what the players are like, why the fans care—our big leagues don't change much except in long, resilient cycles, shuttling back and forth within well-fortified parameters that allow constant tinkering while preserving their essential natures and meanings. For players and fans alike, big-league tingles, sensations, and loyalties should feel classically the same, whether today or in 1894 or (one hopes) in 2094.

My bias here may be quickly stated: I'm a fan, so this book emphasizes the timeless pleasures of these games. Ever since grade school I have happily inhabited the five primary sports domains of playing, cheering, watching, reading, and now writing about them. From so many years of doglike devotion, four decades and counting, I have acquired a visceral, simpleminded trust in these ballgames and their healthy functions. While granting the usual doubts about them, I would maintain that our three favorite American team sports are mostly good for us, offering antidotes to the strains and deprivations of modern life. For me as the writer, this book is another expression of long-held boyish enthusiasms, blithely subjective and opinionated. So I have delved into what interested me, that's all, and wound up with a selective history of big-league baseball, football, and basketball that makes no claims to exhaustive (or exhausting) completeness. My fellow fans are invited to join in the games and have fun.

BIG LEAGUES

Chapter One

Going Airborne:
The Cycles of Sports
History

*

The game pares down to a ball and ballplayers. To a jangling rhythm of possession and release, the ballplayers move the ball around, controlling it for themselves while keeping it from the opponents. The ball is friend then enemy, captive then quarry. In a prudent game, balls and players stay close to the ground. (The coach says: *Don't leave your feet. Don't throw it up for grabs. Keep the ball down. Stay down. Be careful.*) Taking flight is more risky, less in control. But up there the dangers and exhilarations rise together: higher penalties guarding higher rewards. The giddy joy of leaving the ground, soaring and swooping beyond gravity, must also risk a crash. (The law of compensation applied to a ballgame.)

Fans in the stands have always whooped at airborne thrills. Hearing the fans, the big leagues began to soar when the games took to the air. Decades passed before these takeoffs: seventy years for baseball, fifty years for football and basketball. The games moved deliberately, in two dimensions, when held to the ground. Once the third dimension was added, the sudden springing from ground-bound limits, the fans stood up too. Off the ground, the big leagues came of age. The ballgames *looked* transformed—but really were just reverting, turning back to older versions of themselves.

◆   ◆   ◆

No basketball shot is more sensual fun. On the move with the ball, the jump shooter plants a foot to stop dead and leaps straight up off both feet. At the top of the jump—one of the most exquisitely timed moments in sports—at the instant of hanging motionless in the air, when the body is a stable shooting platform neither rising nor falling, the shooter releases the ball, spinning it backward off fingertips. The body's quick conversion of lateral to upward motion and the spring into flight are flat-out jarring explosions, pushed hard and abruptly. Yet the shot is delicate, feathered instead of powered, descending like a snow-flake. When the ball is true, the shooter still feels oddly in con-trol, connected to the spinning ball in flight: an invisible filament unreeling from the last shooting finger to the ball, arcing up and down as it tracks straight to the hoop. Shooter and ball defy gravity together, then fall in sequence.

The jump shot was discovered repeatedly, then forgotten, to be found again. Most basketball breakthroughs have come from players, not coaches—from playing rather than watching. Fool-ing around in practice, or in the timeless solo dance of shooting around, or in the hot glare of a game's crucial moment, a player may try something new. It may be unconscious, not planned or thought out. A sudden moment, an unexpected opening, and the player pulls a move he has never done or seen, leaving him to wonder from whence it came. The essence of basketball has always been jazz improvisation, with the mind yielding to the body and muscle memory. So it went for the six main inventors of the jump shot.

"It started in the air," John Cooper said sixty-three years later. He did not consciously plot it beforehand. At practice one day in 1927, he simply jumped up and fired a new shot. It felt right and—in particular—couldn't be blocked. Cooper was a runty freshman, only five feet eight inches and skinny, playing with older, larger boys on the high school team in Corydon, a farming and coal-mining village in western Kentucky. "In a little town, they'd fill in the team with what they had," Cooper recalled. "That was me, a little scrawny kid. Whenever I got ready to shoot, the bigger kids knocked the ball down my throat." He was getting gun-shy with one eye on the basket and the other on a looming opponent. From this desperation came hurried inspiration. During a scrimmage, a guard on his team lofted a high pass toward Cooper. He leaped, caught it, and then—in his anxiety to avoid a block—shot it, all in one motion, before he landed. "I just didn't come down." That midair accident gave him a more deliberate idea: start on the ground with the ball in his hand, leap straight up, and shoot from the top of the jump. A jump shot.

Two years later, Johnny Cooper's jumper helped him to five hundred points in one season, more than an entire high school team might score at the time. Opponents had never seen a jump shot before and could not stop it. Cooper's magic invention powered little Corydon into the quarterfinals of the already intense Kentucky state high school tournament. There Corydon lost to a team with its own exotic weapon never seen before in those parts: a bounce pass.

Basketball grew by unrelated spontaneous generations, here and there, ballplayers making the game up as they went along. Aside from a few obscure magazines and annual yearbooks, the sport had no national media coverage or audience, no national pro league or college tournament. In thousands of isolated pockets around the country, basketball players found and refound basic techniques, all unaware of how the game was being played even in the neighboring pocket—much less in all the distant pockets. The sport bounced forward in the hands of numberless innovators, most of them now unknown and unknowable.

In basketball textbooks published during the 1920s, three midwestern college coaches—Walter Meanwell of Wisconsin, Craig Ruby of Illinois, and Phog Allen of Kansas—described rudimentary kinds of jump shots. Meanwell called it a one-hand push after a high jump, with the ball banked off the backboard. Ruby called it a two-hand shoulder shot: a player moving away from the basket, toward the left sideline, jumping off his left foot to face the hoop and shooting with both hands from a point to the right of his head. Allen called it a push arch shot: the player with the ball springing up and back off his rear leg, extending his front leg in protection, and shooting a soft, loopy ball to the rim. All three of these recognized college shots, though, were glorified layups, mainly used close to the basket after a lateral jump off one foot instead of a vertical, two-legged leap. The modern jump shot emerged from lower levels of the game.

For Kentucky outposts like Corydon, too small to field a high school football team, basketball stretched from baseball season to baseball season, dominating both fall and winter. Johnny Cooper, born on a farm in 1912, had grown up in town. His father, a strong man fond of sports, worked in the cattle business. A kind of basketball started early, when a Methodist preacher gave the boy a peculiar "out-seam" basketball with raised seams to absorb wear. Cooper first shot it at a barrel hoop attached to the side of a smokehouse. Later he removed the floor from the smokehouse and fashioned the only indoor court in Corydon. At school he would pick a lucky kid to go home with him and play ball inside ("It was too small to play anything but one-on-one"). Protected from the weather, he played constantly, hooked on hoops and moving toward the jumper.

After high school he took his shot to the University of Missouri; cousins had gone there and sold him on the school, though it offered no athletic scholarships. (Adolph Rupp, just starting his basketball reign at the University of Kentucky, drew players only from his eastern end of the state.) To help pay his way Cooper worked in a dairy and at the university bookstore. When he tried out for the Missouri basketball team, his puzzled coach, George Edwards, asked where he had learned that shot. "I thought he really wanted to hear about it," Cooper said later, "but he didn't. He told me that at Missouri they didn't shoot the ball that way." Still skeptical, Edwards sent Cooper into a game against Ohio State. He got the ball, went up looking to pass, found nobody open, and shot it home. "I never heard another word about it from the coach."

Now full grown at six feet, with the speed of a champion 440-yard sprinter and enough spring to get both hands over the rim, Cooper scored almost half his team's points as a sophomore. His 110 points in ten Big Six games tied him for top scorer in the conference. Moving around the foul line, facing the basket, he would catch a pass and launch into flight from his left foot, either at once or after a dribble. Or, back to the basket, he would jump, spin toward the hoop, then release. Holding the ball over his head, he shot with a two-handed motion, but favoring his right hand, which lingered on the ball to the last instant. An all-star in his conference, Cooper was known as Missouri's "jump shot forward." In three years of varsity ball, playing teams from the Big Six, Big Ten, and the West Coast, he never saw anybody else shoot a jumper.

About six hundred miles to the east, though, Glenn Roberts was shooting a similar shot at the same time. He came from a rural, small-town, Upper South background like Cooper's. Both men achieved fame within their own basketball circles for devising and drilling a jump shot. Yet those circles never intersected, and neither ballplayer ever saw or even heard of the other at the time. The "pre-Columbians" of this New World, they made the basic discovery; but the news didn't get out until later.

Glenn Roberts sprang from a hillside farm—eighty acres, planted mainly to corn, on the South Fork of the Pound River—in the western tip of Virginia, halfway between Pound and Flat Gap. Glenn and his six brothers grew tall from the genes of their mother, Orlema, a large woman. "We never played baseball. For us it was basketball, farm chores and school," Glenn remembered. "We didn't have any sisters so we had to help out washing dishes and things like that. Sure, I churned butter. We had to milk and work in the garden." The second oldest child, Glenn walked six miles to the high school in Pound, a town of 150 people, too few to afford a gym. Basketball was played outdoors on an unpaved dirt court. Craving basketball made a boy determined. To get there before school started in the morning, Glenn left home with a kerosene lantern against the winter dark. As the day brightened he left the lantern in someone's barn, halfway to school, to be picked up to light his way home. At school the basketball court, still frozen from overnight, allowed the sharpest game of the day. Later in the day the court thawed and grew sloppy; Glenn and his schoolmates played on it anyway. After a snowfall they cleared it and spread cinders from the school stove. They loved basketball.

In old, reminiscent age, Glenn Roberts was asked where he had found his jumper. Looking back, he stressed the implications of that variable playing surface. "Because of our eagerness for basketball," he said, "we practiced in all kinds of weather. At times it was too muddy to dribble the ball and move effectively especially since we practiced most of the time in our pair of all-purpose shoes." Horsing around before and after school, they played a gunslinger game that rewarded a particular kind of shot: "We would often congregate under our basket and practice in an unorganized way. Whoever recovered the ball after a shot was attempted was on his own to get off a shot at the basket against the combined efforts of everyone else." With nobody throwing picks or passes, how to manage a clear, solitary shot? The informal game and surface launched a J. "It was necessary to devise something besides an ordinary effort to even get the ball to the basket unless you got lucky. By starting to jump as high in the air as I could after recovering the ball and releasing the ball after jumping out of reach of the others I started to get the ball to the basket consistently." (Out in Corydon, Kentucky, Johnny Cooper was shooting *his* first jumpers on a dirt court too.)

Both pre-Columbians rode the shot to celebrated success in high school and college; the lingering puzzle is why they were not more widely imitated even in their own limited spheres. As a senior in 1931, Roberts led his high school team to thirty-five straight wins and the Class C state title. He went on to four high-scoring years—a new national college record of 1,531 points in all, with All-American status—at Emory and Henry College, a Methodist school of four hundred students in Emory, Virginia. He paid his way by sweeping floors and cutting grass. Straight from the farm, he headed for the gym (indoors! a hard, flat wooden floor! no mud or wind or rain!) to the amusement of the basketball coach, Pedie Jackson. "Why, he had on a pair of overalls and every time he bounced the ball it went over his head," Jackson said later, improving the story a tad. "He started shooting goals on the indoor floor and he just couldn't miss them, it seemed." As a freshman he led the varsity with almost nineteen points a game. "Players in every school in this section," a sportswriter reported, "are trying to duplicate Roberts' peculiar unorthodox 'side-jump' shot that has pulled many ball games out of the fire."

Trying to duplicate: it was difficult, suspiciously tricky-looking, and defiant of usual notions of how to shoot; not easy to copy. In college Roberts improved his dribbling and added forward and backward pivots for taking his favorite spots under the hoop and out by the foul line. "We would feed him the ball," a guard on the Emory and Henry team, Sam Neel, later recalled. "He was double teamed most of the time, but he was so mobile and had so many deceptive moves that we were able to get the ball to him." Back to the basket, he held the ball high over his head, waiting to sense a break in the defensive pressure behind him. He jumped straight up off both feet, absorbed the blow from his man, and hung there for a long instant, whirling to face the hoop. In the air he jerked his body, a unique spasm "which one needed to see to believe," said Sam Neel. It resembled, according to Neel, the midair hitch-kick used by long jumpers to stay up. To another observer it looked like "somehow jumping a second time without touching the floor." With his defenders descending he shot a two-hander straight to the rim or, from a near angle, spun it off the backboard, using both hands to apply the snappy English that zipped the ball through the cords.

"I couldn't believe my eyes the first time I saw Glenn practice," said another college teammate, Walter Fielder. "I had never seen the jump shot before. Anywhere from the foul line to the goal, in any direction, he was deadly accurate. . . . I marveled at his jumping ability and his accuracy; it was just unbelievable! There was no way for an opponent to guard him without fouling him." Deliberate and unflappable on the court, six feet four inches and sure of hand, Roberts played a complete game: jumping center, passing and dribbling deftly, ruling the boards. Once he hit ninety-six of one hundred free throws in practice. He led the team to a four-year record of 68-12, with wins over bigger schools like Tennessee and William and Mary. He did every hoop task well, but that unique shot made him special. For "who can guard a man," asked one mystified opponent, "who jumps like a rabbit from a brush pile and, flooey—two points?"

Cooper and Roberts kept burying jumpers after college. For years Cooper played on independent and AAU teams all over Missouri, usually as the high scorer. During the war he served on two Army Air Force teams in Denver and Fort Worth. Roberts played for Dayton and Akron Firestone in the National Basketball League, the major pro loop of the late 1930s. "Against Glenn in our practice sessions we found 'THAT' shot a most difficult one to stop," recalled his Akron teammate Rip Terjesen. (The team included alumni of Notre Dame, New York University, Dartmouth, Monmouth of Illinois, Carson-Newman of Tennessee, St. John's of New York, Akron, and North Carolina State: a wide geographic swath. "It was a shot none of us had seen before," said Terjesen.) Their later careers notwithstanding, both Cooper and Roberts had played their most celebrated ball in college. After graduation their names and fame as the first jump shooters gradually ebbed away. Over the next several years, a few other shooters used jumper variants, in college and AAU play, but without leaving durable impressions.

A decade after the college heights of Cooper and Roberts, four ballplayers—each having found the shot on his own—brought the jumper to the new Basketball Association of America, father of the National Basketball Association, in its first year of operations. Bud Palmer, Belus Smawley, Kenny Sailors, and Joe Fulks all grew up and learned basketball, like Cooper and Roberts, in small towns far from national attention; but they had the good luck as pros to play in plain view on the national stage of the first pro-basketball league to field a full schedule in the major cities of the Northeast and Midwest. Their visible success finally established the jump shot as the airborne future of basketball.

As a small, unmuscled child in the 1930s, Bud Palmer tried shooting baskets by himself but was too weak to throw the ball up to the rim. So he stood almost directly under the hoop, jumped straight up off both feet, flung the ball with both hands—and reached the basket at last. "I used to do this by the hour," he recalled. "I never saw anybody else use the shot." As he grew stronger, he moved farther from the basket and kept shooting it, in prep-school games at Phillips Exeter and then in college at Princeton. "The more I played, the more I realized the value of the shot, which was quite simple. It came off movement so the player guarding me was moving, but I had one enormous advantage. I knew when I was going to jump. Off a fast dribble or quick pass, I would stop, plant both feet and go vertically in the air with both arms completely extended upwards. Off the fast drive, I could get higher off the floor than a straight vertical jump while standing still." Hanging in the air, he waited for his opponent to descend, then shot a one-hander on his way down. With no propelling power from his leap or body weight, he shot a hard, flat arch that left little margin for error. "But let's face it," said Palmer, "it was so damn unusual that I got away with murder. The officials had never seen it. If the player guarding me even touched me, I was awarded the foul." At his mature height of six feet four inches, he was seldom blocked.

One night in the fall of 1946, Palmer went to one of the new BAA's first games in New York and noticed a lot of guys he had played against in the Navy Air Corps, now being paid to play ball. Well, thought Palmer, if *they* can play in this league . . . He asked the Knickerbockers for a tryout ("They hardly knew that we played basketball in the Ivy League"). He made the squad without showing his jumper; the coach, Neil Cohalan, preached the conservative Northeast style of ball control and two-handed sets. But in his first game Palmer went instinctively to his best weapon, missed three jump shots, and was quickly returned to the bench. "What the hell was that?" asked Cohalan, his Irish brogue rising with his temper."What a crazy, dumb shot! Don't try it again or you're through." It took three weeks of practice scrimmages, of gradually showing the shot's potential, before Cohalan let him use it in another game. "I was lucky," said Palmer. "I sank four or five in a row from different parts of the court and different angles. I can still remember an amused, curious murmur from the crowd." He led the Knicks in scoring and shooting percentage that year, then played two more effective seasons before retiring to concentrate on his career in sports broadcasting.

Belus Smawley's version of Johnny Cooper's smokehouse was an abandoned railroad depot in Rutherford County, North Carolina, midway between Charlotte and Asheville. Born in 1918, Smawley was raised on a farm; his father also worked as a mechanic and carpenter. In their teens, Belus and his friends took over an old train-depot building in town. They hung a barrel hoop on the wall, scrounged a near-basketball (smooth rubber, about the size of a soccer ball), and played on Sunday afternoons at the only indoor court in those parts. "I never had anybody really teach me any kind of shot," Smawley said later. "I just came up with my own." Playing without supervision or real equipment, he showed an untutored knack for the game. An AAU team down the road in Spindale, North Carolina, heard about him. The Spindale Firemen, coached by the local fire chief, played in a fast interstate league sponsored by textile mills in both Carolinas. (The Firemen even boasted a real indoor court at the Spindale community center.) Smawley left high school after his junior year to join them, the only high school boy among college-age men.

One night in 1937, in the swirl of a league game, Smawley, without thinking, went up for his first jumper. "I had a big guy playing me," as he later described it, "so I got down on the side, inside a little bit, and faked him and went up, why I shot that shot I don't know, and then from that day on I shot it." It was sheer ad-hoc seat-of-the pants improvising, drawn from the flow of the moment. He then worked on it deliberately, adding details to the spontaneous inspiration. Usually on the move, he would stop on a wing or around the foul circle and fake forward with his upper body. His man caught in mid-decision, Smawley would spring from both feet, fall away from the basket, and shoot with two hands from high over his head. "The big men couldn't knock it down because I was falling away from them."

After two years with the Firemen, Smawley went back and finished high school, then on to Appalachian State, a teachers college in Boone, North Carolina. Still essentially self-taught, he shot sets and free throws with the same odd two-handed, overhead motion of his jumper. His college coach watched him practicing foul shots that way and allowed, "Well, son, as long as you make 'em I won't say a word." The team's offense depended on two other shooters, reliable from afar, so Smawley—at six feet two inches and 195 pounds—played a high double post and went to the boards ("I had to clean up to get shots a lot of times").

World War II, rather than college, pushed him onto a larger court. In the service he played for a crack all-star team at the naval station in Norfolk, Virginia, in 1944. Coached by a peppery young Red Auerbach and bristling with college All-Americans, the team stretched Smawley's game. (Auerbach later remembered Smawley as the first jump shooter he'd seen.) After the war Smawley went home to play for a pro squad in Asheville. The owner of the St. Louis Bombers, a team in the new BAA, had a brother-in-law in Asheville, who saw Smawley play and alerted his relative. Smawley joined the Bombers toward the end of that 1946–47 season. At twenty-eight, the oldest man on the team, he led the Bombers in field-goal and free-throw percentages and averaged 11.9 points a game, second best on the team. He played big-league ball for five years, peaking at 15.5 points a game in 1948–49, sixth in the league that year.

Kenny Sailors owed his jump shot to sharp fraternal games against his big brother, Bud, five years older and seven inches taller. Playing one-on-one with nobody to help him, desperate to get off a clear shot somehow, Sailors had to invent a J to show his brother he could play ("He motivated me a lot," the little brother understated). They lived with their mother on a farm near Hillsdale, Wyoming, about twenty miles east of Cheyenne. Their parents had divorced, and Kenny never knew his father. The family raised corn, hay, hogs, and livestock, with the boys soon learning to work like men. Kenny found basketball in grade school. Sometimes the bus arrived at school early enough to allow keep-away games in the gym. One boy would dribble by himself while five or six others tried to steal the ball. Nobody shot; the point was just to keep dribbling without leaving the court, spinning and faking and juking as long as you could. When another boy stole the ball, everyone chased him, and so on until the bell rang. Later renowned for his uncatchable dribbling, Sailors would trace the skill back to those early games of keep-away in Hillsdale.

One day when Kenny was in junior high, his brother brought home a basketball. They attached a sort of hoop and backboard to the side of a windmill, and went at it. (They played—once again—on a dirt surface, not so good for dribbling and driving, but a softer place for jumping and landing. The lost lateral mobility was gained back in vertical ease.) "My purpose was getting up over the man that was covering me," Kenny said later, "and in those days that was my brother." He found a way: dribble toward his brother to get him leaning backward, weight on the heels, then stop abruptly, bring his feet together, spring backward away from his brother, and shoot at the peak of his jump. The move sliced away Bud's seven-inch advantage.

That jumper, combined with his adroit dribbling and play making, made Kenny the star of his teams in high school and at the University of Wyoming. Always the ball-handling guard at five feet ten inches and 175 pounds, he brought the ball upcourt and usually shot from near the top of the key, in a radius up to ten feet beyond the foul line. Moving toward his man, he would stop and shake the ball from side to side, leading his man to some subtle zig so he could zag. Bringing the ball up on one side of his body or the other—it might be slapped away if held out front—he leaped, raised the ball over his head, and at the suspended instant flicked it from his wrist and fingertips. He cradled the ball with his left hand, pointed his crooked right elbow at the hoop, and shot one-handed. His style exactly anticipated the golden weapon that would soon dominate the game: squared to the basket, a one-handed jumper taken on the move, usually after dribbling, fired at the peak of his jump.

In March 1943 Sailors introduced New York City to the shot of the future. With tight victories over Oklahoma and Texas, Wyoming had won the western regionals of the NCAA tournament, an annual season-ending ritual only since 1939. Now, before a knowing crowd of 13,200 at Madison Square Garden, Wyoming took on Georgetown, the best team in the East, for the national college title. "Sailors was the key man," the *New York Times* reported. "His ability to dribble through and around any type of defense was uncanny, just as was his electrifying one-handed shot." With six minutes left, Georgetown was ahead, 31–26. Then Wyoming, taller and better conditioned, ran 11 straight points to lead by 6. With Sailors controlling the ball, Wyoming downshifted to a slower possession game intended to protect the lead. ("Sailors may very well be classified as one of the all-time college greats," said an expert afterward. "He is a most remarkable dribbler, a fine shot, a good team man and a tenacious defensive guard.") Georgetown crept back to within 3, but Wyoming replied with 9 straight points to win easily, 46–34. Sailors's sixteen points made him the only man on either team to score in double figures. "Our inability to stop Sailors was what hurt us," a Georgetown player said later. "Sailors was quick and had a marvelous jump shot. He could feint, go to the basket, pull up. He hit especially well from the top of the circle." In a special war benefit game for the Red Cross, Wyoming then beat St. John's, winner of the rival NIT tournament. Under the national spotlight of Madison Square Garden, in championship games, the jump shot had finally, emphatically surfaced.

After wartime service in the marines and a final year at Wyoming, Sailors joined the Cleveland Rebels of the new Basketball Association of America in the fall of 1946. The coach, Dutch Dehnert, had played for the legendary New York Original Celtics, who had roared through their barnstorming tours with short passes, spare dribbling, and two-handed sets. Evidently old Dutch had not seen, read, or heard about Sailors's NCAA prodigies of 1943. "Sailors," he demanded after the first practice, "where'd youse get that crazy jumpin' shot?" "Gosh, Dutch, I've been shootin' that quite a while." "Who'd ever teach you a shot like that?" Dehnert asked. "I want to tell you that you'll never make it in this league, dribblin' as much as you dribble and shootin' that crazy jumpin' shot." As it turned out, Dehnert was fired before the season ended. Sailors averaged 9.9 points a game, placed second in the league in assists, and made the all-league second team.

But the Rebels folded after that first season, and that was how Sailors's whole pro career went, as he played well for lousy teams. During two years with the Providence Steamrollers, he led the team in scoring; his 15.8 points per game the second season ranked fifth in the league. But Providence went 6-42, then 12-48, each the worst record of the year, then folded. Sailors went on to the Denver Nuggets and averaged 17.3 points a game, fourth in the league. But the Nuggets went 11-51, the worst record of the year, then folded. On to the Baltimore Bullets, where he played in a backcourt with Belus Smawley. ("It was deadly," Sailors later said of Smawley's jumper, "you couldn't stop him when he was hitting.") Baltimore went 24-42, only the second-worst record of the year, but that was enough for Sailors. Beaten down by all that losing, he retired at thirty and went home to Wyoming. Bad teams and worse luck had kept him out of the play-offs and denied him the full recognition that his skills deserved.

Instead those honors went to Joe Fulks, the first great star and gate attraction of the early BAA. Firing his own version of the jumper, he led the league in scoring for its first two years; his average of 23.2 in 1946–47 beat his nearest rival's by almost 7 points. On February 10, 1949, he hit the stratosphere with 63 points in a game against Indianapolis: a league record that would stand for nearly eleven years. "The greatest offensive player I have ever seen," said Joe Lapchick, who as center for the Original Celtics and a coach in college and pro ball had seen thousands of scorers. "He is to basketball what Babe Ruth was to baseball." His feats left Fulks a popular reputation as the main progenitor of the jump shot—though he, Palmer, Smawley, and Sailors all came into the league at the same time.

Fulks leaped from the jump-shot soil of the Upper South. (Only Sailors and Palmer, of the six principal inventors, came from somewhere else.) Fulks grew up in Birmingham, Kentucky, a hamlet on the Tennessee River, about fifty miles southwest of John Cooper's hometown of Corydon. Joe's father went fishing and hired himself out for farmwork and odd jobs; the family lived in town. Joe, born in 1921, started shooting baskets by lobbing rocks at a tobacco can nailed to a woodshed. Real basketball was played outdoors on the inevitable dirt surface. When he couldn't find a ball, Joe shot brickbats, at some cost to the string nets.

By his mid-teens Fulks had developed a jump shot. Boys from nearby towns who played against him in high school later swore it was the same shot that would lift him to stardom in the NBA. "I tried many times to block it and couldn't," said Joe Jones from Benton. "I'm sure that Joe just developed it on his own," said Leonard Metcalf from Gilbertsville. "He didn't copy it after anybody." As Jones and Metcalf remembered it, anywhere within about eighteen feet of the hoop—either facing the basket or falling away from a turnaround—he would leap from both feet, raise the ball with both hands above his right shoulder, and float a soft, slow shot from his right hand. More than fifty years later, Metcalf retained a sharp image of Fulks surrounded by opponents, "hitting him, beating him, and all of a sudden his hand would come up and he'd let loose with the ball and it would crawl in the basket." The hand would rise above the welter, like a submarine periscope from a stormy sea, and flutter the ball home.

Tall and strong (six feet five inches and 190 pounds when full grown), with enormous hands to cradle and control a basketball, Fulks was the top scorer on his high school team. After his junior year, with Birmingham about to be inundated by the TVA's Kentucky Dam on the Tennessee River, he was induced to come play for Kuttawa in the next county. As part of the transfer, Joe's underemployed father was given a guard's job at the nearby state prison in Eddyville. (Kentucky high school basketball was already a very serious business.) Joe justified the arrangement for Kuttawa by sometimes outscoring the entire team trying to contain him.

In the fall of 1940 he ventured two counties to the south to Murray State Teachers College, a dry campus with 1,132 students and mandatory chapel every Wednesday. "A bashful, retiring country boy," as a classmate remembered him, he was there to play basketball. On a work scholarship, like the other jocks, he swept out a classroom building for his room and board. His classmate Ray Mofield helped write his English themes. "He was a better ballplayer than he was an English student," Mofield said later. "He was devoted to becoming the best basketball player he could be." Mofield and another student would retrieve for Fulks as he practiced shooting on his own, ninety minutes every day, honing his game.

In two years of varsity play he led Murray State with a cumulative 13.2 points a game. Nicknamed "Jumpin' Joe," known for his leaping, he could palm the ball and dunk it, two uncommon skills at the time. The team offense, geared to set him up, deployed a high pivot with Fulks on a wing. He cut across the key while the center, John Padgett, set a rolling block on the defender chasing Fulks, who then took a pass and launched into his jumper. (Padgett remembered the play keenly because Fulks often landed on top of him.) Murray State was limited to a modest local schedule. A major trip brought the team by automobile to the eastern end of the state, where they played Marshall, Eastern Kentucky, and Morehead, one after the other. But Fulks could measure his game against faster company at the annual small-college National Association of Intercollegiate Basketball tournament in Kansas City. In 1943 Fulks had high games of nineteen and twenty-two points and made the tournament all-star team. Belus Smawley, playing in that tournament for Appalachian State, took special notice of Fulks; it was the first time he had seen anybody else shoot a jumper.

A few months later, Fulks left school for the wartime marines. At the base in San Diego he played on a richly stocked service team with Kenny Sailors, fresh from his NCAA glories. Sailors tried to show Fulks the advantages of his squared-up jumper—longer range and a higher jump—but Fulks stuck to his favorite turnaround. Sparked by these two unstoppables, the team rolled to thirty-eight straight wins in a local service league. Then a marine general arrived who had lost a son in the South Pacific. No more nonsense about marines playing ball at home, decreed the general, "and we were gone in two weeks," Sailors recalled.

After rear-echelon duty on Guam and Iwo Jima, Fulks wound up his marine stint supervising a gym and playing basketball again, this time in a demanding Fleet Marine league in Honolulu. Matched against some of the best talent in the country, he led the league in scoring. Somebody told Eddie Gottlieb, the Philadelphia basketball impresario, about this obscure ace. A year later, with the BAA about to launch, Gottlieb phoned Fulks, at home in Kuttawa, and made an offer. Fulks spurned it; service ball had left him a confident sense of how he compared with other famous ballplayers. He wanted more. "If Mikan and Sailors can get that kind of money," he kept repeating, "I'm certainly worth what I'm asking."

"The fellow had his price and he didn't come down one penny," Gottlieb said later. So the city slicker gave in to the hillbilly. Fulks hit 25 points in his first game, 41 against Toronto in January, and a new pro record of 1,611 for the season and play-offs, beating Willie Kummer's old total of 1,404, set back in 1912 in a western Pennsylvania league. With high games of 34 and 37 points in the finals against Chicago, Fulks powered Philly to the first BAA championship. "He turned out to be the biggest bargain in basketball history," Gottlieb concluded in pardonable hyperbole. It was remarkable: a player nobody in the Northeast or Midwest had ever heard of, dominating the new league so easily, using shots few had seen before. He fired the jumper with either hand, both hands, or off his right shoulder with a sweeping hooklike motion. He also hit push shots, conventional hooks, driving layups, tap-ins—"the greatest variety of shots I ever saw," according to Red Auerbach, then starting his pro coaching career with the Washington Capitols.

Fulks played an aggressive but unhurried game. Teammates called him "Dishrag Joe," ever relaxed. On defense, his team's best rebounder, he parked under the enemy basket waiting for a miss. Gathering in the ball, he dumped it to a guard and ran slowly upcourt, hunched over in a tall man's stoop, arms bent at the elbow. No hurry; the offense was waiting to revolve around him. "He makes most of his points on a leaping, twisting shot from a pivot post," a wondering Philadelphia sportswriter noted midway through his first season. "He lets 'em go with either hand, and has an uncanny knack of changing the ball from one hand to the other at the last second and getting it away in the clear without a bit of lost motion. His height, long arms, and the spring in his feet all contribute greatly to his success, but the major factor is a big soft hand with long sensitive fingers that enables him to shoot a 'soft' ball. It seems to merely float lazily off his fingertips, and it either drops clean or practically goes to sleep on the rim."

Granted that Fulks had slow feet and did not play much defense. Sometimes he was selfish with the ball, firing twice as many shots as any teammate. "Shoot, Joe, shoot!" the enemy bench would taunt him if he missed several in a row but kept gunning. In sixty games that first year he managed only twenty-five assists, lowest among the regulars. "But Fulks was in a class by himself with that jump shot," his teammate Howie Dallmar, not a particular Fulks fan, later conceded. "He wasn't a great jumper, but the novelty of it, plus the fact that he put it back over his head, made him impossible to stop. And, he had a great touch." Opponents new to the jumper remembered Fulks as a grim, novel ordeal, a wild creature stalking the court and defying the usual boundaries of the game. "The introduction of the jump shot into the game was very disturbing," said Bob Davies of

Rochester, "because to guard someone like Joe Fulks was very difficult. Suddenly, you had to guard someone shooting on the move. This was next to impossible when we first saw it."

With the advent of Joe Fulks, the jumper had arrived for good. The old horizontal game, a matter of careful picks and floor position, became more open, daring, and vertical. Basketball took to the air. The jump shot led ultimately to more blocks, dunks, and alley-oops. The modern game, the latest evolution from Naismith's peach baskets, became visible.

◆   ◆   ◆

Football went airborne on Benny Friedman's arm. When he entered the National Football League in 1927, the forward pass was an untrusted, underused weapon, deployed with caution and prayer. The football itself, about two inches fatter around the middle and stubbier at the ends than the modern ball, was hard to grip and toss, designed more for kicking than passing. Rules of the game clearly discouraged throwing the ball. A passer had to stand at least five yards behind the line of scrimmage. Roughing the passer was legal, indeed admired as just retribution for a sneaky maneuver. A team was penalized for incomplete passes on consecutive plays, and even forfeited the ball for an incomplete pass in the end zone. Football consisted of running and kicking; pass receivers, hardly necessary, were undeveloped resources deficient in speed, hands, and moves. Except for kicks and laterals, the game was ground bound, a slogging, grinding collision of muscle mass and foot speed.

All this changed because of Benny Friedman, in particular. "I have been told that I revolutionized the game some when I came in," he said in proud old age, knowing pretty well that he had. "At the time everyone was conservative about passing. In fact, the whole offense was conservative. When you were inside your own 30-yard line, you kicked on third down. And you never passed this side of your own 40. When I came into the pros, I decided I would pass wherever and whenever I wanted to." After he had shown the possibilities of aerial football, and how the fans cheered (and paid) for it, the inhibiting rules were changed to invite everyone to throw and catch the ball. Football opened up. More sudden scores and unpredictable thrilling events jolted the pro game and helped secure its future success. Yet today, six decades after Friedman's last game, few football fans know his significance or even recognize his name. He has not been inducted into the Pro Football Hall of Fame, and probably never will be. Friedman is perhaps the least appreciated athlete of such great skill and influence in big-league history.

He rests in obscurity mainly because of missing statistics. The NFL, bravely launched in 1920, remained a leaky, haphazard vessel for years. Schedules fluctuated as teams prolifically came and went. Preoccupied with bailing the boat, the league office neglected to keep the most basic statistics on rushing, passing, and receiving until 1932, when Friedman's career was almost over. For his prime years the official stats page is blank. To the NFL's record keepers today, Friedman does not exist because he has no numbers.

From newspaper accounts and other sources, though, the sports historian David Neft has compiled tolerably complete statistics for the early NFL that show Friedman's ground-clearing domination of his era. From 1927 through 1930 the second-ranked passers in the league, year by year, threw for aggregate totals of 3,770 yards and 27 touchdowns. Friedman in those four years passed for at least 5,653 yards (50 percent more than the runners-up) and 55 touchdowns (more than twice as many). His nearest peers were barely visible in the distance. Friedman twice passed for more than 1,500 yards in a season; even under the soon-liberalized passing rules, no other NFL quarterback managed it until 1942. He threw 3 touchdown passes in a quarter, 5 in a game, 20 in a season: all records, probably, that outlived his era. In 1933, his final season, he played less but still completed 53 percent of his passes, 10 points better than anybody else. "The dead shot Dick of football," one sportswriter called him. "Mighty super-football player of the age," said another. And today he is mostly unknown, a phantom with missing numbers.

The NFL needed some good news when Benny Friedman came along. At the league's pre-season meeting in the summer of 1927, twelve of the twenty-three NFL teams were "suspended," cutting the schedule of franchises in half. But one day later, the Kansas City Cowboys, one of the comatose teams, surprised everybody by announcing they had signed Friedman—the most acclaimed college football player since Red Grange—and were moving to Cleveland. Friedman had grown up there, leading his high school football team to the city title, and now was expected to draw paying customers to his hometown Bulldogs. This unexpected coup energized the droopy league meetings. "With Friedman as the bait," a newspaper reported, "the Clevelanders picked up a choice schedule."

The league's latest savior joined a team of unimpressed midwesterners. Coach LeRoy Andrews, once a tackle for the University of Kansas, drew players from the territory he knew. Friedman was the only Bulldog from east of the Mississippi, the only one with gaudy All-American credentials, the only one who didn't chew Beechnut tobacco. "I had to earn my spurs with my gang," he said later. A few of his teammates, it turned out, could catch passes: Carl Bacchus, an end from Missouri, and two backfield mates, Tiny Feather of Kansas State and Ossie Wiberg of Nebraska Wesleyan. They became Friedman's favorite targets in his first two years.

The Bulldogs opened against the Packers in Green Bay. Under a steady rain, unfriendly to a passing game, Friedman looked nervous at the start. "As we lined up I became aware of the tonnage and talent of the Packers," he recalled. He saw across the line a 255-pound center, other linemen nearly that large, and yet more behemoths on the bench, glaring at him. "That doesn't make the outlook much brighter," he said to himself. After a few plays he sensed that pro ball was rougher, harder, more exact football than he had ever seen. "By the middle of the first period I had thrown only one short completed pass—and I was worried. Touted as a sensation, responsibility weighed on me. I was the bright, particular star supposed to give the customers their money's worth—and there in front of me was a line that an army tank couldn't budge." Benched for two quarters, he returned late in the game and wound up a dismal debut with two successful passes in four throws. In the next game, a scoreless tie against the New York Giants, he was no better, completing three of eight passes.

Starting with the second half of his third game, though, his star began to soar. Against Red Grange's New York Yankees he connected on 7 straight passes, driving the Bulldogs down to the

Yankee 11. He then ran twice, to the 2, from where a teammate carried it over. The Bulldogs lost, 13–7, but the rookie quarterback was playing with more dash and confidence. A week later, in a rematch against the Giants at the Polo Grounds, he started throwing in the second quarter, flicking from one side of the field to the other. The Bulldogs cruised to the only score of the game. "The passing of Friedman overshadowed any other play of the day," a New York scribe reported. "All of his throws were fast and low and right into the arms of the receiver." Late in the final quarter, with the Bulldogs at fourth and goal on the Giant 8, he eluded four pursuers and whipped a perfect strike to a teammate in the end zone—who, exhausted, dropped the ball. When the teams lined up for the next play, the crowd still roared for Friedman. He finished with 13 for 19 passing; at least 3 of the misses should have been caught. Afterward thousands lingered outside the stadium waiting to glimpse Friedman, blocking the path to his taxi, cheering "the most brilliant exhibition of tossing New Yorkers have ever seen."

From that game on, he was the league's hot new sensation of the year. Against the Chicago Bears, in "one of the greatest exhibitions of aerial offensive on record," he took his team 80 yards in 11 plays, mainly with 4 passes, the last for the touchdown. He connected on 14 passes against Frankford, 18 against the Chicago Cardinals. In the Frankford game he also kicked placements, caught passes, played hard defense, carried a punt back 40 yards, and ran 30 yards around right end for a touchdown. "The greatest all around exhibition of football ever put on display by an individual," according to one hyperbolic witness. Why, Friedman was to football what Babe Ruth and Ty Cobb were to baseball, Jack Dempsey to boxing, Bobby Jones to golf: "As far as football goes he has IT and is IT."

Allowing for the excesses of an era of purple sportswriting, even reducing the claims by a few notches, it is still apparent that Friedman was inventing a new style of football. Nobody had ever seen a quarterback throw so often, so well. ("The Bulldogs touchdowns were gained from passes," the *New York Times* explained, ". . . while the Bears, with minor exceptions, played straight football.") He averaged 18 passes and 8 completions a game toward a season's total of at least 1,721 yards: new league records, perhaps, in each category. "Friedman is the greatest forward passer in the history of the game," a Cleveland sportswriter concluded with hometown pride but no fear of an argument. "No other passer has had his accuracy, his judgment of distance, his intuitive ability to pick out the best receiver." Four different versions of an all-league team placed him at quarterback after the 1927 season.

"And how that baby can think," an opponent pointed out. An original football intelligence directed Friedman's brimming assortment of mechanical skills. A particular series of plays against the Bears in 1928 demonstrated his novel touch. The Bulldogs, soggy with red ink, had moved from Cleveland to Detroit and changed their name to the Wolverines, after Friedman's college team at the University of Michigan. (Twenty Detroit businessmen had put up five hundred dollars each to underwrite the city's third attempt at an NFL franchise.) Playing the Bears in Chicago, Detroit moved ahead after Friedman carried 4 times for 30 yards, down to the 1, from where a teammate scored. There it stood until late in the game. With 7 minutes left, Detroit stopped a Bear drive and took the ball on their own 4-yard line. Backs against their goal, they lined up in punt formation on first down. The Bears, not buying the fake, stayed in tight and stopped an off-tackle slant after 2 yards. Second down brought the same play, as the Wolverines gained 3.

Now it was third and 5 on the 9. Friedman was struggling through an off day in the air, only 5 for 13 for 48 yards to that point. For the third play in a row, the Wolverines deployed as if to punt. "In those days," Friedman recalled, "it was automatic that if you had long yardage, you kicked on the third down." This time the Bears bit; two of them faded back for the expected kick. Friedman, barking signals from the single wing, saw them go and changed the call at the line of scrimmage. The snap went to Ossie Wiberg, who mimed a punt and tossed the ball to Friedman. He looked downfield but could not find the primary receiver, who had missed the signal change and was back blocking the tackle, his assignment on punts. Friedman darted about and finally threw to his left end, Lyle Munn, about 30 yards away. Munn caught the pass and made it to midfield. From there the Wolverines stayed on the ground and ran out the clock, winning,

6–0. By throwing on third down from his own end zone, a riskily improper play, Friedman had iced the victory. "Benny was specially dangerous," George Halas of the Bears said years later, "because you never knew when he was going to pass."

Inspired by big games and crucial moments, he played particularly well in New York. Later that 1928 season, in what he remembered as his best pro game, he directed a startling comeback against the Giants. A few weeks earlier, the Wolverines had embarrassed the Giants, 28–0, in Detroit ("Friedman was virtually the whole show," said the *Times*). Now the Giants, defending NFL champs, bigger and braggier than Detroit, expected easy revenge at home. Before thirty thousand fans, the second-largest football crowd ever at the Polo Grounds, the Giants started the fourth quarter leading, 19–7. Friedman, "a veritable man of rubber and iron," rushed for four straight first downs, to the 25. One of his halfbacks, Len Sedbrook, then bolted for the score. The Giants took the ball back and obligingly threw an interception to Tiny Feather. Friedman passed to Carl Bacchus for 15 yards, down to the Giant 10. Three running plays only lost 10 yards. On fourth and 20, his last shot, Friedman faded back, avoided four different Giants, ran to his right, and threw to Bacchus in the end zone. Bacchus caught it and fell over as the crowd exploded. The game ended at 19–19, a moral victory for Detroit. "The greatest all-around pro player of the year," the New York sportswriter Rud Rennie said of Friedman afterward. "From the depths of the grandstand to the heights of the mezzanine one could hear them saying: 'What a man!' . . . After it was all over, oldtime football men said they never saw anything like it."

No wonder that Tim Mara, owner of the Giants, wanted Friedman for his own team. The Wolverines, like the Bulldogs, had lost money—each of the investors got $350 of his $500 back—but, deficits be damned, LeRoy Andrews would not consider parting with his marquee player. So Mara simply bought the whole team, taking Friedman and five others for the Giants. Andrews came along to coach. Friedman was paid $10,000, the richest annual contract in league history.

He earned it. In 1928 the Giants had scored six points a game and finished the season $54,000 in debt. A year later, with Friedman, they flaunted the NFL's best offense at twenty-one points a game, squeaked out a profit of $8,500, and lost a tight championship race to the Packers. This all depended on Friedman's now-routine heroics, such as four touchdown passes in a game against the Bears. In the crowd that day was Knute Rockne of Notre Dame, a hostile skeptic toward pro football (and an ancient, dedicated enemy of Friedman's college mentor, Fielding Yost). Even Rockne, despite himself, was astounded by Friedman's sharpshooting: "It was an afternoon of thrills at the miraculous dexterity of his passing," he said later. "Four yards, ten yards, forty yards—harassed and pounded—he threw the ball from all angles, standing or running at terrific speed, hitting his target right on the button—with never a miss. . . . He could hit a dime at forty yards."

After the 1930 season—Friedman had led the league in passing yardage and touchdowns for the fourth straight year—Paul Gallico of the *New York Daily News* counted no fewer than fourteen separate football skills that Friedman commanded: pass, punt, run the ends, plunge the line, block, tackle, weave through a broken field, drop-kick, placekick, interfere, diagnose plays, direct an offense, spot enemy weaknesses, and not get hurt. A coach might expect a good player to handle, say, four of these tasks. Friedman displayed the whole list.

Gallico offered a case in point. During a game against Providence that fall of 1930 he was sitting on the Giants' bench next to LeRoy Andrews. As his team lined up on offense, Andrews pointed to somebody in the Providence secondary. "He's two yards out of position," said the coach. "Watch Benny now!" Friedman took the snap and drifted toward the sideline, head-faking to his right. Drawing his arm back, still looking to the right, he suddenly whirled, shifted his feet, and threw to the left, to a teammate racing beyond the defender who had wandered two yards out of position. Touchdown, Giants. "Didn't I tell you that play was coming?" Andrews shouted to Gallico over the din. "Benny always comes through. I'll bet there have been more than fifty times since I've been with Friedman as a pro that I've mentally called for a play like that and Benny has seen the same thing and called it for himself." No question about it, Gallico concluded. Benny Friedman was "the greatest football player in the world."

He looked like a muscular rabbinical student, solemn and understated. Friedman was a compact, handsome man, five feet ten inches and 180 pounds, with a wide, squared-off chin, dark olive complexion, and shiny black hair and eyes. His college teammates, acknowledging his speed and hue, had nicknamed him "Flying Ebony," after the horse that won the 1925 Kentucky Derby. In repose the corners of his mouth turned up slightly, implying a subtle smile that lightened his sober demeanor. "He is a queer, brooding boy," wrote Gallico—so somber in mien, his face "sometimes almost a bitter mask." He played seriously, with an alert contempt for half-efforts and inattention that his side might exploit. Friedman could not abide anyone who let a talent go unused or undeveloped. Against stacked odds he had willed himself into being a football player, remaking his body and behavior, devising his own ways of passing, and contending always with offhand assumptions that he was too small, too Jewish, too *something* to succeed at the rough, goyish sport of football.

He was born on March 18, 1905, in Cleveland, the fourth of six children of Russian immigrants who had come to America in their teens. His mother's family, the Atlevoniks, had been wealthy wheat brokers near the Ural Mountains until the day the state confiscated their property and gave them forty-eight hours to flee. They emigrated to Cleveland and opened a fish store on Scoville Avenue. Benny's father worked as a furrier and tailor; the family lived in a working-class, mostly Jewish neighborhood on the East Side. Benny started playing ball in the street with his brothers, feeling the first outside tug that would pull him away from the old-country loyalties inside his home. "My parents are Orthodox Jews," he said later, "and as such adhere strictly to the dietary and sabbatical laws, but the boys like myself who are in athletics cannot and do not adhere. But I do not think that we are losing our religion by giving up these laws. Are we not living like all other American boys and doing as they do?" Addressing the readers of a Jewish newspaper, the adult Friedman thought the point moot because Jews could not assimilate anyway: "As long as we have our characteristics of features and names we will be recognized as Jews whether we hold to our religion or not."

From an early age he went his own way, tenaciously. In grade school, impatient with his natural growth, he started lifting weights. He could not loft a forty-nine-pound barbell until the school janitor showed him a necessary trick with the wrists. To a first-generation child, following the usual pattern of opening himself to new-country ways, America offered available heroes (like Teddy Roosevelt) who had rebuilt themselves with exercise. Benny threw heavy medicine balls and carried a handball to squeeze at odd moments. As a sophomore in high school he tried out for football and was cut after two weeks: the coach said he was too small. It only stoked his fire. He kept exercising, lifting a heavy broom from the end of the handle with one hand, then the other, or raising a chair aloft from the tip of one of its legs, then tossing the chair from hand to hand, catching it by the leg. Trying to widen his football grip, he squashed his hand down on a table, pushing the thumb and pinky into a straight line, holding it there through the pain. His wrists and arms grew engulfingly strong, so a football felt light and easy in his hands. When his family moved, he made the football team at his new high school.

(He maintained those exercises all his life, in defiance of the training orthodoxy of the day that ballplayers should not risk becoming "muscle-bound" or inflexible. A photograph taken in 1927 shows him and two other players, all stripped to shorts, tossing a forty-pound dumbbell. The others appear smooth-muscled, like most athletes of the time. Friedman is all ropes and slabs, taut and defined. Later on, even at the age of sixty-one, dressed in shorts and T-shirt to demonstrate his passing techniques for a photographer, he still looked trimly muscled.)

After quarterbacking his high school team to the city championship, he thought about playing college ball at Penn State. The representative from Penn State decided he was (again) too small. Instead he went off to the University of Michigan with $276 saved from odd jobs such as playing drums in a Chinese restaurant. At Ann Arbor, without a scholarship or much money from home, he collected tickets at a movie theater and worked in a bookstore for forty cents an hour. A cafeteria near school let him eat free meals when the football team won. Eventually a friendly Cleveland businessman and sports lover, Max Rosenblum—"a godfather in fact as well as in name to me"—gave him tuition and spending money.

The hardest moment at college came one day in practice at the start of his sophomore year. Friedman and another boy were warming up, tossing a football back and forth, on the sidelines. The line coach asked the head coach, George Little, for two men to run dummy plays against his starting tackles. "Take those two dummies over there," said Little, jerking a dismissing thumb over his shoulder toward Friedman and his fellow scrub. Friedman heard it, perhaps accidentally, and felt betrayed: not angry but knifed in the back, almost too weak to move his legs. "Here was this coach," he said six years later, still smarting, measuring his sentences. "He had promised to take care of me. I thought he was my friend. And I thought I was pretty good. I thought I was getting somewhere. . . . We went over there where those varsity tackles were and got murdered." The coach's curt contempt hurt more than the ravenous tackles. Why wouldn't Little give him a chance? At five feet eight inches and 172 pounds he was not yet full grown, but he had starred for the Michigan freshmen and expected to play on the varsity. He wondered if Little doubted that Jews could cut it. He thought about transferring to Dartmouth, where the coach encouraged passing.

Finally he got his shot at the end of a famous blowout. On October 18, 1924, Red Grange of Illinois dashed into football history by scoring four touchdowns in the first twelve minutes against Michigan. Little sent in his bench late in the game. On the first play Grange took a handoff and started through the line toward another chunky gain. Friedman sidestepped a guard and tackled him. "When I hit him he seemed surprised," Friedman remembered. "But we were both there, rolling on the ground. Grange had been stopped. I had stopped him." Exhilarated and relieved, Friedman imagined a newspaper headline: GREAT GRANGE STOPPED BY FRIEDMAN OF MICHIGAN. As it turned out, only one sportswriter the next day mentioned the tackle at all, and even he got the name wrong.

The following week, in practice, Friedman was surprised to find himself at starting halfback. On offense against Illinois he had completed one of three passes, to no particular effect. But

Fielding Yost—the athletic director, just retired from twenty-three years as Michigan's legendary football coach—had recognized something in Friedman. Yost ordered Little to play him. Against Wisconsin the next Saturday, Friedman ran for one touchdown, threw for two more, and made three tackles in the backfield. Little praised him afterward, sparingly. When the season was over, Yost fired Little and reinstalled himself as head coach.

Over the next two years Michigan lost only twice and Friedman made All-American. "One of the most accurate passers that ever flipped a football," declared Grantland Rice, the college game's ultimate authority. "He can throw the ball into a tin bucket." Yost showed his young star how to read defenses and invent strategies, how to lead his team with the commanding air expected of a quarterback. Under the old man's guidance ("He taught me all I knew from the ears up"), Friedman once again refashioned himself. "I had to school myself to take charge," Friedman recalled. "I had to change my personality on the field. I learned to bark signals, how to walk, how to hold my head. Yost and I had tremendous rapport. He said I was like a coach on the field."

For the purely mechanical skills, from the ears down, Friedman was always his own coach. In high school he had worked out a unique passing style that he never changed. At the time most football passers threw with a stiff-armed three-quarters motion, like hurling a hand grenade, or a fluttery sidearm, like a discus throw. The exceptionally developed strength of Friedman's wrist and fingers allowed him nearly to grip the pudgy ball and, keeping his arm close to his head, snap the ball overhand like a baseball. "Don't throw sidearm," he insisted. "That gives the ball a curve and the receiver is not sure where it is coming." Ready to pass, he held the ball with his middle three digits on the laces and his thumb splayed along a seam. He stood sideways, with his feet in a line aimed at the receiver, weight on the back (right) foot. As he threw, his weight shifted to his front foot and—in a technique seldom used by any other passer, before or since—he brought his right foot forward, bending and pivoting on his left leg, finishing in a follow-through like a baseball pitcher's. He aimed and threw with his body. This peculiar motion, drawing power and balance from his legs, lightened the strain on his throwing arm and (he believed) improved his accuracy. The step with his right foot also moved him slightly ahead of converging defenders. To finish, the muscled power and relative shortness of his upper body helped him to dive quickly down into a low, protected crouch that avoided injuries from his frustrated rushers, who hoped at least to belt the passer if they could not stop his throws.

In short, quick situations he would throw it hard—like a baseball, or even like a bullet, according to witnesses. More typically, at medium to long distances, the ball spun off his fingertips into a soft, gentle parabola. "A ball should never be thrown with any more speed than is necessary to get it to a given spot," he said. "It should be thrown so that it will drop from its highest arc softly into the receiver's hands. This gives the receiver a better opportunity to judge the flight, and a 'soft' ball that floats in an easy spiral is not apt to be fumbled. It is hard to catch a hard or speedily pitched ball." Bringing the ball past his ear, he cocked his wrist so that the forward point of the ball tilted slightly upward. Following through, his right arm was extended outward, instead of down and across his body, which he thought would drive the pass downward, with a spin difficult to catch. On deep passes he intentionally threw a trifle long to avoid interceptions by the trailing defense and to let his man run under the ball. He aimed for the receiver's face or just to his right. A Friedman pass for distance took a while to get there; the play on the field seemed to slow down, players and fans frozen in the moment, as the ball soared lingeringly toward its target. "When it reaches the receiver it has gone its route," Paul Gallico noticed. "The ball is practically dead. The receiver has merely to reach up and take hold of it like picking a grapefruit off a tree. That is Benny's secret and that is why so many of his passes are completed."

A certain "deliberation"—his own favored term—marked every aspect of Friedman's game. "He is the coolest man I ever saw on a football field," said Yost, who had watched thousands of football players. "He is never ruffled. Regardless of how the play goes, he has never lost his poise. There is never a moment when your confidence in him wavers." Friedman had thought it through. Knowing he could not pass well unless he was relaxed, he willfully suppressed any conscious awareness that snorting linemen were charging toward him. Opponents had to wonder whether he would pass, run, or kick, since he was adept at all three; let them do the worrying. In one Giants game he ran to the sidelines, near a reporter for the *New York World*. The reporter was amazed by Friedman's expression in the swirl of battle: "We could see his calm face as placid as if playing backgammon. Placider."

In those rushed moments, desperate and clattering, Friedman had learned that he must wait—for a hole to appear, or a block to be thrown, or a receiver to break free. Meantime he stayed calm, eyes wide open, not pressing or trying too hard, making instant decisions without the time or need to think much about them. "It isn't speed," Friedman knew. "It isn't power. It isn't quickness at dodging or special footwork tricks. The one thing that separates the good back from the great—from the one that you only see out of 50,000 or more football players—is deliberation."

Deliberately, as always, Friedman wished to please the ticket-buying public. "In professional football," he pointed out, "it's a good day when you satisfy the customers." Fans came to see him: press agents preferred that his team be headlined as "Benny Friedman's Bulldogs" (or Wolverines, Giants, or Dodgers). Crowds loved to see passes and scores, the teams careening up and down the field, thrilling catches and misses—all the emotional lurches of aerial football. During Friedman's NFL prime only Red Grange and Ernie Nevers matched his crowd-pulling capacity. In 1929 the Giants drew 14,000 fans to a game in Providence (a record for that stadium); 30,000 for a game with Stapleton at the Polo Grounds ("The passing of Friedman had the crowd tingling with excitement every moment of the time he was on the field"); 30,000 again to the Polo Grounds a week later, against Frankford ("The Giants could have won by sticking to straight football . . . but, ever a showman, Friedman gave the crowd what it wanted—forward passes"); 26,000 against the Bears in Chicago (the best attendance of the season at Wrigley Field). Evidently fans were buying what Friedman had to sell. "When Benny starts his aerial fireworks, things happen," said Wilfrid Smith, a Chicago sportswriter. "All of which spells excitement, and what more can a grid enthusiast ask?" But the existing rules made an effective passing game impossible for anyone but Friedman and a few others.

After three years with the Giants, after Tim Mara would not let him acquire part ownership of the team, Friedman became playing coach for the Brooklyn Dodgers of the NFL. He tried to improve the woeful Dodgers, who had finished 2-12 in 1931. "Are there any of the graduating football men who weigh 210 or thereabouts," he wrote to Bennie Oosterbaan, his old roommate and favorite receiver at Michigan, "who would like to play, and who you think would be an asset to me? . . . What are your own plans for this fall? You and I in Pro. football would be the sensation of sensations. I need a good big end who can box a tackle and really catch passes." Not even Friedman could make the Dodgers any good; he would soon retire.

As coach of the Dodgers, though, Friedman attended the league's pre-season meetings in Atlantic City in 1932. Just before the expected adjournment, a newcomer, George Preston Marshall, stood up to propose changes in the game rules. A laundry owner from Washington, D.C., with no football background, Marshall had recently bought into a new NFL franchise in Boston. "A hushed silence fell over the meeting," as Friedman remembered it. "Rules changed! *We* didn't make changes in the rules! *We* followed the college game! And then as we realized who it was who had made the suggestion, the stunned surprise gave way to polite, smug laughter. Well, if it wasn't Marshall, the laundryman! Marshall, who didn't know a thing about football. Yet here he was trying to tell some of the biggest minds in the game what to do."

Pro football was too dull and predictable, said Marshall. They were all in show business, and the show needed improvement. The football men laughed indulgently at the upstart. Marshall set his mouth and argued his case for three hours, predicting the advantages of a more open game. Eventually, over the next two seasons, most of his wild suggestions were adopted. The ball was slimmed down for easier throwing. It became legal to pass from anywhere behind the line of scrimmage. Other inhibiting rules were dropped. On plays out of bounds, the ball was brought in ten yards from the sidelines, to allow more room for offensive maneuvers. Friedman voted against these changes, perhaps to protect his own turf from less gifted poachers. In the end, he opposed the revolution he had sparked. From 1933 to 1938, NFL scoring increased by almost 40 percent. By his play on the field, if not by his votes in meetings, Friedman had changed the game.

Looking back decades later, his football contemporaries, at least, still appreciated his special impact on aerial football. "Benny really started the passing game," said Ken Strong. "The first pro quarterback to exploit the strategic possibilities of the pass," George Halas agreed. "Benny demonstrated that the pass could be mixed with running plays as an integral part of the offense." Strong and Halas were not teammates of Friedman's at the time, or particularly friendly with him later on. Their statements objectively reflected his primal role in pro football's conversion to passing.

Benny Friedman stands as an argument for a great man theory of NFL history. Deploying his unique skills and strategies, he was more actor than acted upon. He shaped and reshaped his football environment, until the revised ball and passing rules ultimately cheapened and wiped out the unofficial records he had set under such contrary conditions. "Anybody can throw today's football," Red Grange snorted in the late 1960s. "Now who's to tell what Benny Friedman might do with this modern football? He'd probably be the greatest passer that ever lived."

◆　　◆　　◆

When Babe Ruth hit one right, bat on ball made a unique sound, a dry metallic click like two billiard balls colliding. One of his teammates, sifting memories of Ruth many years later, recalled that distinctive click first: no resounding crack of the bat, like any other hitter, but the oddly understated *tck* of two hard objects of equal force meeting and not giving way. The ball careened off the bat so quickly that fans in the stands saw it leave the infield before they heard the *tck*. Hit so hard, the ball might buck strangely in flight. It could sink and knuckle like a spitball, skidding wildly along the ground, taking squirrelly bounces into the shins and fingers of cowering infielders. "I got a glimpse of a white streak coming straight," said the first baseman Sunny Jim

Bottomley. "I reached out my gloved hand, but the ball was a sinker. It dove two feet. I had just time to put my hand down close to my leg and stop the ball. But that hand was numb for three days."

Out on the mound, a pitcher facing the Babe never felt more forlorn and vulnerable. "Like looking into a lion's jaw," Wes Ferrell remembered. "You were *nothing* out there when Ruth came up. You look around, and your infielders are way back and your outfielders have just about left town, they're so far back. And here you are, sixty feet away from him." The first baseman would yell for an outside pitch, the third baseman for one on Ruth's hands, each hoping he would hit it to the other side of the infield. Pitchers generally tried to foil him with high, slow curves on the inside corner. Shucks Pruett, a pitcher of no other distinction, struck him out fifteen times in their first seventeen encounters with unremarkable little curves. But no pitch worked consistently against him. Luke Sewell, catching a game for Cleveland, was surprised when Ruth missed a pitch by two feet. Sewell checked the ball and found a dirty scuff mark, just right for bending a pitch. "The information seemed too good to waste," said Sewell, "so I strolled out and told the pitcher about it. He examined the ball, adjusted the spot to suit him, cut loose with all the stuff he had and the ball took a terrific break. But Ruth hit it on a line into the bleachers."

A typical Ruth home run sailed high and long, a majestic neck-craning fly ball that stayed up long enough to be savored by everyone but the opposition. He looked for low fastballs that he could golf with his loopy, undercutting swing. Of his longest clouts—one over the right-field fence at Comiskey Park, another beyond the grandstand roof of the Polo Grounds—the most famous came in a spring-training game against the Giants in 1919. It looked at first like a routine long fly to right. Instead of peaking and falling normally, though, it kept rising. "My God," said one of the Giants on the bench, "where is that ball going?" The right fielder gave it feckless pursuit, running so far in the distance that he finally resembled a small boy chasing a bird. The ball cleared a fence nearly 500 feet from home, kept going, and came to rest at a spot later measured as 587 feet away. For the rest of the game, the Giants talked about nothing else.

"But none of those drives," said the Babe, "made any more impression on me than the first home run I ever scored at St. Mary's." A truant child all his life, he could not remember his first home run in the big leagues—but the first one at reform school stayed with him in sharp, savored detail. Barely seven years old, after running feral in the streets of Baltimore, already fond of beer, whiskey, chewing tobacco, and small larcenies, he was newly arrived behind the barred walls of St. Mary's Industrial School. Even the toughest seven-year-old thug must have felt lost and scared among all those older, bigger boys. He turned to baseball. The boys played every day they could, summer and winter, even with snow on the ground, in teams and leagues arranged by skill level. To those hundreds of wild, cooped-up kids, the game offered fun and status, order and release. Little George Ruth went after a place on the team of smallest boys. Standing in against a tall, skinny pitcher ("pretty good for a kid"), he drove a fastball over the right fielder's head, tore around the bases, and slid home to instant acceptance as a real ballplayer. Over the next dozen years he moved up through the ranks of teams at St. Mary's. Playing two, even three games a day, he hit sixty to seventy home runs a season. ("I don't suppose I will ever make that many in the big leagues," he said in 1920.)

John Dunn, owner of the Baltimore Orioles of the International League, heard about the big kid at St. Mary's and went to see him in January 1914. He found Ruth characteristically at play, dressed in overalls and sliding on ice with other boys, looking like a gigantic urchin at the age of nineteen. Presented with a contract, Ruth in wondering disbelief seized his chance to escape St. Mary's, to play ball, to get paid for it! "Gee, there goes our ball club," said the other boys.

Ruth went off to spring training with the Orioles in Fayetteville, North Carolina. On the field, at least, the kid already understood enough baseball to play in the fast International League. "Babe knew how to pitch the first day I saw him," his first catcher, Ben Egan, recalled. "I didn't have to tell him anything. He knew how to hold runners on base, and he knew how to work on the hitters, so I'd say he was a pretty good pitcher—on his own." In practice games he beat three major-league teams and hit a home run more than 430 feet into a cornfield. Off the field he was an uncorked spirit, a wild mustang galloping a new range. Drawn to trinkets and baubles, he wore two large rings on his pitching hand, and a watch bracelet on his pitching wrist, and said they did not affect his throws. He found a horse tied to a post and rode it into a candy store. He mounted a bicycle and ran full tilt into the back of a hay wagon he was trying to pass.

Rodger Pippen, a sportswriter covering the Orioles that spring of 1914, pronounced Ruth "a natural player," a label that stuck to him, for how else could the boy have emerged so complete from St. Mary's? Six feet tall—two inches from his mature height—he walked toward the plate with a jerky motion of one shoulder, then the other, in the lean-muscled gawkiness of an adolescent. "Although in a uniform he has the appearance of being slender," Pippen noted, "George is as muscular as a tiger. He can fight, wrestle, play ball, and, in fact, do most anything in an athletic line." (Except ride a bicycle.) With time he became more than "a natural player." But the essential man always remained a child at immoderate play: a kid in a candy store, on a horse. "Ah, you never have any fun outa life!" he explained to one of his many remonstrators.

Sold to the Boston Red Sox later that year, frisking around the big leagues, Ruth ran into the barnacled presence of Sox manager Bill Carrigan. "He had never been anywhere," recalled his teammate Harry Hooper, "didn't know anything about manners or how to behave among people—just a big overgrown green pea." The Babe expansively flouted Carrigan's rules about play off the field. "I couldn't let him get away with it," said Carrigan, whose nickname "Rough" was richly deserved. "He had to be taught right away that I was the boss and that he must obey orders. Otherwise, he might ruin himself in a hurry and he'd certainly ruin the morale of my ball club." So Carrigan ordered Ruth to room with him on the road. Dutch Leonard, another wayward left-handed pitcher, had already been sentenced to live with the manager. More worldly than the Babe, baiting and leading him on, Leonard would tease him into noisy arguments, then near-fistfights averted only when Carrigan separated them. Straining against his reincarceration, Ruth schemed to escape into his nocturnal amusements. Once Carrigan turned his back just long enough to don a tie; when he looked around the Babe had disappeared. Carrigan spent half the night looking for him. The manager tried his sternest lectures: How would Ruth like it if he stood him up in a team meeting as a player whose misbehavior was costing the Red Sox victories? The Babe promised to behave, but did not. Carrigan next withheld his pay and doled out an allowance of ten dollars a week, supposing that "he couldn't have much of a fling on that amount." That helped a little.

His play on the field would have made the most exasperated manager unreasonably patient. Twenty years old in 1915, he won 18 games, snapping off an unhittable "hook ball" that curled around the edges of the plate. Opposing batters hit just .212 against him, ranking Ruth second in the league to Dutch Leonard. And his hitting foreshadowed baseball's future: in only 92 at-bats, he hit .315 with 4 home runs (three less than the league leader, who had come to bat four times more often) and a slugging percentage of .576 (85 points above the official league leader). In spring training the next year, with Boston's peerless center fielder Tris Speaker holding out, Carrigan thought about switching Ruth to the outfield. But he pitched even better in 1916, with 23 wins, and led the league in shutouts, earned-run average, and opponents' batting average. A year later, he won 24 games and ranked among the league's best pitchers in a half dozen categories. He pitched too well, apparently, to be converted to everyday play in the field.

When his pitching clashed with swinging the bat, though, Ruth preferred to hit. He raged at Carrigan one day; after he had stroked four straight doubles he was ordered to strike out in the top of the ninth to save himself for protecting a slim lead. Whiffing on purpose was intolerable for a man so intent on his passions who so lusted to hit. "I just love to take a swing at that old pill," he gushed. "There's nothing that feels so sweet as a good, solid smash." He announced during the winter of 1918 that he wanted to play every game, perhaps at first base. "When I drive the ball I like to see it sail," said Ruth. "I want to see what I can do with that old batting average."

The world war finally gave Ruth his chance. With left fielder Duffy Lewis and others lost to military service, the Sox were shorthanded. Ruth kept asking to play in the field. "I would be the laughingstock of the league," said the team's new manager, Ed Barrow, "if I took the best left handed pitcher in the league and put him in the outfield." A rarity among managers, Barrow had never played organized baseball. To the Red Sox he seemed not one of their own, a permanent outsider. "He did not know baseball from a player's point of view," Harry Hooper, the center fielder and team captain, said later, "and he let me run the club on the field." Hooper pushed Barrow to use Ruth every day, clinching his case by predicting the slugger would attract more paying fans in that lean wartime season of 1918. Given management's fondness for clicking turnstiles, Barrow at last gave in, skeptically. "Mark my word," said Barrow to Hooper, "the first time he gets in a slump he will be down on his knees begging to pitch."

In early May, pitching and playing first, Ruth hit three homers in three games, then—a month later—four in four games. "Babe Ruth has us all aglow over his prodigious home-run hitting," the *Boston Herald* reported. "Almost before the fan asks 'How'd the Sox come out?' he edges in with: 'Did Babe catch one? Was it a homer?'" Fans started cheering him during batting practice. In a doubleheader against the Browns, playing first, he drew five straight intentional walks. At center field against the Senators in Washington, another skein of three home runs in three games. "I was feeding him slow curves, and he obviously did not like them," Walter Johnson said later. "Frankly, I did not fear him. I had never seen a batter look worse, so I fed him another slow curve. A half-second later I heard a tremendous crash. Then I watched the ball shoot on a line into the bleachers. It was undoubtedly a beautiful drive. The Boston papers all commented on it." Over the last two months of the season, he pitched more—Barrow was asserting himself—and hit no additional homers. In 1919, his first season of playing more than one hundred games, he set a new major-league record of twenty-nine home runs: so grand a total that many doubted he could ever match it.

The next season, sold to the Yankees, he hit fifty-four. Still only twenty-five years old, he was becoming the Babe Ruth of legend, the most famous and recognizable athlete in American history. Fans could pick him out at once from any group of ballplayers on the field: the mincing, pigeon-toed gait, the belly starting to overflow his belt, the massive, rounded torso, the oversized head and the expressive moon of a face, with its great splatted nose and upturned nostrils. (If Ruth ever fell asleep out in the rain, said his teammate Joe Bush, he'd drown.) "His walk is not graceful," Lawrence Perry reported in the *New York Evening Post.* "He is not graceful. He gives one an impression of slothfulness, while his heavy features would not indicate impressive mental alertness. But when he takes his place at the plate a metamorphosis is affected. He is translated into the very embodiment of tigerish grace and energy." When he parked one, said Perry, "you experience the emotions of a man who has picked a winning horse at the race track." One excited fan at the Polo Grounds in 1920 witnessed Ruth's forty-third home run and fell dead from a heart attack.

For many enthusiasts—too many, according to baseball purists—he became the distracting game within the game, more compelling than the contest itself. F. C. Lane of *Baseball Magazine,* a most exacting purist, described a typical afternoon at the Polo Grounds during that breakthrough 1920 season. The game began when Ruth emerged for batting practice; early rooters shouted for him to send one to the bleachers. Settled in the Yankee bullpen for the game, Lane found even in that jaded company a preoccupation with the Babe. The crowd barely noticed when the Yankee shortstop made a difficult stop and throw on a scudding grounder, but roared lustily when Ruth caught an easy fly. "If he had dropped it," said a Yankee in the bullpen, "they would have yelled just as loud." Up to hit, Ruth lined a mere double down the right-field line, not enough to satisfy his admirers. Batting again in the last of the eighth, Ruth struck out, whereupon one third of the crowd, assuming that Ruth would not hit again that day, rose and went home. "Babe Ruth has overthrown all rivals, overturned all precedents," Lane conceded, "and now monopolizes the limelight of the game as no other player, past or present, has ever done."

On his model, baseball went airborne. During the 1920s the two major leagues averaged 1,030 home runs a season, up from 422 a decade earlier. Run production, slugging percentages, and batting averages also rose, though not as much, while stolen bases fell by half. The old "scientific" game of bunts, steals, and low scores was eclipsed. Baseball's rule makers helped by banning the spitter and other trick pitches, introducing a zippier ball with a cushioned-cork center, and insisting that dirty, scuffed balls be replaced during the game. ("Don't think there's much change in the ball," the Babe commented. "Thing that's helped is throwin' so many new ones. Fella can see 'em now.") The game took to the air because of Ruth's thunderous example. Other batters picked up his favorite heavy, long-handled bats, with the weight mainly in the head and a thin handle that allowed a strangling grip. "The boys have nearly all changed their way of hittin' now," said the Babe. "Used to choke their bats. Now they swing from the hips." But none of the imitators approached Ruth's nearly annual feats. He hit 35 more homers than his nearest league rival in 1920, 35 more again in 1921, 19 more in 1924, 28 more in 1926, 27 more in 1928. Even in the new long-ball era he had forced, Ruth still stood alone.

How did he do it? What particular gifts placed him so far beyond every other ballplayer of his time? "I can't explain him," said his Boston teammate Chet Thomas. "Nobody can explain him. He just exists." Many contemporaries described him as a favored child of nature, unaware and unseeing, offhandedly smiting the ball without the need or knack to think about it. "He was like a damn animal," said Rube Bressler, a National League outfielder. "He had that instinct. They know when it's going to rain, things like that. Nature, that was Ruth!" His usual answers to probing journalists fed the general impression of an uncluttered mind. "God knows," he would shrug to any hard question. Did such historical figures as Lincoln, Washington, or Napoleon interest him? "I've never seen any of them." Read any good books lately? "Reading isn't good for a ballplayer. Not good for his eyes. . . . So I gave up reading." Addressing the world as "kid" (pronounced "keed"), he could not seem even to learn anyone's first name. For more than ten years the pitcher Waite Hoyt played with Ruth in Boston and New York. They dressed at adjacent lockers. They caroused and squabbled and made up together. When Hoyt was traded to the Tigers in 1930, the Babe shook his hand and said, "So long, Walter."

Ruth's unwearied pursuit of fun in all forms left an overpowering image of a child at mindless play. He chased pleasures too profligately, and caught them too often, to be taken seriously. His curt, dumb-sounding replies to reporters were often simple evasions to let him escape from a dreary, confining situation and be off into his adventures. He spent all his waking hours trying compulsively to amuse himself. He liked to drink a highball, smoke a cigar, and chew tobacco—all at once, doubtless to the overloaded confusion of his taste buds. "Ruth has the mind of a fifteen-year-old boy," president Ban Johnson declared from the league office. "The American League is no place for a player who dissipates and misbehaves."

What Johnson had especially in mind was the Babe's legendary sex life. Ruth was usually preoccupied, day to day, with plotting his next tryst or savoring his last one. Thinking about it so much, doing it so often, he must have learned a great deal about sex and women. He loved to discourse about them. But whatever he learned is, by the nature of the subject, now lost to history. His main interest outside baseball, the continual focus of his conscious mind, went unrecorded, thus feeding—again—the popular impression of Ruth as a nearly brain-dead chowderhead.

As a sexual gourmand, Ruth was not picky about where he chose to insert himself ("anything that had hair on it," according to a teammate). Understandably fond of his penis, he would often make phallic references in unrelated conversations. "I can knock the cock off any ball that's ever pitched," he would bray. Again, on the way to his hotel: "There will be a stack of mail for me as big as my penis." Or, regretting his billowing paunch: "The worst of this is that I no longer can see my penis when I stand up." It was evidently a remarkable instrument, not in size but in duration and frequency of use. An awed teammate recalled Ruth's unmatched capacity "to keep doing it all the time. He was continually with women, morning and night. I don't know how he kept going." "You never saw him," said his teammate Mark Koenig. "He was always up in the room with his girls." Once Ruth asked the sportswriter Richards Vidmer to come by his hotel suite around nine that evening. At the appointed time they drank and chatted for half an hour before Vidmer realized Ruth had a woman stashed in the bedroom.

"That's why I wanted you to come up," the Babe explained. "I thought I'd need a rest."

His friends learned to arrange themselves around his sexual intervals. Vidmer liked to recount the marathon bridge games in Ruth's room on the road. When the phone rang, Vidmer answered it. "Is Babe Ruth there?" "No, he's not here right now. This is his secretary. Can I tell him who called?" "This is Mildred. Tell him Mildred called." Vidmer would call out the woman's name; sometimes Ruth shook his head. "I'm sorry," in that case, "he's not here right now, but I'll tell him that you called." Before they hung up, though, Babe—unpracticed at saying no—would grab the phone and tell her to come up after all. Babe and Mildred would go into the other room while the cardplayers sat and talked for ten minutes or so. Then the loving couple would emerge, Babe would say "So long, kid," and the bridge game would resume.

According to Waite Hoyt, ballplayers talked more about Ruth's nocturnal feats—his stamina and resilience the next day—than about his home runs. He reminded Hoyt of a large, friendly dog padding around the locker room, hoping to be petted and forgiven without accounting for his recent whereabouts. "It became our custom, when Ruth entered the clubhouse," said Hoyt, "slyly to approach him, look in his eyes and discover the lights of adventure burning there. More often they were merely embers of adventure." Teammates often covered for his lapses. Then, with the ballgame at hand, Ruth would somehow gather himself, stir those embers, and go out to play, eyes clear and senses snapping. Lesser mates could only shake their heads, amazed and envious. "No human could have done the things he did and lived the way he lived and been a ball player," insisted Joe Dugan, the Yankee third baseman. "Hell, Babe Ruth wasn't born. The son of a bitch fell from a tree."

Again the child of nature: for no one so physically endowed could have had a brain too. Could he? People who didn't know him were inevitably surprised when he displayed any wisp of intelligence. He often made shrewd remarks, in private, about New York City and its politics. Facing an audience, Ruth was "probably the best extemporaneous talker in sports," said the sports columnist Joe Williams, not expecting anyone to believe him. "An astonishingly good after-dinner speaker," another observer agreed. "He has perfect poise and presence and a free flow of talk." Easily distracted and quickly bored, with a child's attention span, intellectually lazy and uncurious, Ruth nonetheless knew what he chose to know.

As a ballplayer, for example, he made himself adept at every phase of the game. Hitting might have come naturally to him, but baseball's more arcane skills had to be studied and learned. Not fleet afoot—despite all those clouts to the outer reaches, he never led the league in doubles or triples, and averaged only six stolen bases a year—he compensated on the base paths with smart decisions and deft slides. The umpire George Moriarty pronounced him "the most accomplished slider of any big man I ever saw." Tris Speaker, his first outfielding mentor on the Red Sox, later placed Ruth among the top half dozen defensive outfielders he'd seen. The Babe seemed never to miss the cutoff man or to throw to the wrong base. "The greatest throwing outfielder that I ever played with," said the infielder Joe Sewell. "When there was a man on first and the ball was hit to right field I just went over and put the bag between my feet. That ball would come out of right field on one hop, smack into my glove." The stands would ripple with incredulous laughter at some of his throws, so long and true. Afterward, if asked why he had made a given play, he would explain the options available to him and how he had settled on his choice. He stayed "amazingly well informed on baseball statistics" and could hold forth on other teams and players around the league. "I know that he read the New York newspapers with which I was associated," the sportswriter Fred Lieb recalled, "because he was quick to tell me what he didn't like about my coverage."

At bat, supremely in his element, relaxed and confident beyond arrogance, he was still thinking. "Babe is smart at bat," said his teammate Wally Pipp, careful to add the qualifying phrase, "and whether he admits it or not, he's doping out what the pitcher will give him." He noticed that Paul Zahniser of the Senators and Red Sox declared his pitches in the windup, lifting his hands high above his head for a fastball, but only to his eyes for a curve; so Ruth hit him hard. He learned to handle the high pitches and left-handers, the slow curves and change-ups that once had tormented him. In the batting cage at spring training, he asked for nothing but off-speed pitches. He adjusted. "He could always murder the ball," said Walter Johnson, "but he no longer bites at so many bad ones as he used to do." At first he used a clublike 54-ounce bat. (A typical big-league bat at the time weighed 36 to 40 ounces.) As time passed, and his reflexes imperceptibly slowed, he went to a lighter bat, losing about an ounce a year. By 1928 he was down to 46 ounces—light in his hands, if an unwieldable caber to any other batter.

A persistent interviewer could extract reasonable guesses from him about the secrets of his slugging. The quite persistent F. C. Lane followed him around the ballpark one afternoon. "Ruth is cursed with a perpetual impatience," Lane noted. "He is always in a hurry to get somewhere, it matters little where, so long as it is a different spot from the spot where he happens to be." So, Lane asked the Babe, how did he hit the ball so hard? Ruth scratched his head and ruminated ("the Babe is not over apt at self-analysis," Lane observed). "Well," he offered, "I am not a little guy." True enough; at six feet two inches and up to 256 pounds, he was one of the biggest ballplayers in his era. His father, said Ruth, "was an uncommon strong man and I suppose I inherited some of his strength and perhaps improved on it a little." But height and strength could not explain it, as Ruth pointed out: other ballplayers his size still could not match his slugging, and the boxer Jack Dempsey would flatten even a heavier opponent in the ring.

At that Ruth digressed into his own early ambitions toward prizefighting. "The mind of the big slugger is apt to wander into other channels," Lane noticed, bringing the Babe back to hitting by mentioning his oversized bat. "They tell me I swing the heaviest club in baseball," said Ruth, brightening. "It's really the weight of the bat that drives the ball and I like a heavy bat." He clutched the handle as tightly as he could, following advice given him by Cactus Cravath, the top National League slugger of the 1910s. "The harder you grip the bat the faster the ball will travel," Ruth explained. "When I am out after a homer, I try to make mush of this solid ash handle." He showed his grip to Lane: the muscles on the backs of his hands stood out in knobs and bunches, and his fingers looked embedded in the wood.

With the heavy bat, the steely grip, and his own strength behind it, said Ruth, "the bat overcomes all the resistance of the ball and keeps right on moving after it has struck."

So Ruth did think about his hitting—yet he was probably no more thoughtful than most ballplayers. He had the advantages of height and heft—yet he was no bigger than some others. None of this really explains the mystery of his home-run prodigies. "His eyes," the sportswriter John Kieran offered. "He could read license plate numbers so far away that I couldn't even tell the color of the plate." The great second baseman Eddie Collins took a similar impression of Ruth's eyesight from his duck-hunting trips with the Babe: "We'd be sitting in a duck blind, staring at an empty sky, when suddenly the Babe would slap his gun and remark, 'Well, here they come.' The rest of us would look at the horizon and see nothing. Then, in a couple of minutes, we'd spot the ducks in the distance. But Ruth would always see them first." Perhaps, then, he hit better because he saw better.

In addition, his reflexes and coordination matched his binocular eyes. During the 1921 season—when he hit .378 with 59 homers, 171 RBIs, and an otherworldly slugging percentage of .846, 240 points more than the next guy's—he submitted to three hours of testing at Columbia University's psychology research lab. He jabbed a stylus into a series of holes, tapped a plate as fast as he could, pressed a key when bulbs flashed, read letters as they were blinked at him, counted dots on flash cards, and identified different symbols on other cards. From these tests the psychologists concluded that Ruth's eyes were 12 percent faster than average, his ears 10 percent faster, his intelligence 10 percent above normal; in attention and speed of perception he was 150 percent beyond average; and, overall, he was "90% efficient compared with a human average of 60%," whatever that meant. Clearly a man of rare gifts: a natural, with a functioning brain.

One further explanation may be submitted. Generations of coaches have reassured their charges by claiming that opponents, however formidable, put their pants on one leg at a time, just like everybody else; nothing to worry about. One day a sportswriter watched the Babe dress for a game. He donned his white socks and the long blue woolen hose with the stirrups. Then, before the baffled sportswriter, he turned his pants inside out and lay them on the floor. He pushed both feet through the bottoms of the legs and pulled the legs, from the bottom, up to his knees. Rolling the ends of the legs together with the upper edge of his blue hose, he then took the belted end of the pants and drew them up his legs, turning them right side out in the process. Here was the Babe's real secret: he put his pants on both legs at once.

◆   ◆   ◆

Sports history unreels around a circle, not down a line. The games change in cycles, responding to constant tinkering adjustments, moving back and forth within long-established parameters. "In baseball," said A. H. Tarvin, a veteran sportswriter, in 1936, "nothing occurs that hasn't occurred at least once before—in most cases, many times before." The jump shot, forward pass, and home run all transformed their games, yet in a longer sense merely returned those sports to earlier days. Going airborne finally landed the ballgames back in their pasts. Sports time defies the calendar.

Jump shooters helped basketball recover the open, fluid, inventive play of its beginnings. "Very early in the game, the fast break was tried by all teams," recalled Purdue's coach Piggy Lambert, whose basketball memories went back to the YMCA in Crawfordsville, Indiana in 1897. "There were no set formations. . . . Back in those days, before coaching began to standardize methods of passing and shooting, we saw all types of passes and shots at the basket. Many players used the one-handed shot." The later orthodox style—of ball control, deliberate pace, floor position, short passes, endless weaving, and two-handed set shots—was promoted in the Northeast by such teams as the Buffalo Germans, the Philadelphia SPHAS, and especially the New York Original Celtics, and was then taught elsewhere in the country by coaches impressed with the barnstorming success of the Celtics. But that style of play was never as universal as basketball writers, concentrated in the Northeast, made it seem. Even at the height of the Northeast orthodoxy, in the 1920s and 1930s, teams in the South and West were playing a faster, rougher game, with more fast breaks and running, more varied shots and higher scores. It was no accident that most of the jump-shot pioneers came from outside the Northeast. After the advent of the jumper, even New York adopted the style that other parts of the country had been playing all along—the more open game of the 1890s.

When football first evolved from rugby in the 1870s, the players were spread widely across the gridiron, with lots of open-field running, kicks, and passed-ball exchanges: amounting to spirited, unpredictable action for both players and fans. "It was not unusual," said one veteran, "for the ball to be passed from player to player after a scrimmage until a touchdown or field goal was made." From the 1880s on, massed formations and wedge plays changed football to a dreary series of dull, slogging collisions, with all the players grouped near the ball, and little scoring or visible activity. Football had become deadly boring, and just plain deadly, killing twenty-three players in 1905, then thirty in 1909. The game had to change back. The sudden flurry after 1906 of new rules intended to save football, especially the introduction of forward passing, yielded "a game of more brilliant possibilities," said Walter Camp, football's main arbiter, "less severe pounding, more strategy and of a generally far more open character." Eventually Benny Friedman showed the full potential of airborne football, and the game reverted for good.

Babe Ruth also brought *his* game back to an older style. Only three ballplayers—Billy Hamilton, Harry Stovey, and George Gore—have ever wound up their careers with more runs scored than games played, and all three played in the 1880s and 1890s. Scoring exploded after pitchers were moved back from fifty feet to sixty feet six inches from home plate before the 1893 season. The National League's aggregate batting average jumped from .245 to .280, then to .309 in 1894. The most coveted big leaguer then was a tall, heavy slugger who swung hard, from the end of the bat. "When I broke into the game," recalled John McGraw, five feet seven inches and 155 pounds of punchy pugnacity, "I was considered a freak. . . . Unless a man was a six footer and husky to boot, he wouldn't command much attention as a player. Size and weight were supposed to be necessary because a ball player in those days was primarily a batter, and the bigger a man was the harder he could hit. It was rather primitive reasoning." McGraw and his Baltimore Orioles popularized the newly fashionable "scientific baseball," a game of carefully placed singles, of bunts and steals, hit-and-runs, foot speed, and overwhelming pitching. "Push, poke, shove and chop," as Johnny Evers, one of its masters, described the new style. Scoring plummeted from a National League record of 14.7 runs a game in 1894 down to only 6.7 in 1908. "The passing of the home run hitters was a good thing," McGraw was sure, "for it made the game faster and flashier." But when Babe Ruth appeared, fans at once made clear their preference for airborne baseball. The game returned to slugging and action.

Seen in long perspectives, then, all three of these sports have been at their cores quite stable and therefore familiar. "Nuthin's new in baseball," said the veteran umpire Bill Stewart in 1955. Again and again, an apparent innovation simply returns the game to an earlier time. "I haven't seen a new football play since I was in high school," said Red Grange after fifty years of playing and watching the game. "When they brought out the I formation, somebody asked me if I'd ever seen it before. Well, yes, we used it in the eighth grade. We called it the tandem formation." Most fans and ballplayers, afflicted with short memories and seeing only the games at hand right now, miss the long-term continuities—and so miss a basic cause of their devotion. Everything else in American life changes. We believe in Progress. Our games offer a high, dry rock in the swiftly flowing stream.

Chapter Two

Fans:
A Sense of Belonging

✳

The nation of fans stretches from Nuf Ced McGreevy's saloon to Roger Angell's interior stadium. McGreevy was a primary fan: sport suffused the air he breathed, inflating an impregnable bubble that hovered around him, unbidden, wherever he went. He rooted simply, directly, unconcerned with larger implications. Angell, more complex, was a secondary fan. For him the bubble might be deflated and put away, then restored at will, depending on the company and circumstances. He loved the game and his heroes as passionately as McGreevy did; but he puzzled over— and finally hung his devotion on—those larger implications. Most fans partake of both McGreevy and Angell, in variable proportions. The two, between them, define the terrain for big-league rooters.

Michael T. McGreevy—"patron of all arts and letters that cluster about baseball," according to a contemporary, "and grand exalted ruler of Rooters Row"—ran a saloon and liquor business in Boston at the turn of the twentieth century. His bar, called Third Base, allowed him the freedom and pretext to exult at will in the fortunes of Boston's two major-league baseball teams. Located in the Roxbury section of the city, close to both the National League park on Columbus Avenue and the American League field on Huntington Avenue, Third Base was an overstuffed shrine to the game. A life-sized statue of a ballplayer in a Boston uniform, in full mustache, holding a bat, stood guard above the door. Inside, scattered among the inevitable spittoons, brass rail, and dark paneling, a random riot of noteworthy balls, bats, trophies, and baseball photographs covered the walls and ceiling. The lights, in globes that resembled overgrown baseballs, hung down from bats donated by famous ballplayers such as King Kelly, Cy Young, and Nap Lajoie. The clock behind the bar kept baseball time with a bat-and-ball pendulum. The patrons and the conversation generally circled back to baseball.

Here McGreevy presided, utterly where he belonged, safe at home. He was a small man of medium build and mild disposition, jug-eared and droopily mustached, balding and therefore usually photographed with a hat on; but nobody doubted his authority at Third Base. To seal an argument or separate combatants he would proclaim, " 'Nough said," and that perforce was that. The phrase became his nickname. As an advocate of simplified spelling—an endlessly debated reform in this era of reforms—he rendered it as "Nuf Ced." (In the same endeavor, he changed his name from McGreevey to McGreevy, though the sign outside Third Base retained the original version.)

Nuf Ced inhabited a tight little masculine world, bounded by baseball and politics, lubricated by drink. "Baseball flourishes in Roxbury as in no other section of the town," a Boston newspaper observed in 1908. "That is natural, for baseball and politics go hand in hand—in Roxbury." Ballplayers and Ward 18's politicians mingled easily at Third Base with cops and gamblers. In the neighboring Ward 17, James Michael Curley—the defining Boston politician of his time—was starting his noisy political ascent. McGreevy spent his whole life on this narrow, familiar turf. Born in Roxbury of Irish immigrants, he had grown up with baseball, playing third base in the town leagues at Roxbury's Washington Park. He rooted for the Boston team that won consecutive National League pennants in 1877 and 1878, the team led by King Kelly and John Clarkson in the 1880s, the team that won five pennants in the 1890s. His love for baseball led naturally to the liquor business. "An active interest in athletic exercise," said Boston's Mayor Josiah Quincy in 1899, "and the practice of it, tends to keep a person out of evil paths." Nuf Ced and his friends knew better: for them, sports, saloons, and Irish politics meshed in a seamless culture apparently immune to well-born WASP reformers like Mayor Quincy.

McGreevy's world prospered with the Boston teams until 1920, when the double crime of Prohibition and the evisceration of the Red Sox by a treacherous owner slammed a curtain down. Third Base, raucous echoes and all, became—cruel fate—a mere branch of the public library. Both Boston teams fell to the bottom of their leagues. Nuf Ced's hopes stirred briefly, reminiscently, in 1926, when the Red Sox brought Bill Carrigan, manager in their glory years of the 1910s, back from retirement. "He seldom lost an argument in the old days," McGreevy explained, "because he was generally right when he started arguing." Carrigan then guided the Sox to three more last-place finishes and retired for good. In 1930, sixty-five years old, McGreevy ventured to an Old-timers' Game at Braves Field. Memories flooded back: Jimmy Collins stooping for a ball, Candy LaChance's grin, Freddy Parent sitting astride his bat on deck, Hobe Ferris pulling up his pants, Harry Hooper running, Fred Tenney's backhand stab at first. "What a kick, what a thrill," said McGreevy. "I felt 25 years younger when I saw the old-time stars coming to bat and showing their old-time stuff and old, familiar habits. I want to see them all again." Nuf Ced could only keen over the old days and ways. Without the booked-up saloon or a winning team to cheer for, his devotion dwindled into nostalgia. A primary fan remains ever vulnerable to circumstances beyond anybody's control.

While McGreevy was nursing his memories and losing interest, young Roger Angell, seven years old, went to his first game at Yankee Stadium with his father. (He was impressed—"a very clear memory"—by Babe Ruth's new yellow glove.) For every weary old fan in eclipse, a fresh new fan is born. Seasons turn and the games are renewed. Young Angell lived with his divorced father and older sister in a brownstone on East Ninety-third Street in Manhattan. The father, an ever-young baseball player and fan, took Roger to see the Yankees and Giants and—of course—played catch with the boy. Inspired by Carl

Hubbell of the Giants, his first baseball hero, Roger declared himself a pitcher. At a summer place a few miles up the Hudson River, father and son played long games of pitch and catch fortified by an ancient shed for a backstop; if Roger threw a hard one that popped his glove with authority, the father would nod in silent approval. Roger developed a sweeping curve and even— almost—a difficult screwball, in the Hubble manner. One cold spring day at school he tried a screwball and wrecked his arm, ending his big-league dreams. "I fanned a batter here and there," he said later, "but took up smoking and irony in self-defense. A short career."

He played the game, and went to games, but in particular he read and imagined baseball: his literary tendencies already manifest. With no TV and few games on the radio, a fan in the 1930s had to follow the sport in print. Angell read *Baseball Magazine,* a faithful monthly in a red cover, and the sports sections of four daily newspapers. He started at nine or ten with the box scores, savoring the amazing names never encountered anywhere else: Mel Ott, George Pipgras, Eppa Rixey, Firpo Marberry, Heinie Manush, and (a spray of trumpets) Van Lingle Mungo. Soon he moved on to the bylined sportswriters in the New York dailies, settling on Richards Vidmer of the *Herald Tribune* as his favorite. By 1932 "I was living in the sports pages." All sixteen big-league teams became familiar to him; the powerful Tigers of 1934 and 1935, who swatted aside his Yankees, remained fearsome memories. Yet baseball in no sense dominated his childhood. It merely took a favored place along with other sports, politics, theater and movies, pet animals, and (above all) reading: the usual range of a bookish, urban kid in favored circumstances.

After college and the war Angell settled into a career of editing and writing in Manhattan. For years he seldom wrote about sports. Still an occasional fan, he was driven to uncharacteristic hyperbole by Bobby Thomson's pennant-winning homer in 1951 ("the Greatest Moment in the History of Mankind"). The following spring, he endured the retirement of Joe DiMaggio, "my boy, my nonpareil, my hero." DiMaggio was the first blockbuster rookie to join a New York team after Angell had reached full baseball consciousness. Angell had always checked his name first in the box scores, and then at the end had witnessed his last feat, his double in the eighth inning of the final World Series game in 1951. Angell had watched his whole ballplaying cycle, from rookie to legend to fading veteran. Now he was gone, and base-ball seemed diminished to Angell. The new ballplayers of the 1950s looked by comparison too bland, too much alike, without the star qualities and rough-edged idiosyncrasies of his old he-roes. Then—a cruel, incredible blow—in August 1957 his Giants announced their intended departure to San Francisco. "The End of the World," Angell proclaimed, not exaggerating by much. "I still can't believe it. Me, a Giants fan and therefore accustomed to believing anything." In a sinking gesture of loyalty, he went to the final game at the Polo Grounds, bringing his nine-year-old daughter to her first big-league game—an ironic recapitulation of his own encounter with Babe Ruth's yellow glove, thirty years earlier. The Giants lost, 9–1. The crowd, half filling the stands, was the most subdued he'd ever heard at a game. Afterward, he recalled, "I didn't feel anything—nothing at all."

During these years his most serious literary efforts were oc-casional short pieces of fiction, published in *The New Yorker*. Mostly in a minor key, mostly about affluent, suburban, martini-drinking *New Yorker* types, they were stories of loss, ennui, muf-fled feelings and missed connections, dealing with maturation and stages of life, describing complex, ambiguous family ties. In light of Angell's later career, the most remarkable aspect of these stories was that baseball hardly appeared in them. A son refers to meeting his father for a ballgame; somebody from a train win-dow glimpses three boys playing catch; suburban sons on the phone with their father tell him the score of the game they're watching. That was all—except for three stories about Gloria Kernochan, a devout Giants fan in a frowsy bar on the West Side of Manhattan. She drinks too much, plays baseball trivia with Herman the bartender ("My one true friend"), and sinks into besotted memories of the Giants of the 1930s. On Opening Day she wears a celebratory gardenia corsage and a straw hat with red cherries. "I thought it would never end, this winter," she says. "All those fat wrestlers and those skinny basketball players with the gland trouble." In Angell's genteel fictional world of the 1950s, only someone like Gloria Kernochan—working-class, be-fogged, unaware of realms beyond her West Side bar—was a true baseball fan. For the other characters, sophisticates more like Angell himself, baseball did not much matter.

Finally, in his forties, he turned back to baseball and found his métier. The following events—the context for this shift— overlapped in time, and no clear sequence of cause and effect may be inferred. It appears that writing baseball in some sense rescued him from a middle-age crisis. In the summer of 1963 he divorced his wife of twenty-one years; their daughters were then twelve and fifteen years old. "The girls are old enough to feel the breakup very deeply," Angell's stepfather, E. B. White, noted at the time. A few months later Angell married a woman he had met at *The New Yorker,* where he had worked as a fiction editor since 1956. His domestic upheavals mirrored the politics of the time. A political liberal, he felt challenged and rebuked by the eruptions of the 1960s. "I have few long-term convictions," he wrote for a college reunion. "Like so many people I know, I keep telling myself I should be of more use. I would like to get with it, to be more busily on the side of change, which is the side that has chosen us all. But most of the big questions that bite me seem so clearly to demand the services of experts, officeholders, and the injured that I often hang back. I can't escape the feeling that greater involvement would be self-warming and secretly misan-thropic." He was looking for a new ballgame.

When William Shawn, the venerated editor of *The New Yorker,* first suggested that Angell try a baseball piece, he balked and wor-ried. He didn't know anybody in the game, and few ballplayers had even heard of *The New Yorker.* An outsider, he felt nervous about venturing into clubhouses and asking dumb questions. He was not, could never become, a typical sportswriter. Once, at a spring-training game, he pointed out a migration of Canada geese in the far distance—causing his neighbors in the press box to miss the catcher picking a runner off third. He took co-pious notes on every tiny detail, to the amusement of his fellow scribes. As a sportswriting stylist, he at first betrayed too much of a highfalutin' *New Yorker* influence. "The San Francisco *equipe* is a genetically pure descendant of its dichotomous, death-loving, strong-jawed forebears," he wrote, early on. "When one sees troops with such qualities brought into battle against the massed fieldpieces of the Yankees, one is filled with the same pride, foreboding, and strong desire to avert one's eyes that was felt by the late General Pickett." (The late General Pickett had died in 1875.) These problems aside, though, Angell was a natural. His prose, so spare and restrained in his fiction, became exuberant and playful when applied to baseball; he was having fun.

Over the next three decades, Angell produced the most distinguished body of writing yet published on any major-league sport. Unlike Nuf Ced McGreevy—or Gloria Kernochan—he inhabited a world of vast horizons and high culture, with literary weekdays in Manhattan, weekends in the country, and summers in Maine. At *The New Yorker* he continued to edit some of the best writers of his time. On his office walls hung pictures of the authors V. S. Pritchett, Frank Sullivan, and E. B. White, and of Jim Palmer, the great Orioles pitcher. "Baseball is pretty far from what goes on here," Angell allowed. "One of the great pleasures of writing about baseball is that it provides me with such a radical change." In his baseball pieces he insisted on the primacy of the game itself. He did not, he said, just sit in his office thinking deep thoughts about baseball. But as a secondary fan, he was drawn despite himself toward what the games meant.

◆　　◆　　◆

Primary fans want mainly to cheer on the good guys, the home team. In cheering they also enjoy themselves, feel the gusty release of clapping and yelling, and appreciate the beauty of watching difficult athletic feats performed under pressure. But these are effects, not causes, of what pulls them most strongly to the grandstands, broadcasts, and sports pages: they want to win, and by their devotion they expect to push their team to victory.

To nonfans, the act of rooting looks suspiciously passive and lazy, with all that sitting around, the watching and waiting, the lack of purposeful activity. "Our professional baseball, with its paid players and its thousands of smoking, and sometimes umpire-mobbing, spectators, is doing more harm than good," said a skeptic in 1898. "The spectators are wasting two or three hours of fresh air and sunshine looking at what they ought to be doing." Actually, various studies have found connections between playing sports and watching them. One inspires the other, a reciprocal influence. Having enjoyed the childhood games, adult fans then like to watch them played at pinnacle levels of skill and courage under duress.

Nuf Ced McGreevy was considered "one of the best all-round athletes of his age to be found in Boston." He swam in the ocean every day all winter ("You are not the first one to tell me that I am crazy," he conceded), would bowl at the alley next to his bar, met all comers at handball, and played baseball well into middle age with his own semipro team in the Roxbury League. On spring-training trips with the Red Sox, he was granted a uniform and worked out, in his fashion, with the team. At Hot Springs, Arkansas, in 1906, bedecked in white shoes, blue stockings, a blue shirt, "a dinkey red cap and a smile," he set himself to "doing all sorts of stunts except catching the ball." Placed out of harm's way in right field, he chased a long clout over his head, encountered a patch of mud, flew into a gorgeous dive, and came to rest with sticky yellow clay covering his face. Not a bit discouraged, only forty-one years old, he applied for a place on the team. "I am a good handball player," he deadpanned, "and I have an idea that I can play baseball equally well." Why, he would even shave his mustache to look younger! "We are from Missouri," said the Sox manager. "You are all good players on the train, but it is what you can do on the field that counts." McGreevy was consoled with bogus telegrams from three different teams offering pro contracts. He could, in fact, play passably: once the manager of the Natchez team in the Cotton State League watched him disporting with the Sox and offered to buy "that little fellow with the mustache." The Sox owner "sold" him on the spot for three hundred dollars. His fervent rooting comprised only part of his rounded baseball life.

Rooting is essentially active, not passive. The ballplayers know they are being watched and measured by an exacting audience. Proud of their special skills, wary of public embarrassment, they want desperately to impress and please the fans. "Couldn't wait to get to the ball park and grab that bat," said Lefty O'Doul, who hit .349 over eleven seasons. "Big crowd, sock a triple, nothing like it! Maybe I was a ham. What's the use of doing something when nobody's looking? But a packed ball park, crowd roaring, the guy throws you a great breaking curve, you hit it on the nose and drive it over the outfielder's head. What a thrill!" Jeers might motivate an athlete as sharply as cheers. Hank Greenberg, the best Jewish baseball player of the 1930s, endured more than his share of ethnic insults. As a free-swinging slugger and clumsy fielder, he often heard from the fans about his strikeouts and fielding errors. Sometimes, when the anti-Semitic slurs came cascading down, he bristled and wished he could go fight the abusers. Yet "I found it to be a big help," he said in retrospect. "It would always hit me like a cold shower. It would make me angry, but it would also put me on my toes again. Just *anticipating* a barb from the stands did the same thing."

Management, ever conscious of who paid the bills, also hoped to keep the fans happy—if not with a winning team, then at least with popular ballplayers. The New York Yankees in their early years won no pennants and offered only one legitimate star, Wee Willie Keeler, all five feet four and a half inches and 140 pounds of him. One of the legendary Baltimore Orioles of the 1890s— when he had won batting titles with averages of .385 and .424—he still ranked among the best hitters in the American League. Fans loved his adroitly placed hits and sawed-off scrappiness. So, when a National League club proposed a trade, Frank Farrell, one of the Yankee owners, replied in garbled indignation. "He is the mainstay of my club," said Farrell, "and, were I to let him go, it would be a case of my closing the gates and retiring from business. He is a great favorite here in New York and by me disposing of his services, it would certainly put me in bad with my patrons. Besides there is no power on earth that could get him out of the American League." Keeler finished his career in New York.

A truly engaged fan may expect to influence plays even at a distance of thousands of miles, even when not watching or listening to the game. "Any Believer knows that it *does* happen," insisted William Goldman, the screenwriter and novelist. Goldman had become an immoderate fan when, as a kid in Chicago, he had seen DiMaggio hit a double off the center-field wall of Comiskey Park. His uncle Victor—"the first genuine sports nut I ever knew"—had followed the Chicago Bears since the 1920s, always raving about the superhuman rushing of the great fullback Bronko Nagurski. At Uncle Victor's endless urging, Bill

Goldman and his family started attending Bears games in 1940, three years after Nagurski's retirement. No matter what they saw Sid Luckman or Sammy Baugh or Don Hutson do on the field, Uncle Victor would always say, "You should have seen Nagurski." Goldman came to doubt the refrain. Could Nagurski have been *that* good? Then in 1943, with the Bears in wartime straits, Nagurski came back—just to play tackle, not to carry the ball. Came the last game of the year, which the Bears needed to win to play for the title. Late in the third quarter, the Bears down by ten, their regular fullback was hurt. The great Nagurski trotted slowly out to the huddle. Uncle Victor screamed and pounded Goldman's back, predicting renewed wonders. On the first snap, Nagurski plunged into the line and was apparently stopped for no gain. Goldman turned away, flinching from this sad denouement for the faded star. But the referee marked a four-yard gain. "He sort of fell forward," the guy next to Goldman explained. In that fourth quarter, Nagurski, thirty-five years old, carried sixteen times for eighty-four yards and led the Bears to victory. "Basically the high point of my life," Goldman said decades later, after winning Oscars for *Butch Cassidy and the Sundance Kid* and *All the President's Men*. "The only time, I suppose, anybody ever came through under pressure."

Given that initiation, Goldman believed in the elusive magic of rooting. A literate, civilized man, he lived in New York and cracked jokes about squishily mindless Californians, his movie associates. But "the only subject besides Hollywood that I'm interested in," he insisted, to the peril of his intellectual credentials, "is sports." Sitting through a movie meeting in Los Angeles, he carefully did not watch the silent TV showing a game with his Mets. It was important not to try too hard, not to strain in hubris. Turning, ever so casually, just to glance at the TV, he saw Darryl Strawberry of the Mets hit a home run ("I had gotten Strawberry the homer," he figured). Once out of the meeting, he avoided news of the game until he guessed it was over. Alas, with two outs in the ninth and the Mets up by three runs, some fool called him and amiably mentioned the situation to Goldman. When the Mets were therefore tied in the ninth and beaten in ten, Goldman felt responsible. A fan's power remained so unknowable: your team might lose if you were watching, or if you weren't; if you cared too much, or too little. Who could tell? Goldman could never predict "when I am on my game," he said, "when I am controlling major events around the country, which I can do, I just don't know when." (Actually the point was *not* to know or control. That kept the game interesting.)

When a fan tried too hard, devotion slid over into hero worship, a zombied deification of ordinary mortals. A fan must keep a readiness to boo and bewail. Nuf Ced McGreevy scorned "the worst pest in the family of fans," a type he saw lingering around hotels and ballparks. From his contacts at Third Base, where the ballplayers restored themselves after games, and from his spring-training larks, he knew the athletes as just ordinary oafs off the field with extraordinary skills on it. But the deifiers knew ballplayers only at a reverential distance. McGreevy noticed a certain fan in Pittsburgh who sat near first base and always tried to shake hands with players as they left the field. Once, reaching for a hand, he fell over and cracked his head. (Served him right, McGreevy thought.) At the hotel this fan lay in wait, sending his card, craving the slightest wisp of recognition from men he knew not at all. "I made up my mind," McGreevy concluded, "he was no more than the ordinary class of crank whom some people term a fan."

Consider Woody Allen's adoration of Earl Monroe. Allen first noticed him in 1968, when—a longtime fan of baseball and boxing—he started following basketball too. (The Knicks that year managed a winning record for the first time since 1959; they had not made it easy to become an NBA enthusiast in New York.) When Monroe, then with the Baltimore Bullets, played in New York, Allen rooted for him against the Knicks. "What makes Monroe different," declared Allen, "is the indescribable heat of genius that burns deep inside him." (Get hold of yourself, Woody.) "Some kind of diabolical intensity comes across his face when he has the ball. One is suddenly transported to a more primitive place. It's roots time. The eyes are big and white, the teeth flash, the nostrils flare. . . . The audience's 'high' originates inside Monroe and seems to emerge over his exterior. He creates a sense of danger in the arena and yet has enough wit in his style to bring off funny ideas when he wants to." (Well, yeah, maybe.) After Monroe was traded to the Knicks in 1971, Allen hoped his individual skills and flair would not be subordinated to the team-oriented style played by New York. "Is winning so important that we can afford to sacrifice Monroe's essential gift to the game of basketball?" Allen wondered. "Sacrifices must be made for art."

A few years later, assigned to write a Monroe profile for a sports magazine, Allen took himself firmly in hand and went to Monroe's home on the Upper West Side for a scheduled interview. Granted entrance by Monroe's girlfriend ("an unbelievably beautiful woman"), Allen waited for his hero to show. And waited. And waited. He learned from the girlfriend that Monroe liked to watch TV, eat fish, and read sports magazines. The conversation faded away. After several hours, Allen had to leave for another meeting. Was he annoyed, or disappointed in his hero? Not a bit: "I think to myself, how wonderful. This great athlete is so unconcerned about the usual nonsense of social protocol. Unimpressed by me, a cover interview and all the attendant fuss and adulation that so many people strive for, he simply fails to show up. Probably off playing tennis or fooling with his new Mercedes. Whatever he was doing, I admired him for his total unconcern." Being stood up merely confirmed the great man's stature, that he would slight a mere fan.

Push any enthusiasm too far and the blinders descend. Peripheral vision narrows down to tunnel vision, and enthusiasm crosses the line to obsession. The besetting puzzle for any primary fan is to maintain a sense of proportion. How to cheer without stint, flat out and full-bodied, and yet keep a balanced appreciation for the rest of life? Straddling this tension, male fans may risk the scorn of the women in their lives. After all, only men play in the big leagues; most of the fans who came to love sports by playing ball as kids were boys, not girls; sports pages, publications, and broadcasts are all pitched at men, with the bills paid by beer and car ads. The big leagues are atavistically, hopelessly a man's world. A woman outside this world may find it hostile, excluded by the arcane intricacies of male sports talk.

Yet this quite masculine domain has always harbored a small, growing feminine presence. As early as the 1850s, women showed up to watch baseball games in and around New York. "The ladies (God bless them!) turned out in large numbers," ran an account of a big game in 1858, "and many of them seemed to enter into the spirit of the game in a manner worthy of the most ardent devotees, betting kids [gloves] and other trifles on the result, and applauding heartily a good catch, a good run, and often a noble *attempt*." The first pro leagues after the Civil War attracted rowdy male crowds that smoked, drank, and cheered in unbuttoned masculine vernacular. Tim Keefe, a star pitcher of the 1880s, was so bowlegged that—it was said—his trousers were cut with a circular saw. "Behold!" shouted a Boston fan, HiHi Dixwell, on seeing Keefe pitch for the first time. "What manner of man is this, who carries his balls in parenthesis?" Cringing from such ejaculations, baseball management hoped to attract a more polite audience by making the ballparks agreeable to women. Some owners offered separate women's sections with curtained boxes and cushions. Here smoking was forbidden, and men might enter only if accompanied by a woman. "The ladies are regular and numerous attendants at the grounds," a scribe reported in 1885. "As they took their seats in the grand stand they brought out their score cards and pencils, argued over the merits of the coming players, and consulted little diaries, in which they had entered records of past League games."

Helen Robison Britton, the daughter and only child of a team owner, grew up at baseball games in Cleveland in the late nineteenth century. Her father, a streetcar magnate, owned two forgettable teams and then, after 1899, the St. Louis Cardinals. "I can honestly say that I have always loved baseball," she said later. "My father and uncles talked baseball ever since I can remember. My father early insisted that I should keep score and he didn't have to use any coercion. . . . It is really a fascinating pastime keeping score, and I often wonder if the people who fail to do it don't lose a great deal of the game that they would otherwise appreciate." As a child she played at baseball and tennis, shooting, swimming, and boating as well. After the deaths of her father and uncle, she became in 1911 the first woman to own and run a big-league team. One visitor to her office found "a well appointed, sunny room, with a lady at once keen, attentive, and charming of manner in the seat where you half expect to see the corpulent owner with a fat cigar in his mouth." A suffragist and feminist, she gave the most visible front-office jobs to men, including her husband, but she made the crucial decisions herself. "A woman's influence must inevitably have a refining influence over the game," she said, "and is certain to arouse interest in the sport among women. I hope to make baseball much more popular with women and girls."

The National League's seven other owners, accustomed to a separatist treehouse atmosphere, wondered what to make of Helen Britton. Representing the Cardinals at league meetings, she would sit, front and center, for the group photograph, a stylish intruder against a backdrop of vests and mustaches. They called her, ambivalently, Lady Bee. "I appreciate the fact that baseball is a man's game," she assured them; but she acted otherwise. When the Cardinals dropped to a distant sixth place, forty-one games out, in 1912, she sued to break her manager's contract, fired him, and gave Miller Huggins, her second baseman, his first managing job. He brought the team up to third place, only thirteen games out, in 1914. But her fellow owners tried to force her from baseball on some pretext; the fired manager had many friends in the game. She stayed on until her embarrassing divorce in 1917. (She testified that her husband drank too much, wasted her money, and once broke down the door when he came home late and found it locked.) A woman in baseball, perhaps; but a *divorced* woman in baseball? Retiring from the game, she sold the Cardinals to a safe group of men. "While increasingly popular from a spectator's standpoint, to the ladies," *Baseball Magazine,* noting the sale, declared for the relieved majority, "the business details and general management of a major league club are a man's work."

The double-edged legacy of Helen Britton showed up in the institution of Ladies' Day at the ballpark: women on the edges of baseball. On occasional weekday afternoons, when few paying customers were expected, women were admitted for free. Even without purchasing tickets, they still bought scorecards and refreshments. But they cheered oddly, inappropriately, unlike the regular fans, men and women, who paid their way in to other games. "The free ladies shriek like mad at a ball or strike," a Chicago sportswriter complained in 1930. "They squeal and cheer at a put-out on an easy fly ball that an armless blind man could gobble in his hip pocket. They go into ecstasies over a simple grounder nicely fielded and they go wild over a Cub foul that goes over the fence." They even giggled in unison at one batter who twitched his buttocks before each swing. Ballplayers, on the other hand, did not mind all this uncritical feminine adoration. "While the girls may cheer at anything," said one, "they are at least enthusiastic and add a lot of extra color to a ball game." "It develops new fans," said another, "and women are generally the best fans from a ballplayers' angle. By that I mean, plenty of cheering and no booing." To some ears, though, the random noise interfered with a proper appreciation of the game. Devout fans wanted to abolish Ladies' Days. "A scourge to the working newspaper man," said Stanley Woodward, a veteran scribe, in 1950. "The honeybuns [the what?], admitted free on the theory that they will get the habit and pay on other days, keep up a continual screeching which takes all the order out of baseball." Ladies' Days gradually disappeared during the 1950s.

Genuine women fans—the sort who came often and knew how to comment on developments—included three of the most famous baseball rooters of the 1930s and 1940s. By their trade-marks they were known: Mary Ott, cheering the Cardinals with her horselike neighing ("I like scientific rooting, something that helps the home boys win and makes the other guys sore. I figure if I really work on 'em, I can knock a lot of them pitchers out of the box in three innings"); Lolly Hopkins, traveling the forty-two miles from Providence for every Red Sox home game, raking the enemy through her megaphone; and Hilda Chester, the most celebrated woman fan ever, sustaining the Dodgers with her ever-clanging cowbell. Chester stood out even among the many loud eccentrics in the intimate cacophony of Ebbets Field. She had grown up on Manhattan's East Side, playing baseball with the neighborhood boys. Later she moved to Brooklyn, where she raised her family, sold newspapers, and held various sports-related jobs. "She is stout and pink faced," an amused observer noted in 1945, "with bright, darting eyes, longish gray hair fastened with a celluloid butterfly, and teeth so perfect and prominent that her lips seem always parted and shaped for speech." Though the Dodgers gave her a lifetime pass to the grandstand, she preferred the bleachers. "I can't relax in them fancy seats," she explained.

Waiting for the game to start, wearing a dark print dress and a black hat with a bow ribbon, Hilda Chester looked subdued and maternal, sitting quietly with her hands folded in her lap. The first pitch transformed her. Already substantial, her body grew somehow larger as she bounced in her seat, the eyes distended, the rosy face purpling. She began a husky, exceedingly audible commentary: *"Slow, Ed. . . . Strike!* That's *your* hit! . . . Take yer time, pitcha. . . . God save the King! Hey, King, never mind that blonde over there. . . . *Strike!* That's *your* hit! Strike him out! . . . Don't make no errors, now! Oh-h-h—wotta joik! . . . Ain't it t'ril-lin'? Ah-hah-hah-HAH!" For particular emphasis, she picked up the large brass bell, a gift from the Dodgers, that she kept at her feet. She waved it over her head, clanged it to different rhythms, switched it from hand to hand as she tired. "Make wit' da bell, Hilda!" the fans would yell. "Woik, Hilda, *woik!*" In full deployment she sounded like a small fire engine racing to an emergency.

She especially doted on Leo Durocher, the misbehaving Dodger manager. "Leo is very democratic," she purred. "He always says hello to me." Once he even unwittingly followed her bidding. At the start of the seventh inning of a game in the early 1940s, she called to Pete Reiser as he ran out to his place in center field. ("There could be 30,000 people there yelling at once," Reiser said later, "but Hilda was the one you'd hear.") She dropped him a note for Durocher, which he picked up and stuck in his pocket. The inning over, Reiser ran in, said hello to Larry MacPhail, the Dodgers' general manager, who was sitting by the dugout, and gave the note to Durocher. Assuming the note came from MacPhail—since Reiser had just spoken to him—Durocher read it and soon, as ordered, removed his starting pitcher, who was breezing along. The reliever was shelled and the Dodgers almost lost the game. Afterward Durocher stalked into his office, slammed the door, finally emerged, and said to Reiser, "Don't you *ever* give me another note from MacPhail as long as you play for me." "That was from Hilda," said Reiser, not helping his manager's sulfurous mood. It was a primary fan's dream: to send instructions, *heeded* instructions, to the dope in the dugout.

The sprinkling of women in the stands at baseball games in the 1880s grew to about 10 percent of the crowd in the 1910s and to 35 percent by the 1980s. About the same proportion of women came to basketball games, but many fewer to football games. The violence of football, the cluttered, obscured action when the lines collided, and the severe weather of late fall kept many women from becoming NFL fans. For the same reasons in reverse, women did take to basketball: the action was fast and exciting but not brutal, quite visible and easily understood by newcomers to sports, and the games were played indoors. An informal survey in 1956 found that Celtics fans at the Boston Garden were at least one-third women. Many of these female rooters had played basketball when younger; they had never played baseball or football. They liked the intimate scale of basketball, with all the fans near the action, in a closed building that echoed and contained the noise of rooting. "You feel you are part of the game," said one woman. "Baseball is too far away from the stands. In basketball you get to know the players and it seems like one big, happy family."

With their fans more involved in the game, basketball teams won 67 percent of their home games. The home advantage in baseball and football ran to only about 54 percent. In those two sports, ballplayers rested more often and could pace themselves through the game, needing less of an adrenaline jolt from their more distant fans. Given basketball's continuous, exhausting action, its athletes responded more dramatically to the bedlam of rooting. "It makes you give an extra effort," said Larry Bird. "If there's a rebound or a loose ball, *you* want to get it. The crowd keeps every player mentally in the game. If you're hot, you might make it a little more spectacular. Somebody will cut backdoor and you might put a little more zip on the pass. You might dive for loose balls you don't have much of a chance for, just for the fans. . . . I've always been conscious of having the fans involved. I'll use the press, if I can, to send a message to the crowd that we really need them in the next game. They all read the papers."

Fan support in the NBA might go far beyond polite yelling and clapping. The old Madison Square Garden had guy wires running from the baskets up to the balcony—so fans would shake the hoop when an enemy was shooting free throws. The early NBA included teams in small towns where the fans lay in ambush for anybody from *out there*. Red Auerbach told of a grisly game in 1949 between his Tri-Cities Blackhawks and the Duffy

Packers, the pride of Anderson, Indiana, population 46,820, a town about twenty-five miles west of Muncie. "The Packers' court was dark and dirty and the fans were dirtier," said Auerbach. "It took a solid combination of superior skill, luck and guts, especially guts, to beat the home side." As the teams huddled before the game, somebody from the crowd threw a cup of ice, opening a bloody cut over the right eye of a Blackhawk guard. Later a woman ran up to Auerbach, advised him that he stank, and threw a bag of popcorn in his face. At the end of the game, with the Blackhawks up by two points and fifteen seconds to go, a brave referee called a charge on the home team, sending it to defeat. The Blackhawks raced to the safety of the locker room. The referee, not as fast, was overtaken and clobbered. "I took a helluva chance," he complained to the Blackhawks later. "Where were you bums when I got clouted?"

Syracuse, New York, home of an NBA team until 1963, was so notoriously dangerous that visiting players were known to contract the "Syracuse flu" to escape having to play there. In this blue-collar town, the fans came to spew their frustrations against all comers, especially their hated, privileged downstate rivals from New York City. David used any weapon at hand against Goliath. Fights often flared among players, or between fans and referees. Once a woman in a front-row seat skewered a ref with her hatpin. The "Syracuse Strangler," a burly hooligan, lurked above the runway to the locker rooms, hoping to even scores with anyone who had offended him. Unfriendly calls were a hanging offense. The Strangler managed to hoist one referee by the neck, his feet dangling below, until help arrived.

To support their teams, NBA fans of the 1950s threw coins, bottles, eggs, lighted cigars, oranges, beer cans, bags of peanuts, fragrant fish, shoes, anything throwable. After a tough defeat in St. Louis, the losing coach lingered on the bench with his head bowed. From a dozen feet away, a triumphant sportsman hurled a rotten egg that splattered on the coach's forehead. ("I'm not an egg man at all," the coach protested. "I have never eaten an egg in my life.") On rare but satisfying occasions, the besieged visiting team might fight back. In Philadelphia, a fan of oversized girth and voice liked to sit in the front row under a basket and bellow curses at the enemy. One night in the mid-1950s, the sufficiently provoked Celtics took their revenge: a Celtic stood in front of the loudmouth and looked the other way when Bob Cousy threw him a hard pass. The ball exploded into the fan's face, encouraging him to root more quietly.

But if the Celtics thrived on such fan measures at home in Boston, that was of course different, at least to Celtics fans. Rooters inhabit a world of subjective reality, of cheerful double standards and blithe preoccupation with the particular ox being gored. In 1984 the Celtics met their lovingly hated rivals, the Los Angeles Lakers, in the NBA finals for the first time in fifteen years. Each team was led by a rising superstar: the Celtics by Larry Bird, the Lakers by Magic Johnson, along with a barely diminished thirty-seven-year-old Kareem Abdul-Jabbar. After the Lakers won the first game in Boston, they stayed in town for the next game four days later. Their sleep was disrupted every night as mysterious false alarms set off their hotel's fire Klaxons. The Lakers suspected foul play by local fans; a rumor even spread of an old bald-headed guy with a big cigar, resembling Red Auerbach, prowling the hotel late at night. The sleep-deprived Lakers lost the second game.

Already heated, the series warmed to a flash point in Los Angeles. After the Lakers won the third game by thirty-three points, Bird said his teammates had played "like sissies," without fire or aggressiveness. In the third quarter of the next game, his teammate Kevin McHale submitted a rebuttal. On a fast break, as the Lakers' Kurt Rambis ran to the basket on the right wing, McHale applied a hammerlock and clotheslined him hard to the floor. The Lakers managed only two more fast-break points the rest of the game and lost in overtime. "It was as blatant a cheap shot as I've ever seen," said Lakers coach Pat Riley afterward. "One of my guys wouldn't do that." Aw, "he's just saying that 'cause he got beat," Red Auerbach replied.

They split the next two games, each team winning easily at home, but the Celtics had established a tone. "Before McHale hit Rambis," said Boston's Cedric Maxwell, "the Lakers were just running across the street whenever they wanted. Now they stop at the corner, push the button, wait for the light and look both ways." As the showdown game in Boston approached, Celtics fans were wound tight. "It's the most intense level of interest I've ever seen for basketball in this city," said the manager of a bar on Canal Street. "I think it's the physical aspect," offered a bartender on State Street. "Nobody wants to admit it—it's like admitting you like boxing. But quite a few would like to see a knockout." The Lakers changed hotels but were detected nonetheless: basketball players stand out in any crowd. "As we came down from our rooms the morning of the last game," Abdul-Jabbar recalled, "a mob of Celtic fans was barricading the hotel entrance and the Boston police department had to give us two huge police dogs and six cops on motorcycles for protection. It took our bus ten minutes just to turn out of the hotel drive and into the street." The game, won by Boston, drew the largest TV audience yet in NBA history. "The security force wasn't fully prepared for the brawl-like behavior in the stands," said Abdul-Jabbar. "The crowd hurled trash and wet towels, pelted us with a storm of verbal abuse, and at the final buzzer couldn't be restrained from pummeling us as we left the court. Somebody ripped the glasses off my face and tried for my jersey. I had to defend myself." The fans shared fully with the Celtics in that NBA title.

Nuf Ced McGreevy would have relished the scene; in his time he had pushed a few Boston teams to victory himself. Late in the 1897 season, the Boston Beaneaters went to Baltimore for a series to decide the National League pennant. Over the previous six years, first Boston, then Baltimore, had won three flags in a row. Now Boston hoped to break the Orioles' streak. McGreevy joined a caterwauling collection of 125 "Royal Rooters" that descended on Baltimore with police rattles, fish horns, and a brass band. At the games they shouted:

> Boston, Boston,
> Here we are,
> Here for the pennant,
> Rah, rah, rah!

When a Beaneater made a good play, they passed a hat for him: six times in one game. The teams split two games. With thirty thousand fans on hand, Boston took the third game and pennant, 19–10. "It's a certainty that Boston could not have beaten

Baltimore without them," the Orioles catcher Wilbert Robinson later said of the Rooters. "Little bags of beans pelted every head in sight, and the Boston contingent went mad with joy. But Baltimore was bathed in gloom."

Six years later, Boston's new American League team played Pittsburgh in the first modern World Series. "Why, there is as much difference between Boston and Pittsburgh as there is between a cocktail and a glass of beer," Nuf Ced declared, sure of his professional judgment. "I know good drinks and also good players—give me the cocktail and Boston." After the Pirates won two of three games in Boston, McGreevy led two hundred Boston faithful to Pittsburgh. At their hotel they formed military lines, four abreast, and marched to the park in formation. When their team took the field, Nuf Ced stood up and waved his megaphone over his head, "a signal," according to one sportswriter, "which the 200 others seemed to understand perfectly." They yelled and whistled and clapped. In particular, they sang "Tessie," a popular song of the day, with new lyrics for the Pirates' great Honus Wagner, who was slumping through the series with a .222 batting average:

> Honus, why do you hit so badly,
> Take a back seat and sit down.
> Honus, at bat you look so sadly,
> Hey, why don't you get out of town.

They sang "Tessie" with riffs and variations, over and over. "If a player made a hit it was 'Tessie,'" a Boston newspaper reported. "A good catch brought out 'Tessie,' and so on, until 'Hiawatha' was a welcome sound to Pittsburgh ears compared with that awful 'Tessie.'"

The Boston contingent, players and fans, returned home needing just one more victory for the championship. John Tunis, later the author of a notable series of juvenile baseball novels, came to that game, fourteen years old, with his younger brother. Outside the park, hoping for tickets, they beheld a looming column of marching men led by McGreevy: ward politicians, longshoremen from Atlantic Avenue, bankers and brokers from State Street. For this solemn occasion they wore formal dark suits with high white collars, red rosettes on their chests, and tickets in the hatbands of their derbies. A band inevitably played "Tessie." "Even to our youthful eyes," Tunis recalled, "it was plain that many of the brethren had already visited McGreevy's that morning, for they were in excellent humor, and roared out the refrain."

The Royal Rooters sat in special seats in front of the grandstand. A lone woman, Miss Nelly Riley, braved the foul balls to join them. They cheered and sang hoarsely—"Write it! Write it!" somebody suggested—but effectively. Boston cruised to the first world championship, 3–0. "I think those Boston fans actually won that Series," Tommy Leach of the Pirates said years later. "They started singing that damn 'Tessie' song. . . . Sort of got on your nerves after a while. And before we knew what happened, we'd lost the World Series." Nuf Ced in full bloom.

♦ ♦ ♦

Far above such hurly-burly, safe in the quiet warren of *New Yorker* offices, Roger Angell in the summer of 1981 celebrated, with apologies, his fiftieth anniversary as a fan. "A half-century of vicariousness?" he exclaimed, ducking in advance. "For shame, sir!" His editorial colleagues at the magazine accepted, without encouraging, his sporting habits. (They did notice his offbeat competitiveness at the office. He would challenge people at jumping onto tables, writing notes in the smallest script, or composing palindromes. "Not so, Boston" was the title of his account of yet another Red Sox disaster.) With a nod to his resident skeptics, Angell tried to defend his "foolish servitude" to baseball by invoking a crosshatched latticework of memories and associations, linking his personal history with the game's. "Belonging and caring," he had declared a few years earlier, "is what our games are all about; this is what we come for." Now, marking his five decades, he reverted to the same language: "I belonged and I cared, and because I have been lucky enough to go on caring, I have belonged to baseball now for almost half of its history."

A fan's belonging stretches across four dimensions. Picture an adult fan in the middle of a field, ball in hand, looking for a game of catch. A short, easy toss reconnects the fan to childhood, when the simple pleasures of playing and watching a ballgame first entered a childish awareness. A longer throw takes in family members, real and metaphorical, bound fast to the game. A yet more substantial peg reaches the external community of fans, joined by nothing but pulling for the same team or sport. Finally, a corking heave—drawing applause from onlookers—makes the outer limits, where the game becomes history, and history bounces back to the moment itself, back to that fan in the middle of a field.

As Angell put it, ballgames "connect me on a long straight line to my own boyhood." No matter how elaborated by grownups, it still began as child's play. Children find the game suddenly and rush into a desperate, careening absorption that they may never feel again about anything else. Bridging the time from preschool to early adolescence, the pull of playing ball and rooting may introduce a child's first strong loyalty outside the family. In memory, that first enthusiasm retains its absolute power to transport any unbarnacled adult back to the delightful playfulness of childhood. "We had some merry times among ourselves," said Frank Pidgeon in 1857 of his games with the Brooklyn Eckfords; "We would forget business and everything else, on Tuesday afternoons, go out into the green fields, don our ball suits, and go at it with a perfect rush. At such times, we were boys again." For fans as for players, these sports remind adults to have fun in the moment: to savor life as process instead of outcome, to dream of glorious futures and returning home in triumph. During the New York Knickerbockers' championship season of 1970, Dave DeBusschere noticed the brimming adulation in a young fan's eyes and was suddenly reminded of his own childhood dreams. "Now that a lot of these dreams have become reality," he reflected, "they don't seem quite as rosy, quite as glamorous as they used to. Sometimes I just feel like a businessman whose business happens to be basketball. But the kids remind me that I'm not only a businessman, that I've got some strange power, or appeal, that the average businessman will never know."

On the big-league level, coaches and commentators encase the games in obscure jargons and pretentious intricacies. Most fans and players approach the games more simply, at a level accessible to any child. It pained Angell that "a great many men who play the game—a majority, easily—seem to take only a minimal interest in its nuances and complexities." But most ballplayers are children themselves, playing the game at a child's level and leaving the embellishments to observers. Even Angell sometimes committed such cloying offenses as "the perfection of baseball," "the perfectly observed balance, both physical and psychological, between opposing forces." Nonsense, snorted Keith Hernandez. A raving intellectual among baseball players because he did crossword puzzles and read books about the Civil War, Hernandez was not intimidated by fancy writing, "a vision of the game too romanticized or intellectualized, or both," he said. "Baseball is just baseball. We play the games. Winners and losers are designated. We come back next year. A lot of the stuff written about the 'flawless symmetry' of baseball, etc., etc., falls on deaf ears with the players, and not because we can't understand it. Because it seems overblown, if not misguided." "I hear football fans talking sometimes in that special language they pick up," puzzled Joe Namath, "and, shoot, I don't even know what they're talking about. They've got me doing things I never heard of." "I've been given credit for stuff I don't do," Robin Roberts agreed. "I pitch the same to everybody—low and away, or high and tight. . . . It don't do me a bit of good to tell people this. I try to tell people and they just won't believe me. They want to believe you have everyone taped and baseball is like mathematics or something."

The great danger of rooting as a child is the common risk of never outgrowing it. Children may safely live and die with their heroes because their worlds, relatively uncluttered, have room for the crowding intrusion of fanhood. With age, children normally reduce their rooting levels in proportion to newer interests. A rounded life should put sports in a milder, though still honored, perspective. Any adults who have skipped this transition lead lives out of balance. Jonathan Schwartz, a writer and Sinatra-struck radio personality, grew up in Manhattan, shooting baskets alone on the twelfth-floor terrace outside his apartment. As a child he somehow leaped over the beckoning local teams and attached himself to the distant fortunes of the Boston Celtics and Red Sox. Attending doubleheaders at Madison

Square Garden to catch the Celtics in the first game, he embraced their eruptive coach, Red Auerbach, as "an underdog with a kind of courage I knew I'd never have." Young Schwartz revered and repeated Auerbach's opinions on any subject, from NBA refs to Chinese food. To follow the Red Sox, he would sit for hours in a car on the East Side of New York, where he could pull in a Hartford radio station that carried Sox games. These devotions abated not at all as Schwartz grew up in other ways. He spent thousands of dollars a year on phone calls patched into Boston broadcasts. "I am a member of the Boston Red Sox," he said in dreadful earnest. A lost game would blight the next day: "In the early seconds of waking, it engulfs me, swooping down on my tentative consciousness with a brutal thrust." Oh, come on, Jonathan. It's only a ballgame! It's supposed to be fun! "I am heartsick in the shower, and I feel alone, and later I am fearful of the traffic in the street, and I am haunted by childhood memories." There lay his problem: those childhood memories still dominated his rooting. An adult fan learns to care intensely, like a child, for the moment—and then put it away, like storing a baseball glove for the winter.

As the games recall childhood, they bring up family memories. The first toss of youth usually came from a parent or sibling. So many writers have produced so many sepia-tinted accounts of these initiations that the genre has become a literary cliché: *Fathers Playing Catch With Sons,* as Donald Hall titled his collection of sports essays. Yet the cliché is real enough, tattered simply because the memory is so strong and widely shared, a *Field of Dreams* with hooks for so many millions of nostalgic old ballplayers. The characteristic mood is soft-edged, elegiac, leaning into difficult questions but then pulling back before anybody gets hurt. When fathers and sons cannot figure out what to say to each other, sports lubricate the process. Sports talk is better than no talk at all. The literary genre only hints politely at what was lost or missed; better to focus on the game. The baseball writer Charles Einstein liked to recall a gentle three-generation hoax in his family. In 1932 his father took him to his first big-league game. Just before the seventh-inning stretch, the father announced that he was a magician. "When I say stand up," he told his wondering child, "everybody here will stand up." He did and they did. Then he softly ordered the multitude to sit down, which they did. The son was amazed. Twenty-five years later, Einstein repeated the trick with *his* son. In time that son followed suit with the next generation. (Family continuity at the ballpark.)

Angell dedicated his first book of baseball articles to his eighty-two-year-old father. When he later wrote down his early baseball memories, he was surprised at how the story kept returning to his old man and their baseball connections. Ernest Angell, a Wall Street lawyer, had played nearly every sport but golf. As the national chairman of the American Civil Liberties Union and an inveterate writer of letters to the editor, he toiled for good causes and soldiered on courageously through the McCarthy scares. But he was at his worst as husband to his first wife, Katharine, Roger's mother. Both came from single-parent families (his father had died at sea, her mother of a ruptured appendix). Their marriage, contented for about seven years, disintegrated into ugly fights over his philandering. A man of flaring temper, he sometimes hit her. Once Roger woke up at night to the sound of their squabbling—he shouting, she weeping (a terrifying experience for any child, like hearing the gods in noisy collision); Roger interrupted them by calling out that he was getting a glass of water. Katharine fell into an affair with E. B. White. When Roger was eight, after a final confrontation in which Ernest slapped Katharine and knocked her to the floor, they split up. Katharine and E. B. White were married later that year. Roger and his sister lived with their father during the week, with their mother for weekends, holidays, and summers. For Roger it meant years of loneliness ("I missed my mother") and sad adjustments. He remained on good terms with all three parents, but it could not have been easy. Later came his own marriage, parenthood, divorce, remarriage, and adoption of a son. He knew firsthand how fragile many family ties had become in modern America.

Coming from this background, Angell could especially appreciate the haven of fanhood as a surrogate family. A private man, discreet and tightly buttoned, he sidled up to the notion carefully. Interviewed by George Plimpton in 1977, he said he tried to avoid "large theorizing": "I just can't find the handle on that kind of big, shiny idea." But Plimpton pushed him, and he finally—with reservations—addressed the kinship analogy. Count the reservations: "I *think* we can *almost* say that baseball is *rather like* an enormous and adventurous family," he ventured. *"If it's true* that we have *begun* to lose a sense of our own families in this country, *maybe* baseball provides a *kind of* substitute, or *at least* a *feeling of* something ordered and continuous that is shared by a very large community of people." (Nine hedges.) If that's so, Angell continued, then perhaps sports skeptics who dismissed ballgames and fans so angrily, with such contempt, in fact wished unconsciously that they could gain entry to the warmth of rooting. "They feel left out," Angell suggested. "They may sense that they have been excluded from something in which membership is a privilege and a source of joy."

The ballplayers themselves, such a living presence in Angell's home, so familiar in every detail of their lives, seemed like literal members of the family. In poking around the Yankee clubhouse after games, he had always avoided the grouchy catcher Thurman Munson ("a rough customer—silent and scowling, possibly dangerous"). Yet when Munson died in a plane crash in 1979, still in his prime, Angell was shocked into unexpected grief. He realized that he knew more about twenty or thirty ballplayers than about some of his oldest friends. "I can only conclude that these adopted, seasonal relatives have filled a real need for me, and perhaps for other fans as well," he reckoned. "Belonging anywhere now is terribly difficult, I think, and the old childhood dream of *really* belonging will not go away. . . . We want to know all about ballplayers, because then somehow they will know about *us,* and then we will belong, too."

The "family" matrix expands to nameless strangers and hometown teams. In a diverse society with gaping chasms between rich and poor, sports-mindedness provides one of our more reliable common bonds, "second only to death as a leveler." In 1908 the *Atlantic Monthly,* then a quite genteel magazine, published a sheepish anonymous article by a baseball fan. On his commuting train he read a sporting newspaper that his family would not allow in their respectable home. Leaving the paper on his seat, "I walk from the departing train outwardly stainless." But he envied his fellow commuter, an Italian immigrant in a blue shirt with a flowery silk front, who read the same newspaper and even took it home, unashamed. "Baseball," the fan exulted, "is the best cement democracy knows." In the same way, many male intellectuals, feeling themselves a separate caste with few ties to most Americans, leap gratefully on sports as a chance to be regular guys, to redeem their childhoods as the neighborhood dweebs who threw like girls and were chosen last for games. "For a bookish fellow in a democracy, knowledge about sports seems to me essential," said another closeted enthusiast, writing for the very serious journal *The American Scholar* in 1984. "Sports talk is the closest thing we have in this country to a lingua franca." A sports magazine once sent the poet Robert Frost to cover an All-Star game. "I am never more at home in America than at a baseball game," said Frost. "Beyond this I know not. And dare not."

The modern personality is a free atom, constructing a life from too many choices, selecting even the ties that bind. With the older ties—of family, community, religion, and ethnicity—straining and snapping, big-league sports help to pull people together. A modern American city is never more unified and singleminded than when one of its teams is stalking or celebrating a title. After the Washington Redskins won their first Super Bowl in 1983, the city erupted in sloshed bonhomie. "I'm a prejudiced son-of-a-bitch," said one celebrant. "I hate blacks and chinks and spics and every damn thing. But tonight I've shaken hands with every damn one of them. It's great!" As the Los Angeles Lakers won five NBA titles during the 1980s, the team became a rare binder in the least rooted of American cities. The older Laker fans—such as Jack Nicholson and Lou Adler in their courtside seats, who had nursed the team through the lean years of the 1970s—were joined by trendy multitudes drawn by the pleasures of winning and beating ancient rivals from back East. "The team has gained an emotional hold on the city," Kareem Abdul-Jabbar noticed, "our collective success having forged some kind of unity in this huge and normally fragmented metropolis, and it cuts across cultural and class lines." When the Lakers stumbled in 1992, after the retirements of Abdul-Jabbar and Magic Johnson, the fans drifted away again.

But with the team winning and the fans cheering, even the most sprawling polity may retrieve a measure of the small-town cohesiveness that John Havlicek knew as a child, when the common denominator was sports. Havlicek grew up in the 1950s playing every available game in Lansing, Ohio, a coal-mining town a few miles west of the Ohio River. "Life was pretty simple in the valley," he recalled. "There wasn't a rich person that I knew about in Lansing. Everyone was pretty much alike, and you can safely say the town was one big family. You knew everyone in town and where they lived." Anyone could walk into a neighbor's house and sit down for a meal, no invitation needed. All the males—Italians, Hungarians, Slovaks, Czechs, it did not matter—focused on sports. The coal mines sponsored semipro baseball teams; the high school favored football. For entertainment the men repaired to Cocky Pyle's Texaco station, where the radio blared broadcasts of Cleveland's baseball and football teams. "It was the only thing in town," said Havlicek. "We just hung around Cocky Pyle's drinking Coke, eating candy, and listening to the ballgame." After he went off to college and his career in the NBA, Havlicek came back to Lansing just for visits. But the savored memory of that tight little small-town sporting idyll stayed with him. Big-league fans are reaching for it, however unconsciously, whenever they root for their own local heroes.

"You can't really belong to baseball," said Roger Angell, "unless you belong to a team." The teams of his boyhood later lost his devotion and cast him adrift: the Giants left town and the Yankees won too much. "Something a little sterile about admiring the best," he noted after the Yankees had gobbled five straight World Series from 1949 to 1953; "it lacks kicks." At college in Boston he had attended Red Sox games and felt a stirring for his mother's favorite team. ("I know a New York lady, now in her seventies," he wrote discreetly, "whose heart slowly bleeds through the summer over the misadventures of the Boston Red Sox, a team representing the home town she left in 1915.") He summered in Maine among Sox fans. For years the Red Sox staggered around in mediocrity relieved only by the peerless hitting of Ted Williams. In 1962, though, Angell rushed to embrace the Mets, the wonderfully inept new team in town, who won but forty games and finished sixty and a half games out of first. (Hometown mediocrity was apparently more appealing.) Perceiving "more Met than Yankee in every one of us," spurning "the stolidity, the smugness, and the arrogance" of Yankee fans, he decided "that perfection is admirable but a trifle inhuman, and that a stumbling kind of semi-success can be much more warming." The Red Sox finally snared him in 1967 by winning their first pennant in twenty-one years. At first, as the Sox tumbled into their usual August swoon, "I refused to believe what was happening." Then the Sox won a game after trailing 8–0 and snapped off seven straight victories. "I gave up; from that week on, I belonged." (That word again: he *belonged*.)

In the largest sense, he belonged to a stable historical tradition. Over the years, the big three sports have acquired a massive historical solidity that lets them absorb endless niggling changes and "improvements" and yet remain essentially the same. The games and players are simple; simplicity cannot be picked at without losing its basic nature. The off-field superstructures— business aspects, media relations, coaching, training, scouting— become ever more complex and ponderous. But the most crucial elements—the players, fans, and, in particular, the games on the field—do not change except in minor details. Embedded in modern culture that mistakes change for progress, sports fans are implicit Luddites, heretically doubtful of progress. They want their games to stay as discovered in childhood, as frozen memories to protect from tampering. "The illusion that there was something abiding," said Bart Giamatti, a classical scholar strayed into baseball administration. "I am a simpler creature, tied to more primitive patterns and cycles. I need to think something lasts forever, and it might as well be that state of being that is a game." Ballgames defy the clock and calendar, extending a kind of time travel to any fan with a sense of history. Stop the clock, reverse it, slow it, speed it. "Time is the air we breathe," wrote Donald Hall, "and the wind swirls us backward and forward, until we seem so reckoned in time and seasons that all time and all seasons become the same."

Some observers—fans and players with long memories—witness the continuities. Pudge Heffelfinger, the most celebrated football player of the late 1800s, watched the game for half a century after his playing days. It all looked the same to him. "In some form or another we did about everything that is done in football today," he said in the early 1950s. "Our system of defense and offense was fundamentally the same as it is today. Except for refinements and a closer attention to details, due to larger coaching staffs, it's basically the same game. And all this talk about systems is largely twaddle." Bill Walsh, the most successful NFL coach of the 1980s, was considered a progressive innovator, the winner of three Super Bowls because of his bold breaks from traditional ways. "We continue to find ourselves reaching back into history," he explained. "It is important to remember that so much can be learned from the past." Walsh installed wraparound draw plays from the 1950s, man-in-motion plays from the 1940s, reverse shoulder blocks from the 1930s, and other ancient techniques so old as to lack genealogies. "You know, there is just nothing new in football," concluded Jack Christiansen, an NFL player in the 1950s and coach in the 1960s. "Any time somebody brings up an idea, someone says, 'Hell, we did that forty years ago.' "

Even the volatile issue of money, of playing for pay or playing for sport, stays fixed in time. Weigh, for example, these five random statements on how big money has affected baseball:

"Somehow or other they don't play ball nowadays as they used to some eight or ten years ago," said a ballplayer. "I mean that they don't play with the same kinds of feelings or for the same objects they used to."

"The sordid element of baseball as a business has cast a shadow over the sport," said a newspaper. The players make too much money and become spoiled, "parading about in their automobiles like princes, posing at the cabarets and trotteries as little tin-gods."

"Today the players regard the game in a different light," said a manager. "It is a means rather than the end. It has become a business with the boys, who play for the income."

"The player of today is too unwilling to exert himself," said a retired ballplayer. Once established, he "then falls into an indifferent pace. He somehow becomes very satisfied with himself and coasts along."

"Players are not motivated by winning any more," said a general manager. "They're motivated by money. Alas, baseball is a prisoner of money. In the last two decades, dollars have replaced sense."

These statements were made in 1868, 1915, 1927, 1944, and 1987. This echoing litany reflects not a shifting situation but our permanent unease over paying ballplayers good money to have fun at a child's game. Despite extravagant salaries, and the ever-swelling chorus of laments in the background, the game on the field goes on largely unaffected. There the athletes still play mostly for pride and competition. "I don't want to embarrass myself out there," they invariably explain. The money comes later.

However contrived and commercial, the games as ever seem honest and real to fans. Modern technology has left most of our entertainments canned and predictable. Live theater has turned into movies and filmed TV shows, all edited and polished. Live music is usually heard in recorded form, honed to studio perfection. Only sports remain spontaneously raw, performed live, with the story and outcome unknown by anybody until the game is over. Played against our contemporary shadow worlds of manipulated images and symbols, our sports maintain an unreachable authenticity. The athletes perform in public, visible to everyone, succeeding or failing in clearly defined ways. Everywhere else in American life, from business to politics to the arts, the greatest rewards may go to undeserving louts more lucky than talented because the judgments rendered by the public marketplace are so often capricious and mistaken. But in ballgames, over the long season, the breaks even out as the best teams and players win the garlands. No media spin or legal tap dance can affect the final verdict. They play by the rules while someone keeps score. "It was an honest thing we were doing out there," said the football player Joe Kapp. "I'm not talking about all the hype and hoopla surrounding it. I'm talking about what went on down on the field itself."

Roger Angell, a ballpark classicist like any true fan, clung to what he called "the sunlit verities of the game." As successive waves of innovations intruded on him—league expansions, artificial turf, divisional play-offs, designated hitters, indoor stadia, instant replays at the parks, strikes, lockouts, free agency, inflated salaries, the rampaging effects of TV—he unfailingly scorned them all and fretted. "We are trying to conserve something that seems as intricate and lovely to us as any river valley," he pleaded. "We truly worry about it, grieve for it now." Yet his own prolonged, ever-renewed delight in the game refuted his most mordant predictions for it. Annually, just before spring training, he would think about retiring from his devotion, to try some new challenge instead of the old, familiar turf, and so avoid complicity in the ongoing corruption of the game. "Is there no cure for this second-hand passion," he would wonder, "which makes me a partner, however unwilling, in the blather of publicity, the demeaning emptiness of hero-worship, and the inconceivably wasteful outpourings of money and energy that we give to professional sports now?" After a short time in the preseason sun, though, he would soak up the soothing rituals, the sounds and smells, and feel the old belonging. Despite everything, it was still the same ballgame, the players always young, the sport old but ever new. Play ball.

The pre-Columbians of basketball's jump shot: John M. Cooper of Kentucky *(left)* and Glenn Roberts of Virginia *(below)*, in the early 1930s; they made the essential discovery— but word didn't get out

Johnny Cooper shooting a jumper during his college career at the University of Missouri

Glenn Roberts
finishing his
jumper; from a
semipro game late
in his career

Benny Friedman in his Michigan sweater,
ca. 1926; the first great passer in college
and pro football, and the most
underappreciated star in NFL history

Nuf Ced McGreevy's Third Base saloon, an overstuffed baseball shrine in Boston, in 1903; the largest visible portrait *(to left of moose)* is of King Kelly, the most celebrated baseball player of the nineteenth century

Third Base exterior, bedecked for the first World Series, in 1903; the sign predates Nuf Ced's conversion to simplified spelling

The Royal Rooters at Pittsburgh for the 1903 World Series; Nuf Ced directly behind last player on the right; Boston's ace pitcher Cy Young (who that year won 28 of his 511 career victories), the first player on left, in dark sweater

The stylish Knickerbocker club of New York in 1864; two decades earlier, the
Knickerbockers had invented the modern version of baseball

Arthur Pue Gorman, later the
Democratic leader of the United
States Senate; in 1867 his
Washington Nationals embarked
on the first grand intersectional
baseball tour, suggesting the
feasibility of a nearly national big
league

Teams and grandstand before a NAPBBP game in Boston, 1875; the
Boston Red Stockings, rolling to their fourth league pennant in a row,
and the Philadelphia Athletics *(opposite)*

Action drawings from the first big league, the National Association of
Professional Base Ball Players, in 1874; from opening-day game between the
Philadelphia Athletics and the Philadelphia White Stockings

Walter Camp of Yale,
inventor of American
football and the
game's dominant
figure until brought
down by his hubris
and deceptions

George Halas of the
Chicago Bears; as
player, coach, team
owner, and league
mogul, an NFL
eminence for six
decades

In a typically retiring pose, George Preston Marshall of the Washington Redskins; the clamorous ogre who saved the NFL in the 1930s

Don Hutson of the Green Bay Packers; the greatest player in NFL history, if greatness is achieved by repeatedly exceeding contemporary standards

James A. Naismith, who invented basketball by borrowing elements from the games of rugby, soccer, lacrosse, and duck on the rock

The old basketball, smooth-surfaced and laces ascendant, lopsided and heavy from use; a factor in keeping the game two-handed

BASKETBALL HALL OF FAME

BASKETBALL HALL OF FAME

Chapter Three

Ballplaying Life:
Staying Young

The life starts in childhood and lingers there ever after. The ball rolls toward the child, intriguing in its spin, tantalizing in its course. Hoping to intercept it, the child essays a jerky lunge, misses, tumbles over, but struggles upward to try again. The ball demands primordial timing and rhythm. Human life pulses to cadences of heartbeat, language, and music. To catch the ball—throw it, dribble it, or hit it—the child must pick up the beat of life. Even this early, the ball is not just a ball. The game is more than a game.

The child, all unaware, merely wants to control the immediate ball: an early exercise in mastery. "I can't remember anything that happened before I had a baseball in my hand," said Rogers Hornsby after hitting .358 over twenty-three big-league seasons. "I guess I started playing as soon as I could close my fist over a ball." In time the wayward ball is tamed, grows familiar, and flows easily between the hand of the child and the hand of the mentor. To this the child adds the newfound joys of running and jumping—flying through the air, speeding up earthbound rhythms—and the bracing punch of colliding with other bodies. From playing with a ball, the child starts playing ball.

A lucky child never stops. Magic Johnson found basketball before his tenth birthday. His father took him out to the local schoolyard court in Lansing, Michigan, taught him to shoot layups and use both hands. "I could barely get the ball to the rim, but I loved the game. I was hooked." As one of ten children in a packed house, Magic plotted times just for himself. "I found that with basketball I didn't need anyone else to have a good time, and when I was playing I was having the best time in the world." By the fourth grade he was obsessed with hoops, playing in four leagues at once. Running an errand for his mother or just sitting on the porch, he practiced dribbling. Neighbors complained of the noise. "The game was just in me." In family contests, a brother would impersonate Walt Frazier; Magic was Wilt Chamberlain, the tallest and strongest man in the big leagues. (In downstate Indiana at the same time, Larry Bird was shooting hoops with his cousin. One was Wilt while the other was Bill Russell.)

Heroes matter desperately to young ballplayers. The hero, playing at a rarefied level, does better than anyone—no doubt of that—what the aspiring ballplayer most loves to do. And he does it in trumpeted public, to the cheers of crowds. And he gets paid for it! What a glorious dream! Tris Speaker never saw big-league games around his hometown of Hubbard, Texas, but he adopted the faraway Boston Red Sox and their star pitcher, Cy Young. In a few years Speaker joined the Red Sox himself. Most of the veteran players cuffed rookies as upstarts after their jobs. Young, in his last season as a twenty-game winner, was the first of the Red Sox to befriend the busher: a real hero even up close. George Ruth, a truant child in Baltimore, revered Christy Mathewson of the New York Giants. "Maybe there was a greater pitcher than Matty but I doubt it," the Babe allowed later. "I was a rough kid in those days. Maybe I didn't always know my lessons but I always knew how many games Matty had won and lost. I read everything about him that I could get my hands on." Ruth took to pitching in fealty to his hero.

Hero-worship cuts across races, geographic loyalties, and sports. A kid is a hero-seeking missile, looking for a big leaguer to cleave to. The child's first loyalty outside the family knows no boundaries. Bob Feller, growing up on a farm in Iowa, heard

Chicago Cubs games on the radio and played second base because Rogers Hornsby did. The young Joe Namath, not yet a football star, favored baseball and played the outfield in imitation of his hero, Roberto Clemente. Willie Mays, a young black ballplayer in Alabama with no hope of cracking the segregated big leagues, still fixed on Joe DiMaggio of the distant New York Yankees and became a center fielder in tribute. Bart Starr, later a quarterback, also loved DiMag from Alabama. He would take the bus to visit his aunt Myrtle in faraway Detroit when the Yankees came to town. With just enough money left from his bus fare for a bleacher ticket, Bart went to see his man beat the Tigers. "I watched DiMaggio perform his magic," Starr later testified. "He never disappointed."

Or so the adult Starr remembered it. In fact DiMaggio must have disappointed many times. He could not hit every pitch or catch every hit, though he came closer than most, and looked even better because the Yankees generally won. All these heroes were star performers on winning teams. In every sport, even the best, most winning players must often fail. The young idolaters simply choose to remember the winning homer, touchdown pass, or clinching basket while all the more common failures fade unloved from memory. Heroes neither fail nor age nor die. The image of the hero at his peak stays embedded in time, beyond clocks and calendars. (Sports stop history.) Two decades after his last big-league game, Honus Wagner came back to coach for the Pirates. In his sixties, slowed and thickened with age, he would take practice encores at shortstop. "When he did that," Paul Waner remembered, "a hush would come over the whole ball park, and every player on both teams would just stand there, like a bunch of little kids, and watch every move he made. . . . Gee, we loved that guy."

Any young player with a flair for the ball nurtures the unspoken dream of heroically making the big leagues. A handful of all the dreamers, after years of playing only for pleasure and glory, will reach a defining moment: signing a contract to play for money. The concept defies easy belief. Why should anyone expect to make a living at ballgames? "I still haven't quite gotten over it," said Connie Mack, looking back across sixty years of baseball, "that some men were willing to pay you for playing ball—a game which is so much fun." Bones Taylor came out of Wynne, Arkansas, population 3,500, to play for George Preston Marshall's Washington Redskins. "Playing in the pros was like heaven for this country boy," Taylor reminisced. "To be paid for something you love, well, I never would tell Marshall that I'd do it for free. But at first I think I would have."

For boys up from hard backgrounds, the big show meant even more. Like all ballplayers, they loved the play and the pay for playing; and they with special sharpness appreciated the grimmer alternatives at hand. "Compared to farming," said the pitcher Burleigh Grimes, "or working in the lumber woods or in a steel mill, baseball was a picnic." Tony Lazzeri of the Yankees first toiled in a boiler factory, with its noise, grime, and danger. "It's hard work," he reflected, "fearfully hard for a man who isn't toughened to it. But it makes baseball so much easier in comparison." "When I'd get dead tired from being battered," said Sammy Baugh of the Redskins, "and playing both ways, with a squad of only 23 players, I would remember picking cotton as a 12-year-old boy on my uncle's farm and I wouldn't feel so bad about football." The outfielder Edd Roush grew up on an Indiana farm. Milking cows in the sunless, bitter chill of every implacable winter morning, seven days a week, left him time for ambitious plans: "I was playing ball on the town team and doing pretty well, so one cold dark winter morning I said to myself, 'I'll be a ballplayer.' I didn't expect to ever make it all the way to the big leagues, but I didn't care. I just had to get away from them damn cows."

Stan Coveleski and Red Ruffing, pitchers who won 215 and 273 big-league games, came from even farther down, from below ground. Coveleski, born in Pennsylvania anthracite country between Scranton and Harrisburg, started mining at the age of twelve. For working twelve hours a day, six days a week, he was paid $3.60 ("there was nothing strange in those days about a twelve-year-old Polish kid in the mines for seventy-two hours a week at a nickel an hour"). For much of the year he never saw daylight except on Sunday. Through long summer evenings, though, after work he would throw stones at tin cans. Nothing else to do. With a can placed on a log or tied to a tree, he would stand forty or fifty feet away and plink until darkness. "I did that for so many years I could hit one of those things blindfolded." The semipro baseball team in town heard about his command of tin cans and asked him to pitch. Soon a pro contract took him off to his first train ride, first suit of clothes, and first meal in a restaurant. In 1912 Connie Mack brought him up for his big-league debut. He aimed for the catcher's glove, "and it was just like throwing stones at tin cans."

Red Ruffing grew up in Illinois coal-mining towns. Not fond of school, and with coal in his family, by thirteen he was working underground. "When I hear some of the boys talk about hard work," he said later, proud but not relishing, "when I listen to their wails about a tough boyhood, I have to laugh. Down in the mine at thirteen—not a breaker boy. Down in the shafts, breaking, coupling, hard work." Out of the mine, he played first base and the outfield for the company team. One painfully fortunate day when he was sixteen, a motorman down below ran over his left foot. He lost four toes. After a year of healing, he still couldn't run much, so he switched to pitching. He struck out seventeen in his first game, nineteen in his second. Losing his toes rescued him from the mine, after one final tap. Not yet sure of his prospects after a season in the minor leagues, he spent another winter in the mine. The day before Christmas, his left ankle was nearly severed. He never went back to coal. Free of the mines, Ruffing spent twenty-two years in the bigs. "Baseball put me on the lift," he said from a safe distance, "took me out of the shafts into the sunshine, into a grand game, among grand guys, into a way of living that is remarkable, into real dough."

Ballplayers from immigrant families might haul the extra burden of balking parents. From cultures without sporting traditions, bewildered by American ways of sport, and certain that getting ahead in America demanded hard work and nothing but, these families felt shamed by sons who wasted time playing ballgames. Joe DiMaggio's Neapolitan father would shout for his son to come fishing on San Francisco Bay. Joe would hide under his bed. "And when I gave up shouting," the father recalled, "and go off to my boat Joe would come sneaking out of the house to play baseball. I thought he would come to no good end then." Who could make a living at baseball, the father puzzled; all it did was wear out shoes. "That's crazy," he would scold.

"That's a bum's game." But when Joe and his brothers made the newspapers by playing ball, the old man grew circumspectly curious. He woke Joe at three in the morning, told him to come down to the kitchen for coffee. They sat at the kitchen table till dawn as Joe explained the American game. With his first big money, Joe bought his father a new fishing boat.

Hank Greenberg, the son of Romanian Jewish immigrants, grew up in the Bronx section of New York City. Drawn to baseball early, he built a sliding pit in his backyard and practiced running and sliding by himself, hour after hour. The neighbors scratched their heads. "Why are you wasting your time playing baseball?" asked his mother. "It's a bum's game." The father worried too. "But when the next day came, I was back playing baseball." After his first good year with the Tigers, the neighborhood threw a proud celebration. The neighbors posed for newspaper photographers and said they'd always known he had the stuff. "Look at you," said his mother: "The Napoleon of the Bronx!" ("I was getting paid for fulfilling the wildest dreams of my childhood," Greenberg said later. "Baseball was the most pleasant way to make a living that's ever been invented.")

Ossie Bluege, later of the Washington Senators, was twenty years old, taking accounting courses and playing semipro baseball in Chicago, when a minor-league manager offered him two hundred dollars a month to turn pro. Surprised that he was considered that good, Bluege took the contract home to his father. "He didn't know too much about baseball," Bluege remembered. "He was a strict old German gentleman who believed in hard work and in going to church on Sundays and holding the Bible up in your hands where everybody could see it. He wasn't too impressed with that contract."

"You want to give up all your accounting training, all your schooling?" the father asked.

"Dad, they make five and six thousand dollars a year playing major league ball."

"They pay men that much money to chase that ball around?"

Finally father and son agreed that if he didn't make the big show in three years, Ossie would return to accounting. Next day he took the train to join his new team in Rock Island. At seven-thirty in the morning he was up and ready for work, as usual.

But he couldn't find any baseball people hanging around the hotel lobby. At nine o'clock, worried and wondering, he telephoned his manager, who grumbled at being roused so early. "That's when I began to get the idea," Bluege recalled, "that this was going to be a different life."

Not just paid for play, big leaguers made "real dough," as Red Ruffing put it. Typical salary levels well exceeded what the players could have made otherwise as undereducated young men with few conventional skills. As early as 1868, the top baseball teams in Brooklyn paid wages of $600 to $900 for a six-month season, good money when clerks and manual workers earned less than $500 for a whole year. In 1874 Harry Wright, manager of the Boston Red Stockings, was upset over rising pay scales in the range of $1,200 to $1,800. ("What do the majority of these players do with all that money?" Wright fretted. "Spend it foolishly to the injury of themselves.") Average salaries in major-league baseball—about $1,400 in 1880, $3,000 in 1910, $5,000 in 1923—were generous for the time, and left players free half the year for other work. In 1902 Al Bridwell was earning $150 *a year* at a shoe factory in Portsmouth, Ohio, when he was offered $150 *a month* to play minor-league baseball. He did not have to ponder his decision for long. Three years later he signed with the Reds at $2,100 a year: a fourteen-fold increase over his factory job. In 1922 Earle Combs went home from his first year of pro baseball—in the minors, yet—with more money saved than his father had accumulated after fifty years of farming.

At first pro football and basketball offered less money than baseball. The early NFL teams paid players around $125 a game. The top gate attractions—Red Grange, Bronko Nagurski, and Benny Friedman—made $10,000 for six months of play. When Art Rooney signed Whizzer White (an All-American and future Supreme Court justice) at $15,800 in 1938, other team owners were appalled by so extravagant a precedent. The precedent was duly contained. Sammy Baugh, at $11,000, earned the best NFL salary of the early 1940s. In 1950 the median league salary was about $6,800; backs made more, guards and tackles less. Yet even at these levels, football players earned far more in six months than the average twelve-month salaries of the day.

Before the NBA, pro-basketball teams and leagues came and

went in whimsical succession. Players expected uncertain pay-days. Even so, to play basketball for money still beckoned ball-players, especially during the Depression. When Frank Baird started with the Indianapolis Kautskys, he made $25 a game, "'which seemed like a good bit of money." In the late 1930s Buddy Jeannette played on a team in Warren, Pennsylvania, for $100 a month. The team owner got him off-season work at $15 a week, "the hardest job I've ever done in my life. Warren is an oil area, and we used to go out to the farms that had oil wells and drain them into a pipe that emptied into the refinery. I really had to work for that $15. Playing basketball was nothing com-pared with that."

Sonny Hertzberg played for a New York team in the Amer-ican Basketball League in the early 1940s. At $50 a game and three games a week, he earned more than regular forty-hour jobs were paying. The money was so good that ballplayers com-peted ferally for positions and playing time. If Hertzberg got hot and made a few shots, he could expect defending fingers poked in his eyes, shoving and holding and fistfights. Later Hertzberg went on to the NBA and found raised pay scales and expecta-tions. Kenny Sailors, offered $2,800 in 1946 to teach back home in Wyoming, instead took $8,000 to play basketball. When Belus Smawley finished his first season with the St. Louis Bombers, for which he received $6,000, he went home to North Carolina and taught for $150 a month. The Boston Celtics in 1948 offered $7,800 to their top draft choice, George Hauptfuehrer of Har-vard. Hauptfuehrer decided on law school instead, and it took three years of law school and four years of practice before he made that kind of money outside basketball.

Given the prevailing employment practices of the big leagues, ballplayers were paid remarkably well. For long decades they remained in thrall to the reserve clause (see chapter 9). Without agents on their side, the athletes, young and unsophisticated, dealt unequally with owners, who were mostly older, cannier businessmen and sportsmen. Rookies year by year acted out dra-mas of initiation as the innocent came in from the provinces to meet slick, big-city ways. They should by all likelihoods have routinely been shorn to the skin. Bulldog Turner, out of Sweet-water, Texas, played football at an obscure college in Abilene and was then courted by George Richards, owner of the Detroit Lions. A limousine brought him out to the formidable Richards home. "We went into a big ol' dining room, and there was a great big ol' table," as Turner spun the yarn. "There's nothin' on the table—nothin'. But servants brang you each course. They brang you the service that you were going to use for each course. Well, back home when I sat down to dinner all the food was on the table. You'd pass this and pass that and everybody's up close and you eat. But here we didn't do it that way. . . . They'd get a little ol' dried-up pork chop and set it on a big ol' white plate, you know, and serve it off a big ol' silver service tray. I thought that was a hell of a way to eat." Afterward Richards gave him forty or fifty dollars of walking-around money. "Man, that was the most money I ever saw in my life. And I'm being drove around!" But the courtship failed in the end, and Turner played for the Chicago Bears.

No matter how well paid by standards of the time, ballplayers always groused about stingy pay. Whether they chose to complain out loud sometimes depended on the personality of the man on the other side of the negotiating desk. "Red was very intimidating," John Havlicek recalled of his dickerings with Red Auerbach of the Celtics. "Remember that he was the coach. I had to face him every day and he can be a very irate person at times. I just didn't want any confrontations with him." Vince Lombardi's charges on the Green Bay Packers also tiptoed around the boss's moods. "There was no way I could talk contract with Lombardi," said Jim Ringo. "Hell, I'd go in looking for a thousand-dollar raise, and by the time he got done talking to me . . . I felt as if I should pay him for the privilege of playing at Green Bay." One year Willie Davis, after making the All-Pro team and placing second for the league's Most Valuable Player Award, dared suggest a raise. "Willie, you forgot just one thing," Lombardi rebutted. "Willie, I made you!" Well, yes sir. "After that," Davis concluded, "I knew I'd never win a salary discussion with him. So when the next times came around, I'd just go in, have some small talk and sign whatever he gave me."

Armed with the reserve clause, an owner could simply tell a minion unhappy with his pay to take it or leave it. Both parties knew the money was generous for someone playing a ballgame.

"You have some very wild ideas as to salary," a Detroit Tiger executive advised Matty McIntyre in 1904. "A ball player who can earn $2,400.00 for less than six months work, and easy work at that, is certainly not badly treated, and is receiving about all that is coming to him." Then, after a poor season in 1904—a .253 average with 2 homers and 46 RBIs in 152 games—McIntyre was further insulted. "You will play ball," Tiger owner Frank Navin told him, "if you play in organized base ball with the Detroit club at a salary of Two Thousand Dollars, and you can report or not, as you see fit. You needn't mind suggesting to me how to run the affairs of the Detroit club, as when I want suggestions I will go to someone that I think knows his business." Thump! McIntyre signed for $2,000.

Even Babe Ruth, easily the richest ballplayer of his time, wanted more money. Ruth—or his business manager, Christy Walsh—knew his unique power to sell tickets. Early in 1927, Ruth sent a suspiciously dignified letter to Yankee owner Jake Ruppert, arguing that his salary had remained frozen for five years while the team was carting away lush profits. "If I were in any other business," the Babe's amanuensis noted, "I would probably receive a new contract at higher salary without request. Or rival employers could bid for my services. Baseball law forces me to work for the New York club or remain idle." ("A logical document," the sportswriter John Kieran observed, "which is proof positive that the Babe didn't write it.") The Babe got his raise, to $70,000. Nobody else on the Yankees that year made more than $17,500.

Yet—the essential point—despite these inequities of power and salary, ballplayers could not reasonably complain. The salary explosions of the 1980s—an average baseball salary exceeded a million dollars by 1993—were not as unprecedented as they seemed. Traditionally well paid, ballplayers became *very* well paid, especially measured against what they were equipped to earn in a real job. "I'm living proof that you don't have to be smart to make a lot of money," said Pete Rose. "If I had dug school, I probably would have went to college and played football, and you wouldn't be looking at me here today."

◆　　◆　　◆

"I was not pleased with myself any longer," said Joe DiMaggio as he retired, "and all the fun had gone out of playing the game."

◆   ◆   ◆

However rich and heroic, big leaguers are still children playing with a ball. The game remains fun (even when overflowing with consequences) and simple (even when overcomplicated by coaches and fans). Ballplayers perform best when they're enjoying themselves, in a state of relaxed alertness unimpeded by too much thinking. "You've gotta have a lot of little boy in you," the catcher Roy Campanella explained. Stars perform better, thus have more fun. Having more fun, they play better and become stars. Starhood and fun chase each other around a circle, keeping an adult ballplayer in an agreeably suspended childhood.

"You know, I feel funny playing a children's game in my thirties," the quarterback Fran Tarkenton allowed, "but I do it for one reason. I love it. Nothing in my life compares to the ecstasies I get from this game. And nothing compares to the horrible things." The high of winning needs the stab of defeat; neither would be felt so deeply without the other. Carrot and whip, the goad of winning and losing drives ballplayers beyond pain and fatigue to retrieve a remembered pleasure, to get back that high.

From boyhood they focus on playing their games. Nothing else so engages their attention. On the field, they execute the same moves so many times under so many conditions that playing ball becomes an automatic habit, a routine of muscle memory, like an acquired instinct. By the time they reach the big show, they don't need to think much about what they do. Football players—especially running backs and the defense—take care to avoid what coach Chuck Noll of the Pittsburgh Steelers called "the paralysis of analysis." On a general intelligence test that the NFL gave prospective players, quarterbacks and offensive linemen (who must *act*) graded best while wide receivers, ball carriers, and defensive backfielders (who must *react*) scored lowest. Thinking "gets you caught from behind," said the halfback O. J. Simpson. "I'm not thinking about anything, so hopefully I'm thinking about everything. Pulling in what I need to pull in. You just react instead of consciously thinking about it."

Once into his game, Simpson clicked on an automatic pilot of "instinctive moves without any reason for them."

The defense, reacting viscerally to what the opposing offense does, needs a short memory to avoid dwelling on the last play as the next ball is snapped. Instead of cool analysis, the testy goads of anger and hatred—or any strong emotion—make football defense more effective. "They don't call the middle of the line The Pit for nothing," said the defensive lineman Merlin Olsen. "We really do get like animals. . . . We get so bruised and battered and tired we sometimes wind up playing in a sort of coma. By the end of the first half your instincts have taken over. By the end of the game you're an animal." Fred Smerlas, a nose tackle, could not abide the orderly habits of offensive linemen: always neat and polite, and, worse, they kept everything on hangers in their lockers and exulted in long, dutiful practice sessions. "They don't go to the bathroom without first consulting their playbooks," Smerlas sneered. Whereas defensive linemen wheeled at will and kept everything cluttered but their minds.

It all follows from the pure act on the field. Young Ty Cobb, debuting for his hometown team in Royston, Georgia, felt the bat tingle in his hands when he lined out his first base hit. As the electric impulse thrummed through his body, Cobb sensed a shock of recognition that he had found the right place, doing what he did best. Soon he won a game with another hit and bathed in his first adulation. Looking back late in life, encrusted with battles and honors, he still caressed that early glow: "Once an athlete feels the peculiar thrill that goes with victory and public praise, he's bewitched. He can never get away from it." "I don't know why," said the linebacker Sam Huff, "but I had this burning desire to be somebody; I wanted to be noticed, I wanted to be recognized. Some guys will deny it, but that's what they're playing for."

But the sharpest lure is the game itself: the rough sensuality of body contact, the flow of running and jumping for joy, the challenge of taming the ball, once more, for a moment. "There is this loose projectile flying through space," mused David Knight, a wide receiver, "and it's destined to fall unless you intersect with it. There is an incredible pleasure involved when you and the object meet perfectly." Warren Spahn won 363 games, more than any other left-handed pitcher, yet he most savored the unpitcherly skills. He loved to hit and run the bases but seldom was privileged to do either. "Any kid that plays in the Little League," said Spahn, "knows that the fun in the game is in swinging the bat and in hitting the ball. And when you hit the ball well, it's a feeling that you never forget." (Especially when you can't do it often.)

Ballplayers often claim to play for love, not for money. "The saps pay me for playing ball," said Wee Willie Keeler at the turn of the century. "Why, I would pay my way in to the ball park if that was the only way I had to get in a game." Active ballplayers, pushing their miserly owners for better pay, keep such compromisingly noble sentiments to themselves. Retired ballplayers, looking back rosily and striking the didactic postures of sages, typically claim that *they* played for fun while the mercenary younger generation cares only for money. They deny such ignoble motives in themselves. The claim is made so often, so plausibly, that it sounds sincere. "It wasn't money that kept me around for fifteen years," said Ray Nitschke of the Packers. "The reason I've played football is that I enjoy it. There is nothing I could have done with my life that I could possibly have enjoyed more." The son and brother of lawyers, Smoky Joe Wood spurned a profession and never even bothered to graduate from high school because he had clasped baseball: "I just loved to be out there. It was as simple as that." "I loved baseball," said Lefty Grove, who pitched for Connie Mack's Athletics. "If they said, 'Come on, here's a steak dinner,' and I had a chance to go out and play a game of ball, I'd go out and play the game and let the steak sit there. . . . The truth was, I would have played for nothing. Of course I never told Connie that."

Routinely fun, at rare, unaccountable moments the game takes off into magic and mystery, altering a player's sense of time, tapping into extra powers generally out of reach. These transforming flashes cannot be invoked intentionally. They appear unbidden and then do not come when called. A lone ballplayer may confront an entire team with the help of eerie extra forces. Jim Brown took the handoff from his quarterback, accelerating toward the line of scrimmage. "When I was clutching the football," he recalled, "my instincts were so acute it made no sense. Any movement, any sound, didn't matter where, how slight, I seemed to be aware of. I don't think my senses have ever felt that ridiculously heightened. Physically, I don't know that I've ever felt more vital." On a shared level, an entire team may feel an uncanny connection, knitting together as one organism with a single brain. Larry Bird pushed his Celtics toward this bonded groove: "You bother a guy to make him do something he doesn't want to do and there is a snowball effect for the next four or five minutes. Everybody gets into it and everybody starts clicking. Those moments when everybody is working together on defense are the best times you can have in this game."

The player in the still eye of the storm with the ball in his hand—the quarterback or point guard or pitcher—surveys the whole field before starting play. He feels himself in serene, uncanny command. He notices time slowing down: the more intense the moment, the slower the clock. "I know the defensive line is coming at me just as fast as ever," the quarterback John Brodie told himself. "I know perfectly well how hard and fast those guys are coming and yet the whole thing seems like a movie or a dance in slow motion." Alone on a pitcher's mound, Bill Lee felt paradoxically intense but relaxed, at ease but utterly aware. "Everything is slowed down, yet you are able to perceive things at an incredibly fast rate. Line drives shot up the middle may look hard to the observer in the stands, but they never seemed dangerous when they were hit back to me. They floated to the mound in slow motion." The ball was not a separate, intractable object but a friendly extension of the body. "You are the ball and the ball is you. It can do you no harm."

Basketball players feel these "peak" and "flow" moments with their mates most acutely. Their game features quick ball exchanges between tall, fast teams on a small floor, snapping from offense to defense and back. Any player can get the ball at any moment, and everyone must play responsible defense. It is the most team-oriented of team games. Bill Russell's Celtics, winning eleven titles in thirteen years, was the most dominant team in big-league history. According to Russell, their peaks and flows might last from five minutes to an entire quarter or longer. Both teams had to be evenly matched and play equally well, driving each other, for the magic breakthrough. In the fourth quarter of the final game of the 1965 play-offs, leading the Lakers by sixteen, the Celtics suddenly dashed off twenty straight points. Russell felt not triumphant but let down that the Lakers could not match the Celtics and maintain the flow.

When conditions were delicately right, three or four of the ten players on the floor—the predictable stars, in most cases—would heat up together. "The feeling would spread to the other guys, and we'd all levitate," Russell said later. "Then the game would just take off, and there'd be a natural ebb and flow that reminded you of how rhythmic and musical basketball is supposed to be." With the competition at its sharpest, Russell would feel oddly noncompetitive, rooting for the enemy to keep pace. Straining and wheezing, even coughing up body tissue, he would feel no pain or fatigue. "The game would move so quickly that every fake, cut and pass would be surprising, and yet nothing could surprise me. It was almost as if we were playing in slow motion. During those spells I could almost sense how the next play would develop and where the next shot would be taken. . . . My premonitions would be consistently correct, and I always felt then that I not only knew all the Celtics by heart but also all the opposing players, and that they knew me. There have been many times in my career when I felt moved or joyful, but these were the moments when I had chills pulsing up and down my spine." When the peaks lasted till the end of the game, he did not care who won, though he kept that from his victory-prone teammates. "If we lost, I'd still be as free and high as a sky hawk. But I had to be quiet about it. At times I'd hint around to other players about this feeling, but I never talked about it much, least of all to the other Celtics. I felt a little weird about it, and quite private."

Weird and private: every player had his own unshared perception of how the peak spurted and what it meant. Nobody claimed to know from whence it came or why it went. It seemed a gift from out there, mysterious, an inexplicable force—beyond the particular game and players—that went to the heart of the sport, hinting at what drew the players and fans to the game in the first place.

Bill Bradley felt it one night when his New York Knickerbockers were whomping a hapless team of Houston Rockets.

The Knicks played their own game, not needing the spur of a worthy opponent, helping each other while the Rockets bickered among themselves and yelled at their coach. Bradley's frontcourt mate, Dave DeBusschere, made two jumpers and a drive and then called a backdoor play for Bradley. The three other Knicks cleared the right side of the floor while DeBusschere dribbled toward Bradley in the far right corner, angling as though to set a pick for Bradley's jump shot. Bradley moved toward the screen, sucking in his man, then pushed suddenly off his left foot toward the hoop. DeBusschere dropped a bounce pass and Bradley ran free to the basket. Later another Knick ran the same play with the same easy score. All night long, the ball zipped from Knick to Knick, nobody holding it more than a few seconds, everyone seeking the open man. Plays were run as though no Rocket stood in the way. All the Knicks bounced to the same rhythm. Everything worked.

"The money and the championships are reasons I play," Bradley wrote in his diary afterward, "but what I'm addicted to are the nights like tonight when something special happens on the court." Bradley was a near-intellectual among ballplayers. Often sighted reading a book, even going to museums and plays, he was a Rhodes Scholar from Princeton, later a United States senator from New Jersey. Yet he remained as baffled by peaks and flows as any other jock. "The experience is one of beautiful isolation," Bradley ruminated. "It cannot be deduced from the self-evident, like a philosophical proposition. It cannot be generally agreed upon, like an empirically verifiable fact, and it is far more than a passing emotion. It is as if a lightning bolt strikes, bringing insight into an uncharted area of human experience. It makes perfect sense at the same time it seems new and undiscovered." Verbal description could only hint at the experience; "no one else can sense the inexorable rightness of the moment."

Searching his memory for when he had ever felt so right— "an immediate transporting enthusiasm and a feeling that everything is in perfect balance"—Bradley was carried back to childhood, when he had first found and loved this child's game with a ball. "In those moments on a basketball court I feel as a child and know as an adult. Experience rushes through my pores as if sucked by a strong vacuum. I feel the power of imagination

Ballplaying Life

that creates a sense of mystery and wonder I last accepted in childhood, before the mind hardened." So ultimate a high in playing the game connected him with the child in his adult personality. That spinning whoosh still idled within him, whirring forth at odd moments. "When I play for anyone outside the team, I play for children . . . and through the playing that allows me to continue feeling as a child I sense a child's innocent yearning and love." Back to the child and the ball.

◆　　◆　　◆

The game's decisive everyday imponderables keep a childish sense of wonder, or bafflement, alive in any conscious ballplayer. How to stop a cold streak or start a hot tear, or account for them? Why should a talented, title-bound team bumble away an entire season? How can a journeyman suddenly vault into a single great game, streak, year, then subside again into mediocrity? Nobody knows or can possibly know. Needing some ordering device against this chaos, ballplayers believe in childish rituals and superstitions that no sensible grown-up would admit to trusting. Deploying mysteries to meet other mysteries, the players remain boyish.

"All the time I was in a slump," Babe Ruth complained, "the pitches looked as big as balloons. It looked as though a blind man ought to hit 'em with a toothpick, then I'd swing and top 'em into the ground." The Babe thought he knew a surefire fix for a batting slump: eating raw scallions ("They've never failed me yet"). For routine maintenance, Ruth wore a brand-new pair of sweat socks every game. When Joe DiMaggio entered the clubhouse before a game, he went right to his locker and picked up his glove. From then till game time, no matter what else he was doing, he kept the glove at hand, like a child's favorite blanket. Running to or from the outfield, he always stepped on second; going to bat, he tapped the heel of his right shoe on the top step of the dugout. "I'm not superstitious about anything else," he insisted. "But when I do these things every day . . . I just . . . well . . . I feel right."

Like untrusted children, ballplayers are ordered around by their managers and coaches, told when to play, when to sit, what to do on the field, when to sleep, what temptations to avoid off the field. A typical player's carefully imperfect obedience to all these commands still does not allow a normally adult sense of autonomy. Crucial decisions lie beyond his control or even advice. He knows, is forever reminded, how little talent separates the stars from the spear carriers, and how precarious his place on the team must be. So he is grateful for any edge, any jinx or rabbit's foot, he may contrive. Suspicious? the pitcher Johnny Podres was asked. "No," he replied. "Careful." "It is merely," explained George Moriarty, a teammate of Ty Cobb's, "the business of acquiring habits that set the mind at ease."

Lefty Gomez, the pitching ace of DiMaggio's Yankees, moped through a season-long slump in 1936, besieged by gopher balls, with his earned run average bloating to 4.38. "I don't know what ails me," he cried. "I feel great. I never had better stuff. But I pitch and holler 'hellos' and it comes out 'nerts.' You ask the umpires what they think of my stuff. They will tell you that I do not lack speed or vitality." Next spring he invented a satisfying explanation. (A ballplayer needs only the illusion of mastery. Thinking he can do it, he can do it.) "For years I was a student of all the superstitions with which baseball and ball players are loaded," Gomez announced. "I paid attention to white horses and loads of empty barrels, to cross-eyed women fans, to placing the glove this way and to taking care I did not touch the base line when I walked from the mound to the bench. . . . This year I have abandoned all superstitions, all luck pieces. They did not do me any good last season, so why bother?" And sure enough, in 1937 Gomez led the league in wins, strikeouts, shutouts, and earned run average. Yet he did not recklessly abandon all superstitions. During his roommate DiMaggio's fifty-six-game hitting streak in 1941, Gomez helped out by rankly not changing his underwear for two months.

Personal rituals, a marginally higher order of superstitions, are at least intentional, even if first discovered by accident. Joe Lapchick, coaching the Knicks, forgot to kiss his wife good-bye before a road trip. The Knicks won all three games on the trip, "and I didn't kiss her the rest of the year. When you have a good thing going, you should not disrupt it." Steve Owen, the ensconced coach of the New York football Giants, would take precisely the same route to the Polo Grounds when his team was playing well. Leaving the field, he always walked between the goal posts. Carroll Rosenbloom, owner of the Baltimore Colts, would circle the field before every game, pat Johnny Unitas on the head, accept a piece of adhesive tape from Lenny Lyles, and then repair to his box, having done his bit. Tim Flannery of the San Diego Padres sustained a hitting streak with a postgame ritual of tequila and Chinese food: "The streak had to end or I was going to die."

For players, pregame rituals help to quell butterflies and focus one's mind in the last, jittery moments before the bright lights of play. Joe Fulks would always don his right sneaker first and never touch a basketball in the locker room. Jerry West would tear a stick of gum in half and place the pieces on either side of his locker. Jerry Kramer would use a new roll of adhesive tape to secure his socks, then throw away the rest of the roll before anyone else could touch it. ("I don't know why. It just has to be that way.") Walt Frazier would dress completely, down to his warm-up jacket, before adding his sneakers, then his laces. If he'd played poorly in his last game, he would change the color of his laces, from orange to blue or back. When the Boston Celtics finished warming up before a game, a Celtic—Bob Cousy, later John Havlicek—would take and make the last shot. If a renegade ball boy then threw up a playful shot just before tap-off, a Celtic would have to go back and redo the punctuation. Jim Brosnan, a pitcher known as "the Professor" for his oddly bookish ways, would bind his pregame cud of chewing tobacco with a stick of gum. He would then tear the outer gum wrapper into thin strips, separate the foil from the inner wrapper, tear that into more strips, then cover the shredded paper under a pile of dirt ("I don't consider a game started unless I've done it"). In the big leagues, book learning did not inhibit sacred ritual.

A permanent, offhandedly necessary aspect of big-league life, superstitions reached a loony peak among baseballers from the late nineteenth century into the 1930s. Never before or since have so many big leaguers abided by so many peculiar notions. At the time, players came from odd corners down home and upstate, from diverse ethnic enclaves and folkways. Mass culture as yet lacked the blunderbuss clout to knock off their rough edges and compel a blander uniformity. They brought to the show intact their old-timey beliefs in signs, evil eyes, and mystic gestures.

Nap Lajoie and Eddie Collins, the best second basemen of this era, batted with the help of dirt and chewing gum. On his way to the plate, Lajoie picked up a handful of dirt and dropped it on the umpire's shoes. (Umps didn't give him many walks.) Collins at bat kept his gum on the button atop his cap. With two strikes on him, he put the gum in his mouth to be sure. (He didn't strike out much.) Pepper Martin collected women's hairpins, certain of their power to improve his game. When Christy Mathewson saw a cross-eyed man, he took off his hat and spat into it. His manager, John McGraw, knowing that empty barrels meant base hits, hired a wagonload of barrels to circle the Polo Grounds until the Giants shook their slump. Bat boys were cautioned to keep bats lined up in parallel rows on the ground by the dugout. Crossed bats brought trouble; once they caused Turkey Mike Donlin of the Giants to break a leg sliding into third. But to snap a slump, the Athletics—defying fate—tossed their bats into the air and let them lie where they fell!

In an age less kind to the less fortunate, black people, hunchbacks, and lunatics were considered human good-luck charms, as though their tough breaks in life made a baseball team fortunate by contrast. A team would adopt a black street child, or an older black man, rubbing his head for luck, keeping him around as long as he seemed to help and amused the players. Nuf Ced McGreevy once hired a black mascot to carry a long pole with a large bean pot, the team symbol, dangling from the top. It was good-humored, amiable, but with a mean edge of condescension and dismissal. Thus this imagined doggerel from 1888, racist and innocent:

> I'se a merry little Mascotte coon,
>   An' scatterin' luck I go;
> (I'se little becos' I was picked too soon,
>   And didn't have time to grow).
> De pitcher strikes dem out
>   'Cos he gets his curves from me;
> And whenever I is about,
>   We bag de victory.

Bill "Bojangles" Robinson, the black dancer, blessed his favorite teams with mystic vials of goofer dust. For crucial games he would dance in the dugout and scatter dust over bats and gloves. After a win, he would jump on a rubbing table and give a free show, the players clapping in rhythm. Once, after he celebrated a home run by performing a hornpipe jig on his seat, a grieving fan for the opposition called him a few unfriendly names. "I may be all you say, mister," Bojangles replied, silencing his critic amid laughter, "but it's still a home run."

Black magic sparked one of the phenomenal comebacks in baseball history. At mid-summer 1914, the Boston Braves, managed by George Stallings, dawdled in last place. Stallings deployed his usual superstitions—removing birds and scraps of paper from the field in front of his dugout, holding rigid postures when his team was rallying—but the Braves still stunk until a friend gave Stallings a lucky dime blessed by a Cuban medicine man known as "The Negro Pope." The Miracle Braves immediately went airborne, won the pennant by a mile, and swept one of Connie Mack's great Philadelphia teams in the World Series; thanks, Stallings was sure, to his lucky dime.

Eddie Bennett, the hunchbacked mascot/bat boy of the Yankees, was often the first to shake Babe Ruth's hand after a home run. It was only fair, since Eddie had let the Babe rub his hump en route to the plate. Bennett was a Brooklyn street urchin, an orphan with no interested relatives, crippled by a childhood fall that had left his spine deformed. He played sandlot ball, his back in an iron brace, and hung around the big-league parks. One day in the summer of 1919 he went to the Polo Grounds hoping to sneak into a game between the Yankees and White Sox. Sixteen years old, he looked smaller and younger. Outside the park, Happy Felsch of the White Sox brushed by him, then stopped. "Say, kid," Felsch asked, "are you lucky?" The turning point in Eddie Bennett's life. "Sure, Happy," he said ("I came right back at him kind of quavery, I guess"). The White Sox took him in, touched his hump, and won that day and the next. They passed a hat, collecting sixteen dollars for Eddie, and left town. In Philadelphia, taking no chances, they sent for him. Eddie traveled the American League with the White Sox for the rest of the season, helping them to the pennant. Later he refused to believe they'd thrown the World Series that fall: "They were all such fine guys!"

The next season Eddie joined his hometown Dodgers. They won their first pennant in twenty years and, with Eddie on hand, two World Series games at Brooklyn. Then the Dodgers went to Cleveland—without him—and lost four straight games and the Series. So Eddie's legend grew. In 1921 he moved along to the Yankees, who responded predictably by winning their first pennant ever and entering their first golden epoch. The pitcher Herb Pennock always insisted that Eddie hand him a warm-up ball before starts. Well into manhood, Eddie stayed devoted to the Yankees and modest about his mascoting gifts. "I like to be a mascot first rate. I like to be around with the players," he said. "But it isn't all peaches and cream. When we lose, the mascot feels it as much as the players. True, they don't blame him, but he has sense enough to keep out of their way." The only salaried mascot in the game, at the top of his esoteric calling he lived alone in a rented room and drank too much. Eddie had no life away from baseball. "It's lonesome in the winters," he admitted. "I wish they could play baseball all the year round." A taxi ran him down in 1933, and he died two years later of alcoholism.

Sadder yet was the legend of Charles Victor Faust. For part of one season with the New York Giants, he acted out the game's most appealing scripts: the baseball-struck kid who dreams of the big show, the countrified hick initiated to the big city, the unknown rookie from nowhere who suddenly makes his mark. His teammates drew him in with the usual rough taunting accorded any newcomer. He had his moments, and then was gone. But a jagged crack slices through this classic fable. Not a real ballplayer at all, Charley Faust was crazy. Engulfed by all the laughter around him, he did not get it. The chortling Giants, oblivious to consequences, were toying with a wounded personality, like bad schoolboys at recess twitting an odd kid. "The cold truth of the matter is that Faust never should have been permitted at large," Fred Lieb, a sportswriter then covering the Giants, later concluded. "There is nothing funny in a man who is partly insane."

Faust grew up on a farm in Marion, Kansas, fifty miles outside Wichita, the oldest of six children born to a family of

German-Russian immigrants. In July 1911, the summer of his thirty-first year, he took a train to St. Louis, the nearest city with a big-league team. At the hotel of the visiting New York Giants, he presented himself to John McGraw. In country-earnest language with a German accent, he explained that a fortune-teller had inspired him to join the Giants and become a famous pitcher. How about a tryout? McGraw examined this tall, thin man, the eyes not quite aligned, the expansive gap-toothed smile, the loping gait. What the hell. This could be fun.

At the park that afternoon, Faust came out in his best dark Sunday suit and black derby hat. McGraw squatted down to catch his trial pitches. Faust whirled both arms over his head, like a double-jointed windmill, then lobbed up cream puffs. McGraw got to liking the joke better. Winking at the Giants taking infield practice, he sent Faust up to hit and told him to run on the first fair ball. Charley scorched a dribbler to short and took off. Running and sliding, with the fielders falling over themselves, he made it all the way home, to the delirious appreciation of all. An obvious talisman, he was allowed to sit on the bench as the Giants lost. The next day they gave him a uniform, purposely short in the sleeve and leg, and he again was paced through a hilarious workout. The Giants won the remaining games in the series. As the team boarded its train for Chicago that evening, Faust was there, ready to go. Gosh, said McGraw, he had left Charley's contract and ticket back at the hotel; there was just enough time for Faust to run back for them and still make the train. The Giants watched him gallop away, sure they had seen the last of him.

A few weeks later he showed up in New York, caked with dust and mud. "I'm here, all right," he said, donning his uniform. The Giants won a few games until McGraw, tiring of the joke, barred him from the clubhouse. Faust wept, the Giants lost, and he rejoined the team. "The players believed in him," Christy Mathewson noted, "and none would have let him go if it had been necessary to support him out of their own pockets." Faust grew to like ballplaying life. He took up to five manicures a day and ate pie at every meal. With Faust on hand, jabbering cracked monologues and foretelling events, the Giants swept through a late-season road trip, winning eighteen of twenty-two games to seize the pennant. In the eleventh inning of a game in St. Louis, the Cardinals threatening to win, Faust was warming up in the distant outfield. McGraw sent Matty to fetch him to the bench, where his magic worked better. Faust came loping in, the Cardinals did not score, and the Giants eventually won. "It was as nice a piece of pinch mascoting as I ever saw," Matty smiled.

Charley still hoped to play in a real game. McGraw made out a contract for him on the back of a detachable collar. Faust pitched two innings in meaningless games at the end of the year, allowing two hits and one run; the opponents may have joined in the joke. But his powers vanished in the World Series, which the Giants lost to Philadelphia in six games. The next year McGraw would not give him a uniform. Faust hung around, insisting. The laughter grew thin. The Giants, rolling to an easy pennant, did not need him anymore.

Faust complained to August Herrmann, president of the National League, who asked Giants owner John T. Brush about it. Still kidding, Brush replied that a legitimate "jinx dispenser" should display flashing eyes and curling hair, "and when he [Faust] reached New York neither his eye nor his hair did either of these things." Not amused, Herrmann demanded a serious response. All right, wrote Bush, "I have always felt sorry for Faust. I have never been given to kidding him personally." But "it is simply a physical impossibility to shake him. He follows the Club from one town to another and there seems to be nothing that McGraw can do to prevent it." How to discourage him? "He can not be advised. He has stood at the side of my auto when I was trying to watch the game, an hour at a time and many times repeating over and over again, 'Well I want to sign, well I am ready to sign, well I want to sign,' till it became necessary to get some one to take him away." McGraw had let him pitch for the Giants. He wanted more.

Eventually Faust gave up and wandered to California. He sent McGraw a ninety-six-page letter offering himself once again; after all, he had prepared by climbing a mountain every day. Late in 1914 his family put him in an insane asylum. He died there in June 1915, thirty-four years old. The Giants finished last that year, twenty-one games out: Charley Faust's revenge.

♦   ♦   ♦

"There is little of the serious in a ball-player's makeup," the sportswriter Harry Palmer concluded in 1890. "The life of the average professional ball-player is full of good things."

♦   ♦   ♦

Boys at play on the field, they keep playing off the field, still boys, seeking amusement and easily amused. Play for a living slides over into play as living. The extravagant good fortune of grown-up pay for child's play encourages a child's dream of never growing old, always having fun, a game that keeps going forever. "You don't grow up," said the football lineman Garry Puetz. "You don't *have* to grow up."

Every summer Vince Lombardi rasped his Green Bay Packers into war status at a spartan preseason training camp. For eight weeks the Packers were contained like delinquent children at an isolated playing field and dorm, with an allowance of ninety minutes of free time six days a week, then an extravagant five hours on Saturdays. Lombardi assumed and the Packers understood that not everyone would behave for that long. One year, a half hour after curfew on the second Saturday of camp, a player appeared at the door of the coaches' office. In undershorts and shower clogs, he stood waiting "like a small boy" for the coaches to notice him. Could he have a drink of water? (A restive boy after bedtime.) Sure, said a coach. Thank you, said the player. The coaches heard the shower clogs clump down the hall, then the clink of a coin in the pay phone. "He just dropped a dime in the water fountain," said a coach. "He's going tonight." Somebody checked later that night and found the parched boy and his roommate gone, slaking other thirsts. Lombardi was reminded of what the football coach Lou Little had said: "When I see them on the field they look like gladiators, but when I see them off the field they're just kids." ("It was part of our life," the quarterback Johnny Unitas recalled fondly, "sneaking out if you wanted to risk it. It was a hundred-dollar fine if they caught you, and let's say I got away with it more times than they caught me.")

Arrested in their "terminal adolescent syndrome," happily focused on their various games, most ballplayers were quite simple forms of life. Favorite off-field amusements changed a bit over time, depending on what the players could find, but within a consistent boyish pattern of cheerful emptyheadedness and incuriosity about any world beyond the immediate field of play. "What I didn't know about books would have filled a very large library, and I hadn't the slightest desire to know any more," said Cap Anson, who played baseball from the 1870s through the 1890s. He strayed briefly into two colleges, mostly to fortify the school team, but escaped much improvement. "Maybe one out of a hundred pro football players would go to a library," said Johnny Blood of football life in the 1920s and 1930s. "We played golf, we went hunting, we drank—the ordinary activities of young men when they're at leisure. We had no difficulty passing the day." On NBA road trips in the 1940s and 1950s, recalled Bob Davies, "you either slept or played cards. Not too many of us were readers in those days." "You just go out and fool around, buy records, watch TV," Richard Caster noted of NFL culture in the 1970s and 1980s. Caster did broaden himself to the grand extent of reading a daily newspaper, "something my grandfather told me to do when I was just old enough to read. It's amazing, but just that little bit, reading a newspaper, is something that can separate you from a lot of dudes."

Even Moe Berg, considered baseball's great intellectual, read mainly newspapers, great piles of them every day. His Ivy League schooling and knack for learning languages made him seem a deep scholar. Yet only once over the course of many years did the sportswriter Jerome Holtzman see him with a book in his hand, a Sanskrit dictionary. "Moe certainly wasn't any intellectual in the usual sense," Holtzman decided. "I never heard him engage in philosophical discussions or expound on great ideas or great books." He looked studious only in a group of ballplayers— among whom almost anybody could look studious.

Youthful spirits and blindered horizons leave a ballplayer with a risky sense of proportion, too readily puffed or deflated, his head too easily turned and swelled. A typical big leaguer jumps quickly from bush to plush quarters, from obscurity to limelights. Young and unworldly, he has no frame of reference for the cheers and attention suddenly piled on him. He believes the praise too much. The ballplayer comes to expect free tickets to shows, suits at half price, cars for below dealer cost. He receives and is not required to give. Ever reminded of his eminence, he demands the most attentive service from hotels, drivers, clerks, and food servers. He roisters noisily far into the night and then expects to sleep late, undisturbed. Others check him into hotels, handle his luggage, arrange his travel. And all this on top of the essential privilege of big-league ballplaying. "Vulgarly healthy, frankly outspoken and unawed by any authority or pomp," the sportswriter Hugh Fullerton exasperated in 1910, "ball players are about as spoiled, unreasonable and pampered as a matinee idol."

Like all children, ballplayers dart across a vast behavioral range from annoying to endearing. Spoiled and willful, they yield in a twinkling to boyish pranks, elaborate plots, stupid puns: any broad humor they are supposed to have outgrown. They are out playing with other boys. The laughter makes them bearable again. Honus Wagner claimed that a rabbit once crossed his path when he was chasing a grounder. "In the confusion I picked up the rabbit and fired it to first base. [Pause] I got the runner by a hare." Cap Anson liked to tell a doggy story from the 1892 season. Fans were then allowed to park their carriages in the far outfield, seldom reached by the dead ball, and watch from there. At a game in Boston, an actor named Henry E. Dixey and his pet bull terrier were lounging in a buckboard in left field when the batter hit a hard liner toward them. The ball screamed over the left fielder and hit the dog, breaking his neck. While the dog tumbled down dead, Dixey rose in astonishment, the crowd craned to see, and the batter raced all the way home. It was, Anson later deadpanned, "the only genuine case of making a dog-gone run that has ever come under my observation."

It seemed funnier at the time. Ballplayer humor works best among ballplayers, especially in bored groups away from home, lusting for any shred of amusement. Once the Boston Celtics drove themselves to an exhibition game in western Massachusetts, Tommy Heinsohn riding in a car with coach Red Auerbach. College graduates all, they were playing "an intellectual game" (Heinsohn's phrase) called Zit. The first man to see a cemetery or a dog got a point. To spot a dog pissing meant five points. To spot two dogs in copulation brought the jackpot. After a time, playing Zit understandably palled. The Celtics stopped for a bushel of apples. Boredom sparked inspiration. Bob Cousy's car pulled up alongside Auerbach's and released a volley of apples. The barrage was returned. The cars weaved along the highway. Celtics took bites and stiff-armed the apples like hand grenades, with vocal explosions. Everybody enjoyed the battle until the police siren.

A policeman pulled Auerbach over; Cousy kept going. "What the hell do you guys think you're doing?" asked the cop. "Well," said Auerbach, "we were playing Zit." This did not clarify matters. The cop took the culprits to the local justice of the peace. "They were throwing apples," the officer submitted. What? "We were having an apple war," Auerbach explained. Eventually the justice of the peace, peering hard, saw the humor of the encounter and let the Celtics off.

You had to get away with it. The right aftermath clinched the joke; ballplayer humor could be doused by detection and punishment. Pepper Martin was the sunniest spirit among the rollicking Gashouse Gang of St. Louis Cardinals. At a tight moment in a game, he might stroll over from third base and slap a wad of gum on the pitcher's wrist: a tension-reliever. Martin liked to tie uniforms into knots, nail shoes to the floor, distribute sneezing powder, exploding matches, exploding cigars. Whenever the Cardinals misbehaved, suspicion reasonably hovered over Martin. Partial to water bombs, he lingered one day at the window of a hotel mezzanine—a bag full of water in one hand, a newspaper in the other—waiting for Frank Frisch, the Cardinal manager. Frisch obligingly appeared on the sidewalk below. Martin dropped the bag, tore down the stairs to the lobby, sat down, crossed his legs, and raised his newspaper. And composed himself. Enter Frisch, soaked and sputtering, then furious to see Martin looking so innocent.

The rules of male raillery demanded the roughest jokes about the touchiest matters. The joke tested the toughness of the victim, whether he could air out his private hurt. What to call a player with bad skin? Pizza face. How about someone prone to pulling hamstrings? Hammie. A man of loony lapses? Psycho. Eppa Rixey, proud son of Virginia, heard enemy dugouts whistling "Marching Through Georgia," a theme song of Sherman's pillage to the sea. "That song doesn't make me mad," said Rixey. "The thing that makes me mad is that they *think* they're making me mad." Danny Murtaugh, ugly by any standard, sat in a hot thermal bath with his teammates. "Danny, you sit here long enough," one suggested, "and your face will get as soft as putty, then we'll remold it." "I'll try it," Murtaugh agreed, with no choice but to play along. "Anything would be an improvement."

Art Donovan, a tackle for the Baltimore Colts, was fat, inattentively dressed, and terrified of small, furry animals. His teammates made sure he knew they knew about all these traits. In training camp a joker shot a groundhog and placed the remains, with half the head blown away, in Donovan's bed. He found the gift, screamed, and spent that night sleeping on the floor of another room. Next day, he opened his locker and flinched at the groundhog hanging from a string. Donovan bolted the premises, knocking down the equipment manager, and was almost hit by a car.

Not funny, he thought, not like the coat story. Donovan cherished a favorite sport jacket, fraying at the cuffs and collar, which he stubbornly wore on every road trip. It fit him well, he figured, and that was hard to achieve on a man called "Fatso." But in a hotel lobby, two Colts came up behind him and ripped the coat from his broad back. "It was funny and everybody laughed and all that, and I took the jacket and threw it in the trash can at the hotel." A few hours later Donovan passed through the lobby and found his jacket adorning a statue of a naked lady. Again he threw it away. After the game the next day, a bellboy brought him a package, COD, three dollars due. The jacket. Donovan flung it out the bus window. The night before the next road game, another bellboy in another hotel with another COD package. The jacket. Donovan threw it down a laundry chute. Two weeks later, at home in Baltimore, again the jacket. Donovan asked his wife to burn it. Eight months later, at a Shriners gala, Donovan as the guest of honor was presented with: the jacket.

Within the team, players agree to be amused by almost any lurch at humor, no matter how lame, stale, or hurtful. It is part of the unwritten team compact: *While we play for the same team, if you take the trouble to tease me, you must want to be my teammate. So I'll play along.* Locker rooms overflow with prickly jests that would be gross insults outside the team. "A harsh clubhouse is a happy clubhouse, in my experience," said the first baseman Keith Hernandez. "The reason is simple: We're not going to joke with a player we're not comfortable with." None of Joe DiMaggio's teammates called him "Joltin' Joe" or "The Yankee Clipper." Those were merely newspaper nicknames. The Yankees knew him as "Dago," "Dag" (pronounced Dayg) for short. When Phil Rizzuto joined the team, the two became "Big Dago" and "Little Dago," "and you can see that they took it as a compliment," according to Leo Durocher, looking back after fifty years in the game. "For as long as I have been in baseball, every Italian has been called 'Dago,' and every Jew has been called 'Hebe.'" The terms sounded meaner, though, when yelled from the enemy dugout. "Given a certain inflection," Durocher conceded, "it can be a sign of affection. Given another inflection, it can be something else again."

The team is a portable cauldron of peculiar folkways and cryptic humor. Ballplayers spend half the season away from home, thrown together more than they as unteamed individuals would freely choose. Until the 1960s they traveled mostly by train. The run from St. Louis to Boston took over twenty-four hours; men went to bed with wet towels over their noses to screen the soot. "It wasn't the greatest sleeping," said the outfielder Bob Cerv. "You'd have to be pretty danged tired to go to sleep with that clicking." Sometimes it helped to repeat a ballplayer's name—Heinie Manush, Heinie Manush—to the rhythm of the clicking rails. The team reposed in hierarchy, spread through two or three Pullmans. Stars got lower berths in the middle of the first car, the spot with the best ride. Other regulars, then benchwarmers, then rookies took upper berths at distant points in the immutable pecking order. A good teammate bore a swaying upper berth as he bore an insult too close to home: part of teamness.

They dawdled through long days on the train with card games and chitchat. A particular student of the game, such as Ted Williams, might hold technical seminars. The clock was turned off. There was nowhere to go, nothing to do; just ride the rails. "We learned to know our teammates intimately and developed team spirit," said Jimmy Dykes, recalling the best parts.

"Give me the comfort and ease of a Pullman chair car, the chatter, the gags, the absence of worry, real or imaginary, the passage of idle time." On a trainload of Cardinals in 1942, the veteran Estel Crabtree initiated a rookie to big-league humor. A passenger could leave his shoes just inside the curtain of his compartment, to be picked up and shined by the porter during the night. Crabtree told the rookie that someone had been stealing shoes, so he must guard them, piled together in the rookie's compartment. Came the night and the porter on his rounds. The rookie pounced, grabbed the porter in a bearhug, yelling, "I got him! I got him!" The other Cardinals laughed all the way to breakfast.

"I've always had this thing for trains," said Johnny Blood of the Packers. "They bring something out in me." After the last game in 1930, the Packers toasted their second straight NFL title on the train back to Green Bay. Spirits were raised. In the club car at the front of the train, Blood tossed wet napkins at Lavie Dilweg, a large end. Dilweg bristled, which only brought more wet napkins. Dilweg went for him and Blood, smaller but faster, took off. "We just went racing through car after car, the people looking up wondering what the hell was going on." Blood dashed through the last car and onto the rear platform; no more running room. Dilweg roared in triumph as he burst through the final door. Blood sprang to the railing, then to the roof of the car. The train careened along. "I looked back down and you should have seen the look on his face. He just stared up in disbelief." Blood yelled, "So long," and ran the top of the train, jumping from car to car, all the way to the locomotive, where he surprised the crew. He hid there till they reached Green Bay.

In road cities teams staked their claims to hotel lobbies. Lolling in comfortable chairs for hours before and after games, commenting on the passing scene, smoking expansively and looking for fun, ballplayers met their publics, told stories, and settled bets. "Lobby sitting takes much patience, concentration, endurance and even alertness," an observer noted. "No man can be a great sitter if he is restless and a squirmer." Perhaps for these reasons, baseball pitchers—Lefty Grove, Lon Warneke, Charlie Root—excelled as sitters, showing a pitcher's tenacity and patience. They rose from bed early to claim the best chairs, then rested for the game. Grove ("a lobby jokester with rare timing and a trigger brain") delighted in tripping the unaware. At six feet three inches and 190 pounds, he got them to enjoy it. Warneke liked to drop a fat wallet on the rug, with string attached, and yank it from anybody who reached for it. No seasoned lobby sitter dared close his eyes. That risked hotfoots, spitballs, newspapers aflame. They were ballplayers.

Freeze that tableau: the playful boys grouped in a lobby. Within that circle, time stops. The tobacco smoke, curled and hovering, hangs rigid. Everyone holds still. Outside that circle, the real world remains complex, unpredictable, ever changing and daunting. Ballplaying life beckons, simple and safe. "Day after day we were always the same," recalled Pat Jordan, a minor-league lobby sitter who never made it to the bigs. "We were always in the same pose, the same chair, talking about the same things," said Jordan, yearning for the lost chances. "We never grew. We didn't have to. As long as we remained 'in baseball' we could postpone the unpleasantness of growing. . . . Sitting in those lobbies, we never wanted to leave."

"Sometimes we'd forget there was a real world out there," said Lloyd Waner of the Pirates. "Remember, we went from the hotel to the ball park, back to the hotel, and then onto the train for the next go-around. All of our reservations were made for us, all of our meals were paid for. Did that for six months." After which Lloyd and his brother Paul would go back home to Oklahoma, to the Dust Bowl and the Depression, "and then we would realize how bad things were."

Bill Bradley, full of books and long-term ambitions, shared little ground with his Knick teammates except basketball. That common purpose kept the team close, to a point. Teammates were loyal and honest with each other, communicating clearly and simply, feeding "relationships which are close and real but never intimate." Friendships were shallower but tidier than in the real world. Ballplaying life was both more and less than real life. "We travel from city to city," Bradley noticed, "sometimes as if we were unaware of a larger world beyond our own. Every city we enter is full of crises and problems that never reach us in a hotel room." For big leaguers, "every day is a struggle to stay in touch with life's subtleties."

Most simply avoided the struggle, or didn't notice it. They had a game to play. During the game, nothing else seemed so real or important. Before and after the game, the engine merely idled, leaving time to kill.

◆　◆　◆

"The professional ballist has a hard time," a Buffalo newspaper bantered in 1885. "He rises every morning at 10 o'clock, takes a snug breakfast in the cafe, reads the Metropolitan newspapers, strolls out in the corridors and smokes a Reina Victoria, takes a nap before dinner, dines at 2 o'clock and strolls out to the ball field about 3 o'clock. . . . His income, compared with that of others in the same stratum of society, is simply princely. The small boy worships him, the young girls dote on him, and his friends and neighbors look upon him as immense, perfectly elegant, the howlingest kind of a swell. . . . He's criticised by the newspapers and hissed at by the spectators in the grand stand. He's sensitive, very sensitive—men of refined natures are apt to be—and these things grate on him harshly."

◆　◆　◆

The beckoning dangers of ballplaying life were ample free time and a lust to make it fun. "He's apt to become a bum," Benny Friedman said of a typical football player. "Outside of a couple of hours of light practice a day all he's got to do is hang around and twiddle his thumbs between games." "The only trouble with being a pro football player in New York was that you were bored to death," Tuffy Leemans of the Giants agreed. "You had too much leisure time on your hands."

Faced with this awful condition, ballplayers amused themselves with the dangerous fun of drink and sex. Each of these masculine pleasures was agreeable in moderation but deranging in excess. Ballplayers generally disapproved of moderation. They won by taking chances on the field; here again an attitude carried over into life when the game finished. A little peril sharpened the experience. How far was too far? At what point did bold turn reckless turn self-destroying? Finding out was part of the thrill. Playing hard risked losing the game, even the ultimate game, but it made winning yet more savory.

"Promise me one thing," Connie Mack's mother implored him when he signed his first contract in 1884. "Promise me that you won't drink." Mack never did, which made him strange among ballplayers. From the start, baseball had played with booze. The first clubs in New York topped off games with convivial dinners. Saloons served as clubhouses. The sporting underground of the late 1800s was always well oiled, fans and players alike. Old ballplayers retired to tending bar and telling stories. While the National League tried feckless measures to dry out, the American Association—the other major league of the 1880s—was known as "the Beer and Whiskey League." Beer barons ran its affairs as the stands roared with gambling and drinking. One rainy day after a wetter night, Pete Browning of the Louisville club bought a fishing pole and sat on the front porch of the Midland Hotel in Kansas City, dangling his hook and line in the muddy water of the gutter. The Louisville manager, quite perturbed, left him in Kansas City.

Nobody ever *had* to drink, but ballplaying life did in ways demand liquids. Young men, sweating hard under tight pressures, naturally grew thirsty. They veered through extreme emotions that called for cushioning or enhancement. "The games present us with excuses to take a drink," the pitcher Bill Lee noticed. "If we have a good game, we want to celebrate. If we were horseshit, we want to forget. Young players drink to fit in, to take part in the camaraderie and relieve the boredom. When a player sees his career coming to an end, it's a more dangerous time. He tends to drink a lot more than he used to, knowing that his days in the sun are almost at an end and there's nothing he can do about it."

On the baseball model, football and basketball players also raised their glasses. "Hell, we'd all get drunk after a game in those days," Clarke Hinkle said of the NFL 1930s. "[Packer coach Curly] Lambeau would say. 'The lid's off, boys, but stay out of jail.' " "After every game," Toy Ledbetter of the Eagles said of the 1950s, "we'd unwind and get drunk on our kiesters. Not everybody, but probably 70 percent of the team, and we'd all go together." These postgame blowouts aside, football's physical demands controlled hard, habitual drinking. A suspected lush might, in practice, have to perform the dread "roll drill": lie down and roll the length of the practice field until dizzily nauseated. Only quarterbacks like Bobby Layne, protected from hard contact, could swill at will, year after year. "I drink for the same reason I keep company with girls," Joe Namath insisted. "It takes away the tension." Once his roommate, convinced they were sloshed too often, persuaded Namath to stop drinking from Tuesday till the Sunday game. The Jets, favored that week by 19 points, lost as Namath threw 5 interceptions. Too much tension. So Namath drank steadily through the next week, then was not intercepted as the Jets won. (He played only once under a hangover. He threw 14 for 21, 3 touchdowns, 287 yards, for a win. "To this day, I don't know what happened during that game," he puzzled. "I guess my receivers must have had a helluva day.")

Basketball, requiring players to run miles every night, also by its nature weeded out drunkards. They might still play, but not for long and not at their peak. Joe Fulks had started drinking Kentucky bootleg whiskey in high school. He averaged almost twenty-four points a game during his first three pro years, twice leading the league in scoring, but then tailed off. "The bottle," his boss, Eddie Gottlieb, said later. "That was the trouble with him. Eventually it ruined him. . . . He could have played a couple more years if that didn't take something out of him." At thirty Fulks enjoyed his last good season. Two years later he was down to eight minutes a game, then gone from the league. "He was a free spirit," Gottlieb decided. "Free spirits are happy. He wasn't drinking because he was unhappy. He liked Kentucky bourbon."

Beyond these inherent limits imposed by the games themselves, coaches and managers could little affect what players drank, though they felt obliged to try. Red Auerbach allowed beer but not whiskey; Joe McCarthy allowed whiskey but not beer, which he thought would give a man "beer legs" and make him sweat too much. (Auerbach—"Don't ask me why"—also banned waffles or pancakes within twelve hours of game time.) Coach Al Cervi of the Syracuse Nationals decreed only two cans of beer for his players on trains; so Johnny Kerr toed the letter of the law with two one-quart cans of Foster beer before bedtime. John McGraw called every move on the field but gave up elsewhere. "What's the use of telling a player what time he should go to bed or what he should drink?" he asked. "If I've got to force a man to take care of himself, then he will be no good, anyway." Miller Huggins imposed a five-hundred-dollar fine on the Yankees for excessive drinking. Babe Ruth didn't notice.

Baseball's rulers, setting an example, talked one way and drank another. As a federal judge, Commissioner Kenesaw Landis dealt strictly with violators of Prohibition while in private he continued tippling his favorite illegal bourbon. At a drenched party in 1922, he jested a toast: "Gentlemen, let us drink to the Eighteenth Amendment." Ban Johnson, the purse-lipped founder of the American League, thundered warnings to his players about the dangers of drink; he was himself often drunk in public, slurring soggy rants at banquets. After one such evening, perhaps unsure of where he found himself, he urinated in a hotel elevator. Another time, he managed to find his way to the right room number, in the wrong hotel. A knowing sportswriter imagined a colloquy at a meeting of baseball's high commissioners in 1918:

Garry Herrmann: "We have assembled here, gentlemen, to open a new case."

Ban Johnson: "Um hum. I trust the case does not contain less than twelve quarts—"

Raucous laughter. Booze and baseball were entwined in a sloppy embrace. What else were fans supposed to drink with their peanuts and hot dogs? Team owners (like Horace Stoneham of the Giants) and general managers (like Larry MacPhail of the Reds, Dodgers, and Yankees) were often notorious lushes. Beer companies owned teams and sponsored broadcasts of games. In 1954, only two teams—the Giants and Pirates—did *not* include brands of beer among their radio sponsors. Alcohol in one form or another trickled into every corner of the game.

For some ballplayers this meant drowned careers and brief lives. Bugs Raymond, a spitball pitcher, lurched through three teams in six years. "They used to say he didn't spit on the ball," a teammate recalled; "he blew his breath on it, and the ball would come up drunk." Raymond was finished pitching at twenty-nine, dead from a blow by a baseball bat at forty. Rube Waddell, the most extravagantly gifted pitcher of his era, led the American League in strikeouts seven times. His pitching hand, big enough to hide a billiard ball, could engulf a baseball with his fingers touching the palm behind it; so Waddell could twist off any spin to the ball he wished. He would whirl through a bizarre windup, arms flailing against the sky, bringing the ball to a dead stop at his belt, then release a fastball unrelated to the busy windup. When his pitch was hopping right, Waddell's catcher could see inches of daylight between the ball and the futile swings of the enemy. "How good he'd have been if he'd taken baseball seriously is hard to imagine," Sam Crawford said later. According to Connie Mack, his most patient manager, Waddell had four passions: fishing, drinking, fires, and baseball. "In about that order. Only, sometimes he reversed the first two." Mack finally gave up and exiled him to the St. Louis Browns. Waddell played his last good season at thirty-two and was dead five years later. "He burned his life away," *Baseball Magazine* keened, "when he should have been in his prime, a cruel April jest."

If a great ballplayer unaccountably lost his skills too early, drinking might lurk behind the seemly explanations offered the public. In 1941 the Dodgers' Pete Reiser, twenty-two years old, hit .343 and led the league in doubles, triples, runs, and batting average. But after coming back from three years in the wartime army, he was known mainly for injuries and colliding with out-field walls: a sad case of blighted promise, it was said, because he played too hard. In fact, Reiser had devoted his war years to playing baseball for army teams, running up debts, getting divorced, and drinking. In 1944 the Dodgers loaned him $1,250. A year later, with that debt unpaid, Reiser asked Dodger president Branch Rickey for another $2,000. Rickey gave him a lecture instead. "For some time past, and from more than one source, there has come to me stories, really ugly stories, about yourself," Rickey told his ballplayer. "These stories have to do with your drinking, mainly that. . . . You know just as well as I do that you were supposed to have a great future ahead of you in baseball, and why you will kick that future around like a boy with a football is mystifying, of course, to those who have never seen it done. I have seen it done a good many times. I have seen some great athletes go to hell pretty fast." No loan and no further sympathy for Reiser. Back in the big leagues—only twenty-seven, moving into what should have been his peak seasons—Reiser averaged just .272 for the rest of his career. He played too hard, on and off the field.

Few ballplayers earned or seized a second chance. Rabbit Maranville, an agile little shortshop, drank and clowned his way through fifteen seasons in the bigs. "A good deal of the time I had half a snoot full," he said later. Once he dove into the aquarium of a dignified hotel and came up with a celluloid goldfish wiggling in his mouth. In his condition, it seemed a brilliant jest. Finally, in 1927, his habit sent him down to the minors. After a week's binge he vowed to drink no more, like many ballplayers after many binges. Maranville stuck to it and thus played seven more years in the majors. "I can't shake out of my system all the booze I've lapped up through a dozen seasons," he said. "I'll admit now that I never liked the taste of the stuff. I drank for the sociability with a crowd of good fellows. . . . Let me have six or eight beers or a few whiskies and I was primed. The only thing that interested me then was getting a few more." If only, he mused, somebody had broken a bat over his woozy head; if only liquor had habitually made him sick, so that he could have awakened the next day with a reproaching hangover. Instead he got away with it for fifteen years.

From the arid wisdom of his later career, Maranville remembered trying to reach Grover Cleveland Alexander, the most notoriously pie-eyed pitcher in baseball history. Teammates for three years in the 1920s, they would sit together in a hotel room, the one remonstrating, the other intermittently focusing on the conversation. Couldn't Alec see the writing on the wall? "Alec would strain his eyes in the direction I pointed, and shake his head. Then I'd say to him, 'I can read it plain as print, You're through.' . . . Alec would listen to me and agree, 'Yes, yes.' He'd 'yes' me to death. He meant well, big Alec. There never was anything the matter with his guts. He had more courage on the diamond than anybody I know. But there was something lacking in his spine."

Still, Alexander pitched for twenty years in the big leagues, winning 373 games—only Cy Young and Walter Johnson won more—with a lifetime earned run average of 2.56. His most storied feat, striking out Tony Lazzeri in the 1926 World Series, came after an all-night bender. In 1927, forty hard years old, he still won twenty-one games for the Cardinals. If he had never touched booze, just how much better could he have played? "He was the greatest pitcher I ever knew," even the dried-out Maranville conceded. "I saw Mathewson plenty of times and faced him. He was a more intelligent fellow than Alec, but Alec had it on him as a pitcher." Not a simple, tragic saga, Alexander's career may as plausibly stand as an oblique argument for the healthy, stats-enhancing advantages of alcohol abuse.

No tense ballplayer can romp on the field. At times, for some athletes, alcohol may relax, embolden, sharpen. "I can't hit the ball until I hit the bottle," said Pete Browning. Cy Young in his prime would down a few belts in the clubhouse before starts. "From the park to the nearest saloon," John McGraw said of his old Orioles, "there was a beaten path that these players took as soon as they could get dressed." Well slaked, the Orioles won three straight pennants in the 1890s. Branch Rickey, no friend of booze, liked to remind clucking observers that his best team ever, the Gashouse Gang, included nine hard drinkers. Bill Lee noticed that he might pitch *worse* after a sober, restful night: "On the other hand, there was many a time when I got to the stadium with my head on fire, still smelling of last night, and I'd go out and twist the opposition into pretzels. . . . When you're hurting badly enough you don't think about pressure. Your body is like an open wound, so your instincts take over, and this is still basically an instinctive game."

Over a long career, Paul Waner hit .333 and won four batting titles. Using any bat that came to hand, flicking his wrists, he sprayed hard liners all around the outfield. He kept his secret, a pint of whiskey, in an ice chest in the dugout. "Paul thought you played best when you relaxed," his brother Lloyd explained, "and drinking was a good way to relax." Waner drank before, during, and after games, alarming the Pirate management. Under pressure, he agreed to lay off for the 1935 season. His pickled body could not withstand a drought; his average sank 41 points to .321. Drinking again the next year, he won the batting title at .373. "I sometimes think it helped me," he later said of his boozing. "I was more daring against pitchers and running bases and hitting the wall for a fly ball." In 1938 the Pirates, expecting to contend for the pennant, again requested sobriety. Waner hit only .280, his first season below .300 in thirteen years.

Even ballplayers of dry general habits could still benefit from a slump-breaking jag. If a man looked stale late in the season, John McGraw would prescribe a bottle of champagne. Charlie Gehringer, wound tight in a long slump, took a purposeful bender with his roomie and two lady friends. They drank beer and danced all night. Next day Gehringer felt shaky and achy. He hid in a corner of the dugout, far from the manager's suspicious eye. "But I played, and it was uncanny! I hit the fences with four straight line drives. I was so relaxed!" Keith Hernandez tried the same fix: "The idea is to get so wasted you can't get tied up rehashing past mistakes, and you wake up with a clean slate—in a stupor, granted, but with a clean slate." He stayed up all night drinking Scotch and listening to music. In that afternoon's doubleheader, he broke free with six hits, his slump drowned.

Conversely, sobriety and clean living might not enhance play on the field. "The ones who drink milkshakes don't win many ballgames," Casey Stengel was sure. Sober ballplayers might think and remember too much, lose their nerve, tense up at crucial points, forget to have fun: and so lose the game. "All the players on our team at present have exemplary habits," said Frank Navin as his Tigers bumbled to seventh place in 1904, "and it don't seem to do them any good, so I don't know that I care so much about the player's habits, if he is not too bad, as long as he delivers the goods on the ball field." The next year, the Tigers drank freely and rose to third.

For every player wrecked by drinking—Hack Wilson, Don Newcombe, Sam McDowell—the record shows others helped (or at least not harmed) by it. Honus Wagner liked to top off a game with six beers at a saloon, and he was merely the best National Leaguer of his time. Babe Ruth drank more and hit more than anybody. In the great Yankee tradition, Mickey Mantle later imitated Ruth in both respects. Could they have played as well sober? The question lingers with no possible answer, an enduring mystery of ballplaying life.

In his besotted early days, Rabbit Maranville went celebrating one night with teammates at the home of a liquor importer near

Boston. Used to beer, he was dared into trying Scotch and champagne chasers. He woke the next morning with sparks flying from his whirling head. The manager made him play. At bat in the tenth inning, he still did not notice the first pitch, a strike. Then, "I saw the pitcher start to wind up and I started to swing at his motion when ball and bat met and it sailed over the left field fence." A teammate advised him to run around the bases, which he managed to do. He hit only three other homers that year. "I never did see the ball I hit," the Rabbit always insisted. Yet he, or the hangover, did hit it.

Baseball and booze wound through a complicated history. Like some players, no generalization about it can stand up. Judgments depend on how well the man has been playing. "A buffoon is a drunk on a hitting spree," Leo Durocher explained. "A drunk is a pitcher who's lost his fast ball. A confirmed drunk is a pitcher with a sore arm. An incurable drunk is a pitcher who hasn't won a game all season." Beyond that, no one can say.

◆　◆　◆

"I like women," Joe Namath proclaimed, surprising nobody. "I can't imagine anyone who doesn't enjoy sex, who doesn't want sex all the time."

◆　◆　◆

The ballplaying boys played their most adult games with girls. Linked with drink, major-league sex was an athlete's reward for good play, his consolation for failure, his initiation on the way up and his reassurance on the way down. "Boys, I'm just going to say one thing to you," a minor-league manager told his charges, holding his thumb and forefinger an inch apart. "I want to remind everybody that you're just this far away from big-league pussy."

Ty Cobb, seventeen years old, wanted to sign his first contract. Cobb's father worried that his son would tumble into the carousing sins of ballplayers. "I was a simple-minded country boy from an excellent home," Cobb said later. "I had been well brought up. I used neither liquor nor tobacco. And I had been taught a deep respect for the church and for the finer things of life." From his first game in organized ball, Cobb started spiking this polite background. He fought with everyone, friend and foe, and bristled at trifles. In 1905, eighteen years old, he was sold up to the Tigers. "I note what you say regarding his disposition," his new manager thanked his former owner.

By his second year in the bigs, Cobb had succumbed to the prevailing amusements. "He does not associate with good people," Frank Navin of the Tigers complained to Ban Johnson, "and the women who are his friends are of the worst class in the city. As an illustration, he left a couple of passes one day at the box office for some women who came to get them. One of the detectives of our city happened to be standing around the office and asked what player left the passes for those women. He found out it was Cobb, and when Cobb 'was called' for it, he tried to bluff it through that the women were all right. He even tried to bluff the detectives through, until they agreed to show him on the register where they had been arrested for almost all the crimes on the calendar a number of times." Cobb's conduct so upset Detroit management during spring training in 1907 that Navin considered waiving him to the minors as punishment. "It seems hard to think that a mere boy can make so much disturbance," Navin puzzled. "He has the southern aristocracy notion in his head, and thinks he is too good to associate with ball players. He will not allow any of the older members of the team to make a suggestion to him." Yet Cobb looked so promising— "he has a chance to be one of the grandest ball players in the country"—that Navin kept him. That year Cobb, at twenty, led the league in hits, RBIs, batting, slugging, and steals, so Navin liked him better, regardless of the women he courted. As with liquor, good play on the field might compensate for almost any play off the field.

Marv Fleming, a tight end, acquired a yen for women early. In high school and college, coaches warned that his passion for dalliance could wreck his ballplaying. Fleming played his own games and still joined the champion Packers. "My *real* introduction to pro football as a rookie," he recalled, "came not on the field, but in a motel room in Dallas during the 1963 preseason." The Packers, in town for an exhibition game, relaxed nightly with beer and women. At one gathering, somebody suggested a sex party. A Packer All-Pro—"a real leader"—stripped to his underwear and started dancing with his girl, but the others held back. A catalyst named Connie was called in. "Connie took off her blouse, then her skirt, and pretty soon there were clothes and naked bodies all about the room. I was sitting there taking it all in, and thinking, 'Wow, I don't believe this.' I knew Green Bay was a great team. I knew the players were idolized. But I'd had no idea life could be this easy." Fleming felt like a big leaguer.

For his idol and model the rookie settled on teammate Paul Hornung, the Golden Boy, the most storied Lothario in the NFL. Whenever the Packers pulled up to a hotel, a beautiful woman would await Hornung in the lobby or in a convertible outside. "See you later, fellows," Hornung would say, leaving the other Packers to wish. Trolling at night, a group of teammates would stick near Hornung, knowing he would attract talent. After Hornung left with his selection, the rest descended on the quite adequate leftovers. "The married guys were out almost as much as us bachelors," Fleming noticed. "This upset me at first because I thought the husbands should be at home with their wives instead of encroaching on my territory. But after a while I realized there was plenty of companionship for everybody."

Married or single, most ballplayers chased women as though they were loose balls to be pounced upon. Married men typically split their sex lives—reasonably good husbands and fathers at home, bad boys on the road—and hoped the two would never intersect. "Even though my body keeps ending up in the wrong place," one man insisted, "my heart is always in the *right* place." Bill Russell quaintly stayed faithful to his wife for his first two seasons with the Celtics. "The other Celtics, who were curious about my personal life, thought I was square." On the road he kept to his hotel room; at home he played with his electric trains. Eventually he grew restless; "I heard too much from my teammates about how they spent their spare time." One night he told his wife he was going out. He found a partner that first time and never returned to monogamy.

Even the most unlikely studs, enduring the boredom and isolation of road life, might spear the easy fruits dangled before them. The stolid Lou Gehrig lived with his mother and amused himself decorously. Yet away from home, according to the sportswriter Fred Lieb, "he shyly admitted to me an occasional sexual adventure." Only his shyness in the telling distinguished him from his roistering mates. Bill Bradley, beside whom Gehrig seems a rococo libertine, heard the other Knicks joking and leering about road coups. He sat in his hotel room, reading books, listening to the radio, arguing with his roommate about the TV—feeling bored and disconnected. Under these pressures, "what normally would be out of the question for me becomes acceptable," Bradley noted, squirming. "Normal shyness would prevent me from entering a stranger's hotel room, but on the road there seems to be nothing to lose. Everyone in the hotel sleeps under the same roof for one night and moves on. Loneliness can be overcome only by reaching out for contact. . . . The percentages are that if a man spends enough nights in hotels he will meet a woman with whom for that night he will share a bed." (An oblique confession by a future politician.) Road flings were brief and intense, Bradley noticed, offering an emotional complement to the quick high of the official games in public. "But during those brief encounters life seems fuller on the road; whatever their duration such moments are genuine, alive, exciting, troublesome, dangerous, sad": all of those at once, over in a flash.

On the record, management had to disapprove of ballplaying sex. Athletes were not supposed to offend their admirers, especially innocently idolizing children. Bed checks and curfews, enacted for show, merely challenged players' imaginations. Paul Hornung remembered a chilly night on the road: he and roomie Max McGee were entertaining women in their hotel room when a coach knocked on the door. The women decamped to the veranda while the coach came in and chatted, wondering why he smelled perfume. After he left, the cooled-off women, teeth chattering, were whisked from the hotel. Another time, a bed-checking coach found Hornung and McGee in bed together, naked, their arms around each other. "Would you just please turn off the lights and shut the door," they deadpanned, "we're busy now." The coach retreated, flabbergasted. "But that didn't stop him or the other coaches from taking bed check every damned night," Hornung groused.

They had to maintain appearances. After a detective hired by the Yankees reported that Babe Ruth had accommodated six women in one night, manager Miller Huggins fined him five thousand dollars, a huge sum at the time, for unspecified crimes. The Babe paid up and kept plowing his way around the league. If the Yankees were playing sloppily, Huggins would suspect excessive carousing. "So he'd call a meeting and lay down the law—maybe even fine us a few bucks," catcher Benny Bengough recalled. "Then, for the next two or three nights you'd see the whole gang around the hotel lobby, behaving like good little boys. But soon after that they'd be off again, having a good time. But you can't say very much to a guy who's hitting .350." Later the Yankees put a private eye on Mickey Mantle. "Threatened to show the report to my wife," Mantle said later, more amused than offended. "Hell, the only thing on it was that I was comin' in at one in the morning, and she already knew that."

As in the drinking issue, management was afflicted with its own hypocrisies. Albert Spalding—quondam star pitcher, owner of the champion Chicago White Stockings of the 1880s, sporting-goods entrepreneur—struck all the right postures. He lived in a plush neighborhood, belonged to snooty clubs, and aspired to the Chicago social register. We do not intend, he declared, "to entice young men into a business that will demoralize them. . . . We are trying to elevate them and with it the game." Playing a different game on the side, Spalding kept a mistress who bore him an illegitimate son. After his wife's death, Spalding married the mistress and moved out to California to join a religious cult. He could not square how he talked with how he lived.

Leo Durocher managed the Dodgers with all the overtly buttoned zeal that Branch Rickey expected. A player caught too much on the town would be whipsawed at the next practice by Durocher's deft fungo bat, as he made the offender lunge for ball after ball placed just out of reach. One carouser, detected again after repeated warnings, was fined one thousand dollars and condemned to the lowly Phillies. Meantime Durocher himself rotated a string of compliant showgirls shuttling to meet him around the league. "Leo kept all these lovelies moving from stop to stop as skillfully as he herded his runners around the bases," recalled Harold Parrott, the Dodger road secretary in charge of these maneuvers. "The ladies never crossed paths, and no two of them ever arrived embarrassingly at the same place at one time."

According to Hy Turkin, a New York sportswriter, Durocher even seduced his players' wives—and then at the ballpark teased the players about these conquests, loudly and obscenely. Yet most of his players revered Durocher and hoped to imitate his playing techniques.

They hardly needed his lecherous example. Players were so randy, popping with the animal spirits and heedless explosiveness of young men, and women were so there, so willing. "For a young ballplayer," Ted Williams remembered, "there's never any shortage of available girls around a ball park. A lot of them move in pretty hard, and after a while a ballplayer learns to move pretty good himself." The women usually were pros in the nineteenth century; but soon dedicated amateurs took over. "The saloon and the brothel are the evils of the baseball world at the present day," Spalding's *Guide* fretted in 1889. (Spalding did not mention his own mistress.) A sporting house would welcome a whole team of sporting men with a lubricious dinner and party. Even celibate ballplayers, if any, might come for the beer and company. In Philadelphia, the Athletics favored a bountiful auxiliary, "The Big Bosom Girls." Wilbert Robinson of the Athletics used a tape measure to check on qualifications. Prostitutes often came out to the park to pick up tickets (as in Ty Cobb's case) and cheer on their customers.

In the early NFL, Green Bay was the favorite recreational stop on the schedule, especially the whorehouses in the northeast section of town, especially one at 801 and 803 Reber Street. Johnny Blood, the train-struck halfback, liked to read Shakespeare and discuss economics when sober. After a few pops he studied pornographic novels and bought out whorehouses. "He'd pay the madam for *all* the girls," according to his teammate Clarke Hinkle, "'and have all the girls to himself. Now I'm sure he couldn't service all of them, but that's just the kind of guy he was. They all liked him, too, wanted to talk to him and have fun with him."

Baseball teams training or playing exhibitions in pre-Castro Cuba would sample the wide-open pleasures of Havana nightlife, the casinos and floor shows running flat out under American gangsters and Cuban tinhorns—and one cathouse in particular. "You never saw anything like this place at 258 Colon," said one ballplayer, the memory still glowing across decades. "The most beautiful girls in Havana. They had music, soft lights, drinks, and about fifteen rooms. Guys would come back from the ball park, have a drink at the hotel, and head straight for 258 Colon. Some of them just about had their laundry sent out from there. They'd stay till four or five o'clock in the morning and then go back to the hotel."

These commercial exchanges aside, ballplayers usually got laid for free, or at most for the price of drinks and dinner. Big leaguers had their privileges. At a party celebrating the 1928 pennant, Babe Ruth stood on a chair—beer in one hand, sandwich in the other—and announced, "Any girl who doesn't want to fuck can leave now." Few left. Clarke Hinkle remembered women cruising by the team's hotel, in Packards and other fancy cars, "just wanting to be with the Green Bay Packers. I'm telling you, it spoiled you, because you had the pick of the most beautiful gals in town." The wife of another football player, stubbornly innocent, was astonished by the female aggressions when she went out with her husband: "As soon as they find out he's a pro football player they fall all over him, even in front of me. I never realized before that just like men go for a woman's shape a woman goes for a man's physique. I've had women come up to me and tell me what a physique my husband has. They never tell me until they find out he plays pro ball."

As for the willing women in question, their motives were left unexplored. Ballplayers seldom asked or cared. The women often remained anonymous, known generically as Sadies and Annies, sometimes by more specific nicknames. The Hook and The Nook hung around Ebbets Field in the 1940s—a peril to whatever remained of any rookie's virtue. A few years later, The Hook, The Crook, and The Snook would meet a favorite married football player at Grand Central Station. The man would pretend to place a phone call while one of the women squeezed into the booth with him and his teammates chortled. Chicago Shirley, the most accomplished baseball Annie, hit on every team in both leagues, a legend for her persistence and catholic taste.

It was so easy. "Open your door," noted the Boswellian pitcher Jim Bouton, "and you're liable to be invited to a party down the hall." Women called, left messages, sent letters, flowers, undergarments. At the game, a player would scan the stands for talent, "shooting stingers" (sticking out his tongue) at prospects. If the woman smiled back, bingo. At Comiskey Park in Chicago, a serious fan could penetrate the bullpen through a maintenance door and tickle a pitcher's fancy during the game. "The first time I sat out there and checked out this sexual circus," Bill Lee relished, "I thought, Now I know why everyone is so hot to get up to the big leagues."

Bill Bradley, who thought in patterns, noticed cultural affinities between ballplayers and pretty young women. Both were popular objects, rewarded and limited by their physical gifts, at once idolized and trivialized by the general public. Unacquainted with complexities beyond the skin-deeps of face and body, both skirted "a dangerous vanity." Both lived hard and fast, needing to squeeze everything in quickly, knowing that time could only diminish their gifts. Both knew only the moment, nothing before and after: play it now. Athlete and beauty would logically conjoin.

Probably so. But in the sexual moment, they usually attracted each other for simpler, raunchier reasons. Lynda Huey, a former cheerleader and athlete, had sex with many jocks before withdrawing from play in her early thirties. She liked the association with fame and what she called "the vicarious exhilaration of getting close to someone else's victory." She thought of herself as a fellow athlete, an equal. Common sports groupies, preoccupied with hair and makeup, bored and repelled her. ("Did I look like one of them? In some ways *was* I one of them?") Yet in explaining her itch for jocks, she struck a literal bottom line: "There ain't *nuthin'* like the cheeks of an athlete. Those firm, rounded buttocks out there in the huddle. Those gorgeous gluteals climbing into the starting blocks. . . . I'm a *cheek freak.*"

Detroit Shirley, in the tradition of her Chicago namesake, spent about nine years "fucking around with the athletes," as she put it. It started when a boyfriend took her to a certain Detroit bar festooned with ballplayers. "It was a real sewer hole," she said later, but "when I saw all the athletes there and I saw all the things that were going on in the bar, I liked it, so I went back and tried to make friends with them et cetera." Since it was fall, she began with football players, then changed teams with the seasons. Versatile and skilled, she could play any game ("I'll do anything. Way-out sex, things like that, anything"). After surveying most of the talent on all American League and most National League baseball teams, all the *better* football teams—she had standards—and most hockey teams, "baseball players are my favorite," she decided. "Football players are lousy. For one thing, baseball players like orgies and football players don't. Not that I'm an orgy person, but baseball players are just more sexually acclimated. They don't have the hang-ups that other people do. They can go with somebody, without somebody, with any kind of situation, they can cope with it sexually. Football players aren't that flexible."

Shirley acknowledged the secondhand strut of watching a famous ballplayer on TV and knowing she had "seen" him: "It sets me apart. It makes *me* a little better, I guess." But what really drove her back to that jocky bar was a well-researched physical preference like Lynda Huey's. "Athletes are the most virile men around. Other men just can't compete with them," she explained. "They're just special. I don't know how else to say it. They have that supremacy . . . I don't know . . . because they are athletes. They're better sexually, at least baseball players are. . . . They're ego-trippers, and I like that." In retirement, a bit hard-faced but still with a tight, supple body, she expected to miss all those jocky muscles. She recounted her feats with a quiet pride and muted laughter, stressing that no athlete had ever *bought* her favors. In fact, "some guys I met I would gladly pay and I never said that in my life." Baseball players, presumably.

Men from other sports preened their own notions about who performed best. "Women love those football players," Jim Brown was sure, Detroit Shirley notwithstanding. "Guys who play football have that manly, physical image—the gladiator—and women go crazy for it. Talk all you want about brain power, but the intellectual gets the secondary women. It's the physical giant who gets the premium women." In five years with the Dallas Cowboys, Hollywood Henderson had sex with (he guessed) more than a thousand women. "I don't know whether it was my good spirits," he mused, "my sense of humor, the way I looked, my frankness or my general approach, but women always seemed to like me. . . . Ladies around the country find ways of getting through to professional athletes and I was easy to find, didn't have to ask me twice." In the spring after his rookie year, still discovering the riches that awaited him, Henderson and his roommate, Too Tall Jones ("He liked to fuck, eat and play football"), were treated to their first orgy, just the two of them and about nine women at somebody's house. On a capacious waterbed covered in red velvet, the women pulled off Henderson's clothes and licked him from toe to toe. "I was hooked. Hooked! You don't get this one time and try to live without it. . . . I had never done anything like it; roll off of one girl, roll onto another."

Thus inspired, the roomies held their own orgy at home. They handed out cutoff Cowboy T-shirts as door prizes. Women padded around the house garbed in the T-shirts and nothing else. "We were standing around smoking a couple of joints, drinking beer and peppermint schnapps, and I was a little apprehensive. I knew what I wanted to happen but I wasn't quite sure how to get it there." Eventually Henderson settled on a prospect—"the one with the long legs and the flat stomach"—and took her to his bedroom. And left the door open.

Basketball players put up their own claims. "I guess I'm something of a sex symbol to a lot of girls," conceded Wilt Chamberlain, on his way to a claimed twenty thousand lovers since age fifteen. He got hundreds of mash notes a month:

"I admit a strong interest in seeing your new house, especially the sheets."

"I would really appreciate it if you would send me your oldest and rattiest jock strap."

"I am waiting and I am moist."

Ever willing, Chamberlain would accommodate his fans in tough circumstances, such as in the backseat of a little Ford Falcon, or under a blanket on an airplane. But he picked his shots carefully. Over seven feet tall, he liked women about five feet four to five feet six, and valued legs and derrieres over breasts. "I've generally found that extremely tall girls just don't seem feminine enough for me," he said, drawing the line at anyone less than a foot and a half shorter. He rated women's looks on a twenty-point scale. Here too he was picky; in decades of unsleeping scrutiny he had never spotted a twenty, only a few nineteens. He virtuously declined married women and those of sporting habits. "I sure as hell don't insist on virgins, but I won't take some other athlete's hand-me-down fuck."

Chamberlain recalled playing only one NBA contest that was affected by his shots off the court. After a game in Boston, he scheduled one woman at midnight, two more at two A.M. They all ate breakfast together. That afternoon in Milwaukee, a woman phoned his hotel and offered herself on her lunch hour. "It was a very nice visit," Wilt bragged, "even if I was a bit weary that night when the Bucks blew us off the court by 21 points."

Players wished to believe that women usually improved their games. Hollywood Henderson claimed that sex the night before left him better rested and less nervous; "the times I didn't get any I didn't play well the next day," unaccustomed as he was to celibacy. A slumping ballplayer might try to break out by sleeping with an ugly woman, or one of another race. In 1942 one of the Dodgers sent a chorus girl to wear out a Cardinal pitcher before a crucial start. After she kept him up all night, he went and threw a two-hit shutout. She tried again, and he threw a three-hit shutout. "That looked like pretty good medicine for a pitcher," noted Kirby Higbe of the Dodgers, "and I asked why they didn't try it out on me." The 1971 Houston Astros had a song:

> Now Harry Walker is the one
>   that manages this crew;
> He doesn't like it when we drink
>   and fight and smoke and screw;
> But when we win our game each day,
>   Then what the fuck can Harry say?
> It makes a fellow proud to be an Astro.

But the Astros finished only fourth in their division, four games under .500.

Harry Walker might have thought he knew why. "It ain't sex that's troublesome," said Casey Stengel, "it's staying up all night looking for it." In 1909 Frank Navin of the Tigers gave up on a pitcher, George Suggs, after he had appeared in only fifteen games over two seasons. "He does not drink," Navin said of

Suggs, "but he is insane about women. In fact he is a regular 'Stanford White' and has not the strength or vitality to pitch over five or six innings. . . . I do not think he will ever do any one much good." Shipped to Cincinnati, Suggs won fifty-four games in the next three years, averaging a workhorse 277 innings per season—probably without much changing his sexual habits.

The real dangers of ballplaying sex came off the field. A few big leaguers were murdered or killed themselves over women. Eddie Waitkus of the Phillies was shot by a woman in a Chicago hotel room in 1949. Others might pick the wrong quarry. Once a group of baseball writers were loitering on a train when the door burst open and Babe Ruth, breathing hard, ran through, followed too closely by a dark-haired woman with a knife. She couldn't catch him. Later that same season, Ruth was chased from a Detroit hotel by a man waving a gun. In the 1950s, Toy Ledbetter of the Philadelphia Eagles was courting a woman, a "good-looking shiny thing," he said, "and come to find out she was a racketeer's girlfriend. He was down in Mexico or some-where until something blew over. I was just a hick kid from Oklahoma, and all I knew, she was good-looking and we were getting along just fine." NFL Commissioner Bert Bell called him in and commanded, "I want you to stay away from that broad," and that was that.

Random, prolific sex always carried the threat of incurable disease. Some early baseball players—Hoss Radbourn, Pete Browning, and others—died young of syphilis. Newspapers would gently describe an amatory ailment as malaria or rheu-matism. Jimmy Dykes remembered a teammate on an overnight lake steamer from Cleveland to Detroit who "won a beautiful blonde from strong competition" and was disabled for weeks afterward. In spring-training sermons to his teams, Branch Rickey liked to preach an admonishing story: "I lost two pen-nants in St. Louis because of unnecessary disease." One year, long before penicillin, the Cardinals were battling near the top in August when "a great player . . . nobody on the team more vital to me than he" was lost to a sexual malady. The Cardinals fin-ished third, and "I haven't any doubt that we could have won if he had stayed on his feet." Years later, the same situation, again with an infielder. The man nearly died and never played baseball again. "All because of idleness—not knowing what to do with unexpected leisure," Rickey wound up, making his point. "Damn leisure! A rainy day has lost me two pennants." Later, in the age of AIDS, ballplaying sex again became lethally dangerous.

Most ballplayers could limit the physical harm but not the emotional costs. Ballplaying sex ultimately wrecked countless marriages and left children without fathers at home. Of the hundreds of basketball players Wilt Chamberlain had known, he could think of only one, Paul Arizin, with a reputation for marital fidelity. "The toughest thing about the major leagues," said Mike Hegan, "is explaining to your wife why she needs a penicillin shot for your kidney infection." Ballplayers tried to control the damage by not taking wives on road trips or allowing them into favorite bars, lest they see and talk too much. On one level or another, fought out or not, the wives still knew.

Ballplaying sex was a horny adolescent's dream: intercourse on demand with new and comely partners, no responsibilities, no commitments. Women as toys, ornaments, and scabbards, not as fully human peers. At age thirty-seven, Wilt Chamberlain had never lived with a woman for more than three weeks, had never even told a woman, "I love you." It kept a man young, and childish.

◆　◆　◆

Consider the chastening saga of John Clarkson and King Kelly, the best baseball battery that ever played itself to death. Clarkson was the finest pitcher of the nineteenth century, Kelly a star catcher and the first glittering popular idol in baseball. Opposites in temperament and background, for five years in the 1880s they formed an odd but peerless tandem. Linked in games and then in death, they were among the earliest casualties of ballplaying life, double-edged testaments to the dangerous fun of stardom.

Mike Kelly surfaced as a bumptious twenty-year-old rookie with Cincinnati in 1878. On the team's first visit to Boston, Kelly—already known as a base stealer—tangled with Tommy Bond, the league's best pitcher that year. "Wait till he tries to steal a bag on me this afternoon," Bond told a teammate before the game. "I'll kill him, sure, before he reaches the base." Kelly heard about it, vowed to show him, but managed only one scratch hit. Bond challenged him from the mound: "You're going to steal it, are you?" Kelly took off for second but catcher Pop Snyder threw him out. The Bostons, rolling toward a pennant, laughed at the squashed rookie. "I felt pretty bad that night," Kelly said later. Next day, with Bond again pitching, Kelly made no boasts but got three hits and three steals. Turning the screw, he even filched third while Snyder was lobbing the ball back to his pitcher. The Boston fans remembered Kelly.

In his second year Kelly hit .348 and placed among the league leaders in a half dozen offensive categories. That fall, on a barnstorming tour through California, Cap Anson signed him to play for his Chicago White Stockings, thus setting up a collision between a free spirit and a martinet. "There are few more unyielding disciplinarians than Anson," a sportswriter remarked. As Chicago's playing manager, Anson flogged his team, berated umpires, and sneered at enemy crowds. A big, tough man, over six feet and 220 pounds, he was baseball's first splendid ogre.

"I was a bit afraid of Anson when I first met him," Kelly recalled, precisely what Anson intended. When the team gathered in Chicago on the first day of April 1880, Kelly expected easy gym workouts to trim the winter's lard. "You haven't any idea what Anson meant by training," Kelly said later. "It almost makes me shiver to think of it." After a light breakfast, they all trooped to the ballpark for a limbering one-mile walk, and a trot of fifteen miles. After lunch and a rest, back to the park for a practice game. "It was a real game, too," Kelly winced. "No knocking up the ball and catching it was allowed. . . . When you hit a ball, even if it was gathered in by the pitcher, you would have to run to first base like a deer. If one didn't do it, the 'old man' would be after him very strong. For a few days we were all broken up under this treatment." After a week they got used to it and started having fun. Even Anson smiled, a little, after striking out in practice. "Sometimes he is apt to be a bit harsh," Kelly decided. "He watches every point in the game. Nothing escapes him."

Chicago won five pennants in the next seven years as Kelly became baseball's most riveting attraction before Babe Ruth. On the field Kelly seemed more than the sum of his parts; he had none of Ruth's unique and comprehensive skills. Kelly hit well, but not as well as Anson, Dan Brouthers, Roger Connor, and other contemporaries. Buck Ewing, Kelly's great rival, was technically the best catcher of the time. Receiving pitches, Kelly showed the hands of a stonemason and was prone to passed balls, often four or more a game. Throwing to bases, his arm was strong but erratic. Whirling for pop fouls, he often turned the wrong way. If tired or hurt, he essayed other positions. In the infield, "the grounders climbed him and insulted him." Wandering the outfield, he could not judge a fly hit in front of him, "though he would generally manage to get pretty close in under it," in Anson's generous memory. "In such cases he would remark with a comical leer: 'By Gad, I made it hit me gloves, anyhow.'"

On the base paths, though, Kelly was supremely in his element, the best base runner anybody had ever seen. Again he transcended the limits of his own body. Large for his time, nearly six feet and 190 pounds in his prime, with his legs often wounded from catching without shin pads, he could not run fast. He excelled at starting and finishing, stealing an edge before and after his lumbering gait down the line. He studied the pitcher, took a daring lead, accelerated quickly, and slid inventively, avoiding a sure tag with a twist or a fake. "Slide, Kelly, Slide" became a catchy hit song and a durable baseball mantra for decades afterward. Kelly may have invented, and surely popularized, the "Chicago slide" later in general use: the runner sliding on his hip, one leg doubled under, the other extended to hook around the bag, the upper body held out of the baseman's reach. To this sliding staple he added endless riffs and variations, "a regular boxer with his feet." For three years in a row he led the league in runs; in 1885 he scored 124 runs on only 126 hits. Stolen-base stats were not kept until 1885; Kelly averaged 62 steals a season for the next five years—extraordinary for a slow man with vulnerable legs.

He stole with his brain, not his legs. "I have known all the great players since the game became a professional affair," said Alfred Spink of the *Sporting News* in 1910, "and I can recall no one of the lot who compared with Kelly when it came to . . . quick wit and quick thinking, ability to see and to do the right thing at the right time." He helped develop basic techniques of the game: exchanging signals with pitchers and other players, hitting behind a runner on first, shifting his feet at bat to hit to the opposite field, sacrifices and hit-and-runs. Faking a dash home from third on a batted ball, he would leap forward, bellow, stamp his feet, kick up the dust so the rattled infielder threw home while the batter made first. With enemy runners on first and third, Kelly and his favorite second baseman, Fred Pfeffer, would kill a double steal. Kelly would flip his mask into the path of the runner coming home and zip the ball to Pfeffer, standing well in front of second. "All you had to do," the scatter-armed Kelly said of Pfeffer, "was to throw anywhere near the bag, and he would get it—high, wide, or on the ground. What a man he was to make a return throw; why, he could lay on his stomach and throw 100 yards then." Pfeffer in turn remembered Kelly as a playing coach in the outfield, with the entire game splayed before him, yelling instructions and warnings, always pushing and conniving.

It was smart, legal baseball, playing the game right, but Kelly did not stop there. To the rapture of his fans and the fury of his enemies, he tiptoed across legalities, stretching and ripping the rules, testing the lone umpire who could not watch the whole field. Kelly stories of faked catches and phantom balls, repeated and embroidered over the years, leaped easily into myth. A few may be verified. At a game against Boston in Chicago in May 1881, he scored the winning run with what became his most famous trick. "It was strongly suspected," the hometown *Chicago Tribune* winked, "that Kelly, in his eagerness to reach the plate from second, somehow forgot to go by way of third, but slighted that bag entirely by some ten or fifteen feet." The stolen run counted because the umpire was watching the play at first. Later that season Kelly repeated the theft in Boston, not for the last time. "How a Boston audience would shout and roar," Kelly savored, "with mingled feelings of anger and joy, when I would cut the third bag on my way home. It almost reminded one of hundreds of insane people let loose."

Wherever he went on the field, whatever he was doing, the crowd watched him, expecting some never-seen feat. His unpredictability kept the other team on edge, wondering. Racing for a foul ball near a fence, he caught it, leaped the fence, and held on. "Never touched me," he shouted. Trundling toward home with the catcher squatting low to tag him, Kelly hurdled the catcher and landed on the plate. Playing a shallow right field, he scooped up a ground single and threw the runner out at first. Running the bases, he would falter as though lame, relaxing the fielders, then speed up to take the next base.

Late in the 1882 season, the Providence team came to town leading Chicago by four games. Chicago trailed by a run in the ninth when Kelly reached first. The next batter, Tom Burns, sent a sharp grounder to George Wright at short for what looked like an easy double play. "I never ran so hard in my life," Kelly said later. "I reached the bag a second before George, and then like a flash, he raised his arm to send the ball to the first base, to cut off Burns. Somehow or other an accident occurred at that moment." Uh huh. "My arm went up in the air, and it caught George on the shoulder. The result was, that when the ball left George's hand it went away over into the grand stand." Kelly scored, soon followed by Burns; game over. Chicago won the next two with Providence, which then swooned into a slump. Chicago swept to its third straight pennant. Harry Wright, the Providence manager, blamed "Kelly and his infernal tricks."

He was the King of baseball, loved and hated by fans beyond any ballplayer of his time, "one of the jolliest fellows in the world." His cascading wit and undentable affability cushioned almost any provocation he might devise. "He tortures the opposing players, the crowd and the press," a sportswriter noted, "and the more they resent this treatment the more he enjoys it and dances with glee." Posing and swaggering, "kicking" (arguing) with umpires, he teased the crowds into a roiling mass nibbling from his hand. A personal following came out to see him at every ballpark in the league. "The game concluded, the rush of all is around Kelly," said a sportswriter, "and ludicrous mistakes are sometimes made in the endeavor to identify him, though he has just come off the field. A howling, insulting mob follow him to the bus, and on the way not a word escapes his lips. . . . Uncomplimentary remarks intended for Kelly's ears are heard all the way along the route. In the hotel corridors the question 'Where is he?' grows very tiresome. He does not cater to newspaper men for puffing. He sizes a man up quickly, and has a brusque way that many do not like. More who know him are aware that he has many excellent qualities."

"People go to see games because they love excitement and love to be worked up," Kelly understood. "The people who go to ball games want good playing, with just enough kicking to make things interesting thrown in." Advertisers paid thousands of dollars for his endorsements. Dressed in the latest, snappiest clothes, his picture peered from billboards and magazines. Fondled and cosseted, anything but an innocent, he yet seemed uncorrupted by adulation. With his hands and legs often banged up, he still came out to play. Teammates noticed that he never complained about lousy hotel rooms, upper berths on trains, or too many exhibition games. He was everybody's friend on the team. Anyone could nick him for a loan.

On the field, he was the smartest, fastest thinker of his time. When John Clarkson, a rookie pitcher, joined Chicago for the last two months of the 1884 season, Kelly showed him how to win in the National League. By now Kelly knew the particular weaknesses of all the enemy batters, so he did the rookie's thinking for him. Kelly taught him details of team play, such as signaling the next pitch to the fielders behind him, and added dubious touches of his own, such as quick-pitching a batter while Kelly distracted him with chat, or wearing a large, shiny belt buckle that might be flashed into a batter's eye from the pitching box.

Clarkson hardly needed such tricks. The league had just formally allowed the overhand pitching motion. Clarkson's best pitch—learned a year earlier, with the Saginaw team of the Northwestern League—was a hopping overhand fastball, flung from a box then only fifty feet from the cowering batter. "John could shove them over so fast," said his Chicago teammate Billy Sunday, "that the thermometer would fall two degrees when the ball whizzed past." As a rookie, Clarkson appeared in fourteen games, winning ten, and—a harbinger—led the league with almost eight strikeouts per nine innings pitched. In one game he whiffed seven straight batters. He was a prototype of the new style of overhand power pitchers. Fred Pfeffer later challenged older hitters from the 1870s to "take a bat some pleasant afternoon, when they are quite well, and face John Clarkson's cannon-balls when he feels first-rate. I want these gentlemen to discover from experience just how much the science of pitching has improved since that old-time, underhand delivery."

In 1885 Clarkson won 12 straight games, threw a no-hitter, and wound up with 53 victories, best in the league. (Hoss Radbourn had set the record with 60 wins in 1884.) Clarkson also led the league in games, starts, complete games, innings, shutouts, strikeouts, and even assists and total fielding chances: an uncommon statistical sweep. Chicago took the pennant and repeated the next year, as Clarkson won 36 games and Kelly, at .388, won his second batting title. Clarkson and Kelly now formed the best battery in baseball on the best team in baseball. When his youthful fastball waned, Clarkson improved his curve and control. For the next six years he averaged 34 wins a season. He finished at 327-178 for his career, a winning percentage of .648, with a lifetime earned run average of 2.81. According to his Total Pitcher Index, a complex statistical formula that weights various team and league factors, Clarkson was easily the greatest pitcher of his era, with a wider margin of supremacy than any other pitcher in any era.

The twin terrors of baseball, Clarkson and Kelly could scarcely have less resembled each other. Clarkson, four years younger, came from Cambridge, Massachusetts, the son of a wealthy jewelry manufacturer. Two of his brothers went to Harvard. "He is a young man of rare intelligence," purred a sportswriter in *Harper's Weekly,* "and good social standing." As a boy in his Cambridgeport neighborhood, he had started with three old cat (a precursor of baseball) as soon as he could lift a bat. He played his first organized ball for the Webster Street grammar school's team, then graduated to the Beacons, a top amateur club in Boston. After a brief stint with the Worcester team in the National League in 1882, he joined Saginaw, where his manager, Arthur Whitney, taught him the overhand style. Striking out ten and twelve batters a game in the Northwestern League, he got Cap Anson's attention.

The best pitcher he ever managed, Anson said later, but not the most easily managed. Clarkson did accept Anson's lessons about covering first on grounders to the right side of the infield. Yet he was difficult and moody. Expecting to pitch every game, he sulked when he did not. (In 1885 he appeared in 70 of Chicago's 113 games.) At some unreachable, unconscious level Clarkson apparently doubted his own talent. Taking no chances, he wanted to throw every ball over the heart of the plate. Anson told him to shade the corners, good advice that Clarkson resented. Eventually Anson figured out that his ace bloomed only in the sunshine of unclouded praise. "Scold him," said Anson, "find fault with him, and he would not pitch at all." But stroke him after a win, "and he would go out the next day and stand all the batters on their heads."

Kelly, in contrast, harbored no doubts or insecurities that anyone could detect. Always laughing, in command of any situation, self-assured beyond belief, he could not be rattled. "No occasion was too desperate," said an observer, "no subject too serious, for him to 'josh' about." Kelly had been toughened by a harder road upward than Clarkson's. Born in a rough immigrant section of Troy, New York, he was raised in a fatherless family. At nine he was the fastest runner at school—his only distinction as a schoolboy. Growing up in Paterson, New Jersey, near the baseball hotbed of New York City, as a teenager he briefly toiled in a mill for three dollars a week, hauling baskets of coal from the basement to the top floor. Next he worked as a paper boy, rising at four in the morning to go fetch his newspapers in Manhattan, which at least left the afternoons for baseball. At fifteen he joined a hometown semipro team. A few years later, on a team in Columbus, Ohio, still so poor he was playing in socks, he went on strike for a five-dollar advance to buy baseball shoes.

Money management always puzzled him. King Kelly spent time and cash recklessly in the sporting underworld of saloons, brothels, theaters, and racetracks—the careening demimonde that he had entered so early, and never wanted to leave. Kelly was a handsome man, with dark hair and a thick mustache, and eyes forever twinkling and japing. Arrayed for the adventures of the evening, he affected a twirling cane, an ascot anchored with an enormous jewel, and pointy patent-leather shoes. Friends engulfed him anywhere he went. Snapper Garrison, a top jockey, dropped him occasional tips on horses, so Kelly occasionally won his bets. His theater buddies gave him parts in modest productions—*Rag Baby* and *O'Dowd's Neighbors*—in which his personality and fame made up for his singing and dancing.

Pursuing any amusement, he drank, and drank. (Even during some games: "It depends on the length of the game," he explained.) "The man never lived," said Anson, "'who could drink King Kelly under the table." Forty years later, one sportswriter recalled a scene in a bar on lower Fifth Avenue in Pittsburgh. Kelly strode alone into the joint crowded with sporting men and threw a fifty-dollar bill on the moist mahogany bar. "Drinks for the house, Jack," said he, "and when the fifty is gone let me know." No wonder they called him King. At rare moments, Kelly's head would clear, and he might contemplate sobriety. Once in St. Louis he ordered a soft drink, declaring he was off whiskey for life. The bartender served him with crepe paper dolefully placed around the rim of the glass. Kelly soon was back to booze.

Most of his Chicago teammates followed their leader. The pennant-winning club of 1884 played hard and died younger, at an average age of fifty-five, than any big-league baseball team in history; three men expired in their twenties, four others in their thirties. "Good habits on and off the field are what we want of professional ball-players," Anson hoped. Not even Anson, with his formidable presence and will, could make his charges behave. One evening on the road, a sportswriter covering the team was working in his hotel room when a group of players dropped by, as though for a casual visit. Anson meantime kept watch for delinquents at the hotel's bar and front door. Up in his room, the sportswriter asked what was afoot and was told to keep writing. A porter then wheeled an eight-gallon keg of beer into the room. The reporter's scribblings gave way to a long, wet game of poker. For several nights this routine continued, with an unknowing Anson down at his post, satisfied that his boys had at last reformed. One evening a poker player wandered to the window and noticed Anson sitting by the entrance, four stories below. Inspired by beer, he dropped the keg on the sidewalk near Anson. "With a report like the discharge of a fourteen-inch gun," it bounced twenty feet in the air and sent Anson diving for cover. Anson never found the culprit, though he had his suspicions.

Albert Spalding, the team owner, also tried to rein the boys in. "What are you running here?" Kelly replied. "A Sunday School or a Base Ball club?" Spalding began to get letters from fans about his players, telling "stories of drunkenness and debauchery," describing "scenes of revelry and carousing that were altogether reprehensible and disgusting," as he remembered them. When newspapers published some of the luscious details, and even criticized Spalding's management, he had to act. Spalding hired a Pinkerton detective to tail the players on their nocturnal wanderings through Clark Street and the tenderloin districts. The detective handed in a report one inch thick with embarrassing details on seven players in particular. Spalding assembled the team and read the report. Grim silence, broken by an uncontrite Kelly: "In that place where the detective reports me as taking a lemonade at 3 A.M. he's off. It was a straight whiskey; I never drank a lemonade at that hour in my life." Losing the game, Spalding told the guilty seven to decide on their own punishment. Since the Pinkerton had charged $175 for the report, the seven came up with $25 apiece to pay for it. With that mild rebuke, case closed.

Immune to reform, Kelly could only be removed. In the 1886 World Series against St. Louis, champs of the American Association, Kelly—"in no condition to play," according to Spalding— hit weakly and bumbled the final throw home that gave the championship to the Browns. "He was of a highly convivial nature," Spalding said later, "extremely fascinating and witty, and his example was demoralizing to discipline. Particularly was his influence objectionable upon the younger members of the nine. Everybody in Chicago liked Kelly; all the players desired to be where he was." Kelly had his own complaints. The greatest star in the game, he was paid $2,500 in 1886. At least thirteen other ballplayers enjoyed fatter salaries that year. (Dan Brouthers and Hoss Radbourn each made $4,000, Buck Ewing $3,500.) Spalding had also fined Kelly for drinking, money that Kelly wanted back. So when Boston offered to buy Kelly's contract in the winter of 1887, Spalding and Kelly were both willing.

Only two years earlier, Detroit had bought Buffalo's "Big Four"—Brouthers and three others—for the sensational total of $7,500. Now Boston purchased Kelly alone for $10,000. The sale and the price staggered the baseball world, which already extended far beyond the tight circle of cities with major-league clubs. In San Francisco, the canceled check for $10,000 was displayed in a store window, then removed because milling crowds blocked traffic. "Oh, I'm a beaut," Kelly informed his new fans in the Boston bleachers, "you can bank on that—a regular ten thousand dollar beauty. I come high, but they had to have me." His salary, with a new advertising deal thrown in, was doubled to $5,000. Back in Chicago, Spalding added a temperance clause to his contracts and offered bonuses for total abstinence. "We don't intend to again insult ladies and gentlemen," he spat into the wind, "in this city or any other by allowing men who are full of beer and whiskey to go upon the diamond in the uniform of the Chicago club."

A year later Spalding sold Clarkson, also to Boston, also for $10,000. The local hero had returned home. HE IS OURS, trumpeted the front-page headline in the *Boston Globe*. "Everywhere they were talking about Clarkson last night," the *Globe* reported. "In the clubs, in the theatres, in the hotel lobbies everywhere, John Clarkson signing with Boston was the topic of conversation." "It's the only $20,000 battery in the world, and Boston has got it," said one of the proud (if depleted) team owners. "Our pair of $10,000 beauties will beat the world this summer."

Sure enough, Boston started the season with a 9-game winning streak. Clarkson beat Philadelphia in the first game, throwing a no-hitter for five innings. Next game was Kelly's, with 2 homers, a double, and 6 runs batted in. Clarkson then shut out Washington for 11 innings until Kelly's hit and baserunning scored the winner. "Clarkson's command of the ball is wonderful," said the *Boston Herald*. "He watches the bases very sharply. . . . A thoroughly intelligent and scientific pitcher." Finally, after Clarkson's fifth win in the streak, the team lost to New York. But the Bostons slumped under .500 for the rest of the season as New York won the pennant. In 1889 Kelly, still commanding the base paths, stole 68 bases and led the league with 41 doubles. Clarkson won 49 games, best in the league, and also led in strikeouts, shutouts, innings, and earned run average. Yet the team finished second, only a game behind New York. Still no pennant in Boston for the $20,000 battery.

The King never stopped drinking and losing money. "A big-hearted, open-handed, kindly chap," recalled Jim Hart, one of his Boston managers, "the easiest man imaginable to manage as to the ordinary laws of baseball and the hardest to discipline that I ever had under my control. . . . His earnings belonged to everybody and anybody but himself." At paydays he often received canceled receipts instead of cash. Fans in Boston gave him a house in Hingham and a fine horse and carriage; he didn't own them long. Toward the end, Kelly advised a hopeful young ballplayer to stay in college and become a doctor instead. "And I want you to promise me," he added, putting his arm around the young man's neck, "you'll never take a drink."

Posing for the Boston team photo in 1892, Kelly looked old, jowly, and sluggish, his belly drooping over his belt. Boston took the pennant, but without much help from the King, who hit only .189 in seventy-eight games. In the World Series against Cleveland he got no hits but flashed an old Kelly trick, one last time. With a Cleveland runner on third and two outs, the batter grounded to short. The batter was called safe at first, but Kelly threw his glove to the ground, pretending the batter was out. The runner heading home saw Kelly drop his glove and slowed up, assuming the inning was over. Kelly whirled to the first baseman, called for the ball, caught it bare-handed, and tagged the runner out.

Two years later Kelly was dead. Out of baseball, he had opened the inevitable saloon in New York and resumed his theatrical career. In November 1894 he took a boat to Boston to appear at the Palace Theater with the London Gaiety Girls. (He was going to recite "Casey at the Bat," the immortal poem inspired by his career.) A cold caught on the boat turned serious, and he died in a few days. The doctor called it pneumonia. Everyone knew he had drunk himself to death, only thirty-six years old.

John Clarkson had just finished his own baseball career. Especially when standing next to his tipsy catcher, Clarkson had seemed a model of restrained conduct. "His temperate habits and the excellent care he takes of himself always keep him in good condition," noted one sportswriter. "John Clarkson is not merely a great ball player; he is a modest, unassuming gentleman." "He is a fit representative of the base ball player of today," declared Jake Morse of the *Boston Herald,* an early historian of baseball. "He is quiet, gentlemanly and intelligent, inobtrusive and undemonstrative, just the man to make a host of friends."

His problem was less public, less acknowledged than Kelly's. Clarkson succumbed to ballplayer sex. Married since 1886, at some point late in his career he contracted syphilis. (Years later, the Chicago sportswriter Hugh Fullerton claimed that both Clarkson and Kelly had been sold to Boston because of "a woman," no details provided.) In 1895, out of baseball, Clarkson and his wife settled in Bay City, Michigan, where Dr. Charles T. Newkirk specialized in the treatment of venereal diseases. For a few years Clarkson ran a tobacco store in Bay City. Declining slowly, in 1902 he was sent to the Michigan state hospital for the insane in Pontiac. Eventually he returned to Massachusetts to live with his parents. He died in February 1909 at McLean Hospital, a mental institution, so deranged at the last that he was strapped to his bed. The death certificate listed pneumonia as the primary cause, along with "general paralysis," a common syphilitic euphemism of the time.

The $20,000 battery, killed by ballplaying life.

◆　　◆　　◆

Like the games, the life does not change. The ballplayers are always young and simple, amusing themselves with drink and random sex. Society at large, out there in the real world, runs through cycles—now more tolerant, now less—toward such amusements. Ballplayers do not care. Safe in their bubble, protected by adulation, they follow their impulses, part of a classic tradition of which they realize little. They look neither backward nor forward. Eyes on the ball, they watch the play right here, right now. They live supremely, recklessly in the moment.

Chapter Four

Baseball:
"This Well Known
and Old Fashioned Game"

A child's game of ancient and obscure origins, baseball was first played by adults on a regular basis around 1825, in the booming village of Rochester, New York. (The modern history of the game began when grown-ups took it up as a scheduled, predictable diversion; from that moment, big-league ball became possible.) A young printer in Rochester, Thurlow Weed, later remembered those games played in Mumford's meadow, an expanse of eight or ten acres bordering the Genesee River. "A base-ball club, numbering nearly fifty members, met every afternoon during the ball-playing season," Weed recalled. "Though the members of the club embraced persons between eighteen and forty, it attracted the young and the old." Among the "best players," Weed listed eight names: a merchant, three doctors, and four lawyers. In those particular players and place, the essential elements of nineteenth-century baseball were already visible.

The true birthplace of the modern game was—not coincidentally—America's first inland boomtown, a gigantic village in the throes of giddy expansion and transformation in the 1820s. (Baseball developed in counterpoint to the swelling, clattering cacophony of nineteenth-century progress.) Rochester rose at the intersection of two waterways, the Genesee River and Erie Canal. An aqueduct finished in the fall of 1823 carried the canal across the Genesee, smack in the middle of town; at 802 feet, it was the longest stone bridge yet built in the United States, and a pride and wonderment for this newborn frontier metropolis. Now traffic through Rochester could flow west to Buffalo and Lake Erie, and east all the way to Albany, the Hudson River, and finally New York City. "Every thing in this bustling place appeared to be in motion," noted a British visitor, Basil Hall, in 1827. "The very streets seemed to be starting up of their own accord, ready-made, and looking as fresh and new, as if they had been turned out of the workmen's hands but an hour before." The town population leaped from 331 in 1815 to 4,274 in 1825, then to 7,669 two years later. Every adult resident had come from somewhere else.

Thurlow Weed and his fellow baseball players, the rising leaders of the town, were typical of the enterprising folk drawn by Rochester's eruption. Weed, on his own since childhood, had arrived in 1822, learned the newspaper business from the local editor, and become absorbed in politics. Later, as editor of the *Albany Evening Journal* and mentor to William H. Seward, he would become a national political boss of unsurpassed power and shrewdness. Thomas Kempshall, the merchant-ballplayer, had come to Rochester as a penniless British immigrant, seventeen years old, and worked as a carpenter, then clerked in Ira West's dry-goods store. West made him a partner; a year later Kempshall bought the business. In 1827 he and Ebenezer Beach put up the largest flour mill in the country. One of Rochester's richest men, Kempshall later served as mayor and as a Whig congressman. Of the lawyers on the baseball club, Fred Whittlesey, a Yale graduate from western Connecticut, also later went to Congress, while Addison Gardiner and his law partner Samuel Selden both became judges. All these men—along with the other lawyer, James K. Livingston, and the three doctors, George Marvin, Fred Backus, and A. G. Smith—worked at self-bossed, sedentary jobs that allowed them the energy and flexible schedules to go play baseball on pleasant summer afternoons.

The deeper reasons for those games must be inferred. Most

of the boomtown's residents had grown up in more settled circumstances amid old-stock Yankees. The work of canal-digging had brought Irish laborers, the largest immigrant group in Rochester, with their Roman Catholic church and fraternal Hibernian Society. Fourteen different religious persuasions in Rochester offered services. But hoteliers and tavern keepers in town were letting their church memberships lapse. Nearly one hundred places were licensed to sell drinks; the fretful Protestant middle class started urging temperance. Crime increased, a robbery here, a stabbing there. Members and enemies of the Masonic fraternal order squared off after a mysterious kidnapping and probable murder.

Rochester was disintegrating into the hopeful, jangling disorder of headlong progress. "We have seen our village, from a log hut or two, in the deep and lonely forest, rise like the work of magick, in a few years, to the form of a busy and populous city," said one of the older citizens in 1827. "We have seen the forest yielding to the fruitful field, and the fruitful field to streets crowded with commerce, and wharves covered with the merchandise of every nation." But now, "our future prosperity depends on the tractability of a mass of mind, a host of mingling opinions, passions, virtues, and vices, thrown together from every corner of the globe. Shall it rise through years to come in moral and social order and beauty?" Soon Rochester would be swept by more than its share of religious revivals and enthusiasms, then social crusades and utopian experiments.

Already, in the Rochester of the 1820s, one could discern the looming, unsettling nineteenth century in America: migration from country to town to city, the transportation revolution, restless mobility, industrialization, westward expansion, the shift from muscle work to head work, immigration, secularization and revivalism, cultural diversity, political upheaval and reform. So Thurlow Weed and his friends among the young elite, cutting a pattern for men of their age and class, went out and played baseball.

◆　　◆　　◆

The game they played was probably town ball, also called base, goal ball, and (later) the Boston game or the Massachusetts game.

(Most of the ballplayers in Rochester were migrant New Englanders.) Lacking, as yet, any written rules, town ball was an oral tradition passed along the generations, with many variants in styles and terminology. Usually it involved four bases, with a fifth base, where the batter stood, midway between first and fourth, somewhat behind the baseline between them. Thus bulged outward on one side, the bases might comprise a square from twenty to (more typically) fifty feet wide, or a forty- by fifty-foot rectangle, or an irregular polygon in which the batter ran about twenty feet to first, forty-five feet to second, thirty-five feet to third, and fifty-five feet to fourth or home. (The point was to reach first; then the fun began.) The bases might be five-foot stakes, flat stones, old tin plates, or trees and hitching posts if the game was played on a street in town. The ball, softer and larger than a modern baseball, was usually made from twine or yarn wrapped around a springy core—cork or rubber were best—and covered in leather by a shoemaker or compliant mother; in a pinch, a sturgeon's cartilaginous nose or the thick end of a corncob would do. The bat might be a tool handle, wagon-wheel spoke, sawed-off wagon's tongue, or even a stout tree limb custom-hewn and turned for the game. No manufacturer sold such sporting goods as yet; everything had to be scrounged.

The play on the field looked like rudimentary baseball grafted onto a child's version of hunting and an elaborate game of tag. The batter stood at one edge of a boxy infield (instead of standing at the point of a diamond, as in modern baseball). The other team's thrower (also called the feeder or giver), from the middle of the field, served overhand pitches to the batter (striker, knocker, or batman). Aside from the catcher, the other defensive players (scoots or scouts or shackers) arranged themselves all over the field. With no foul territory, any batted ball was fair. Short scoots stood near the bases or behind the pitcher, long scoots farther away, and a back scoot or two to reinforce the catcher. A fence scoot might sit atop a distant but reachable barrier to retrieve balls that went over it. Nobody bothered to guard the bases because no outs were made there. Instead the striker was retired after three whiffing swings, or if a struck ball was caught on the fly or after one bounce, or—the most distinctive feature—if the striker was hit (soaked or patched out) by a scoot's throw before he could reach the next base. Even with the soft ball, a good soaking might sting.

For ballplayers still so close to the farm and frontier, accustomed to guns and hunting, the act of soaking must have reminded them of a hunter's drawing a bead on his quarry, nailing a target in flight. Sometimes the duck was sitting. One thrower for a town-ball team in Boston later recalled his version of a pickoff: noticing a runner standing too far from first, he faked a pitch to the striker and—in the absence of a balk rule—soaked the runner hard in the stomach. "It did not hurt him much," the thrower recalled, not much, "but the surprise and dismay upon his face at thus suddenly finding himself put out caused much laughter. It was a risky shot, but the game was a close one and I took the chances." Town ball by its nature favored the strikers, with barrages of hits, scurrying action, and funny bounces on irregular terrains. In some versions, if a struck ball was lost in tall grass the striker could keep rounding the bases, scoring repeatedly, till it was found. The field, extending in all directions, encouraged hitting; a striker might choke up on his bat and tick or even stroke the ball backward, past the catcher and back scoots. But—a solitary advantage for the thrower—innings could pass quickly because only one striker had to be retired before the teams switched sides. Runs, called tallies, were recorded by notching a stick. The game ended when a team reached a certain number of tallies, perhaps fifty, perhaps one hundred. Poor hitting could mean a very long game stretching over two days.

Rochester's town-ball players knew the game as part of the English cultural inheritance brought over from the old country. In the southern counties, both east and west of London, that provided most of the emigrants to New England, bat-and-ball games had long, vaguely recorded histories; few chroniclers took serious notice of childish pastimes. The first written use that anyone has discovered of the world *baseball*—by a Puritan minister in Maidstone, thirty miles southeast of London, in 1700— was merely an irritated note in passing that certain people were profaning the Sabbath by playing the game on Sunday. A children's book published in London in 1744 pictured a group of kids playing "base-ball," with posts for bases, a child ready to strike a thrown ball with his hand, and this play-by-play:

> The Ball once struck off,
> Away flies the Boy
> To the next destin'd Post,
> And then Home with Joy.

Another old folk game, called stool-ball in the western counties and bittle-battle in southeastern England, added a stick-wielding batter to the essential mix of ball and bases.

For boys in colonial New England, the act of hitting an object with a stick weighted at the business end was an everyday task: chopping wood, hammering nails, digging or grubbing out roots with a mattock, and swinging a sledgehammer to drive a wedge or sink a fence post all demanded similar dexterities of hand-eye coordination. To these mundane tasks of "batting" a stationary object, the challenge of hitting a moving target (a thrown ball) added a sporting aspect. Thus New Englanders of the 1700s in playing their traditional ball-and-bat games were using skills already honed elsewhere. In 1791 the Reverend William Bentley of Salem, Massachusetts, took note in his diary of the "Puerile Sports usual in these parts of New England." Boys took up "the Bat & Ball" as summer began to cool: "The Ball is made of rags covered with leather in quarters & covered with double twine, sewed in knots over the whole. The Bat is from 2 to 3 feet long, round on the back side but flatted considerably on the face, & round at the end, for a better stroke." The game they played might have been cat ball, a particular favorite because of its expandability. Only three ballplayers were needed for one old cat, which consisted of two bases, a pitcher, catcher, and batter. After hitting the ball, the batter would try to run to the pitcher's base and return before being soaked; if he was put out, the three traded places. Another batter made the game two old cat, and so on to three old cat and four old cat. When even more ballplayers showed up, on special occasions like holidays, a barn-raising, or town meeting day, they played town ball. (Hence the name: the game was usually played *in town*.)

The most obvious English ancestor of town ball was the game of rounders, especially popular in the west of England. Its origins lost in prehistory, perhaps derived from games brought by Norse invaders, rounders shows up in scattered English sources from the 1600s on. Four stones or stakes, thirty-six to sixty feet apart, were placed around a circle. The batter stood in front of a hole about a foot wide and six inches deep. The pitcher (the pecker or feeder) tossed the ball gently to the batter. ("The feeder is generally the best player on his side," according to one observer, "much depending on his skill and art.") If the ball got past the batter and went down the hole, the batter was out. If the batter hit the ball, he ran clockwise around the circle of bases, avoiding a thrown ball from a fielder. The batter was also out if he missed two (or three) swings, if a batted ball was caught, or if a fielder threw the ball into the hole—"grounding" it—while the runner was off base. Circumnavigating the bases scored a rounder; the teams changed sides after everybody was put out. Henry Chadwick, later the codifier of American baseball, played rounders as an English schoolboy in the 1830s. "It was simply a game to occupy about an hour or two," he recalled, "and the fun consisted in hitting the runner." Except for the hole in the ground, rounders shared many elements with town ball. *The Book of Sports* by Robin Carver, published in Boston in 1834, gave the rules of "base, or goal ball" by reprinting, nearly verbatim, rules for rounders published in London in 1829. Carver's book included a picture of a game in progress on Boston Common, with the State House in the background: the first illustration, apparently, of an American baseball game.

Centered in New England and its migrant outposts, town ball by the late 1700s had already spread as far south as Pennsylvania and New Jersey. (Continental soldiers at Valley Forge played it occasionally in 1778, as did Princeton students a few years later.) Other scheduled, organized gatherings of adult town-ball players began soon after the games in Rochester had started. In the spring of 1831, a group of young Philadelphians, all over the age of twenty-five, crossed the Delaware River to the village of Camden, New Jersey. With only four participants on hand, they played two old cat at a field on Market Street. Their boyish memories stirred, so they recruited a regular party of fifteen to twenty for Saturday games of town ball in Camden—to a chorus of hoots and catcalls. "The players were frequently reproved and censured by their friends," one historian said later, "for degrading themselves by indulging in such a childish amusement." They joined up with another group, originally formed to play town ball on the Fourth of July each year, and in May 1833 organized the Olympic Ball Club of Philadelphia, the first baseball club with a written constitution and field rules.

Like the Rochester ballplayers, the Olympics drew from a young elite of merchants and other solid citizens bound for notable careers in Philadelphia business and professional circles. "A conservative and temperate body of gentlemen," as one member recalled them in 1861, "who enjoyed mixing their sports with good conversation, wit, food, and drink." (Once a member was expelled for suggesting too strenuously that liquor be banned from club functions.) Each year on July Fourth, the club president would read the Declaration of Independence, leading to songs, a speech, and a ballgame. Baseball was already meshing with politics, patriotism, and liquid bonhomie. The Olympics played games among themselves and with newer town-ball teams, the Excelsiors and Athletics of Philadelphia, and other clubs in Camden and Germantown; but not *too* seriously. They played for fun and companionship, and, incidentally, to win. "Respectability has always been the ruling desire," a member said later. "One of the commendable objects of the club, always kept in view, has been to make it socially agreeable." At ease among their carefully chosen peers, more serious about baseball than they realized, they retrieved an inchoate *something*, dimly remembered, that was missing from the rest of their lives.

◆　◆　◆

The modern history of baseball is traditionally dated from several teams of the mid-1800s in the New York City area. By then it was not uncommon for adults to play the old, familiar game on a regular basis. When teams from New York and Brooklyn met on October 21, 1845, newspapers reported "a friendly match of the time-honored game of Base," "this well known and old fashioned game." The newspapers hardly needed to explain a game already considered old-fashioned in 1845. One of the New York clubs, the Knickerbockers, fiddled with the rules and produced a new variation on town ball. No surprise there either; the many extant versions and names of town ball testified to the statutory looseness that ballplayers had always brought to it. But unlike other revisionists, the Knickerbockers wrote down the rules for their game and played it, year after year, gradually converting other clubs to the new style. So town ball evolved into baseball.

Alexander J. Cartwright, the seminal figure among the Knickerbockers, was born in New York in 1820, the son of a Nantucket sea captain. He worked as a teller at the Union Bank, and later ran a bookstore and stationery shop on Wall Street with his brother. About 1842 he joined a group of occasional town-ball players on a field at Twenty-seventh Street and Fourth Avenue in Manhattan; two or three men would set forth on a pleasant morning and collect enough hands for a game. Soon encroaching urbanization sent them seven blocks north to another field in the Murray Hill neighborhood, then across the Hudson River to the more rural Hoboken. Progress chased them back to the country.

These migrating ballgames led to certain improvements. The extent of Cartwright's particular role in these alterations is usually assumed but not proven. He later referred to the "dear old Knickerbockers" as "the first Base Ball Club of N.Y." and was proud of his part in their founding—but he did not claim to have invented a new game. According to a brief history of the Knickerbockers published in 1868, Cartwright merely "proposed a regular organization, promising to obtain several recruits." The club was then formally organized by Cartwright and others on September 23, 1845, with Duncan F. Curry, William R. Wheaton, and William H. Tucker as officers and with Wheaton and Tucker as the rules committee; Cartwright was not among them. But in 1877 Curry told a different, improved story: "Well do I remember the afternoon when Alex Cartwright came up to the ball field with a new scheme for playing ball," he recalled. "His plan met with much good natured derision, but he was so persistent in having us try his new game that we finally consented more to humor him than with any thought of it becoming a reality. . . . When we saw what a great game Cartwright had given us, and as his suggestion for forming a club to play it met with our approval, we set about to organize a club." No doubt Cartwright did suggest a formal organization. (According to his grandson, he "often spoke of the beginnings of the National game . . . how he started the Knickerbocker Club.") The Knickerbocker game variations, though, were probably the joint inspiration of several ballplayers on the field, all of them thinking it through, trying different rules and dimensions, poking at this old-fashioned game.

The Knickerbocker version rotated the town-ball infield 45 degrees, dropped its fifth base, and placed the batter at fourth, now called home, with foul lines stretching past first and third. The distance from home to second, and from first to third, was stated as 42 paces; so the batter ran 29.7 paces from base to base. (A standard military pace at quick time was 30 inches, at double time 36 inches. By those definitions, 29.7 paces converted to either 74 feet 3 inches or a bit more than 89 feet, close to the modern baseline of 90 feet.) The batter swung at balls "pitched, and not thrown," delivered with a stiff-armed underhand motion, as in pitching horseshoes or tenpin bowling. As in town ball, a batter was out after three missed swings, or if a batted ball was caught on the fly or after one bounce. Any number could play, and the pitcher could stand anywhere he liked. But soaking was banned: "A player running the bases shall be out, if the ball is in the hands of an adversary on the base, or the runner is touched with it before he makes his base; it being understood, however, that in no instance is a ball to be thrown at him." The teams switched sides after three outs, not one, and the first team to score twenty-one runs (counts, or aces) won the game.

Thus, in broad strokes, the Knickerbockers laid out the game of modern baseball, more fun for both players and spectators than town ball. The usable field had been quartered, allowing fans to sit much closer to the action, where they could see, hear, and be heard more, and so more pointedly affect the play. Compressed in this sense, the game also spread out. The bases were twice as far apart, the infield four times larger; the smaller, harder ball, now too dangerous for soaking, could be thrown and hit much farther. ("They put so much into the balls to make them lively," said one early convert, "that when the ball was tossed to you like a girl playing 'one-old-cat,' you could knock it so far that the fielders would be chasing it yet, like dogs hunting sheep, after you had gone clear around and scored your tally.") With outs now made at the bases, fielders had more to do and fans saw more varied action.

The essential, aggressive act of the game switched from soaking to batting. Both offense and defense gained: the batters in facing underhand pitches designed to be hittable ("like a girl playing 'one-old-cat' "), and the fielders by throwing *to* a stationary, receptive teammate, not *at* a moving, dodging runner. New situations called for more complicated strategies. The game took on modestly cerebral qualities. ("It exhibits more physical skill and mental activity, with considerable powers of the mind.") Three outs per inning created fluid yet known situations posing the eternal baseball question, ever on the minds of both teams: How many outs are there? Played for only twenty-one aces, instead of fifty or more, the contest ended in a few hours—a manageable chunk of time in scheduled urban settings. Baseball was now faster, quicker, more complex, satisfying on more levels; a game for both players and fans, a public spectacle as well as private amusement.

The Knickerbockers played the new game among themselves in the fall of 1845 and spring of 1846, testing and tinkering, then in an arranged match with the New York Club, one of the informal town-ball teams around town. The New Yorkers took to the game all too readily, winning, 23–1. "The chief trouble was that we had held our opponents too cheaply," Duncan Curry explained later, "and few of us had practiced any prior to the contest, thinking that we knew more about the game than they did." Then, too, the enemy pitcher "was a cricket bowler of some note, and while one could use only the straight arm delivery he could pitch an awfully speedy ball." (Players on the field could already bend almost any rule.) Perhaps embarrassed, the Knickerbockers didn't play another interclub game until five years later. By then Alex Cartwright had lit out for California in the gold rush of '49, playing the new game on the trek west, armed with a rule book and a baseball from the games on Murray Hill. ("Many is the pleasant chase," he said in old age, "I have had after it on Mountain and Prairie.") He wound up in Hawaii, where he sold insurance and evangelized the Knickerbocker version.

The game itself, the play on the field, was always its own best argument. The Washington Club, later called the Gothams, started playing baseball at a cricket field in Harlem in 1850. Their games with the Knickerbockers, well reported in newspapers and attended by up to a thousand fans, led to two more Manhattan teams, the Eagles and Empires, by 1855. The *Spirit of the Times*, a major sporting paper, gave "baseball" an entry of its own in its annual index, after previously listing it as a subheading under cricket. Upon seeing a game between the Eagles and Knickerbockers in November 1854, John Suydam organized the Excelsiors of Brooklyn, a team first known as the Jolly Young Bachelors' Base Ball Club. (The old informal town-ball games had often pitted bachelors against married men.) Baseball kept evolving: now nine men to a side, the pitcher in a box forty-five feet from home, contests ending after nine innings instead of twenty-one runs. The game spread onward to Philadelphia, then to Boston. A response to urbanization, it logically was centered in the three principal cities of the country.

Baseball's arrival in Boston may illustrate the process of conversion. As a national force the Hub was now entering its long Indian summer, losing commercial and political leadership to its disapproved rival down on the Hudson. Vigorous town-ball teams in Boston—the Olympics, Elm Trees, Green Mountains, and Hancocks—spurned tamperings with their own game, "the Massachusetts game," especially by advocates of anything called "the New York game." Ned Saltzman, a twenty-five-year-old second baseman for the Gothams in New York, brought the game along when he moved to Boston in 1857. Employed at his trade as a watch-case maker, he started playing baseball with his shopmates on Boston Common, then organized the Tri-Mountain Club, the first baseball team in New England. "It gave an equal share to all those engaged," one member later said of the new style, "to test their abilities as ball players." As the resident expert for his own team, Saltzman got to pitch and catch as well as play second. For a season they played New York ball only among themselves; no other Boston team would try the new game.

In September 1858 the Tri-Mountains played a team from Portland, Maine, led by Sam Crowell, captain of a coastal steamer running between Portland and New York. This first interstate contest in New England illustrated the wild, swooping lurches through which a game in those days might swing. Nobody as yet wore gloves or any protective equipment; one of the Portlands had to leave the game in the first inning with a ball-struck hand. (The regulation ball of 1858 was an ounce and a half heavier and an inch greater in circumference than the modern baseball.) On a parchingly hot day on Boston Common, the Tri-Mountains led, 5–4, after 3 innings, scored 11 runs in the fourth and 13 more in the fifth, yet finally lost, 47–42. According to one teammate's later recollection, Sam Crowell—who weighed 220 pounds—"helped himself to too much ice water," or perhaps to something stronger. With the bases full, his mates had to revive him and lug him to the batter's box. His senses briefly focused by the occasion, Crowell hit the first pitch over the left fielder's head into the distant Frog Pond. He staggered all the way home. The crowd took note. Many local town-ball players watched the game "with a dignified tolerance befitting those who 'guessed' that the old game was good enough for them," as one of the skeptics, Jim Lovett, later told the story. "But some who came to scoff remained to pray. . . . The pitching, instead of swift throwing, looked easy to hit, and the pitcher stood off so far, and then there was no danger of getting plugged with the ball while running bases; and the ball was so lively and could be batted so far!"

Already known as "the national game" and "national pastime," by 1860 baseball was being played in (for example) Rochester, Cleveland, Detroit, Cincinnati, Chicago, Pittsburgh, Baltimore, and Washington, D.C., and in such distant outposts as Wisconsin, Minnesota, Missouri, Louisiana, Texas, and California. The National Association of Base Ball Players, founded in New York in 1857, soon embraced some eighty clubs. In May 1860 even the Philadelphia Olympics converted, wrenchingly, from town ball. (Most of the older members then quit among "mutterings both loud and deep.") Town ball persisted in isolated pockets here and there; Ty Cobb played it as a kid in Royston, Georgia, in the 1890s. But after only fifteen years, in any town that considered itself up to date, this new version of the "old fashioned game" had triumphed.

Spreading with such speed, its demographic base inevitably broadened. The Knickerbockers of the 1840s, like the Rochester town-ballers of the 1820s and the Philadelphia Olympics of the 1830s, were British-descended men of relative education and economic potential. About two thirds of the Knickerbockers were doctors, lawyers, and others in white-collar occupations—not old, landed wealth, but an ambitious middle class, new to the city, in peppery motion. Their surviving letters about club matters, precise as to language, grammar, and spelling, reflect a high level of literacy. Their jobs offered intellectual demands without physical outlets, hence a need for exercise; and in an expanding, splintering city, their upward-heading social aspirations needed ties with peers. These two linked motives, physical and social, run through the early years of baseball. "Its members have from its inception been composed mostly of those whose sedentary habits required recreation, and its respectability has ever been undoubted," one contemporary said of the Knickerbockers. "No person can obtain admission in the club merely for his capacity as a player; he must also have the reputation of a gentleman." Such dignified postures, declared for the record, need not be unduly believed. No doubt the Knickerbockers in private indulged the usual masculine frailties. ("We are all moral young men," a prospective member teased, "and read our Bibles regularly.") But they clearly were not typical Manhattanites of their day: and playing ball was a happy act of defining solidarity against the roiling diversity of New York City at mid-century.

The Knickerbocker pattern held elsewhere in baseball for most of the 1850s. In New York, Brooklyn, and Philadelphia, 62 percent or more of the ballplayers worked at white-collar jobs. John A. Lowell, the leader of Boston baseball after Ned Saltzman, started his own engraving business. In Albany, a team of clerks played baseball for relief from their indoor labors. Even on the Brooklyn Eckfords, a team founded by naval mechanics and shipwrights in 1855, about a quarter of the members worked at nonmanual jobs. As urbanization and industrialization transformed work into tightly scheduled jobs performed indoors and sitting down, people naturally compensated by seeking outdoor, muscular play. A popular song about baseball celebrated this impulse:

Come jolly comrade, here's the game that's played in open air
Where clerks and all the indoor men can profit by a share
'Twill make the weak man strong again
'Twill brighten every eye
And all who need such exercise should catch it on the "Fly."

Aside from its own intrinsic beauties, baseball thrived in the 1850s by comforting certain new middle-class anxieties. Nearly half the population in the Northeast lived in cities and towns, in circumstances that their rural ancestors might have found dangerously unnatural, frazzling to nerves and deadening to muscles. "It is the universally-acknowledged fact," said Catharine Beecher in 1856, "that the present generation of men and women are inferior in health and in powers of endurance." The prescribed remedy, regular exercise, became intentional and fashionable for the first time in America. This "constantly increasing taste for athletic exercises," as *Harper's Weekly* called it, included adult ballplayers, new public gyms, walkers and runners, sailors and shooters, a public health movement, school training, and "muscular Christianity." Not for the last time, a fad settled on America by promising to restore something lost in the offhand wake of progress. "It has been supposed that a race of shopkeepers, brokers, and lawyers could live without bodies," Thomas Wentworth Higginson wrote in the *Atlantic* in 1858. "Who, in this community, really takes exercise? . . . The professional or business man, what muscles has he at all?" So go back to the old games, said Higginson: "To almost every man there is joy in the memory of these things; they are the happiest associations of his boyhood. It does not occur to him, that he also might be as happy as a boy, if he lived more like one."

Baseball was essentially an act of retrieval, an effort—however dimly realized or unconscious—to balance the losses and commotions of modernity. In a revealing flight of hyperbole, Dr. J. B. Jones, a prime organizer of baseball in New York, pictured the game rescuing "thousands upon thousands of the sedentary from their death-dealing cloisters, with their pale, wan countenances, emaciated forms, tottering steps, and listless eyes." (So much for modern progress.) Nineteenth-century progress was roaring down the track, dazzling and unstoppable, slowed not at all by its incidental "death-dealing" side effects. Swept up by this juggernaut, stoking the engine yet not quite sure about it, Americans developed a sentimental, revealing affection for anything labeled "old." The songwriter Stephen Foster, hit maker of the 1850s, kept plucking this popular single chord (my old Kentucky home, old Black Joe, old Uncle Ned, old dog Tray, the old folks at home, the old plantation, farewell old cottage, on and on). The word's peculiar emotional freight all by itself could stir a twinge, even a nudging, rueful sniffle. Baseball, the old game at home now slightly improved, thrummed the same nostalgia. Even with the Knickerbocker variations, it was still "the old fashioned game of Base Ball," as the *Spirit of the Times* called it (once again) in 1854. Another pop song of the 1850s suggested this mood:

> Here's a health to our *Base Ball*, and honor and fame,
> For 'tis manly and hearty and free;
> Oh long may it flourish, our *National Game*—
> Here's a health, good old base ball, to thee.

Baseball would never lose these flashbacking associations. On some level, a ballgame always meant going back to youth: of the person, the culture, and the country.

Baseball by 1860 had already grown beyond its origins. The old mansion was permanently under renovation. Earlier the cost of lavish postgame dinners, a politely celebrated feature of interclub matches, had discouraged less wealthy ballplayers from joining teams. But more frequent games meant a cloying surfeit of celebrations. As such dinners became less inevitable, members could expect to pay less to play, just the annual club dues and the cost of their uniforms. New occupational groups formed teams in New York: firemen (the Mutuals), cops (the Manhattans), barkeepers (the Phantoms), food-service workers (several teams), and others edging down the class ladder. Sporting papers began to fret, in middle-class tones, about raucous postgame celebrations, "the indulgence of a prurient taste for indecent anecdotes and songs—a taste only to be gratified at the expense of true dignity and self-respect." As time passed, the game's exploding popularity for Americans obscured its original meanings. No longer merely a game for office-bound gentlemen, baseball was too relentlessly popular.

◆　　◆　　◆

Professionalism now lifted the game to its next level. During the 1860s, delayed only slightly by the Civil War, baseball for its finest players changed from recreation to occupation, with the best hired teams ultimately traveling not across town, or from Brooklyn to Hoboken, but thousands of miles to play other crack hired teams in distant parts of the country. A typical ballpark, no longer an open field free to any onlooker, became a fenced enclosure, with admission fees, seats, and even a grandstand roof. Architecture reflected organization: a team's once loose structure took on the form and—to some extent—the purposes of a business enterprise, with the sound political connections that any shrewdly conducted business would covet. As a social bonder, the game sprawled out laterally, transcending the old team ties of friendship-occupation-neighborhood to the wider, more diverse dimensions of city and region. A town's baseball team became a matter of civic pride and sharp competition with other aspiring towns. Ballplayers felt the exacting attention of a larger public. When played and watched for pay, and mobile beyond the pulls of merely local geography, baseball edged closer, an easy toss, to the approaching concept of big-league ball.

The boldest originator of these redefinitions was Arthur Pue Gorman, an underappreciated figure in baseball history. The briefness of his baseball phase and the unrelated prominence of Gorman's later political career have helped to obscure the baseball interests that so occupied him before his thirtieth birthday. Best known as a conservative Democratic senator from Maryland, "the handsomest man of his time," Gorman first came to national political notice when he managed Grover Cleveland's successful run for the presidency in 1884. Twice, in 1892 and 1900, he was himself a serious candidate for the White House. On issues he was unpredictably independent, an ally of southern segregationists on one hand and of northern anti-imperialists on the other. As the acknowledged Democratic leader in the Senate, a shrewd and cynical judge of motives and measures, he buried himself in the details and bargains of legislation, to the ultimate cost of his reputation for honest public service. ("One of the ablest members of the United States Senate," *The Nation* allowed, but "a skillful manipulator of men and marshal of the forces of corruption.") When he died in 1906, the obituaries skipped over Gorman's baseball youth to dwell on his mature political life.

Yet those baseball days provided his self-education in leadership and management, showing Gorman at his best in a young man's idyll of enthusiasm and innovation. He was born in 1839 near Baltimore, the son of a granite contractor who helped build the Baltimore and Ohio Railroad. Young Gorman started political life as a congressional page at thirteen. Quickly adept at finding patrons in high places, he drew the interest of Senator Stephen Douglas, who brought him into the household and made him a private secretary. He toured with the Douglas party during the Lincoln-Douglas debates of 1858. Back in Washington a year later, now a Capitol messenger at age twenty, he started playing baseball on the spacious lawn that stretched south of the White House down to the Washington Monument and the Potomac River. An informal local club, the Potomacs, had just introduced New York ball to Washington. Gorman picked up the new game and helped form another team, the National club, in that spring of 1859. They adopted a uniform of long blue pants, a white shirt with blue shield, and a white cap. "A majority of its members were far advanced in life," said a contemporary, "only playing ball for exercise, and to have a pleasant time socially." But Gorman took the game more seriously.

Baseball at that moment had just started accidentally turning pro. In August 1858, in New York, a crowd had for the first time paid to see a baseball match. This all-star game between players from Manhattan and Brooklyn took place at a neutral site, the Fashion Race Course near Flushing, on Long Island. Facing the expense of grading the track's infield into a roughly acceptable baseball diamond, the game's organizers decided to charge spectators fifty cents a head. Fans from the city had to take the Fulton

Ferry, then a steamer to Hunter's Point, then the Flushing Railroad to the game. Still the crowd was huge—perhaps ten thousand fans, according to the *New York Herald*. (Harry Wright, a ubiquitous figure in the early history of pro baseball, played right field for the New York team.) If baseball could attract thousands of dollars, it suddenly took on new potential and dimensions.

The National Association's gentlemanly ban on paid ballplayers was brushed aside, an ideal no longer enforced. The first pro star was Jim Creighton, the best pitcher anyone had yet seen. Hired by the Brooklyn Excelsiors in 1860, he led them to eight straight wins on a tour through upstate New York all the way to Buffalo; then, after a week back home, on to games in Baltimore and Philadelphia. (Tested only by the rough Troy Haymakers, the Excelsiors blew away eight opponents by a total score of 260–69.) Taking note of Creighton's professional example, the Mutuals, founded in the Williamsburg section of Brooklyn in 1857, became a favorite plaything of William Marcy Tweed, the extravagantly corrupt Tammany boss. As president of the Mutuals after 1860, he put his players on city payrolls, usually in the street-cleaning department. Strengthened by those embezzled jobs, the Mutuals became the most popular team in New York and the biggest draw at the Elysian Fields in Hoboken. Other teams, lacking Boss Tweed's access to the public trough, depended on now-paying fans. After William Cammeyer built an enclosed field and clubhouse in Brooklyn, teams began to play for a share of the receipts there and at other fields in the borough.

In Washington, Arthur Gorman found in the Treasury Department the ever-generous sponsor he needed for his National club. Treasury's main office building, just east of the White House, looked out on the baseball games that dotted the White House lawn late on pleasant afternoons. It was natural that Treasury employees would drift into the games after work. Edward F. French, a Treasury clerk, helped Gorman start the Nationals and served as club president from 1862 through 1865. His father, E. B. French, also friendly to baseball, was head of the Second Auditor's office in Treasury, with many clerical jobs ready at his fingertips. The entire Treasury Department—expanded fivefold under the pressures of the Civil War—was a vast, undisciplined patronage empire of ten thousand jobs, the biggest civilian employer in Washington, rife with doubtful appointments and sometime corruption. Lincoln's first two Treasury secretaries, Salmon Chase and William Fessenden, let subordinates administer the department; and the next secretary, Hugh McCulloch, appointed in March 1865, was a baseball fan.

Dozens of the Nationals, such as the fastball pitcher Billy Williams and the ace catcher Harry Berthrong, received undemanding Treasury jobs that left ample time to play ball. Of the other Nationals, true amateurs employed outside the Treasury, few appeared to be men of wealth. Richard Cronin, for example, had a shoestore, H. H. McPherson was a druggist, Dayton Ward was a bookkeeper at the First National Bank, and George Hibbs ran a coal business, then worked in a clothing store. Somewhere—perhaps from wealthier members of the club, perhaps from caches in the easygoing labyrinth of Treasury—Gorman found major additional sources of money. In 1865 Al Reach of the Brooklyn Eckfords, considered the top baseball player at the moment, was courted by several pro teams. Gorman made him the richest offer, but Reach joined the Philadelphia Athletics so that he could still live at home on Long Island.

During the war the Nationals played mainly among themselves, "simply to keep the club from disbanding," scheduling only three or four match games a season with amateur teams from Washington and Baltimore. (Gorman spent the war safe in the congressional post office, becoming postmaster of the Senate at age twenty-six.) After the war ended, Gorman arranged twelve games in the summer of 1865—the first National matches to be covered by Washington newspapers. First they breezed through four local teams. E. A. Parker, the second baseman (and a clerk in the Internal Revenue section of the Treasury), hit well—making eight runs and no outs in one game—and Gorman roamed center field adeptly. The clerking battery of Williams and Berthrong looked unbeatable. Against the Pastimes on August 2, Berthrong "made a most brilliant play, leaping the rope and taking the ball in the midst of a crowd of spectators." ("In activity and judgment in catching foul balls," Henry Chadwick said later, "we know of no one who surpasses Berthrong.") After the Nationals beat the Jefferson club, 34–13, they claimed the championship of the South and promoted themselves to faster company from the North.

On August 28 and 29 they entertained two of the best pro teams in the country, the Philadelphia Athletics and Brooklyn Atlantics. Among more than four thousand spectators at the first game were Treasury secretary Hugh McCulloch (on hand to see his employees in action), three major generals, and President Andrew Johnson's private secretary. "The most numerous and brilliant assemblage ever before gathered at a match outside of New York," the reporter for the *New York Herald* concluded. "Great interest was taken in it by hundreds who never saw a game played before." The Athletics hit 18 homers and whomped their hosts, 87–12. Dick McBride, their pitcher, threw even harder than Williams, and a peculiar "twist" in his deliveries kept the Nationals hitting pop-ups. The Nationals were expected to fare even worse against the Atlantics, undefeated since 1863 and considered the best team in all of baseball. The crowd was bigger, estimated at six thousand fans, including President Johnson. (It was the first intercity baseball game seen by a president.) Gorman and Berthrong played well; "Gorman was repeatedly applauded for taking the ball on the 'fly' on the outer verge of the centre field." After six innings the Nationals led, 17–12. Then the tiring Williams lost his fastball. The Atlantics started poling the ball, scored 21 runs in the next two innings, and won, 34–19.

Later in 1865 the Nationals beat a crack New York team, the Brooklyn Excelsiors, in Washington by a score of 36–30. "The Nationals have improved so much in their play of late as to make them second to few clubs in the country," a local reporter exulted. "The Nationals play a more dashing and brilliant game than any of the first-class clubs that have visited this city during the present season." (A pardonable hometown exaggeration.) At the banquet that evening, J. B. Jones of the Excelsiors invited the Nationals to come play in New York.

Exactly what Gorman wanted to hear. Assuming the presidency of the Nationals in 1866, he planned a demanding tour for the first week of July: the Nationals would play six games in

six days in Philadelphia, New York, and New Jersey. The club
now fielded two distinct teams, amateurs and professionals.
Their diamond south of the White House, true to this double
identity, offered both ticketed seats and unenclosed areas open
to all. The pro squad had added more ballplaying Treasury
clerks, notably Goodrich Smith at shortstop, the slugging George
Fox at third ("a good player in this position," according to Chadwick, "but with more careful play he might be better"), and Sy
Studley and H. C. McLean in the outfield. Gorman had so improved the Nationals that he no longer played well enough to
start for his own team as it headed north. "We expect them to
return with laurels on their brows," a Washington paper announced. "We expect to greet them as champions of the United
States."

In Philadelphia they were again baffled by Dick McBride and
lost to the Athletics, 22–6. More than ten thousand fans, the
largest baseball crowd yet in Philadelphia, came to the Athletics'
grounds at the corner of Fifteenth and Columbia streets. After
beating a lesser local team, the Nationals went on to New York,
where they looked tired from travel and ballgames and lost badly
to the Unions of Morrisania and the Brooklyn Excelsiors. "A
brilliant social tour," a Washington reporter wrote home, "if not
a professionally victorious one." The Excelsiors took them on a
long carriage drive around Brooklyn, introduced them to the
mayor at City Hall, gave them a lavish midday dinner, then
another feast after the game. The Nationals returned to their
hotel long after midnight and—perhaps inevitably—lost again
the next day, to the Gothams. On the way home they beat a team
in New Brunswick, New Jersey, their second win in six games.
Later that season the Excelsiors returned to Washington for a
game on September 18. "The opinion had become general that
on their own ground the Nationals could not be vanquished,"
said a Washington paper, but the Nationals lost, 33–28. They
still could not meet the best New York and Philadelphia teams as
equals; in eight games over two years they had won only once.

For Gorman personally, though, both his income and his
baseball reputation were ascending. In September 1866 he followed his ballplayers into the green fields of the Treasury, as he

was appointed collector of internal revenue for the southern counties of Maryland, a more lucrative position than the Senate post office. Later that fall he was elected president of the National Association of Base Ball Players at its tenth annual convention in New York: the first man from beyond the Northeast to hold the office. Elected with him as corresponding secretary was Charles E. Coon of the Washington Empire club, yet another Treasury clerk. Contained briefly by the war, baseball was bursting open in the years after Appomattox, with 91 clubs from 10 states and the District of Columbia represented at the NABBP meeting in 1865, then 202 clubs from 17 states and the District a year later. This growth and Gorman's election were both taken as signs of national reconciliation, reassuring evidence "that sectionalism is unknown in our national game," as the *New York Clipper* put it.

Riding these crests, in 1867 Gorman organized the ambitious tour that would earn him a place in baseball history. The Nationals embarked on a three-week, five-state, ten-game swing through the Midwest and Upper South, a total of three thousand miles at a cost of five thousand dollars: easily the most challenging and literally "National" ballplaying expedition yet, the first time a team had gone that far, to different sections of the country, to play baseball games. The only comparable previous tour, by the Excelsiors in 1860, had covered about twelve hundred miles within the mid-Atlantic states. Gorman's vision was born of necessity; he had nowhere else to take the Nationals. They too easily beat the nine other organized teams in Washington. (Again their playing field marked their progress: in June 1867 they moved into Washington's first real ballpark, at the corner of Fifteenth and S streets, near the State Department, with refreshment booths, a roofed grandstand, and an enclosing eight-foot fence.) They could not, it was clear, beat the crack teams in Philadelphia and New York. So they headed west.

To bolster the Nationals, Gorman had hired George Wright, soon recognized as the best all-around player of his time. For Wright, one of the new breed of "revolving" pros who saw baseball as a job, not as long-term membership in a social club, it meant his fifth team in four years. Still only twenty years old in

1867, schooled by the best teams in New York, he could handle any position but excelled at shortstop. His "phenomenal" arm let him play a deeper short than any contemporary, increasing his range on balls hit to his left and right and on pop-ups over his head. He typically caught grounders with his heels together, his gloveless hands held well in front to give with the impact. He moved smoothly, easily, deft in every motion. "Knowing his own power of swift throwing," Henry Chadwick noted, "he would wait until sure of his aim, and then let the ball go like a rifle-shot." He was equally gifted at hitting and thinking, finding the cracks in the rudimentary rules of the time by (for example) catching a fly in his cap, or intentionally dropping a ball to double up the runners on base. Wright was medium-sized, five feet nine and a half inches and 150 pounds, slightly bowlegged, with a bushy shock of dark, curly hair, sideburns sometimes below his ears, and a small mustache. Nobody could miss the transparent delight he took in his multiple talents. "His wits were always about him," his fellow ballplayer Sam Crane recalled. "He was invariably upon his mental tiptoes, and whenever he would pull off one of those grand, unexpected plays that were so dazzlingly surprising as to dumfound his opponents, his prominent teeth would gleam and glisten in an array of white molars." Gorman must have gone deep into whatever coffers the Nationals could tap to get Wright. The planned western tour, offering a chance to travel the country and play before new fans, no doubt sweetened the offer.

The Nationals left Washington on July 11 in their own private railroad car on an express train to Columbus, Ohio, some 550 miles away. Of the starting nine, only Williams and Parker hailed from Washington; the others were New Yorkers, itinerant pros. The whole party—of ballplayers, club members, Charles Coon of the Empires, Henry Chadwick of the *New York Sunday Mercury,* and assorted friends, about forty in all—was led by Frank Jones, head of the Treasury's redemption division and the current president of the Nationals. (Gorman, busy with work, would join the team in Chicago.) Given the reputations of Wright and the other pros, and the plain audacity of the tour, it was already drawing national attention. "The result of the games played will be looked for anxiously," said the *New York Tribune*. The Nationals met no real competition until Chicago, their last stop. After waltzing by Columbus, 90–10 ("very good for a commencement," a Washington paper admitted), they went on to Cincinnati.

The team there, founded a year earlier by a group of lawyers and now led by George Wright's older brother Harry, was considered the champions of Ohio. They played on a new field on the west side of Lincoln Park with a high fence, roofed seats for women fans, and a two-story clubhouse for the ballplayers: some ten thousand dollars' worth of improvements. The admission fee was raised to twenty-five cents to hold the crowd down to manageable size; yet more than five thousand paid up. Harry Wright retired the first two National batters and then faced his brother.

"There you are, are you?" Harry offered.

"I am here," said little brother, "and I don't want any of your nonsense; so just give us a ball, will yer?" Harry threw and George hit a ground-ball single. For three innings the other Nationals founds Harry Wright's pitching "very troublesome." But then they pulled away, the crowd grew quiet, and the Cincinnatis lost, 53–10. After beating another local team, 88–12, the next day—a game mercifully called after six innings—the Nationals took an overnight boat ride down the Ohio River to Louisville. On a cool, clear moonlit night, with piano music and dancing in the cabin, the ballplayers savored the river cruise, such a restoring contrast to the hot noise of a railroad car. "The excitement in regard to this Club," the *New York Tribune* reported, "increases as they progress on their tour."

Dipping below the Mason-Dixon line only two years after the war, the Nationals encountered their first hostile crowd. The game at Cedar Park in Louisville drew battalions of unreconstructed Confederates who razzed the Nationals as just another bunch of invading Yankees. The park was small, with fans crowding the field and impinging on foul territory. Rowdy boys clumped in seats near the catcher and in trees beyond the outfield. (Henry Chadwick deplored "the ignorant portion of the foreign element" with "their partisan yells and cheers," annoying the well-behaved majority.) Such rebel animosity must have puzzled the Nationals, usually regarded as a southern team, but it didn't hurt their hitting. They scored 22 runs in the eighth inning and won, 82–21; Wright hit 3 homers.

Back in the Union, they next beat the Western club in Indianapolis, 106–21, a slugfest lasting over four hours. "The play of the Nationals, especially the fielding, was most excellent," the *Chicago Tribune* noted. The Nationals also piled up 15 home runs, 6 by Wright; one of his clouts, a low, bounding ball, jumped the left-field fence and was lost in tall grass more than 600 feet from home. After a supper donated by the gallantly battered Westerns, the Nationals took a night train to St. Louis, where they clubbed the Unions, 113–26, and the Empires, 82–26. The Nationals told the Empires that two of their men were "the best players in the West," not extravagant praise considering that so far the Nationals had won seven games by a total margin of 614–126. The other teams could hit and catch reasonably well, but they could not come near the Nationals' skill at throwing the ball. Everywhere the games had drawn immense, unprecedented crowds—three thousand in St. Louis at grounds that could comfortably accommodate one thousand—with many baseball fans coming from distant towns and villages, curious to see how the game was played at this level.

In Chicago the Nationals formed the centerpiece of a state baseball convention and tournament. The forty-three clubs represented at these meetings showed how deeply the New York game had already penetrated small-town America. The clubs came from all over Illinois, mostly from the upper half of the state, but also from the distant Mississippi River towns of Quincy, Alton, and Cairo. Chicago was home to nine clubs; Waukegan, Aurora, and Monmouth each sent delegates from two teams. Railroad lines into Chicago offered reduced fares for the convention. The city bulged with baseball. A new diamond for the big games had been carved from the infield at the Dexter Park racetrack, six miles south of the Loop, accessible by streetcars and railroads from the city.

After long, run-filled games on successive days in St. Louis, the Nationals trained the three hundred miles to Chicago, arriving tired. Their first game, against the Forest City club from Rockford, Illinois, on July 25, was supposed to be easy, merely a setup for their major test two days later against the Chicago

Excelsiors. (Forest City had lost twice to the Excelsiors earlier in the summer.) The Dexter Park field, so newly graded, was soft and bumpy—a tough adjustment for the Nationals after the hard, lively surfaces they encountered elsewhere on the tour. Under a dark, drizzly sky, the first Forest City batter lofted an easy pop fly to Wright, who dropped it: an omen. The runner went to third on passed balls and came home on a wild throw. After another run the Nationals actually trailed, 2–0. They came to bat against a tall, skinny pitcher, Al Spalding, still a few weeks from his seventeenth birthday. He knew the reputations of Wright, Fox, Berthrong, and the others, and he was petrified. "It was the first big game before a large audience in which I had ever participated," Spalding said later. "A great lump rose in my throat, and my heart beat so like a trip-hammer that I imagined it could be heard by everyone on the grounds." As for his teammates, "every one of them was so scared that none could speak above a whisper. The fact is, we were all frightened nearly to death."

The nervous young pitcher walked his first batter and allowed the Nationals 3 runs in the inning. But Forest City scored 8 runs in the second and led, 15–8, after three. Despite an occasional good play—"Wright jumping into the air for a high ball and holding it with great cleverness"—the Nationals looked ragged, slipping around the wet field. In three different innings they were even held scoreless. Billy Williams was wild, serving up 33 called balls to only 6 for Spalding. Wright relieved Williams to pitch the sixth inning; Forest City fell on him for eight more runs. Slowed by two rain delays, the game slogged on. The fans, not believing what they were seeing, kept waiting for the Nationals to explode. "No one had an idea," the *Chicago Tribune* reported, "that the Forest City nine—a club coming from a town in the interior of the State—would . . . wrest from them the palm of victory." After the sixth inning, down 6 runs, the Nationals looked faded and beaten. In the eighth, Forest City turned a pitcher-to-second-to-first double play, then threw out the next batter at second. "The crowd fairly yelled their delight." Forest City won, 29–23, and was carried off the field. "The invincibles are at last beaten," a Washington sportswriter wired home, "by an Illinois county club."

While the Nationals retired to their rooms at the Sherman House to rest up for the Excelsiors game two days later, the male population of Chicago quivered in wait. "The universal tendency was towards base ball," the *Tribune* noted. "Laboring men, men of business, young men and pale office boys devoted much of their time and thoughts to the approaching event. Staid men of family, well along in years, were inquiring of the younger regarding the game and how it is played." Around the Sherman House, anyone wearing a Nationals badge was admired, then besieged. Gamblers offered bets of fifty to three hundred dollars on the Nationals but found no takers. On the morning of the game, "the match, and nothing but the match, occupied every one's mind. One heard of it at the breakfast table, and when he went along the street the people he passed were talking about it. . . . It crept into saloons, was heard at the courts, in the stores and out-of-the-way offices, intruding upon and overturning business." A fan making his way to Dexter Park found an animated, motley throng of people, horses, and carriages surrounding the green field, with all the colors bright and blazing under a hot July sun. Temporary seats collapsed, an occasional horse bolted, but in the snapping excitement nobody seemed to mind. Paying fifty cents a head, the crowd was estimated at ten thousand, the biggest yet for baseball in Chicago.

Batting first, the Nationals made 2 outs to the noisy pleasure of the fans, then tallied 7 runs. The Excelsiors were held scoreless. The Nationals piled up 26 runs in the next two innings. The crowd began to wilt in the broiling sun. To the Nationals, used to summers in Washington, it seemed a cool and pleasant day. Williams, well rested, mowed down the Excelsiors. The crowd settled into a deep silence. Playing their best ball of the tour, the Nationals won, 49–4. Wright led his team with 8 runs scored. Seeking an explanation, the next day the *Chicago Tribune* accused the Nationals of throwing the game to Forest City to set up betting bonanzas against the Excelsiors.

"They are professional athletes," the *Tribune* said of the Nationals, "while the Excelsiors are but amateurs. That which is the business of the one, is the recreation of the other." Reduced to "a regular confidence game," baseball had been "abused and prostituted, a healthful game perverted into a gambling operation, as demoralizing as racing or cock fighting." Arthur Gorman and Frank Jones called on the *Tribune* office and, lying plausibly, convinced the editors that the Nationals were not professionals or gamblers but average good citizens: clerks and students who happened to play crackerjack baseball because they practiced longer. The *Tribune,* on second thought, withdrew its charge. The Nationals played one more game, beating the Atlantics of Chicago, 78–17, and then took a twenty-four-hour train ride home, fatigued and sunburned.

In those three weeks the Nationals, justifying their name, had shown that a nearly national baseball league was possible. A pan-American constituency for baseball was waiting, at least in that chunk of America east of the Mississippi and north of the Mason-Dixon line. Networks of railroads could now carry teams thousands of miles in reasonable comfort and fighting trim. Faraway fans recognized and would pay to see the fabled players from the East. A nationwide baseball public looked for the scores in newspapers. The national game was assuming national dimensions. One year later, on Gorman's model, three teams from New York and Philadelphia toured the Midwest while several midwestern clubs came east. A year after that, the Cincinnati Red Stockings—led by Harry and George Wright—dropped the usual amateur pretenses, declared themselves professionals, and went undefeated on a fifty-seven-game national tour all the way to California. (The stinging loss to the Nationals, its only defeat in 1867, had inspired the Cincinnati team to shed its amateur ideals.) And two years after that, the first big league was launched.

♦   ♦   ♦

"The evolution of the game of Base Ball," Al Spalding wrote in old age, forty-four years after he beat the Nationals, "from its crude form in the earlier days to its present degree of perfection, has been largely wrought through observation and experience of incongruous rules by players themselves."

♦   ♦   ♦

What the players could *not* do was run their own professional league. On St. Patrick's Day in 1871, representatives from ten pro clubs met at Collier's Saloon, on the corner of Broadway and Thirteenth Street in New York City, to launch the National Association of Professional Base Ball Players. The first slate of officers—from Philadelphia; Cleveland; Washington; and Troy, New York—reflected the new league's determined nationalness. A club could join the National Association by paying an entrance fee of ten dollars. In the absence of a league-mandated schedule, each team was to arrange to play five games with every other team. The club with the most wins in the fall would be awarded a pennant purchased with those entrance fees. Their work done, the founders then retired to the "hospitality" provided by Boss Tweed's New York Mutuals.

Rising above the dubious founding site and host, Harry Wright embodied the National Association's best chances for success and esteem. After his triumphs with the Cincinnati Red Stockings, Wright had moved the team name, two of its best players (brother George and Cal McVey), and its odd uniform of knickers and long red socks to Boston in 1871. He brought along Al Spalding and two teammates, Ross Barnes and Fred Cone, from Rockford's Forest City club. As the most respected manager in baseball, of undoubted integrity, Wright took on the main responsibility for scheduling the new association's games. "Base ball is business now, Nick," he wrote to Nick Young of the Washington Olympics, "and I am trying to arrange our games to make them successful, and make them pay, irrespective of my feelings." He wrote polite, graceful letters, sprinkled with literary allusions and even an implausible pun in pseudo-Latin ("Soc et tu em"). Nobody could have better represented the association than this tall, handsome man who looked more like a clerk than an athlete. But even Harry Wright could not make it truly respectable. When the Philadelphia Athletics won the association's first pennant, the flag was hung with others in a saloon. Wright preferred "some place where *all* who wish could go and see them," he said. "To elevate the National game we must earn the respect of all . . . to make the game a success—financially and otherwise. (Which it was *not* last year.)"

Part of the problem, it soon developed, was that Wright had fielded too good a team in Boston. After placing second in 1871, the Red Stockings won the next four pennants, peaking at an intimidating record of 71-8—undefeated at home—in 1875. Every year Boston's Al Spalding led all pitchers in games won. "On receiving the ball," a New York sportswriter noted of the Spalding style, "he raises it in both hands until it is on a level with his left eye. Striking an attitude he gazes at it, two or three minutes in a contemplative way, and then turns it around once or twice to be sure that it is not an orange or coconut. . . . After a scowl at the shortstop, and a glance at home plate, [he] finally delivers the ball with a precision and rapidity of a cannon shot." Improving every year, Spalding won 20, 37, 41, 52, and 57 games in five seasons. At bat, the Red Stockings deployed the association's three top hitters in 1873—Ross Barnes, Deacon White, and George Wright—then four of the top five—those three plus Cal McVey—in 1875. The association became known as "Harry Wright's League." Boston so dominated the competition that fans lost interest and stayed home. "There's no use going," people said. "Boston's sure to win."

But the players themselves dealt the most killing blows to the association by controlling its affairs to their own unbridled satisfaction. Bob Ferguson, a playing manager for three association teams, served as the compliant player-elected president from 1872 to 1875. (A light-hitting, sticky-fingered third baseman, Ferguson went by the imperishable nickname of "Death to Flying Things.") He donated an administration too friendly toward his fellow ballplayers. With no reserve clause, they freely broke contracts, switched teams, shopped around their services, and thus jacked up salaries to ruinous levels. Cap Anson, fresh from a farm near Marshalltown, Iowa, made $66 a month playing for Rockford in 1871. The Athletics lured him away for $1,250 a season, more than triple his pay at Rockford. To keep Anson, the Athletics were paying him $1,800 by 1875. Unable to match such generosity, member clubs came and went; only three of the original teams played all five seasons. Seven of the thirteen teams in 1875 failed to finish the season.

Ballplayers drank, fought, and gambled at will, confidently free of punishment. Gamblers, sometimes including uniformed players, plied their trade openly in the stands, sowing rumors of bribes and fixes. At the Capitoline grounds in Brooklyn, a gamy section of the grandstand became known as the "Gold Board," bristling with bookies in full cry. "The spirit of gambling and graft held possession of the sport everywhere," Spalding recalled. The Mutuals and Haymakers, in particular, were suspected of throwing games. The *New York Times,* pursing its lips, described a typical professional ballplayer in 1872 as "an eminently undesirable person," "a worthless, dissipated gladiator; not much above the professional pugilist in morality and respectability."

William A. Hulbert, the assertive president of the Chicago White Stockings, was perturbed by all these conditions, not least the domination of the league by Boston. Addressing that problem first, during the 1875 season he secretly signed four of Boston's best players—Spalding, Barnes, White, and McVey—to play for Chicago in 1876. A Chicago paper soon leaked the big news. "Boston is in mourning," said a newspaper in nearby Worcester. "The famous baseball nine, the perennial champion, the city's most cherished possession, has been captured by Chicago." That winter, amid rumors of punitive action by the association over such an egregious theft, Hulbert avoided retaliation by simply pocketing his ball and starting his own pro league.

Business-minded men from eight teams launched the National League of Professional Base Ball Clubs in February 1876. The new name was significant; this would be a league of clubs, not of players. Power now shifted from players to owners: well-established men such as Walter N. Haldeman, president of the *Louisville Courier-Journal,* and Morgan G. Bulkeley, a banker from Hartford, later a Connecticut governor and United States senator. Hulbert's thirteen-point plan of organization restricted new memberships, enforced territorial monopolies, called for a regular league schedule to start the season, held players more tightly to their teams, discouraged games on Sunday and gambling and liquor sales at ballparks, and generally implied a tighter ship. Entrance fees increased tenfold, to one hundred dollars. The strongest association teams at once switched to the new league, leaving the association dead and deserted.

Hulbert dominated the league until his early death from heart disease, at age fifty, in 1882. For five years most teams lost money, and every season brought a new roster of league clubs. Hulbert persisted, enforcing rules, still boss of the White Stockings yet a fair league president as well. "Strong, forceful, self-reliant," as Spalding remembered him. "I admired his business-like way of considering things." Born in Otsego County, New York, Hulbert had been brought to Chicago as a child. If he ever played baseball, it did not become a matter of record. After attending Beloit College he started working in a wholesale grocery, later shifting to a coal business. A prominent member of the Chicago Board of Trade, he was a familiar operator at the Exchange. Evidently he came to baseball less as a fan than as one of the new breed of urban boosters, using his team (and league) to promote his burgeoning hometown. "I would rather be a lamp-post in Chicago," he liked to say, "than a millionaire in any other city."

Hulbert's gift to baseball was to impose commercial standards of rationalization and order on the unruly sport. After the 1876 season, he expelled the Philadelphia Athletics and New York Mutuals—two of the strongest, most popular teams in the league—for failing to play their final scheduled games in the Midwest. A year later, he ejected Cincinnati's cellar-dwelling team for not paying dues and dropped lifetime bans on four Louisville players for gambling and throwing games. At the end, in his last official act, he banished ten reeling players for conspicuous drunkenness. "Arbitrary and severe though he may have been at times," Cap Anson said later, "yet the fact remains that he was the best friend the ball players had ever had." The structure and survival of the National League are preeminently Hulbert's legacy.

◆　　◆　　◆

On the field, though, the players had the game in hand. Because they best knew and loved baseball, the game evolved essentially through their play, with rule makers then responding to their initiatives. Baseball history can be understood only by lingering near the diamond, down in the grass and dirt, listening to the chatter and ball sounds. New styles of playing came to the game in the same way that professionalism had entered it: started by the players, rules be damned, then after much resistance codified off the field by managers, owners, and rule makers. As Spalding perceived in his lifetime of baseball, the players were always pushing against the rules, poking and tinkering, with the consistent purpose of making the game faster, more demanding, and more fun.

Stay near the field. Back in the 1850s, ballplayers after a certain critical mass of games and practice had improved their fielding enough to render obsolete the old rule of making an out by catching the ball on one bounce. Aside from insulting a man's ball-hawking mastery, a touchy point, the rule allowed absurdities such as a batted ball that slammed onto a hard infield and sailed over the infielders' heads, to be caught in the outfield, retiring the batter. By 1858 James Whyte Davis of the Knickerbockers was proposing his "fly rule," mandating that balls must be caught "on the fly" to make outs. Davis arranged an exhibition game between the Knicks and Excelsiors, using the fly rule, in June 1858. All the ballplayers seemed to like it. Yet it sparked bitter arguments at meetings of the National Association of Base Ball Players, as opponents linked it with cricket (an effete *English* pastime) while advocates insisted it would make baseball more adult, less a child's game. The convention of 1860 wrangled over the fly rule before voting it down, 87–55. "One of our best ball players remarked to us," a reporter noted, "that if the clubs would send *players* to the convention instead of *talkers* the rules of the game would be made more satisfactory to the practical members of the Base Ball fraternity." Then delayed by the war, the fly rule finally passed in 1865. "It did more to improve the game," George Wright said later, "than any other change in the rules."

Baseball moved on in a rhythm of challenge and response, an endless dance between offense and defense, keeping the two in near equilibrium lest the game lurch out of balance. As the fly rule helped hitters, pitchers—formally restricted to stiff-armed, underhand motions and no funny spins—rebutted with illegal deliveries and trick pitches. Given the permanent shortage of good pitchers, umpires did not stop them. Both Dick McBride's "twist" ball—the pitch that had kept the Nationals popping up— and a drop pitch thrown by Phonney Martin ("Old Slow Ball") of the Brooklyn Eckfords anticipated the curveball that Candy Cummings started fooling with around 1866. A slight man, five feet nine inches and only 120 pounds, with long wrists and fingers, Cummings discovered that by holding the ball in his fingertips he could snap off a horizontal spin that sent the pitch on a long, sailing curve, away from a right-handed batter. Cummings and then Bobby Mathews both curved their way to success in the National Association. "It was so contrary to all preconceived notions of what a respectable baseball should do," one man recalled, "that half the baseball world wouldn't believe until they had seen it, and then had their doubts." Batters "simply watched them go by and went to the bench, bewildered."

Cummings managed to twirl his curve with a legal underarm motion. But most pitchers had to release the ball from a higher point to make it bend. Gradually, long before the rules legalized what was already happening, pitching became throwing, with the arm rising higher and higher, delivering a faster, livelier challenge to the batter. The National League in 1876 required that the pitching hand must pass below the hip. Two years later, below the waist. (Pitchers took to wearing their belts well above their stomachs.) By 1883, below the shoulder; and a year later, no limits at all. For some stars, disinclined to adjust, these new styles meant shortened careers. Al Spalding pitched one season in the National League and then retired at twenty-six to tend to the White Stockings and his thriving sporting-goods company. After hitting .353 during five years in the National Association, George Wright at age twenty-nine moved on to the National League, where in seven seasons he never hit over .300. Curves and in-shoots bothered him; he grew gun-shy at the plate, a bit frightened by the ever faster, less predictable pitching. Average runs per game dropped from 11.8 in 1876 to 9.3 in 1880. Run production improved briefly after pitchers were moved back five feet, to fifty feet from home. But pitchers soon adjusted. In 1884 the flamethrowing Charlie Sweeney of the Providence Grays struck out a record nineteen batters in one game—not with his heat but with "ins and outs, drops and rises . . . the most deceptive curves imaginable."

The new pitches made a catcher's job an even grislier test of manliness. With nobody on base or fewer than two strikes they could stand back and receive pitches on one bounce. Otherwise they crouched behind the bat naked of glove, mask, or any protection, sometimes reduced to shielding head and chest with their arms. Silver Flint in thirteen years of big-league catching broke every joint of his fingers at least once. Other fielders were scarcely less endangered. "We had a trick of making a spring-box of the fingers," Cap Anson recalled, "the ball seldom hitting against the palm, and we could haul down even the hottest liners that way, though broken fingers happened now and then. The hands of the infielders were awful sights, as a rule, but they stuck to their work even when bleeding fingers were useless at the broken joints." A hard throw to a first baseman could split an inch-long gash between fingers; the man would just tie the two fingers together, temporarily closing the wound, and stay in the game. It became part of the ballplaying code: to succeed at this *hard*ball test, ballplayers were tough and proud of it.

So the first man to don a glove had to be tougher still. Before 1870 two battered catchers, Doug Allison of the Cincinnati Reds and Nat Hicks of the New York Mutuals, may have used gloves occasionally. Other such innovators have no doubt been lost to history. In 1875 Charlie Waitt, an outfielder–first baseman for St. Louis, injured his hand. To keep playing he took an ordinary leather glove and cut out the back for ventilation. Hoping to avoid much notice, he chose a flesh-colored glove. Other players nonetheless leaped on this cowardly device, hooting and jeering. Waitt wore it anyway. Catchers and first basemen followed suit, then other infielders, and finally outfielders. The gloves at first mainly protected palms. With fingers cut off to allow throwing, ballplayers usually wore them on both hands. Somebody—perhaps Arthur Irwin, an infielder of the 1880s—invented a larger, thicker glove, padded in the palm, to be worn on the off hand. Not merely protective gadgets, gloves changed the game. Fielding now sharpened. With no fear of the ball, a player could charge a hard hit (instead of bracing and "giving" with it), take the ball in front, and throw it faster, with his body behind the motion. Following a design by the catcher Harry Decker, the glove vogue quickly reached excess, with big, padded mitts two or even three feet across. The last bare-handed fielders retired in 1894. In 1895, the first time the rules had ever mentioned gloves, the National League decreed that catchers and first basemen could wear mitts of any size and weight, but everybody else was restricted to gloves of ten ounces and fourteen inches around the palm. Once again, the game had changed before the rules did.

Off the field, owners came and went—businessmen, politicians, confidence men—a banal, anonymous bunch, generally not of much historical significance. Three rival big leagues, daring to challenge the National League's control of baseball, were launched and sank; one, the American Association, endured ten years of unequal competition. The most significant baseball figures of the late 1800s were two managers, Cap Anson of the Chicago White Stockings and Ned Hanlon of the Baltimore Orioles. One of the dominant players of this era, Anson with his short, careful swing won two batting titles, led the league in RBIs seven times during the 1880s, and hit over .300 for his first twenty big-league seasons. "I was as full of animal spirits as is an unbroken thoroughbred colt, and as impatient of restraint," he said of his younger days. "The pranks that I played and the scrapes that I got into were, some of them, not of a very creditable nature."

This changed in 1879 when, at twenty-seven, Anson became Chicago's playing manager. Now supposed to apply discipline instead of receive it, he was known as a relentless scold and taskmaster, leading his men by fear and example. He adopted new techniques: spring training, signals, the hit-and-run, platooning, and a pitching rotation. (The demanding new pitches and overhand style meant that a single pitcher could no longer hurl every game for his team.) A canny judge of fresh talent, Anson relentlessly bent young ballplayers to his style and will, at least on the field. "There are many players who do not like Anson, yet the longer men play under his captaincy, the more unwilling they are to play under anyone else," noted the sportswriter Harry Palmer of the *New York Herald*. "He is matter-of-fact, calculating, and practical to a degree rarely met with. Once convinced that a man is in pain or in distress, the 'Old Man' will do anything and everything, in his unassuming, practical way, for the sufferer; but he is a hard man to convince."

His best players were the pitcher John Clarkson, the catcher-provocateur King Kelly, and the "stonewall infield" of Tommy Burns at third, Ned Williamson at short, Fred Pfeffer at second, and himself at first. Before Anson, a typical infield bunched toward left field, where most batters hit the ball. Anson had all his infielders range more widely from their bases, and he shaded the shortstop toward second and his second baseman toward first. Thus the whole infield became more balanced, mobile, and impervious—or else they heard from Anson. "The secret of success with Captain Anson is confidence," Pfeffer observed. "A man in this profession cannot have too much confidence in his own prowess." Williamson at short moved quickly and threw hard, yet the ball came softly, easy to catch, into Anson's hands. Acknowledged as the finest such unit yet in baseball, the stonewall infield led Chicago to five pennants in seven years. They could hit too: in 1884 the top five RBI men in the league were Chicago's infield, plus King Kelly.

The White Stockings were the most famous, glamorous team baseball had ever seen. At every stop in the league they collected slavish fans hoping for a chance to celebrate them. They rode to the enemy ballpark in open carriages, not in a closed omnibus like other teams: they wished to be admired. With their eponymous white socks, they might appear in wide Dutch shorts, or skinny black tights, or wildly checkered bathrobes, or even dress suits with boiled white shirts. Nobody could intimidate them. Late in their pennant-winning season of 1886, on a road trip to Washington, Anson finagled an invitation for his team to the White House. (Presidents had been meeting championship baseball squads since Grant.) President Cleveland greeted them in a Prince Albert coat, tightly buttoned, looking "much stouter," Kelly thought, "than the photographs we had seen of him." Anson shook his hand first, then Kelly. "The President's hand was fat and soft," Kelly noted. "I squeezed it so hard that the President winced." And so through the other players, each delivering a firm grip oblivious to presidential discomfort. "President Cleveland looked glad and happy when it was all over." He talked baseball for half an hour, recalling his own ballplaying days as a young man in Buffalo. "The President didn't shake hands again when we parted," Kelly noticed.

Ned Hanlon was a journeyman outfielder, a .260 lifetime hitter who in a dozen years never led the league in any category. Hired to manage the woeful Baltimore Orioles in 1892, he inherited not much talent except the catcher, Wilbert Robinson, and an underused nineteen-year-old utility man, John McGraw. "I decided we had too many big, clumsy fellows," Hanlon said later. He wanted guys who could run, bunt, hit, steal, and—in particular—think fast and nick the corners off the rules. Over the next two years Hanlon arranged larcenous trades for Hugh Jennings, a shortstop, and the outfielders Joe Kelley and Willie Keeler. All three bloomed and thrived in Baltimore. The Orioles finished last in 1892, eighth among twelve teams in 1893, then won three straight pennants. In 1894, with every regular batting over .300, they hit .343 as a team. Not the best team of the 1890s—Boston won two more pennants—the Orioles were the rowdiest, the most exciting and influential aggregation of their time. "Only a few ever gave him credit for his really masterful work in building up a team," McGraw later said of his mentor. "A greater organizer and builder than a field general . . . Hanlon had little to do other than to encourage us to keep on. He had built well."

In his "Big Four" of McGraw, Jennings, Kelley, and Keeler, Hanlon in effect had four managers on the field, all of them popping with tricks and strategies. They called their own signals, ranging at will with their speed, always pushing and taking risks. After a rule change in 1893 moved the pitcher back to sixty feet six inches from home, the Orioles joined in the general explosion of offense, adding their own special touches. With the pitcher now ten and a half feet farther away—thus less able to field bunts—they had Thomas J. Murphy, the invaluable Orioles groundskeeper, grade the base path downward to first, with ridges toward third and first to keep bunts from rolling foul. The infield dirt, mixed with clay, offered a hard, fast track when wet and rolled, good for a running game and the bounced hits that became known as Baltimore chops. Although weak at pitching, fielding, and first base, the Orioles still pestered the enemy into exasperated defeats. Seven consecutive batters might bunt. At bat, McGraw would flick fouls down the third baseline—twenty-four in a row, on one occasion—until he got the pitch he wanted. "They took every chance," the sportswriter Hugh Fullerton noted, "stole on the wrong ball, hit at the most unexpected times, and bunted when the play seemed to be to hit." In 1896 they stole 441 bases, 91 more than any other team. Their style of

speed, sacrifices, punched hits, reckless daring, and heady team-
work became known as "inside" or "scientific" baseball. It would
dominate the game's theory and practice for the next two decades, especially as preached by McGraw in his long tenure as
manager of the New York Giants.

On another level, Baltimore's style was fortunately less con-
tagious and durable. Always scratching for an edge, the Orioles
fought, cursed, and cheated, "playing the dirtiest ball ever seen
in the country," as the authoritative *Sporting News* objected at the
time. They hid spare baseballs, to be discovered at needful moments, in the long outfield grass provided by Thomas Murphy.
They tripped runners on the base paths, spiked them, held their
belts, stepped on their feet, got in their way. Umpires were force-
fully advised of their failings. "I have never seen such a torrent
of vulgarity, profanity, and brutal senseless abuse heaped upon
an umpire," said a Cleveland newspaper after a series with Baltimore. "They were mean, vicious, ready at any time to maim a
rival player or an umpire, if it helped their cause," said John
Heydler, an umpire in the 1890s and later president of the National League. "The worst of it was that they got by with much of
their brow beating and hooliganism." At a game in Boston in
May 1894, McGraw started fighting with the enemy third baseman. As the benches emptied, the battle spread to the crowd.
Somebody set the wooden stands on fire. The ballpark burned to
the ground, along with 170 other buildings nearby: Oriole baseball at its hottest.

Such riotous scenes helped secure the success of the American League, the first permanent rival to the National League.
"CLEAN BALL is the MAIN PLANK in the American League
platform, and the clubs must stand by it religiously," founder
Ban Johnson told his clubs as the American League started operations in 1901. By then the game, excesses aside, had grown to
its full-blown modern form. After only fifty-five years of the
Knickerbocker variations, all the essential rules and dimensions,
plays and techniques, glories and abominations—so familiar then
and ever since—were in place. Baseball settled into a long, stable
future, deriving its most powerful meanings from the simple fact
that it did not change except in minor details. Starting in 1903,
the same sixteen teams played in the same ten cities for the next

fifty years. Few other American institutions could exhibit such apparent tranquillity and permanence.

◆   ◆   ◆

The historian Warren Goldstein has suggested that professional baseball can claim two histories, linear and cyclical. The linear record traces the game's material evolution through organizations and institutions, as measured by the omnipresent balance sheets of salaries, expenses, and profits that seem to demonstrate progress, or at least change over time. The cyclical record, harder to track and analyze, pulses to baseball's emotional relationships, repetitive and generational, where not much ever changes—and fans like it that way. The game circles back on itself, recapitulating its own history, as new fans—no matter how ignorant of baseball history—feel the same tugs and swoops that fans have always felt.

In these terms, the *linear* history duplicates American life. In April 1889, at a fancy banquet at Delmonico's in New York, Mark Twain celebrated baseball as "the very symbol, the outward and visible expression of the drive and push and rush and struggle of the raging, tearing, booming nineteenth century." Thus the Knickerbocker game changed baseball from a pleasant, easygoing pastime into a faster, more complicated contest, reflecting the headlong pace and schedule of an urban-industrializing America, demanding sound business management. "Professional baseball is now reduced to a business problem," said the directors of the Worcester Ruby Legs in 1882, "and to be successful the same principles must be applied to its management as are applied to any well managed and successful corporation, woolen mill, or machine shop." From this management perspective, baseball should express and reinforce the values of rationality, money, competition, and statistic-worship that were overtaking the American nineteenth century. Indeed, the big leagues depended on, could not have existed without, the new technologies of railroads, telegraphs, and high-speed printing presses—and, later on, of radio, TV, and airplanes. ("If sport arose as an antidote to industrialism," the historian Dale Somers has noted, "the disease contributed mightily to the cure.")

Yet the *cyclical* history of baseball inverts American life, turns it inside out, addressing fans, effects, and motives, while the linear history deals with management and techniques. Baseball owners might have hoped to run tidy businesses, but many other employers avoided hiring workers known to play baseball from fear that they might imperil "all regular business habits," as one complained. Baseball was "a curse," said a Newark newspaper in 1868, encouraging "strong, muscular, lazy boys, whose sole ambition is to be good ball players, to forsake their work." For most players and fans—if not for management—baseball was always essentially a recreation: play, fun, something apart from the ordinary schedules and business of life. American progress rushed down the track, always faster, more uprooting and atomizing, and mesmerized by the new. Baseball remained a way station, content to stay in place, traditional and respectful toward the past, a matter of connection and continuity: in every sense, a rebuttal of American modernity. At its deepest levels, emotional and cyclical, baseball offered Americans a refuge from real life.

Chapter Five

Football:
Variations on Campball

Askirl of bagpipes, high and wild, announced the biggest football game of 1815. In the Scotch Border county of Selkirk, south of Edinburgh, this game—"the greatest match at the ball which has taken place for many years"—renewed ancient rivalries among clans and parishes. On the eve of the contest, proclamations from Selkirk's church steeples suspended all laws in the county for the next twenty-four hours. People came from distant dales, up to twenty miles away, and spent the night in the heather. Selkirk was returning in play to feudalism.

On game day, December 4, the panoply resembled preparation for battle: before two thousand spectators on the plain of Carterhaugh, the Duke of Buccleuch's war banner was displayed for the first time in a century or more. Walter Scott, poet and novelist of old Scotch folkways, and sheriff of Selkirk by the grace of his patron Buccleuch, proudly watched his teenage son—armed and mounted, dressed in forest green and buff, a heavy gold chain and medal, and a green bonnet topped with an eagle's feather—carry the Buccleuch banner emblazoned with "Bellendaine," the ancient war cry of the Scott clan. Companies of men stalked across the field in a bristling display of old weapons and armor, shouting and cheering, pumping the crowd. A feudal ceremony was performed. Scott, who lived like a medieval laird at his Abbotsford estate in Selkirk, contributed a song, "Lifting of the Banner":

From the brown crest of Newark its summons extending,
  Our signal is waving in smoke and in flame,
And each Forester blythe, from his mountain descending,
  Bounds light o'er the heather to join in the game;
Then up with the Banner! let forest winds fan her!
  She has blazed over Ettrick eight ages and more;
In sport we'll attend her, in battle defend her,
  With heart and with hand, like our Fathers before.

More than a game, the match renewed grudges nursed and handed down for more than three centuries. At the battle of Flodden Field in 1513, the English army had destroyed Scotland's King James IV and ten thousand of his men. According to the traditional account told in Selkirk ever since, the men of Selkirk had defended their king bravely while Lord Home of Yarrow had declined to fight, leaving the battle and taking his force back to Scotland. Among Selkirkmen the memory rankled ever after; Scott had revived it, once again, in his long narrative poem *Marmion,* published in 1808. In the fall of 1815 the current Duke of Buccleuch teased the current Earl of Home (his brother-in-law) about his ancestor's craven retreat. The earl, smarting, suggested a grudge match of football between Selkirk and Yarrow. "A desperate contention is expected," wrote Scott, blissfully immersed in the preparations. "Lord have mercy on their necks and legs, their shins are past praying for."

A belligerent throng, perhaps seven hundred, even eight hundred men in all, took the field. "Our game was not well arranged," Scott admitted later, in private. "We had not reckoned on half the numbers that came and found grave difficulty in settling which should play on each side. Selkirk and Yarrow were the districts named but all the other dales-men joined." To identify themselves the Selkirks wore slips of fir, the Yarrows sprigs of heath. The Duke of Buccleuch threw up the first ball; for ninety minutes of "severe conflict" the two sides kicked and pushed, tackled and fought, until Robert Hall, a mason from Selkirk, drove the ball across the Yarrow goal. For the second game, "still more severely contested," fifty men from Galashiels switched to the Yarrow team. "After a close and stubborn struggle of more than three hours, with various fortune, and much display of strength and agility on both sides," George Brodie from Greatlaws upon Aill-water scored for the Yarrows. As twilight fell, the day disintegrated into squabbles about how to divide the teams for a deciding match. So they arranged a third game, between picked teams limited to one hundred men each, to be played sometime between Christmas and New Year's. "They maintained the most perfect good humor," Scott wrote for an Edinburgh newspaper, "and showed how unnecessary it is to discourage manly and athletic exercises among the common people, under pretext of maintaining subordination and good order."

Thus the official version for publication. That night, the gentry drank and danced till dawn at the Duke of Buccleuch's country home at Bowhill. But among "the common people," the night brought drunken fistfights and showers of thrown stones. Certain individuals were burned in effigy. Men from both sides were cast into the river. In prudence, the third match was never played. When Washington Irving visited Scott two years later, he was told that "the old feuds and local interests, and revelries and animosities of the Scotch, still slept in their ashes, and might easily be roused." In fact, "it was not always safe to have even the game of foot-ball between villages;—the old clannish spirit was too apt to break out."

◆   ◆   ◆

Football came down the centuries less as an agreeable recreation, like baseball, than as an expression of durable animosities between longstanding rivals. The essential point was to smite the enemy, not to play the game. Traditional football by itself was too rough and risky to attract many players without the extra, emboldening goad supplied by smoldering feuds and hatreds.

In its simplest form—two mobs of people trying to kick or carry a ball in opposite directions—rudimentary football was played for centuries in many cultures scattered across Europe,

Asia, and pre-Columbian America. It first showed up in the British Isles, perhaps derived from the French game of *soule,* about two centuries after the Norman Conquest. From the early 1300s on, it was repeatedly, ineffectively banned by English monarchs and local governments: sometimes in rebuke of all sports, more typically because of football's associations with civil disorder and damage to life and property. It awoke and provoked sleeping dogs. A Nottinghamshire chronicler in the late 1400s condemned football as "more common, undignified, and worthless than any other kind of game, rarely ending but with some loss, accident, or disadvantage to the players themselves." Disapproving authorities kept hoping that football players would take up archery, or perhaps handball, instead.

The problem of historical evidence here is that the early players themselves left virtually no record of their field-level attitude toward the games. The laws and chronicles were written by football skeptics; so the available sources stress the violence without conveying the attractions of the sport. That the game survived repeated censures suggests, by itself, the ballplaying enthusiasm that must have sustained the combatants. A rare early expression of football ardor appears in Alexander Barclay's epic narrative *Amintas and Faustus,* written around 1514:

> They get the bladder and blowe it great and thin
> With many beanes and peason put within;
> It ratleth, soundeth, and shineth clere and fayre
> While it is throwen and caste up in the ayre.
> Eche one contendeth and hath a great delite
> With foote and hande the bladder for to smite;
> If it fall to ground, they lifte it up again,
> This wise to labour they count it for no paine;
> Renning and leaping they drive away the colde.
> The sturdie plowman, lustie, strong, and bold,
> Overcommeth the winter with driving the foote-ball,
> Forgetting labour and many a grevous fall.

By this dissenting account, football was fun, "a great delite," just a vigorously warming manly exercise in cold weather.

On ceremonial occasions, though, it took on quite serious

purposes. All through the British Isles, an annual game—on Christmas Day, New Year's, or (most typically) Shrove Tuesday—allowed permissible combat between rival demographic groups, parishes, towns, or sections of towns. When played on Shrove Tuesday, "the British Mardi Gras," the games offered a last, frolicking blowout, traditionally fueled by wanton pancakes and fritters, before the sober denials of Lent. Unhindered by rules or referees, with the ball kicked, thrown, or carried, the play roared through streets, bounced off shuttered windows and closed shops, and spilled into waterways, heading for some arbitrary goal distant enough to prolong the game for hours. "All was fair at the ball of Scone," shrugged one football proverb. The players—hundreds, even thousands, in a single match—were mostly young men, but sometimes included women and children. For the game between the Welsh parishes of Cellan and Pencarreg, in South Cardiganshire, the men removed their coats and waistcoats, the women their dresses and (sometimes) petticoats, and everybody dove in. The fishwives of Inveresk, near Edinburgh, played their own game: "As they do the work of men, their manners are masculine," a chronicler recorded in 1795. "On Shrove Tuesday there is a standing match at foot-ball, between the married and unmarried women, in which the former are always victors."

Designed to ventilate a whole year's worth of grudges in one day, the games were exuberantly rough, punctuated by fistfights, barked shins, rearranged faces, and other sideshows. The Shrove Tuesday game in Derby, between the parishes of St. Peter and All Saints, began at noon in the marketplace. A large ball was tossed into the crowd. When a knotted mass of the quickest, strongest players formed around the ball, everybody else pulled and hauled, trying to direct the human tide goalward. Two or three hundred men might wind up in the river, ducking each other. "Broken shins, broken heads, torn coats and lost hats are among the minor accidents of this fearful contest," a town historian noted, "and it frequently happens that persons fall in consequence of the intensity of the pressure, fainting and bleeding beneath the feet of the surrounding mob. . . . Still the crowd is encouraged by respectable persons attached to each party . . .

urging on the players with shouts, and even handing to those who are exhausted, oranges and other refreshment." A Frenchman passing through Derby on game day remarked that if Englishmen called this playing, what could they possibly call fighting?

British colonists in America, beyond these old feuds, played football less often and more amicably. In 1685 the adult males of two Massachusetts towns held a match, but it did not become an annual ritual. An English visitor to Rowley, Massachusetts, a few years later watched "a great game of football," he noted, "to be played with their feet, which I thought was very odd; but it was upon a broad sandy shore, free from stones, which made it more easy. Neither were they so apt to trip up one another's heels and quarrel, as I have seen 'em in England." Yet football remained irreducibly rough and a worry for moral guardians: no other ballgame was so dangerous. "Unfriendly to clothes, as well as safety," noted the Reverend William Bentley of Salem. "In Marblehead, even heads of families engage in it, & all the fishermen while at home in this [fall] season. The bruising of shins has rendered it rather disgraceful to those of better education."

The game still needed built-in rivals to sustain itself. In the early nineteenth century, as the folk custom of Shrove Tuesday games withered away, the main locus of British football shifted to private prep schools: a bracingly competitive arena in which young men measured each other daily for toughness and athletic skill. Football rules varied from school to school; at Eton and Charterhouse, the small, enclosed fields meant a game of kicking only. At Rugby, a larger field encouraged more running and tackling. One November day in 1823, as a bell started to peal the five o'clock hour that ended the game, a Rugby student named William Webb Ellis—in inspired desperation—picked up the ball, flouting the rules, and ran with it. The practice caught on at Rugby, then at other schools. (And was not so heretical after all, since Shrove Tuesday games had included ballcarrying.) Generations of schoolboys in England and America learned of Rugby football from the book *Tom Brown's School Days,* published in 1856 by Thomas Hughes, an old Rugby boy. The book, with its stirring accounts of football games, was so popular that, by inference, it has been linked to the revival of football in American colleges from the 1860s on: ballplaying thus inspired by book reading.

Yet football was already a continual tradition in American colleges, occasionally stamped out but always revived. Football was a relief from books, not a consequence of them. As early as the 1730s, freshmen at Harvard were supposed to provide "bats, balls, and foot-balls" to upperclassmen. Students were expected to bond with their classmates, and against men of other classes, with a ferocity now difficult to grasp or explain. By the early 1800s at Harvard, and later at such schools as Yale, Princeton, Brown, Rutgers, Amherst, Bowdoin, and West Point, an annual football game between freshmen and sophomores became a blood ritual of displayed courage and loyalty. One Harvard man fondly recalled the "opportunity it gave us, and the commensurate excitement, of kicking and pounding one's very best friend." Held on the eve of classes, or the first Monday of the term, the game guaranteed the sophs the tactical advantage of knowing their classmates; the unacquainted frosh could not tell friend from foe, and usually lost. A student described the 1853 game at Yale:

There were yellings and shoutings and wiping of noses,
Where the hue of the lily has changed to the rose's,
There were tearing of shirts, and ripping of stitches,
And breaches of peace, and pieces of britches.

The players were often drunk as well. No wonder that students relished these games, or that the Harvard and Yale faculties had abolished them by 1860. Students persisted with less formal, less conspicuous games through the fall season. No mere faculty could stop footballers intent on their play.

In high schools and prep schools, meantime, male students essayed their own notions of football. As with baseball, two distinct indigenous folk versions of the game emerged in Boston and New York; neither version, locally invented, much resembled Rugby football or was visibly influenced by *Tom Brown's School Days*. The New York game deployed teams of twenty men each, divided into ten roaming "runners" and ten "position" players responsible for assigned areas of the field. Each team tried to kick a round, black rubber ball at any height, even on the ground, between two goalposts. (Rugby players kicked an egg-shaped ball between goalposts and over a crossbar ten feet from the ground.) Carrying and passing the ball were forbidden, but "batting" was allowed: holding the ball in his left hand, a player with a motion like an overhand baseball throw would wallop the ball with his closed right fist. A well-batted ball went nearly as far as a kick, with more accuracy, and could even score goals. Instead of arm-tackling, as in Rugby, body contact was restricted to running body-blocks ("butting") delivered by the shoulders and upper arms. The play was continuous and exhausting, halted only after a goal. "For fifteen minutes at a time," one man recalled, "our runners would continue sprinting, like hounds in the traces of a flying fox, from one end of the ground to the other. And also dodging, twisting, turning, kicking sidewise and backwards as well as forwards, and ever and anon driving the ball swiftly with the unerring bat, we position players defended our own goal or threatened that of the enemy"; till at last somebody scored, "and we all crossed over and found time to pull a few breaths and take account of bleeding shins or bruised bodies." Play then resumed until the next goal. Starting with the Princeton-Rutgers game of 1869, colleges in and near New York City played occasional intercollegiate matches of New York football.

The Boston game used the same round rubber ball but otherwise was quite different. Boston high school boys of the 1860s played fall games during recess on Boston Common and, after school, on a vacant lot in the Back Bay. The ten or fifteen players on each team would arrange themselves into "tenders" to protect the goal (an imaginary line across the whole width of each end of the field), "half tends" at midfield, and "rushers" up front. The ball was mainly kicked, but under certain conditions it could also be picked up, thrown, or carried. Tackling was allowed, even of players without the ball. "Lurking" near the enemy goal was defined as offside. Anybody holding or running with the ball had to stop and kick it, or pass it to a teammate, when a chasing opponent yelled that he had halted pursuit: an odd feature that worked on an honor system. "The severest penalty was the taboo for unfair play," one of these ballplayers, Morton Prince, said later. "The style of play as developed under these rules and by tradition was thoroughly open, and remarkably individual, leaving nearly everything to the initiative, skill, and agility of each player." In the fall of 1862 a group of recent high school graduates in Boston formed the Oneida Football Club, one of the first American football teams organized outside of school. For four years the Oneidas won every game, its goal line uncrossed by the enemy.

When these Boston schoolboys went on to Harvard, they found their favorite fall game still outlawed. (This ban had made the Oneida Club necessary.) Finally, in the fall of 1871, football was revived at Harvard by men who had played the Boston game in high school. Nearly every afternoon that fall, they played pickup matches on the Cambridge Common, safely outside Harvard Yard and the faculty's reach. A year later they boldly established a Harvard team, and the faculty relented.

Football still depended on the animosity of ancient foes. The game matured in America after it was grafted onto the oldest college rivalries. Harvard and Yale, the most venerable pairing, could not play each other until their different versions of the game were reconciled. In 1873 Harvard declined a football conference with Yale, Princeton, Columbia, and Rutgers because those schools all played New York ball. Instead, in May 1874, Harvard tried two games in Cambridge against McGill, a Canadian college: one by Boston rules, the other by Rugby rules. (Rugby, which prohibited batting and butting but allowed ball-carrying, resembled Boston's game more than New York's.) The Boston game, with its limited pursuit and code of honor, could only work between teams that knew each other, or at least agreed to behave like gentlemen. For opponents that lacked those understandings, the Rugby style of clean pursuit and tackle added visceral thrills while averting arguments about when runners were stopped. Harvard saw the advantages of the Rugby game and converted to it for a return match in Montreal in the fall of 1874; three touchdowns and victory over McGill, formerly their mentors, sealed Harvard's decision for the Rugby style.

Loyal to a less similar game, the New York ballplayers took longer to come around. Harvard and Yale, feuding adversaries since 1701, first engaged at football in November 1875. Special "concessionary rules" compromised the different games: Harvard allowed batting and Yale allowed running with the ball. A delegation of 150 Harvards trained down to New Haven for the contest. In the crowd, watching intently, was a high school senior, Walter Camp, catching sight of his (and football's) future. The Harvard boys—"agile, athletic youths"—took the field blaring in rampant crimson caps, jerseys, and stockings, and immaculate white knickerbockers: a cleaner, crisper version of a standard baseball uniform. The Yale boys, without uniforms, began to droop. "Yale had no idea of the possibilities of the running game," Camp recalled. "Our men seemed like snapping wolves in their vain attempts to catch the runner and ball together, for we had no notion of that style of play." Harvard runners swept dodging down the field, using their hands and arms to deflect tacklers. "After the first few moments of dazed and pained astonishment, the superiority of the Harvard team became so manifest that the Yale crowd were actually forced to laugh." (Through clenched teeth, presumably.)

After the game, Yale was embarrassed into converting to Rugby; the other New York colleges soon followed. Yale sent off to England for regulation Rugby balls. When they did not arrive, Yale was forced—oh, the shame of it—to borrow one from Harvard, along with a set of Rugby rules. "I can see now the antics which that Harvard ball played with us," said a Yale man. "The leather egg never did anything twice alike."

The next fall, Walter Camp began his football life at Yale: he would dominate the game for the next three decades. Gene Baker, captain and founder of the Yale team, recruited a squad to avenge the loss to Harvard. "Upper-class men were hard to persuade," Camp noted, but "freshmen were eager to be accommodating." Baker drove them hard. For two hours each afternoon they practiced on a small, unforgiving field bounded by curbstone, a high picket fence, and a pile of rocks; then, at nine o'clock at night, they gritted into a briskly paced three-mile run on the gym track. Afterward Camp would sometimes stagger home, fall on his bed, and sleep in his clothes. "Baker, seeing that the sport had a great fascination for me, made me more or less of a confidant." They could not, said Baker, hope to match

Harvard's skills at kicking and passing. In fact, Harvard did once again control the ball, keeping it in Yale territory for most of the game. But nobody scored until Oliver David Thompson kicked a twenty-five-yard goal for Yale. With Thompson's teammates distracted by hugging him, Harvard picked up the ball and ran it home—but the referee called it back. Harvard later tried another kick but missed, and the game ended. Victorious Yale would not lose another Harvard football game until 1890.

A complete athlete, Camp played every available sport well. But this new game became his particular passion. He walked around the campus, football in hand, bonding to it. "He seemed to know every inch of its surface," a teammate remembered, "and it seemed almost as if the ball knew him. It would stick to his palm, like iron to a magnet." The Rugby game kept the ball in the air, on kicks and passes, so dexterous ballhandling mattered. Camp—swift and tough at six feet, 170 pounds—liked to run down the sideline, holding the ball with one outstretched arm, warding off tacklers with the other, shifting the ball from hand to hand as play demanded. He and Chummy Eaton ran in tandem; when one man was almost caught, he would loft an overhand toss to the other; the ball went back and forth for chunky gains. "It was a pretty game to play, and a pretty game to look at," recalled the teammate.

Most of the time, anyway; playing Columbia in 1876, Camp tackled a runner, cracking his head on the frozen field. The man lay stunned and bleeding. "I ran up to the captain," Camp recalled, "and said that I wished to be taken out, as I had killed a man and could not play any more." The dead man came to and resumed the game, leaving Camp's devotion unsullied by death on the field. Camp played for four years as an undergraduate, and two more as a desultory medical student, before finally retiring *as a player* from the Yale team. But he stayed devoted to the game: an ardor with profoundly ambiguous implications for the future of football.

◆　◆　◆

As the sport developed, it could reasonably have been called Campball, a synthetic derivative from invention and new rules. Rugby was a game of oblique angles and diagonal movements.

The ball went from man to man, downfield but also toward the sideline, as each ball carrier in turn would lateral outward to a teammate when trapped. No interference ran ahead of the ball: the ballcarrier was always the point man, with the other players splayed out and churning behind him. Tackles were clean and solitary, more like roughly glancing brushes than mass head-on collisions. With many kicks, passes, and fumbles, the ball changed hands often, making the action visible and variable to onlookers.

Conceiving a different game, for reasons that he never made explicit, Camp gradually imposed his vision on everybody else. It had started with a schism between linemen (then called "rushers") and backs on the Yale team of 1879. As Camp's teammate John Harding remembered it, the linemen "were unanimously of the opinion that the kicking, dodging and passing open game was the game we should strive for and that it was the duty of the half-back and backs to end their runs with a good long punt, wherever possible, and give us a chance to get under the ball when it came down." The backs, by contrast, preferred "a running mass play game" of ball control and few kicks and passes, especially in sloppy weather. At a tense team meeting late in the season, Camp as captain spurned protests from linemen over the lack of kicking. When the linemen, bigger and more numerous than the backs, insisted on their preferred style, Camp said he was quitting the team and left the room. The others quickly decided "we could not play the open game without Camp as captain," Harding recalled. "Some one was sent out to bring Walter back; matters were smoothed out; we played the open game and never lost a touchdown during the season."

Camp was stubborn. As a player, he had excelled at the very game—of passes, individual heroics, balls in the air—that he now wished to reform out of existence. He envisioned a team game, more orderly and controlled, with louder collisions and a single organizing intelligence directing the play. At annual meetings of the intercollegiate league (formed originally by Yale, Harvard, Princeton, and Columbia), he pushed through new rules, working steadily toward his vision. He made the field smaller, with each team cut from fifteen to eleven men, yielding a tighter arena more suited to coordination. In Rugby football, the ball was put into play by a disorderly scrum: between two massed lines of players, the ball—possessed by neither team—was kicked about until it emerged and was picked up, by somebody, in unpredictable circumstances. "This pushing, puffing and panting was manifestly senseless," one early player recalled.

So Camp in 1880 invented the line of scrimmage: one team *in possession of the ball* put it in play to itself, initially by a toe-snap, later by a hand-snap from center to quarterback. Now a team knew it was getting the ball and could arrange itself beforehand into a devised play. Set to receive the ball, the quarterback could direct his team with secret vocal signals. Bodies now bumped together in massed, head-to-head alignments. Instead of glancing tackles in the open field, knots of players butted heads, like locomotives colliding, in more dangerous, full-bore contact. For the linemen, at least, weight and strength became more effective than speed and skill with the ball. Baseball, the rival team sport of the day, had evolved as a player's game, invented on the field; after the scrimmage and snap were installed, football evolved as essentially a coach's game, directed and refined by strategists on the sidelines.

The new system made ball possession so important that free passing gradually disappeared. Play grew more restricted. Under the new rules, a team could keep the ball indefinitely, barring a punt or fumble. In the climactic game of the 1881 season, Princeton held the ball the whole first half, Yale for the entire second. Neither team scored or even made a substantial gain: a dreary bore for everybody. Camp's invented scrimmage line was generating unforeseen side effects. Casting about for a remedy, Camp—instead of then returning to the Rugby scrum, an option apparently not considered—came up with another innovation, the system of downs. As first introduced, if a team did not gain five yards, or lose ten, in three plays (downs), it had to relinquish the ball. (The field thus acquired yard lines, and football became the gridiron game.)

Each reform changed the game and demanded more reforms; offense and defense had to be kept in fragile balance. Because the downs rule weakened the offense, interference was informally allowed as a new challenge to the defense. In Rugby, no teammate was permitted to convoy the ballcarrier; in American football, the same principle gradually withered away. As early as 1879, Princeton deployed a man on each side of the runner, shielding him with their bodies only. A few years later, the shielders had moved out ahead of the runner, using their arms and hands to shed tacklers. The old offside rule was not withdrawn, but it was no longer enforced. Barely a decade old, football had lost this final vestige of the Rugby game.

Camp and the Yale team, reinforcing each other's success, smoothly dominated football. Crushed opponents could only resort to accusing Yale of dirty tactics such as doubled fists, or jumping on downed men with knees flourishing ("means which gentlemen would never stoop to"). Over its first decade of intercollegiate football, Yale lost only 3 games. A not untypical team went 13-0, scoring 698 points and allowing none all season. With records like that, who could question Camp's wisdom, or dedication? His entire adult life was organized around football. Employed by a watch company, he worked briefly in New York and as a traveling salesman, then settled into a long career with the firm in New Haven, where he could stay close to the Yale team. "There is only one man in New Haven of more importance than Walter Camp," wrote Richard Harding Davis in *Harper's Weekly*. "I think he is the president of the university." Camp also maintained an enormous correspondence with football enthusiasts around the country. Anyone interested in the sport would naturally contact him. ("Will you kindly furnish me," wrote an instructor at Notre Dame, an obscure Roman Catholic college in Indiana, "with some points on the best way to develop a good Foot Ball Team.") He sent forth missionaries into unfootballed fields. As the game spread and flourished, at least eleven of his Yale boys became the first football coaches at other colleges.

Grounded in Yale's lopsided victories, Camp's prestige vaulted beyond the field into less quantified dimensions. His personality demanded respect and agreement. Vigorous and opinionated, brimming with manly vitality, shining "the two most luminous and gleaming eyes I have ever seen in a man's face," as one Yale quarterback put it, Camp could dominate any room. Yet the ultimate source of his power was not coercive but moral: his reputation for righteous disinterestedness. The most ardent of Yale loyalists, he could still be tapped to referee a game between Yale and—even—Harvard, and pull it off with unchallenged fairness. Who would accuse him of cheating, or even shading a call for the Old Blues? Walter Camp was a gentleman, so everyone agreed. (When his power over football later waned, it was only after events had tarnished his apparently impregnable moral authority.)

In 1888, presumably to help the defense, Camp legalized tackles below the waist, down to the knees. When applied, this new rule doubled back on itself, spawning an era of brutal mass momentum plays by the offense. The low tackle, sure and deadly, discouraged running in an open field; so the offensive line contracted, the men bunching shoulder-to-shoulder, while the backs drew in closer to the line. A few years earlier, Princeton and Lehigh teams had toyed with "wedge" or "V trick" formations in which several players formed moving assault teams of blockers. The legalized low tackle soon made such mass plays fashionable for most teams. George Woodruff, a Yale man coaching at Penn, installed his soon-imitated flying interference: just before the snap, the left end and left tackle would pull and run through the backfield to the right. Joined by the fullback and right halfback, the four abreast would slam at full speed into the right side of the line, followed closely by the left halfback with the ball. A lone defender could be trampled.

A rougher offense inevitably begat a rougher defense: force on force. Pudge Heffelfinger, Yale's legendary guard, devised an appropriately harsh response. With a running leap, knees drawn up and brandished, he would thump the lead man in his chest, collapsing the wedge; or he might simply vault the interference and land on the ballcarrier. Such maneuvers led to more fights and injuries, sometimes to deaths. The simple addition of low tackles had brought new levels of brutality and dirty play to the game—exactly what Camp had not intended. "We were past masters at tackling around the neck," said John Heisman, looking back at the 1890s. "There was a rule against it, but that rule was, I am sure, broken oftener than any other in the book. . . . Fact is, you didn't stand much chance of making the line those days unless you were a good wrestler and fair boxer."

Lorin Deland of Harvard, an unlikely football strategist, took the mass momentum fad to its bizarre extremity. A Boston lawyer, a literary fellow and chess expert, Deland had never played football. He saw his first game by accident in 1890. Like many other observers, then and later, he was struck by parallels between football and battlefield strategy in war. Rereading his books on Napoleon, Deland applied the principle of massing one's strength at the enemy's weakest point. Though barely aware of the rules of football, he convinced the Harvard team to unveil his flying wedge in the Yale game of 1892. With Harvard in possession, its heavier men retreated to near the right sideline, twenty yards behind the scrimmage line, while the lighter men clumped to the left, fifteen yards back. At a signal the two groups ran hard to the ball, formed an interlocked V, and plowed through the left side of the line. Instant impact: on the first try, the ballcarrier was pulled along for thirty yards, finally tripping over one of his own teammates. The new play was pronounced a vigorous success. Given sensational notices in the national press, the flying wedge was soon adopted, or attempted, by every self-respecting football team.

The mass plays ignited howling debates about the dangers of football. Players in the 1890s donned little protective gear beyond thin pads and occasional shin guards or nose guards. "One who wore home-made pads was regarded as a sissy," Heisman recalled. Thundering downfield and scattering tackles, the mass plays were rough on heads and limbs. If a borderline psychopath such as Frank Hinkey of Yale wanted to hurt an opponent, the new style gave him too many chances and pretexts. ("We were plenty scared of him ourselves," Heffelfinger said of Hinkey, as kindly as he could. "He was a morose, introspective type, given to brooding spells. He seldom uttered a sound, never laughed at our jokes, took out his repressions on the football field. But, boy, was he rough.") Responding to the flying wedge's thudding effectiveness in 1892, Hinkey kneed a Harvard man in the stomach, and jumped with both feet on another man as he lay on the ground. After a game in 1894, "no father or mother worthy the name," said the *New York Evening Post,* "would permit a son to associate with the set of Yale brutes on Hinkey's football team."

Camp named Hinkey to his annual All-America team three times and defended football against all its critics. Many sportsmen, even those who had never played the game, agreed with him. "We were tending steadily in America to produce in our leisure and sedentary classes a type of man not much above the Bengal baboo, and from this the athletic spirit has saved us," Theodore Roosevelt assured Camp in 1895. "Of all games I personally like foot ball best, and I would rather see my boys play it than see them play any other." Roosevelt spoke for many of his ethnic class who saw in football a redemption from fin-de-siècle ennui and "race suicide" by the waning patricians. The old blood, so the argument ran, could be purified and renewed in the annealing fires of the gridiron. "It is a good thing," said Roosevelt, "to have the personal contact about which the *New York Evening Post* snarls so much, and no fellow is worth his salt if he minds an occasional bruise or cut. . . . I would a hundred fold rather keep the game as it is now, with the brutality, than give it up." In his own strenuously sporting life, Roosevelt had been knocked out at polo and had broken his arm and nose in riding to hounds; "it seems to me that when I can afford to run these slight risks college boys can afford to take their chances on the foot ball field."

Yet the mass momentum game was worse than violent; it was boring. On play after play, Richard Harding Davis reported, fans could see only "two lines of men breaking away suddenly and making for a bunch of three or four, who run shoulder to shoulder until one of them goes down, and there is a confused mass of legs, and the lines form once more, and the same thing happens again." Years earlier, watching the outmoded game, fans could savor balls in the air, long solitary runs, tackles in the open field. "But to-day the men are as confidential as two partners at whist; they hand each other the ball as though they were ashamed of it," and nobody in the stands could tell where it went. As a former player and permanent fan, Davis urged a return to "the old days of long passes," when "the spectator could understand what it was all about."

Granted that football veterans, yearning for their youths, inevitably preferred the games of *their* day to any modern improvements. But less prejudiced observers also came to similar conclusions. In 1893 George Wright, the old baseball player, saw a couple of Harvard games and was moved to write Camp a grizzled admonition. Given his interest "in all manly athletic games," said Wright, he urged the abolition of mass and wedge plays to avoid injuries, "at the same time adding greatly to the life and spirit of the game." Spectators wanted "a chance to see the ball now and then, and not to have it smothered in the centre most of the time." Consider, Wright suggested, the difference between a baseball game dominated by the pitcher and catcher, and one with lots of batting, baserunning, and plays in the field: "You know the game that most pleases the spectator, and so it would be in foot ball; and I hope my dear boy you can frame rules for next season that will come near to pleasing all." Walter Camp ruled football. Ultimately he had only to please himself.

◆　　◆　　◆

At this point, with the game in its dullest, bloodiest phase, pro football first appeared. It grew accidentally from gentlemen's clubs and their losing struggles with the ideals of amateur sport. Amateur athletic clubs, proliferating in cities during the decades after the Civil War, offered the same mix of sport and social selection that had animated early baseball teams like the Knickerbockers. In their plushest form, these "athletic associations" maintained clubhouses, redolent of sweat and cigars, with a gym, perhaps a pool, and males-only social rooms. They sponsored teams and matches in the older, patrician games of track, cricket, and water sports, and in the newer fads of baseball and football. As these clubs competed with each other, and started nursing grudges and traditions, a manly will to win overcame the abstractions of Greek ideals. The Amateur Athletic Union (1888) was supposed to set standards of conduct; when San Francisco's Olympic Athletic Club lured athletes to its teams by getting them jobs, the AAU in 1890 declared such practices merely "semiprofessional," a new category, and thus squeakily permissible by amateur standards. This evasive ruling in effect gave any willing club permission to hire the best players, quietly. Overlooking the frauds and lies involved, this process did at least democratize football.

Consider Big Bill Thompson and Pudge Heffelfinger, teammates on one of the first semipro football squads. Later notorious as the underworld's favorite mayor of Chicago, Thompson led a wild, intractable youth, disciplined only slightly by sport. Born to wealth, at fourteen he quit school to become a cowboy in Wyoming. When he turned twenty-one his father bought him a thirty-eight-hundred-acre ranch in Nebraska. After three years of agreeable profits, Thompson gave up ranching and came home to Chicago following his father's death in 1891. Still only twenty-four years old, with a decade of ranch life behind him, he had nothing much to do. Others managed the family's two million dollars in real estate. Bored and restive, Thompson mostly hung out at the Chicago Athletic Association. There Eugene Pike, Yale 1890, got him interested in water polo and other sports. Thompson, tall and toughened by those cowboy days, acquired his nickname and started playing tackle for the Chicago AA football team, an eager neophyte again. Most of his team-mates were veterans of college ball. The playing manager, Billy Crawford, took the team on an ambitious eastern tour in the fall of 1892, paying generous expenses to his best players. (Crawford already nursed dreams of a "professional football league" embracing cities from Chicago to New York.)

Among the Chicago AA's most expensive players, presumably, was Pudge Heffelfinger, who had wandered a quite different route to that semipro tour of the East. Pudge and Big Bill had nothing in common save the inevitable Yale football connection. Heffelfinger, the most celebrated gridiron star of the nineteenth century, had grown up in Minneapolis, showing precocious football gifts. His father owned a shoe factory and dealt, badly, in real estate. At Yale Pudge's team lost two games in four years and he was elected class president for life. Nothing after his graduation approached those heights. He lingered another year, eligible for football by enrolling in Yale's law school. Urged to join his father's business, he learned that the family was broke. For years, in fact, his father had submitted false statements to secure credit and saving loans. So Pudge spurned the family and accepted an offer from the Great Northern Railroad. But his promising title translated to a dreary office position in Omaha. He missed the game. When the Chicago Athletic Association invited him on its eastern tour, six games in twelve days, he was ready. Heading east to play football in that fall of 1892, he must have felt the old college glories stirring again.

Evidently the Chicago AA's terms gave him a keen sense of his market value in football. The tour over, he was persuaded to play one game in Pittsburgh for more money than most American workers were making in a year. The Allegheny Athletic Association, founded in Pittsburgh around 1890, was yet another Yale football colony. The Allegheny AA had been organized by Oliver David Thompson and John Moorhead, Jr., football teammates of Walter Camp's at Yale. Both were wealthy Pittsburgh bluebloods: Thompson was the son of an attorney and congressman, Moorhead the son of an iron merchant who sat on corporate boards. Thompson had starred at Yale, "the best all-round athlete in college in our time," famous for kicking decisive field goals against Harvard and Princeton in 1876 and Harvard again in 1878. After college he went home to Pittsburgh, joined his father's law firm, and led what he later called "a life absolutely without incident." Starting the Allegheny AA gave him a chance to recover, in safely limited doses, the sharply savored athletic highs of his college years.

At first the Allegheny AA played truly amateur football, just for fun, and without much skill. In October 1890 its team lost to Princeton's lowly scrubs, 44–6. Local bragging stakes were raised when a new rival, the Pittsburgh Athletic Club, fielded its own football team. After challenges back and forth, the two clubs played a 6–6 tie on Columbus Day in 1892. Afterward, a revelation: the Pittsburgh AC had fielded a pseudonymed ringer, A. C. Read, captain of the Penn State team. The Allegheny AA piously condemned the ploy and then engaged its own ringers for the rematch a month later. Because the Alleghenys kept honest records, Heffelfinger and two teammates, Ed Malley (a shot-putter from Detroit) and Sport Donnelly (a former Princeton star), may be regarded as the first *documented* cases of playing football for money. All three received twenty-five dollars from the Allegheny AA for expenses; Pudge also got five hundred dollars, an enormous sum reflecting his unrivaled reputation.

Amid mutual charges of deceit, the game on November 12, 1892, was first canceled, then played with the understanding that all bets—perhaps a total of $10,000—were off. On a cold day with snow on the ground, before three thousand paying fans, Pudge earned his fee by picking up a teammate's fumble and running twenty-five yards around end for the only score. It was a rough game with many injuries: an ambiguous precedent for the future of pro football. But even after paying $575 to its professionals, a 25 percent cut of all receipts to the visiting team, and other expenses, the Allegheny AA still made $621 on the contest. The Alleghenys had won both on the field and at the gate. (A few weeks later, Pudge went to the Harvard-Yale game, his first as a noncombatant in six years. Overcome with enthusiasm, and perhaps other intoxicants, he wandered out onto the field and was restrained by three cops. It was hard to leave. Next fall, he played a few more games for the Chicago AA and then headed west again, to try coaching the new football team at the University of California. Finally he came back home and took on the doomed family business. But he still helped out with the football team at the University of Minnesota—where the coach was, of course, a Yale man.)

Growing beyond the amateur clubs, semipro football teams were soon sponsored by churches, companies, and small communities craving recognition. Amateur pretenses dwindled steadily away. In Chester County, west of Philadelphia, small towns took to football as a formalized excuse for beating up men from other communities. Phoenixville, a tough mill town on the Schuylkill River, launched a team in the fall of 1893 under playing coach Ed Hicks, a dentist. For prospective ballplayers, prior football knowledge mattered less than other qualities. Billy Beard was husking corn when three representatives of the Phoenixville AA rode up on their high-wheeled bicycles. "They dismounted on the rail fence," Beard recalled, "and asked me if I wanted to play football. I never saw a football, I admitted. That didn't matter, they said, 'We understand that you're pretty good with your mitts.' " And furthermore, " 'We'll pay you top wages, $1.65 a day.' That was wonderful money those days." Another raw recruit, John Austin, made his first touchdown by passing the goal line, heaving the ball over the crossbar, then catching the ball and downing it. "But how was any of us to know," said Austin. "We had never seen any of those funny looking balls before." Serious football was no longer the exclusive domain of college boys.

"Phoenixville was noted for roughness," quarterback Jimmy

O'Donnell later bragged. "Opposing teams whose members expected to return home all in one piece generally gave this town
a wide berth. . . . And most of the players who said that were
toughened college stars. As for us, we were just trying to teach
the other towns a little respect for one of the greatest little bor-
oughs in existence—Phoenixville." In a game against Norris-
town, somebody's cleats ripped off Bill Austin's right eyebrow.
He tied it up with his handkerchief to keep it from dangling into
his eye, and finished the half. To counter an enemy's V-wedge,
one sacrificial soul would lie flat in front of the wedge's apex.
The wedge would trip and crumble, leaving the ballcarrier naked. John Stoker liked to tackle a troublesome enemy by catching him in the small of the back so that he spun in midair and
landed in a heap, "looking like he had lost all interest in living."

During the West Chester game of 1894, Mike Grady (a baseball catcher who had just finished his rookie year with the Philadelphia Phillies) dove, cleated feet first, into the neck and face
of Phoenixville's J. R. Dunbar, who protested. "I'm only trying to
break your neck," Grady explained, "you ——— of a ———."
Dunbar's teammates took note. After the next play Grady was
carried off the field, and the game went on, adorned by fistfights.
Phoenixville won and fled a caterwauling mob back to its hotel.
"Inside the hotel, after another fight, the men stuck me under
the table until I cooled off," Billy Beard remembered. "Soon the
cops came and 'escorted' us—first to jail by mistake—then to our
train. The mob followed us all the way out of town. They tried
their darndest to bottle up our train by wrecking it. They put
stones and everything on the track. . . . They heaved beer bottles
through the windows, breaking the lights on every car in the
train. I'll say we ducked!" (The scene recalled the aftermath of
the game between the Selkirks and Yarrows in 1815: local pride
in football eruption.)

The notorious brutality of semipro football allowed ballplayers to ventilate old grudges—beyond the four-year constraints of
college ball. After a vicious game between Penn and Lafayette, a
Lafayette player joined the Greensburg AC just to get back at a
Penn player who was supposed to play for the Pittsburgh AC
against Greensburg. It didn't work out, as the Penn man prudently did not appear for the game, leaving the Lafayette man

unrequited in revenge. Hector Cowan, a former Princeton star playing for the Cleveland AC, had better luck against the Crescent Club of Brooklyn. An old enemy from Yale was playing for the Crescents; "on a long end run I took after him," Cowan noted, "caught him from the side, threw him over my head out of bounds. As we were both running at the top of our speed he hit the ground with considerable force. I felt better towards him after this game."

Football was drifting farther and farther from polite amateur ideals. Under AAU pressure, the Allegheny AA did not field a team in 1895. But Big Bill Thompson, now captain of his Chicago AA squad, assembled by unpublicized means a crack team for the 1896 season, with college stars from Yale, Purdue, Michigan, Illinois, Williams, Penn, and Princeton. They sailed through their local schedule and arranged to meet the Boston AA on Thanksgiving Day for what was declared a national championship. Just before the game, Chicago was forced to drop six players for accepting free meals from a Chicago AA member—surely the least of their amateur sins. Chicago won anyway, before eight thousand fans in a steady rain, on touchdowns by Phil Draper, a fullback from Williams, and Fred Slater, an Illinois halfback. Draper, in "one of the most marvelous performances in the history of football," no less, caught a punt at midfield, dodged and bulled through most of the Boston team, and fell triumphant between the goalposts. The action on the field could not justify the chicaneries off it. A few months later the Boston AA dropped its football team. Thompson retired from football and was elected a Chicago alderman in 1899, beginning his dubious political ascent. The frauds of his football career foretold his later depredations as a gangster in Chicago politics.

From the shady twilight tolerated by the AAU, semipro football now shifted to explicitly professional teams. One crucible became the steel and mining towns around Pittsburgh, an area that would later produce many noted players. The Greensburg team hired men like Lawson Fiscus, who had briefly studied at Princeton, and Adam Wyant, who had played four years for Bucknell and two more for the University of Chicago. In nearby Latrobe, Greensburg's natural rival, an editor named David Berry started a team and proclaimed it through his newspaper, the *Clipper*. Over six seasons Latrobe won forty of its fifty-five games against the best teams available.

In 1902 Berry persuaded the state's major-league baseball teams—the Pirates, A's, and Phillies—to underwrite pro football squads. They grandly called themselves the National Football League, with Berry as president. A few baseball stars, including Christy Mathewson and Rube Waddell, played pro football that fall. "They care no more [about] professionalism in the colleges here than we do," Willis Richardson, coach of the Pittsburgh team, told a college friend. "A man will play on a professional team one year and the next, loom up as an amateur college star. . . . They regard it as a business, pure and simple, and think nothing of a man taking money for his talent, before he completes his college course. Such a bunch of men you never saw." This "National Football League" played out its modest schedule, lost money, and disappeared after one season.

Tom O'Rourke, a New York boxing promoter, had what he thought was a better idea: an indoor pro football tournament at Madison Square Garden, played during the week after Christmas in 1902. (An indoor game in Chicago on Thanksgiving Day of 1896 had drawn a profitable crowd to see Chicago and Michigan contend for Midwest supremacy.) Whatever the scheme's commercial potential, O'Rourke himself could only hurt the reputation of pro football. With his partner Big Tim Sullivan—a Tammany warhorse and underworld figure—O'Rourke staged boxing shows, lawful and otherwise, at their Lenox Athletic Club. At various times he was accused of fixing fights, making illegal side bets, and bribing politicians to keep boxing legal in the state. As a necessary adjunct to these endeavors, he ran a whorehouse, the Delavan, at the corner of Broadway and Fortieth Street in Manhattan. His entry into pro football merely confirmed the ethical anarchy engulfing the game.

A local team, the Orange AC of New Jersey, was favored to win the 1902 tournament. But the Syracuse AC, for what must have been a hefty price, engaged the services of Pop Warner, a protean figure in football's evolution. Then thirty-one years old, he had played at Cornell and coached at three colleges before landing in 1899 at the Carlisle Indian School in Pennsylvania. Joining Syracuse for a week of practice, he brought along his brother Bill and two of his best Carlisle players, the brothers Hawley and Bemus Pierce. Syracuse had also hired two fleet halfbacks, Billy Bottger of Princeton and Phil Draper, late of the Chicago AC. Other college veterans from Williams and Columbia filled out the squad.

In the first game—the debut of pro football in New York City—Syracuse met a New York team dominated by eight men who had played college ball for Penn. About thirty-five hundred curious fans showed up. The Garden's wooden floor had been removed, leaving a sticky dirt surface that kept the players slogging and slipping. The field was only about seventy yards long and thirty-five yards wide, further limiting mobility. The action ran mostly to mass plays over guard and tackle. Frustrations showed up in occasional fistfights. In one mass play Pop Warner's head was cut, but he kept playing. Phil Draper made the best run of the night: a breakaway dash of thirty yards, heading for a touchdown, till he was caught from behind by a thrilling tackle; "the spectators cheered both players for their clever work." Pop Warner, more hurt than he acknowledged, missed three field goals, but Billy Bottger managed a touchdown for the only score of the game.

Syracuse swept by another opponent into the final game against Orange. It drew a football-wise crowd sprinkled with judges and politicians. Pop Warner, still hurting, did not appear. (Blondy Wallace, who had played for New York against Syracuse, took his place; rosters were flexible.) A kick in the face broke Bemus Pierce's nose. Otherwise Syracuse rolled over the local favorites, 36–0. "Whenever the big fellows from Syracuse exerted themselves," the *Times* reported, "and tried for gains they invariably got them, and with the exception of a couple of fumbles, they played an excellent game all through." Billy Bottger scored three touchdowns. Phil Draper also ran well and boomed a surprise punt fifty yards downfield. Only one man was knocked out; another, cut over the eye, finished the game swathed in a bandage. The experiment was pronounced a success.

And repeated a year later, this time during the week before Christmas, and under the more seemly auspices of the Watertown, New York, Athletic Association. Known for its paper mills,

Watertown was an industrial community of about twenty thousand people at the eastern end of Lake Ontario. Football had come to Watertown in 1892 when the local YMCA secretary, Walter B. Street, who had played the game for Williams College, coached the first high school team in town. As more ringers joined the squad for big games, it evolved into a semipro team called the Red and Black. At the turn of the century Mayor James Black Wise, a wealthy manufacturer of machine hardware, took a well-heeled interest in the team. Under his generous management, Watertown soon boasted one of the best pro football squads in the country. For the Madison Square Garden tournament in 1903, Watertown deployed Carl Kruse (an All-American tackle from Northwestern), the well-traveled halfback tandem of Draper and Bottger, and alumni of Annapolis, Williams, and Bucknell teams. Sparing no expenses for the hometown glory he expected, Mayor Wise announced prizes of $1,250 for the winners and $750 for the runners-up. To improve the footing, five hundred loads of dirt were spread over the Garden's subsurface, then steamrollered down.

In the first game, played to a small crowd of two thousand, Watertown met unexpected resistance from the Oreos of Asbury Park, New Jersey. After a scoreless first half, the Oreos' rooters—who filled several large sections of seats—offered "all sorts of odds" to Watertown bettors. The game turned on a trick play. Twenty yards from a touchdown, the Watertown quarterback, E. C. White, took the snap and threw a long lateral to a back at the left end of the line, who then ran nearly to the goal line. This long pass, recalling the open football of the 1870s, seemed barely legal in 1903. The Oreos yelled their protests, but the referee—hired, after all, by Watertown interests—allowed the play. Bottger then carried it in, the only score of the game. The Oreos howled even louder; one belted a Watertown player. A scuffling crowd collected, bringing cops and brandished nightsticks from all over the Garden. With no penalties called, play resumed. "Slugging in the game was a common feature," the *Times* reporter noted. "Every man on the teams was apparently willing, if not eager, to give a little more than he received."

Watertown was expected to clinch its title three nights later against the Franklin, Pennsylvania, AC, a team dominated by

Blondy Wallace and other veterans of the previous year's New York squad. Instead Franklin won, 12–0, ripping through Watertown's line "almost at will." The newspapers offered no explanation; but according to the story handed down in Watertown ever since, five crucial members of the Watertown team missed the game because concerned gamblers had taken them out for a spree the night before, leaving them unfit for combat (or perhaps bribed not to appear). Mayor Wise therefore lost the ten thousand dollars he had bet on the game. Many fans of the Red and Black had to wire for money to get home to Watertown. The switch of sponsors from Tom O'Rourke to Watertown had not, after all, raised the ethical tone of pro football. Crowds were thinner too. So ended the Christmas pro football tournaments at Madison Square Garden.

◆　◆　◆

"A gentleman does not make his living from his athletic prowess," said Walter Camp. "He does not earn anything by his victories except glory and satisfaction."

◆　◆　◆

While pro football floundered in red ink, the Harvard-Yale game of 1901 sold more than thirty-four thousand tickets for gross receipts of $61,859. No professional contest could approach those figures. The leaders of college football strenuously deplored play for pay, yet tolerated, indeed encouraged, loping professionalism in their own "amateur" game: hired coaches, ever more imposing stadia, recruiting with cash, cheating on entrance exams, winked-at eligibility standards, special tutors and breaks for jocks, and control of athletics by coaches and alumni instead of by students and faculty. Charlie Daly put in four years as quarterback for Harvard, then two more years for West Point—a parlay so routine that it escaped comment. In one season Fielding Yost played for two college teams and the Allegheny AC; when, as a coach, he switched from Stanford to Michigan in 1901, he brought along three of his best players to his new job. (It was, after all, a *job*.) Pop Warner's Carlisle squads engaged the top college teams that dared meet them. "Carlisle wasn't nothing but an eighth-grade school, but they called us a college," Indian Joe Guyon said later. "Of course, some of us were pretty old by the time we got there." Guyon played two years at Carlisle, went backward to prep school, then on to Georgia Tech. (Yost, a repentant sinner after a reforming spasm hit Michigan, would not schedule Carlisle because "Warner does not in any way discourage professionalism among his men.")

Yale as ever led in these charades. Utterly in charge, Walter Camp modestly attributed Yale's athletic conquests to "the czar principle" at work. Students—the founders of intercollegiate sports—had long since been subordinated. The Yale Financial Union, consisting of Camp and the student managers of football, baseball, track, and rowing, pooled funds flowing to and from these major sports. While student managers came and went, Camp stayed on as treasurer, controlling the money year after year. He also oversaw the Yale Field Corporation, acting for alumni who owned and maintained the football field, and was a favored member of President Arthur Twining Hadley's inner cabinet. "Somehow, without exercising any great amount of political talent or pull," Camp explained to a Stanford administrator who had wondered how Yale did it, "I have in the vernacular 'corralled' all the offices in sight. . . . Between you and me it has proven wonderfully successful both from an economical stand point and a stand point when measured by athletic victories." (And then, remembering himself, "and finally and best of all from a stand point of keeping the tone of our athletics good.")

The Financial Union usually ran an annual surplus which Camp deposited into a secret reserve fund. Only he could tap this fund, answering to nobody save a seldom-consulted "investment committee" of three, one of whom, a local banker named Pierce Welch, himself borrowed more than $28,000 from the fund. Camp tapped the fund to pay a salary to Mike Murphy, the athletic trainer, and an annual $5,000 to himself for his part-time work supposedly undertaken for sports and Yale only. (A Yale full professor made about $3,500 a year.) In annual reports Camp hid these wages under expenses for "maintenance of the field." The accumulating surplus, never mentioned in the yearly reports, had piled up to $96,323 by 1905. It was a reserve fund of marked liquidity, with $41,000 distributed into four active accounts at New Haven and New York banks. Occasionally

Camp had to meet private rumors circulating among Yale men about this swelling sum. Undergraduate managers, Camp confided in 1900, could merely act in the short term. He needed to control long-range planning. Furthermore—the clinching argument to any Yale audience—"Harvard has a great many more rich graduates than we have" who in recent years had donated "a field, two fully equipped boat houses, two launches, and I hesitate to say what else. . . . Yet we are expected to compete on an equality with them." Nothing mattered more than victories over Harvard; Yale left the details to Camp.

For example, the All-American career of James J. Hogan. Born in Ireland, the son of a stonemason, and brought to Torrington, Connecticut, as a child, Jim Hogan had graduated from high school and started working for a hardware company when somebody noticed his football potential. A scholarship to Phillips Exeter was arranged. One of his teachers at Exeter remembered "the noble fight he made to get an education . . . always on the edge of his seat fighting for every bit of information that he could get and determined to master any particularly difficult subject. It was interesting and almost amusing at times to watch him. One could not help respecting such earnestness." Captain of the football team, he graduated from Exeter and—Camp's directing hand may be assumed—enrolled as a freshman at Yale, one month short of his twenty-seventh birthday.

A grown man among boys, 210 pounds and two inches under six feet, Jim Hogan was one of the great tackles in Yale history. Thick in the chest and neck, with his sleeves rolled above his muscular forearms he swung his mitts like flails against the enemy. Carrying the ball in tackle-back formations, he was "almost irresistible," with "overpowering strength in his legs." In crises he would bellow and cry, a bit of a showman, pushing his teammates to play harder. "He was a hard, strong, cheerful player," one observer noted; "that is, he was cheerful as long as the other men fought fair." Camp made him a first-team All-American for three years. As a senior Hogan was two years older than the Yale coach.

"We do not make exceptions to rules," said Camp, for public consumption. "Hence our men are not eligible if they have received money or compensation for ball playing." What, then, to make of this poor boy's plush life at Yale? Hogan lived in a suite at Vanderbilt Hall, the most opulent Yale dorm, and ate free meals at the University Club. A scholarship paid his tuition and gave him one hundred dollars a year. He made extra money from selling scorecards at baseball games, and on every pack of American Tobacco Company cigarettes sold in New Haven. After his last football game, Camp sent him with Mike Murphy on a two-week vacation to Cuba. (The cost of five hundred dollars was hidden under "miscellaneous expenses" in Camp's accounting.) A pampered favorite with the faculty, Hogan still plugged away at his books, made the coveted Skull and Bones society, and ranked in the top third of his class. But a nonathlete of similar academic promise would never have enjoyed such privileges. Long before official football scholarships, he was paid to play football.

Such shenanigans—common at any college that took football seriously—along with the ever-thudding brutality of mass plays pushed the game into its gravest crisis. Though the flying wedge had been outlawed, other techniques—especially the tackle-back formation devised by Camp as graduate guru to the Yale team—kept football mired and slogging in the center of the field. "Fateful, monotonous, stupid," one observer implored Camp. "We are tired of this contest of ponderous tortoises. Give the hare a chance." Twenty-one men and boys died playing football in 1904, then twenty-three more in 1905: only a few in college play, but college football governed the game. Columbia, Stanford, and California all abolished their teams. Alarmed observers demanded a more open game. Colleges outside the Northeast demanded representation on Camp's tightly held rules committee. To all this Camp offered small changes and soothing words, leaving his mass game intact and deadly. Ever since college he had staked his football life to Campball, his invented preserve, and he would not budge now.

But suddenly, he could *be* budged. In the summer of 1905 and again early in 1906, just as the football crisis was tightening, muckraking articles in the *New York Evening Post* and in two national magazines, *McClure's* and the *Outlook*, revealed the messy details of football affairs at Yale: the annual surpluses, the secret fund, the loan to Welch, the hidden salaries of Camp and Murphy, Hogan's pamperings and his free trip to Cuba, and the general air of "lavishness and luxury." Other publications passed along the juicy revelations. THE GREAT MONEY POWER AT YALE, one headline blared. "The possibilities for scandal in such loose conditions of accounting," another paper editorialized, "have been such as to take one's breath away." Enemies on the Yale faculty, restless for years under Camp's jock hegemony, now stood up, ammunition in hand. Under pressure, as part of what he called a "retrenchment" Camp took a pay cut to $3,750, then to $3,250. Jim Hogan, itching to reply in public, was kept quiet. President Hadley allowed a few reforms, though he still insisted the faculty had no jurisdiction in athletic matters. A few years later Camp resigned as treasurer of the Yale Field Corporation. His moral authority, always the ultimate source of his power, had suffered permanent damage.

With Camp wounded, football reformers settled on a startling innovation, the forward pass, as the best way back to a more open game. Camp would not hear of it. Teddy Roosevelt called men from Harvard, Yale, and Princeton to lunch at the White House and told them to put football on "a thoroughly clean basis." Camp treated it as advice from a Harvard man. So Chancellor Henry MacCracken of New York University convened a rump conference of colleges not represented on the rules committee. (Earlier in that fall of 1905, a player for Union College had been killed in a game against NYU.) Captain Palmer Pierce of West Point emerged as leader of the secessionists. After rumblings back and forth, the old rules committee and the new group merged to form what became the National Collegiate Athletic Association, with Camp replaced by a reformer on the joint rules committee. Following recommendations by men from Penn and Annapolis (and quiet enabling maneuvers by Harry Williams of Minnesota, one of Camp's boys), the NCAA then legalized the forward pass and, over the next few years, added other field-openers: no pushing or pulling of ballcarriers, no interlocking arms or pass interference, and four downs to make ten yards instead of three to make five. Initial restrictions on the pass were gradually lifted. Football became less brutal—up to a point. Camp, ever the good sportsman, stayed involved at the highest levels of football, but his reign had ended.

As teams learned to use the forward pass, football returned to its old style, with the action spread across the field, longer solitary runs and tackles, balls in the air, and more visible thrills for fans. Schools outside the Northeast—especially Chicago, Oklahoma, and St. Louis University—first made regular use of the new weapon. The pass came east, emphatically, in November 1913 when Notre Dame played at West Point in what Camp called the "most startling" game of the year. Palmer Pierce must have rued what he had wrought back in 1906: Army, heavily favored, lost, 35–13, as Notre Dame completed 13 of 17 passes for 243 yards. On one crucial, telling play, quarterback Gus Dorais sent Knute Rockne deep. "I started limping down the field," Rockne recalled, "and the Army halfback covering me almost yawned in my face, he was that bored. Suddenly, I put on full speed and left him standing there flat-footed." He caught a 40-yard pass in the end zone. "At the moment when I touched the ball," said Rockne, "life for me was complete."

◆   ◆   ◆

"One of the impressive features in the evolution of foot ball," wrote Parke Davis, a gridiron historian, in 1926, "is the periodic appearance of some play of the early days . . . to be discovered by some modern tactical student and suddenly brought forth."

◆   ◆   ◆

A reasonably stable pro football league emerged finally from the town teams of Ohio. The earlier semipro teams, when conceived amid lingering amateur ideals by college-bred gentlemen, had not survived the transition to full-blown professionalism. The Ohio town teams, founded by local boosters to hammer ancient rivals, and fully if modestly professional from the outset, were sustained by simpler, monolithic purposes. The athletes, typically blue-collar local boys instead of expensive college mercenaries, played for their teams year after year, building continuous traditions and needs for revenge. They were pushed by football's sharpest, hoariest motivator: a hard, nasty pleasure in belting old enemies. That goad sustained the Ohio town teams for two decades and eventually formed the core of a new National Football League.

The Shelby Blues, started around 1900, drew mainly from employees of the Shelby Steel Tube Company. "There was not a player on the team that ever went to college," one Shelby fan recalled, "and some of them did not get very far in grade school." They practiced after work and played any opponent they could find on Saturday—usually at home because Shelby offered the only field in those parts with chalk lines. Occasionally they hired an outside ringer such as Charles Follis, a black halfback, or Branch Rickey, who had played football and baseball for Ohio Wesleyan. "When I found I could get up to a hundred and fifty dollars a game, I grabbed it," Rickey said later. "I was strong, fast and healthy." A ferocious competitor at end, Rickey broke his right leg just above the ankle in one Shelby game and refused to leave until he was carried off the field. With the town population under five thousand, the games pulled crowds of twenty-five hundred to stand along the sidelines. Lacking a grandstand, the richer fans would draw their buggies close to the field. It was football without frills. The all-purpose water bucket offered a big sponge and a restoring mixture of water and rolled oats. A thirsty player would suck from the sponge; the same sponge would wash off a bleeding cut, then be thrown back into the bucket; the next man would squeeze out the blood, resoak the sponge, and suck. "You should have seen that water at the close of the game," a water boy remembered, "but those were the good old days."

The Columbus Panhandles were formed about 1902 by men who toiled for the Panhandle division of the Pennsylvania Railroad. (This connection got them free railroad passes to away games.) The key Panhandle figures were Joe Carr, a machinist who moonlighted as a sportswriter for the *Ohio State Journal,* and Ted Nesser, one of six large football-playing brothers born to German immigrants in Columbus. The Panhandles, too, had not learned the game in college. ("I have been playing foot-ball for quite a number of seasons and we allways have conferance Officials," Nesser wrote to Walter Camp. "One thing they cannot make plain to me is the oppertunity for making fair catch. . . . They claim the signal is not neccesary [Nesser's spelling]. Who is right?") With six Nessers on the field, averaging more than 220 pounds each, the Panhandles heaped family pride on top of community loyalty, a double dose of belligerent cohesion. Joe Carr, team manager for twenty years, remembered a characteristic gesture at a game in 1908: Ted Nesser, injured early, sat on the bench in agony, swathed in blankets, with two bones of his left arm protruding from the skin. Urged to go see a doctor, he stayed through the game. "I ain't going to desert the boys," he explained. "They like to know I'm here." Al Nesser, the youngest brother, never wore shoulder pads or a helmet to shield his balding skull. Such Nesserian toughness set standards for the other Panhandles. "In many ways a unique team," Carr said later, "we often approached greatness."

The sharpest rivalry played out between two towns in Stark County, south of Akron: Canton, the county seat, with a population of around fifty thousand, and Massillon, seven miles to the west, a quarter the size of Canton and ever conscious of that disparity. In 1903 Edward Stewart, editor of the *Massillon Independent,* created the Massillon Tigers essentially in order to engage Canton's Bulldogs at football. "The crowds were mostly rubber, steel, and factory workers," one Massillon player recalled. "The games were played on baseball fields with stands on one side and a rope stretched across on the other; that was standing room only, where most of the betting took place." Grounded in local talent and hatreds, neither team had much luck with hired guns. In 1905 Canton paid Willie Heston, a Michigan halfback of large reputation, a rumored six hundred dollars for one game against Massillon; the Tigers won anyway, 14–4, and claimed a third straight Ohio title. A year later Canton tried again with Blondy Wallace, the itinerant footballer. Massillon won yet again as Wallace fomented a betting scandal and left town hurriedly. Embarrassed and broke, the Canton-Massillon series subsided for a few years, then inevitably revived in 1911. (In the hoodlum football tradition of Big Bill Thompson, Wallace later wound up as an accomplished bootlegger in Atlantic City.)

Canton took a giant step toward bigger things in 1914 when Jack Cusack, the team manager, found an angel in a local brewer named J. J. Frey. With a ten-thousand-dollar line of credit at the Canton Bank, Cusack in 1915 hired Jim Thorpe, the most famous athlete in America. An All-American at Carlisle, then the star of the 1912 Olympics, Thorpe had just finished his third season as a light-hitting reserve outfielder for the New York Giants. At football, his metier, he excelled in every phase of the game as a crunching runner and tackler, a peerless punter and dropkicker of field goals. "Jim would shift his hip toward the guy about to tackle him, then swing it away," his teammate Pete Calac recalled, "and then, when the player moved in to hit him, he'd swing his hip back, hard, against the tackler's head and leave him laying there." On defense he tackled "like a steam roller," throwing his body into the opponent's back, ramming at kidneys and ribs with his heavy old leather shoulder pads that felt like iron to the victim. Thorpe became the first consistent gate attraction in pro football, with his name billed above his team's, more famous than any squad he might play for. "The big Indian hated practice and generally would go coon hunting instead. Often he didn't even know the signals," said his sometime teammate Fats Henry. "But how he enjoyed the game in his early years! I can still hear that deep-throated laugh of his as he crashed through, flattening everything in sight."

Thorpe earned his $250 a game for Canton. Averaging 1,200 fans a game earlier in that 1915 season, with Thorpe they drew 6,000 at Massillon—the Tigers won, 16–0, as Thorpe slipped on a wet field—then 8,000 for the rematch in Canton. There he kicked two field goals and, after howling arguments, Canton finally beat Massillon, 6–0. Given that boost, Cusack in 1916 hired what was probably the best football team yet assembled, with Thorpe, his Carlisle mate Pete Calac, and other college stars from Harvard, Wisconsin, Syracuse, and Dartmouth. The line averaged 213 pounds from end to end. Thorpe unloaded an 85-yard punt as Canton beat the Columbus Panhandles, 12–0. They played a scoreless tie in Massillon, then clobbered the Tigers in Canton, 24–0, before two raucous crowds of 10,000. For the season they went undefeated in ten games, outscoring the enemy, 264–7. Pro football had reached a newly respectable level of skill and popularity. On the model of baseball's National League, then entering its fifth decade, the leaders of Ohio's town teams started talking, once again, about a pro football league of national scope.

Delayed by the world war, the National Football League came to flickering life in the summer of 1920. On August 20, meeting at Ralph Hay's automobile agency on McKinley Avenue in Canton, men from the town teams of Akron, Dayton, Cleveland, and Canton formed a loose association to cooperate in scheduling, and promised to limit salaries and not to steal each other's players. Over the next six weeks they pulled in ten other teams from Ohio, Indiana, Illinois, and western New York. Joe Carr of the Columbus Panhandles, one of these fourteen charter members, was by seniority the obvious choice to administer the new league. "We need the biggest possible name to serve as president," Carr demurred, so the job went to Jim Thorpe instead. Thorpe did publicize the league on the field, playing for seven teams in eight years, but he avoided his slight presidential duties. (One applicant for an NFL franchise found Thorpe playing billiards at a Louisville hotel. He was too busy to talk, said Thorpe, and suggested that the man not apply for league membership.) In 1921 Carr took over as league president for one thousand dollars a year to start, and stayed on until his death in 1939.

Aside from Carr, the new league's main stabilizer became George Halas and his Chicago Bears. As player, coach, and executive, Halas was a thundering presence in the NFL for more than sixty years, the individual most responsible for the league's survival and ultimate prosperity. Born in Chicago to Roman Catholic immigrants from Bohemia, raised in a Bohemian neighborhood, he and his brothers were sent to public school "to speed our development as Americans," he said later. His father worked successively as a newspaper reporter, tailor, landlord, and saloon owner. In the classic pattern repeated by many new Americans, sports beckoned young George out of old-country ways. His warmest early memories were of street softball games on mild summer evenings, under gaslight, with manhole covers and sewer grills for bases. He played college football at Illinois for Bob Zuppke, a noted coach; his older brother Walter, also an Illinois alumnus, later coached under Rockne at Notre Dame. Both college connections served Halas well in the NFL.

In 1920 A. E. Staley, a starch manufacturer in Decatur, Illinois, hired Halas to start a football team designed to advertise his business. The players all worked in the plant and practiced for two hours a day on company time. "We were starch workers first and football players second," George Trafton recalled. "I received a salary for paddling starch. And I mean there was no kidding around. I had to work." The Staleys placed second to Akron in the new league's first season. A year later, when Staley dropped the team, Halas moved them up to Chicago. Playing at Wrigley Field, home of the Cubs, Halas piggybacked on the popular baseball team by calling his boys the Bears. Trafton, whom Rockne had expelled from Notre Dame for playing semi-pro football on the side, became the prototypical Bear: a mean, dirty, very effective center hated and feared throughout the NFL. At six feet two inches and 235 pounds, he waged noisy domestic battles with his first wife, was known as the best bar-room fighter in Chicago—"You've got to quit being a fool," Rockne scolded him—and later opened a famous boxing gym on Randolph Street: a Bear to the heart.

Another original member of the Staleys, Guy Chamberlin, compiled a remarkable coaching record over the first decade of the NFL. A tall, handsome end from Nebraska, he played and coached the Canton Bulldogs to undefeated seasons in 1922 and 1923. Despite two straight NFL titles the Bulldogs tumbled into debt and were bought, for only twenty-five hundred dollars, by a Cleveland sports promoter named Sam Deutsch. Chamberlin and six other Bulldogs moved on to Cleveland, where in 1924 they won another league championship and went broke again. In the ever-foundering young league, adding and deleting teams each year, even the best teams might go under. Chamberlin and his star tackle, Link Lyman, shifted to the Frankford Yellow Jackets of Philadelphia, the first strong NFL team in the East. The Yellow Jackets went 13-7 in 1925, then 14-1-1 in 1926 for Chamberlin's fourth title in five years of coaching. A year later, after a grim season with the Chicago Cardinals, Chamberlin left the league for good, still only thirty-three years old. His career winning percentage of .763 remains the best in NFL history.

Two developments in 1925 implied a more stable future for pro football. The NFL added its first permanent team in New York City, potentially the richest football market in the country. It turned on another Ohio connection: Harry March, a doctor raised and schooled in Stark County, then briefly associated with the Canton Bulldogs, had moved to New York after the world war. "If professional football goes in the Middle West," some-body asked him, "why won't it go here?" Why indeed? March went to see Tex Rickard, manager of Jack Dempsey and lord of Madison Square Garden, who passed him on to Billy Gibson, manager of Gene Tunney and well-connected sportsman around town. Gibson wasn't interested either, but loitering in his office when March came along was Tim Mara. A bookie and horse racing man, Mara had never seen a pro football game. But an NFL franchise cost only five hundred dollars, petty cash for such a high roller. "The Giants were founded on brute strength and ignorance," Mara liked to recall. "The players supplied the strength and I supplied the ignorance." Mara left the team management to March and concentrated on promotion. A big, ruddy-faced man in a derby hat and a coat with a velvet collar, Mara talked up this new toy on his endless rounds of parties, saloons, and racetracks, handing out tickets at half-price or no price. ("You could tell him he had to make germs the most popular thing in town," said his drinking buddy Toots Shor, "and he'd find a way . . . a promotional genius.")

Red Grange, the most celebrated football player yet, also joined the NFL in 1925. A lean six-footer, more grace than power, at Illinois he had established a unique running style: cruising along apparently at three-quarter speed, as a tackler closed in he would juke and wiggle, swerve and swoop, changing directions without losing momentum and leaving the tackler lunging at nothing but air. "He ran with such little effort that he appeared slow," recalled his college coach Bob Zuppke, "and not until one noticed the violent effort of his pursuers was it noticeable how fast Red really was." It looked magical, beyond understanding or description; the "Galloping Ghost" drifted through broken fields like a disembodied spirit, setting incredulous fans to howling and wondering. Such mysterious feats (How did he *do* that?) made him an unmatched gate attraction.

After Grange's last college game in November 1925, Halas— using his Illinois connections—signed him for the Bears. On Thanksgiving Day against the Chicago Cardinals, they drew 36,000 (the biggest pro football crowd yet) to the last NFL game of the season. In early December Grange and the Bears ground through a barnstorming tour of the East and Midwest, eight numbing games in twelve days. Tim Mara had lost forty thousand dollars on the Giants that first year; Grange pulled a stupefying crowd of 73,000 to the Polo Grounds, the biggest throng that had ever witnessed a football game in Manhattan. "Grange played through the first period and part of the second without performing any astonishing feats," Damon Runyon reported. But late in the game, when the Giants tried a pass, "the muddy lean-flanked figure of Red Grange came from nowhere. He reached up and grabbed the ball in the air, whirled and sprinted across the New York goal line for a touchdown. No New York player was close to him as he loped along, his knees lifting high with every stride and his hips swaying." Mara was persuaded not to fold his football hand just yet.

According to the legend later stoked by Halas in particular, this Grange tour established the NFL as a visible, financially solid big league. Actually its effects were ambiguous. After peaking at the Polo Grounds, the barnstormers limped through the remaining stops, cold and hurting. On their special Pullman the trainer might work through the night patching the boys together for their game the next day on some frozen field. In Boston an injured Grange couldn't do much; when he flipped the ball to the referee, scornful fans cheered sarcastically for the completed pass. Only five thousand showed up at Pittsburgh as Grange left the game early. In Detroit, when they announced he couldn't play, thousands demanded refunds. Many newspapers denounced the tour for exploiting Grange and not delivering the promised show.

Afterward the NFL remained a precarious operation for years to come. Twelve of twenty-three franchises were "suspended" to start the 1927 season. Later that year, only eighty-three paying customers braved harsh weather for a Bears game at the Polo Grounds. ("Halas and I thought of calling it off," Mara remembered. "Then we decided to play just for the fun of it.") Fun or not, the Giants lost fifty-four thousand dollars in 1928. Even with the Bears, the trainer would have to wait for the first dozen tickets to be sold on game day, then take the cash to go buy tape for the team's ankles. Teams still had to arrange their own games; the league office issued no schedule and kept no official statistics. The NFL continued to lurch from game to game, year to year.

The signing and selling of Red Grange also handed live ammunition to the enemies of pro football. In luring Grange to leave college before graduation, Halas had broken an NFL rule that was supposed to mollify guardians of amateur football. Coach Zuppke refused to speak to Grange for years afterward. Given the shady history of pro football, critics could reasonably warn of gamblers, fixes, and other debaucheries. Football had always depended on visceral, emotional motivations, on love of alma mater or hatred for a neighboring town. How, then, asked the critics, could mere paid mercenaries care enough to play the game hard and well? "The professional game is not worth watching," said the *Outlook* in 1926. "What the promoters have failed to realize is that they have taken hold of a game that is essentially rooted in amateurism." Coach Amos Alonzo Stagg of the University of Chicago revoked the varsity letters of any of his boys who turned pro. Once, finding his team on an eastbound train with the NFL's Chicago Cardinals, Stagg locked the doors between the two squads to avoid professional contamination. "It is purely a parasitical growth on intercollegiate football," said Stagg, the game's grand old man. "Football on such terms is a travesty, a Shetland pony rodeo, a vegetarian guzzle."

Joe Carr did his best. Not a college graduate, he contended with "too many college men on newspapers who thought we were a menace," he said later. "It was slow work convincing them we had a legitimate venture and a great sporting show." From the league office in Columbus, the hometown he never left, Carr enforced rules and led cheers for his ever-changing roster of NFL teams. Also involved in pro basketball and minor-league baseball, he could tap into connections among sportsmen and sportswriters all around the country. Quiet, diligent but colorless, he lacked flair and vision; he had the soul of a bookkeeper. "Joe Carr's a nice guy and he's good with paperwork," said an unfriendly team owner, George Richards of the Detroit Lions, "but what this league needs is a promoter, a man with new ideas and contacts to get things rolling." Carr by himself could never achieve his ambition of lifting the NFL to parity with major-league baseball.

The league's problems came down to the game on the field. The single-wing offenses used by most teams kept the action bunched in the middle of the line, with few long runs or passes.

Aside from the pioneer passer Benny Friedman, few quarter-backs dared put the ball in the air, where fans liked to see it. The NFL generally played a ground-bound, low-scoring, crowd-boring game. In 1931 half the squads averaged seven points or fewer per game. Dwindling crowds during the Depression cut into NFL franchises; from twelve teams in 1929, the league fell to its all-time low of eight teams in 1932. That season an average game yielded a total of only sixteen points for both teams, the lowest scoring level since 1926. After a dozen years, the NFL was tottering.

◆   ◆   ◆

Amid trumpets and fanfare of his own devising, George Preston Marshall arrived to save the league. A grossly obnoxious person-ality—bullying to subordinates, stingy to his players, and a spoiled, willful child at league meetings—he was still the show-man the NFL needed. Part Barnum, part Rasputin, he blew into pro football in 1932, just when it had bottomed out, and remade the game in his own noisy, commercial image. "Football is a game of pageantry. . . . Its great success is due to the color sur-rounding it. It needs music and bands," he preached. "Two teams scrimmaging without music and bands is like a musical show without an orchestra." Always a fan, never a player, Mar-shall saw the game from the perspective of customers in the stands waiting to be entertained. With unique insight and head-long forcefulness, he delivered what the fans wanted.

Growing up in the small town of Grafton, West Virginia, Marshall had launched his first promotion at age eleven. By placing an ad in his father's newspaper, he sold a rabbit worth $.40 for $1.25. A few years later, his destiny already apparent, he was shilling a semipro football team. (On some games he cleared twenty-five bucks.) When the family moved to Washing-ton, Marshall—still in his teens—mounted the stage, playing hammy roles at theaters here and there. The lure of greasepaint and footlights, and a knack for playing to an audience, never left him. Only twenty-two when his father died in 1918, Marshall took over the family laundry business in characteristic fashion. "I wrote advertisements that were designed to amuse as well as to sell," he recalled. "We decked our employees in blue-and-gold

Football

uniforms, with plenty of paint to match on our branch offices. I grabbed all the publicity that I could get." On a slogan of "Long Live Linen," the business grew to fifty-three stores and seven hundred employees cleaning more than fifty thousand shirts a week. Not wishing to deprive the public of the sight of Marshall in full cry, he worked in an office on the first floor of a downtown building, with a huge window facing the street so that passersby could see him dictating, telephoning, and plotting his next moves. On the side he played in Democratic politics, inhabited nightclubs and society columns, married a Hollywood actress, was often glimpsed at racetracks, published a Washington newspaper, and ran four theaters and a pro basketball team.

The NFL had never seen anybody like him. Buying into the shaky Boston franchise in 1932, he came to his first league meeting and outlined the wholesale changes he had in mind. The football men laughed at the laundry man, but he eventually got his way. Marshall and George Halas, "bosom enemies," formed a contentious alliance that came to dominate league affairs. "When I knew he had a particular project in mind," Halas recalled, "I would start off ahead of time by playing it down, even though I believed in it and knew that eventually I would vote for it. I would touch on the subject and talk about the weaknesses of it and why it would not help the game. Then Marshall would get up at his end of the table and rave and rant, which I enjoyed so much." Once the team owners labored for days over the league schedule chalked on a blackboard; Marshall, not pleased, stood up and erased it, wiping out the only copy and sending everybody back to two more days of work. If the others balked at some Marshall idea, he would table the matter, then spring it again at the end of the meeting. Tired and ready to go, the others would shrug—the hell with it—and agree.

By such maneuvers Marshall made NFL football a more commercial product. The league issued its first schedule and set up a climactic play-off game for the title to conclude the season. To encourage aerial displays, various inhibiting rules were dropped, and the ball was slimmed by about two inches around the middle. (This new passer's ball meant the end of drop-kicking.) Balls out of bounds were brought in ten yards for the next play, and goalposts were moved from the back of the end zone to the goal

251

line. Substitutions became freer. Communications between coaches and quarterbacks were allowed. Roughing the passer was prohibited. An annual all-star game, the Pro Bowl, was launched. A college draft each year gave the weakest teams the first shot at the best new talent. Almost all these improvements were Marshall's inventions. In their wake, scoring increased from nineteen points a game in 1933 to twenty-seven points a game five years later. More action on the field meant better action at the box office. From an average crowd of five thousand or less early in the decade, attendance climbed to nearly twenty thousand a game by 1939. The league's roster of teams finally stabilized. The NFL had reached "an established place in the field of professional sports," Joe Carr said shortly before his death in 1939, "as important in its way as the American and National baseball leagues."

For a while Marshall had less success with his own team. To coach his Boston Redskins he hired Lone Star Dietz, of Indian ancestry, and outfitted the team in feathers and war paint for photographs before the first game. Then they played, still in war paint. "The paint bothered some of the boys because it clogged their pores," recalled Cliff Battles, a Redskin halfback. "The whole thing was so overdone it was embarrassing." Marshall sat on the bench yelling orders, orated at halftime, sent players into the game with heartfelt, baffling instructions. The Redskins kept losing. After running through four coaches in five years, and a total loss of eighty-five thousand dollars, he brought the Redskins home to Washington. He gave them a marching band, 150 strong, in costumes of burgundy and gold with white feather headdresses from Hollywood, and fancy halftime shows. More to the point, he drafted Sammy Baugh out of Texas Christian University. (When Baugh flew to Washington, Marshall had him emerge from the plane in full cowboy regalia to greet the press.) The best NFL passer since Benny Friedman, Baugh led the Redskins to a championship in 1937. Marshall was hooked for life; the National Football League survived.

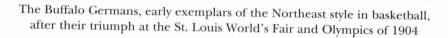

The Buffalo Germans, early exemplars of the Northeast style in basketball, after their triumph at the St. Louis World's Fair and Olympics of 1904

The SPHAS of the South Philadelphia Hebrew Association, Jewish hoop champs of the Northeast in the early 1920s; Eddie Gottlieb *(last player on right)* later became a basketball impresario and the dominant figure in the early NBA

The New York Original Celtics, the best basketball team of the 1920s, and foremost proponents of the Northeast style. *Left to right:* Johnny Beckman, Nat Holman, Chris Leonard, owner/embezzler Jim Furey, Joe Lapchick, Dutch Dehnert, and Pete Barry

Barnstorming through basketball America, the Celtics passing time in yet another hotel room. *Left to right:* Beckman, Dehnert, Barry, and Lapchick

The Harvard football team of 1893;
William H. Lewis, the first black All-
American, is the third from left in
back row, in dark sweatshirt

Fritz Pollard of Brown, in 1916 the
second black All-American; later a
star halfback and coach in the early
years of the NFL

The New York Renaissance Big Five—the Rens—the best basketball team of the 1930s. *Left to right:* Fat Jenkins, Bill Yancey, John Holt, Pappy Ricks, Eyre Saitch, Tarzan Cooper, and Wee Willie Smith

Action from a Rens–SPHAS (Hebrews) game at the Renaissance Casino on Thanksgiving night, 1937, won by Rens 32–26; Willie Smith leaping over a SPHA for the tip

The two major figures in the reintegration of baseball: Branch Rickey, general manager of the Brooklyn Dodgers, who always sought ballplayers who could run; and Jackie Robinson in his minor-league uniform (a publicity still from the 1950 movie *The Jackie Robinson Story*)

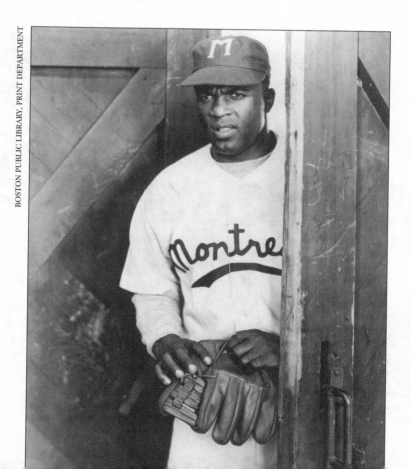

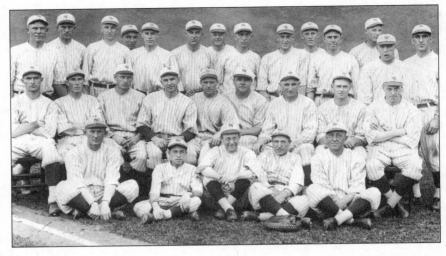

The 1921 New York Yankees, the first Yankee pennant-winner; Babe Ruth, fourth from right in second row, hit .378 with 59 homers, 171 RBIs, and an .846 slugging percentage; manager Miller Huggins in middle of first row; at his right hand, mascot/bat boy Eddie Bennett

Ed Barrow, Yankee general manager; the canny front office behind the Huggins and McCarthy teams of the 1920s and 1930s

Lou Gehrig's powerful hands and forearms ("I'm an arm hitter"); the grip that produced the third-best career slugging percentage in baseball history

In uncharacteristic repose, Vince Lombardi of the Green Bay Packers, who dominated pro football in the 1960s by exploiting the cycles of sports history

The Packers in 1962, NFL champs for the second year in a row, on their way to five titles in seven years; here behaving like ballplayers

The man with sixteen NBA titles, Red
Auerbach of the Boston Celtics, blissfully
engaged in running the Celtics bench and
berating a zebra

Bob Cousy, the best guard of
the 1950s, reaching for a ball
late in his career

Bill Russell, the first great
hoopster who could
neither shoot nor dribble,
led the Celtics to eight
titles in a row and eleven
in thirteen years

Chapter Six

Basketball:
A Scientific Game

Pro basketball took its initial shots during the first decade of the twentieth century, in the northeastern part of the country, especially the hooped states of Pennsylvania, New Jersey, and New York. In those years a half dozen regional leagues drew up schedules and struggled through a few seasons before flickering out. The game, still so new, had already assumed its basic form: two five-man teams trying to throw a large ball through a horizontal hoop suspended ten feet from the floor. Two aspects at once distinguished the game from baseball and football, its only rivals as popular American team sports. Basketball was played indoors, during the winter, in varied settings of gloriously diverse eccentricities. And basketball, devised in 1891, had no hoary folk-game traditions behind it, no slow evolution from centuries of sport; so nobody knew how to play it, leaving all the details of this invented game in a perpetual, unlimited state of tinkering and reinvention.

The ballplayers on a typical pro team of the early 1900s were men of average size or a bit less. A stray big guy might play guard, the main defensive position; height was not yet deemed a particular advantage on offense. In full uniform the teams looked heavily armored, with padded pants, tights or knee socks on the legs, long-sleeved smocks, pads at the elbows, hips, and knees, and perhaps nose guards or mouthpieces. The standard basketball shoe, a canvas high-top, had a rubber sole stippled with holes for traction. Many starting teams played the whole game, with only one or two forlorn subs on the bench hoping to get in. During a fast game the elaborate uniform, shoes, and pads absorbed sweat, gaining weight as the players tired, dragging them down and slowing the pace.

The ball, a few ounces heavier and a few inches fatter around than a modern basketball, grew stretched and lopsided under hard use, leaving an unwieldy puzzle for shooting or dribbling. Its resistance to easy control encouraged a two-handed game. The inner bladder's inflation valve, pushed down and laced over, left a lump that might make the ball bounce oddly or yaw in flight. Players would try to center the lump and laces in their hands before shooting or passing. Bouncing on unkempt floors, the porous leather cover picked up dirt and sweat, blackening and slicking with age. "When you shot the ball, you could see it going up by leaps and bounds depending on how the air would hit the laces," recalled Joe Schwarzer, a veteran of the early New York State League. "If it hits the rim on the laces, God knows what would happen. So when you shot, you wanted the ball to rotate just once, and you didn't want the laces to hit the rim."

On offense, the early pros deployed few types of passes but many kinds of shots. Most passes were two-handed, from the chest; long baseball passes or bounce passes in close action were uncommon. Except for leaping one-handed layups, players usually shot from a balanced, stationary position with both feet on the floor. Launching the quarrelsome ball, they tried one-handers, two-handers, overhead pumps from under the basket, underhand sets from distance; but, as yet, no hook shots or jumpers except in an atypical, unrepeated moment of inspiration. On the rare occasions when somebody scored, play stopped while the ball was fished from the unyielding net and brought out to a center jump. The center would tell his teammates by signal or gesture where he planned to tip the ball, and the game would resume. In the "guards down" play, a favorite, the center tipped to a forward while both guards broke for the basket; the forward passed to one guard, who dribbled down and dished to the other guard for a layup. This play might surprise the opponents because guards usually stayed back to concentrate on defense. Aside from these recurrent tap-offs, teams used few strategies or set plays. Everybody was still making the game up in flight, reading game situations as they developed, responding by recently honed instincts.

The playing court offered none of the relative uniformity of a baseball diamond or football gridiron. Lacking arenas built specifically for basketball, the early pros played in Masonic temples and YMCA and settlement-house gyms, with overhanging tracks and gymnastic equipment scattered around; in National Guard armories, vast and musty halls often unheated and ill lit; on the stages of theaters and auditoriums, with short courts and an easy tumble into the orchestra pit; in dance halls, slipping and sliding on the polished floors; and in boxing arenas, with a pugilistic crowd yelling for blood. Backboards were made of wood, metal, glass, or chicken wire, each surface lending its own quirk to the game. The basket might be hung six inches from the backboard, or twelve inches, or even (in the New York State League) suspended from a pole with no backboard at all. The variable playing floor might be bordered by hot radiators or dotted with posts, pillars, or wood-burning stoves: all ideal for setting implacable picks on the opposition. ("Post" plays started with a literal post.) Low ceilings or flush walls were sometimes in play, depending on the local rules; a trick shot would bounce the ball off the ceiling down to the hoop, or its vicinity. On other courts, a shooter would have to thread the ball through rafters to reach the hoop.

Such unpredictable venues gave the home team special advantages. A visiting team faced an odd, unfamiliar court—and a forceful crowd *within walls*. The home fans, their cheering contained and echoed indoors—unlike the outdoor din at baseball and football games—were close and involved, all of them on top of the action. Aside from firing palpable gusts of crowd noise, they might shine mirrors into the eyes of the shooters, flip cigars and cigarettes at the enemy, poke them with parasols and hatpins, throw bottles and bottle tops, or shake the backboards to rattle unfriendly foul shooters. Basketball fans came to the game expecting to participate, to help the right team win.

In part to minimize such interference, some early pro leagues played in a cage: a fence of rope or wire mesh, ten to twenty feet high, closely bordering the court on all four sides. Thus contained, the ball seldom went out of bounds and courtside fans were protected from diving ballplayers. (Otherwise the first team to touch the ball *after* it went out of bounds got possession, leading to wild scrambles off the court.) "The ball is continually before the eye and always in play," a cage advocate explained. Cages did encourage a faster, less interrupted game. Players learned to use the cage wall as a second surface, bouncing passes and shots off the netting, even climbing walls for acrobatic scores. One man remembered a crowd-prodding feat by Andy Suils and Jack Inglis during a pro game in Carbondale, Pennsylvania: "Suils threw a very high lead pass. Inglis leaped into the air on the left side of the basket, grasped the net enclosing the court and, flexing his left arm, raised his entire body higher into the air. He turned to his right, caught the pass from Suils with his right hand and with the same motion shot the ball cleanly through the basket."

But the cages also encouraged brutal play. A defender could force his man against the netting or a splintery support post, grab the wire on either side, and pin him there for a jump ball. The metal cages, in particular, left burns and cuts. Honus Wagner, the great Pirate shortshop, played pro basketball in Pennsylvania leagues to balance his beer drinking in the off-season. "Basketball was just a sport for me," he said, "and I got a lot of fun out of it." When he came to spring training covered with wire burns, though, the Pirate owner asked him to confine himself to the gentler sport of big-league baseball. Early pros remembered, wincing, the sheer pain of playing cage ball—scraped and bleeding, tears in their eyes—with few respites from the furious, continuous action. Confined to the cage, with a yowling crowd outside, they might feel like death-sport combatants on display. "You could play tick-tack-toe on everybody after a game," said one man. "You were like a gladiator, and if you didn't get rid of the ball, you could get killed."

Whether played in a cage or not, early pro basketball was fiercely rough and dangerous. Rowdy play offended fans and helped kill off leagues. "If the officials are not backed up," an observer noted, "the games become regular indoor football contests, players being injured and spectators becoming disgusted." Some leagues allowed a two-handed, discontinuous dribble; a strong man could bull his way down the court, backing in, dribbling, picking it up, dribbling again, till he reached the basket. Only a full-bore fistfight would move the ref to toss players from the game. With no disqualifications for committing too many fouls, everybody fouled at will. The refs overlooked most contact anyway. A defender could virtually jump on his man, or swing his arms violently around the head of anybody with the ball. "When a guard met a forward, or any other player, head-on—no hipping or shouldering—just plain front to front—it was not called a foul," one man remembered. "All that was necessary was to make the play on the ball . . . you could play the ball and put all you wanted in back of your play. If the player who was dribbling happened to be right in back of the ball—that was his fault."

◆   ◆   ◆

This was not the game Jim Naismith had in mind. To a greater degree than even Alex Cartwright or Walter Camp, Naismith had *invented* a sport, intentionally, self-consciously, with prescribed qualities to meet stated needs. Baseball and football, childish pastimes of checkered reputations, had become respectable as adults took to them. Basketball, first played by adults with serious purposes, was born respectable but then outgrew it.

Naismith's creation was a byproduct—and the most popular, durable legacy—of the powerful Protestant evangelical movement known as muscular Christianity. Proclaimed in the late 1800s by such prominent preachers as Dwight L. Moody and Henry Ward Beecher, this movement—catching and building on the athletic waves of the time—adopted sports as the sign and vehicle of a full-bodied, vigorous Protestant faith. Muscular Christians built YMCA gyms, integrated sports into school curricula, preached the manliness of hard competition and fair play, and so added sweating and grunting to the routine tasks of the faithful. Like many other young people of sporting taste and deep belief, James Naismith was drawn by the movement's compelling double lure of fun and righteousness.

Soberly earnest and striving, the young Naismith was a product of hard circumstances. Born in 1861 in a small town in southern Ontario, the son of a Scottish-immigrant carpenter, then orphaned at eight, he grew up on an uncle's farm near Almonte, Ontario. With his schooling interrupted by farmwork, he was twenty-one when he graduated from high school. Strong from the farm, he played rugby football at McGill University, then worked out in a gym while attending a Presbyterian seminary in Montreal. He hoped to preach but lacked, it turned out, the necessary ease and eloquence in a pulpit. "There were other ways of influencing young people than preaching," he decided. "In games it was easily seen that the man who took his part in a manly way and yet kept his thoughts and conduct clean had the respect and the confidence of the most careless. It was a short step to the conclusion that hard clean athletics could be used to set a high standard of living for the young." In the fall of 1890 he enrolled at a YMCA training school, a citadel of muscular Christianity, in Springfield, Massachusetts. There he played on a football team coached by Amos Alonzo Stagg, fresh from his sporting feats at Yale. "Jim, I play you at center," Stagg told him, "because you can do the meanest things in the most gentlemanly manner."

Luther H. Gulick, the son and grandson of missionaries, and a tireless evangelist for muscular Christianity, hired Naismith upon graduation to teach at the Springfield school. Late in the fall of 1891, Gulick assigned him a task that had frustrated two other instructors. A class of eighteen future YMCA directors, seasoned men in their late twenties and early thirties, had become bored and grumpy in gym class with the usual routine of indoor games and exercises. "Those boys simply would not play drop the handkerchief!" Naismith recalled. "What could we give them? There was no indoor game that would invoke the enthusiasm of football or baseball." He tried indoor versions of football, baseball, and a dozen other games; all proved too rough or too dull. He needed a game of contained vigor: fast and exciting to engage older men who would have preferred football, but safe for a small gym, a hardwood floor, and Christian principles.

Instead of merely offering a workout, Naismith was determined to appeal to ballplaying instincts. The given framework, then, was two teams with a ball; a large ball, he decided, thus softer and less dangerous—a soccer ball would do. If the target were a horizontal goal, above their heads, they would have to shoot the ball with delicate lobs, not hard pegs. (Here Naismith remembered a game from his childhood—duck on the rock—in which the players lofted rocks in gentle arcs to dislodge a larger stone target.) For the arrangement of players on the floor and an initial method of putting the ball in play, Naismith drew on elements of rugby and lacrosse, familiar Canadian games. But the most crucial element was pure, original inspiration. To avoid hard contact on a hard floor, Naismith decided the ball could only be advanced by passes from one man to another. "Don't let him run with the ball," Naismith said later, "and there is no need for tackling. This was the new principle that was needed and it was an innovation in ball games."

Naismith asked the school janitor for two boxes, eighteen inches square, to serve as goals. The janitor had no boxes but came up with two peach baskets, which Naismith tacked to the overhead running track, which happened to be ten feet off the gym floor. In the first game, in December 1891, one William Chase made hoop history by scoring the first and only basket. Within a few days the new sport was drawing spectators to daily lunchtime contests. A group of young women teachers at a Springfield grade school, walking by the gym and intrigued by the shouts and laughter, watched a few games and asked Naismith for lessons. Invented for men, basketball at once engaged women too, spreading quickly to Smith and other nearby women's colleges.

Basketball exploded, blowing away most other indoor games. At first the new sport was picked up and broadcast by the built-in international YMCA network of gyms, missionaries, and publications. The eighteen original hoopsters went off to YMCA jobs, bringing the word. The physical director of New York's Central Twenty-third Street Y, James H. McCurdy, happened to be in Springfield that first winter and took basketball home to Manhattan. "The game has been started as a substitute for football, with an attempt to eliminate the roughest features of that sport," the *New York Times* explained a few months later. (HAS BECOME POPULAR IN GIRLS' COLLEGES, a headline elaborated.) By the following winter ten teams were playing at the Central Y, with other squads at three Y branches elsewhere in the city. "The skill lies in passing the ball quickly from one to another, so as to get it down to the opponents' goal," said the *Times*. "If a player is at all slow, it will be snatched away in a twinkling by one of the other side." In a well-played game with proper defense, the winners might total six points, "but poorer teams may roll up twenty or more."

After playing in early games in Springfield, Amos Alonzo Stagg took basketball to the new University of Chicago, where he was hired to coach football in the fall of 1892. At Chicago's Garfield Boulevard YMCA, Herb Reynolds and his friends read about the game in a Y magazine. "Not to be behind Springfield," they hung up a wastebasket and, "mauling each other around the gym floor," passed and shot an old boxing glove. "We got action, all right, and that determined us to follow it up." Transferring to Chicago's Central Y, Reynolds ascended to regulation baskets and a soccer ball. "We were every week happy and riotous, developing the new game, with a bunch on the floor, if not on their feet, playing." They started a league with teams from Hull House and the University of Chicago; the Central Y went undefeated, and Reynolds became one of the first basketball lifers as player, coach, and referee.

As these early enthusiasts fiddled with the game, Naismith's original vision was modified. Because fans in overhead galleries might deflect enemy shots, backboards were added behind the baskets, leading in turn to the new playing technique of banked shots from close angles. Fouls at first had awarded the fouled team a point; in 1894 Naismith devised the foul shot from twenty feet, then from fifteen. The original team of nine members was cut to seven, then to five. ("We looked with suspicion at the new departure, fearing that it would slow up the game," Herb Reynolds recalled. "It was a great surprise to us when it proved instead to speed play.") And—most significantly—dribbling was allowed, first an "air dribble" by tapping the ball in the air, then by bouncing it on the floor. "It is not a foul to bounce the ball and catch it while running," Naismith ruled in 1895, "thereby making progress." In actual play, advancing the ball with passes only had proved too restrictive. Now, by dribbling, a ballplayer could in a sense run with the ball; so the game grew rougher as dribbler and defender bumped and clutched.

For many muscular Christians, basketball was becoming both too popular and too boisterous. They wanted a polite game. "The new principle involved here," urged Dudley Sargent of the Harvard gym, "is an attempt to introduce some of the Christian graces into an athletic contest." In small, crowded gyms, advocates of Indian clubs and floor exercises could not compete with the new converts to basketball. The hoop game spilled over the whole gym as balls and players careened around; when fans grew excited, and teams warmed to the battle and picked at each other, Christian graces might be neglected. "Basket ball fiends should never be allowed to monopolize the floor except at the regular times allowed for them," Luther Gulick warned in 1895. "It should never be allowed to run itself, nor should it be run by a group or clique of self-appointed enthusiasts; it will soon run wild." Too late: the game was already running wild. In 1896 the YMCA of Camden, New Jersey, banned basketball as "too brutal a game to be played by a Christian organization"; some other Ys around the country agreed.

Naismith himself demonstrated the difficulty of containing basketball ardor within the rules. While he nurtured the game and handed down rulings, he only *played* basketball twice, in 1892 and again in 1898. His old rugby and football instincts asserted themselves; he fouled too much. Even Naismith, who had designed the game to eliminate hard contact, could not play it that way. In theory he always urged what he called "scientific" basketball: a game of tight teamwork, little fouling, and passing instead of dribbling. In practice the game assumed its own definitions.

The would-be definers were most offended by professional basketball. "The kind of basket-ball developed by these men is exceedingly bad," said Gulick in 1897. "They play to win merely." But amateurs in their headlong zeal showed hardly less restraint. "We went into action equipped like trench raiders, masked, padded, and expecting the worst," Herb Reynolds remembered. "I have lost teeth, had my nose broken twice, and was never free from cut and contusion, while playing the game. My father stormed about my crippled muscles, and the rest of the home circle made caustic comment on my almost constant black eyes during playing season." Barely a decade old, the hottest new sport in America, Naismith's inspiration had already grown beyond anyone's control.

◆　　◆　　◆

As pro baseball and football had risen from amateur athletic clubs, pro basketball took off from the YMCA's good intentions. The first pro hoopsters learned the game in Y gyms. Then, pushed by the sober second thoughts of the muscular Christians in charge of those gyms, and pulled by the wonderful candy-store notion of play for pay, the best YMCA teams turned pro, or at least semipro, and went barnstorming. In the Northeast, these early pro teams evolved a distinctive style of basketball: the "short passing" game of pivot plays, prudent shots, adroit screens, limited dribbling, and—the signature—frequent, quick, careful passes. This style reduced overdribbling and rough contact (the worst aspects of early basketball) and became the game's first orthodoxy, a regional variation that eventually spread through much of basketball America.

No single inventor of the short passing game can be identified. The style first appeared, spontaneously and concurrently, in two of the finest pro teams at the turn of the century: the Buffalo Germans and New York Wanderers. Based at opposite ends of New York State, the two teams never played each other. But by touring widely through the Northeast, and occasionally beyond it, they brought their brand of ball to isolated places hungry for basketball instruction. With basketball governance and rule-making split among four or five jurisdictions, and no single authority assuming the early role of the YMCA, the Germans and Wanderers offered the first wisps of coherence and continuity to a sport in expanding chaos.

Fred Burkhardt, one of Naismith's eighteen original ballplayers, had taken the game in 1892 to his first job, as physical director at a Y branch in a German neighborhood of Buffalo. Of the teams under his supervision, a squad of fourteen-year-olds emerged in 1895 as the undefeated champs of a junior league in the city. The "Germans" lost no outside games for two more years, graduated to adult competition and kept winning, and so grew beyond the founding Y on Genesee Street. The team's top scorer and dominant personality was Allie Heerdt; he and Ed Miller, another original member, paced the Germans through their glory years. In 1901, after toying with the local opposition for years to a cumulative record of 87–6, the Germans vaulted onto a larger stage at a world's fair in Buffalo.

Among the athletic events at the Pan-American Exposition, a basketball tournament sponsored by the Amateur Athletic Union presented seven teams from Massachusetts, New Jersey, and New York. On an outdoor grass court, forty feet by sixty feet, the Germans beat the favored Entre Nous team from Paterson, New Jersey, 16–5, and rolled over four other opponents to the final day of the tournament. By accident or collusion they were then nearly cheated of the title. Heerdt, Miller, and a third team member—still only seniors in high school—were delayed by final exams. Against St. Joseph's, another team from Paterson, the Germans had to start the game with just three players on hand. After seven minutes, and only one point scored by each team, Ed Miller appeared and dove into the game in street clothes. Allie Heerdt joined him a few minutes later. After donning uniforms at halftime, they led the Germans to an especially savored victory, 10–1. "It remained for a Buffalo team, practically unknown theretofore," reported James Sullivan of the AAU, "to win the coveted trophy." Posing for a victory photograph with banner and trophy, the Germans looked muscular, self-assured, and *very* serious.

They repeated this triumph three years later at another world's fair, in St. Louis. Again playing outdoors—through the moist heat of a Missouri summer—the Germans flattened six teams from Chicago, San Francisco, St. Louis, and New York City by margins up to *eighty-nine* points. They met Herb Reynolds's vaunted Central Y team from Chicago in the final. For two months the Chicago team, anticipating the outdoor clay court in St. Louis, had practiced in heavy, cleated shoes. But a soaking rain on the final day sent the title game indoors to Washington University's gym. "Our two months in heavier footwear had slowed us up," Reynolds recalled, "our team-work went glimmering, and we were fairly beaten," 39–28. "That the team representing this city is the greatest in the world is now an assured fact," crowed a Buffalo newspaper. "They have beaten every team that amounts to anything this side of California."

Testing that boast, the Germans spent the next winter on the road from Portsmouth, New Hampshire, to Kansas City, Missouri. Taking time from their day jobs (a pastiche of trades: bookkeeping, medicine, sales, steamfitting), the Germans officially turned pro that winter of 1904–1905. With a six-man squad, the sixth man often serving as referee, the Germans won sixty-nine of eighty-seven games in this first grand basketball tour. To many isolated basketball outposts they brought the short passing game—and a seasoned knowledge of dirty tricks too. "How they could perform! They were a willing and rough-and-ready lot," recalled Phog Allen, whose athletic-club team played them in Kansas City: "All the artistry of swinging an adept hand, clutching an opponent's thumb as he rushed by, giving an opposing player a forward tug in order to pull him over and off his feet at the proper time, cleverly slipping an alien foot sideways to push a competitor's rear foot against his front one while he was running and, thereby, causing him to trip and go headlong, and blocking so cleverly at times that the opposition was confounded and blamed itself for being so awkward and so dull." Allen went on to a major hoop career as coach at the University of Kansas and as a powerful force in basketball governance. Looking back at the Germans three decades later, still annoyed by their rule-bending, he yet acknowledged their historical significance: "They liked the freer style of play and were the genuine originators of the short pass and pivot and block."

Allie Heerdt kept the Germans playing together into the 1920s. At home in Buffalo they were underappreciated—perhaps because they won too much—so they played mostly on the road, barnstorming through western New York and northwestern Pennsylvania. In 1907 they added their first man over six feet tall: Ed Miller's kid brother Harry, a giant at six feet three inches, joined to play center. For three years, from 1908 to 1911, they went undefeated in 111 straight games, averaging 54 points to the enemy's 18. Heerdt by himself made 21 points a game during the 1910–11 season. "They are the most wonderful athletic machine the world has ever known," the *Cleveland News* concluded. The best pro basketball teams of Philadelphia and New York City might have argued the point. Constrained by their day jobs, and with Buffalo a long train ride from the eastern seaboard, the Germans joined none of the pro leagues of the early 1900s; and during their 111-game streak they played no teams from the Eastern, Central, or Hudson River leagues, the major pro loops of the time.

In faster company, the New York Wanderers won nearly as often. Organized in 1896 to represent the Twenty-third Street YMCA in Manhattan, they were led by center John Wendelken, guard Bob Abadie, and their star, Sandy Shields, a quick, strong forward. After punishing local Y and college teams for two seasons, they won a national AAU tournament in New York in 1898 and turned pro. The Twenty-third Street Y responded by suspending their memberships and banning them from the gym; the homeless team became known as the Wanderers. They played all over the Northeast, always away from home, for average takes of twelve to fifteen dollars apiece after expenses. It was a hard regimen: after a regular day's work or study, a quick supper and train ride to the game, forty minutes of rough action, then a bath or shower or not, the train home, and to bed by two o'clock. "We were all well trained, both spiritually and physically (thanks to our YMCA association)," John Wendelken said later, "hence all members of the team were clean-living, strong, healthy individuals, always in the proverbial pink."

In 1900 they joined the National Basketball League, the first pro circuit. Launched two years earlier by sportswriters from Philadelphia and Trenton, the NBL did not quite deserve its striving name; all member teams except the Wanderers were based within forty miles of Philadelphia. They endured the brutal pro game of the time, in a metal cage around a floor sixty-five feet by thirty-five feet, with wire screens for backboards. The Wanderers played the full league schedule of thirty-two games and as many independent contests too; over New Year's Eve and Day of 1901, they managed four games in twenty-four hours. Trenton won the NBL championship of 1900. The following season, the Wanderers were slogging along with a middling record when they hit a groove for three weeks in mid-season, winning sixteen games in a row to take the league title.

The crack competition of the NBL pushed the Wanderers to sharpen their game. Their twice-weekly practices started with thirty minutes of "Slugee," a frenetic, nonstop ballhandling exercise. With unlimited numbers on each side, the idea was to keep legal possession of the ball without shooting. "Everybody ran all over the court, covering, pivoting, dodging, passing, feinting," Wendelken recalled. "This developed the legs, improved the wind, ballhandling, coordination, alertness and speed"—and encouraged passing, not dribbling. The Slugee session was followed by a half hour of shooting and then a regular game, with no score kept.

One night, in a league game at Camden, the Wanderers first devised a pivot or bucket play. They called it the double cross: "Getting hold of the ball we executed a series of rapid fire, short running passes, in the middle or back court," as Wendelken described it. "Suddenly one man, usually Shields, would dart for the foul circle and hold the ball in front of the foul line, juggling it from hand to hand or rolling it on the floor in front of him." Two teammates would crisscross past him, sloughing off their defenders, and break for the basket. Shields would dump a bounce pass to one of them for an easy score; or, if they were covered, would rise from his crouch, pivot, and shoot. Thus the short-passing style acquired its basic maneuver: a hard, slicing play off a pass, not a dribble, that opened the clogged floor to various options. "This play was invented by the New York team long before other outfits adopted it," Wendelken later insisted.

Devised by ballplayers, the Northeast style gained a relentless advocate and publicist in William J. Scheffer, a sportswriter for the *Philadelphia Inquirer*. Sometimes called "the father of pro basketball" in Philadelphia, as a teenager in the early 1890s he had helped form the city's first teams, the Penn Treaty Wheelmen and others. His Philadelphia League, launched in 1902, evolved under his direction into the Eastern League, the most stable pro loop of the 1910s. For fourteen years the Eastern League ran a schedule of teams in the Philadelphia hoops orbit, drawing crowds of up to five thousand. A noted referee as well, Scheffer preached the beauties of the professional Northeast style from the bully pulpit of the *Reach Official Basket Ball Guide,* an annual yearbook published by a sporting-goods company in Philadelphia. (The competing *Spalding Guide,* issued in New York, ignored pro basketball.) Celebrator and scold, instructor and executive, Scheffer was the best friend in print of professional hoops.

As he taught it, basketball was a "scientific" game of speed, stamina, passing, and limited contact. The center needed leaping ability, not for shooting or rebounding but to control the ball at the center jump after each score. "Forwards must be quick starters and fast on their feet, so as to escape from their guards and get the ball on the jump off," Scheffer wrote in the 1910 *Guide.* "They must be fast, as speed, and the endurance to maintain it for 40 minutes without a stop, is what wins games." For the guards, defensive players mainly, "height is desirable, providing it does not interfere with speed, because the forward has a harder time breaking away from a tall guard, for a try at goal." Passing instead of dribbling kept the game cleaner. Scheffer's Eastern League played a gentler style than the New York State League, its main rival. "Hugging around the cage, holding when the referee don't get a chance to watch and so much dribbling and running as is done by the New York State Leaguers is not a scientific game by any means," said Andy Sears, a star guard for the Eastern League's Reading team, as quoted (and probably elaborated) by Scheffer in the 1914 *Guide.* "I like the passing game and signals bringing it down to a scientific basis, like in the Eastern League. . . . It is better all around to have each player doing his best on an open floor, instead of going in to kill each other." (Scheffer's vision of scientific basketball essentially repeated Naismith's founding concepts, even his use of the adjective, with a few modifications. "It is getting more scientific every year," Scheffer declared in the 1915 *Guide.* "The different codes of playing are gradually getting down to one style of play," for basketball "was never intended to be a rough game, but a scientific educator.")

In its speed, passing, and aspirations to clean play, the Northeast style was a small man's game, spread out laterally on the floor, close to the ground instead of up near the hoop. The short passing techniques made stars of darting little waterbugs like

Harry Hough and Barney Sedran, who zipped around and through the lumbering heavy-foots of the time. Hough, hailed as "the greatest basketball player" by one sportswriter in 1909, learned the game in his hometown of Trenton, New Jersey. Only five feet two inches and 135 pounds, he survived twenty-one years of pro basketball with larger, angry defenders keying on him. In one game against the New York Wanderers, Bob Reed shoved him repeatedly into the wire screen; finally the screen broke and a protruding wire opened a two-inch gash in Hough's side. Another night, Hough scored twice on Winnie Kincaide, who was fifty-five pounds heavier, ten inches taller, and noted for his defensive grit. Enraged, Kincaide picked Hough up and threw him to the floor—three times. "But Hough only bounced up like a rubber ball and gave the giant the laugh."

Hough provoked this furious attention with his speed, evasive dribbling, and phenomenal shooting touch. A favorite move was the carom shot: in motion, with his defender closing, he would slam the ball against the screen, slip by the defender, catch the rebound, and shoot it through. "The little wonder's greatest specialty is in caging the ball while on the run," an observer noted, "but he secures goals from almost any position. He is a wonderful shot with either hand, and when a man is covering him, so that it seems impossible for him to shoot . . . he is most dangerous." With his team ahead late in the game, he would untouchably dribble out the clock, leaving exasperated pursuers in his wake. After leading two leagues in scoring, "the great Hough," "the invincible Hough," "the world's star" was paid three hundred dollars a month in 1908 by Pittsburgh's South Side team in the Central League—the top salary in pro basketball. William Scheffer later included him on a short list of the five leading basketball players of all time.

Barney Sedran, five feet four inches and 118 pounds, came from the settlement-house leagues of New York's Lower East Side. In his neighborhood of Jewish immigrants, he played on a famous team called the Busy Izzies, all of them tough little guys like Sedran. For three years he led his college team at CCNY in scoring, "drifting around the court like an anemic ghost." A consistent winner, he then played on ten championship teams in fifteen years of pro ball, usually ranking among the league's top scorers. In the fierce New York State League, his Utica team—which included Marty Friedman from the Busy Izzies—won the 1914 title; shooting at a basket with no backboard, he made seventeen field goals in one game. "This combination worked together like machinery," Scheffer wrote approvingly in the *Reach Guide,* "using a short pass, and every man was fast." Crowds usually loved the David-and-Goliath spectacle of a small man running riffs and inventions on the larger, slower opposition. Once, condemned to a jump ball against Stretch Meehan (who was a mere fifteen inches taller), Sedran faked the jump, ran between Meehan's legs, and intercepted the uncontested tip.

Eventually the Northeast style spread beyond its base and began to dominate organized basketball. The early pro game by its nature encouraged cross-fertilizations and uniformity because players moved around so much, jumping teams and contracts. A typical pro might play for several teams in several leagues in a single week; he changed teammates but encountered familiar techniques. An entire team might play together one night and then, under a different name, play as another team in another league the next night. (Hough and Sedran were teammates for one year on the Eastern League's Jasper Jewels.) Touring pro teams repeatedly brought the style beyond the Northeast; in 1915 one New York squad, the New York State League champions from Troy led by center Ed Wachter, won thirty-eight straight games through the Midwest, while another, the Nationals from the Rockaways, won forty-four of forty-five games, all the way to San Francisco. All those losing teams naturally tried to copy the Northeast style that had beaten them. Individual pros also coached college and amateur teams, preaching the gospel of the short pass, and wrote textbooks. (Hough coached at Pitt, Allie Heerdt at Niagara and the University of Buffalo, Wachter at Harvard and four other colleges.) And Scheffer hammered away every year in the *Reach Guide.*

Though most prevalent in the Northeast, the short passing game reached distant hoopsters as well. As Phog Allen, out in Kansas, declared in 1924, it had become "the dominant style of the present day." The Northeast game emphasized patient team play, with endless weaving, everyone in motion, until a clear shot developed. It discouraged individual moves and unorthodox shots, especially one-handers from a distance. A good short-passing team would weave, set picks, work the pivot—everybody in motion together—to spring an easy shot close to the hoop; eventually, if nothing opened up, someone would try a long two-handed set, pushing the ball from the chest. That technique with two hands became "almost the basic shot of the game," according to a basketball textbook published in New York in 1921. (One-handers were correspondingly improper.)

◆　　◆　　◆

But outside the founding, forming Northeast, out there in basketball America, the scattered history of one-handed shooting reveals the Northeast style as not so universal as generally supposed, then or later. The two-handed set, the siege gun of basketball, could not escape the defects of its virtues. The shooter aimed from a solid base, feet balanced and aligned, the arms gathered close to the body, the trunk bowing and straightening up as the ball was released. But the solid base took time to set up and deliver, and the shot at chest level, dead in front of the body, offered itself too easily to blockers. Two hands, mustering twice the power of one, allowed a long shot with fingertip touch, not a coarse heave, even from distant points. But if the shooter moved while shooting, especially from side to side, one hand might override the other and send the ball astray; two hands doubled the possibility of misfires. Vulnerable to disruption, the two-hander had to wait for the busy horizontal movements of the Northeast style to carve out the floor space and time (one beat, two beats) that the shot required.

Daring and unorthodox, a one-hander was quicker, more flexible, more mobile and harder to block. One hand, one beat. Instead of two hands gripping the sides of the ball, the shooter balanced the ball on one hand and placed the shooting hand behind the ball, aligned directly, center on center, with the basket. In this posture, the shooter could twist and duck, then fire from unexpected angles, the legs and body still pushing behind the release. Movement made the shot harder to block—and to shoot. When taken in motion, the classic form sent the shooter jumping laterally off one foot (usually the leg opposite the shooting hand) toward the hoop, across the key, or at some angle in between. To compensate in flight for this motion required a delicate kinesthetic adjustment, like target-shooting from a speeding car. Versatile and varied, the one-hander was also easy to miss, easy to look bad when missing. The two-hander by contrast looked so solid, so deliberate and intentional. Northeast orthodoxers scorned the one-hander as a trick shot, self-indulgent and show-offy: a crowd-pleasing device used by unsound barnstorming teams such as Ole Olson's Terrible Swedes. Based in Coffeyville, Kansas, during the 1920s, the Swedes dared behind-the-back passes and long one-handers from the corners. The Swedes were mere vaudeville, retorted advocates of the short pass; an entertainment novelty, not a *real* basketball team.

Here and there, however, generally in places far from the Northeast, one-handers flourished among serious college basketball players, some quite famous—even during the height of the short-pass orthodoxy.

- At the University of Tennessee in the early 1920s, David Beane shot a one-hander in his single year of varsity ball. "He was the one player of that time," recalled a teammate, "who used a one-handed shot." (At least in those parts.) "The rest of us just put it up there any way we could, but David had real touch, real skill."
- Chuck Hyatt, the most celebrated amateur hoopster of the 1920s, shot his one-hander from down near his belt buckle. A favorite move was to dribble to his right, dart quickly to his left, and fire a sweeping left-hander facing the basket. At Pitt from 1928 to 1930, he made first-team All-American for three years, twice leading the nation in scoring, pulling his team to two national titles and an overall record of 60–7. Doc Carlson, the Pitt coach, liked a freewheeling offense and did not constrain his star. A complete, versatile player at six feet and 170 pounds, Hyatt used other shots and was not especially identified with one-handers. After a long, honored career in AAU ball, he placed fourth in a sportswriters' poll taken in 1950 to name the best player ever.
- At the University of Illinois in 1928, a coach named Coleman Griffith predicted the one-hander would soon replace two-handers because it needed "less adjustment and coordi-

nation." Another Illinois coach, J. Craig Ruby, described a one-hander from around the foul line in a coaching textbook published in 1931. Back to the basket, the shooter pivoted on his left foot away from his guard. Turning his head to the left, sighting toward the hoop, he dropped his left hand from the ball and completed the pivot motion by shooting with a rapid, bent-elbow release. According to Ruby, this one-hander—a kind of choked-up hook—was better protected by the body, and more quickly released, than a two-hander.

• Lindy Hood, an All-American at Alabama in 1930, made most of his points one-handed. A giant for his era at six feet six inches, Hood pushed the ball with a shot-putter's motion, released from the palm, thus sacrificing control for power. Another Bama basketeer, Zeke Kimbrough of the class of 1934, later followed Hood's style. "I'd take the ball home in the summer and practice the one-handed shot by the hour," Kimbrough recalled. "Most everybody was shooting two-handed when I came to Alabama, but a lot were shooting one-handed when I left."

• Aggie Sale in 1932 was Adolph Rupp's first All-American at Kentucky. A strong dray horse, six feet four inches and 200 pounds, Sale grew up on a farm twenty-five miles west of Lexington, often slighting his chores to practice on an outdoor court. His favorite flip shot resembled Ruby's one-hander from the foul line, except that Sale turned to his right, not his left, and so shot in a backhanded motion against the momentum of his turn. The authoritative *Converse Basketball Yearbook* could barely contain itself: "He was the greatest one-handed shot in the country," it said of Sale in 1932, "equally deadly with right or left hand and hit best when closely covered." Later on, after forty years of Kentucky basketball, when Rupp got to recalling his best players he usually mentioned Sale first.

• At the University of Wyoming from 1931 to 1934, Les Witte also made All-American and placed sixth, fourth, tied for first, and first in scoring in the Rocky Mountain conference. "Witte was the cleverest player to show in the conference in a long time," said the *Spalding Guide* in 1932. "This boy's dribbling, pivoting and feinting, and his lefthand arch shots, could not be stopped." Teammates predictably imitated his one-hander. Indulged by the coach (his brother Dutch), Witte reached a career total of one thousand points and was called One-Grand Witte.

And the one-handed canon goes back even farther. With due credit to these athletes and coaches, the true pioneer of the one-hander was an earlier, more obscure college ballplayer named Charles Gray. At the University of Idaho from 1914 to 1917, Gray led his team in scoring and twice made All-Northwest squads. He used the one-hander so effectively that it became a tradition in the Northwest—a safe three thousand miles from proscription by the Northeast orthodoxy. "The one-hand push shot is a product of the Northwest," claimed Hec Edmundson, basketball coach at the University of Washington, in 1931. "Its value is unmistakable, even though it is not yet in universal use." Charles Gray's historical significance, then, is not merely that he shot one-handed (others, better known All-Americans, did too); Gray also generated a regional technique that persisted for decades after his playing days and ultimately emerged to national acceptance.

Born in 1894, Gray grew up on a farm with nine brothers and sisters in the small town of Genesee, in the Idaho panhandle, a few miles south of the University of Idaho at Moscow. He started playing basketball in high school. "Since he was usually smaller than the opposing players," his son recalled, "he had to depend on speed and quickness to try to offset their size advantage. He said his size was also why he used the one-handed shot. He felt he could get the ball in the air faster." On his own, innocent of formal instruction, Gray devised a quick, flexible style of ballhandling. Catching the ball with both hands, he would roll his left hand underneath and place his right hand on the top rear of the ball. From this position he could shoot, dribble, or pass without telegraphing the move. He shot with a spinning motion of his left hand, guiding the ball with his right, sending it off in a pronounced overspin that helped it curl over the front rim. Playing for his high school's first basketball team—the coach's wife stitched the uniforms—as a junior in 1912, Gray led Genesee to the state high school title, scoring ten of Genesee's eighteen points and hitting two foul shots in overtime to clinch it.

He went on to the University of Idaho to study agriculture and play ball. One day Hec Edmundson, then coaching track at Idaho, noticed Gray scrimmaging in the college gym. "He'd get up there and push the ball up and in one-handed," Edmundson recalled. "That was so unorthodox that it occasioned much discussion; but Gray was a deadeye on those close one-handers, so of course they let him continue. There was some copying, but not a great deal." Still undersized, only five feet eight and a half inches and 138 pounds when full grown, he skittered around the court, the best shot on his team. "Charles Gray was everywhere," the Idaho student newspaper said of a game against Oregon State in 1915, "and he shot free throws as easily as most men could hit a flying elephant with an eight gauge shotgun." In his senior year he averaged four baskets a game and shot 72 percent from the line: impressive stats for the era.

The Fox brothers, Alex and Rich, followed Gray at Idaho in the early 1920s. Alex Fox, the best foul shooter in the conference, was known for his speed, dribbling, movement without the ball, and deadeye shooting from anywhere. He made the All-Pacific Coast first team in 1922. "I can still see him coming down the floor," an opponent remembered, "stopping well out beyond the foul line, casting off with one hand and the ball dropping through the net."

When Hec Edmundson in 1920 started his long coaching career at the University of Washington, he brought along the one-handed gospel. It was soon picked up by coach W. D. Fletcher at the University of Oregon as well. In a basketball textbook published in Seattle in 1931, Edmundson described his favorite version of the shot. From fifteen feet or less, always on the run, the shooter leaped from the left foot—for height, not distance—raised the ball to shoulder level, dropped his left hand, and shot with the fingers of the right hand splayed behind the ball, gently depositing the shot "as carefully on an imaginary shelf, which is the top plane of the basket, as he would a fragile object on a real shelf. He attempts to reach just as high as he can and just rest the ball on the shelf." The one-hander had become so locally popular by 1931 that Edmundson even noticed "a marked tendency to overuse this weapon of attack among the teams in the Northwest." During the 1930s the shot spread down the West Coast, then eventually to New York. It was, Edmundson said later, "the one definite contribution of the Pacific Northwest to basketball."

Another challenge to the Northeast style, the fast break, emerged from college teams in the Rocky Mountain conference in the late 1920s. The short-pass game valued ball control above all other virtues; guards brought the ball upcourt slowly, carefully, and then waited patiently for a "good" shot to appear. The fast break, first unleashed by Montana State in 1927, then copied by Brigham Young and other schools in the conference, combined a rebound, an outlet pass, and a headlong rush to the other end of the court: all done as quickly as possible. Skeptics called it the avalanche system, pell-mell, wild and woolly, race-horse, fire-horse basketball. "The orthodox belt-buckle-to-belt-buckle short pass is rarely used," conceded G. Ott Romney, coach at Brigham Young, in 1932. "On the contrary, the long hook pass and the baseball catcher's peg for fifty to eighty feet are used frequently. Great versatility in shooting is encouraged, and a great deal of one-handed handling of the ball. . . . Shooting of all varieties is taught and encouraged, and every shot is considered an optional pass. The players are allowed to do some unorthodox shooting." Crowds responded to the speed and high scoring, the flat-out dashes up and down court, the constant action and whooshing conclusions. The fast break was adopted by a few other coaches, notably Frank Keaney at Rhode Island State and Herbert Read at Western Michigan, but remained principally identified with western basketball.

One-handers and fast breaks represented the future of pro hoops. They arrived slowly east of the Rockies, awaiting the cultural diffusions of more national basketball media and intersectional play. For the time being, back in the Northeast, the pro game was locked into short passes and two-handed sets.

◆   ◆   ◆

The Northeast style peaked with the New York Original Celtics, the best pro team of the 1920s. The Celtics passed the ball. (And passed it, and passed it.) "Make the ball sing!" was their axiom. "There is no mad rush up the floor," one sportswriter noted. "Then, all at once, something happens! Suddenly what was a moment before five men now seems to be eight. . . . The ball slips through the ozone invisible to the naked eye. Ordinary opponents have been known to go off Easter egg hunting, un-able for the life of them to find the leather." The Celtics whipped it around, snappy but well under control, always looking for an open layup or two-hander, with everybody in motion and wait-ing for the opposition to be bored, distracted, or outlasted. The top draw in basketball, they attracted crowds of 10,000 at Mad-ison Square Garden, a two-game crowd of 23,000 in Cleveland, and made up to $5,000 a game. In 1922–23 they played 205 games in 114 cities, losing only 11 times. Touring victoriously through the East, South, and Midwest, teaching their game in preseason coaches' clinics, they pushed the Northeast style to its pinnacle of success and popularity. As the *Converse Basketball Yearbook* concluded in 1924, "The Original Celtics have probably done more to advance basketball than any other aggregation."

A very New York story, the Celtics came up from a settlement-house team on the Lower West Side. Their four best-known players—scorer Johnny Beckman, defender Dutch Dehn-ert, playmaker Nat Holman, and center Joe Lapchick—were all first-generation Americans, born in New York of immigrant Eu-ropean parents and raised in neighborhoods of newcomers. None was Irish, but the team had begun in Hibernian hues. Its name derived from Celtic Park, in the Chelsea neighborhood near Twentieth Street on the Irish West Side. An early backer, a bootlegger named Donovan, was killed one night on Tenth Av-enue in a Prohibition feud. The team was then managed by the Furey brothers, Jim and Fat Tom. Jim Furey stocked the Celtics with top talent at top dollar—apparently by embezzling nearly $190,000 from the clothing store he served as head cashier. (For this creative exercise in sports management, Furey eventually did five-to-ten at Sing Sing.) A few of the Celtics also worked for bookmakers in the off-season. "We were rough-cut all the way," Lapchick recalled. "Except for Nat Holman, a two-malted-milk man, we drank redeye Prohibition whiskey out of water tumblers (though even when we were drinking, we talked of nothing but basketball). We so dominated the game we could get away with breaking training."

A solid neighborhood team, the Celtics went big time in 1920 when Jim Furey hired Johnny Beckman and Dutch Dehnert. Beckman, a vagabond pro since 1913, was already known as "the most dangerous shot in the game to-day." Growing up in West Side church leagues, he had once posted fifty-seven points for St. Brendan's. An inch or two under six feet, the fastest man on the court, Beckman played a slashing, relentless, fatigueless game of drives and long, dropping sets. During the 1915–16 season, at age twenty, he had toiled for fifteen different teams in three leagues, a withering total of 174 games in 195 days. Three games in a single day merely tested his stamina. He would come home from road trips looking thin and beat-up, with broken digits and sprained thumbs, and then play some more. On the Celtics he became the leader, trainer, holler guy, and scold. His cold-steel intensity and mental toughness, no matter the opponent or game situation, would not acknowledge most injuries. "What's the matter?" he would sneer, his "mean fighter's eyes" flashing at any teammate claiming to be hurt. "No guts?"

Dutch Dehnert, like Beckman the son of German immigrants, had grown up on West Forty-first Street. The family lived above his father's bakery. Basketball for him started with two ash cans on opposite sides of the street and a nonbouncing rag ball, sewed up by somebody's mother. This game reverted to Naismith's original vision of all passing, no dribbling. "When I got hold of a *real* basketball," Dehnert said later, "whoa, that was wonderful." He played his first indoor hoops—in socks because he had no sneakers—at the Christ Church House on Thirty-sixth Street. (His father could not understand: "What are you, crazy? You fellas jumpin at a hoop? What are youse doin out there?") By age twenty Dehnert had joined Wilkes-Barre in the Penn State League and Utica in the New York State League, making five bucks a game plus food and expenses; "I was a big shot then." Solidly built, not a shooter, on the Celtics he rebounded, passed, and defended. Usually he drew and quartered the other team's best scorer. One night Dehnert's man kept clawing at his face and eyes. Calling for a hard pass to the pivot, head high, Dehnert ducked and the man was knocked cold.

With Beckman and Dehnert added, the Celtics staged a show-down against their only peer among New York's pro teams: the Whirlwinds, an East Side squad led by Marty Friedman, the ageless Barney Sedran, and Nat Holman, a young flash. In April 1921 they met in a best-of-three series for city supremacy. The games sparked so much interest that gamblers tried to fix them. Before eleven thousand fans jammed into an armory, the Whirlwinds took the first game easily, 40–29; high scorers were Sedran (10 points), Holman (22), and Beckman (25). A few days later the Celtics won the second game, 26–24, a rough contest decided by foul shots. The Whirlwinds were outquicking the Celtics, as Sedran and Holman repeatedly beat their men to the ball. So before the third game could be played, Jim Furey opened his checkbook—or perhaps the till at the clothing store—and stole Holman and the Whirlwinds' center, Chris Leonard, for his own team. The rubber game, impossibly tilted, was not played.

Now the Celtics' playmaker, charged with getting the ball to Beckman, Holman came from an impeccable New York hoops background. He grew up on the Lower East Side, one of ten children; his big brother Morris was captain of CCNY's team in 1918. Nat started playing basketball at school before his tenth birthday, then moved on to local settlement houses. Dazzled by the Roosevelt Big Five, one of many teams led by Sedran and Friedman, he was soon asked to join them. (Years later, Holman still considered Sedran the best all-around player he'd seen: "What a man he was!") After high school Holman took a teaching degree at the Savage School of Physical Education, where John Wendelken of the old New York Wanderers taught anatomy and, informally, basketball too. Under Sedran and Wendelken, Holman had learned basketball from two prime instigators of the Northeast style. Holman in turn inspired generations of smart, short, quick Jewish ballplayers in New York. "The Jew is fast, generally short, strong, with great competitive spirit and alert mentally," he said later. "It's the driving little man, with speed and classy ball handling, who makes basketball." A superb faker, adept at drawing fouls, Holman shot a line-drive set (useful in gyms with low ceilings) and generally controlled the ball.

Joe Lapchick, another established pro, joined the Celtics in

1923 to play center. The son of Czech immigrants, he had grown up in the Hollow, a Slavic section of Yonkers. His first version of basketball, on a corner lot, used a cap stuffed into a discarded soccer ball; you scored by tossing it onto the roof of a shed. Quitting school at fifteen, Lapchick went to work as an apprentice machinist. But his height, an uncommon six feet five inches, attracted basketball offers. Skinny and gangly-clumsy, he worked on his coordination in solitary drills late at night, when nobody could watch or mock him. On a cinder road behind a carpet mill, "I would run at full speed, stop suddenly, change direction, pivot, run backwards, and shadow box. Slowly but surely I began to improve." Signed to four different teams at once, when game dates conflicted he would play one manager against another, squeezing them for seventy-five or even one hundred dollars a game. (At his day job he made fifteen dollars a week.) "I began to really live it up," he recalled. He would drive his new car to a game, park right in front of the hall, throw his equipment bag toward a group of kids, and escort the boy who caught it into the game for free.

Lapchick had made himself a special basketball talent. At his height he could usually control any tap-off; and, unlike other men his size at the time, he could also run and handle the ball, and even shoot a bit. Crowds loved his juggling one-handed fakes and passes, the ball rolled "so securely against his forearm," one sportswriter noticed, "that he can swing it around as easily as if it had handles." When the Celtics beckoned, "My heart was jumping so hard I could scarcely sign the contract," Lapchick remembered. "The Celtics were the biggest name in the history of the sport, and they lived the part. Their entire lives were wrapped up in basketball." A crisp, edgy focus kept the team taut. In learning the team's switching defense, Lapchick heard sharply of his game blunders: "When a fellow made a mistake, the rest of the Celtics hollered at him and chewed him out until he got it right. No floor instructions, just hints." Winning was easy fun, a zesty treat. "The teams who bowed gracefully, we treated nice and held the score close. Those who challenged us and were a bit antagonistic—well, we showed them who was boss." After an infrequent loss, sharper for its rarity, "our dressing room was an awful place," like a den of starved wolves. "Recriminations were vicious, profane and sometimes physical."

They won with a more skilled execution of the traditional Northeast style. All five men took part in the offense, running figure-eight weaves in a lulling rhythm, then sudden give-and-gos: a man passed off, broke for the hoop, got a return pass and layup. The Celtics rediscovered the pivot play (and thought they had invented it themselves). Dutch Dehnert stood at the line, his bulk securing the floor space, and took a pass; Beckman and Holman zipped by him, scraping off their guards; Dehnert would dish or (rarely) shoot. Or the two best offensive players, Beckman and Holman, ran their own "buddy" plays. Their favorite deke started with two body fakes: Beckman lazed in a corner, apparently at rest, while Holman played with the ball near midcourt, not looking at him. Beckman came slowly out of the corner, then suddenly reversed and broke for the basket, where Holman's overhead pass met him shoulder-high. Sometimes Beckman jumped, caught, and shot in one crowd-exhilarating motion. Game after game, the Celtic trademark was hard, deft passes. "The greatest ball-handling team I ever saw," said Lapchick after a lifetime of hoops, including coaching at big-time college and pro levels. "But there was no 'showboating.' Every pass and every move had a purpose, and the technique broke the backs of practically every team we met." Meantime Dehnert and Leonard anchored the defense; "no one scored any baskets," said the *Reach Guide* in 1925, "unless they thought it might cheer up the opposition."

Holman—the most articulate and studious of the Celtics, the only one exposed to higher education—became a forceful guardian of the Northeast style. Midwestern ballplayers, he wrote in the 1923 *Converse Yearbook,* were well conditioned but needed to pace themselves better and not run flat out all night. They needed to use bounce passes and defensive switches. They risked too many long shots and slow, loopy, interceptable passes; "the short, snappy pass with players coming in toward the ball is the most effective style." Impatient and undisciplined, midwesterners shot "from the most difficult angles even when not properly 'set' for a shot." Back East, said Holman, "when a player is not set for a shot or is forced into an awkward angle, rather than take the slim chance, he throws the ball back to one of his mates, and the play is started over again." Thus the deliberate, slow-break, orthodox-shot game. Holman taught this Northeast gospel as Celtic, coach for four decades at CCNY, power in the National Association of Basketball Coaches, and author of influential textbooks. These versatile, prominent roles, wrapped around what the New York sportswriter Stanley Frank called "the most dominant personality the game has ever known," gave Holman, and thus the Northeast game, unmatched impact.

The American Basketball League—launched in 1925, with the Celtics in their prime—demonstrated the power and limits of the Northeast style. Propelled by the explosion of big-time sports in the 1920s, the ABL was the first pro basketball loop in major-league cities across several regions of the country, with exclusive contracts and salaries up to ten thousand dollars for the five-month season. It was founded by three entrepreneur-sportsmen, not basketball men per se: George Preston Marshall, the Washington laundry tycoon, before his invasion of the National Football League; Max Rosenblum, owner of a Cleveland clothing store, and a patron of football and baseball; and George Halas, owner of the NFL's Chicago Bears. All three were already sponsoring independent pro basketball teams that had run out of local competition. Six other established pro teams—from Detroit, Fort Wayne, Buffalo (coached by Allie Heerdt of the Germans), Rochester, Brooklyn, and Boston—completed the starting year's schedule. NFL president Joe Carr, free after the football season, administered the new league for its first three years.

Though five of the initial nine teams were based well west and south of New York, Northeast players and techniques generally dominated the ABL. The Cleveland Rosies were coached by the fiery Marty Friedman, who brought out his fellow New Yorkers Honey Russell, Carl Husta, and Nat Hickey. They played a passing game, with sudden breaks to the basket. The Washington Palace Five, named for Marshall's laundry, were led by Ray Kennedy, Rusty Saunders, and George Glasco: three of the league's top six scorers that first year, and all from the Northeast. Even the Chicago Bruins engaged three lesser-known eastern college veterans. Only the Fort Wayne Hoosiers notably displayed local stars and styles, with Homer Stonebraker from Wabash College and Frank Shimek of the University of Iowa. Stonebraker liked to launch an astounding underhanded two-handed set, often from *beyond* midcourt, fifty feet out; once he hit five in a single half against the Celtics. Occasionally the Hoosiers could push another ABL team into a looser style; playing the Bruins at home in 1926, they won a high-scoring game, 49–33. "Both teams played the western brand of basketball," noted the *Chicago Tribune*, "featuring long passes, and popped at the net from long range." But this was atypical enough to draw comment. By Stanley Frank's estimate, more than 80 percent of the ABL's players came from the Northeast. They naturally played the game they knew.

Earlier the Celtics had helped to bury the Eastern League, the oldest pro loop, by winning the 1921–22 title, then taking thirteen straight the next season and quitting the league just before its collapse. Barnstorming richly, leery of lesser competition, they stayed out of the ABL in its first season. But the ABL survived that year, with predictable shakeouts, and added Eddie Gottlieb's Philadelphia Warriors, the best pro team in Philly, for the next season. Five games into the 1926–27 schedule, the Celtics joined the ABL, enticed by a special deal: for road games the Celtics got thirty cents a ticket and a three-hundred-dollar guarantee; other league teams made twenty cents and two hundred dollars. The ABL's biggest draw, the Celtics pulled three thousand fans to a January game in Chicago. (Showing their usual "wizardly mastery of the ball," the Celtics won, 42–26, "faultlessly shooting the ball back and forth with the speed of a baseball . . . until Beckman and Holman were in position to lay it against the backboard.") The Celtics waltzed through the ABL, going 80-15 in two seasons, including play-offs, and won two league titles. With fans bored by such competitive imbalance, the ABL's leaders broke up the Celtics before the 1928–29 season. But Max Rosenblum brought four of them—Beckman, Dehnert, Lapchick, and Pete Barry—to Cleveland, which then won its second ABL title.

The ABL struggled through six seasons, never reaching big-league status. The league office's expenses ran to only $11,662 in 1928–29—but that still exceeded income by $3,421. Marshall folded his team early in 1928; Rosenblum followed him in December 1930. "Fans have shown by their lack of attendance," said Rosenblum, "that they are disinterested in professional basketball." Only Chicago, Fort Wayne, and Rochester lasted all six ABL seasons. The Depression cut deeply into league attendance. But the league's larger problems were rough, monotonous play and few new stars. In its last year the ABL tried to limit body contact, abolish the pivot play, and restrict teams to three veterans on the floor at once, but it was too late. "Professional basketball, as a money-maker, apparently has had its day," Phog Allen concluded a few years later. "The inaction of the [ABL] players proved their own Waterloo. They tried to save themselves from any excessive action in the game by expert ball handling and manipulation and, consequently, in time, they played to empty seating galleries."

As a college coach at Kansas, Allen might have harbored an outlander's suspicion of the Northeast pro game, skewing his judgment. But even Joe Lapchick, from the perspective of three decades later, reached a similar verdict. "Professional basketball faded because of the style of play," Lapchick wrote. Great passing aside, "It was stagnant and uninteresting basketball. The pro players lost their pep, and new faces were slow to appear. Even when new and faster players appeared, they were frozen out by the oldtimers who liked the possession game because it preserved their legs and their tenures in the game." Northeast basketball had dominated the American Basketball League, and finally helped to kill it. The pro game returned to barnstormers and regional leagues.

◆　　◆　　◆

A basketball revolution was nonetheless coming. During the 1930s, a string of new rules—three seconds in the lane, ten seconds to get the ball past half-court, replacing the center jump after each score with a quick inbounds pass—made the game faster, a continuous flow less broken by stops and starts, with more shooting and scoring, less passing and weaving. The ball itself became zippier, about two inches smaller in circumference. An improved manufacturing technique produced the molded basketball, a perfect sphere without laces or a protruding valve that kept its shape and feel in heavy use. The molded ball bounced and fired more truly, and was easier to shoot and control with one hand. The new game and new ball reached a newly national audience. Starting in 1934, intersectional college basketball games, well attended at Madison Square Garden and other major arenas around the country, showcased fast breaks, one-handed shooting, and other game-loosening methods, popularizing these challenges to the Northeast style.

The celebrated advent of Hank Luisetti at Madison Square Garden in December 1936 merely confirmed, under a New York spotlight, where basketball was already heading. Luisetti was not even the first one-handed shooter to shine in New York. The previous spring, in a series of Olympic tryouts at the Garden, Hec Edmundson's team from the University of Washington had displayed the one-handers that had been a Northwest trademark for two decades. Ed Loverich of Washington had one-handedly scored twenty points in one game, and made the tournament's all-star second team. The sportswriter Arthur Daley had noted, in the *New York Times*, "the startling one-hand shooting of the Washingtonians from all parts of the floor." But Luisetti's performance eight months later got more publicity, and it has left him with a durable—if undeserved—reputation as the originator of one-handed shooting.

Like most basketball pioneers, Luisetti thought he had made it up himself. As a kid in San Francisco, fooling around with older boys at a playground on Russian Hill, he had discovered a basic advantage of shooting with one hand. "I was small, playing against high school kids," he recalled. "The only way I could shoot was to throw the ball up with one hand. I couldn't shoot with two hands. They'd block it." Luisetti then taught the shot to his teammates at Stanford. It was not, as sometimes described, a jump shot from a vertical leap off both feet, but rather a running move from a lateral jump off one foot. This horizontal motion, not height off the floor, made the shot all but unstoppable—especially by eastern teams that hadn't seen it before.

On a Christmas tour, Stanford came to New York in December 1936 to play Long Island University, which boasted a forty-three-game winning streak and a six-feet-eight-inch center. A full house of 17,623 expected another win for LIU, but Luisetti scored 15 points and Stanford breezed, 45–31. The local sports-writers, steeped in the Northeast game, thought they had witnessed a revelation, a new kind of basketball. "Overnight, and with a suddenness as startling as Stanford's unorthodox tactics, it had become apparent today that New York's fundamental concept of basketball will have to be radically changed," declared Stanley Frank in the *New York Post.* "Every one of the amiable clean-cut Coast kids fired away with leaping one-handed shots which were impossible to stop."

Luisetti's true significance derives not from that peculiar shot but from his entire panoply of skills. Luisetti was the first modern basketball player, not merely a scorer but gifted and graceful in every phase of the game: tall enough at six feet two and a half inches to rebound, springy enough to block shots and hang in the air on drives, agile enough to dribble through traffic, play defense, and make steals, and with the court sense to pass and set up his teammates; and he had a certain effortless, undefinable, good-looking presence that drew fans' attention to his every move. In the Garden crowd that famous night was Max Zaslofsky, then a college ballplayer, later a pro star. "I watched this man handle himself," he recalled. "I saw how fluid and acrobatic he was in everything he did. . . . He was uncanny the way he moved and everything. I was deeply impressed with him. You could call him something of an idol." Another future pro standout, Jim Pollard, then playing high school ball in Oakland, went to Stanford games to see Luisetti. "He had great style," Pollard said later. "He was a great guy to watch. He had that charisma about him that everybody liked. . . . He was my hero when I was a kid." So Pollard started shooting a one-hander in fealty.

A few diehards still clung to the Northeast style. "I'll quit coaching if I have to teach one-handed shots to win," said Nat Holman. "Nobody can convince me a shot predicated on a prayer is the proper way to play the game." After Stanford returned to the Garden a year later and beat his CCNY team, Holman started coming around. Physical skills—height, jumping, drive, conditioning—became as important to the game as basketball skills, and all but the most stubborn eastern fans took to the new style. "Two years ago I thought the deceptive hipper-dipper we always used in the East was the nuts," said Clair Bee, LIU's converted coach, in 1939. "Now I want the drive and speed emphasized by the West. It may not win more games for me, but the fans think it's more exciting, and that's the answer." "I do not like one-hand shooting, but it is here, and here to stay," added Frank Keaney of Rhode Island State. "Players enjoy it, get fun from it, and the averages of baskets made is in their favor!"

◆　　◆　　◆

Thus the state of the game when pro basketball resumed following World War II. After seventy years of baseball's National League, and twenty-six years of the National Football League, a stable national league for pro basketball was finally launched in the fall of 1946. The Basketball Association of America, a bastard child, sprang from the unlikely parentage of pro hockey and the Hearst press. Max Kase, sports editor of Hearst's *New York Journal-American*, conceived the BAA and drew up its charter. In major cities of the Northeast and Midwest, pro hockey teams—members of the National Hockey League and the lesser American Hockey League—controlled large indoor arenas that generally stood empty when their teams were away. Kase's idea was to fill those empty dates with pro basketball. The hockey moguls fell in line, along with the Hearst newspapers in six of the new BAA's cities. "We feel that we certainly have a little obligation to the Hearst papers," said Al Sutphin of the Cleveland Rebels at a BAA directors meeting in August 1946, "inasmuch as they are the real fathers of this idea of the basketball league."

This interfolded, ready-made structure of arenas and friendly press lacked but one seemingly crucial element: basketball experience. The new BAA commissioner, a New Haven attorney named Maurice Podoloff, was president of the American Hockey League. "I know nothing about basketball," admitted Walter Brown of the Boston Celtics; this ignorance did not preclude Brown from a leading role in the BAA. Even the New York Knickerbockers' Ned Irish, who had been running college basketball shows at Madison Square Garden for a dozen years, understood the game's promotion but not its technical aspects. (Focused on his college doubleheaders, Irish had effectively inhibited pro basketball in New York. When his Knicks played the

Chicago Stags in November 1946, it was the first big-league pro basketball game at Madison Square Garden since 1929.)

Eddie Gottlieb, coach and part-owner of the Philadelphia Warriors, was the only true basketball man among the BAA founders. From his three decades as player, coach, and entrepreneur, he knew—or had met—every aspect of the sport. Almost by default, he became "the brains of the league," said the sportswriter and NBA chronicler Leonard Koppett. "Gotty knew the game—how to sell tickets, how to get the arena cleaned, how to promote, how to sign up talent. . . . When anyone inside the league or outside had a question, they went to Gotty." Each season, from a desk strewn with notes and odd bits of paper, he laboriously assembled the league schedule. For twenty-five years he chaired the league's rules committee, tinkering and refining the pro game. To this formal control of schedules and rules, Gottlieb added the personal power of his tenacious personality and grumpy vision. "You could not win an argument with the man," said Dolph Schayes, a star player in the 1950s. "He was brilliant, opinionated, and when you disagreed with him, you got the feeling he was thinking, 'How can you be so stupid not to see that I'm right?' " More than anyone else, Gottlieb nursed and poked the new league through its early years. "He acted as if he ran the team, the building, even the league," noted the referee Norm Drucker. "Everyone just accepted that as fact."

Gottlieb's basketball roots went deep, to his childhood in an immigrant Jewish neighborhood of South Philly. Born in Kiev, Russia, he learned basketball at South Philadelphia High School from a coach named Mike Saxe. He attended a teachers college and taught school briefly, but by age twenty had ventured into sports promotions, notably a semipro basketball team, the SPHAS, sponsored by the South Philadelphia Hebrew Association. Their uniforms of blue and white displayed Hebrew letters on the chest. Coached by Saxe and captained by Gottlieb, the SPHAS first featured Chick Passon at forward and Babe Klotz at center. In 1921–22 they went 70-13, challenged other Jewish teams to play for the Jewish championship of the East, and beat the only two clubs (from Wilkes-Barre and New York City) that responded. Later Gottlieb quit playing and took the SPHAS uptown to a home court with three thousand seats in the ballroom of the Broadwood Hotel. (Gil Fitch of the SPHAS would change clothes after the game and direct the dance band.) A power in local pro leagues, the SPHAS played a classic Northeast style. "We moved as a team, not as individuals," recalled Shikey Gotthoffer, who joined the SPHAS in 1934 for thirty-five dollars a game. "We played on the supposition that if all the men were advancing, they had to guard us that way. When we came sweeping down, we came down with full force. They didn't know where the ball was going to go or who was going to handle it. The ball always moved—it was always off the floor."

Utterly immersed in the game, running his business affairs from his pockets and his hat, never moored to the security of a real job or an institutional coaching position, Gottlieb had to stay current to survive. For the BAA's first season, he stocked his Warriors with college stars from Philadelphia and New York. But he also drew two starters from distant points and ballplaying styles: Howard Dallmar, a six-feet-four-inch forward from Stanford, and Joe Fulks, the jump-shooting prodigy from Murray State in Kentucky. Gottlieb had never seen a jumper before Fulks came to his first practice. Recognizing at once the future of pro basketball, Gottlieb built his offense around Fulks, the league's top scorer and first star. This odd couple—the short, rotund, urban ethnic and the tall, small-town, hillbilly WASP—led the Warriors to the BAA's first title. At the championship banquet afterward, inspired and inspirited, Fulks rose to impersonate his coach. "You all know what kind of a coach Eddie is," he said. "He's the nervous kind. This is how he was the night we made a poor pass with half a minute to go when we were ahead by twenty-two points." Fulks sat down, mussed up his hair, pulled his necktie from side to side, smacked his palm on his forehead, held both hands over his eyes, and kvetched, in a Yiddish-South Philly accent by way of Kuttawa, Kentucky, "Even if there is only half a minute left, there shouldn't be such a pass." (Gottlieb led the laughter.)

For three years the BAA competed with the National Basketball League, a pro loop based mostly in smaller midwestern cities. Founded in 1938 by industrial-league teams in Akron and Fort Wayne, the NBL had struggled through the war with semipro players employed in defense industries. After 1945, still shut out of most major cities, the NBL showcased some great ball-players. Leroy Edwards of the Oshkosh All-Stars, now tailing off at the end of his career, had led the NBL in scoring three times with his strength and deft hook shot. (Adolph Rupp, briefly Edwards's college coach at Kentucky, always called him the best pivot man he'd ever seen.) Bobby McDermott of the Fort Wayne Zollner Pistons had gone directly from high school on Long Island to pro ball. The finest outside shot in basketball, he could hit his two-handed set from anywhere inside half-court; Dutch Dehnert once saw him make thirteen such howitzers in a row. Bob Davies of the Rochester Royals was a slick playmaking, jump-shooting guard. In high school he had seen Hank Luisetti pull a behind-the-back dribble in the game sequence of a for-gettable Hollywood movie; Davies practiced the flashy maneuver and, as a pro, made it his trademark. And George Mikan of the Minneapolis Lakers was the most coveted prize in the game: the first basketball player to combine serious size (six feet ten inches, 245 pounds) with reasonable speed, coordination, and shooting touch—and a ferocious, sharp-elbowed will to win. In his first two pro seasons Mikan led the NBL in scoring and pushed his teams to championships.

Based in different cities—except for rival teams in Chicago and Detroit in 1946–47—the BAA and NBL competed for ball-players, not fans. Each league needed the marquee names to draw paying customers. The BAA, though, had locked in the major urban markets. "We had the players; they had the are-nas," Bob Davies said later. "So we joined them." Before the 1948–49 season, three of the NBL's top four teams—Minneap-olis, Rochester, and Fort Wayne—jumped to the BAA's greener pastures. The BAA players, Davies noticed, were bigger and stronger, but not as fast or as agile as the NBL's. A year later, the two leagues merged under a melded name, the National Basket-ball Association. Minneapolis and Rochester, two old NBL teams, dominated the NBA for the next five seasons. After some nec-essary winnowings, the league began to stabilize. In the fall of 1952 the NBA for the first time started a season with the same teams in the same cities as the year before.

One particular innovation, without model or precedent in basketball history, secured the league's future. As successive challenges to the Northeast game had made clear, fans wanted action: dashes up and down court, shots and scores, daring plays invented on the spot, risks taken and delivered. But coaches wanted to win, and that sometimes meant slowdowns and freezing the ball with a lead. "Teams literally started sitting on the ball in the third quarter, especially with a 15-point lead," recalled Bob Cousy of the Boston Celtics. "The game was stagnant." This approach bottomed out in a ridiculous encounter between the Pistons and Lakers in Minneapolis on November 22, 1950. Fort Wayne got an early lead, then held the ball and declined to shoot, even with open layups. The Lakers stayed under their basket, refusing to engage the stall. Fans booed, read newspapers, threw garbage on the floor, aimed missiles at the Piston coach, demanded their money back. Fort Wayne slunk off the floor with a 19–18 victory. In the next few years, the NBA tried to outlaw such tactics with new rules on fouls in a quarter and in the last few minutes of a game. "No one would listen to me," recalled Danny Biasone, owner of the Syracuse Nationals. "I said forget all these different rules about fouling, what we need is a time limit. Make them shoot the ball and we'd be all right. After they tried about everything else, they were willing to look at my idea."

An idiot savant in basketball terms, from one of the league's smaller cities, Biasone had never played the game. His Eastwood Recreation Center—a ten-lane bowling alley upstairs, a restaurant downstairs—had earned this Italian immigrant a modest fortune. "For much of my life," he said later, "I was a nobody, a broken-down bartender." Civic pride, not a passion for hoops, had brought him into the NBL. Given the natural upstate rivalry between Syracuse and Rochester, he had bankrolled a basketball team essentially because he wished to compete with Rochester's team, the Royals. "Danny was a small Italian guy," recalled Johnny Kerr, one of his ballplayers. "He wore long, double-breasted coats, Borsalino hats and smoked filter cigarettes. As he talked, he left the cigarette in his mouth and bit down on the filter. . . . He sat on the bench during games, usually next to the coach, with that cigarette clenched between his teeth. He'd yell at the officials, but seldom said anything to his coach during games." "A very quiet guy," as Red Auerbach of the Celtics remembered him. "I think he was embarrassed about his command of the English language, but he was a gentleman and he was a thinker."

Somehow Biasone calculated that a team ought to shoot within 24 seconds of getting the ball. (As he explained it, this was based on a team's taking 60 shots a game; 120 shots in 48 minutes meant one every 24 seconds. But in 1953–54, even with late-game stalls, NBA teams already averaged 70 to 80 shots a game. Biasone pulled the number 60 from thin air.) In any case, 24 seconds was about right, long enough for teams to work the ball and wait for a good shot, but short enough to keep the game moving. In 1954-55, the first season with a 24-second clock, NBA teams took about 10 more shots per game. A team's average points per game went from 79 to 93, then to 99 a year later, and kept climbing. Biasone's shot clock was "the single most important rule change in the last fifty years," Auerbach said four decades later.

At the end of its first decade, the NBA had at last established basketball as a big-league sport. Attendance averaged about 5,000 a game, up from 3,300 in 1946. Most ballplayers made between $9,000 and $12,000 for the six-month season; top stars like Cousy earned up to $20,000. The eight NBA teams were playing the best basketball in the world. The league still had difficult times ahead, but Eddie Gottlieb knew, better than anybody, where pro basketball had come from. "I been in this business for 30 years, and any young fellow goes into basketball promoting is crazy," said Gottlieb in 1956. "But it ain't as bad as it was. In the old days my Philly team had its home court at the Broadwood Hotel. It was the ballroom. I'd book a game, a band, a girl singer, and hope the people showed. We don't need girl singers no more."

Chapter Seven

Black Power, Black Speed

In America the first discernible black athletes surfaced during slavery. This absurd reality, of slaves at play, wriggled through random cracks in a peculiar institution not generally conducive to games and leisure for African Americans. "Our sports and dances was big sport for the white folks," recalled Will Adams, a formerly enslaved Texan. "They'd sit on the gallery and watch the niggers put it on brown." Black sports began in thralldom, with white people looking on, betting and provoking, laughing and cheering. The owners wanted a contest like a horse race or cockfight—an amusing showdown among prized possessions. (White promoters, black athletes.) "I was tough and strong. I could outrun a wild animal, barefooted and bare headed," said Charles Hinton of Arkansas. "Old marster would have my father and Uncle Jacob and us boys run foot races. You know they was testin' us, and I know I was valued to be worth five hundred dollars." Whether in slave or horse, the owners looked for fast bloodlines.

Until adolescence, most slave children worked sparingly in the fields. With time to themselves, kids could shoot marbles and arrows, throw horseshoes, race in games of tag and prison base, ride stick horses, play early versions of baseball, "run around and kick their heels." In Spartanburg County, South Carolina, Lorenzo Ezell would walk a half-mile to the white school at lunchtime "to run base when dey play at noon." Slave children played usually for fun, but sometimes for whites, thus raising the stakes to dangerous levels. During the Civil War, Confederate troops bound for Louisiana stopped for the night at the Solman plantation near Alto, Texas. "We had the big races," remembered Preely Coleman, ten or twelve at the time. "There was a mulberry tree we'd run to and we'd line up and the sojers would say, 'Now the first one to slap that tree gits a quarter,' and I nearly allus gits there first. I made plenty quarters slappin' that old mulberry tree!" (It almost got him killed by other slaves: "So the chillen gits into their heads to fix me, 'cause I wins all the quarters." They threw a rope over his head, choked him, and dragged him down the hill to a spring. "But we meets Capt. Berryman, a white man, and he took his knife and cut the rope from my neck and took me by the heels and soused me up and down in the spring till I come to. They never tries to kill me any more.")

Even this early, in such desperate circumstances sports could turn deadly earnest. Denied so many other outlets, rewarded for displays of athletic gifts, the best slave performers preened and strutted their physical feats. "I was as lively as a young buck," recalled Josiah Henson of himself at fifteen on a Maryland plantation, "and running over with animal spirits. I could run faster, wrestle better, and jump higher than anybody about me." They vied for whatever status the owners allowed. Before mechanization, in a rural world powered only by muscle, foot speed took on practical uses as well. C. B. McKay of Jasper, Texas, nicknamed "Racer," later claimed he could catch a rabbit just by running it down. Another Texan, Green Cumby, raced and trained for nighttime visits, without the required pass, to his girlfriend on a nearby plantation. The feared patrollers, mounted and ornery, never caught him despite many chases. A popular slave song described such encounters:

> Run, nigger, run; patter-roller catch you;
> Run, nigger, run; it's almos' day;
> Run, nigger, run; patter-roller catch you;
> Run, nigger, run; you'd better get away.

Adult slaves toiled dawn to dusk every day but Sunday, with occasional half-Saturdays off and about four additional holidays a year. While the more pious slaves kept the Sabbath holy, most looked for day-of-rest amusement in gambling, dancing, drinking, and sports. "This is often encouraged by slaveholders," noted Henry Bibb of his enslaved adolescence in Kentucky. "When they wish to have a little sport of that kind, they go among the slaves and give them whiskey, to see them dance, 'pat juber,' sing and play on the banjo. Then get them to wrestling, fighting, jumping, running foot races, and butting each other like sheep." To spur fights the whites would offer bets and booze, or perch a chip on a slave's head and dare another slave to knock it off. They wanted a dirty, bloody bout, with kicking and head-butting, but if it turned truly dangerous they stopped it: protecting their property. "De nigger fights am more for de white folks' joyment," recalled John Finnely of Alabama, "but de slaves am 'lowed to see it."

Christmas was a time apart, an extended holiday that might last till the New Year, with rare feasts and presents from the owners. A lulling, deceptive contrast to everyday bondage, this annual blowout—careening with play and celebration—helped to reconcile both blacks and whites to slavery. Frederick Douglass, reflecting on his slave years in Maryland, later saw the whip in the master's extended hand: "A slave who would work during the holidays was considered by our masters as scarcely deserving them. He was regarded as one who rejected the favor of his master. It was deemed a disgrace not to get drunk at Christmas." The master wished to feel generous and kindly, at least once a year. This annual benevolence helped still any lingering qualms over the business of owning humans. As for the slaves, said Douglass, the Christmas holidays ranked "among the most effective means in the hands of the slaveholder in keeping down the spirit of insurrection" by functioning as "conductors, or safety-valves, to carry off the rebellious spirit of enslaved humanity." All parties implicitly understood this exchange. "And woe betide the slaveholder," said Douglass, "the day he ventures to remove or hinder the operation of those conductors!"

In slave sport, then, the games were already more than

games. Competing with each other, even pitted against animals, slaves were playing unplayfully for stakes that might last a lifetime. As a young man Henry Coleman would race against horses in South Carolina. "I wuz de swifes runner on de plantation," he said in old age. "De white fokes used to bet amongst dem selves as much as $20.00 dat I could outrun dat horse." The race started with the crack of a whip: a hundred yards down, a hundred yards back. "Quick as de whip popped, I wuz off. I would git sometimes ten feet ahead of de horse 'fore dey could git him started. Den when I had got de hundred yards, I could turn around quicker dan de horse would, and I would git a little mo' ahead. Course wid dat, you had to be a swift man on yer feets to stay ahead of a fas horse." If pleased by the race, the whites would give him some of the betting money. "Dey nebber got mad when I come out ahead. After I got through, my legs used to jus shake like a leaf. So now, I is gib plum out in dem and I tributes it to dat."

◆ ◆ ◆

For eighty years after slavery, black baseball rode the whims of white America's racial priorities. If a larger issue could be served by shunning blacks, so be it. Hostile to blacks, or merely indifferent and unthinking, white baseball sacrificed black ballplayers as the historical circumstances demanded: first to postwar reconciliation, then to the hoped-for harmonies of racial segregation. Sport, at its best an inverted refuge from everyday life, in this case moved in lockstep with societal trends of the day: a too-precise reflection of American travails. The baseball diamond was merely a four-pointed leaf in an accelerating whirlwind, as black chances in American life plummeted through the late nineteenth century. In sports as in society, blacks were granted no significant voice or power over the process: unwelcomed, then excluded, they retreated to their own athletic world, separate and unequal. However inexcusable to a modern perspective, all this looks inevitable within its historical context. This fatedness lifts a sad story into the hardened, deepened domain of real tragedy: not merely the product of wrong choices that could have gone differently, or a few villains pulling strings, black baseball was squeezed among relentless social forces drawn from entrenched, intractable histories, beyond individual will or control, even beyond anybody's comprehension at the time.

In 1866, at its tenth annual convention, the National Association of Base Ball Players elected Arthur Gorman of Maryland as its first president from beyond the Northeast. Only twenty months after the last shot of the Civil War, Gorman's election seemed proof to one hopeful observer "that sectionalism is unknown in our national game." The NABBP's next convention, a year later, dealt with an apparent threat to this fragile national reconciliation: the black Pythian Club of Philadelphia applied for membership. "If colored clubs were admitted," the association's secretary argued, "there would be in all probability some division of feeling, whereas, by excluding them no injury could result to anybody, and the possibility of any rupture being created on political grounds could be avoided." So the nominating committee unanimously banned any team with a black member. "No injury could result to anybody"— except to black ballplayers and their fans, who could be disregarded. For the whites, a rough sectional squabble, fought once again over blacks, had been avoided; no rerun so soon of the war. The Union was preserved. On much larger stages, this simple trade-off, North-South amity at the expense of blacks, littered national politics for the next thirty years.

Pro baseball dominated the game from the 1870s on. While the National League remained blackless by informal agreement, scores of lesser leagues needed baseball talent. At least seventy black players earned places in some twenty pro leagues during the late nineteenth century. Bud Fowler, the first black to breach white organized baseball, learned to play in small towns of central New York and started pitching for a white team in Chelsea, Massachusetts. In 1878, twenty years old, he threw an exhibition shutout against the National League's strong Boston team, which later that season won its second pennant in a row. Fowler became an itinerant all-purpose utility player, appearing for many teams for brief stops in many leagues, picking his way through an unpredictable tangle of racial mores. "One of the best general players in the country," said the national magazine *Sporting Life* in 1885, "and if he had a white face he would be playing with the best of them." He settled at second base, a reliable .300 hitter with fast feet. "Fowler has two strong points," a Denver paper deadpanned: "He is an excellent runner and proof against sunburn. He don't tan worth a cent."

Fleet Walker caught for Toledo's 1884 team in the American Association, the other major league of the time, and so became the first black big leaguer—sixty-three years before Jackie Robinson. Articulate and sophisticated, the son of a physician, Walker had attended and played baseball for two white colleges, Oberlin and the University of Michigan, before turning pro. When the Toledo team in 1884 ventured to Louisville, below the Mason-Dixon, Walker met withering enmity and was held out of later games there. In Richmond, Virginia, a letter threatened "much bloodshed" if Walker appeared. His own teammates had doubts too. Tony Mullane, "the Count from County Cork," won thirty-seven games for Toledo in 1884 and later called Walker "the best catcher I ever worked with." And yet, said Mullane, "I disliked a Negro and whenever I had to pitch to him I used anything I wanted without looking at his signals." (At second base, Bud Fowler wore wooden shin guards because of too many hostile white runners sliding in spikes high.)

The beleaguered blacks in organized ball were playing in a darkening landscape, the game getting late, dusk closing in and the whites going home. Grim blows rained down on blacks through the 1880s. As part of the national trade-off, the federal Civil Rights Act of 1875 was declared unconstitutional by the Supreme Court in 1883. Lincoln's party in 1884 lost the White House for the first time since the war. The South's previously unofficial apartheid became rigidly legalized. Even in New Orleans, the most tolerant city in the Deep South, the interracial baseball games of earlier years had ceased by 1890. Up North, following the 1883 Supreme Court decision, well-intentioned state laws forbade racial discrimination in public accommodations; but custom and resistance left these laws unenforced as informal segregation spread across the country. Among labor unions, the integrationist, tolerant Knights of Labor yielded leadership to the segregated American Federation of Labor. Lynching reached its grisly heights, with a black killed by mob violence every other day. Pushed back on their heels, harried and besieged, blacks would soon accept the pliant, desperate racial leadership of Booker T. Washington.

The black presence in whiteball peaked and retreated in 1887. Bud Fowler started the season as the best batter and base thief for the International League's Binghamton, New York, team. A local paper praised him for "developing new possibilities in the art of base running." But a few teammates turned on him, and Fowler—.350 average and all—was forced to quit. Soon the International League directors, informed "that many of the best players in the League were anxious to leave on account of the colored element," prohibited future signings of blacks. Similar incidents and shutdowns spread across baseball that summer of 1887: in Missouri, Ohio, Ontario, New York, New Jersey. Though a few ballplayers on white teams lingered into the 1890s, organized baseball was closing down for blacks.

So the game for African-Americans turned to all-black teams. The first amateur black squads had appeared after the Civil War. "By 1880," the black writer James Weldon Johnson re-called, "nearly every city and town in the South had its coloured baseball club." These amateur teams drew mixed audiences of whites and blacks to major games against rivals from other cities or states. The Memphis club was especially proud of its crack battery of Higgins and Gwin; Higgins later signed with a white team in Rochester. The first professional black teams—the Orions of Philadelphia and the Black Stockings of St. Louis—started playing in the early 1880s, just as the wave against blacks in whiteball began building. The long career of Sol White, later the first historian of black baseball, illustrates the separating drift of the times. Born in Bellaire, Ohio, in 1868, he started formal baseball with white teams in his hometown. As a teenager he played third base for several clubs in the white Tri-State League. After the convulsions of 1887, except for a brief stint with Fort Wayne in the Western State League, he played only for black teams, notably the Cuban Giants, the most celebrated black squad of the late 1800s.

The Cuban Giants began as a summer fling among waiters at the Argyle Hotel on Long Island's southern shore; the hotel fielded the team to amuse guests. A white businessman from Trenton, Walter Cook, then bankrolled a real pro team, with ballplayers drawn mostly from Philadelphia and the District of Columbia, under a black manager, Cos Govern. Passing as "Cubans" to blur their blackness, traveling in a private railroad car to avoid the vagaries of Jim Crow, they toured the East, South, and Midwest, meeting white teams, even occasional big leaguers. In 1888 they lost only 23 times in 129 games—"more by carelessness," explained the black *New York Age,* "than actual superiority of their opponents." That summer they won a tournament in New York against three other black pro squads, the Pittsburgh Keystones, the Norfolk (Virginia) Red Sox, and the New York Gorhams. "It is the general opinion," said the *Age,* rubbing it in, "that the Red Sox should never leave Virginia to play ball." The tournament's best player, second baseman George Williams of the Cuban Giants, accepted an engraved silver ball as the winner's trophy.

Serious athletes, the Cuban Giants also "brought something entirely new to the professional diamond," according to Weldon Johnson: baseball comedy. As a baseball-struck teenager, Johnson had learned to throw a curveball from one of the Giants; by the turn of the century, he was a songwriter and bon vivant in New York, stroking his way around the sporting circles of theaters, clubs, and ballgames. With a professional eye he could recognize the thespian tricks of good comedy. "The coaches kept up a constant banter that was spontaneous and amusing," Johnson wrote of the Cuban Giants. "They often staged a comic pantomime for the benefit of the spectators. When the team was in the field, the catcher habitually indulged in a continuous monologue in which he counselled and encouraged the pitcher or got off remarks not wholly complimentary to the batter. Generally after a good play the whole team would for a moment cut monkey-shines that would make the grand stand and bleachers roar." To varied degrees, most other black teams copied these vaudeville routines. Aside from drawing customers, the comedy served the critical purpose of lightening the atmosphere when black teams beat white teams; it was prudent that the whites not take their defeats too grimly. The comedy also fed a black image comforting to whites, of happy "darkies" laughing and hooting in broad stereotypes of eruptive good humor. "The negro ball player has ever 'known his place,' " *Baseball Magazine* later remarked. With his "glorious good nature and clean comedy" on the field, "he has never grown fresh or bumptious, never presumed upon his good fortune, never figured in race riots or 'black uprisings.'"

Most of the black teams were at first owned by white entrepreneurs—who, it may be presumed, also encouraged the comedy routines. (White promoters, black athletes.) J. M. Bright, owner of the Cuban Giants after 1888, was "extremely selfish in his financial dealings and naturally shrewd," according to Sol White. "He generally got what he asked for." Other white owners treated their ballplayers more fairly. Walter Schlichter, founder of the Philadelphia Giants, was himself an athlete, a swimmer, boxer, sculler, and sprinter; knowing sports from the inside, "Slick" dealt with his Giants as fellow jocks. Sol White called him "my ideal of an owner of a colored baseball team." In 1907 the *New York Age* declared the Philadelphia Giants the best team outside the white majors. Jess McMahon, a white boxing promoter in New York, owned shares in two black teams, the Lincoln Giants and Lincoln Stars. They played at McMahon's Olympic Field at 136th Street and Fifth Avenue in Harlem, and later in the Bronx. The powerhouse Lincoln Giants went 88-17 in 1911 with such stars as shortstop John Henry Lloyd (who hit .475 that year), catcher Louis Santop (.470), and pitchers Smokey Joe Williams and Cannonball Dick Redding: four of the greatest names in black baseball. Two years later, the Lincoln Giants won merely 101 of 107 games, including a sweet 9–2 exhibition victory over Grover Cleveland Alexander and the Phillies. Though he did resist pressure to employ black umpires, McMahon generally kept a good reputation among black sportsmen as "a square shooter" who "knows the colored sport problem as well as any white man in the United States."

John W. Connor was the first significant black owner of a black team. A native of Portsmouth, Virginia, "Uncle Jawn" had migrated to New York and prospered with his Royal Cafe on Myrtle Avenue in Brooklyn and (later) the Royal Garden nightclub at the corner of 135th and Lenox in Harlem, when that neighborhood started turning black. Well connected to politicians, Connor moved easily through the sporting underworld. His Brooklyn Royal Giants, named for his Cafe, started in 1905.

Chappie Johnson, whose blackball career began in the 1890s, later called Connor "the father of modern Negro baseball" because he had paid living wages to his men, thus forcing other owners to match him. His teams were the first black squads to carry three changes of uniforms, including coats and sweaters, and the first to play at Ebbets Field and the Polo Grounds. His later team, the Bacharach Giants of Atlantic City, was for a time the best in black baseball.

Connor fought and lost to his bête noire, Nat Strong, a white booking agent in New York who had been promoting black baseball and other sports events since the early 1890s. By 1910 Strong had, through a ruthless system of favors granted and withheld, seized control of most blackball games in the New York area. During the 1911 season he gave Connor's Royal Giants such poor bookings and cuts of the gate that the team lost money. A year later the *New York Age* reported efforts "to have all the colored clubs controlled by white managers." Just before the 1913 season, Connor temporarily quit baseball; Strong then, in a sequence implying cause and effect, took over the Royal Giants.

Eventually Strong held interests in five black teams. Some blacks made profitable peace with him. Ed Bolden, black owner of the Hilldales of Philadelphia, deferred to Strong in exchange for choice weekend dates. "The white promoters run the teams . . . and make money, which comes in a large measure from the pockets of Negroes," said the black sportswriter Lester Walton in 1918. "Invariably they seem to be actuated by a spirit of selfishness." ("I have been known to colored people who patronize colored amusements for many years," Strong replied, none too convincingly. "I know where I stand among the colored folks.") With his associate Max Rosner, Strong owned Dexter Park in Brooklyn; yet his Royal Giants never played there, hence never as the home team had to split the receipts with a visiting club; but Strong collected such fees from other teams. "For Strong," noted Rollo Wilson of the *Pittsburgh Courier,* "it is all coming in and nothing going out." Wilson and another leading black sportswriter, Fay Young of the *Chicago Defender,* scorned Strong as a parasite, "one of the sinister influences which have retarded the development of the game."

Strong at least made Rube Foster look good by contrast. The

only black man in blackball with power to rival Strong's, Foster was founder and boss of the Negro National League, the first successful black loop. As pitcher, manager, owner, and league mogul, he forged the most significant career of anybody in black baseball—and still died young, only fifty-one years old. Part of the coming wave of southern black migrants to northern cities, Foster was born in a small Texas town in 1879, the son of a presiding elder of the Methodist Episcopal Church. As with many white contemporaries, the game lured him from middle-class respectability. "I left school at the eighth grade to try and make a living at baseball," he recalled. "Rode freight trains, have been barred away from homes on account of it, as baseball and those who played it were considered by Colored as low and ungentlemanly." A touring black team in Hot Springs, Arkansas, discovered him and brought him north. With a thunking fastball and mean disposition, and one of the shrewdest baseball minds of his time, he pitched adeptly for black teams in Chicago, New York, and Philadelphia. In 1906 he led eight dissatisfied members of the Philadelphia Giants out to Chicago. Four years later he managed these Leland Giants to a record of 123-6, with 21 straight wins on an eastern tour.

On that reputation-building crest, in 1911 Foster started his own team, the Chicago American Giants, with a white partner, a tavern owner named John M. Schorling. As the son-in-law of White Sox owner Charles Comiskey, Schorling brought useful contacts in whiteball. He also provided his team a home field at Schorling Park, where they played every Sunday. Thus—a quiet irony—white money backed this blackest force in blackball. Foster and Schorling remained partners for fifteen years, splitting the receipts equally, never quarreling because Schorling prudently left the baseball decisions to Foster. For a decade the American Giants were the top club in blackball; but Nat Strong still hogged eastern bookings and profits. So in 1920 Foster launched his Negro National League, comprised of the best midwestern clubs. At Foster's insistence, every team in the league except J. L. Wilkinson's Kansas City Monarchs was controlled by black men. (Black promoters, black athletes.) Strong then replied by starting his own Eastern Colored League, with whites owning four of the six teams.

Foster now entered his brief prime. Commanding and imperious, he was an immense dark-skinned black, six feet four inches and 250 pounds after he quit playing, a fleshy presence with an ever-puffing pipe and hooded, inscrutable eyes. At league meetings he held noisy court, dispensing decisions and dominating any room. "A loud-voiced man with a smelly pipe," as Rollo Wilson of the *Pittsburgh Courier* described him. "The Master of the Show who moves the figures on his checkerboard at will. . . . The King who, to suit his purpose, assumes the robes of his Jester. Always the center of any crowd, the magnet attracting both the brains and the froth of humanity. Cold in refusals, warm in assents. Appraising his man the while he dissembles. Known to everybody, knows everybody. That's Rube." For home games Foster still managed the American Giants. From the bench he called each pitch, moved his men around, dictated every play: always in charge. Unlike most black managers, he also enforced dress codes and curfews. "I associate with my players," he explained. "I go into their homes, study their dispositions and habits, find out the things that appeal to them most." As a result, "I have broken up many of their bad habits."

In his own way, Foster was no less a boss than the hated Nat Strong. Every club in the Negro National League had to pay the American Giants 5 percent of its gate receipts. Foster dictated bookings and a haphazard schedule, never slighting his own team. Over the first six years of the league, the Giants grossed $514,000; other clubs lagged far behind, with the Monarchs at $248,000, the Detroit Stars at $165,000, and others less. So much richer than their rivals, the Giants could pay top salaries to the best players and so usually won the pennant. But color mattered: although a boss, Foster was at least a *black* boss, with his white partner, Schorling, kept in deep background. "If Rube Foster is a czar," said Fay Young of the *Chicago Defender*, "we need a few more czars in his line."

As the seasons passed, black teams on Foster's model developed their own style of baseball. It was serious, even dangerous hardball, full of beanings, brushbacks, spikings, and intimidations, played to win. Thin on the bench and in pitching depth, blackball generally ranked a notch or two below whiteball, but the best half dozen black clubs surely could have played in the white majors. This dangling might-have-been sharpened the stakes when black teams met barnstorming teams of white big leaguers. By John Holway's reckoning, blacks won about 60 percent of these interracial showdowns. "I guess we tried probably harder than they did, because we had something to prove," said Pat Patterson of the Monarchs. "We usually would beat them because of that. They were just out there to get their money. . . . We proved that a ball player is a ball player." "We played hard all the time 'cause we wanted to *win*," agreed Buck Leonard of the Homestead Grays. "It was a matter of pride. I wouldn't say they [the whites] *always* put forth their best efforts, but we did have some very good games."

White observers at black games encountered a kind of hyper-baseball—faster, rougher, more daring and exuberant than whiteball. "They play baseball with a verve and flair lacking in the big leagues," a white sportswriter concluded. "They look like men who are getting a great deal of fun out of it but want desperately to win, sometimes too desperately." To some unknowable extent, perhaps, psychological compensations affected play. On the road, the blackballers spent long, dreary hours cooped up in buses and cars, sleeping in snatches, never sure of finding food and lodging that would accept them. Brimming with the geysering energy of young, athletic men, confined and too often abused by white society, they hit the ball field busting out, tired but with an edgy, irritable force usually transmuted into rough playfulness. On the diamond they were released, at play: a safe stage and haven from the bizarre, offhand insults of racial America. "Their baseball is to white baseball as the Harlem stomp is to the sedate ballroom waltz," wrote Ted Shane in the *Saturday Evening Post*. "They whip the ball around without looking where it lands, and woe to the receiver if he isn't there instinctively. They play faster, seem to enjoy it more than white players. . . . Players clown a lot, argue noisily and funnily."

And, said Shane, "they undoubtedly are better base runners than their white confreres." Ballplayers themselves, contemporary observers, and later historians have all agreed: what most defined black baseball was fast runners, in the field or on the bases. A baseball child of the early 1900s, Rube Foster always taught the "scientific" game—bunt, run, steal, hit-and-run—that dominated the majors before Babe Ruth. Even after the big leagues turned to longball, Foster kept preaching the old gospel. As the *Chicago Defender* observed in 1922, the success of the American Giants was "built upon speed and a system of ability to think and take advantage of such." If the Giants got a man on first, they expected him to score. They would routinely bunt on third strikes, take unlikely extra bases, pull double and triple steals. At their peak, recalled Dave Malarcher of the Giants, "we had seven men in the lineup could run a hundred yards in around ten seconds. All speed, and with Rube directing it, it was something. Rube telling us what to do—push it here, hit it by the first baseman, hit over there."

In part because Foster so bestrode his sport, the speedy style of his team came to characterize most of black baseball. "Everywhere you go," Piggie Powell recalled of his playing days, "they had five or six *fast* men on there, could lay the ball down and get away." On the New York teams of the 1910s, the fleetest feet belonged to Louis Santop and Spottswood Poles of the Lincoln Stars and Jessie Bragg of the Lincoln Giants. In the Eastern League of the 1920s, the Hilldale club of Philadelphia deployed such burners as Judy Johnson, Frank Warfield, Clint Thomas, and George Carr. "That was our game," Johnson later told a white interviewer, "run, steal, make them make mistakes. Well, most Negroes can run—I guess you've noticed that." Even Josh Gibson, the burly slugging catcher, was "one of the fastest big men I ever saw," according to Carl Hubbell, and once led his league in steals. The slugging outfielder Oscar Charleston, perhaps the best all-around black ballplayer, was also unexpectedly fast. "We'd run you to death," Piper Davis told white opponents. "I'd played against white boys and I saw their type of ball. . . . Our game was always 'run and hit,' 'run and bunt.' " "People came to see us because we were fast," Art Mitchell agreed, "because we hustled, and because we scrapped for runs."

Competing in this fleet company, the outfielder Cool Papa Bell could outrun anyone—"perhaps the fastest player in any league, white or colored," a writer in *Baseball Magazine* suggested in 1929. No other player so embodied the essence of blackball. On defense, his speed let him play a daringly shallow center field. "Cool Papa apparently believes," said the *Pittsburgh Courier* in 1933, "that any ball hit in centerfield should be caught." His whooshing quickness inspired many unlikely stories. He could steal two bases on one pitch. He could stroke a sharp grounder through the middle and get hit by the ball as he slid into second. He could turn out a light and jump into bed before the room was dark. Legends aside, he could and did score from first on a bunt, from second on a fly ball. Once, on a rain-softened field, he was timed at 13.1 seconds around the bases, better than the big-league record of the time; on a dry field, he said, he could do it in a scorching 12 flat. "I don't know *where* he got that speed from," his teammate Bill Drake said later. "He'd just be standing there like that, and then he'd be gone. A lot of fellows got to lean off. He'd stand up straight, like nothing was going to happen, and was off just like a streak of lightning." From the 1920s on, most white ballplayers stopped running, swung from their heels, and played a sloggy longball. The blacks kept running.

◆　　◆　　◆

A theme emerges from the historical evidence: black speed afoot. Preely Coleman running to the mulberry tree for quarters, Green Cumby escaping on foot the mounted patrollers, Henry Coleman outracing horses, Bud Fowler "developing new possibilities in the art of base running," Rube Foster preaching and winning with the gospel of speed, Cool Papa zooming around the field, feet barely touching the ground. "Now, Mr. Foster," asked a white baseball magnate, "how do you make 'em *move* so on the bases?"

Exactly; everyone could see the overpowering speed of the black ballplayers. The baffling, necessary questions were why and how they ran so fast. Sports were raising a new, dangerous notion for whites: that blacks, this supposedly inferior race, might actually excel at something beyond their storied music and dancing. From the 1890s on, a few black athletes—the boxer Peter Jackson, the cyclist Major Taylor, and especially the white-whomping heavyweight champ Jack Johnson—beat white competition often enough to suggest the grim possibility of black athletic superiority. In the summer of 1911 Clark McAdams, a white editorial writer for the *St. Louis Post-Dispatch*, noticed that a local black baseball team—the St. Louis Giants—had beaten every white team in town save the big-league Cardinals and Browns, who refused to risk playing them. "Colored baseball, like colored pugilism, is to supercede the white brand," McAdams predicted. "The colored people play it so much better that the time is apparently coming when it shall be known as the great African game."

Fine so far. But McAdams went on to explain this racial gift as a function of the black man's more primitive, animalistic nature: "Less removed from the anthropoid ape, he gets down on ground balls better, springs higher for liners, has a much stronger and surer grip, and can get in and out of a base on all fours in a way that makes the higher product of evolution look like a bush leaguer." Already, in 1911, this early claim for black athletic gifts carried a glistening double edge; the praise was quickly withdrawn by its apparent implications, overtly stated or not. If black baseball teams beat white boys, that proved the race's evolutionary closeness to apes. On the other hand, if blacks lost to whites, that also proved the race's inferiority. The whites comfortably had it both ways.

Sprint events in track and field offered the most precise comparative tests of black and white foot speed. In 1914 Howard Drew of the University of Southern California, the first champion black sprinter, tied the world record of 9.6 seconds in the 100-yard dash. Blacks also won a string of AAU races in New York. "The negro's proficiency in athletics," said the *New York Times,* ambiguously, in the fall of 1914, "has become a source of much speculation and discussion in athletic clubs." During the 1920s Ned Gourdin of Harvard and DeHart Hubbard of Michigan set world records in the long jump. (As to the continued black victories in sprints, and the dearth of black hurdlers and distance runners, Gourdin denied the common explanation that "in keeping with our emotional nature we can only work in spasmodic efforts.")

From the 1930s on, black sprinters paced American track teams at the highest levels of competition. Four blacks made the 1932 United States Olympic team; Eddie Tolan won gold in the 100 and 200 meters. Ten blacks made the 1936 team; led by Jesse Owens, they brought home eight gold medals. "In the brief span of four years the Negro has lifted himself to a dominating position in track and field," declared the black sportswriter Roi Ottley in 1936. "The Negro is not only keeping pace, but he is frankly surpassing the efforts of his white brothers." Yet amid the celebrations, the general American glee at spoiling Hitler's Olympics, the old questions surfaced: How did they do it? Was it only a matter of training and dedication? Did they have a natural edge? A black sportsman in New York, Harry F. V. Edwards, a former sprinter on the 1920 British Olympic squad, recognized the usual implications and offered a clear-eyed prediction. "For years it has been said that Negroes can sing and dance," Edwards pointed out. "From now on we will hear the platitude that all Negroes can run and jump."

Given the power of black stereotypes to mold the thinking of both races, the idea of black athletic superiority could offhandedly encourage the oldest, most harmful racial myths: the notions that black people were inherently stupid and lazy. For many thoughtful observers, black and white, to admit any physical differences somehow opened the door to other, less flattering distinctions. "If the notion of race-linked black physical superiority is accepted," said one black sociologist, "race-linked white intellectual superiority becomes at least plausible." In their alleged duplication of the speed and strength of lower animals, perhaps black athletes had to admit an animal's intelligence too. And if blacks had inborn athletic advantages, then perhaps they won without training hard or thinking much, without truly earning their victories. This raised a touchy point with Cool Papa Bell, who liked to credit his brain along with his feet. "I would be alert on the bases," he later insisted. "A lot of fellows could do the same things I did if they were alert. A guy drops the ball and *then* they run. I was always looking for a break. It wasn't that I was that much faster than the other guys, it was just the way I played." Many other black champions have echoed Bell, preferring different explanations for their feats than unearned "natural" advantages.

These troublesome implications must ever be kept in mind in any responsible discussion of black athletes and foot speed. Yet the historian's task is to hold the implications down, for the moment, and to look at the sporting evidence on its own merits. To inch one's way across such a tightrope demands a delicate balancing act: remember the racial context, those ever-beckoning complexities, but let the sources speak for themselves without the shapings of ideology. Primary empirical facts must be weighed more heavily than secondary speculations. Stay close to the game. Leave the discussion till later.

◆　　◆　　◆

When the Michigan football team came to play Purdue in 1892, they brought a star black halfback named Jewell. "Kill the coon!" shouted the Purdue crowd. "Kill the coon!" Early in the game, Jewell was buried under a pile of tacklers, then carried off the field unconscious. The Purdue crowd stood and cheered.

◆　　◆　　◆

Black football arose virtually independent of its historical context. While black baseball reflected the rise and fall of racial segregation in America, events in one matching events in the other, black football went its own historical way: more a matter of individual personalities than of broader social currents. The game of football itself, spread by elite white colleges and athletic clubs, and more expensive and dangerous than baseball, was for decades little known or played among blacks. Early black footballers, then, were hardy anomalies playing for white teams in white leagues.

William H. Lewis, the first black football player of national reputation, started playing the game by accident. His football days, significant as they became, were merely a brief—though telling—episode in an extraordinary career stretching from the remnants of slavery to high appointive office in Washington, prominence as a criminal attorney in Boston, and pioneering membership in the American Bar Association. Bill Lewis was born in Norfolk, Virginia, in 1868, the son of former slaves of mixed ancestries. His father was a Baptist preacher. As a child Bill liked to attend murder trials in Portsmouth, absorbing his first lessons in the law. By peddling matches and other odd jobs, Lewis paid his way through a black teachers school in Petersburg, Virginia. His academic record attracted white patrons and brought him, a few months short of his twentieth birthday, to Amherst College in Massachusetts: a vaulting passage from segregated Virginia to a patrician white northern college with lingering abolitionist traditions.

A very serious young man, Lewis had never played sports down home. At Amherst he was nonetheless obliged to try out for the freshman-class football team; class spirit allowed no slackers. As the heaviest man in a lightweight group, he was placed at "center rush," the ball snapper on offense and the point man on defense. Agile, muscular, and smart, Lewis picked up the new game quickly. A year later he beat out the incumbent center, a man fifty pounds heavier, and then starred for three years of varsity football. As popular on campus as any white football hero, he made good grades, honed his oral arguments in debating societies, and was elected football captain and class orator. The law schools of both Harvard and Yale wanted him; graduate students were still eligible for intercollegiate teams. He chose Harvard, "a step which was greeted with great delight by the football men at Cambridge," according to a newspaper account.

At Harvard he made Walter Camp's All-America team, the first black so honored, in 1892 and 1893. "I had the age on the others," he said later, "being about 24 years old, and a fat kid of 19 didn't bother me much." On offense, he snapped the ball cleanly to his quarterback in the precise maneuvers required by the massed plays of the day. A photograph shows him crouched over, left hand on the ball, right elbow resting on his right knee, the fist clenched and head up; when he delivered the ball he raised his free hand to protect his face. On defense he was one of the first linemen to pull and roam the secondary, anticipating the range of a modern middle linebacker. "He was not so large," said a contemporary, "but he was like a piece of tempered steel." Playing at around 175 pounds among linemen averaging over 200, he handled their weight and strength with foot speed and guile. On kickoffs he would career down the field, often beating supposedly faster men who were supposed to arrive first, and pounce on the ballcarrier. Caspar Whitney of the *Harper's Weekly* sports department watched his feats in amazement. "A very fine muscular development," Whitney wrote of Lewis in October 1892, "and he is quick, often successful in stopping plays some distance from his position. He keeps his eye on the ball and gets into every play." "To watch him in a game is a sight of itself," wrote Whitney a year later. Strong in every phase of the game, Lewis was "not only the best centre of this year, but the best all-around centre that has ever put on a college jacket." (A decade after his last game, an all-time squad compiled by the *New York World* still placed him at center.)

Lewis hung around Harvard football for a few seasons after he finished playing, coaching defense and driving the boys hard. In 1898 he devised a special strategy to stop Penn's dreaded "guards back" formation. When the Penn guards pulled out, the tackles shifted to their place in the line while the ends replaced the tackles. Lewis put Harvard's defensive halfbacks directly behind his tackles; on the snap of the ball, the Harvard halfbacks shoved their tackles onto the lighter ends moved in opposite them, disrupting the formation before the backfield reached the line. Walter Camp, no less, overlooked his college connection and considered Lewis "a great student of the game and Harvard's most reliable defensive coach." When Camp revised his Spalding football textbook in 1903, he had Lewis write a new chapter on "Defense."

Years later, after appointment as the first black assistant attorney general, Lewis declared football the most valuable part of his college days because it had taught him "to regard with indifference trifling insults or severe physical hurts." The worst insults came off the field, where Lewis could not physically retaliate. In the spring after he was first named All-American, a barber in Harvard Square refused to cut his hair. Football players then led a student boycott—"as his friends, we strongly resent any such treatment"—until the barber relented. Later, at a team meeting, somebody referred to a troublesome opponent as a nigger. After an awkward moment, Lewis broke the tension by asking, "Why the devil didn't you kick him in the shins?" By such accommodations, usually as the only black in the room, Lewis made his way upward, first in football, then in politics and the law. He and Booker T. Washington, his useful political mentor, understood each other.

Though occasional blacks continued to appear on white college teams, especially in the Ivy League and Big Ten, twenty-three years passed between Lewis and the next black All-American. Fritz Pollard was a quite different personality:

northern-bred, focused on football from an early age, and not a student at all but an itinerant pure halfback, offering his wares in a too-free market. Born in Chicago in 1894, the son of a barber, Pollard attracted his first football notices as a schoolboy. For three years after high school, he attended—or at least practiced with the football teams of—five different white colleges: Northwestern, Brown, Dartmouth, Harvard, and Bates; then a detour back to remedial studies at a high school in Springfield, Massachusetts, and finally to Brown again, in the fall of 1915. This wandering course reflected both Pollard's coveted skills and the sadly flexible standards at the colleges that wanted him. As a Brown freshman Pollard managed eight D's and two flunks, which still left him barely eligible for his great season of 1916.

What contemporaries most remembered about Pollard's game was his blazing, unprecedented speed. "When he came by me," said a Brown quarterback, "it was like a cyclone and it was like somebody had hit me and took it [the ball] out of my hand. The fastest man to cross the line that I had ever seen to that day." Only five feet seven inches and a muscular 165 pounds, Pollard would shoot through the smallest holes in the line: "You couldn't see where he went through—he could just smell it." Once he was in the open field, nobody could catch him; when tacklers drew near, he would fake, execute a cross-step dodge, and whiz off in another direction. "It wasn't a question of tackling him," said a frustrated opponent. "The problem was getting near him."

On successive weekends in 1916, Pollard all but singlehandedly beat Yale and Harvard, accounting for 63 percent of Brown's total yardage in the two games. Against Yale he caught a punt at midfield, evaded the ends, started right—drawing a pack of Yalies in that direction—juked his cross-step, "switched to the left, where he outstripped every Yale pursuer in a desperate sprint for the Yale goal line, sailing across with the second touchdown for the visitors," the *New York Times* reported. "This heartbreaking performance nailed the lid down on Yale hopes." He also recovered three fumbles and made a touchdown-saving tackle. A week later he helped beat Harvard, 21–0, the worst defeat yet for any Harvard team under coach Percy Haughton. "He was the sensation, the spectacle, and all else of the game," said the *New York Sun* of Pollard, "effective in every department of play, exhibiting not one weakness," unleashing "the straight arm, a baffling change of stride and extreme speed."

In effect, Pollard was already a professional football player. As game day approached, he would tell interested businessmen in Providence that he wouldn't play unless his bills were paid; so the businessmen coughed up. Poor grades kept him off the Brown team in 1917, and Pollard soon began an overtly pro career of many short-term engagements. Blacks had played professionally for Ohio's town teams since at least 1902. When the National Football League was launched from those Ohio teams in 1920, blacks as a matter of course were admitted to the new league. Pollard played for four NFL teams in seven years, flashing his expected slippery quickness, usually serving as the team's coach: the first black to lead a team in a white big league. For the Akron Pros in 1920, he made the first all-league team at halfback. Opponents keyed on him, a marked man. Unfriendly crowds might chant: "Get that nigger!" Sometimes Pollard would dress for a game at an undisclosed location and appear just before kickoff to avoid problems. When tackled he would roll on his back and bicycle his legs, cleats brandishing, to discourage pilers-on. "It would get a little rough," Pollard said later, "but I never tried to mix up with the other team. I'd just grin if they called me names and jump up and try to run through 'em again."

Aside from Pollard, twelve other blacks played in the NFL from 1920 to 1933—as many as six in a single season. The best known were Paul Robeson, who had made All-American at Rutgers in 1917, and later became a celebrated singer, actor, and political activist; Inky Williams, an All-Pro end for Hammond in 1923; and Duke Slater, a tackle from Iowa who played with distinction for ten NFL seasons. After 1926, no more than two blacks played in the league at any given time. As the NFL grew beyond the founding Midwest, it included teams based in cities closer to Dixie, and drew more white players from the South and Southwest. This expansion complicated the issue of blacks in the league. When Rock Island played in Kansas City, Duke Slater stayed on the bench, banned by the home team. In 1926 the New York Giants refused to play Canton at the Polo Grounds because the Bulldogs included a black man, Sol Butler; after a delay, Butler withdrew and the game went on. (The *Chicago Defender* blamed a few of the Giants, notably Steve Owen and Cowboy Hill from Oklahoma and Cecil Grigg from Texas.) Meantime teams in some of the smaller midwestern cities, more willing to play blacks, quit the NFL as it went big time.

After 1933, no blacks played in the NFL for the next dozen seasons. This informal ban ran against other social currents of the day. At a time of sweeping reform and political liberalism, the American apartheid was starting to crumble in the 1930s. Pressures to integrate white baseball were building, from whites and blacks alike. Yet in this promising era, with old fault lines cracking open, pro football slammed a curtain down. "There are many sane arguments against playing colored men in games requiring personal contact," said Harry March of the Giants in 1934. "There are so many Southern boys in the League that much feeling is sure to result. Then, too, the management is frequently embarrassed by the refusal of dining cars and restaurants to serve the colored players and of hotels to give them the desired accommodations which the white players receive." True enough; yet managements had contrived to live with that embarrassment until then.

The NFL went lily-white not for general historical reasons but because of the overwhelming personal influence of one man, George Preston Marshall. Of border-state origins and racial sensibilities, Marshall had entered the league in 1932. Five years later he moved the Redskins from Boston to his home city of Washington and began a Confederate marketing strategy, aiming his radio broadcasts and publicity at the white South—which still lacked any NFL teams of its own. When the Redskin band played "Dixie" at halftime, the symbolism was inescapable. Given these circumstances, Marshall would not abide an integrated NFL. By deploying his noisy assertiveness at league meetings, and because of his crucial friendship with George Halas, Marshall usually could impose his will on other league owners. Apparently no formal agreement was ever necessary. Everyone knew how Marshall felt, and nobody risked a public fight about it. The NFL faded to white.

◆　　◆　　◆

Black basketball took a third historical course. Squeezed from the big leagues, black baseball had settled into the lower reaches of the race's class structure, bordering the demimonde of the sporting underworld. Black football emerged fitfully with occasional black stars on white college teams: solitary blacks on a pale background, far from a soulful racial context, and then professionally banned by one man's marketing whim. By contrast, black basketball began in the upper reaches of African-American society. Well distant from both the sporting underworld and the white colleges, in only three decades it matured—leaping and bounding—from its first dribbles in high society to domination of the best white teams, thus compiling one of the quickest, least-known success stories in black sports.

Serious black basketball began with the St. Christopher club of New York, a product of muscular Christianity and a Manhattan real estate boom. The St. Christopher team was sponsored by St. Philip's Protestant Episcopal Church, the richest black congregation in America. Founded in 1819, admitted to the white Diocesan Convention in 1853, St. Philip's had followed the cross-town migrations of New York's black community. By 1886, when Hutchens C. Bishop became rector, it was already known as "not only the most fashionable church [in New York City] . . . but the wealthiest," with a "reputation for exclusiveness" and the only rented pews of any black church in the city. The first black student and graduate of the General Theological Seminary, the leading white school for Episcopal preachers, Bishop in 1889 moved his flock to a church on West Twenty-fifth Street. After two decades there, with local real estate values ascending, the light-complexioned Bishop sold the West Twenty-fifth Street property for some $600,000 and—passing as white—bought land and apartment houses in Harlem, which he then conveyed to St. Philip's. Now richer than ever, the congregation in 1911 settled into an impressive new English Gothic church on West 134th Street. The new parish house, on West 133rd Street west of Seventh Avenue, included a gymnasium and athletic equipment.

To a unique degree among New York's black churches, St. Philip's had the resources to sustain an elaborate sports program. Everard W. Daniel, the curate at St. Philip's, preached and lived the tenets of muscular Christianity. "We believe in all forms of athletics," said a church statement, "as aids not only to the vigor of the body, but also to mental alertness and moral soundness." Daniel took vigorous charge of the church's St. Christopher athletic club, adding track and basketball teams, using sports to reach young people. "He was a big brother to all of younger Harlem," the black sportswriter Lester Granger said later, "and his tall figure and scholarly face with its genial smile were familiar at every gathering where the affairs of boys and girls were discussed." St. Christopher became the largest black athletic club in the city, peaking at nearly a thousand members, with an athletic council of older men dispensing money and advice. Its teams "never wanted for anything in the line of paraphernalia"; once, facing a basketball game on an unexpectedly slippery floor, they simply went out and bought the latest model sneakers for the whole team. With St. Christopher thus raising the ante, its main local rivals—the Smart Set of Brooklyn and the Alpha Physical Club of New York—had to follow suit, and lesser clubs fell into line. Black amateur sports in New York entered their prime decade.

Basketball games, with dances afterward, became fashionable occasions for New York's polite black society of the 1910s. "Here was the game which both sexes could enjoy," recalled Romeo Dougherty, sports editor of the *Amsterdam News,* "which also gave all hands their best opportunity for mingling socially." When the St. Christopher "Red and Black Machine" set forth to meet the Alphas, in their uniforms of blue and white, thousands of rooters accompanied the teams up to the Manhattan Casino on 155th Street. "And on those nights when that far famed cheering section from the church started the works, answered by the wearers of the blue and white," said Dougherty, savoring the memories, "it made the blood of all present thrill, driving the populace to wild enthusiasm when the teams took the court and played as only amateurs can play."

During the 1913–14 season St. Christopher hired a white basketball coach, Jeff Wetzler, a German Lutheran who worked at a local city recreation center. ("The outstanding coach among the Negro teams," according to Dougherty. "Jeff was totally color blind.") Wetzler's prize prospect, Clarence "Fat" Jenkins, eventually became the finest all-around black hoopster of his generation. Only sixteen years old in 1914, coached by Wetzler since he was a little boy and still years from his prime, Jenkins was already a schoolboy champion in the 100-yard dash. Attending Stuyvesant High School, he played baseball and track for his school and club basketball for St. Christopher. Jenkins's nickname must have been bestowed in irony: he was lean and compact, usually the fastest man on the court. On the baseball diamond, left-handed but too short to play first base, he became a skilled outfielder who later starred in the Negro leagues. Under Wetzler's coaching, on New Year's Day of 1914 St. Christopher beat Alpha, 24–19, at the Manhattan Casino; "the biggest thing in the basketball world," a sportswriter for the *New York Age* called this annual showdown. Later that season St. Christopher also beat Howard University, the best black college team, by an easy 29–17 score and so claimed national black supremacy in the sport.

The Monticello club of Pittsburgh might have argued the point. Cumberland Posey, Jr., Monticello's leader and best player, came from the same upper-class background as the St. Christophers. His father, one of the wealthiest black men in Pittsburgh, operated river steamboats and coal barges, dabbled in banking and real estate, and was president of the *Pittsburgh Courier*. His mother, a teacher and artist, was the first black graduate of Ohio State. Cum Posey, Jr., flirted with higher education—briefly attending three white colleges—before settling into a sporting life of baseball and basketball. "Fragile in appearance and innocent in looks," according to Rollo Wilson of the *Courier*, "he was a natural athlete and a born leader who found self-discipline and routine irksome." About five feet nine inches and 145 pounds, Posey copied the speedy, high-scoring basketball style of Harry Hough, the skittering little white pro who played for Pittsburgh's South Side team in 1908. (Posey regarded Hough as the best basketball player he'd ever seen.) In the spring of 1911, after flunking out of Penn State, Posey helped launch the Monticello club with his older brother See. "Considered throughout the country as one of the fastest boys playing the game," as the *New York Age* noted in 1912, Cum Posey roamed the court on elusive, untiring legs. "I had Posey that night," one opponent recalled. "At least, I was supposed to have him. I don't believe I saw that bird after we shook hands at the start of the game until the first half ended."

Easily the best black team in Pittsburgh, the Monticellos had to seek worthy rivals elsewhere. In March 1912 they beat Howard, 24–19, in "a clean yet furiously played game." Cum Posey led his team with 15 points. It was only Howard's third loss in three years; so Monticello grandly claimed "the colored basketball championship of the country." (Such claims piled up redundantly.) A year later the Monticellos came to New York during the Christmas holidays and beat the Alphas, 40–24, and the Smart Set, 27–14. But in February the Alphas traveled to Pittsburgh and hung on Monticello its first defeat of the season, 24–19. A few weeks later Howard beat them badly at the Manhattan Casino in New York, 33–17. The *Age* praised Posey as the best black player in basketball, but dismissed Monticello as merely "a one man's team."

So, in the fall of 1913 the Posey brothers quit Monticello to start their own team, the Loendi Big Five, officially an amateur club but with creeping professional tendencies. Within a few years, from varied sources, Posey had assembled the kind of team that only money could buy: from black colleges, George Gilmore of Howard and Pimp Young of Lincoln University; from the Homestead steel mills, Greasy Betts, a champion sprinter at 100 and 220 yards; and for center, James "Legs" Sessoms, at six feet seven inches the tallest man in black basketball. Gilmore, in particular, played the game on Posey's demanding level. Nearly unbeatable during the world war, the Loendis inevitably claimed the chimerical national black championship.

The amateur phase of black basketball—of muscular Christianity, social status, and the game, officially, for its own sweet sake—was yielding to professionalization. The pro issue had splintered the St. Christopher team in the fall of 1914. Will Anthony Madden, the team manager, departed with two of his best players, the center Walter Cooper and Edgar Perkinson, a high-scoring forward, to form a nascently pro club, the Incorporators. (Fat Jenkins stayed with St. Christopher.) The new team soon boasted its own uniforms and training quarters with a swimming pool and handball court; "The showers are a joy forever," Madden noted. In two years the Incorporators went 40-2 and, of course, claimed the national title. Cooper, strong and springy, usually topped his team in scoring. Sure of his touch from the foul line, he would shoot, turn around, and start walking upcourt with the ball still in the air. "Cooper stands head and shoulders over every other colored basketball player in the world," said Madden with proprietary pride in the spring of 1916. "Furthermore, he has met and defeated many of the best white centers. . . . His ability to ring baskets from the field is so remarkable that it is almost uncanny; and when it comes to shooting under fire he is a genius." However—a coach's classic complaint about his best scorer—"I cannot say that I am entirely satisfied with Cooper's passing."

A short, aggressive man with a Napoleonic personality, Madden soon antagonized his colleagues in New York's black hoop circles by his choice of friendly referees and his suspicious ways with money. The other teams united against the Incorporators; finally his own team turned on him, and Madden was driven from the game. But the play-for-pay drift he had introduced to New York went on without him. Walter Cooper shifted to the Alphas, an overtly amateur team, and then—in revealing litigation—sued them for wages secretly promised but not delivered. Amateur black basketball faded out; even St. Christopher no longer sponsored a team. The old intercity rivalries among Monticello, Lincoln, Howard, and the New York teams, for which clubs would entertain each other with elaborate social weekends built around the games, now pared down to mere contests for cash. "Instead of being met at the station by a committee from the club and escorted to breakfast and lodgings," Rollo Wilson keened, "no one knows whether you have arrived till you put in your appearance at the hall. After the combat you collect your money and vamoose. It's a cold-blooded business proposition."

In these circumstances Bob Douglas launched his Renaissance Big Five, the finest black basketball team ever. At their peak in the 1930s, touring the country to play white teams before white crowds, the Rens in general won amicably, letting the outclassed opposition down easily. But anyone who messed with them might have his jaw broken. The Rens merely reflected the spirit of their owner. An immigrant from the British West Indies, Douglas had

arrived in New York in his teens. He worked as a doorman—
twelve hours a day, six or seven days a week, for four dollars in
wages—then as a messenger and porter for a music trade paper.
He saw his first basketball game in 1905, when he was twenty-
one. "I thought it was the greatest thing in the world," he recalled. "You couldn't keep me off the court after that." Small but
feisty, he joined the Spartans, a top amateur club, eventually
becoming the team captain, then manager. "I wasn't a real good
player but I was rough," he allowed. "We played the game almost like football. I only weighed 150 pounds but when I hit
you, you felt it. And I didn't let anyone get past me to the
basket." As a manager he modeled himself on John McGraw of
the New York Giants, another tough little guy, and earned a
reputation for unforgiving discipline. When Hobey Johnson, the
star and captain of the Spartans, missed too many practices,
Douglas barred him from the next game. "One of the most de-
ceiving fellows in the world," Romeo Dougherty said of Douglas.
"He has little to say at any time, and by his carefree manner and
almost apologetic smile you would be inclined to take him for a
tender. Yeah, but what a surprise is in store for you when you
rub him the wrong way and arouse his ire."

In the fall of 1923, accepting the professional drift of the day,
the Spartans turned pro. In return for using the Renaissance
Casino at 138th Street and Seventh Avenue as its home court,
the team was renamed the Renaissance Big Five. Two key players, both well-traveled, joined the Rens in 1924, lifting them to
parity with the best white clubs. Pappy Ricks had starred for
teams in New Jersey, then for Cum Posey's crack Loendis; the
Pittsburgh Courier had called him "the most dangerous shooting
forward in the country, inside the 15-foot mark." For the Rens,
Ricks was the designated set shooter, the only player Douglas
allowed to shoot at will from distance. As he released the ball,
Ricks would holler, "Two!" and head upcourt with the serene
confidence of a pure shooter. Fat Jenkins, already a veteran of a
dozen seasons of big-time black ball, became the Rens' floor
leader and on-court coach. In team photos he looked serious,
knowing, in charge. Many observers described him as the fastest
man in basketball, black or white: "like a streak of greased lightning," said one, "or a whippet getting around the floor, and he

followed the ball with uncanny skill and precision." The shortest man on the team at five feet six and a half inches, he played the tallest, most relentless defense. Of ascetic habits, he neither smoked, drank, nor chewed tobacco, and kept playing two pro sports well past his fortieth birthday.

For a few years the Rens stayed near home, barnstorming around the New York area, with regular holiday and Sunday night games at the Renaissance Casino. Crowds of thousands, in tuxedos and evening gowns, would light up the Casino for the game and the dance afterward. In 1925–26 the Rens took two of five games from the Original Celtics, then at their peak, and beat strong white pro teams from Kingston and Paterson. They won 26 straight that year, finishing at 77-15 for the season. "The team has become an institution in Harlem," declared the *Amsterdam News*. "The colored fans find in it a vent for their emotions and an outlet for their pride in race."

Around 1930, as the Depression settled into Harlem, local crowds dwindled away. So Douglas bought a bus (dubbed the Blue Goose) and sent his team on the road, with Fat Jenkins as the acting coach. In 1929–30 they went 112-20, with only 31 of those games at the Casino; in subsequent years they came home even less. For this itinerant squad, venturing into unknown towns with unpredictable racial attitudes, Douglas added two strong rebounders and enforcers. Tarzan Cooper, schooled by high school and pro teams in Philadelphia, was a muscular six feet four inches. Under the hoop, pushing for rebounding position, opponents just rolled off his back. Joe Lapchick of the Celtics later praised Cooper as the best center he'd ever guarded. Wee Willie Smith, whom Douglas spotted in a preliminary game in Cleveland, stood an inch taller than Cooper. He became the team's policeman. "The toughest, meanest basketball player I ever faced," said John Wooden, whose Indianapolis Kautskys met the Rens when they came through Indiana. "He wasn't dirty, just tough and mean. . . . He weighed about 220, had a beautiful build, was quick, with lightning reflexes, had great balance, and was truly a superb athlete." To amuse crowds Smith might show off by palming the ball, an uncommon skill at the time.

Their lineup set, the Rens played a classic Northeast short-passing game, with the tempo turned up. Back in 1923, Douglas

had engaged Nat Holman, the foremost advocate of the Northeast style, to coach the Rens for three days. Holman cut the
squad down from thirty to eight men, picking his kind of ballplayers, and preached the Celtics' gospel: pass the ball, don't
dribble, keep it moving; no dubious shots; work together as a
team. To which the Rens added their own touch: "sustained
speed," as A. E. Francis of the *Amsterdam News* put it, "controlled
speed, and then some more speed. There is no team in the
business who can stand up under the devastating fire of the
Renaissance offense without withering." Sportswriters exhausted
their imaginations in trying to describe the Rens on a roll. Like
whipping a baseball around, said one. They passed the ball as if
it were attached to their hands by elastic bands, offered another.
A third, after watching Cooper in the pivot, said it was like
hurling golf balls against a concrete wall, with Cooper as the wall,
and the balls bounding back with the speed of bullets. "It was
almost impossible to follow the flights of the ball with any degree
of accuracy," A. E. Francis concluded, "and the darting and
shifting of the men were so phantom-like they appeared like
shadows."

Over the decade of the 1930s, the Rens were the best basketball team, white or black, pro or amateur. In 1932–33 they won
eighty-eight straight games, doubling the Celtics' pro record.
Out on the road, they would establish base camps at black hotels
in certain cities—Chicago, Indianapolis, Kansas City—from
which they made forays of up to two hundred miles each way for
contests. Contending with all those strange courts and stranger
referees, they remarkably won more than 86 percent of their
games. In a one-point loss to the Chicago Bruins, eighteen fouls
were called on the Rens, none on the Bruins. The *Chicago Defender* whiffed "a rank smell" to the contest. Against the Celtics in
Cleveland, twenty-seven fouls on the Rens, seven on the Celtics.
"The referees gave us nothing," one of the Rens said later.
"Sometimes we had to fight just to stay alive. Willie Smith may
have broken a lot of jaws, but he never started a fight." They
picked their way carefully through white America, not running
up scores, letting the opposition look good (and thereby encouraging a return match), behaving themselves off the court. "On
the rare occasions when we got to stay in a nice hotel," a Ren

recalled, "those of us who stayed sober would stand watch until the drinkers came back to make sure they didn't create any disturbance. All those hotels needed was one mistake so they could say that they had tried, but they couldn't have our kind around."

The Rens' only rival among black teams was the Harlem Globetrotters, founded in 1927 by Abe Saperstein, a white sports entrepreneur in Chicago. (White promoter, black athletes.) Like the Rens, the Globies played mainly on the road, mostly against white teams, with only occasional stops at their nominal home, the Savoy Ballroom in Chicago. Saperstein at first drew his best players from alumni of Wendell Phillips High in the black South Side: Inman Jackson (a six-foot-four-inch center with large ball-palming hands), his buddy Toots Wright (a defensive ace), and Runt Pullins ("the Bronze Nat Holman," a high-scoring little guard). The Globetrotters toured the country, playing night after night, winning with a looser style than the Rens' that included long passes and peculiar shots. The *Chicago Defender* attributed their nightly success to precise passing, exceptional ballhandling, and "extraordinary speed afoot."

Their commercial success depended as much on their comedy routines. In the minstrel-show tradition of the Cuban Giants and other black baseball teams, the Globetrotters spiced their serious play with goofball antics. Inman Jackson would glaze an opponent's eyes with a whirl of pantomime passes, then rest the ball on the man's head, leave it there for a beat, and pluck it away. Another Trotter would throw a ball with so much spin that it bounced back to him, leaving his man in mid-lunge. With the game on, the whole team might shoot craps or play cards, or mime a baseball or football game. A Globie would drop-kick a shot from seventy feet. Harmless fun on one level, when performed in loud, broad stereotypes these tricks made many blacks wince. "I won't let my team fake games and out-and-out clowning is no good," Saperstein explained. "The only answer is a blend of basketball and entertainment. I am the only one in the business who seems to realize this." Apparently impressed by the Globetrotters' gate receipts, the Rens added a few trick passes and plays, and briefly hired Rabbit Bethards, a player skilled at clowning. But their limited comedic efforts never overcame the ballgame. "Abe Saperstein died a millionaire because he gave the white people what they wanted," Bob Douglas said later. "I could never have burlesqued basketball."

Unfriendly rivals, the Rens and Globetrotters didn't play each other until March 1939, at the debut of a pro tournament in Chicago. The grandly named "World Tournament," attracting top pro teams from the Midwest and East, was sponsored for a decade by the *Chicago Herald-American*. The only two black teams among eleven entrants in 1939 met in the semifinals; Bob Douglas even came out from New York to coach his team, pacing the floor in front of the bench, chewing up a half-smoked cigar. The bionic Fat Jenkins, soon to turn forty-one, held the Trotters' Henry Rusan, who averaged 17 points a game, to a single basket. All the Rens played tight defense, limiting the Trotters to long shots, and won, 27–23. Their final opponent, the Oshkosh All-Stars, had finished second that season in the National Basketball League. Led by 12 points from Pop Gates, a Rens rookie out of Benjamin Franklin High in New York, the Rens ran off 11 straight points and took the title, 34–25. They finished the year with 122 wins in 129 games.

The 1940 World Tournament expanded to fourteen teams studded with thirty-three college All-Americans. After flogging their first-round opponents by 21 and 24 points, the Rens and Globies met again in the quarterfinals. The Rens were riding a fifty-game winning streak. Both teams played grim, careful games, with none of the showmanship that had punctuated their waltzes through the first round. The contest snapped back and forth until the Trotters' Sonny Boswell hit two free throws with forty-five seconds left for a tight 37–36 victory. In the semifinal against the Syracuse Reds the Globies trailed, 8–0, and went seventeen minutes without a bucket, but came back to win, 34–25. For the final, against the hometown Chicago Bruins, local bettors left the Trotters 3–1 or 4–1 underdogs. Trailing by 8 with five minutes to go, the Trotters ripped off five baskets in two minutes. At the gun, a Bruin fired from midcourt; the ball hit the rim, bounced high, hit the rim again, and rolled off; the Trotters won, 31–29. In two years the World Tournament had anointed two black pro champions.

"Basketball is NOT a white man's game," exulted Fay Young

of the *Defender* afterward. "The pale faces just don't know how to play it."

◆　　◆　　◆

As the course of racial integration accelerated toward Jackie Robinson, the disorderly culture of black baseball took on interracial significance. If whites wondered how blacks might perform in the big leagues, they looked for clues in the Negro leagues. On the field, blacks obviously could play the game; off the field, they left more dubiously mixed impressions.

Within the race's class structure, pro baseball had settled into a twilit realm between the honest working class and the sporting underworld. Middle-class black magazines such as *Opportunity* and the *Crisis* paid little attention to the Negro leagues; and the athletes, as ever, spurned middle-class amusements. For nocturnal recreation most ballplayers descended to the demimonde of nightclubs, gambling joints, and cathouses. Many black jazzmen—Louis Armstrong, Fats Waller, Count Basie, Lionel Hampton, Cab Calloway—were great fans of blackball, sometimes even buying into teams. Linked by their callings, jazzmen and ballplayers both "played" for a living, and kept playing other games after work. Both lived on the road, performing for only a few hours a day, far from domestic restraints, with glamorous girlfriends and certain secrets to hide from the straight world. "The professional players were a rough bunch," recalled the shortstop Tweed Webb. "I didn't drink or smoke, and I didn't like the women that hung around the players."

So black ballplayers often found trouble, with women and the law. "Our baseball players," said Rube Foster, "are harder to handle than the white players." In 1925 Dave Brown and Frank Wickware of the Lincoln Giants were separately charged with murder; one disappeared, one was cleared for lack of evidence. In 1926 Dobie Moore, the star shortstop of the Monarchs, was shot in the leg by a girlfriend, ending his career; and Dimps Miller, the Monarchs' only left-handed pitcher, was shot in the pitching arm by his wife. After the season, Rollo Wilson of the *Courier* reported a rumor that five Monarchs were being dropped for unruly conduct. "It's a sad truth," said Wilson, "that if Negro baseball were purged of its bad actors, there would not be left men enough to man one league." At a Hilldale game in 1929, a woman involved in the local numbers racket was murdered by her common-law husband; later that season, three of the Hilldales got into a brawl outside a Philadelphia whorehouse, leaving one player with a fractured skull. A few years after that, Lemuel Hawkins of the Monarchs killed a man following an argument over a card game.

Black sportswriters kept scolding the ballplayers, deploring "the many shortcomings and unreliability of colored clubs," urging them for the sake of racial pride and discretion to behave themselves: to no apparent effect. "Players have refused to keep in shape," wrote Fay Young after the 1927 season. "Some would be seen on the streets in the early hours of the morning with a hard game to be played later in the day. Whisky, such as it is, white mule and riotous living have shortened the life of a good many men." In June 1929 Roy Poindexter, ace pitcher for the Memphis Red Sox, lost a tough game in St. Louis. That night, in their hotel room, his teammate J. C. McHaskell started teasing him. "Well, Friday is ladies' day at the park," McHaskell twitted, "and you ought to do better with the girls all there." So Poindexter pulled a revolver and shot McHaskell in the foot. (Bad luck pursued both men. That winter, McHaskell suffered an accident at his packinghouse job; the same foot was crushed, then infected, then amputated. And Poindexter, a year after shooting his teammate, got into a fight in Washington and was stabbed to death.)

Employee relations in the Negro leagues displayed a similar flaring, unpredictable volatility. "We always had contracts, but they didn't mean much," recalled Cool Papa Bell. "They wouldn't pay you your money, and that was that. You'd just go somewhere else." In the off-season players might dicker with various teams, sign a contract or two, collect advance monies, and then show up, or not. Owners would make trades and announce them to the sporting press, knowing the players might not switch teams as directed. Defaulting owners and wandering ballplayers generally ignored the mere scraps of paper that bound them. "They were regular contracts. But we didn't pay much attention to them," said Bill Yancey. "If I was unhappy I said the hell with this and I jumped."

The owners themselves were often underworld figures, fellow denizens with their ballplayers of the black demimonde. Barron Wilkins, the "king of Harlem's underworld" until his murder in 1924, was a silent partner behind most of New York's black teams. He owned a tony underground gambling joint, the Exclusive Club at the corner of 134th and Seventh, that catered mainly to whites. A political power at election time, generous to cops, Wilkins was known to blacks as "the man with the big bankroll." The Detroit Stars were owned by Tenny Blount, a power in black policy gambling. "He was one of the squarest men," said Turkey Stearns, one of his ballplayers. "I never worked for anyone better. If you worked, you got paid." In Pittsburgh, the Homestead Grays were bankrolled after 1933 by the gambler Sonnyman Jackson, whose holdings included a poolroom, gambling houses, a tavern and restaurant, and hundreds of jukeboxes.

Led by Gus Greenlee, the Negro National League of the 1930s was dominated by team owners based in numbers gambling. Greenlee—"Big Red"—had migrated to Pittsburgh from North Carolina, started out in beer bootlegging, then seized control of the city's numbers games by the threat and application of muscle. He lavished money on his Crawfords, buying them a new ballpark, a fancy bus, and three sets of uniforms. "He looked like the racketeer that he was," said his second baseman Dick Seay. "Dressed neat, big expensive hats, always a big crowd around him." "And his heart was as big as his automobile," added Ted Page. Greenlee's fellow numbers kings/owners in the Negro National League included Alex Pompez of the New York Cubans, Abe Manley of the Newark Eagles, Tom Wilson of the Baltimore Elite Giants, and Ed Semler of the Black Yankees. Aside from the intrinsic pleasures of a baseball spotlight, these teams offered their owners legal covers and money-laundering devices for their illegal enterprises. The numbers games had no connection with sports betting, so the presence of gangster-owners in blackball spawned few rumors of fixed games or bribed players. But this massive underworld presence did reinforce, again, the wayward reputation of the Negro leagues.

The only blackball star familiar to white fans was Satchel Paige, one of the great pitchers in baseball history. In the summer of 1940 alone, *Time, Life,* and the *Saturday Evening Post* all ran amused, admiring Paige pieces. *Life*'s photos showed him playing pool, tinkling a boogie-woogie piano, ensconced in a barber's chair attended by a manicurist, shoeshiner, and barber, and decked out in a fancy suit, shoes, and hat, reclining on the fender of his big red Packard. Few pitchers have ever boasted his combination of speed, control, and longevity. "Satchel kicked his foot away up here like Dizzy Dean, then he'd throw around that foot," said Newt Allen. "Half the guys were hitting at that foot coming up. We had a hard time *bunting* Satchel's throws, much less hitting them." Slim but amazingly strong, with long arms and fingers, Paige could apply enough backspin on the ball to make it seemingly rise two to four inches. Joe DiMaggio was not the only big leaguer who called him "the best pitcher I ever batted against."

This most celebrated black ballplayer was, alas, a walking stereotype of annoying, erratic habits. A loner who seldom hung around with other ballplayers, Paige lived out of his cars, went fishing or courting whenever the urge struck him, and ignored clocks and calendars for his own private schedule. "I'm Satchel," he explained. "I do as I do." His ever-changing teammates, at least, excused his lapses once he wandered onto the field and started throwing smoke. "You'd forgive him for everything because he was like a great big boy," said Jimmie Crutchfield. "He could walk in the room and have you in stitches in ten minutes' time. He'd warm up by playing third base or clowning with somebody and then he'd go out and pitch a shutout. How could you get mad at a guy like that?" Owners could and did. Paige left them hanging too many times, holding the bag, waiting for Satchel. "We must have discipline on and off the field," said Abe Manley, after Paige had twice jumped his contracts, "and such is hard to maintain with a Satchel Paige around." For most whites, Paige epitomized black baseball. His image—so gifted on the field, so ungovernable off it—did not appeal to the moguls of white baseball. Paige confirmed what they already wished to believe about black ballplayers. In the end he probably retarded big-league integration.

White baseball had its own gamblers, bad actors, and confidence men; but not to the same degree, apparently, as black baseball. And in white America, black transgressors usually paid more dearly for the same sins committed by whites. "We have to be more careful than white baseball," urged Rollo Wilson. "They'd be saying colored people don't know how to behave themselves." The rough folkways of blackball handed whiteball a convenient pretext for remaining closed to blacks. In 1946 the big-league owners endorsed a secret report that opposed baseball integration. "A major league baseball player must have something besides great natural ability," the moguls agreed, in private. "He must possess the technique, the coordination, the competitive attitude, and the discipline."

The Negro leagues did, in fact, lack discipline. The problem of integrating the big leagues took in culture, and perceptions of culture, as well as the simpler, obvious issue of skin color. In guarding their gates, the white moguls were assuredly racist; but it was a complex racism, thus more difficult to overcome. "There was one requirement in the major leagues that we didn't have, and that was your character," said Buck Leonard of the Homestead Grays, from the wisdom of old age. "If you could play ball, regardless of your character, you could come in our leagues. You could be a drinker, you could be staying with another man's wife, you could be a gambler, whatever you wanted to be—if you could play ball, you could stay with us. Some of our good ballplayers wouldn't have met the major-league requirements."

◆   ◆   ◆

Branch Rickey was no racial crusader. A conservative midwestern Republican FDR-hating teetotaling Methodist WASP, he took little interest in social or political causes. His racial and ethnic attitudes were utterly conventional for a white Protestant of his generation. He could make offhand reference to someone "of Jewish extraction and characteristics," and he told occasional black-dialect jokes. "Did you ever hear the story," he wrote in confidence in 1941, "of the fat, old colored woman who was in a high state of agitation listening to the parson's sermon on the subject of the devil? In a great climax the parson said, 'The debbil am a big, black man with long horns and a forked tail,' and just then the old colored lady let out a big poop. The parson immediately squinted one eye and pointed his finger. 'Yes, and sister Johnson, sittin' way back dah in the corner, if you f . . . when you hear me describe the debbil you sure will s . . . when you see him.' " Such casual attitudes, though, hardly contained one of the most complicated, layered personalities in baseball history.

Always in control, veiling his moves behind a rumbling cascade of vaguely impressive language, Rickey liked to upset the expectations of anybody trying to figure him out. Deeply, notoriously religious, a famed Sabbatarian, he even adjusted his piety to baseball circumstances. As a young ballplayer he had promised his parents he would never play or watch a game on Sundays. "Honestly I'm just about ready to declare myself something besides a ball player," he wrote home from spring training in 1906. "It is a sort of disgraceful profession. A few men make it so. . . . I get more and more disgusted and every time I have a good thought I get more disgusted." A weak-hitting catcher, he appeared in 120 big-league games spread over four seasons. (His major achievement embarrassed him ever after: one sore-armed afternoon, he allowed a record thirteen stolen bases. "I had a truly great arm," he later insisted; "that was the special thing that marked my ability as a Major Leaguer . . . and an accurate arm—known everywhere—and those who knew me in that day would so testify.")

His own Methodist faith and habits seldom wavered. Recovering from tuberculosis in 1909, he followed doctor's orders to drink a daily quart of beer to gain weight—and then never touched beer again. As manager and general manager of the St. Louis Cardinals, he kept his Sundays holy—yet easily abided the un-Christian tendencies engulfing him. "I have been pedestalized as a sort of pussycat religionist, some sort of a Sunday School purist because I didn't play ball on Sundays," he noted. "I think I am a liberal about the employment of one's time on Sunday." In private, Rickey played cards, made personal bets of up to five thousand dollars, even boldly ventured into drinking joints; "I've been to saloons lots of times," he bragged. He not only tolerated but doted on Pepper Martin, Dizzy Dean, and Leo Durocher: three of the most unbridled spirits ever in the game. Rickey took laughing, exasperated pleasure in all three. "I've been your friend," Martin once wrote him, "and your the only friend I've had in baseball." When Rickey bought Durocher for the Cardinals in 1933, the high-living ballplayer owed thousands of dollars in gambling debts. Rickey put him in private bankruptcy, gave him ten bucks a week, and paid off his debts with the rest of his salary. Durocher kept messing up; Rickey kept forgiving him. "Manager Durocher is valuable on the field, in uniform," Rickey explained. "Originally unmoral, he has acquired some concepts of right thinking but not many."

At his core Rickey was not Methodist or Republican or WASP but a baseball man. After spending his entire adult life in the game, he brought Jackie Robinson to the Dodgers for sound and sufficient baseball reasons, nothing more. Celebrated as a judge of young talent, he looked for athletes who could run, throw, and hit, insisting on players capable of at least two of the three. Hitters and pitchers might blow hot and cold, but a fast runner was always fast. "I have had some responsibility in the field of choosing teams with good legs," he said later. "Always the team had speed afoot. I'm unable to tolerate a team that cannot run." During his seventeen years as general manager of the Cardinals, his boys had placed first or second in the league in stolen bases twelve times. The Cardinals filched the 1931 and 1942 World Series by outrunning the opposition.

Switching to the Dodgers after the 1942 season, he inherited a roster of plodding heavy-foots. "The team is simply a no-good team. The boys cannot run," Rickey confided to his daughter Mary in June 1943. "It is not my kind of team at all, but there isn't anything I can do about it now." Not even Rickey could rebuild his team in the midst of World War II. In 1944 the Dodgers fell to seventh place and stole only forty-three bases, less than half the Pirates' league-leading total of eighty-seven. Where could Rickey find his preferred ballplayers with good legs? Well, everybody had heard about the speed of the Negro leaguers. . . . Rickey started to plot, hiding his intentions behind a verbose flurry of feinting diversions.

For years he had been thinking about breaking baseball's color line. "I wanted to introduce a Negro player in St. Louis," he said later. "I had no control of the club in that respect." In fact, black fans could not even buy grandstand tickets in St. Louis but had to sit out in the bleachers; Rickey tried but couldn't change that policy either. Soon after arriving in Brooklyn, Rickey advised his board of directors that he might recruit blacks. "If you're doing this to improve the ball club, go ahead," he was told. "But if you're doing it for the emancipation of the Negro, then forget it." Rickey's ancient nemesis, baseball commissioner Kenesaw Mountain Landis, had fought back the mounting integrationist pressures from sportswriters, black groups, and a few renegade baseball men such as Bill Veeck. But Landis helpfully died in 1944, and his successor, Happy Chandler, was more amenable. In the spring of 1945, Rickey confided to Red Barber, the Dodger broadcaster, that he planned to sign a black. "I don't know who he is or where he is," said Rickey, slowly and intently, "but he is coming." (Barber, from the Deep South, went home and told his wife he would have to quit the Dodgers; then he slept on it and decided to stay.) The choice of which particular black ballplayer remained crucial to the experiment.

Jackie Robinson was not a typical Negro leaguer; that was the point. Born in January 1919, twenty-five days after the death of Theodore Roosevelt, he was named Jack Roosevelt Robinson, and he coincidentally shared certain qualities with the great TR: intensity, competitiveness, a flaring pugnacity, outspokenness, a relentless love of sports, a worldly idealism, a strong self-contained sense of himself, and the courage to pick and pursue a difficult course. After graduating from a mainly black high school, he attended Pasadena Junior College and UCLA, where most of his classmates and teammates were white. A four-sport star at UCLA, in March 1942 he sought a tryout with the Chicago White Sox in spring training. The *Pittsburgh Courier* described him as "a veritable blur on the paths, a slick shortstop and a good hitter," but the White Sox weren't interested. During a wartime stint in the still-segregated army, he continued to beat against racial barriers. Stationed at Fort Riley, Kansas, he came out for the base's crack baseball team, which included Pete Reiser and other big leaguers. "You have to play with the colored team," Robinson was told. "That was a joke. There was no colored team," Reiser later recalled. "He stood there for a while, watching us work out. Then he turned and walked away. I didn't know who he was then, but that was the first time I saw Jackie Robinson. I can still remember him walking away by himself."

Out of the army in 1945, he signed with the Kansas City Monarchs—the first Negro leaguer from the relative toleration of California, and the first to have attended a major white university. "He had a different baseball background from most of us in the Negro American League, because he had played under white coaches," said his teammate Othello Renfroe. "A highly intelligent guy, didn't drink, didn't smoke, didn't run after any women." Quick to anger, unreconciled to Jim Crow, he bristled easily at small discriminations on the road. Friends worried about his temper. Those coiled emotions, so precariously contained, exploded in games. His flat-out ferocity on the field startled and puzzled other ballplayers. "Jackie was a real fireball who loved to win," recalled Quincy Troupe. "He really had a sharp tongue and I wondered who was this young cat raising all that sand."

Wendell Smith of the *Pittsburgh Courier* suggested Robinson to the Dodgers. Rickey had his scout Clyde Sukeforth check him out. Sukeforth liked what he saw—the baseball skills plus the evident toughness, intelligence, and pride—and brought him to Rickey's office in August 1945. It was a meeting laden with theater and history: the sixty-three-year-old white man, unreadable behind his bow tie and famously bushy eyebrows, and the twenty-six-year-old black man, eager and curious, full of hope and mistrust. Rickey stared at Robinson, who stared right back. "Oh, they were a pair, those two!" Sukeforth recalled. "I tell you, the air in that office was electric." For three hours Rickey hogged the floor, as usual, enticing Robinson but warning him of the racial abuse he would face, of how he would have to remain stoically quiet no matter the provocation. When Robinson got to speak, Rickey admired his smarts and strong personality, but fretted over his combativeness. "He had more and deeper racial resentment than was hoped for or expected," Rickey recalled. "He was anything (one would think) but ideal for this 'experiment.' " Still, Rickey went ahead and announced the signing in October.

After a year in the minors Robinson joined the Dodgers in 1947. A small Dodger rebellion against his presence was quelled when Pee Wee Reese, a Southerner from Kentucky, didactically accepted him. The shortstop and team captain, Reese invited

Robinson to dinner and teased him in the rough ballplayers' badinage that meant inclusion. The other Dodgers then followed suit. Opposing teams, though, took longer. Granted that bench jockeys always railed at the opposite dugout, couching their insults in the most offensively ethnic terms available; but for Robinson, the solitary black, the abuse cut with sharper edges. "We used to knock him down almost every time he came up to home plate," recalled Richie Ashburn of the Phillies. "We'd try to hit him hard on double plays. It was terrible, the things he had to go through. But every time we knocked him down, he got up and he hit a line drive somewhere. And I said to our players one day, 'Maybe we ought to stop knocking this guy down, he's killing us.' "

Robinson did bring the Dodgers the speed Rickey sought. "Be a whirling demon," Rickey told him. "I want you to run wild, to steal the pants off them, to be the most conspicuous player on the field." In a game against the Giants that first season, he doubled, took third on a fly, then stole home. Seizing his lead from a base, he remained in constant, noisy motion, stirring up dust and pebbles, bouncing around and upsetting the pitcher's concentration. Against the Pirates one day, he drew a pickoff throw to first; the throw went astray and rolled not more than six feet from the bag. "He saw where that ball was a split second before I did, and that's all he needed," said the first baseman, Elbie Fletcher. "By the time I picked it up I didn't even have a play at second on him. That's how quick he was. Unbelievable reflexes. And alert, always alert." In pregame meetings the Cardinals went over not only how to pitch him but how to control him on the bases—the only player granted such deference. Robinson led the league in steals as a rookie, and again two years later. In 1949 no less an authority than Ed Barrow of the Yankees declared Robinson the swiftest man in baseball. (The old Negro leaguer Judy Johnson recognized his style. "We were daring," Johnson said of his own playing days. "Negroes can run—we had to run—and we kept that up. We'd run, drag, push. . . . Jackie Robinson brought all that stuff back into the big leagues." Integration of the majors killed the Negro leagues, but their brand of ball lived on.)

◆　　◆　　◆

With much less commotion, the other big leagues were integrated at about the same time. The National Basketball League had included blacks since 1942 with no particular on-court difficulties. The newer Basketball Association of America held out for a few years—apparently in obeisance to Abe Saperstein, whose Harlem Globetrotters played in profitable doubleheaders with BAA teams—but was then integrated after folding into the NBL. Chuck Cooper and Earl Lloyd, the first blacks in the merged National Basketball Association, attracted little comment when they entered the league in 1950. "I never had problems with other NBA players, and neither did Chuck or any of the other blacks," Lloyd recalled. "I stepped on the court and the world kept spinning. No one said a word—fans, players, anybody."

The National Football League was reintegrated in 1946. The Cleveland Rams had migrated to Los Angeles and hoped to play in that city's huge municipally owned Coliseum. Local politics then broke pro football's ban on blacks. Aware of the NFL's whites-only employment practices, the Coliseum commissioners made it clear that the stadium was unavailable to the Rams unless they added a black player. A predictable storm broke when the other NFL owners heard of the Rams' intentions; no doubt George Preston Marshall of the Redskins made the most noise, as usual. The Rams went ahead and signed Kenny Washington and Woody Strode, local heroes who had starred for UCLA's football team. (Washington had been a backfield mate of Jackie Robinson's.) Over the next decade, most other NFL teams were also integrated. Marshall's Redskins clung to the barricades, the last sulky holdout, until 1961—finally yielding to pressures from the federal government and the civil rights movement.

In varying degrees but repeating patterns, black athletes transformed all three sports. Of the black stars soon flooding into baseball, especially into the National League, Willie Mays displayed the most remarkable panoply of five crucial skills. Nobody else could run, throw, catch, hit, and think with Mays. "Willie seemed to have it all," said his teammate Bill Rigney. "Even in his first year, he'd get on second base, say, and right away he'd steal the catcher's signals—within a minute he'd see the combination. He *knew*. No matter what was going on, he

knew what it would take to win the game. . . . It impressed me
that there could be a player so young who seemed to know
everything." Mays also broke one of the oldest baseball axioms:
heavy hitters, it was thought, could not run well, and whippets
could not thump the ball. (Babe Ruth, Jimmie Foxx, and Mel Ott
had finished with six times as many home runs as stolen bases.)
Alone among the great sluggers in baseball history, Mays wound
up with more than half as many steals as homers. His contemporary Mickey Mantle, whose speed was sometimes equated with
Mays's, averaged only 8.5 steals a season, with a high of 21, and
never led the league. Mays averaged 15.4 steals each year, with
a peak of 40, and led the league four times.

Jim Brown entered the NFL in 1957 and was the league's top
rusher for eight of the next nine seasons with his fullback's size—
six feet two inches, 230 pounds—and his halfback's speed and
moves. Like Mays, Brown was a light-footed slugger. "He was
the smartest runner I've ever played against," said the Green
Bay linebacker Ray Nitschke. "He was an artist—a brilliant football player who could not only beat you physically but mentally."
Carrying the ball in one hand, like a halfback, he tracked his
blockers and used them well. He knew how specific opponents
tended to tackle, and how to counter them. Thinking like a
halfback, he preferred to display his speed and shiftiness, jumping and cutting and spinning. When he had to, when head-on
collisions were unavoidable, he belted tacklers with his shoulder
and one of the most effective forearms ("The Blow," he called it)
ever seen in football. "He was so fast and so strong," recalled the
linebacker Sam Huff. "You'd hit him and it was like hitting a
tree; nothing would give. Three or four of us would gang-tackle
him and think we had him, and all of a sudden he'd feel like he
was going down. You'd relax a little to brace yourself for the fall,
and he'd just gather himself and go into a gear nobody else has
ever had—before or after, I guarantee it. He was the finest football player I have ever seen."

Bill Russell joined the Boston Celtics in 1956 and led them to
eleven NBA titles in the next thirteen years: the most extraordinary run of any team in big-league history. Oddly agile for a
man six feet nine inches tall, he could spring without dipping his
knees and bending his upper body, and so could wait until the

last instant, *after* his man released a shot, before jumping to block it. With his uncommon lateral mobility, Russell would leave the basket and pluck stray rebounds up to ten feet away. "He was the smartest guy I ever saw on a basketball court," said his opponent Dave DeBusschere. "Sure, he had quickness, reaction, all the tools he needed," agreed his coach Red Auerbach. "But most of all, he was a thinker. If you faked him a certain way and wound up making a basket or grabbing a rebound, he'd file it away in his mind, and you'd never fool him the same way again." For most of his career, Russell was the tallest *and* fastest man on the Celtics. They ran a speed drill in practice: from one baseline, dash to the near foul line and back, then to midcourt and back, to the far foul line and back, and, finally, to the other baseline and back. In this grueling test of stopping, starting, reversing, and flat-out speed, Russell beat all his teammates, even the quickest little guards.

These three great black ballplayers were all much smarter than most jocks, and they applied their intelligence to their games with exhilarating effect. All three also brought physical gifts never before seen in their leagues. Willie Mays, the first slugger who could run; Jim Brown, the first fullback who could run; Bill Russell, the first center who could run. Is there a pattern here?

♦ ♦ ♦

From the perspective of the 1990s, it is apparent that blacks have sped up the three major-league sports and now dominate most speed maneuvers and statistics. In baseball, blacks revived the stolen base, a nearly extinct weapon, and delivered the game from the lumbering doldrums of the home run. First Maury Wills, then Lou Brock, then Rickey Henderson set new records for stolen bases, and no whites have led either league in steals for decades. Pushed by black burners, average thefts per club went from only 43 a season in 1955 to 127 two decades later. "I'm not a great runner," Pete Rose apologized, "but I'm not bad for a white boy." In football, no white ballcarrier has led the NFL in rushing since Jimmy Taylor interrupted Jim Brown's skein in 1962. Blacks now control all the "speed" positions in the NFL (running back, wide receiver, defensive secondary) and have added unprecedented mobility to other positions as well. A stray white wide receiver like Ricky Proehl of the Phoenix Cardinals may now encounter racial taunts from opposing black corner-backs. ("*Hey, slow white boy!* You ain't going anywhere today. You ain't catching nothing!") In basketball, a black sport at every level of the game, Fay Young's exulting declaration of 1940 has been confirmed. Virtually all the best hoop runners and leapers are African-Americans, from Michael Jordan down. When a rare white leaper like Rex Chapman appears, and the black Charles Barkley says, "He's got black legs," everyone knows what is meant. For most fans and ballplayers alike, black speed and spring are givens, so obvious they hardly merit discussion. As the basketball writers Bob Ryan and Terry Pluto have noted, it is evident to any NBA observer that an average black player can run and jump better than an average white. "People in basketball don't really care *why* that is," according to Ryan and Pluto. "They just know it's so, and they act accordingly."

Attempts to probe the *why* usually provoke ferocious contro-versies. Careful, well-researched attempts to explain black speed—a 1971 *Sports Illustrated* article by Martin Kane, and a 1989 NBC documentary by Tom Brokaw and Jon Entine—met firestorms of off-the-point criticism that scorned reasonable ev-idence of differences in black muscular and bone structure. The white broadcaster Jimmy the Greek Snyder was fired by his net-work after his off-guard explanation that blacks had been bred in slavery for their physical prowess. ("I agree with that," said the black halfback Tony Dorsett. "Maybe Jimmy shouldn't have said what he said, or maybe he should have said it in a different way. But what he said is what a lot of people think.") Indeed, Snyder was only restating a theory previously advanced by the black psychiatrist Alvin Poussaint, among others. More prudent ob-servers play it safe and avoid the *why*. In his book *Elevating the Game: Black Men and Basketball,* the black writer Nelson George amply demonstrated what he called "the jumping ability and quickness African-Americans brought to the game" without ven-turing near an explanation for them. The issue of black speed has become a contemporary version of the emperor's nudity, widely noticed but seldom addressed.

This peculiar disjunction derives in intellectual circles from the gulf of specialization separating physical scientists and social scientists. In general, neither field knows what the other field knows. Modern research by physical scientists has shown certain biological distinctions among races; that blacks, for instance, are more resistant than whites to malaria and yellow fever, less resistant to tuberculosis and pneumonia. Yet most social scientists, in their efforts to refute societal racism, assume on faith, as a matter of willed belief, that no significant physical differences among races can be proven. As good political liberals, in any discussion of nature versus nurture they favor environmental explanations over biology and genetics. Thus, to account for why blacks now comprise 77 percent of the NBA but less than 20 percent of big-league baseball, they note that constricted black neighborhoods have room for more basketball courts than baseball diamonds. Yet black neighborhoods don't have many football fields either, and the NFL is 68 percent black. (A better guess is that, relatively speaking, basketball and football reward explosiveness—two teams chasing a ball up and down a field, darting and leaping—while baseball rewards more stationary skills—the pitcher, batter, and catcher monopolizing play, all rooted to their spots, while the other fielders mostly stand and wait. Foot speed matters more in basketball and football.)

The theme of black speed runs through most of the history of black sports in America. It is dangerously easy, though, to overstate the point. Every black athlete cannot outrun every white athlete. (Yankee manager Casey Stengel, when presented with the lead-footed catcher Elston Howard, had put it crudely: "They gave me the only nigger that can't run.") Black athletes themselves know their successes did not come without effort, as a mere birthright of mindless "natural" athletic gifts. "As if I had never worked hard to get where I did," said Willie Mays. "A lot of thinking also went into how I played." "I had a mental capacity at home plate that nobody seemed to appreciate," Henry Aaron agreed. "They said that hitting was just something that came naturally to me. . . . I thought about baseball constantly, and I made it a point to learn what I could from older players."

The issue is often framed too simply: *either* blacks are inherently faster and springier *or* they are spurred to athletic excellence by societal unfairness and the lack of other options *or* they work and think harder than lesser athletes. None of these explanations by itself can adequately account for the overwhelming black presence in the big leagues. Surely all three are true to some degree, with the relative proportions varying so much, so unknowably, from individual to individual as to render large generalizations impossible. The sad, lingering irony is that blacks have assuredly shown and developed these glorious knacks for speed and jumping—yet now, given the complexities of American racism, may feel reluctant to claim them. For many blacks and well-intentioned whites, a genuine black gift has doubled back on itself and looks like a liability, to be denied and explained away. Blacks and whites, fans and ballplayers, should all simply admire these marvelous feats without the tug of the troubling implications. But this seems impossible: another loss snatched from success in the ongoing tragedy of American race relations.

Chapter Eight

National Teams:
Yankees, Packers, Celtics

*

The big leagues depended on local pride. Fans cheered for their teams mostly because of geographic proximity; in rooting their boys home—a revealing phrase—they affirmed their region, their city, and ultimately themselves. A cheerful, sometimes belligerent provincialism powered this fandom, sustaining it through both the usual sloughs of defeat and the rare, crowing championship. These attachments helped compensate for the atomizing, alienating tendencies of modernity. A society of freely contracting individuals—forever cashing options and moving around, with ever-shorter attention spans—needed any available glue. The teams of the big leagues helped knit together fractious, dispersing communities.

A few teams transcended these local attachments and took on national constituencies. Such national teams might ride to country-wide adoration with the help of an especially eminent ballplayer (like Babe Ruth) or an unusually famous coach (like Vince Lombardi). But a national team had to win repeatedly, year after year, in an unprecedented string of success: often enough for fans in distant regions to notice, then spurn their local heroes and adopt a faraway team. For many American rooters, such consistent, implacable winning might overcome even the deepest provincial attachments. A tradition of triumphs could overwhelm one form of community in favor of another, larger, synthetic version: the national society of Yankee, or Packer, or Celtic fans. The lure of the privilege of shouting "We're number one" could leap any barrier, overpower any loyalty—as long as the national team kept winning.

◆   ◆   ◆

The New York Yankees were founded by two criminals, Big Bill Devery and Frank J. Farrell. The sleek, all-conquering teams of later years began in tawdry deceptions and boodling crimes against the people of New York. Devery and Farrell owned the Yankees for a dozen years with no pennants. Their major achievement was an elaborate scheme for stealing the opposing catcher's signals. Their star ballplayer, gifted and charming, was the most brazenly corrupt hooligan ever to despoil any big-league team; he and these Yankees belonged together. Finally Devery and Farrell fell to quarreling, stopped speaking to each other, and sold the team. They left behind a tradition of inept, outlaw stupidity that could only make future Yankee management look inspired by comparison.

One was a cop, the other a crook, but who in New York at the turn of the century could tell the difference? Big Bill Devery, who later prided himself on never having read a book, had grown up on the North River waterfront of the Lower West Side. After a brief fling at bricklaying, he joined the police force in 1878, prowling the docks. "If you want to see the real people of this town," he liked to say, "come over on Double Fifth Avenue—that's what I call Tenth Avenue." As a captain in the 1890s, running precincts in the Tenderloin and Hell's Kitchen, he was repeatedly charged with blackmail, extortion, and neglect of duty—but always wriggled free. As his crimes went unpunished, he grew complacently candid ("Every man of sense looks out for his own interests"). His gleeful, shameless wickedness and booze-loosened quotability beguiled local newspapermen such as the young Lincoln Steffens. One day Devery strolled by a protected whorehouse and was solicited by a hooker; he was so shocked, so offended, that he increased the house's monthly payoff to the cops. "He was not lacking in a certain kind of genius," said his frustrated foe, the Reverend Charles Parkhurst, "but it all ran on depraved lines. His precinct was an open advertisement of his character."

His devotion to duty was rewarded in 1898 when he became New York's chief of police. Devery looked the part, weighing more than 250 pounds, with the face of a retired prizefighter. A photograph shows him in a derby and three-piece suit, his paunch straining the vest, his doubled chin resting in a high wing collar, the eyes wary and curious above a walrus mustache. "He was no more fit to be a chief of police than the fish man was to be director of the Aquarium," Steffens recalled, "but as a character, as a work of art, he was a masterpiece." He centralized graft, setting regular schedules for gambling joints, prostitutes, and horse-betting "poolrooms." Every night he met his clients quite openly in the Tenderloin to get his shares. After three profitable years as chief he bought real estate worth $640,000— only a fraction of his take. "The Brigand in Politics," the *New York Times* called him when he ran for district leader in Hell's Kitchen: "Unfitted for any useful vocation, trusted by no one with anything at risk, and lacking every mental and moral quality which would commend him to public confidence, Mr. Devery wants to be as near as may be to the 'cow' at milking time, and if possible to hold the pail."

Shared business interests had drawn Devery and Frank Farrell together in the 1890s. Farrell owned a busy saloon and horse room at the corner of Thirtieth Street and Sixth Avenue—half a block from Devery's Nineteenth Precinct police station. Small and quiet, neatly dressed but with a shadowed look to his eyes, Farrell tried to stay anonymous while Devery preened and capered for the newspapers. Their careers ascended together; Farrell in gratitude bought Devery a house at 310 West Twenty-eighth Street, where New York's police chief lived for free on a gambler's largesse. This odd arrangement helped to make Devery and Farrell major issues in New York's city elections in the fall of 1901. Police scandals and gambling raids—one had found a check for seventy-four hundred dollars cashed by Farrell—

spawned a brief, poignant spasm of public outrage that elected a reform mayor (Seth Low) and a crusading district attorney (William Travers Jerome).

New York's reformers had come and gone for decades, diverting but then boring the electorate, leaving no permanent improvements. When Mayor Low fired Devery, the worried police stopped protecting gambling—for a while. To meet this crisis, Farrell in August 1902 opened a fancy new gambling house at 33 West Thirty-third Street with special security devices, a double iron gate at the front and a secret button that killed the lights and closed all windows and doors. At the top of four elegantly decorated floors, a hidden iron door led to the adjacent house, where the top two floors offered faro tables, roulette wheels, and other amusements. Well-dressed men and women, including some prominent citizens, were seen entering 33 West Thirty-third. "I don't know anything about it," said the local police captain. DA Jerome, more curious, raided and closed the house three months later. Farrell denied everything, bought another house at 66 West Forty-fifth, and started to outfit it for gambling.

In these circumstances Devery and Farrell became the first owners of New York's American League baseball team. For two years Ban Johnson had been plotting to add a New York club to his new big league. Devery and Farrell were rich and willing; nobody knew how long Low and Jerome would keep disrupting business as usual, so the underworld needed new enterprises. After prospering under Devery's benign chiefship, Farrell had bought the Empire City racetrack in Yonkers for about $217,000, and his own lawyer placed Farrell's net worth at $750,000 or more. But the two men were too notorious to be identified as the new baseball magnates. Even as the final deal with Johnson was cut, Farrell was being sued by a man who said he'd lost $11,000 at gambling in Farrell's fixed games. (After repeated efforts to avoid testifying, even missing a court date, Farrell took the stand, insisted he was just a horse bettor, had maybe once seen a roulette wheel in Saratoga Springs but wasn't sure, and certainly knew nothing about gambling.) So Ban Johnson—a man of declaimed righteousness, given to noble homilies about the evils of gambling—made secret arrangements with Devery, Farrell, and their friends. The new team was announced with Joseph Gordon, an obscure coal dealer, as president; no mention of Devery and Farrell.

Farrell now tried to become respectable. Late in 1903 he sold the gambling house at 66 West Forty-fifth Street. A few years later he dumped Gordon as team president and assumed the title of the job he already had. "I decided that I should get some of the glory," he explained. "I had put up the money and done a lot of work." He encouraged the newspapers to call him a "sportsman" instead of "the celebrated Poolroom King." Though he still bet on horses, and shared bets and tips with his fellow magnate Frank Navin of the Detroit Tigers, Farrell did manage to acquire a more proper fame. "Frank Farrell has done much for baseball here," said the *New York Tribune* in 1911, "and deserves whatever reward a championship team would bring."

Behind the scenes, though, Farrell and Devery imprinted their boodling tone on the team. From their box near the dugout they stayed close to their boys, on and off the field. Hal Chase, their pet ballplayer and fan favorite, spent most of his bizarre career in New York only because he danced through the same shadowy worlds that Farrell and Devery inhabited: they all deserved each other. The fifth son of a prosperous lumber dealer in Los Gatos, California, Chase had started playing with his older brothers as soon as he could hold a ball and glove. He always outran other boys his age. At home, to protect his throwing arm he declined to chop wood. (His mature game, of speed and willfulness, was already apparent.) He arrived in New York in 1905 with a cardboard suitcase, oddly cut clothes, and a peculiar flat pancake glove. "A fresh-faced young man," as John McGraw's wife Blanche remembered him. "He was a bright and attractive boy of twenty-two, alive with youthful love of the game. John often talked baseball with him." Playing first base, he already moved one jump ahead of his teammates: in an early game, with a runner on second he dashed toward home as the pitcher wound, picked up the bunt a few feet from the plate, and threw to third—where nobody was covering. "In less than a week Hal Chase was the baseball sensation of the season," a local scribe recalled. "In the end everybody agreed that it was not possible to understand a raw boy who broke into the fastest company in the business, ready-made."

As a sophomore Chase hit .323 and placed among the league leaders in six offensive categories. A year later he batted safely in twenty-seven straight games. Fast on the paths, he averaged thirty steals a year with New York; the novelist James T. Farrell remembered seeing him single, then steal second and third— and repeat these feats a few innings later. But game after game, it was his fielding that astounded observers. When a ball was hit to him, fans would stand up, expecting a surprise. Nobody before Chase had played such a mobile first base. Poised for the pitch, he usually stood far from the bag, into short right field; sometimes he stole singles by trap-hopping liners out there and flipping to the pitcher at first. A baseball rarity who batted right but threw left, he excelled at the 3-6-3 double play. Lean and supple, he ranged all over the field, snaring foul pops behind the catcher, backing up other bases, tagging out runners across the diamond. With a strong, accurate arm, he would snap the ball to third if a runner rounded it by a few steps. Bunts remained his special delight—once his teammates adjusted to his style. At Philadelphia one day, with a man on first he flew across the infield, pounced on a perfect bunt twelve feet up the third baseline (beating the catcher, pitcher, and third baseman, all of them closer to the play), threw to the shortstop covering second, who threw on to the second baseman covering first: double play. He pranced around, overflowing with zest and brio, happy and smiling, enjoying himself on every level; "a girl in the grand stand may improve his game," it was noted.

So quick, so smart, so magical; and so corrupt. The raw kid from California folded all too easily into big-city life. A cardsharp and pool shark, he freely caroused and gambled (Frank Farrell could hardly disapprove). A teammate once stood behind him during a team poker game and saw the three kings in Chase's hand mysteriously become four kings, without a draw, as he won a pile. The professional gamblers who clustered at the ballpark made him a regular customer—and a co-conspirator. "I used to bet on games," Chase later admitted. "My limit was $100 per game and I never bet against my own team. . . . I had to have a bet on the side and we used to bet with the other team and the gamblers who sat in the boxes. It was easy to get a bet." In fact he did bet against his own team; from 1908 on, he was too often accused of intentional mistakes at first base, of throwing games and offering bribes to teammates to collude with him.

His style of play both encouraged and concealed such accusations. He gambled on as off the field: taking risks, trying difficult, unorthodox throws, playing close to the edge. Ranging so far from the bag, he often caught balls on the run, fully extended, with one hand; if he dropped a crucial toss, it might still look honest. But Chase committed too many errors for so skillful a fielder. In 1908 he placed ninth among all American League first basemen, with a .977 fielding percentage and twenty-six errors—a lot for his position—in 106 games. "I remember a few times I threw a ball over to first base," recalled the Yankee shortstop Roger Peckinpaugh, "and it went by him to the stands and a couple of runs scored. It really surprised me. I'd stand there looking, sighting the flight of that ball in my mind, and I'd think, 'Geez, that throw wasn't that bad.' Then I'd tell myself that he was the greatest there was, so maybe the throw was bad. . . . What he was doing, you see, was tangling up his feet and then making a fancy dive after the ball, making it look like it was a wild throw."

Regardless of what his managers told him, Frank Farrell always backed his star with blind or conspired faith. In August 1908, upset over a newspaper report that the manager doubted his honesty, Chase left the team to play for an outlaw club in California: a grave offense to the guardians of organized baseball. Yet he was welcomed back the next spring with a silver loving cup. A lesser player under more stringent management would have been banned. His next manager, George Stallings, duly accused him of trying to throw a game. Chase took his case to Farrell, who stayed in character, fired Stallings, and named Chase manager. "God," a teammate said later, "what a way to run a ball club!" A subsequent Yankees manager, Frank Chance, told sportswriters that Chase was again muffing pegs and tanking games. When one of the writers printed a milder version of Chance's remark, Farrell lit into the man: "That was a terrible thing you wrote about Chase," he said.

An incident at the end of the 1909 season epitomized the Devery-Farrell regime. Somebody in Washington had tipped Detroit's manager, Hughie Jennings, about suspicious circumstances at the New York ballpark. During a game on September 25, Jennings sent his trainer, Harry Tuthill, out to center field to investigate. "Mr. Farrell has always been a good friend of mine," Tuthill later reported to Ban Johnson, "and I do not wish to make any statements whatever of the occurrence, as I do not think he is in any way to blame, but as you insist on a statement, I will give you the exact facts in the case." Tuthill discovered a box about six feet square attached to the back of an advertising sign and protected by barbed wire. He climbed up, poked around, and entered the box. "The operator had evidently heard me trying to get through the barb wire before I succeeded in doing so, and he escaped. In this cubby hole I found all the daily papers of that date, a half empty bottle of beer, two one-inch holes bored in the fence close together, evidently for the purpose of using field glasses." A handle operated a signal on the other side of the fence; the operative with binoculars would steal the catcher's signs and then flash the next pitch to the New York batter. Tuthill broke off the handle and returned it to Farrell. (The Yankees had improved their home record that year from 30-47 in 1908 to 41-35.) The league office sputtered, the Yankee management denied all, and the episode subsided.

Even such petty crimes could not produce a winner. After climbing to second place in 1910, the Yankees finished sixth, eighth, seventh, and sixth over the next four seasons. "The Yankees at that time were what we used to call a joy club," Roger Peckinpaugh recalled. "Lots of joy and lots of losing. Nobody thought we could win and most of the time we didn't. But it didn't seem to bother the boys too much. They would start singing songs in the infield right in the middle of the game." Hal Chase was finally traded in 1913, for two nobodies, but his spirit lived on. By now the owners were having no fun. Tired of losing games and money, they sold the Yankees early in 1915 to Jacob Ruppert and Tillinghast Huston.

Ruppert, the dominant and then (after 1923) sole owner, inhabited a different world from the team founders'. The Yankees' social standing leaped from Double Fifth Avenue to the real Fifth Avenue, where Ruppert lived alone, except for servants, in a fifteen-room apartment. The team henceforth went first class, in railroad sleeping cars and good hotels, with uniforms dry-cleaned each day: everything in sumptuous Ruppert style. Forty-eight years old in 1915, shrewd and demanding, known as "the Colonel" after a political appointment in his youth, Ruppert had inherited a brewing fortune and multiplied it with his own real estate operations. He looked cold and immaculate, always well tailored and valeted, with appraising, unblinking eyes and a disciplined Teutonic mustache. Immersed in his business dealings, he left most baseball affairs to his capable management and treated the Yankees as a hobby—a very serious, high-stakes hobby. "The Colonel rode in a Pierce-Arrow the size of a pullman car, all gleaming bright as if it had been bought new that morning," recalled his pitcher Waite Hoyt. "Once in a while he would take a few of us to the ballpark in it and would try to discuss with us the team's prospects and even make mild jokes at our expense. (A typical Ruppert 'joke' was to take two or three pitchers in the car with him and in a conversation about our prospects, agree that we should have a good season 'because we have good hitters, anyways.')"

Occasionally, if a player balked at signing a contract or needed reprimanding for some lapse, he would be summoned to Ruppert's ornate office at the brewery on the Upper East Side. The player would wait in an anteroom with white marble walls, hat in hand, then make his way through wide corridors, on rugs that felt like soft grass, past mahogany desks to the boss's baronial inner sanctum. Clerks came and went, silent and preoccupied. Heavy bronze statues anchored the lush carpet. On the dark, wainscoted walls hung hunting trophies and a photo of Ruppert and his father from the 1890s, when Jake was an eligible bachelor around town (a bit of a playboy, in fact, known as "the Prince of Beer"). Sunk into a massive, deeply cushioned chair, the player would feel small and out of place: exactly the intended effect. "If a man cleared his throat," Hoyt noted, "he felt as if he had laughed out loud in church. The Colonel could really intimidate a baseball player from his big Mussolini-type desk, sitting stern and stiff as a true Prussian colonel and never seeming to be the least bit moved by any sad story the player might offer."

A commanding businessman, Ruppert didn't know much about baseball. As a child he had played a rich boy's version of the game, organizing his own team with other kids in the neighborhood around Ninetieth Street. "I had a little menagerie of my own, some pigeons, guinea pigs and so on," he reminisced. "On Saturday mornings I had to take my music lesson. Then the members of the team used to come to see my menagerie. It was a great treat for them and their pay for playing ball." (For playing ball with the rich kid, that is.) "In the afternoon we had a game. I played the outfield, myself. It was my ambition to catch behind the bat, but I could never seem to make it. All the boys were anxious to play." They had to let him play somewhere, so they stuck him in the outfield. He grew up a Giants fan, sometimes hanging around their ballpark with other boys, hoping for a ball to clear the fence.

Ruppert's adult baseball interest waned as he bred show dogs and trotting horses and built his collections of jades, Chinese porcelains, Indian relics, and first editions. Before buying the Yankees he had only seen them play twice—to watch Ty Cobb and Walter Johnson with their visiting teams. "Baseball sort of bored me," he said later. A friend took him to the 1913 World Series, the Giants against the Athletics, but he left in the seventh inning "and I didn't feel I ever wanted to go to a ball game again." Then Ban Johnson introduced him to Till Huston and talked them into rescuing the Yankees. Ruppert was appalled by the team's financial affairs: "I never saw such a mixed-up business in my life—liabilities, contracts, notes, obligations of all sorts. . . . There were times when it looked so bad no sane man would put a penny into it." But they went ahead, bought the team, and in a few years lost more than $300,000 on the investment.

Three smart moves built the Yankee dynasty. First, Ruppert over Huston's objections hired Miller Huggins as manager. For a dozen years, until his death in 1929, Huggins guided the team through its initial phase of greatness. He was a tiny man, listed as five feet five inches and 140 pounds but probably smaller, with hunched shoulders and a sad, tired poker face. He stalked up and down the dugout—worried and fidgety—yelling orders in his high, squeaky voice ("Coive him! Coive the busher!"). Rodent allusions pursued him; when he emerged from the dugout, creeping timidly across the grass, enemy fans would laugh, "Here comes the mouse!" Sportswriters found him accessible but not interesting. "He is as cold as an Arctic iceberg," one concluded; "as methodical as a milkman and about as much given to enthusiasm as a hitching post." He looked like anybody, or nobody. Once, on a train, some guy bragged that he knew Miller Huggins; Huggins bet him five bucks that he didn't. "The trouble with me is that I have no personality," Huggins lamented. "I wish I had the knack of salving newspaper men. But I haven't and that's all there is to the story." Charged with directing bigger, louder, more famous men, he relied on will and brains with none of the usual trappings of leadership.

He had always been a plucky little guy, picking his way carefully around large objects to avoid being squashed. Born of British immigrants in Cincinnati in 1880, he started playing baseball anywhere he could. "I was too short to pitch or thought I was," he recalled. He had a strong arm, but broke it at fourteen by falling from an apple tree. The arm never fully came back, relegating him to second base. He took a law degree, passed the bar, and practiced miserably for six months. (Fred Lieb remembered him as "more erudite than 95 per cent of his fellow players.") Baseball pulled him, not unwillingly, from the law. Aggressive and fearless, he survived thirteen seasons in the National League. As a mere rookie, he started riding the home-plate umpire one day in St. Louis. "Say, young busher," replied the ump, "if you want to talk to me come out of the grass so that I can see you." He hit passably, ran well—six years of thirty or more steals—and ranged so widely at second that he was called "The Rabbit" and "Little Everywhere." In 1911 baseball writers voted him the sixth most valuable man in the National League, just below Honus Wagner and Pete Alexander. The best part of his game was cerebral. He played smart, like a future manager. His height and persistence drew many walks; he led the league four times, once with a batting average of only .248. At second, "a hustling, yelping, gingery field leader," he schemed and chattered relentlessly. Huggins managed the Cardinals for five years, got fired, and was beckoned forward by Jake Ruppert.

In New York he changed his managing style from bunt, squeeze, and run to longball; the Yankees already favored sluggers. "A manager has his cards dealt to him, and he must play them," he said. "New York is a home run town." Ever the second baseman, he still coveted a tight infield, especially around second. And he never relinquished a protective, sentimental affection for short ballplayers. "Little guys like us can win games," he told his protégé Leo Durocher. "We can beat 'em"—tapping his head—"up here." A budding manager, Durocher sat beside Huggins in the dugout and wrote down all his moves in a little black book. Durocher noticed how Hug treated different men as their personalities demanded—scolding or encouraging, whatever worked—and how he never, ever let up. ("I come to play!" said Durocher five decades later. "I come to beat you! I come to kill you! That's the way Miller Huggins, my first manager, brought me up, and that's the way it has always been with me.")

Huggins insisted on dugout decorum: players had to sit up straight—with no slouching or feet up or even resting chins in hands—and keep their heads in the game, talking nothing but baseball. If anybody's attention seemed to wander, Huggins would ask him the count on the batter. Beyond that schoolmasterish quirk, "the best government is the least government," said Huggins. He used few signs and kept the game and his strategies simple. In ballplayers he looked for "disposition" (a favorite word), by which he meant tenacity and love of the sport, so that playing hard came easily and unforced by the manager. "I'm not interested in baseball theories," he said. "One little fact that can happen any day on the field will upset a whole ton of theory." He believed only in percentages, the law of averages, the most likely outcome based on his experience. He traded ballplayers shrewdly, patiently arranging complex multiclub deals, and making few mistakes. "An odd little man," Waite Hoyt later said of Huggins, but with "a marvelous determination and a knowledge of baseball and baseball players such as no one else I ever knew could match. He was, in my experience, the greatest manager who ever lived."

Huggins talked Ruppert into a second crucial move when the owner asked his manager what he needed to win a pennant. "Get Babe Ruth," said Huggins. In 1919, playing for the Boston Red Sox, the Babe led the league in runs, RBIs, and slugging percentage—and set a new major-league record of 29 home runs. Only twenty-four, still years from his prime, he was already the runaway sensation of baseball. Ruppert contacted the Red Sox owner, Harry Frazee, a wildcat theatrical producer with cash-flow problems. Frazee wanted $450,000—more than Ruppert and Huston had paid for the whole Yankee team, and nine times the previous record price for a ballplayer. Ruppert went back to Huggins. "He agreed that it was a lot of money," Ruppert recalled. "He pointed out this and that, and we discussed the whole thing until the $450,000 grew smaller and I felt the same as Huggins about it."

Ruppert gave Frazee about $125,000 in cash (the announced purchase price) and a loan of $325,000 secured by a mortgage on Fenway Park, where the Sox played. (The loan was kept secret until revealed by the league office a year later.) Everybody benefited from the exchange except the Sox and their fans. Frazee, who lived and worked in New York, pacified his creditors and now got to see Ruth play more often than when the Babe had toiled half the season up in Boston. The secret loan, instead of an outright payment, meant a better deal for the Yankees too: over the next few years, as their manpower needs demanded, they would drain the best talent from the laden, indebted Red Sox and give only small change and throwaway players in return. In 1920 Ruth hit 54 homers and helped the Yankees draw an unprecedented 1.3 million fans, some 400,000 above the old record set by the Giants in 1908. Though still pennantless, Ruppert felt better about his extravagant investment. (Frazee became a favorite drinking companion of the Yankee owners, and no wonder; when Huston sold out, a rumor even floated that Frazee had bought his share.)

After the 1920 season, in his third, clinching move, Ruppert hired Ed Barrow as business manager from (where else?) the Red Sox. Fifty-two years old in 1920, Barrow had pursued an odd, not especially distinguished career in baseball. As a kid in Des Moines, Iowa, he had excelled at boxing—"As far back as I can remember, I was always pretty good with my fists"—and only dabbled at baseball. He pitched for a local pickup team until he hurt his arm at seventeen or eighteen and never played again. The toughest boy on the field, he always liked to manage teams, and nobody dared deny him. As a minor-league manager in the 1890s, he won some pennants and discovered Honus Wagner throwing chunks of coal along a railroad track near Pittsburgh. The Detroit Tigers promoted Barrow to a brief fling in the bigs: he managed them to a fifth-place finish in 1903, then—with his team at 32-46—was fired halfway through the next season. (During his short stay in Detroit, Barrow already showed the fastidious attention to detail that would mark his long tenure with the Yankees. Ordering the team's coats before the 1904 season, Barrow demanded a short, loose garment, not more than twenty-eight inches long in the smaller size and thirty inches in the larger. "I want a big loose fitting jacket of short length," he specified. "I would esteem it a great favor if you would closely observe these few things, as nothing looks *worse* than a long, tight fitting, narrow shouldered coat.")

Barrow didn't get back to the major leagues until fourteen years later. He managed a few teams, tried the hotel business for two years, took charge of the foundering International League; he seemed stuck. "The big man of the minor leagues," *Baseball Magazine* called him early in 1918. Would he ever get another shot at the bigs? "It sounds like the argument of a failure, but the fact is I have never had a good chance," Barrow offered. "I have never had a first rate opportunity to break into major league baseball." And furthermore, his pride still flickering, "I found reasonably big things in my own small circle," and "I could do bigger things than I have yet done if given the opportunity." His break finally came when Harry Frazee made him manager of the Red Sox. Barrow took the club to a World Series victory in 1918—a quick dash to the pinnacle of baseball—but then, as Frazee bled the team, the Sox fell to sixth and fifth in the next two seasons. When Ruppert offered him the job in the Yankee front office, a move that surprised observers, Barrow gladly stepped from a falling to a rising star.

After those long years of bush-league obscurity, Barrow took firm charge of his new situation, sketching in clear lines of authority. A large, forceful man of about 250 pounds with a rugged, heavy-browed mug, a prickly temper, and still-adept fists, he inspired deference. He was sometimes called Simon, as in Legree. After Huston's departure in 1923, Barrow steadily added to the power of his office. Ruppert gave him carte blanche: "If Ed says so, it's so, and it goes!" Barrow made the clubhouse off limits for himself and his owners; that was Huggins's domain. During games he sat obscurely in the back of the grandstand, missing nothing, planning up to two years ahead. If players wanted to see him, they came to his office. (They learned to avoid him on mornings when he hadn't shaved; stubble on the Barrow face implied the temperament of an awakened bear after a hard night.) At the ballpark Barrow deployed a small force in civilian clothes to eject professional gamblers: "We threw them out. Bodily. And then their hats after them," Barrow recalled with satisfaction. "They are jackals." As gestures to the paying customers, he added numbers to uniforms and distance signs to outfield walls, and let fans keep foul balls into the seats.

Along with Branch Rickey, his only peer at building and maintaining championship clubs, Barrow became the prototype of the modern general manager. Before Barrow and Rickey, field managers generally controlled player moves, trades, and salaries; after them, such matters shifted to the front office. Rickey considered Barrow the great master of what Rickey called "team balancing": offsetting weakness here with strength over there, and bringing together all the necessary elements for success, from the stars to the bench, and keeping them supplied year after year. As the Yankees built their dynasty, Barrow for a quarter-century was the only common element, the one individual most responsible for the accumulating triumphs. "You are the Number One baseball executive and administrator in all the history of baseball," Rickey once told him. "And I am not going to wait until you're dead to say it."

The dynasty began with the first Yankee pennant in 1921. Jake Ruppert, who expected to win every year, took home his initial flag after seven seasons of waiting. Capping a tight race, the Yankees had met the pursuing Cleveland Indians in a New York showdown late in September. With his team up by a run in the ninth, the Colonel, beside himself, came down and sat, eyes averted from the field, with his bullpen pitchers. "I tell you," Ruppert cried in his German-inflected English, "I win the pennant, I give you the brewery! Somebody please! Tell me what's going on!" When the Yankees won, clinching the pennant, Ruppert almost had to be helped up the stairs; but the brewery remained in his hands. They lost the World Series to the Giants in 1921 and again in 1922. In 1923 they moved into their new Yankee Stadium, the grandest ballpark yet built, and easily won a third straight pennant. With a team dominated by Red Sox alumni, they finally beat the Giants in the Series as well.

After finishing a close second a year later, the Yankees toppled into seventh place in 1925 amid metastasizing discipline problems. A few of his stars had always fought Huggins's leadership. The testy pitcher Carl Mays, ace of his staff in 1920 and 1921, infuriated Huggins with his selfishness. He became expendable later by pitching badly. "I hope I will be traded," said Mays late in 1923, ". . . so I won't be bothered by the little Shrimp." Huggins gladly waived him to the National League. Bob Meusel, the slugging outfielder, had the best arm in baseball; even Ty Cobb wouldn't run on him. Yet Meusel often looked bored and lazy, cruising at half-speed and refusing to dive for balls at his feet. "Hustling is rather over-rated in baseball," said Meusel. "It's a showy quality that looks well but counts for little unless it produces the goods." Huggins, whose entire playing career was built on grit and hustle, could not comprehend Meusel or induce him to stop loafing; and he hit too well—leading the league in homers and RBIs in 1925—to be dumped. Babe Ruth seemed unreachable for the same reason. The Babe ignored orders, expansively broke training, and told reporters "the Flea" (as Ruth called Huggins) should be fired for incompetence. After many provocations, Huggins in August 1925 suspended him and fined him five thousand dollars, a year's salary for most of the Yankees. Ruth bellowed, then backed down. The team kept losing. "I've called them everything, and they don't even get mad," Huggins told Barrow. "They just don't care any more." Okay, said Barrow: "We'll get a new team."

The Red Sox had nobody left, so Barrow and Huggins used expert scouts and Ruppert's bottomless checkbook to rebuild the Yankees. Bob Connery, Huggins's closest friend, had been his chief scout with the Cardinals, then came with him to New York. Connery was best known for discovering Rogers Hornsby in Denison, Texas, in 1915. ("I wasn't so much impressed with his hitting," Connery later said of the greatest right-handed hitter in baseball history. "What I saw was a loose gangling kid, with a good pair of hands, a strong arm, and a world of pep and life on the field.") Connery found many other big leaguers after Hornsby—"more star ball players in the rough than any other scout," one baseball writer declared in 1925.

Paul Krichell, the other noted Yankee scout from this era, had met Ed Barrow in the minor leagues. Barrow hired him to scout for the Red Sox, then brought him along to New York; after the season the two men would go turkey-shooting in South Carolina. Otherwise Krichell spent his life on the road, attending ballgames at every level, charming and schmoozing, talking about prospects at dinners and social events, getting tips in bars and barber's chairs. "There is no set formula," as Krichell explained his trade. "A player with a pronounced weakness may become a star in the major leagues. But he can't climb to the top if he has more than one flaw in his equipment." Temperament mattered, but nobody could see inside a young player's head. "So, how well does he like to play ball? Does he really love the game?" Krichell pursued his guesses well enough for Barrow to call him "the best judge of ballplayers I ever saw."

Krichell accidentally encountered Lou Gehrig at a college ballgame at Rutgers. He had gone to see somebody else, but noticed the big first baseman playing for the Columbia team. So he went back, to a game on the Columbia campus, and Gehrig obligingly hit a four-hundred-foot homer that bounced off the library steps. Krichell told Barrow he had found "the next Babe Ruth," brought him to the Yankee office, and signed him for a fifteen-hundred-dollar bonus. A muscular innocent, still unformed as both ballplayer and personality, Gehrig moved into the Yankee lineup three years later. He looked clumsy and hesitant at first base, reluctant to roam from the bag for grounders. One day Huggins criticized him for not cutting off an outfield throw, allowing Ty Cobb to reach second and then score. Gehrig, it turned out, had never heard of cutoff plays; on the way home from the game, his teammates showed him the rudiments right there on the sidewalk. Another day, after popping up in a crucial situation, Gehrig started weeping, audibly, on the bench. Huggins turned around, growled, "Come ON!" and looked back at the field in disbelief.

This man-child could always hit, though: grasscutters into the right-field corner, whistling liners to all fields, smoking home runs that left the park without peaking. He stood at the plate, feet far apart, then stepped into the ball with a short stride, generating power from his slabbed shoulders. "Babe gets his entire body behind his blow," Gehrig explained. "I'm an arm hitter. . . . It's the strength you have in your grip, in your forearm, more than anywhere else." Many home runs were just lucky, he added. "But there's nothing lucky about a solid smash, straight out over the diamond. It means only one thing, that the batter has connected just right. I believe they ought to keep a record of a batter's line drives." The most remarkable aspect of Gehrig's record of playing 2,130 straight games was the unflagging level of daily excellence he maintained. Though sometimes tired or hurt, "The Iron Horse" didn't show it. He hit consistently, .340 over his career, especially when it mattered: in his 14 full seasons Gehrig averaged an extraordinary 141 RBIs a year. His lifetime slugging percentage of .632 has been surpassed only by Ted Williams and the Babe.

Bob Connery signed the outfielder Earle Combs after he hit .380, with 42 stolen bases, for Louisville in 1923. Up with the Yankees, Combs started slowly, pressing to justify the fifty thousand dollars that Ruppert had paid for him. "But he has shown me that he has the proper disposition for a star," Huggins declared. "Good natured, laughing and full of youthful exuberance." He settled in, hitting .342 in 1925, then .356 two years later. The swiftest man on the team, once timed at ten flat in the 100 in full uniform, he whizzed around the vast center field at Yankee Stadium. (Joe McCarthy, his manager at Louisville and later on the Yankees, called him "the fastest human being I've seen in a half-century of baseball.") Leading off, crouched into his stance, Combs rifled liners through the box and set the table for the sluggers following him. Over his first eight full seasons he averaged 125 runs scored a year. His only flaw was a weak arm that looked even worse in that peerless outfield. "I could name at least a dozen outfielders in the American League whose throwing arms are not a bit better than mine," Combs insisted. "You never hear of them, however. I have to compete with Babe Ruth and Bob Meusel."

When Tony Lazzeri tore up the Pacific Coast League in 1925, Paul Krichell and two other Yankee scouts looked him over.

Krichell then signed him for $50,000 and five throw-in ballplayers, a total value of about $75,000. Lazzeri had come up from a tough childhood in the Cow Hollow neighborhood of San Francisco. He fought his way through the local kids, played baseball in Golden Gate Park, and stayed in school mainly to pitch for the team. At fifteen he was finally expelled from school, to his relief, and went to work with his father as a boilermaker's helper. The heavy, noisy work built up his shoulders and forearms but left him deaf in one ear. He still played semipro ball on the side. After three years at the ironworks, about to become a full-fledged boilermaker, he was offered a minor-league contract. He spent four seasons in the bushes, mainly with Salt Lake City, and reached the Yankees in 1926: still only twenty-two, but older than his years, with a mature face and a grim, silent presence.

Miller Huggins paid Lazzeri his ultimate compliment. "He has the right disposition for a ballplayer," said the manager. "He had to work hard in his younger days and he appreciates what baseball has done for him." Lazzeri arrived with the skills to play anywhere in the infield: a powerful, loose-jointed arm, equal agility to his left and right, and a sure glove. He also hit better than most second basemen, averaging .313 and 105 RBIs over his first five seasons. What most intrigued observers, given his youth, were his baseball intelligence and habit of command. "He's got a surprising head on his shoulders," noted the umpire Tommy Connolly. "I never saw a young fellow like him." Lazzeri took charge of the green Yankee infield in 1926, with another rookie, Mark Koenig, at shortstop and the still-callow Gehrig at first; the only veteran was Jumping Joe Dugan at third. Off the field, partly because of his semideafness, Lazzeri seldom spoke. ("Interviewing that guy," said one scribe, "is like trying to mine coal with a nail file and a pair of scissors.") On the field he came to vociferous life, moving fielders around, yelling at the pitcher, scolding and encouraging. Watching Lazzeri, Huggins must have been reminded of himself. Another smart second baseman, always thinking, Lazzeri noticed tiny subtleties such as the slightest change in a pitcher's motion. Even as a rookie, he functioned as the unofficial Yankee captain. "He was the making of that club," Ed Barrow said later, "holding it together, guiding it, and inspiring it."

These new Yankees, dependent on Huggins's favor and grateful for his tutelage, caused fewer discipline problems. "He taught me everything I know," said Gehrig. "I don't think anybody could bring along a kid player like Huggins could," said Lazzeri. "Barrow could make you feel like a midget," said Koenig, "but Huggins made you feel like a giant." The team started winning again, rolling to another string of three pennants beginning in 1926.

The 1927 Yankees, often called the greatest team in baseball history, piled up 110 victories and could have won more; they clinched early, on September 13, and after coasting in still finished 19 games ahead of the nearest pursuer. They hit .307 as a team and paced the league in virtually all hitting and pitching categories. (Meusel managed only .337, the worst average in the outfield.) Ruth set his record of 60 homers—more than any other American League *team* hit that year. Combs led the league in hits and triples, Gehrig in doubles and RBIs, Ruth in runs and slugging. The league's top four pitchers in winning percentage were all Yankees: Waite Hoyt, Urban Shocker, Wilcy Moore, and Herb Pennock. Moore and Hoyt had the league's best earned run averages as well. Surprising nobody, New York swept the World Series that fall, and again a year later. All this winning made the team harmonious; the harmony helped it win. "One of the things that inadvertently meshed was the personalities of the fellows playing on that club," Hoyt recalled. "We all got along. We had inordinate pride in ourselves as a unit."

The rise of the Philadelphia Athletics (Jimmie Foxx, Lefty Grove, Al Simmons) and the death of Huggins in 1929 brought this Yankee epoch to a close. The next phase started in 1931 when Barrow hired Joe McCarthy as manager. Like Barrow, McCarthy had toiled for years in bush-league obscurity, and both men conveyed a deadpan sense of power held in reserve: a similar unflamboyant strength that didn't need to trumpet itself but might smolder, then flare when required. McCarthy came to the Yankees after five years with the Chicago Cubs as a known disciplinarian. Serving notice, he banned shaving and card playing in the clubhouse, eating hot dogs and peanuts in the dugout, and fraternizing with the enemy. (At Yankee Stadium, he had a new door installed so that the visiting team could reach the field

without violating the Yankee dugout.) On the road, everybody
except that day's starting pitcher had to appear for breakfast, in
coats and ties, before eight-thirty; McCarthy sat behind a newspaper, noting arrivals and how alert they looked after the last
night's adventures. At the ballpark, he enforced a serious clubhouse, no pranks or hollering or singing, quiet and purposeful.
"It was all business before a game," a Yankee recalled, "and
there wasn't a whole lot of hell-raising after one either. McCarthy simply wouldn't allow it." These stringencies brought no
immediate success but established a long-term professional sobriety. McCarthy won one pennant in his first five Yankee seasons—and then seven in his next eight.

As a baseball strategist he was conservative and old-fashioned,
building the team around reliable pitchers and a sound double-
play combination, sprinkling his offense with unexpected bunts
and squeezes. Three of McCarthy's Yankee clubs even led the
league in stolen bases. He told his players *what* to do, expecting
them already to know *how*. "One thing that always impressed us
about McCarthy was that he managed with the utmost simplicity," Waite Hoyt reflected. "Occasionally he played a hunch—
and the success of those hunches gained him a reputation for
being smart." Instead of holding team meetings, he sat back in
his office, talking with the coaches who kept him informed and
conveyed his instructions. For touchy exchanges a player might
be summoned to a private audience. "He seemed always to know
just how to talk to you," Tommy Henrich recalled. "He knew
when to jump on you, when to be your friend, when to give you
a pat on the back, when to leave you alone. Best manager I ever
knew or heard about." Young ballplayers especially remembered
his deftness: patient and encouraging, or threatening to send the
boy back down to Newark, whatever worked. "He had a way of
sticking the ice pick in you when it was real cold," Spud Chandler
added. "But he had a reason for it. He always had a reason for
everything he did."

Paring baseball to its essentials, McCarthy had little use for
distractions or public relations. During the season he allowed
himself no hobbies or diversions and read only box scores. At
some cost to his reputation, he steadfastly withheld the inside
tips and quotations on which sportswriters fed. "Let me worry

about that," he would say, ending the interview. The stonewalled writers took refuge in calling him a push-button pilot who managed by rote, without thinking. "The scribes find Joe a bit on the difficult side," one noted. "There's no exchange of confidence. . . . Joe could make it easier for himself if he would—well, shall we say 'loosen up a bit.' " Only his baseball intimates, other men directly involved in the game, knew his stupefying command of facts and lore. In a private, arcane baseball conversation, somebody else would grope for an obscure name; McCarthy would supply it. "The greatest baseball memory I've ever known," Barrow noted. "Actually it was astonishing." In many respects—keeping the game simple and well anchored at the keystone, the delicate sense of player psychology, skill at developing youngsters, reticence with the press, the compulsive everyday attention to detail—McCarthy not coincidentally resembled his fellow second baseman (and Barrow employee) Miller Huggins.

McCarthy's Yankees won with five great ballplayers—Gehrig, Red Ruffing, Lefty Gomez, Bill Dickey, Joe DiMaggio—and bunches of good ones. This second Bronx dynasty improved on the first in one crucial area. Having once defined pitching as 70 percent of a team's effectiveness, McCarthy grounded his juggernaut on mound skill. Huggins's six pennant winners had led the league in staff ERA only twice; McCarthy's eight winners did it seven times—and placed second in 1941 by .01 of a run. Such accumulating consistency, year after year, could not have been accidental. (But, then, seven of those eight teams also topped the league in runs and homers: they rolled on by commanding both halves of the inning.)

Red Ruffing, a tall 205-pound horse who had left four of his toes in an Illinois coal mine, blossomed late as a pitcher. Over his first eight big-league seasons—six with the Red Sox and two with the Yankees—he finished with an ERA under 4.00 only once. Then, at twenty-eight, he matured to become the ace of the Yankee staff and stayed under 4.00—three times under 3.00— for the rest of his career in New York. "A big guy, I mean *big,* but a real easy-going style, like he didn't give a damn," Ted Williams recalled. "But his ball used to . . . in the last six feet it kind of oomed, built up on you, and was right by you." At first a pure smoke-and-curve pitcher, Ruffing accidentally picked up a slider by unconsciously changing his grip on the ball, and added a screwball and other slop as his speed waned. He also batted so well, better than most pinch hitters (over .300 eight times, with 36 career homers), that he kept himself pitching through the late innings of tight games. Devoid of temperament, wedded to a strict routine of diet and warm-ups on starting days, and seldom injured, he continued to win into his late thirties: a true McCarthy ballplayer. "He said hello to me the first day of training camp," Ruffing said of his manager, "and said good-bye to me the last day of the season. In between, he just put the ball in my hand and that was all I wanted."

Lefty Gomez began life as a right-hander, fell off a horse and broke his right arm, started throwing left-handed, and thereafter worked hard to become everybody's notion of an eccentric southpaw. In 1930 the Yankees bought him from the San Francisco Seals for thirty-five thousand dollars. After first refusing to shake hands with the rookie, Herb Pennock—the staff's veteran lefty—taught Gomez the accumulated wisdom of two decades in the bigs, going over the strengths and weaknesses of every hitter in the league. McCarthy improved Lefty's control by changing his sidearm motion to straight overhand. Gomez won 21 games his second season, then 24 the next. But he showed a southpaw's expected inconsistency. He went 26-5, then 12-15; led the league with a 2.33 ERA, ballooned to 4.38 two seasons later, and back to 2.33 the following year. Responding to these fluctuations, or perhaps causing them, Gomez fiddled constantly with his mental approach and pitching motion. "I've been getting too smart," he typically announced. Wishing to be accepted as a real pitcher, not a mere thrower, he developed his curveball. "And all it's done is to make trouble for me! I get some hitters out with it and then I switch to my fast ball and it always seems that just when I switch is the time when they are laying for me to switch and they mallerate my fast ball. The trouble is now I got too much stuff." He told himself to "just go out there and give 'em that old fast ball with a hey-nonny-nonny and a hot-cha-cha like you used to."

Aside from these spasms of overthinking, Gomez puzzled his manager with distinctly unMcCarthylike behaviors: chinning himself on the dugout roof, blocking the boss's view; wanting to wear suspenders so that he didn't waste energy tugging at the pants slipping down his skinny hips ("it is no end distressing and takes my mind off my pitching duties"); appearing in the dugout with a cane, tin cup, and dark glasses and telling the umpire he had graduated from umpire school; pausing in a World Series game to watch an airplane fly by; suddenly, pointlessly, tossing the ball to Lazzeri at second, because Lazzeri was supposed to be so smart, and Gomez wanted to see his reaction. The southpaw remained a blithe, garrulous intrusion on this too-serious, tight-lipped team. "You could take only so much of Lefty," McCarthy said later, not getting the joke. "A nervous fellow on the bench, boiling over with energy and enthusiasm. He was calm and collected on the mound, but on the bench he was always trying to get my okay to go to the bull pen if we were losing or in a tight game. He'd pound his glove, mutter about going in there and stopping them, and pretty soon he'd be almost sitting in my lap." No other Yankee risked such presumptions with the boss. But he led the league twice in victories, three times in strikeouts and shutouts, started five of the first six All-Star games, and went 6-0 in the World Series. And he was, after all, a left-hander.

Bill Dickey moored the pitching staff, catching at least one hundred games a season for a record thirteen years in a row. "Dickey and I know each other so well," said Ruffing, "we have been working together for so long, that we have a perfect understanding." The son of a conductor for the Missouri Pacific, Dickey had grown up in Little Rock, Arkansas. (McCarthy disapproved of southern ballplayers, expecting them to act headstrong and hot-tempered, but made an exception for Dickey.) When he ascended to the Yankees, he looked too tall, thin, and vulnerable for the ground-hugging, dirt-eating, collision-prone life of a catcher. A Yankee pitcher criticized him for setting too high a target. But he had compensating skills; Dickey already boasted a gunning arm from a smooth, quick release. "He's got young, limber knees," noted the umpire Bick Campbell. "He bobs up like a shot out of his crouch and rears up like a monument and lines that ball down to second pretty." Quick-handed, he went through the entire 1931 season without a passed ball. Along with Mickey Cochrane, his only equal as a backstop in the 1930s, Dickey soon pioneered a style of swifter, more agile catching. They replaced the old cumbersome chest protector, and its hindering groin flap, with a smaller protector and a metal cup in the jock. They adopted a smaller, more flexible mitt no bigger than a first baseman's. Anticipating a technique not in general use until decades later, with nobody on base Dickey learned to catch one-handed, saving injuries to his oft-injured throwing hand.

"A good catcher," an old baseball hand said of Dickey in 1937, "and a great hitter." He batted well from the start, .310 or higher in his first six full seasons, but without much power. When he started pulling the ball, his slugging percentage, never before over .500, suddenly leaped up around .600. At his peak, for the Yankee teams that won a then-record four straight World Series from 1936 to 1939, he averaged .326 with 26 homers and 115 RBIs—while he was catching 128 games a season. His .362 in 1936 remains the best modern average for a catcher. These feats were sometimes overlooked because of Dickey's colorless, matter-of-fact personality. "Of all the star ballplayers in the game at the moment," wrote Stanley Frank in 1939, "Bill Dickey is the man nobody knows." Steady and dull, he had no flash, no personal magnetism, no eccentricities or stories to tell. Even his blandly handsome face and regular features made him less memorable. On the road he roomed with Lou Gehrig; in the evening they decorously stayed home to read and play honeymoon bridge. (When Dickey fell into a slump one year, Ed Barrow told him to have a drink before every game.)

Joe DiMaggio was only twenty-one when he came up in 1936. "He seems to be very hard to get acquainted with," Jake Ruppert noticed. In spring training McCarthy put him through private outfield drills but otherwise left him alone, then and later. Like Tony Lazzeri, his fellow San Francisco Italian, DiMaggio arrived young but fully formed, preternaturally mature, with his own style of playing. At the plate he stood, bat high and motionless, with his legs wide apart, barely lifting his front foot as the pitch approached; he thought this restricted movement let him better follow the ball's line of flight. "That's the only way I can bat," he said. "It is natural for me. I don't think I shift my left foot more than three inches when I swing." He liked a top-heavy bat, "kinda thick out at the end, with most of the weight there. It keeps me

from swinging too fast, and when I do connect, the ball travels."
DiMaggio started quickly and did his best hitting before his
twenty-seventh birthday. Over his first six seasons he averaged
.345 with 33 homers and 143 RBIs. In his last seven seasons—
one before the war and six afterward—he seldom regained the
early heights, reaching those averages only once in each category. (But he had fashioned one of the great debuts in baseball
history, better than those of Ruth, Cobb, Hornsby, or Joe Jackson, comparable only to the .352, 33, 125 compiled by Ted
Williams in *his* first six seasons.)

Although his hitting tailed off, DiMaggio's fielding and baserunning remained impeccable. He moved so smoothly, without
flourishes, that even when flat out he seemed to be running in
slow motion, deliberate and contained; always contained. "I'm
pretty much on my toes," he explained, "even if it doesn't seem
so. I know that when I run, these long legs of mine make me look
as if I were loping along. But I can travel fairly well." Gliding
around center field, cutting off doubles in the alleys or charging
singles like a shortstop, he uncorked the finest outfield arm Mc-
Carthy had ever seen. During his rookie year, before opponents
fully appreciated that arm, Detroit came to New York for a
crucial series. In the ninth inning, with one out, the Tigers got
the tying run on third and the potential winning run on first.
The batter hit a long fly to left-center; DiMaggio caught it over
his shoulder, running away from the plate. The safe move would
be to concede the run and throw to second, holding the Tiger on
first. Instead DiMaggio shifted his feet like a veteran and threw
home on the fly—he meant to bounce it—easily doubling the
runner from third and ending the game. Mickey Cochrane,
watching in the Tiger dugout, later called it "the greatest throw
I ever saw." Afterward McCarthy doled out his usual circum-
spect praise: "What are you trying to do, Joe? Show me how
strong you are?"

The best, most famous player on the best, most famous team
in baseball, blessed and cursed to spend his career in the publicity carnival of New York, DiMaggio retreated behind a shy
man's wall of dour unapproachability. Except for Lefty Gomez,
his roommate on the road, even his teammates seldom saw
DiMaggio outside the clubhouse. Gomez always wondered why

McCarthy had paired them. ("We were opposites. I talked all the time, and Joe never talked at all": which may explain it.) Only Gomez was allowed the privilege of teasing DiMaggio, calling him a funny name and extorting a laugh; nobody else dared try. Less recognizable than his roomie, Gomez could without commotion stop at newsstands to buy DiMaggio's favorite *Batman* and *Superman* comic books for him. "He's always relaxed," Gomez noted. "And how that feller can sleep." Although mute off the field, DiMaggio still set the standards and tone for the Yankees. His legs were usually scraped raw from sliding so hard. If he went hitless in a loss, DiMaggio would sit unmoving before his locker for thirty or forty minutes afterward, blaming and torturing himself. His teammates noticed—and absorbed the implicit lesson. "The strongest drive for winning of any player I ever played with or against," Tommy Henrich said later. "That inner toughness put him above all the other greats."

In essence, DiMaggio was simply a McCarthy Yankee. They played the game at a smart, full throttle, without any fuss, and then went home. Babe Ruth's roistering spirit—and the older shades of Big Bill Devery and Frank Farrell—no longer hovered over the team. In July 1939, as part of Gehrig's retirement ceremony, the 1927 Yankees were brought back to the stadium. The current Yankees, sweeping to their fourth straight pennant, were being favorably compared to the best Huggins team. Jumping Joe Dugan (a pickled carouser in the old days) watched in amazement as the '39 ballplayers sat soberly by their lockers, going about their business like clerks in an office. "This Yankee club may be greater than the 1927 team," said Dugan. "I doubt it very much. Let that go. But we certainly had a lot more fun."

◆　　◆　　◆

Vince Lombardi told the Green Bay Packers: "We're going to be the Yankees of football!"

◆　　◆　　◆

The Packers dominated pro football in the 1960s by exploiting the cycles of sports history. Vince Lombardi had waited a long time for his shot in the bigs. For more than two decades, while he labored at high school ball and assistant-coached in college and the NFL, he watched football styles appear and recur. Though later most familiar to fans as a ranting maniac on the sidelines, bellowing threats and orders through his gleaming alligator teeth, he was in fact a serious football historian. ("A really formidable intelligence," noted Herbert Warren Wind in *The New Yorker*. "When Lombardi talks about football, he is cogitative, analytical, and almost scholarly.") As a student of gridiron history, Lombardi understood that inventing something new and unstoppable in the game might just involve retrieving something old and forgotten. After Lombardi assumed control of the Packers in 1959, he summoned his quarterbacks to a special camp in early June. "We're going to take a giant step backward, gentlemen," said the coach.

The Packers were then an old, proud franchise fallen into desperate straits, ready to try anything. The team was itself a giant step backward: the last survivor from the modest hinterland town teams that had launched the NFL in the 1920s. Green Bay, Wisconsin—on Lake Michigan, a hundred miles northwest of Milwaukee, with a population in 1959 of about sixty thousand—held on as the smallest, northernmost, and coldest NFL city. Those dubious superlatives, alas, then exhausted the team's bragging rights. Over their last two seasons the Packers had won only four of twenty-four games, the worst record in the league. A misbehaving player on another team might be threatened with exile to Green Bay, the football Siberia. But in their glory days, before the end of World War II, the Packers and their ancient rivals, the Chicago Bears, had commanded the NFL. Each team won six titles before 1945, more than any other franchise, and their annual showdowns rocked and bloodied the frozen turf. Vince Lombardi's task in 1959, then, was to restore this old-fashioned team through old-fashioned means to its old-fashioned eminence.

The Packers had been founded and then coached for twenty-nine years by a Notre Dame dropout named Curly Lambeau. Toiling at a grubby job for the Indian Packing Company in his hometown, Green Bay, and missing football, Lambeau decided to start a semipro team in 1919. His employer provided a practice field and five hundred dollars for equipment, so they called themselves the Packers. Like other town teams of the day, the

Packers were an instant civic institution, a kind of Rotary Club in cleats that advertised the town and expected its support. One Packer—Verne Lewellen, a star punter and running back—was even elected Green Bay's district attorney in 1928. The local paper, the *Press-Gazette*, helped launch the team and remained its faithful cheerleader and publicist; the Packers, according to later grumbles, were the only NFL team with their own newspaper. Small-town loyalties ran both ways, though. As the biggest heroes in town, Packer ballplayers cut easy swaths through Green Bay women—but also might be reported by fans if they were seen drinking at the wrong times or in the wrong places. The team nearly expired from money problems at least three times, only to be saved by civic pride and public subscriptions. The citizens of Green Bay literally owned the team, as the team owned the town.

This symbiotic embrace demanded a habit of winning. Lambeau was a stern, demanding coach, distant from and unloved by his charges. "I don't think Lambeau had a friend in the world, as far as football players were concerned," said his fullback Clarke Hinkle. "Yet all of them respected him." Winning always overrode mere sentimental affections: over their first twenty-seven NFL campaigns, the Packers suffered only one losing season. They took three straight titles from 1929 to 1931, the first league team to achieve such a sweep. And they won with an exciting, high-scoring aerial offense. An early advocate of throwing the ball, Lambeau once ventured forty-five passes in a single game. After retiring himself as quarterback in 1927, he brought in adept passers (Red Dunn and Arnie Herber) and receivers (LaVern Dilweg and Johnny Blood) to keep balls in the air. A favorite play started with a fake handoff to the fullback, then a pass to Blood in the flat. Even Clarke Hinkle, the team's top rusher, also threw and caught passes. The Packers were known for daring, unexpected gambles, such as a long pass from their own one-yard line. Sometimes, just before a snap, the giant tackle Cal Hubbard (later a noted umpire in baseball's American League) would shift to end, making him an eligible receiver. "Why beat your brains out running against a pro line?" Lambeau explained. "It's easier to throw the ball and save your players. It's better business to pass the ball. It's better show business, too." In different ways, Lambeau as coach, Benny Friedman as player, and George Preston Marshall as owner and league mogul together converted pro football to the passing game.

Don Hutson—the first modern receiver, and one of the greatest players in NFL history—joined the Packers in 1935. At Alabama he had made All-American and caught two touchdown passes in a Rose Bowl game. Lambeau saw that game and contacted him; Hutson had never considered pro football or even heard of the Green Bay Packers. In training camp he looked frail for the NFL, lightly padded and only six feet one inch and 180 pounds. But he ran the 100 in 9.7 seconds—a mere blink slower than Jesse Owens's 9.4 world record at the time. Hutson arrived as an NFL star in his second pro game, against the Bears in Chicago. On their own 17, the Packers lined up with Johnny Blood split wide to the right and Hutson on the left. Blood took off down his sideline, drawing the attention of the Bears' secondary; Hutson lost one defender by faking to the outside and lulled the safety by slowing to a near stop. The safety looked away as Hutson sprinted into open territory. Arnie Herber lofted one of his long, floating passes, and Hutson ran under it for an 83-yard touchdown, the only score of the game. "It worked just like in practice," Hutson said later. "I was never one for being nervous."

In eleven seasons Hutson doubled and tripled contemporary notions of what pass receivers were supposed to achieve. He repeatedly broke the old records of 26 catches and 432 yards in a season, peaking at 74 catches and 1,211 yards in 1942. He led the league in receiving eight times, in touchdowns nine times: feats that remain untouched. His career mark of 99 touchdown passes stood until 1989. Hutson was lucky to play with skilled passers—Herber and then Cecil Isbell—and a coach who loved to throw the ball. Granted these fortunate breaks, he still by himself invented and refined the position of wide receiver. Self-coached and self-contained, never upset or excited, he terrified opponents. At Wrigley Field in Chicago, in tense situations the Bears fans would shout, "Stop him! Stop him!"—and everybody knew who "him" was.

Taking off from the line, Hutson ran with a gliding, deceptive gait, little knee or arm action, feet close to the ground.

Known as the only man who could fake in three directions at once, he cut at hard, sharp angles instead of the smooth waves and circles more typical at the time. ("I believe," he later allowed, "that I went in more for the faking—more for the deception— than previous pass receivers had.") Once he literally faked a Bear out of his shoes. On short-yardage plays he buttonhooked and dropped to his knees for a quick, low pass. Hutson's usual deadpan expression never changed with a ball in the air; a defender watching his eyes saw nothing suspicious. An uncanny judge of a football's flight, he sometimes cut away from a throw, luring the defender, then zipped back at the last instant. Jumping for a ball, he scissored his legs, hung in the air while the defender descended, and flicked out his long arms. If he caught it, no opponent could run with him. One time he sped into the end zone, hooked an elbow on the goalpost, and spun around for the touchdown throw. His speed, moves, and sticky hands, taken together, were unprecedented and overwhelming. In 1944 Arthur Daley of the *New York Times* called him "the most extraordinary athlete football has yet produced." (Five decades later, a book-length history of pro football by Peter King of *Sports Illustrated* still ranked Hutson as the best player of all time.)

After Hutson retired, the Packers tumbled into mediocrity. Lambeau under pressure fell to squabbling with his board of directors. They questioned his dictatorial style and spending habits, his divorces and Hollywood wives, his summers in Malibu, and (in particular) his losing football games. The Packers went 3-9 in 1948, then 2-10 a year later, the team's worst record yet. Lambeau was fired, but new coaches didn't help. In the 1950s the Packers twice finished at .500 but otherwise produced losing records each year. Formerly accustomed to first-class hotels and the best gear, the Packers even *looked* bedraggled. At training camp in 1953 Jim Ringo, a rookie center, fished a left shoulder pad from one pile, a right shoulder pad from another. "I managed to patch myself together," Ringo said later, "and thought, 'So this is professional football.' We had better equipment at Syracuse." The fretful board of directors hovered around, interfering with the coaches, complicating the situation to no purpose. The Packers bottomed out at 1-10-1 in 1958. Vince Lombardi arrived a few months later and announced that he would run the team without advice from the directors. Desperate for former glories, they meekly agreed.

The new coach was no less assertive with his ballplayers. Before the first training camp, Lombardi summoned Jim Ringo to Green Bay from his home in New Jersey. "Who the hell does this guy think he is?" Ringo wondered. Grumbly and skeptical, he went out to the Packers' office and found Lombardi enthroned behind an enormous desk. The coach described his plans, how they would achieve this and that; Ringo lost patience, called him Vince, and said he'd heard that same stuff from two other Green Bay coaches. "He hit the desk so hard," Ringo recalled, "that an ashtray flew up in the air and broke into a million pieces. At that point I started to call him 'Sir.' " Lombardi ran a training camp straight from Bataan. Not prepared for the new regime, players passed out, threw up, lost an average of twelve pounds a man. On the second day of workouts, Lombardi found twenty victims in the trainer's room. "What is this, an emergency casualty ward?" he roared. "I have no patience with the small hurts that are bothering most of you." Next day, only two men dared approach the trainer. The coach was getting their attention.

Lombardi's proclaimed giant step backward reinstated the running game on a team historically known for passing, and installed as the bellwether play an old offensive setup that had passed out of fashion since the 1930s. Lombardi thus dropped the Packers into the endless cycle of offensive football strategies—a cycle that went back to the earliest days of Campball. The classic T formation had first appeared, of obscure parentage, sometime in the 1880s: the quarterback about a yard behind center, the fullback behind him, the halfbacks on the fullback's flanks. This T evolved into the deadly mass formations of the 1890s and early 1900s, then yielded around 1910 to the single wing invented by Pop Warner at Carlisle. For three decades the single wing, with its variants the double wing and the Notre Dame box, remained the choice of most coaches. Warner's single wing started from a conventional T; just before the snap, the left guard shifted to the right of the line, putting four linemen on that strong side; the right halfback spread to a wing position beyond and behind the right end. The snap went six yards through the air, usually to the left halfback. While the right halfback ran downfield, for a pass or decoy, the other two backs blocked into the strong side of the line with the left half following them, to run or pass. The man with the ball thus hit the line well convoyed, with time to survey the field and pick a course. But the ball went six yards back, then six yards forward before it even reached the line; long gains were rare because plays developed slowly and the defense could clearly track the ball. It was plain, power football, without much faking or deception. Most NFL offenses sputtered in the 1920s and 1930s because they were playing ground-bound, conservative ball-control single wings.

Alone among NFL teams, George Halas and the Chicago Bears kept using the T formation. Ralph Jones, whom Halas had known since his college days under Bob Zuppke at Illinois, tinkered with the classic T when he coached the Bears for three years in the early 1930s. The Jones variations made the T faster and less predictable. Jones spread the line and backs a few yards wider, loosening the defense and leaving play less bunched in the middle of the field. The quarterback moved up close behind the center, touching him, taking the ball directly so that the center—instead of peering backward through his legs for the long pass to the backfield—could keep his head up and block more effectively. The quarterback might then run, pivot to hand off, or drop back to pass, faking one or more of these maneuvers before committing himself, freezing the defense for a precious moment before it could charge. As another field spreader, Jones put a back in motion, running laterally toward a sideline while the quarterback barked signals. The man-in-motion was at first only a decoy who never got the ball. In a game against the Packers in 1930, though, the Bear quarterback on a sudden inspiration threw to Red Grange when he went in motion. ("We often made up new plays in the huddle," Grange said later.) It worked, spreading the defense even wider, opening the line for quick openers through the middle and fullback bucks toward the end.

This new T was further refined by Clark Shaughnessy, one of the most fertile minds and strangest personalities in football history. Among the convivial, well-lubricated fraternity of football coaches, Shaughnessy neither drank nor smoked and disapproved of both. Obsessed with football, he didn't notice friends passing on a sidewalk and would interrupt family dinners to go diagram a new play. He liked to retire at seven o'clock, then rise at three in the morning to think without distractions. Sober in every sense of the word, shy and solitary, he puzzled other coaches. "They spoiled a great funeral director when they made a coach out of him," Bob Zuppke joked. "He is a clean man, who sips buttermilk." In the late 1930s, unhappily coaching at the University of Chicago, Shaughnessy moonlighted with the Bears. "When George Halas didn't laugh at me or my theories I naturally warmed up to him," Shaughnessy recalled. "He didn't make fun of me." For the Bears Shaughnessy devised novel blocking combinations and codes for signal-calling. In particular, he added a counter play to the man-in-motion that made a defense overshift to one side just before the play unfolded at the opposite end. When Shaughnessy moved on to Stanford in 1940, he brought along his revised T. The Stanford ballplayers, raised on single wings, doubted a formation that sent the runner into the line with no blocker ahead of him. "The T looked new," Shaughnessy noted, "to these young bloods of today who couldn't remember as far back as 1908."

After Stanford won nine straight games and upset Nebraska in the Rose Bowl, and the Bears humiliated the Redskins, 73–0, in the 1940 NFL title game, football stampeded back to the T. With the Jones and Shaughnessy improvements, it replaced the overt power of the single wing with speed and deception. The ball reached the line so quickly that a blocker didn't need to flatten his man; instead he could merely brush-block him for an instant while the ballcarrier, nearly at full speed for the handoff, whooshed into the secondary. After quarterbacks learned the delicate spins and fakes, and the quick drop backward before passing, they preferred the T because they no longer were expected to block for ballcarriers. A few skeptics remained; old Pop Warner scorned the revived T as the "Interference follow me" system. But fans embraced the faster, more open game, the apparent up-to-date modern fashionableness of the T. It all looked quite familiar to football observers with long memories. "The new T is a variation," Bob Zuppke commented in 1946. "Ignorance makes fans think it is new. In fifty years they will rediscover the football of today and claim it as new." By the

1950s every NFL team had replaced the single wing with some version of the T, usually the standard pro set—two running backs behind the quarterback, receivers flanked left and right, and a tight end near the tackle—devised by Shaughnessy as head coach of the Los Angeles Rams in 1949.

Cutting against this grain, at his first meeting with the Packer offense in 1959 Lombardi diagrammed a single-wing play, the power sweep, that would become the signature of his Green Bay teams. "If we're going to be successful offensively," the coach stressed at that first meeting, "this is one play we're going to have to run and run successfully." It worked in part because of its novelty; the typical pro defenses of the time were designed to stop T formations, not a relic from the single wing. Lombardi had kept the sweep in mind ever since college, when as a guard for Fordham in the mid-1930s he was impressed by the Pittsburgh single-wing teams coached by Jock Sutherland. In his own coaching career he had mostly taught the T and its variants. When he moved up to the NFL as an assistant for the New York Giants in 1954, he included the sweep among his offensive plays. The skeptical Giants doubted the sweep, argued with Lombardi about it, and finally accepted a compromised version.

By the time he reached the Packers, Lombardi had the sweep all worked out and brooked no arguments about it. He would stand at the blackboard for hours, blissfully covered with chalk dust, going over each man's assignments against any imaginable defense, demonstrating blocks and swinging his elbows around, bellowing and gritting his teeth in enthusiasm, discussing every option and variation, repeating and pounding it home. At its best, the Green Bay power sweep combined the force and massed blocking of the single wing with the speed and deception of the T. "We line up our quarterback behind center in the T-formation manner," Lombardi explained, "yet we are less a T than a single-wing team." His favorite version, the 49 sweep, sent the left halfback running with the ball toward the right side of the line. He did not go naked; in the single-wing tradition, the two guards pulled from their down positions and preceded the halfback into the line. (This demanded fast guards and a slow halfback for them all to meet at the crucial moment.) The quarterback took the snap, faked a handoff to the fullback—who dove between the right tackle and tight end to nail the defensive end—and stuck the ball in the left halfback's stomach. From that moment, every Packer except the quarterback had a blocking assignment. The two most difficult blocks put the center on the opposing left tackle and the left tackle on his defensive counterpart. If it all worked right, the left halfback saw an opening around the right end. (Lombardi's celebrated "run to daylight" approach sent the ballcarrier wherever a hole appeared, not to a rigidly predesignated spot on the line.)

The sweep's success depended on deft personnel and execution. Right tackle Forrest Gregg—whom Lombardi later called "the finest football player I ever coached"—was a master of footwork and blocking techniques. He took out the middle linebacker and then sometimes ranged downfield as well. Of the pulling guards, Jerry Kramer excelled at leading plays, Fuzzy Thurston at pass blocking, so they compensated for each other's weaknesses. The tight end, split out three yards to the right, had to neutralize the other linebacker. The ballcarrier cut inside or outside—ran to daylight—depending on where the butting tight end and linebacker went. The Packer tight end, Ron Kramer, was perhaps the most gifted athlete on the team. Strong, agile, and smart, at six feet three inches and 250 pounds he ran the 40 in 4.6 seconds—only a tenth of a second slower than the quickest little Packers. But he acted enigmatic, quiet and pensive to a worrisome degree. Teammates wondered if he took football seriously enough. For a time he was benched after not running his pass routes as taught. Eventually Lombardi—a peerless motivator—reached Kramer, harnessed his latent talents, and pronounced him "as fine a blocker as I have ever seen."

The two running backs either carried the ball or blocked for each other. Jim Taylor, the fullback, had a slow first step and ran the 40 in a sluggish 4.8. Among the Packers he had to overcome an initial reputation for stupidity; he couldn't seem to remember names or plays. A teammate would throw teasing double-talk at him and Taylor would nod, a dummy without a clue, pretending to understand. But he was cast-iron strong—a year-round weight lifter long before such dedication became typical—and mean. When a tackler closed on him, Taylor lowered his shoulders and swung his free forearm like a punishing mace. In short-yardage situations he churned forward, snorting and determined, all but inexorable. "We'd line up and defy the other team to stop us," Taylor said later. He relished contact, sometimes colliding intentionally when he could have sidestepped an opponent. At first reluctant to block for the sweep, he also soon bent to Lombardi's will. One opponent, Art Donovan of the Baltimore Colts, remembered Taylor as "a fullback with the mind-set of a polar bear on Dexedrine." On the sweep, said Donovan, with the halfback lugging the ball and Taylor bearing down, "just as I was about to make the tackle this Clydesdale impersonating a fullback would literally burrow me into the ground."

Left halfback Paul Hornung rode the sweep to stardom as the team's "Golden Boy" and best-known player. A Heisman-winning quarterback at Notre Dame, he smoothly folded into the Packer sweep as an option ballcarrier who could run or pass and doubly worry the defense. Like Ron Kramer, he had seemed undedicated early in his NFL career. A notorious sybarite, tending to overweight, with his shirt off Hornung looked soft and puffy, devoid of visible muscles. On the field he was not especially fast or strong. Following Thurston and Jerry Kramer into the line, though, he didn't need blazing speed. He tracked his blockers well, poised and balanced, and sharply cut back against the flow when pursuers overran him. As a former quarterback he made cool option decisions and threw smart, accurate passes. Prodded by a sense of the moment, Hornung played best in clutch situations, crucial games, and anywhere near the end zone. "While you have to whip him a little, he is no malingerer," Lombardi said of his favorite Packer. "In the middle of the field he may be only slightly better than an average ballplayer, but inside that 20-yard line he is one of the greatest I've ever seen. He smells that goal line." Also the team's placekicker, he scored 33 points in one game, booted 96 consecutive extra points, and set the NFL single-season scoring record of 176 points in 1960.

Lombardi freely slashed away at the roster handed to him in 1959; fifteen members of the 1-10-1 1958 team had departed a year later. Yet Ringo, Gregg, both Kramers, Taylor, Hornung, and a dozen other presentable players were already Packers before the advent of Lombardi. (On the first title team in 1961, fourteen of the twenty-two starters predated the Lombardi era.)

The Packers needed only a better coach, not a better team. "Basically, the talent was there when Coach Lombardi came," Gregg said later. "We had a good mixture of youth and age, but one thing we had a lot of was young players who just needed direction." Lombardi injected "discipline, conditioning, and attitude into the mix, and he kind of pulled everything together," said Gregg. "That's what had to be done."

Discipline had defined Lombardi's whole life. It came without effort to him, naturally and unforced, woven into the entire fabric of his daily existence. He imposed discipline on the Packers simply by imposing himself on them: rigid, obsessed, and ferocious, but therefore consistent, thorough, and indomitable. He'd been born in the Sheepshead Bay section of Brooklyn in 1913, the son of an immigrant from Salerno, and grew up in striving middle-class circumstances. The father, a wholesale butcher, was strong-willed, explosive, harsh in judgments, and a daily communicant at mass. "He was a very basic man," recalled Lombardi, utterly his father's son. "There was only right and wrong, and he believed that you only did the right thing all the time." After public grade school, Lombardi spent the next quarter-century as a student, athlete, teacher, and coach in Roman Catholic schools. At Fordham, an undersized guard on a famous line, he studied hard and helped other football players with their courses. He seemed especially pious. "We all thought he was going to be a priest," said a classmate. Coaching and teaching at a parochial high school in Englewood, New Jersey, he scorched and then patted his players, taught them to arrive on time (even a bit early), to play with small hurts, and to run to daylight. "All the students were afraid of him," one recalled. "But also everybody loved him, if you can imagine this love/fear relationship." The future coach of the Packers was already manifest.

Biding his time in high school ball, dreaming of returning to Fordham as head coach, he twice applied to coach at Notre Dame and never even got acknowledgments of his letters. "It's easy to have faith in yourself and have discipline when you're a winner," he later reflected. "What you got to have is faith and discipline when you're not a winner." In 1949, thirty-six years old, he moved up to become an assistant coach under Red Blaik at West

Point. Military order and Blaik's ramrod style well suited Lombardi. He adopted certain Blaik mannerisms—ambling across the field, hands held behind, head down and thinking—and later often invoked this mentor to the Packers. "He worked on me and molded me and fashioned my entire approach to the game," Lombardi said of Blaik. "He took me in and taught me everything I know. Not only football, but life, and how to handle men, and how to win." Though doubtless sincere, so fulsome a tribute was overstated by several notches. Lombardi's personality and coaching habits had clicked into place well before Blaik entered his life. His five years at West Point were important for other reasons: as a crucial leap toward the big time, and as confirmation—needed though unadmitted—of his talents and ambitions. Blaik gave him the confidence and visibility to go on to the Giants, and then to the Packers. The Green Bay position meant his first head-coaching job beyond high school; he brought along his old blackboard habits.

"I am a teacher first and a coach second," said Lombardi. He taught his lessons in meticulous, repetitive detail, explaining not just what the Packers must do but why. The teacher laid down rules: Packer sport coats and ties on the road and at meals, a five-hundred-dollar fine for sitting or standing at bars, certain watering holes off limits entirely, and unforgiving punctuality. The players learned to arrive on "Lombardi time," fifteen minutes early. Overweight players trimmed down, or else, and nobody dared complain of minor injuries. "Pain is only in the mind," the coach taught. "You can tell yourself it does not hurt, and it will not." At meetings they laughed when he laughed, and stopped laughing when he stopped. In practice he imposed his favorite torture, the dreaded grass drills: the players ran in place; on the command "Down!" they dropped to the turf and lay prone; on "Up!" they leaped up and resumed running; up and down, up and down, perhaps for just five minutes, but then maybe eighty or a hundred reps without a break, to the limits of endurance and beyond until the coach grew bored and relented.

Lombardi operated from a grim but effective theory of football motivation. "To play this game," he believed, "you must have that fire in you, and there is nothing that stokes that fire like hate." He lavished abuse on his charges, keeping them fruitfully worried about their jobs. After chewing a man out in public, he might apologize in private; players wished it were the other way around. At film meetings he reran all the mistakes, over and over, embarrassing the culprits into better play. After a victory, with everybody relaxing and congratulating themselves, he might storm into the locker room and leave the players wondering if maybe they had actually lost the game. At practice he roared and chided without mercy, reaching for threats and insults, his great raspy bark of a voice commanding the field. "It's hard to resist hating him," noted Jerry Kramer, the team's Boswell. In hating and fearing the coach, they pulled together and tried to *show* him—exactly the effect Lombardi wanted. "It's ridiculous," wrote Kramer, "the way supposedly adult individuals cower and hide from one short, fat Italian." (They took refuge in private Lombardi jokes. Coach got into bed and his wife said, "God, your feet are cold." "Dear," Coach replied, "in the privacy of the house, you may call me Vince." Coach had an accident; he was hit by a motorboat while walking across the river. A player died, went to heaven, and saw a short guy yelling at some angels playing football. "Oh, that's God," it was explained. "He thinks he's Vince Lombardi.")

The teacher kept the lessons uncomplicated and easy to learn. "Some people try to find things in this game that don't exist," Lombardi often said. "Football is two things. It's blocking and tackling." They practiced the same few plays hundreds of times until every detail became automatic, unthinking, with every man assigned a role and responsible for it. In a game the Packers used only fifteen or twenty plays, fewer than most NFL teams. They sacrificed surprises for consistency, aiming for a modest workmanlike ideal of predictable performance and thus few mistakes. The Packers could go an entire season with only two or three botched plays. Opponents knew the sweep was coming, jabbered warnings to each other, but could not stop it. "The Packers were very direct," said an opponent. "You knew what they were going to do." The coach, team, and style of play boiled down to two qualities: discipline and simplicity. "I have been called a tyrant, but I have also been called the coach of the simplest system in football," Lombardi bantered. "The perfect name for the perfect coach would be Simple Simon Legree."

It didn't work for everybody. The ballplayers who could take it—who understood and accepted the coach's intentions—stayed and became famous. The others fell away and disappeared. (Especially in sports, history belongs to the victorious.) Quarterback Bart Starr, drafted in the seventeenth round in 1956 from a winless Alabama team, played an invisible backup role on the Packers for most of four seasons. A devout Christian, quiet and self-effacing, easily injured, average-sized and weak-armed, he showed neither the skills nor the temperament to become a great quarterback. "I wasn't mentally tough before I met Coach Lombardi," Starr said later. "I was too nice at times. . . . He taught me that you must have a flaming desire to win. It's got to dominate all your waking hours." When the coach lit into him, Starr felt his toes burn as his whole body registered the blow. Lombardi noticed, pulled back, and tried more positive reinforcement on him. (He didn't treat everybody the same.) The coach went through other quarterbacks and finally settled on Starr by default. In a Bears game late in 1960—with the team still unconvinced of his guts and durability—the linebacker Bill George sacked Starr, cutting his lip, and yelled, "I'm going to take care of you, Starr, you pussy." Starr spat blood and nailed George with a few unChristian epithets (the first time Jerry Kramer had ever heard him swear). Then he threw two touchdown passes and led the Packers to an easy win. "I began to believe in Bart Starr that day," Kramer noted.

The Packer defense, under assistant coach Phil Bengston, inevitably reflected Lombardi's faith in football fundamentals. Bengston, silent and cerebral, stayed cool under most pressures. (The coaching staff had room for only one Lombardi personality.) His players knew when Bengston was angered because his voice got a bit louder; that was all. Setting up, they used the standard 4-3 alignment, with variations, devised by Tom Landry for the Giants in the 1950s. "It wasn't complicated; it was just thorough," said one stymied opponent, the quarterback John Brodie. "Because they were so well prepared and so on top of what offenses were doing, they held to one basic formation and made adjustments inside it." Unlike the offense, the defense was built with new Packers, not incumbents. For strategic and morale purposes, Lombardi put his best athletes on defense; consigned to the grubbier, unglamorous, and anonymous jobs in football, they at least knew their unit included the swiftest, strongest players on the team. The defensive linemen—unkempt and snarly compared to their offensive counterparts on the Packers—were smaller but faster than most of the enemy linemen they encountered.

Since NFL offenses were typically loaded to their right, the Packer defense was stacked on the left. Willie Davis, the left end, was traded to the Packers after two nondescript years with the Cleveland Browns. Under Lombardi's lash, he became All-Pro and the only unstoppable man on the defensive line. Not particularly big for a pro lineman at six feet three inches and 245 pounds, he excelled at lateral pursuit, turning end runs back toward the middle of the field. His exceptional balance made him hard to knock off his feet and out of the play. Herb Adderley, the All-Pro left cornerback, was drafted from Michigan State in 1961. Opponents so respected him that sometimes Adderley went two or three games with no passes thrown into his zone; he would roam the field at will and still finish the afternoon in a clean uniform. The Packer trade-off, of speed for size, gave up short rushing plays but usually contained long gainers and cheap touchdowns. "The Packers were not physically bigger or faster," Davis said later. "We were not anything but guys who were willing to work hard enough to get themselves ready to play. And, with Lombardi in charge, maybe sometimes it was not an option."

Behind the line, the Packer defense was anchored by Willie Wood at safety and Ray Nitschke at middle linebacker: the two most ferocious competitors on the team. If any Packer missed a tackle, he expected to flinch from Wood's wrath. "Next to Lombardi, in fact," Jerry Kramer noted, "Wood scares his own teammates more than anybody else does." Nitschke had come to the Packers in 1958 as a muscle-bound delinquent who picked fights and drank too much. The coach landed on him hard. (Nitschke later put it carefully: "Lombardi didn't think I was the kind of player who needed compliments, and I guess he was right.") After a few years, marriage and Lombardi's hectoring transformed Nitschke into a disciplined All-Pro linebacker, the quarterback of the defense. He played in a caterwauling fury—one of the league's hardest tacklers—with a pain threshold high enough to extract even the coach's approval. Against the Lions in 1963, Nitschke broke his forearm, stayed in the game, broke his nose, and then came out. The angry aggressions of his youth tumbled forth on the field, any field. "He can be absolutely murderous during practice," Kramer noted. "He seems incapable of letting up, even against his own teammates. . . . I don't feel there's any reason for him to hit me in the head with a forearm during dummy scrimmages." (Nitschke had lost his father at three, his mother at thirteen. Like many of the Packers—including Hornung, Jerry Kramer, Davis, and others—he had grown up without a father, and so was ripe for a strong paternal figure. "We were Lombardi's family," Nitschke later reflected. "Black or white, young or older, hairy or bald like me, we were his sons.")

During the week before a game, Lombardi and his staff spent Monday, from nine in the morning till midnight, studying Sunday's films. On Tuesday, after a win the offensive and defensive units watched film separately; after a loss everybody sat together, the better for the coach to shame those responsible. "It was murder," Forrest Gregg recalled. "It was one of the toughest things about playing for him. He'd point out every mistake. Nobody was spared. . . . He'd show everyone what a donkey you were." Practice then offered the hope of redemption and expiation earned by pain. The sessions were crisp, all planned out and exactly timed, and quite serious. In the bitter weather of late fall in Green Bay, nobody expected to have any fun. "No other team in pro football works as hard as we do," Jerry Kramer moaned. "Of course, no other team wins so often, either." On Thursday Lombardi would speak cordially to his wife for the first time that week; that night, the assistant coaches could expect to enjoy their first evening since Sunday with their families. On Friday the tension started building toward Sunday. Bart Starr, the most studious Packer ("the smartest quarterback I ever saw," according to Lombardi), immersed himself in films and playbooks, getting ready. "The heart of his system was preparation," Starr said later. "He prepared us beautifully for every game, for every eventuality. . . . Thanks to Coach Lombardi, I knew—I was positive—that I would never face a situation I wasn't equipped to handle." On Sunday, just before the game, Lombardi faced his team. Depending on his sense of the moment, he might deliver fire and brimstone, or a quotation from St. Paul, or just a joke to break the tightness. "He always knew exactly how to treat us," Kramer noted. "He played us like a virtuoso."

The Packers rose quickly to the top of the league and stayed there: a winning record in 1959, a near miss in the 1960 title game, then a 37–0 dismantling of the Giants for the 1961 championship. "You can't realize how much joy there is in this team," said a Green Bay fan, "until you know the heartaches and despair of the past." The Packers won again in 1962: Taylor led the league in rushing, Starr in passing, Wood in interceptions. Lombardi later called the 1963 team his best ever, though it lost two games, and the Western Conference championship, to the Bears. After an off year in 1964, the Packers took three titles in a row—the first such streak since the Green Bay skein of 1929–31. They won the 1967 title on the last play of the famous "Ice Bowl" game, as Starr snuck in for the winning touchdown against Dallas. Afterward, "it was something to see," Nitschke recalled, "that locker room full of big, tough guys, hugging each other and slapping each other's backs and crying from happiness. What a feeling there was among us. What a great joy it was to be there." They capped the 1966 and 1967 titles with easy victories in the first two Super Bowls against the American Football League. Under Lombardi they had started as David and wound up as Goliath.

In poor health, Lombardi retired himself to the Packer front office after the 1967 season, and two years later he was dead. No NFL team has ever matched his run of five titles in seven years. Over that stretch they won 78 percent of their regular-season games and eight of eight in the postseason. Lombardi and nine of his Packers later made the Pro Football Hall of Fame: four from defense (Davis, Nitschke, Adderley, and Wood) and five from offense (Gregg, Hornung, Starr, Taylor, and Ringo). Surely the finest team in NFL history, they played out the American dream by way of Poor Richard: the newcoming outsiders, unprivileged, who rose by simple schoolbook maxims—hard work, grit, and blood—to unprecedented and unmatched heights.

And they were fortunate to play in the 1960s, when pro football popped from the tube into the national sports consciousness. A Gallup Poll in 1961 asked Americans to name their favorite sport: 34 percent said baseball, 21 percent football. A decade later, another Gallup Poll found those figures flipped: 36 percent football, 21 percent baseball. Average attendance at NFL games went from 30,257 in 1960 to 52,381 in 1970. The first Super Bowl drew 65 million TV viewers, the largest audience yet for any game in any sport. Lombardi's Packers were both cause and beneficiary of this televised surge toward football. As millions of new fans around the country tuned in to the grid game, they reasonably adopted the best team of the day, that squad in the snappy green-and-gold uniforms from the little town in Wisconsin. When TV networks broadcast Sunday doubleheaders, they aired the local team first, then the Packer game second. Lombardi was perhaps the most prominent sports personality of the 1960s: while fans spoke of Ruth's Yankees and Russell's Celtics, it was always Lombardi's Packers. In the decade of football's grand expansion, they were the national team.

◆　　◆　　◆

"We've got one of the greatest sports names in the world," said Red Auerbach of the Boston Celtics. "People say we're on a par with Joe McCarthy's New York Yankees and Vince Lombardi's Green Bay Packers."

◆　　◆　　◆

When the National Basketball Association was launched in 1946, Red Auerbach still had red hair. Only twenty-nine years old, flourishing quite modest credentials, he had talked his way into a head-coaching job with the Washington Capitols for the league's first season. Competing against older, more celebrated coaches—including such veteran pros as Eddie Gottlieb, Dutch Dehnert, and Honey Russell—young Auerbach whipped the Capitols to a 17-game winning streak and a league-whomping record of 49-11. (No NBA team had a better season until twenty years later.) Auerbach stayed involved with the NBA for the next five decades: the only founding father still active into the 1990s. As coach, general manager, and gnarly guru of the Boston Celtics, he masterminded the most consistently successful basketball

franchise in history. At their peak from 1957 to 1969 they were
the best pro team, in any sport, ever. Along the way, Auerbach
annoyed many observers—even some Celtics and their fans—
with his sometimes churlish behavior, his childish rages and
triumphant cigars, petty complaints and grating self-
congratulations. Yet these all seem trivial when measured against
the consistent excellence of the Celtics. Auerbach's long string of
achievements remains unrivaled in big-league annals.

Aside from his own substantial gifts of intellect and temperament, Auerbach came to the NBA in 1946 with the ready-made
advantage of an uncommon blend of basketball backgrounds:
raised and schooled in the stern disciplines of the Northeast
style, he had already played and coached the best techniques
drawn from the rest of the country. Few coaches of any age in
1946 were so broadly, nationally gauged in hoops as the twenty-
nine-year-old redhead. He was a Brooklyn boy, born and raised,
with a personality formed more by the rough streets of his
Williamsburg neighborhood than by parental shapings. "I'm just
the opposite of the way my father was," Red said later. "He was
a very friendly guy. He liked people. People liked him." Hyman
Auerbach, a Russian Jewish immigrant, ran a deli, then a dry-
cleaning business. As a boy Red picked his way carefully through
the simmering factions—Italian, Irish, Jewish, Polish—of multi-
ethnic Williamsburg. The local school was only three blocks from
the headquarters of the notorious Italian/Jewish underworld
gang that newspapers called Murder, Incorporated. "Nobody
seemed to have any money," Auerbach recalled, "except the guys
in the rackets." (His amiable father even befriended the gangsters.) One day when Red was nine or ten an Italian kid picked
a fight; after verbal exchanges the other boy suddenly surprised
and staggered him with a sucker punch, then beat him up. Auerbach never forgot the lesson: throw the first punch, and sort
things out afterward. He went through life with his fist half-
cocked.

"I can't remember when I didn't love basketball," Auerbach
said later. "There wasn't a tree in sight at my school. Everywhere
you looked, all you saw was concrete, so there was no football, no
baseball, and hardly any track there. Basketball was our game."
Hyman Auerbach wondered why his second son stole so much

time from books to shoot hoops. Of medium height, Red became a typical New York ballhandling guard: tenacious on defense, adept at passing and two-handed sets. Captain of his high school squad, he made the all-Brooklyn second team (an honor that would later amuse the Olympians and All-Americans among his Celtics, but of which Auerbach remained defiantly proud). Nat Holman contacted him about playing for CCNY, but Auerbach didn't have the grades. So he enrolled at Seth Low Junior College in Brooklyn. One night Red's father came to see his first basketball game ever. Against a zone defense, Red spent the evening in the backcourt, moving the ball around, scoring little. "You're in the living room, and all the action's in the kitchen," Hyman told him afterward. "No wonder you couldn't score!"

During his second year at Seth Low, a lucky break: the George Washington University basketball team came up to New York to play Long Island University. After a scrimmage against Seth Low, George Washington's coach, Bill Reinhart, offered Auerbach a scholarship. Red thus came under the prolonged tutelage of the man he would later credit with "probably the greatest brain in the history of basketball." A three-sport star at the University of Oregon, Reinhart had coached there for a dozen years before coming to George Washington in 1935. He brought along the western style of fast breaks and one-handed shooting. The George Washington team itself included players from Indiana and Oregon as well as New York. Cracking into this established unit that had already played together for two years, Auerbach intruded a leaning, grabbing New York defense that provoked four fistfights in the first two weeks of practice. ("But I had come off the streets, so they didn't bother me. I'd play real strong defense, and if it aggravated them—too bad!")

Yet the roughneck from Williamsburg was not too arrogant to learn a new kind of basketball. After growing up on New York ball, Auerbach soon recognized the limitations of the Northeast style. "There is a notable deficiency in the art of offensive rebounding, fast breaking, running lay-up, and general aggressiveness," Auerbach wrote a few years later. "A common fault is to overweave. . . . The remark is often made that if someone were to put two more baskets on the sides of the court, the Easterners would be the best ever. Seriously, the players should know where the basket is, and move with that thought in mind and not move merely for the sake of moving." Whether in set plays, rebounding, or transition, Reinhart taught a single maxim: go to the hoop. The Reinhart fast break featured a quick outlet pass from the rebounder to a guard, the forwards filling their lanes at top speed, and everyone passing the ball on the run without much dribbling. Already headed toward a coaching career, Auerbach absorbed Reinhart's methods—especially his fast break and the relentless physical conditioning it demanded—and applied them to every team he ever handled.

During the war he coached high school teams in Washington until he was drafted into the navy. His first published article, a matter of puffed pride for this nonstudent in his family, appeared in the March 1943 issue of the *Journal of Health and Physical Education* under the byline of A. J. Auerbach. (It described an indoor obstacle course laid out around the edge of a basketball floor.) Assigned to wartime phys-ed duties at the Norfolk Naval Base in Virginia, Auerbach encountered college basketball stars and techniques gathered from around the country: Johnny Norlander of Hamline in Minnesota, Bob Carpenter of East Texas with his sweeping hook, Bob Feerick of Santa Clara with his sidearm one-hander, and Belus Smawley of Appalachian State with his jump shot. In the midst of the world war, busy with other tasks, Auerbach again found his hoop horizons widening. On his own time he assembled semipro teams, made important contacts with an arena owner in Washington, and so was ready when the Capitols' coaching job came his way in 1946.

"I borrowed a leaf from Bill Reinhart's book," Auerbach recalled, "and decided to draw my men from the whole wide country. New York and the Northeast had the ball handlers and the smart defensive players, the Midwest had the drivers and runners, the South had the one-hand jump shooters, and the Far West had the big tough rebounders. I wanted a heterogeneous squad that would give me a diversified game." From his navy teams he took Feerick, Norlander, and Bones McKinney of North Carolina. The other two starters for the Capitols were John Mahnken, whom he had seen play for Georgetown, and Freddie Scolari of San Francisco, recommended by Feerick. In addition, "I had to have a Jewish smart ballplayer, so-called," so he made Irv Torgoff of Long Island University his sixth man. ("The shrewdest guy I ever met," Scolari later said of Auerbach. "He was cocky, arrogant and sometimes extremely difficult to like. In fact, I never really got to like him until years later.") This oddly assorted team dominated the league's initial season but unexpectedly lost to Chicago in the first round of the play-offs.

For a decade that was how Auerbach's NBA coaching career went: only one losing record (with the Tri-Cities Blackhawks in 1949–50), usually finishing among the league's top teams, but his squads never won a title. In 1950 he took on the ample challenge of coaching the Boston Celtics, one of the worst NBA teams. The Celtics in four seasons had finished last, third, fifth, and last in their division, lurching to a cumulative record of 89-147. Walter Brown, the principal owner, was universally admired for his reckless generosity and public spirit; but he was a hockey/baseball/track man who knew nothing about basketball. Forty-five years old in 1950, Brown had followed his sports-promoter father as manager of the Boston Garden. At one point somebody had suggested that Brown stage college-basketball doubleheaders at the Garden, as Ned Irish was doing with great success in New York. "It looks like a silly game to me," Brown replied. "We can't afford to put on events that nobody will look at—and nobody watches basketball in New England."

Brown was, however, notably softhearted—the sort of man, it was said, who would only bet on horses named for his mother. Once his fellow hockey moguls talked him into a fling at pro basketball, Brown clasped the Celtics to his bosom in a stubborn, indulgent, even dangerously self-jeopardizing embrace. As the Celtics kept losing games and money, his initial partners pulled out. Friends advised him to cut his losses; Boston just wasn't a basketball town. "And I wanted him to give up, too," his wife, Marjorie, recalled. "We had just finished paying off our home. Now he was thinking of mortgaging it and putting up our stock if necessary. He was prepared to put everything he had into the Celtics because he believed in them." He did mortgage the house and sell his stock, and borrowed what he could. The game, team, and ballplayers had hooked him. He went to Celtics games at the Garden as a fan, more concerned with the score than the gate receipts. Recognizing a soft touch, players hoped to dicker with him, not Auerbach, at contract talks. "He was a hero-worshipper, and that bothered me," Auerbach said later. "To me, players are players, and that's what they get paid to be. They are not people to be adored and admired by their bosses! . . . When he started to fall in love with the players, someone had to crack the whip or we'd have ended up with a bunch of happy guys in last place."

Over his first six seasons in Boston, Auerbach snapped his whip and made the Celtics respectable, finishing at .500 or better, placing second or third in their division each year. With Bob Cousy and Bill Sharman paired at guard, the team was strongest in the backcourt. Cousy, the best NBA guard of the 1950s, had come to Auerbach unbidden and unwanted: a simple stroke of plain dumb luck. A local college hero, Cousy had starred at Holy Cross in nearby Worcester with a flashy, crowd-wowing game likely to click NBA turnstiles. Auerbach felt pushed to draft him; under such pressure, his Williamsburg instincts aroused, Auerbach pushed back and drafted somebody else. So Cousy was taken by Tri-Cities, which traded him to Chicago, which folded. Names were then picked from a hat, and the disappointed Celtics got Cousy. (He wasn't delighted either. "I had never seen an NBA game," Cousy said later. "The NBA was Mickey Mouse.")

For several seasons Auerbach and Cousy circled each other, more alike than they cared to admit, two first-generation New York boys bristling with pride and glints in the eye. Cousy was born on the Upper East Side of Manhattan, the son of French immigrants. His father drove a cab. Until the age of five he spoke only French; he always had trouble pronouncing the English letter *R*, as his Celtic teammates often reminded him. After discovering basketball in the eighth grade he announced his retirement from baseball to concentrate on hoops. He started to wake up an hour early to shoot before school at the playground across the street. Cousy matured into reasonable height (six feet one inch) and speed with three crucial physical gifts: large hands and long arms for a man his size, and uncanny peripheral vision, so that he could see the whole court and whip passes without, apparently, looking at his target. To these skills he added a showman's extravagant, risk-taking flair. In the heat of a game, colorful moves—dribbling through his legs, passing from his ear, threading the ball through an opponent's legs—came to him spontaneously, all but unconsciously. Though not the first NBA guard to unleash behind-the-back dribbles and passes, Cousy used them more often, to better effect, and made them his signature.

Auerbach had to be convinced. At first Cousy seemed disinclined to switch on defense or to set picks for his teammates. Even his offense looked shaky; too many of Cousy's passes went unexpected and astray, bouncing off a man's head if he turned to cut for the basket, or trickling off fingertips out of bounds. "We had to tell him to cut out the whipped cream," recalled his teammate Sonny Hertzberg, "and just make it bread and butter." As late as Cousy's fourth season in Boston, Auerbach publicly criticized him for showboating and throwing the ball away; Cousy, stung, said he might ask to be traded. As Cousy later figured out, Auerbach had noticed that he played best when he was angry: " '*I'll show this guy,*' I used to mutter, then the next night I'd try to show him." Coach and star reached a testy understanding. Instead of bawling him out in public, Auerbach took him aside for quiet instructions. Measured public praise by the redhead meant even more to his playmaker after so many grousing complaints. "Cousy can dribble from the front," said Auerbach in 1953, "either side or the back without breaking his stride, twisting his body or changing the cadence of his dribble. I've never before seen a basketball player who could do that."

At the peak of his game, leading the league in assists for eight straight years, Cousy was an absolute magician on the court. "I have my own world, a lighted patch, 90 feet by 50 feet," he said later. "I control the ball. I control my team. . . . In that lighted patch, I control life." Though often the Celtics' top scorer, he shot poorly, even by the standards of the 1950s, with a career field-goal mark of only 37 percent. He never developed a jumper. Instead he took more difficult shots—long looping sets, off-balance running one-handers, and hooks from odd angles. The hard stop, planted foot, and upward leap of a jump shot did not fit his rhythm. He flowed like molten lava running downhill, no sharp starts or stops, not even jagged darts from his established course, leaping laterally instead of vertically in continuous, graceful forward motion. Nobody had ever led a fast break so deftly. Commanding the center of the floor, seeing everything, he head-faked the defenders and dished to a wing or took it in himself, snapping the ball about in one of his meat-hook hands. Receiving an inbounds pass in his backcourt, he knew without turning around where the Celtics were downcourt; sometimes he would just flip it two-handed over his head, backward, into the hands of a breaking, perfectly led teammate. Dribbling upcourt, he could with one hand zing the ball nearly the length of the floor, directly off the dribble, in one motion. "And he'd whip the ball, about waist high," a teammate recalled. "It would go through about four different guys right into your hands. I never figured out how he was able to do that."

Bill Sharman, his running mate at guard, complemented Cousy's skills and style. They meshed well because they played so differently. Disciplined, methodical, predictable as an Auerbach tantrum, Sharman excelled at jump-shooting and defense. He took a beautiful jumper, squared to the hoop and under control, never varying the form. A passion for repeatable order extended to every detail of his life. He practiced seriously, even in shooting games of HORSE, and predictably led the league in foul-shooting. (At the line he was blissfully in his element: just Sharman, the ball, and the hoop in a closed universe.) On the road he unpacked his suitcase, put everything in the closet and dresser in a set order, then put everything back in the suitcase in the same order. On game days he napped, ate, and used the bathroom at unchanging times, and invented the pregame shoot-around later established as a standard NBA practice. In the locker room he performed stretches and calisthenics, again years before those became a normal routine, and reviewed index cards of reminders (how to hold his hands on defense, where to place his feet on the foul line, noted habits of the enemy). He combed his hair carefully and got mad if anybody mussed it. Always in tireless shape, one of the first habitual year-round joggers in the NBA, Sharman beat his lagging defenders by running them to exhaustion. "He never took a bad shot," recalled Cousy, who was often accused of that sin. "He was in constant motion, running the court in a circle and running his defensive man into picks. Eventually, he either ran his man into the ground or wiped him out on a pick and was open. Then his shot was automatic."

And basketball was only his second choice for an athletic

career. Growing up as the best athlete in Porterville, California, Sharman excelled at all sports but dreamed baseball dreams in particular. At USC he broke Hank Luisetti's conference-scoring record in basketball. (John Cooper, one of the two main inventors of the jump shot, was then teaching at USC. During lunchtime Cooper and Sharman would compete at shooting games for Cokes.) Signed by the Brooklyn Dodgers, Sharman spent three years as an outfielder in the minors, hitting in the high .200s; the Dodgers brought him up late in the 1951 season, but he never got off the bench. Committed to baseball, he decided not to play pro hoops. So in the fall of 1951 he asked Auerbach for a twelve-thousand-dollar salary, more than he expected to get—but Red agreed to it. He spent his first Celtic season as the sixth man, still focused on baseball. That winter, hoping for a trade to a less talent-laden team, he sent Branch Rickey of the Pittsburgh Pirates a laborious, three-page handwritten letter. "I feel this is definitely my last year of professional basketball (Because season is too long and overlaps into spring training)," Sharman wrote. "I love baseball and I am *very very ambitious* about making the major leagues." Nothing doing; he was stuck with the Dodgers. After another season in the minors he quit baseball and resigned himself to the Celtics.

Paced by Cousy and Sharman, the Celtics led the league in scoring for five straight years but still could not survive the playoffs. They needed help up front, especially a rebounder. Three new arrivals in the 1956–57 season finally lifted the team to a championship level. Frank Ramsey, a versatile swingman, came from a blooded Kentucky basketball background: born in Corydon (John Cooper's hometown), All-State in high school and All-American for Adolph Rupp in college, he had captained the 1954 Kentucky team that won twenty-five straight games. After one injury-ridden season with the Celtics he served two years in the army and belatedly emerged, twenty-five years old and primed for the NBA. Not tall or strong or a gifted shooter, he ran in a peculiar pigeon-toed, stiff-butted gait that looked absurd. "But he got things done on pure Kentucky grit," a Celtic recalled. "He was only six foot three, but he'd crash right in there, get offensive rebounds, dribble past everybody and lay the ball in, and nobody could ever figure out how." Ramsey looked

innocent, like the hayseed he was not, and got by on temperament and guile. Ever aware of what the refs could see on a given
play, he would hold on defense and cheat on fast breaks by
taking off with an enemy shot still in the air. Adept at drawing
phantom fouls, he would spread his arms in an underhand scoop
layup to get hacked, or fake a shove in rebounding position and
fall down dramatically, or jump into his man, bump and shoot.
"All the pros know about this sort of thing," he allowed—yet few
performed such tricks as well as Ramsey.

Tommy Heinsohn made Rookie of the Year by averaging
sixteen points and ten rebounds a game for the Celtics. Another
Holy Cross alumnus, strong and mean at six feet seven inches
and 220 pounds, in his crew cut and ferocious game face Heinsohn resembled a displeased marine drill sergeant. His game was
never bashful. To understate the matter, he was not reluctant to
shoot, especially a long hook from the corners and a flat, line-
drive jumper from anywhere. Teammates called him "Gunner"
and "Ack-Ack" and teased him without mercy. "He never shoots
without the ball," Cousy pointed out in his defense, sort of. Auerbach made him the team scapegoat, responsible for whatever
went wrong on the court, though Heinsohn usually hustled and
often led the Celts in scoring and muscle. (Yet he should have
played even better than he did. He rebounded well whenever
the mood struck him, but not consistently. On the road, he broke
training and kept late hours. "If they didn't close the coffee
shop," Cousy noted, "Heinsohn would stay up all night, just as
long as he had one listener left with one eye open." Often overweight, a two-pack-a-day smoker, he would retire at the early age
of thirty.)

Bill Russell, the third addition in that season of 1956–57,
delivered the special skills the team needed to reach unscaled
heights. Russell was the first great basketball player who could
neither shoot nor dribble (the most basic court talents), the first
whose game was built on rebounding, shot-blocking, thinking,
and intimidation. He did not, as often claimed, revolutionize the
game of basketball; nobody since Russell has dominated the
same way, to the same degree, though many lesser athletes have
imitated parts of his game. He was sui generis, a primal hoop
force who invented his own style and commanded his era as no

one in the NBA ever had. Anchored in the pivot, surrounded by a changing cast of teammates that left no survivors from his first championship team on his last championship team, Russell led Boston on the longest sustained run of titles in big-league history. And he never did learn to shoot or dribble.

He had come out of nowhere, a gawky late bloomer whose career took off from the lucky accident that he graduated from high school in January of his senior year. Russell was born in 1934, into the strict segregation of rural Louisiana, and was brought to Oakland, California, at the age of nine. After his mother died when he was twelve, Russell and his older brother were raised by their formidable father, gruffly loving and distant. As an adolescent, deep in teenage angst, Bill could not seem to connect with anyone or anything. "Everybody I encountered felt that there was something wrong with me," he recalled. "Worse, I *agreed* with them. I was clumsy at everything. . . . I was insulted all the time." Like many other smart introverts, he consoled himself with an active, prudently concealed inner life fed by books and almost daily trips to the public library. One day in his junior year, as he walked down a hall between classes at McClymonds High, he was overcome with an inexplicable sense of well-being. "Hey, you're all right. Everything is all right." The feeling flooded through him, without cause or premeditation: the closest he ever came to a religious experience. His interior, where he spent most of his time, suddenly and permanently felt different.

As a senior he made the basketball squad, barely, but didn't shine for the top high school team in northern California. A reedy six feet five inches and 160 pounds, in his best game he scored merely fourteen points. Upon graduation in January 1952 he was nonetheless picked to join a barnstorming team of California high school all-stars. The sponsor wanted to include somebody from the famous McClymonds champs; that meant Russell, the team's only January graduate that year. His former teammates twitted Russell about his unmerited all-star status. As the tour wandered by Greyhound through the Northwest up into British Columbia, Russell—focused on basketball as never before—was snared by the imaginative, intellectual aspects of the game. He studied his more accomplished teammates: the cutting and faking of one, the positioning and rebounding of another.

One night, while he was observing from the bench, "something happened that opened my eyes and chilled my spine." Russell watched a teammate pull a favorite move, then closed his eyes and literally saw the play again, unwinding like a movie on his eyelids; if he missed any details, he watched the game some more and replayed it again. Then he imagined himself making the same maneuver. (It first happened, characteristically for Russell, inside his head.) When he got into the game, he tried it for real: a simple sequence of taking an offensive rebound, darting quickly to the hoop, and scoring. And it worked! "I was so elated I thought I'd float right out of the gym. Every time I'd tried to copy moves in the past, I'd dribbled the ball off my arm or committed some other goof. Now for the first time I had transferred something from my head to my body." For the rest of the tour he talked and thought nothing but hoops. "Hey, you can jump," a teammate told him. Russell discovered a previously unnoticed knack for jumping high and blocking shots. His teammates started referring to blocked shots as "Russell moves." His basketball world opened and beckoned.

Back home, Russell finagled a tryout at the University of San Francisco, which led to a basketball scholarship. Ross Guidice, the freshman coach, spent hours with him in private sessions, teaching him a hook shot, explaining screens and passes. As a sophomore Russell was raw but talented enough to attract the appraising eye of Bill Reinhart. Still coaching for George Washington, Reinhart saw Russell at a tournament in Oklahoma City and alerted his old ballplayer Red Auerbach. "I knew there was no more acute judge of basketball talent," Auerbach recalled, "so I had to sit up and take notice when the coach started talking, in his sure, quiet way, about Russell's potential." Go see him play, Reinhart urged. Over the next two years, Russell grew to his mature height of six feet nine inches and led USF to fifty-five consecutive wins and two NCAA titles. Saddled with one of the last draft picks in 1956, the Celtics seemingly had no shot at the most coveted college ballplayer in the country. Auerbach schemed and dealt; with Walter Brown's help he got the team holding the first pick to forego Russell, then traded up to the second pick and seized his prize.

Playing for the gold-medal United States Olympics team in the fall of 1956, Russell missed the first third of the NBA season. On December 19 he signed a Celtics contract for seventeen thousand dollars, the most ever paid an NBA rookie. A reporter asked him about his shot; "It's atrocious," said Russell, not kidding. "I can't shoot at all." The most anticipated athlete in Boston since the advent of Ted Williams, he debuted in a nationally televised home game against St. Louis on December 22. Entering with five and a half minutes left in the first quarter, he looked lost and tentative, not sure of where to go. He went one way and slammed into a pick, turned another way and hit a second pick. He missed a shot, committed a foul—and then, after two and a half minutes, gathered his first rebound. For the game he shot only 3-for-11 from the floor and 0-for-4 from the line. "We've got boys on our high school team," said a woman fan from New Hampshire, "who shoot better than he does." At least he nailed 16 rebounds in just twenty-one minutes on the floor. "Bill was so excited that all I had to do was fake a shot and he was up in the air and I was open for a layup," the opposing center, Charlie Share, said later. But on their next encounter, "the move that worked the first time didn't. He remembered and adjusted—that was what made him great." In his third game, for forty-two minutes he shut out the high-scoring Neil Johnston, blocking his supposedly unstoppable hook shots. In his fourth game he grabbed 34 rebounds, only 5 fewer than the NBA record at the time, and set a new mark with 16 boards in the first quarter.

Nobody Russell's size was supposed to be that quick and agile. "He moves so fast out there," Bob Cousy noticed. "I don't know of anyone who is fast enough to get away from Russell." His extravagant physical gifts—lateral mobility, leaping, instant reflexes, the ability to spring without gathering himself—at first obscured his basketball intelligence. Tutored in nuances by the Celtics' incumbent center, Arnie Risen, he learned quickly. Supposing that he must score, he took too many hopeless twenty-footers until Auerbach forcibly changed his approach. Forget the points, said Red; just get us the ball. Because of his late arrival and special status, Russell was spared the usual rookie chores of carrying bags, fetching Cokes, and paying cab fares. No ordinary rookie, he was coddled and protected. The coach's main contribution was to inject a little Williamsburg pugnacity. "My biggest problem with Russell was getting him mad," Auerbach recalled. "He bounced off more elbows and shoulders and hips than anyone else I ever saw, but he didn't do anything to stop it." One night, with New York's center Ray Felix abusing Russell, Auerbach called time and exploded at his center: "What's the matter with you? If you hit this guy you'd murder him." The next time Felix pushed an elbow in his face, Russell knocked him cold with one punch. Word got around.

Russell made the Celtics champs by dominating the defensive end and both backboards. His teammates steered opposing drivers toward the lane because he was waiting there. The first great shot-blocker, he seldom just batted the ball out of bounds—a showy play that made crowds whoop but gave possession back to the enemy. Instead he deflected it toward teammates or tipped the underside of the ball so that it popped up to be recovered. On rebounds, his mobility zipped him to the best floor position, and then his height, spring, and strong hands took the board. When an opponent shot, the other Celtics were freed at once to switch to the fast break. Russell got the ball and threw a hard baseball pass to the outletting guard as the break stormed downcourt. "In effect, Russell was making me play faster than I really was," Heinsohn said later. "I could cheat the court . . . because we *knew* Russell would get the rebounds. All we had to do was fly." The veterans, Cousy and Sharman, especially appreciated Russell's game. After years of stellar play leading nowhere, the star guards—expecting at last to win—could relax and thus play even better. "You could gamble, knowing he was there to cover your mistakes; more important, knowing he had the willingness to cover them," Cousy recalled. "There was less pressure now, and that meant my own playmaking instincts could express themselves better. If you have the opportunity to do your own thing, you're going to do it better when everything's loose, when everything's flowing."

A harbinger of the league's future, Russell was the first notable black star in the NBA. (Maurice Stokes had played well for three years, though without Russell's impact, and then retired after a catastrophic, paralyzing head injury.) Russell's career in Boston coincided with the rise of the civil rights movement; his first game, in fact, took place one day after the final legal victory in the Montgomery, Alabama, bus boycott that sparked the movement and brought Martin Luther King to national prominence. While Russell was inside playing ball, a social revolution was unfolding outside. The team itself reflected the course of desegregation. As a rookie Russell was the lone black on the team. "I would speak only when spoken to," he said later. "I would not be unfriendly, but at the same time I did not want the reputation of being just a joking, laughing Negro." After a game, the white sportswriters—unaccustomed to interviewing any black, let alone one of Russell's depth and complexity—would bypass his locker and head for Cousy, a reliable fount of quotations. Russell resented such slights and so became even less accommodating to scribes. Over the next few years, though, three other important black players joined the team: Sam Jones, a fast shooting guard from a black college in North Carolina; K. C. Jones, one of Russell's best friends, a playmaker and implacable defensive guard who had played with him at USF; and Satch Sanders, a peerless defensive forward from New York University.

With other blacks on the team, Russell felt less isolated and could unbend, a little. Auerbach appreciated the situation; he had a firm rule against socializing with players, lest his decisions be complicated by sentiment, but made an exception for Russell. Invited to dinner at Russell's home, concerned that a refusal might be misinterpreted, Auerbach showed up at the party—astonishing other guests aware of his no-socializing policy. As victories and titles piled up, the Celtics developed the easy, rolling camaraderie typical of a winning team. In the masculine style, they kidded around roughly, picking on sensitive areas and toughening them by exposure. Ramsey sometimes stuttered; so his teammates bribed a waitress to bring him four glasses when he ordered "Tw-two Cokes." Sanders and K. C. Jones teased Russell about his walk, his striving wardrobe of capes and odd headgear, his clanging free throws, even the way he rubbed his beard. Sanders would burlesque—and defuse—Russell's penchant for somber brooding by sitting, chin in hand like Rodin's "The Thinker," scowling absurdly. Russell had no choice but to laugh at himself. K. C. Jones, a gifted mimic, would convulse the locker room by imitating Auerbach's walk and talk; one day when he was doing Red he looked around and found the coach glaring at him. "We never had a clique, we never had a quarrel," Russell said later. "A man might be a black super star or a white super star. It made no difference." In fact, "We loved each other. That gave us something that carried us."

All the elements were now in place for the Celtics' amazing streak of eight straight titles (and eleven in thirteen years). A snapshot album of the team at its peak in the early 1960s would begin with Auerbach's usual horrific preseason training camp. "Reinhart taught me," Auerbach noted, "to have my team in top shape for the opener so we could just run and hide from the rest of the NBA." The coach greeted his charges with a standard speech: you are the champions, so everyone will be gunning for you; last season's reputation will bring no victories; is this the year you get soft and lazy and stop paying the price? "Then I'd run their asses off," Auerbach recalled fondly. The sessions ran twice a day, one task dovetailing into the next, with few breathers or even water breaks. "We jogged a little," Heinsohn recalled, "then we did calisthenics—jumping jacks and all that crap. Most of all, we ran. Boy, did we run!" Auerbach had the sessions all planned and timed, with shifting tortures so the team wouldn't know what to expect next. If Red was distracted during push-ups, everybody slacked off except Sharman, who kept pumping away. They ran long passing exercises, chasing after full-court throws; two-on-two fast breaks, up and down the floor; an especially fiendish drill in which the players, with hands behind their heads, jumped and reached, jumped and reached, hopping the length of the court, then returned—hopping backward. The first man who dropped out had to run sprints in penance. Then they scrimmaged hard for ninety uninterrupted minutes. The afflictions concluded with height-segregated sprinting races; the winners—usually Russell and Sam Jones—got to sit down while the others kept running.

By the third day every muscle in a man's body ached. Just

getting out of bed and dressing took heroic effort. At his first Celtics camp, Heinsohn showed up on the third day expecting sympathy, got none, and was matter-of-factly set to work. The team veterans took gleeful pleasure in the disbelieving shock of newcomers. Willie Naulls joined the Celtics in 1963 after seven solid years in the NBA. "I thought Auerbach was absolutely crazy," Naulls said later. "I never did that kind of running before in my career." In one afternoon session, Red ran them around for a while, then without a pause ordered push-ups. Naulls fell to, threw up, and fainted into his own vomit. Russell, greatly amused, took him by the feet and dragged him into a corner while push-ups continued. The story passed into Celtic lore, re-told with laughter for seasons to come. "A lot of them puked and fainted, but that was their problem, not mine," Auerbach shrugged. Veterans could barely enjoy their off-seasons because of dreading the approach of camp. "It was a weight on my mind all summer long," Sanders recalled. "It was the same thing, year after year. No matter how much work you did during the sum-mer to keep in shape, you still had to face the tension, pressure and pain of Auerbach's camp." Nobody challenged the coach because all this suffering brought indisputable results. In the early 1960s the Celtics dashed off to such starts as 25-5, 29-5, and 34-4, leaving the league in their wake.

The unforgiving rigors of training camp carried over into regular practice sessions during the season. Practices were sharp, even bloody, as Auerbach encouraged a constant pitch of combat readiness. The subs, knowing they could start for other league teams, wanted to prove themselves and earn more playing time. That meant hard, competitive scrimmages; two men might dog each other and finally trade punches. "Red loved it," Cousy noted. "The rougher it got, the better he liked it." Russell aver-aged forty-five minutes on the floor each NBA game, more by far than any other Celtic, and he hated practices. Resting from his long games, in scrimmages he often loafed, slogging the tempo for everyone else. "You big schwartzer sonofabitch!" Auerbach would yell. "You're ruining it for everybody. Now start moving." Russell would measure the coach with his long, baleful stare—but he never barked back. Eventually, as the NBA titles accumulated, Auerbach relented. Russell was frequently excused from practice, or sat out with a minor injury, or just officiated at scrimmages. "The last thing I wanted out of him," Auerbach said later, "was for him to leave his game on the practice court. The idea is to win games, not to make Russell tired in practice."

For all his choleric reputation, Auerbach in private showed a quite delicate, modulated grasp of human psychology and motivation. He consciously stoked his image as the tough guy from Williamsburg. "We have a great deal of respect for Red," said Naulls, "and a considerable amount of fear, too." His more abused players vowed, on retirement, to belt him; but they didn't. In pep talks he sometimes ranted and roared, but more typically was calm and restrained, pointing out facts in an even tone. "Within the unit," said Cousy, "he was often a pussycat." He read people brilliantly, matching his approach to a given personality: stroking one, threatening another, tweaking a man's pride, leaving someone else alone. He might warn Russell before practice that he would rake him as an example to the others, so Russell wouldn't take it literally. Auerbach was kindest to rookies and benchwarmers, assuring them of their importance though they seldom played. He encouraged private team meetings, where the players could ventilate and criticize each other without the coach present. When practice became too intense, Auerbach might order giddy scrimmages between the big men and little men, with Cousy wheeling in the pivot and Russell bringing the ball upcourt, tricky-dribbling in his fashion. "Basketball is a game of touch," Auerbach pointed out. "If a player becomes too hypertensive, it's no good."

They played home games at the Boston Garden, a dirty, smoky, rat-graced arena built over a railroad station. Designed for boxing matches, the Garden offered hoop fans poor sight lines and many seats with partial views of the floor. The Bruins, Boston's hockey team, were the older, more favored tenants, so they got the best dressing room. The Celtics made do with a miserable little hole, about fifteen feet by twenty feet, underneath a staircase. Because the ceiling sloped, tall guys dressed in the front, small guys in back. The facilities included two showers (with erratic hot water and a clogged drain), one john (without a door, and often flooded by overflow from the shower), a urinal and a sink, and no lockers, just a board on the wall with nails and hooks for hanging up street clothes. Here the world champions donned their uniforms. (Cousy once complained to Walter Brown but was told that the Celtics couldn't afford any improvements.) The trainer's room resembled a tiny Pullman kitchen, with one table and a narrow aisle. Russell sat on the table getting his ankles taped; if he felt dreamy, he might close his eyes and imagine himself a Roman gladiator about to enter the arena. Before an important game, he threw up; for a very important game he threw up twice. Ramsey sat in a corner, saying nothing, working himself into a game state. Sharman did his stretching exercises and drank some tea, which puzzled Auerbach. Heinsohn smoked a cigarette and paced back and forth. Cousy sat with his head down.

Just before game time, Auerbach addressed his troops. A hoops fundamentalist, he approached basketball as a simple game often jeopardized by needless complications. He paid no attention to statistics, trusting only what he could see on the court with his own eyes. "The biggest danger in coaching is overcoaching," Auerbach believed. "The worst thing that can happen to a coach is to fall in love with the sound of his own voice." So he varied his pregame speeches, speaking for two minutes or ten, or not at all, "and they'd get motivated by the fact I wasn't talking to them." To explain why this particular game was important, he waxed loud or soft, soothing or berating, whatever he had not tried recently. In general he ignored matchups, not deigning to respond to the other team in any detail, focusing instead on what he expected from the Celtics. "If Red said to do it," Ramsey recalled, "we did it, because we knew he knew what he was talking about. It was as simple as that."

They emerged from the dusky catacombs through a center door onto the Garden floor. Under bright lights, in the pregame buzz, the old arena almost looked pretty. The famous parquet floor, a deep amber glow, consisted of 264 panels, each five feet square, built from thick oak planks cut against the grain for strength. Loose screws, soft spots, and wide gaps between panels made dribbling an adventure, though Cousy seemed unbothered. The team ambled through warm-ups, capped when a Celtic made the last practice shot. If that last shot was missed, Auerbach sent the man back to put it in: a Celtic tradition/suspicion. After a final word from the coach, the starters touched hands in a semicircle and went to center court. While the others slapped each other and pumped themselves, Russell walked out slowly—apparently bored, arms folded—and cast scornful looks at the enemy. "It was an act I developed over my first two or three seasons, and almost always somebody fell for it," Russell said later. "My little show was aimed at the guards and forwards on the other team; I wanted them to drive on me and try to beat me all night . . . because then they wouldn't be playing their game."

Once the ball was tossed up, Auerbach entered his own special zone. He excelled as a bench coach and strategist. "I thought I was the best," he later claimed, not unreasonably. Tracking the score, time, and foul situation, understanding the personalities of everyone on the floor (even the referees), he settled into the flow of the contest and made constant shrewd adjustments. Every move had a sound reason: a time-out, a substitution, or a strategic, motivating tirade at the refs. Flogged by their coach and strengthened by the blood and sweat of training camp, the Celtics pushed the tempo at both ends. They looked to fast-break whenever they got the ball, even after a made free throw. The worried opponents shot and stepped backward, instead of toward their own offensive board, to return soon enough on defense. Back in position, they had to face Cousy bearing down on them. "If I had my man beaten by a quarter-step," Heinsohn recalled, "I never had to look for Cousy; I'd just take off for the basket and the ball would be waiting for me when I arrived. Bang! Right on the money, every time. That's how good he was." They kept the pressure cranked up on defense as well. Auerbach made them hold their arms high, obstructing the passing lanes, switching and running like crabs without crossing their legs, never relaxing; and Russell always looming in the lane. "You had to be so careful with the ball," one opponent sighed. "I remember thinking I never saw so many arms and hands in my life! . . . It was like playing against eight guys at once."

Auerbach maintained the tempo by shuttling in fresh legs from the bench. The sixth man—Ramsey and, later, John Havlicek—was a faster, more skillful player than the fifth starter.

Instead of a letdown, Auerbach wanted the first substitution to jolt the pace even higher. Ramsey sat on the bench next to Auerbach, his warm-up jacket open and ready to be flung aside, and entered the game with his shooting arm unholstered. Havlicek, a bionic athlete from Ohio State who neither sweated nor tired, writhed on the bench, restless to play—which Auerbach noticed and used. "Red knew I was antsy, and sometimes he would keep me out just a little longer than he normally would," Havlicek said later. "He'd look at me, and I'd be looking right at him. It was a little game he'd play to get me a little more fired up than usual, and it worked." With Cousy and Sharman winding up their careers, Auerbach spelled them with the Joneses at guard, expecting no letdown. Sam became a crack scorer with his then-unorthodox caromed jumper; K.C. glued himself to his man in the backcourt and stayed so lockstepped close they seemed to be dancing. Auerbach wanted a distributed team effort, with balanced scoring, everybody contributing and feeling useful. Sanders and K. C. Jones, like Russell, were poor shooters not expected to score; they had other jobs. During these years the leading Celtic scorer—Sharman or Heinsohn, then Sam Jones or Havlicek—never finished higher than fifth in the league in points per game. Top guns, Auerbach believed, were liable to become prima donnas, not true Celtics.

On offense, if the break stalled and nothing opened up, they chose from only seven set plays, each with options. (Keep it simple.) For the "1" play, Russell set up in a high post at the top of the key and took a pass; the playmaking guard ran and stood next to him; the shooting guard sloughed his man on the double pick, got the ball, and took a perimeter jumper. Or the "1" with an option: if the other team overplayed the shooter, Russell gave the ball back to the playmaker, now freed to wheel for a driving layup. In the "2" play, the playmaker passed to a forward in the corner while Russell came out and set a pick on that wing; the playmaker ran into the pick, got the ball back, and went inside (a "2-I") or outside (a "2-0"). So it went, all basic stuff, only one or two passes leading to a shot; the coach thought more passes meant wasted motion. All seven plays significantly involved Russell. Though he seldom shot, he still played central roles in the offense. Auerbach wanted to keep him interested and active at both ends of the floor. "He knew where everybody on both teams was better than any big man I've ever seen," Havlicek noted. "He made the best pass more than anyone I have ever played with. . . . His ability as a passer, pick-setter, and general surmiser of the offense has always been overlooked." (Russell placed among the league's top ten in assists four times—an unusual feat for a center.)

The seven plays never changed. Opponents learned them, started moving into appropriate defensive positions before the plays even unfolded, but still could not stop them. At one point Sharman—always thinking, a future coach who would win titles in three different pro leagues—urged Auerbach at least to change the numbers on the plays. Red couldn't see it, thought it a pointless complication, but agreed to a trial "to prove to them that I was right and they were wrong," as he later claimed. So "1" became "2," "2" became "3," and so on. Next game, Cousy yelled a number and three Celtics set up in one play, two in another. Cousy tried the new numbers twice more, to the same confusion. Auerbach called time, told his boys to lower their heads and shut their eyes, and gently slapped them—*bap, bap, bap, bap, bap*—in the mouth with the back of his hand to clear their minds. They returned to the old, familiar numbering. (Keep it simple.) "And then they were fine again," Auerbach reminisced. "You see, you got to have a dictator."

A dictator, but one who listened well. When he called a time-out, the Celtics in the game stood around him in a circle, paying attention. Nobody was allowed to sit down, no matter how tired he felt. "I wanted to show contempt for the other team," Auerbach later explained. "They needed rest. But we were in superb physical condition. The Boston Celtics were not tired." (At least the coach was not.) No player in the huddle spoke unless spoken to. Auerbach ticked off his points, checked his players for un-tucked shirttails or twisted shirt straps, and sent them back into the fray. Late in a game, though, with the score close and the crowd howling, he called time and was open to suggestions. "Anybody got anything?" he led off. For a few moments he stood unwontedly mute as players offered ideas: one guy was open; another one's man looked tired; why didn't they run the "4" play with the first option? Then Auerbach raised his hand for silence and said, "Everybody listening? Okay. Here's what we're going to do." If he used somebody else's plan, that man bloomed with pride and tried even harder to make it work. "We were all allowed to have creative input," Heinsohn recalled. "We weren't just robots, just hired hands waiting to be told what to do."

Whatever they tried probably worked; in the early 1960s the Celtics won 85 percent of their regular-season games at the Boston Garden. Toward the end of the contest, when victory looked assured, Auerbach lit his notorious cigar and sent in the bench, another win packed away. Up in the smoky rafters, the championship banners were multiplying.

◆　　◆　　◆

The Yankees have won twenty-two World Series, the Packers eleven NFL titles, the Celtics sixteen NBA banners: the top totals in each sport. Money—the windfalls of rich owners and New York crowds—helped the Yankees keep winning, but it doesn't explain their success. Other baseball teams (such as Phil Wrigley's Chicago Cubs and Tom Yawkey's Boston Red Sox) spent as freely, to no point. The three national teams kept winning because of smart management and strong coaches who imposed their wills on ballplayers. A long-tenured power in the front office—Ed Barrow (and later George Weiss), Vince Lombardi, Red Auerbach—kept planning ahead and picking the right talent, with the ownership relegated to business details. Fundamentalists on the bench—Miller Huggins, Joe McCarthy, and (again) Lombardi and Auerbach—who grasped the eternal simplicities of their games made the ballplayers focus on a few necessary essentials: conditioning, basics, teamwork. "Vince Lombardi has been honored for everything," Bart Starr said later, "except the quality that was probably more important than any other—his continual emphasis on the need for us to help each other."

Since Lombardi's departure in 1967, the Packers haven't come close to renewed glories. The Yankees picked up following World War II and won twelve more World Series, the last in 1978. After Auerbach left the bench, the Celtics under Bill Russell's coaching won two additional titles—then five more without Russell, the last in 1986. In the decades of mediocrity since Lombardi, the national constituency tuned in to the Packers in the

1960s has switched to other channels. The sustained eminence of the Yankees and Celtics has left them the sole truly national teams in their sports. Anywhere these two teams play, pockets of Yankee and Celtic fans show up to cheer, braving the hostility of the local faithful. National fandom is a portable loyalty, carried anywhere the fan goes, jeopardized only by a beloved team that fails too long to win.

Chapter Nine

Big Money

S ports fans are inherently conservative in their rooting, skeptical of the usual American versions of progress and clinging to what's old and familiar. Once beyond adolescence, they often prefer an imagined golden age of the past: when athletes played the game for pure sport, the action on the field was cleaner and sharper, and star ballplayers in some more innocent era—the imaginer's childhood, usually—were heroic, straight-living "role models" for the kids who worshiped them. None of that was ever true, but fans wish to believe it all. Piling on this determined yearning for a fantasized past, fans cling yet more tenaciously to ballgames as they are now. Sensing, however unconsciously, that sports offer them a rare anchor against the storms of modernity, fans don't want their games to change in even trivial details. Almost any innovation—in rules, structures, even ballparks and uniforms—may call forth keening laments and predictions of doom for the big leagues as we've known them.

Money—the deadly serpent slithering into this fanciful green garden—especially intrudes on fandom's instinctive Luddite resistance to change. Fans have always been uncomfortable about big-league salaries. After all: here are ball*play*ers, overgrown children in most cases, *play*ing a child's game that is inherently fun, basking in the applause and fame, showing off in front of hordes of people who want to adore them. And yet: they expect to be paid for it? Worse, to be paid big money for it? To make *millions of dollars a year* for playing a ballgame? The notion is manifestly absurd. The big leagues are obviously doomed.

◆　　◆　　◆

The money explosion began in the 1960s, pushed by ballplayer discontent and pulled by vaulting television revenues. Traditionally well paid by contemporary standards, big leaguers grew restive when owners fed them ever smaller shares of the general pie. Back in the nineteenth century, baseball teams had spent more than half their total expenditures on player salaries. That proportion steadily dwindled away, to less than 25 percent by the 1950s, though ballplayers kept getting small raises in absolute numbers. At a time of galloping postwar inflation, the minimum pay scale in big-league baseball, set at five thousand dollars in 1946, increased by only a thousand dollars over the next twenty years. The money ballgame then changed, needed to change, when players—frustrated by the entrenched power arrangements—turned to unions and agents for help.

Until then ballplayers in all three pro sports had been locked into baseball's peculiar reserve rule. Established in the 1880s by team owners to prevent costly bidding wars and contract-jumpings, the reserve rule bound a player to his club until it chose to trade, sell, or release him. The owner had absolute control over wages and working conditions; no matter how discontented, a player could not quit his team and hope to be hired anywhere else within organized baseball. An apparent violation of fair employment practices and of federal antitrust law, the reserve rule was unaccountably upheld three times by the Supreme Court. In decisions marred by contortions of logic that defy comprehension, the high court agreed with the owners that baseball was a unique public enterprise, endangered by a free market and thus exempt from the usual antitrust standards.

The reserve rule always depended less on strict legal logic than on whose ox was being gored. Abstract principles yielded to self-interest; the owners had the richest interests, and who dared tamper with baseball? John Montgomery Ward, baseball's first labor leader, initially opposed the rule as a ballplayer. A star pitcher and shortstop, in 1885 he founded the Players' Brotherhood, a fraternal group and incipient union that fought the recently imposed reserve clause. "It has been used as a handle for the manipulation of a traffic in players, a sort of speculation in live stock, by which they are bought, sold, and transferred like so many sheep," Ward declared in *Lippincott's Magazine.* "Like a fugitive-slave law, the reserve-rule denies him [the ballplayer] a harbor or a livelihood, and carries him back, bound and shackled, to the club from which he attempted to escape." Ward then helped found the Players League, a utopian fling that attracted the National League's best ballplayers, unreserved, to its single season in 1890. But when the new league foundered in red ink, Ward and his fellow rebels slunk back to the National League and its reserved contracts. His union ardor ebbing out, Ward shifted over to management, guiding two National League teams of the 1890s. Later he served as the league's general counsel and owned the Boston Braves; from these perches the reserve rule looked different. "Base ball to be a success needs firm administration and regulation," Ward agreed in 1913. "In my experience I have never been able to see where ball players were oppressed. . . . The present form of regulation is good." (Or so it seemed to Ward from the other side of the desk.)

For almost a century the baseball owners ran their duchies as they pleased. Pitching for the Red Sox, Ray Collins won 19 games in 1913, 20 in 1914, but after a poor season in 1915 was offered only $1,200 for the following year. He had also angered management by advising other players to hold out for better pay. Collins refused to accept the proffered $1,200; the Red Sox refused to trade or release him; so he had to quit baseball, only twenty-seven years old and with a splendid career ERA of 2.51. In 1929 Lefty O'Doul hit .398, the best in the bigs, with 32 homers and 122 RBIs, and set a new National League record of 254 hits. For these feats the Phillies gave him a raise—of $500. A ballplayer entering salary discussions had nobody on his side; a holdout of even Joe DiMaggio's stature usually found the owners, fans, and press arrayed against him. Management warned ballplayers not to compare salaries among themselves: knowledge meant power. "We were like kids going into war with a popgun," said Pee Wee Reese of his dealings with Buzzie Bavasi of the Dodgers. One year, after signing Tommy Davis for $50,000, Bavasi had a fake contract made out to Davis with his pay stated as only $18,500. When Ron Fairly came in to talk salary, Bavasi put the fake contract visibly on his desk and left the office for a moment. Fairly took the bait: he peeked at the fake contract, then signed for $18,500, glad to be paid as well (he thought) as Tommy Davis.

During these years the players' only leverage derived from the dangled competition—actual or anticipated—of rival leagues outside organized baseball. In 1947, worried about enticing offers made by the upstart Mexican League, the owners established a limited pension plan for their players. The Mexican League soon disappeared, like other rival leagues before it, so the reverting owners planned to abolish the pension and divide the accumulated funds. But Bob Feller, the American League player rep, heard of the reversion plan and leaked it beforehand to the Associated Press. The owners were embarrassed into retaining the pension, increasing its stake from TV revenues, and even tripling their own contributions to it. Building on this modest coup, in 1954 Feller and a few other stars—including Stan Musial, Robin Roberts, and Ralph Kiner—established the Major League Baseball Players Association, the first durable attempt at a ballplayers' union since Monte Ward's Brotherhood. Over the next dozen years the Players Association focused on improving the pension plan; but in general it was too much a company union, dominated and underwritten by the owners, to raise pay scales significantly.

This all changed with the advent of Marvin Miller in 1966. At a time of generalized assertions in American life, ballplayers now stood up and realized their latent powers too. Fifty years old in 1966, Miller had spent a quarter-century in labor advocacy, mainly as chief economist for the Steelworkers Union. A dedicated trade-unionist and liberal Democrat, sharp of tongue and judgments, he was appalled by what he found when he was hired to direct baseball's Players Association. "They were the most exploited people I had ever seen," Miller said later, because of yawning chasms between prevailing salaries and the players' true value to the owners. Yet the owners did show a redeeming quality, he recalled: "Most of them weren't very bright, and the people they selected to carry on baseball's operations were, with a rare exception or two, not all that bright either." As a sleek monopoly, baseball had never had to live by its wits or develop competitive intelligence. Over the next few years Bowie Kuhn, the hapless baseball commissioner, offered Miller an ideal foil: bumbling and flailing around while Miller stood off to one side, then inserted his rapier at the right moment. "If Bowie Kuhn had never existed," said Miller in triumph, "we would have had to invent him."

The Players Association under Miller became the most successful American labor union since World War II. Victories piled up: in 1966, a new benefit plan covering pensions and insurance; in 1968, the first collective-bargaining agreement in any sport; in 1970, a guarantee of impartial binding salary arbitration; in 1972, the first strike. Even before free agency, the average baseball salary grew from $19,000 in 1967 to $46,000 eight years later. Players now entered contract talks well armed, with expert agents and lawyers at their elbows. The first serious legal challenge to the reserve system, by the outfielder Curt Flood, lost on a narrow 5–3 vote by the Supreme Court, but Flood's suit eventually opened the way to arbitration for other players. The landmark grievances filed in 1975 by the pitchers Andy Messersmith and Dave McNally then blew the remaining lid off, ending the reserve clause in baseball and freeing established players to sell themselves on an open, soon overheated market. For a few years in the 1980s, the owners tried to rein themselves in by refusing to bid on free agents. The ploy backfired; it restrained wages just briefly and, in the end, cost the moguls $280 million in fines for illegal collusion. Meantime—and necessarily—rising revenues pulled and prodded the exploding salaries. Network-television contracts brought baseball an annual $16.6 million in 1970, $47.5 million in 1980, $365 million in 1990. Ballplayer wages grew by 13.8 percent a year from 1976 to 1991, to an *average* salary of more than a million dollars—but revenues meanwhile rose 11.7 percent annually, close enough to the salary spiral to keep teams reasonably solvent and players happy.

In the National Football League, wage levels ascended without free agency—but with the scales balanced by even more money from network TV. Ever since the 1920s, the NFL's owners had imposed their own version of the reserve rule to hold salaries down. Given the league's prolonged struggle to survive, most players accepted whatever crumbs they were thrown. In 1931 Mel Hein signed to play for the New York Giants at a Depression-level $150 a game. Seven years later, after small raises for making All-Pro center six straight times, and after leading the Giants to the NFL title in 1938, Hein requested a jump to $300 a game—and got it only after threatening to switch to the Los Angeles Bulldogs, an independent team outside the NFL. Salaries improved when the league matured after the war. As a rookie with the Philadelphia Eagles in 1949, Chuck Bednarik made $10,000 plus a $3,000 bonus—which left him the fourth-highest paid man on the team. Paul Hornung, a touted Heisman winner, got $15,000 and a $3,000 bonus from the Green Bay Packers in 1957 ("For those days," he recalled, "it wasn't bad"). Jim Brown negotiated his rookie contract with the Cleveland Browns in 1957—$10,000 and a $5,000 bonus—with the help of an agent, Kenny Molloy: perhaps the first time an NFL player had dared bring expert assistance to the table.

More typically, NFL salary talks in these years were just a player and a general manager in a room, staring each other down. When the GM was also the coach, that left the player yet more vulnerable. "I rather looked forward to it," Ray Nitschke later said of his contract squabbles with Vince Lombardi of the Packers. "Our discussions would get pretty loud. . . . We'd get sore at each other. But it was all part of the game." Only Nitschke, a man of legendary pain threshold, could have enjoyed such a process. In 1962 Jerry Kramer placekicked for the Packers and was named an All-Pro offensive guard; so next year he asked Lombardi for a raise from $13,000 to $19,000. If he didn't get it, Kramer figured, he would jump to the rival American Football League. Lombardi offered him $15,000. Kramer turned it down and went to training camp without a contract. A harsh taskmaster in even the happiest circumstances, Lombardi fell on his holdout without mercy, roaring insults to everything Kramer did or attempted in practice. "Move, Kramer, move," he screamed, "you think you're worth so damn much." The assistant coaches dutifully followed suit, sniping away at poor Kramer, tattooing his backside. Even his teammates started twitting him, "and the teasing didn't sound like teasing to me because I was getting so much hell from all angles."

The Packer linemen enjoyed a congenial ritual the day before a game: they threw passes among themselves, each man getting to play quarterback (the lineman's dream) until a pass fell incomplete. But on the day before an exhibition game in 1963, as the linemen started horsing around, an assistant coach told Kramer he couldn't even play at quarterback—because of his holdout. Besieged and seething, pushed beyond endurance, Kramer nearly slugged the coach. Then, demoted to the dangerous kickoff team for the game, Kramer ran out his frustrations by tearing downfield ahead of the pack and hitting everyone he could reach. Lombardi noticed; a day later Kramer signed at $17,500. He earned the raise, if only for braving Lombardi's wrath.

Even the most timid attempt at collective action could enrage the free-market martinets who ran the NFL. In the preseason of 1951, Sammy Baugh and a few teammates on the Washington Redskins formed a players' committee to call on George Preston Marshall and request payment for exhibition games. (They had heard that the Chicago Bears and Detroit Lions were getting such extra pay.) When Baugh—a veteran star, and Marshall's pet ballplayer—started to speak, Marshall stormed from the office; after being retrieved, he listened in sulfurous silence to the committee's pleas. "We're not going to give you a thing," he then replied. "If any of you don't like it"—he pointed toward the stadium gate—"that's the way out of here." End of discussion.

Thus the NFL Players Association was founded under armed, fretful secrecy. In January 1954, on the weekend of the Pro Bowl in Los Angeles, a daring group of NFL stars—Kyle Rote and Frank Gifford of the Giants, Norm Van Brocklin of the Los Angeles Rams, Eddie LeBaron of the Redskins, and about a dozen others—met quietly in a small room at the Ambassador Hotel. Abe Gibron, the burly offensive guard with the Cleveland Browns, set the meeting's tone when he stood up, pulled a gun from his jacket, and slammed it down on a dresser. "I know we all may get in trouble for being here," said Gibron. "But goddammit, we have to get a union. We have to be together, and, dammit, we *will* be together!" Duly cautioned, the men at the meeting agreed to recruit their teammates, in private, for the nascent union. They went public in December 1956 by meeting openly in New York and squeaking their demands: recognition of the union by the owners, fifty-dollar pay for exhibitions, paid expenses and time limits for training camp, and a minimum salary of five thousand dollars. The owners grumbled but accepted the whole package within a year. Soon they even started to fund a pension plan.

Yet it was TV, not the Players Association, that made football players rich. In the 1960s, its fifth decade, the NFL at last came of age—mainly because of television. The medium itself had matured at the right time, with the ongoing refinement of color technology, wider distribution of color sets in homes, better sideline cameras and mikes, and the crucial inventions of instant replay and super-slow motion. With these improvements, it turned out that football showed up especially well on TV: the two teams in bright, colorful uniforms, on a (more or less) green field, with cameras scanning the bands and panoply in the stands. Not everyday occasions, NFL games generally took place on Sundays, in a weekend mood, with people at home and looking for amusement. The scale of the game well suited a TV screen. Lined up for the snap, both teams fit neatly into the camera's middle distance, close enough for intimacy (the frozen breaths, the quarterback's barks, the grunts and collisions) but distant enough for a comfortable sense of proportion. Football's recurrent crises—four downs to make ten yards—presented a gripping series of small dramas, with tensions building to quick, repeated resolutions. The regular intervals between downs left space for replays and comments, savorings and armchair strategies. TV analysts, needing to fill airtime and justify their function, sometimes made the games seem too intricate for gridiron purists. "Football is a simple game," Vince Lombardi snorted. "Television has most of the people believing it's something complicated." Probably so; but what TV meant for everybody in the NFL was exposure and money. The annual NFL telecast rights fees paid by the networks went from $4.65 million in 1962 to $185 million in 1970. In those eight years each team's share of the TV pot leaped from $330,000 to $1.8 million; but the average player salary was only raised from $20,000 to $23,000.

The NFL Players Association, dormant since 1957, was revitalized by such discrepancies. Informed as well by the new militancy of the baseball Players Association, in early 1968 the football union hired a professional staff and presented twenty-one issues to the owners. "The pension payment was the biggest bone," recalled John Gordy of the Lions. "What we were trying to do was to make football's pension plan equitable with baseball's." In protracted negotiations, stretched numbingly over months, the players sat across a conference table from the owners and their expert arbitrators. Gordy tried always to have a bigger-name player sit behind him, so that when the owners launched a protesting speech they would see Bart Starr, say, glowering at them from the shadows. The hardest adjustment of these sessions was for athletes trained in instant, violent retaliation to learn when *not* to speak, when not to challenge doubtful assertions, so that matters might subside. Of the NFL brass, only the formidable Lombardi impressed Gordy at the table. "Now here I was opposite him and still feeling this awe, and knowing I couldn't act scared," Gordy said later. "Suppose I opened my mouth to say something to Lombardi and out came this little canary noise?" With training camps about to open in July, the owners gave ground on every issue but the pension. A poll of the players stiffened their position, so the owners closed the camps. After a lockout of ten days the players won: a minimum salary of $12,000, better pay for exhibitions, and a doubling of the annual pension-fund contribution to $3 million.

The NFL's TV contracts, rewritten every few years, kept setting records. With the deals signed in 1977—for an annual total of $646 million, and $5.8 million per team—football's TV income for the first time exceeded its take at the live gate. Pro football had become the first television sport, underwritten mainly by the tube. By 1982 average player salaries had reached $100,000: a fivefold increase over 1962. But that year's new TV contracts yielded $2.1 billion in all, and $13.6 million per team: a fortyfold increase over 1962. No wonder the players struck that fall for fifty-seven days, from September 21 to November 17, in what became the longest strike in big-league history. "It *caused* the strike," one NFL executive said of the 1982 TV deal. "When those players read about $2 billion in the paper, there was no way they weren't going to harden up and try for their share." In settling the 1982 strike the players emerged with further gains in pensions and severance pay, but they deferred—again—any action on establishing free agency. (Baseball players by then had been hauling in the rewards of free agency for six years.)

During the 1970s and 1980s, the NFL Players Association went after short-term goals without confronting the reserve system. On the other side of the bargaining table, football's pooled TV revenues left the owners uncommonly united, at least on some points. They formed a tougher negotiating monolith than the bickering bozos of baseball did. By doling out better pay and limited versions of player mobility (the so-called Plan B), the football moguls ultimately staved off full-blown free agency until 1993. Then it landed on them, hard, with an earned vengeance.

◆　　◆　　◆

Pro basketball took a third, more effective route toward big money. As in baseball and football, the most prominent (and therefore most job-secure) NBA stars founded a rudimentary union in the mid-1950s. Bob Cousy of the Boston Celtics, the instigator, started talking informally to other players during the 1953–54 season. They began with small details—the erratic, excessive fines levied by the league office, and an NBA schedule that jammed games together, leaving too little time for sleep and travel—instead of the larger issues of wages and player freedom. In the summer of 1954 Cousy wrote to top players on the eight NBA teams about forming a union; all assented except Andy Phillip of the Fort Wayne Pistons, who feared the response of his owner, a crusty manufacturer named Fred Zollner. "I've never had a union in my shops," Zollner told Cousy, "and I won't have a union on my ball club." The others went ahead and organized the NBA Players Association at the league's All-Star game in New York in January 1955.

The union lurched forward in jerks and spasms. In December 1955, a few days before a nationally televised Celtics-Lakers game in Boston, a rumor started that Cousy would torpedo the game by calling a sit-down strike. The league office, neglecting to verify the rumor with Cousy, announced that it would ban any strikers for life. "We are not thinking in terms of a strike at any time," Cousy insisted. "I will admit that the players, in our own meetings, have discussed the chance that it may, at some time, be necessary to ask for a strike vote. But that would be the last recourse." The game was played on schedule, but the episode got the owners' attention. Shortly after the 1956–57 season, they made their first concessions to the Players Association: a more generous play-off pool for the players to split; seven dollars per diem for food on the road; limits on fines, exhibitions, and training camps; moving expenses for players traded during the season; a procedure for appealing league decisions; and an agreement to meet with player reps at the annual league meetings. (Still no mention of wages or pensions.) Cousy took well-earned satisfaction in these small changes, but he'd grown discouraged as a union organizer. Most of the players ignored his letters requesting dues, and two teams—the Philadelphia Warriors and Rochester Royals—dropped out of the union en masse. So Cousy passed the thankless job on to his Celtic teammate Tommy Heinsohn.

Instructed by baseball's pension plan, in the early 1960s Heinsohn started to hold organizational meetings with visiting teams in Boston. He appointed strong team reps, such as Bob Pettit of the St. Louis Hawks, to act as shop stewards, and collected dues assertively, even barging into enemy locker rooms to prod laggards into paying their twenty-five bucks. Heinsohn kept pushing the owners for a meeting on creating a pension fund. The owners ducked, evaded, and finally agreed to a sit-down at the league meeting in New York in November 1963. Player reps flew in from around the country, at their own expense. Through a long afternoon they waited in a hotel lobby to be beckoned forward. They were proud athletes, the best basketball players in the world, with crowded schedules. The call never came. The owners ignored them—a catalyzing strategic mistake. In a rump session on the spot, the players agreed not to play the All-Star game set for Boston that March without real progress toward a pension. Heinsohn alerted his owner, the universally respected Walter Brown (one of the few NBA moguls who had actually supported the Players Association). "I don't have a pension," Brown replied, "why should you guys have one?"

On the day of the All-Star game, a blizzard descended on Boston, snarling arrivals and pushing tempers yet higher. During the afternoon Heinsohn kept calling the owners and the new NBA commissioner, J. Walter Kennedy, and getting nowhere. "We were not militant people by nature or background," Heinsohn said later, "but were forced to challenge the owners' one-way attitude." He gathered both squads into the Celtics' dressing room and called for a strike vote. The first vote went 11–9 against striking: not what Heinsohn wanted. So they voted again, this time 11–9 for the strike. Heinsohn left to deliver a final ultimatum to Walter Kennedy. The players sat there, careers and livelihoods on the line, not a bit sure of what they were doing, in a mood of tightening nervous tension. Well, we have to understand their position, one player offered. Shut up, he was told. Bob Short, the Lakers' owner, pounded on the door, threatening his players—Elgin Baylor and Jerry West—with permanent unemployment. Someone delivered a message to Baylor: Mr. Short wanted West and him to come outside. "You go tell Bob Short to fuck himself," said Baylor. Just before game time, Walter Kennedy came into the room and promised he would deliver a pension plan. So they took another vote, decided to play the game, and a few months later the owners conceded the start of a modest pension fund.

Once again, a new league became the ballplayer's best friend. The American Basketball Association, eleven teams in non-NBA cities, tossed up its first red-white-and-blue balls in the fall of 1967. "We thought that the ABA was a maverick league, a gimmick league," recalled the NBA veteran Wayne Embry. The ABA never reached the promised land of a network-TV contract. Game crowds averaged about three thousand less than for the NBA. In nine precarious seasons of dying teams and shifting franchises, the ABA lost around $40 million before merging its remnants with the NBA. But by bidding recklessly for college ballplayers and throwing money at established stars, the ABA shifted the NBA's balance of power away from management. The NBA Players Association proceeded to win a collective-bargaining agreement, severance pay, first-class airplane seats, disability and medical insurance, better playing conditions and pension benefits, and much fatter paychecks. The average NBA salary during head-to-head competition with the ABA went from $20,000 in 1967 to $107,000 in 1975: more than twice what baseball and football players were making at the time.

NBA salaries, in fact, were outrunning league revenues. After the football decade of the 1960s, ad agencies and sportswriters predicted a basketball boom for the 1970s; but it didn't happen. The NBA's TV contract was switched from ABC to CBS in 1973. ABC then ran other sports programming on Sunday afternoons, opposite NBA games, and beat their ratings. The NBA's TV-audience share of 26 for the 1976–77 season dribbled away to just 18 four years later. Basketball's drawing power on television was so diminished that CBS bumped the final game of the 1980 play-offs from prime time to a late-night tape-delayed slot; fans in the East and Midwest couldn't see the game live. A year later, seventeen of the twenty-three NBA teams lost money. A half dozen franchises nearly went under. Instead of a boom, pro basketball had tumbled into a deepening crisis of red ink and fan apathy.

Now an ironic twist: these hard times wound up saving the league by forcing workers and bosses to cooperate. David Stern, an adroit lawyer who had worked intermittently for the NBA since 1967, became its general counsel in 1978, then executive vice-president for marketing and broadcasting two years later, and finally league commissioner early in 1984. Adept at both selling and negotiating, Stern oversaw a crucial labor agreement in April 1983 whereby the owners accepted free agency and revenue-sharing while the players accepted the novel concept of a salary cap that guaranteed them 53 percent of the league's gross revenues from tickets and TV. "The players and management were in the gutter together," an official of the Players Association said later. "Everyone saw how necessary it was for both sides to work together to survive." The salary cap, imposing an aggregate wage ceiling for each team to apportion as it chose, meant a fair and public share of gross incomes for the players. The cap also made them active partners with the league. If the NBA flourished, they knew they would too.

For the first time since the advent of the twenty-four-second clock three decades earlier, the league took practical steps to improve the product offered to fans. From the vanquished ABA—the derided "gimmick league"—the NBA borrowed three-point shots, new statistical categories (turnovers, blocks, and steals), and the showcase of an All-Star game weekend, with its rousing three-point and slam-dunk contests. In regular game competition, the three-point shot spread the action more widely across the floor—longer shots, longer rebounds—opening the lane for more drives and dunks. Instead of the big men who had previously dominated the NBA with their effective but limited moves, the game in the 1980s rewarded faster, more agile guards and forwards, sending passes and players careening up and down the court. To spur scoring the league also installed a new rule against illegally clumped defenses, and tacitly allowed palming the ball and an extra step on drives to the hoop. By design, the NBA now presented a swifter, more varied game that fans wanted to see.

And by luck, the NBA soared in the 1980s with three great ballplayers, quite different in styles and personalities but quite alike in fundamental aspects. Magic Johnson joined the league in 1979 as the first six-foot-nine-inch point guard in history. Nobody that height had ever so smoothly led a break or run an offense. He defied a near-century of accumulated basketball wisdom: playmaking guards were supposed to be little guys with low centers of gravity, trading height for agility, skittering around the court close to the floor (the better to pounce on loose balls). Comfortable in any of the five established hoop positions, Magic shattered the usual categories. In the final play-off game of his rookie year, with Kareem Abdul-Jabbar disabled, Johnson started at center and sealed the NBA title for the Lakers with 42 points, 15 rebounds, 7 assists, and 3 steals. Just three years earlier, he had led his Lansing, Michigan, high school team to the state championship. One year earlier, as a sophomore he had taken Michigan State to the NCAA title. And now, only twenty years old, when he should have been a college junior he stood at the pinnacle of pro basketball.

The youngest man on his team, Johnson became its assertive, acknowledged leader. The Lakers called him Earvin (his real name) or "Buck." (Buck was a rarely bestowed honorific among black athletes. Willie Mays and Reggie Jackson had proudly been Buck to their teammates.) Vocal and expressive, on the court he gestured and hollered instructions to the obedient Lakers. Their signature fast break began, often enough, with a rebound by Johnson; he averaged seven or eight a game, extraordinary for a guard. Instead of the usual sequence of rebound and outlet pass, he simply plucked the ball and started dribbling upcourt. If a distant Laker were cutting for the basket, Magic might zing an unlikely forty-foot *bounce* pass that settled agreeably into the cutter's hands. On the run, Johnson looked stiff-legged, heavy-footed, and not especially graceful, yet he arrived in the fore-court as quickly as anyone. If he broke into the lane, he could whirl through his favorite spin move and muscle the ball over his shorter opponent. With Johnson dealing assists, the Lakers got many layups and easy shots; over his first seven seasons they led the NBA in field-goal percentage five times. When the break stalled, he stood outside and easily lofted an entry pass over his man into the post. A point guard his height had clear advantages worth imitating. Yet he remained sui generis because few men that size could run, dribble, and pass with Magic.

Larry Bird could dribble and pass with him, at least. Magic and Bird—both six feet nine inches, with modest athletic gifts—were paired from their first encounter, in the 1979 NCAA title game. They entered the NBA together, on opposite coasts, and led their teams to the two best records of the 1980s. For ten straight years, the NBA finals offered the Lakers or Celtics or both. Johnson would lie awake at three in the morning, eyes open, puzzling about how to beat Bird. Always pitted as rivals, at first the two superstars hated each other, declining even to shake hands or nod hello at the opening tap. But shortly after the 1984 season, which had been capped by a bitter Celtic-Laker show-down in the finals, Bird and Johnson shot a TV commercial together. With little alternative, they started talking and—sur-prise—liked each other, sharing more common ground than they suspected. Both from modest origins in the small-town Mid-west, still close to their families, teachers, coaches, and old friends, they left the big city and went back home every summer, small-town boys to their cores.

They relaxed enough to kid about Bird's anomalous position

as a palefaced eminence strayed into the NBA's black elite. "White men can't jump? He was living proof," Johnson joked later. "Some white men don't move too quickly either. A lot of players run faster, and yet Larry always seemed to beat them up the court." Bird was not entirely ungifted: his strong hands and wrists made him one of the best rebounding forwards ever; a bit left-handed off the court, he shot mostly right-handed and played an exceptionally ambidextrous game; he was blessed with the vision, coordination, and reflexes to dish and deal on the break at a nearly Magical level. No frontcourt man had ever passed or set up plays so well. (He often functioned as a point forward.) Few players at any position could match his shooting range. To develop these skills Bird drew on his soon-legendary mental toughness and gritty devotion to practice. He played a cocky game, with a woofing, hard-edged attitude, making sure that enemies understood all their many deficiencies. "Look in his eyes," said his opponent Dominique Wilkins, "and you see a killer." On game days he came out to warm up before anybody else, just a ball boy and Bird taking a hundred shots or so until his teammates appeared. Red Auerbach, still quite involved with the Celtics in his seventies, declared Bird the best-motivated athlete he'd ever seen. "I've always thought of basketball as a black man's game. I just tried to do everything I could to fit in," Bird said. "I've proven that Larry Bird, a white boy who can't run and jump, can play the game of basketball."

Michael Jordan played the blackest game of all. He came into the NBA in 1984, five years after Johnson and Bird, but soon blew past them and everyone else as the first hoopster in two decades—the first since Elgin Baylor and Oscar Robertson—to combine supreme athletic gifts with superlative basketball skills. Jordan won seven straight scoring titles, matching Wilt Chamberlain's record, and finished at 32.3 points per game, the best career mark in NBA history. He zoomed around the court, obviously quicker and springier than the most determined defender; nobody could stick with him. His tongue-wagging, inexorable swoops to the hoop thrilled fans and even modified TV's coverage of the sport. Before Jordan, elevated cameras had followed the main action from a distance, with sideline, floor-level cameras relegated to close-ups and reaction shots. "We changed it with Michael," recalled Don McGuire, a television sports producer. They started putting a sideline camera on Jordan when he was fifteen or twenty feet from the hoop, "and following him as he drove. You could count on him doing it a lot in a game. No one had ever gone to the basket like that." If the lane was jammed, opponents converging on him, Jordan dished expertly to the open man or (more often) took a gorgeous, classic jump shot: disciplined and unchanging in its mechanics and release, the ball arcing high and spinning straight to the net. Stoking all these talents was a demonic, unthrottled will to win, to play every minute of every game hard. Even in routine scrimmages with his Chicago Bulls teammates, he kept proving points, reminding them all how good he was. "He used to get upset if he didn't feel the games were being called correctly," said a Bulls executive. "He was just obsessed with winning and showing he could prevail."

So intent on victory and demonstrating his skills: and Jordan waited seven writhing years for a title. It could not have been easy on him. Johnson had won in his first year, Bird in his second. The most airborne basketball player ever, Jordan was for a time dragged down by journeymen teammates. His first three Bulls teams never finished over .500 and won but one of ten play-off games. Skeptics wondered if Jordan was merely a brilliant solo performer, another Pete Maravich, without the mysterious knack—so prominent in Johnson and Bird—of lifting his team to near his own level. After Scottie Pippen and Horace Grant joined him in 1987, the Bulls started winning and eventually took three straight titles, the best streak since the Celtics of the 1960s.

Victories, at last, combined with his uniquely exciting style on the court—accessible even to someone new to basketball—to bring him an unprecedented celebrity beyond the game. Handsome, well spoken, and expertly marketed, Jordan became the most famous athlete in the world, a ubiquitous corporate spokesman who floated across boundaries of race, gender, and nation. At his peak he made $4 million a year playing basketball—and about $30 million more off the court. Big leaguers often complain about the cost of fame in the loss of privacy, the newfound inability to move easily through the everyday world. For Jordan in particular, his notoriety, though sought and welcomed for its rewards, became a public prison: relieved, ironically, only under the bright lights and clamor of an NBA ballgame. "When I'm out there, no one can bother me," he said. "The game is one of the calmest parts of my life. No one can come onto the court. No one can cross those lines. It's a very calm place."

Johnson, Bird, and Jordan arrived in the NBA as instant, full-blown stars—and only got better. They won eleven titles among them and three MVP awards each, but they never stopped thinking and working on their games to keep winning, and to keep up with each other. Magic taught himself to make effective passes without needless, risky flourishes ("In my first couple of years I was a bit of a hot dog"). He learned a hook shot and improved his outside one-hander. Before 1988–89, he had clanked a career 19.2 percent on three-pointers; that season he somehow improved to 31.4 percent. Bird, the third-best foul shooter in league history, led the NBA four times from the line. "Larry Bird was hitting in the 90 percent range," Magic said later, "so that became my goal." Johnson practiced and practiced—and shot .911 in 1988–89 to lead the league. Over his first four seasons, Bird averaged 5.4 assists a game, more than acceptable for a forward; then he improved to 6.6, 6.8, and 7.7 a game. One year he heard that rival coaches were saying he only moved left with his jumper. "I went home that summer," he recalled, "and worked every day on going to my right. There's no problem now." After winning his second NBA title in 1984, Bird felt tired for the first time in his basketball life. So he spent the summer lifting weights and running the back roads of Indiana. Jordan, for his part, was such a comprehensive scoring force that critics could only carp about his defense. So he dug in, led the league in steals, was named defensive player of the year for 1987–88, and made the All-Defensive first team six straight times. "When I block a shot I feel so good about it," he said. "I like to see some guy going up to make a basket, and he thinks he's going to make a beautiful play, and he doesn't see me coming. And I swat the ball away and his beautiful play is over. . . . The big guys, especially, really get pissed off."

After their ceaseless work and self-improvements, sparked by the mutual competition among them, what finally united this

great trio of ballplayers was the rare completeness of their games.
All previous NBA stars had shown at least one major flaw: Joe
Fulks played little defense, George Mikan was too slow, Bob
Cousy took too many bad shots, Bill Russell couldn't shoot at all,
Elgin Baylor had no left hand, Oscar Robertson wouldn't fast-
break, Wilt Chamberlain embarrassed himself at the line, Kareem Abdul-Jabbar retired from rebounding, Bill Walton kept
getting hurt, and Julius Erving was harmless beyond twenty feet.
Johnson, Bird, and Jordan had none of these problems. Fans
responded knowingly to their comprehensive skills; they evidently wanted to see not specialists but versatile, relentless poly-
maths who tried hard and succeeded at every phase of the sport.
Jordan, "only" six feet six inches and 200 pounds, even looked
normal-sized among his towering NBA cohorts: another key to
his universal appeal. "Today, a team doesn't need a great center," Johnson concluded. "Guys like Larry Bird, Michael Jordan,
and me have changed the game. These days it's possible to dominate from anywhere on the court." (But the cycles of sports
history keep turning; big men would no doubt again have their
day.)

Like the NFL, the NBA at last came of age in its fifth decade. By any measure, esthetic or financial, the 1980s were
prime times for the NBA. While pro football's TV ratings
dipped 14 percent, and baseball's by 21 percent, pro basketball's numbers soared upward 21 percent. The annual NBA
take from network and cable-television contracts reached $175
million by the end of the decade. Average game attendance
during the decade increased 42.6 percent overall, setting new
records in seven straight years. Most pertinently of all, gross
revenues—which included burgeoning sales of NBA-licensed
merchandise—leaped from $110 million in 1980 to $1.25 billion ten years later. Given their guaranteed 53 percent share of
the loot, this meant bonanzas for ballplayers. An average salary
reached $700,000 in 1989. Then Jon Koncak of the Atlanta
Hawks, a big white stiff with career stats of only 6.2 points and
6.1 rebounds a game, signed a six-year contract worth $13 mil-
lion. "What was I supposed to do?" asked Koncak amid the en-
suing alarmed outcries. "Say no?" Building on that inflated
precedent, many other NBA players and agents became richer

than ever. "Let's face it," admitted Xavier McDaniel of the Seattle Supersonics. "We're all overpaid."

◆　　◆　　◆

Off the field, big money unhinged many ballplayers. Most of them had grown up in modest circumstances where people spent whatever money they had because they barely had enough. Savings and prudence were alien concepts. Even ordinary players now went overnight from the privations of college or the minor leagues to sudden fortunes in the bigs. They wanted, at once, the gaudiest, shiniest toys they could buy. Ballplaying life itself encouraged an ethic of playing the game right now, without much thought about yesterday or tomorrow. Careers were short, uncertain, and always vulnerable to crippling injuries. (Put the ball in play and let's go.) As ever, big leaguers were just overgrown children amusing themselves at a child's pastime: but now more willful and spoiled than ever. All their nearby parental figures—coaches, team executives, money managers, even agents—now made less money than they did; and wealth of course defined status and deference. Why should a ballplayer listen to them, or to anybody? Do millionaires take advice from working grunts?

Many rich ballplayers, then, developed addiction problems fueled by too much cash and too little maturity. The outfielder Jack Clark signed a new contract with the Boston Red Sox in December 1990. During fourteen workmanlike seasons with four different teams he had batted over .300 twice, hit more than 30 home runs once, and knocked in more than 100 runs twice. His career averages were quite ordinary: .270, with 19 homers and 66 RBIs a year. The Red Sox nonetheless guaranteed him $8.7 million over three years, with incentives that could raise the total to $11.2 million. In 1991 Clark had a .249, 28, 87 season: not bad, though less than the Sox had hoped for the $4.4 million they paid him that year. Two-thirds into the next season—he was hitting .211 at the time, with only 3 home runs and 26 RBIs—Clark filed for bankruptcy, under a declared net indebtedness of $6.7 million. "It gives me a fresh start," said the ballplayer. "This shows everybody what can happen to you if you don't manage your money well."

Indeed. It turned out that Jack Clark was addicted to cars. He owned at least *twenty* of them: including a couple of antiques from the 1930s, five classics from the 1950s, four late-model GM vans, two late-model Lexus plushmobiles, three 1992 Mercedeses together valued at more than $350,000, a 1989 Ferrari Mondial worth $200,000, and, the glossiest bauble of all, a 1990 Ferrari F-40 worth $717,000. (It did 0 to 60 in 3.8 seconds, with a top speed of over 200 mph.) "Jack likes speed," said one of his many car dealers. "Jack liked cars." Clark also bankrolled his own racing team on the fuel-car circuit, throwing more than a million dollars into the effort. Now he owed $400,000 in back income taxes; $113,000 to various charge accounts; $164,000 to his agent; and $50,000 to his overwhelmed financial adviser, Mark Gillam. "You can only give so much advice," Gillam later explained. "Jack's a very amiable person, he'd take the advice in stride and say, 'That's a very good idea.' But the execution didn't always follow." Actually, it never followed. In the spring of 1992, with his financial affairs already crashing down around him, Clark bought a new $2.4 million house in California. He even insisted on major alterations to the home, costing additional hundreds of thousands of dollars. "When Jack Clark was around the property," said the astonished builder after the fall, "he gave no indication at all that he was a man running out of money." Bankruptcy left Clark broke and embarrassed, and not a bit apologetic. "I don't have any regrets," he said. "I haven't done anything illegal and I haven't hurt anyone." (Except all those creditors to be paid off on fractions of a dollar.) Did he have exorbitant tastes? he was asked. "Yeah," he allowed, still without a clue. "Why and how this happened is something I haven't been able to sit down and analyze yet."

The most famous ballplayers ran the heaviest risks. Higher pay scales and yet more arrogant doses of star hubris, when applied to a dangerous enthusiasm, might pull a man down to derangement and ruin. Not the best baseball player of his era, Pete Rose was perhaps the most exciting. "I don't *like* Pete Rose, exactly," said the old pitcher Smoky Joe Wood, "but he looks like he plays the game the way we did. He'd play for the fun of it if he had to." Celebrated for running out walks and bowling over a catcher in a mere All-Star game, Rose always played at full throttle, with a pure, transparent enthusiasm. One of the best defensive players ever—as judged by the criteria of versatility, durability, and effectiveness—he made only twenty errors in eight outfielding seasons and won Gold Gloves at four different positions. He took four batting titles, the last at age forty. He set career records for two-hundred-hit seasons, games played, at-bats, and (sweetest of all) hits, finally overtaking the supposedly uncatchable Ty Cobb when he was forty-four. At the top of his game, Rose stroked and fed catchy lines to sportswriters, who fawned over him and protected him too long. To fans he looked guileless and real, a throwback (as Smoky Joe suggested) to the good old days. (As practicing antimodernists, fans always liked throwbacks.)

Teammates saw the private Rose, selfish and disagreeable. "The statistic I'm most proud of," he said in public, "is that I've played in more winning games than any man on earth." Actually he cared more about hits and his place in baseball history than about team victories. He disliked giving himself up by hitting behind a runner; it might hurt his batting average. After a game, his mood depended on how *he,* not the team, had done. This blithe self-absorption extended beyond baseball. A flagrant woman-chaser even by ballplaying standards, he openly kept girlfriends in every league city and in the usual off-limits of his hometown as well, to the shame of his long-suffering wife. (His manager Sparky Anderson never had to wonder about Rose's whereabouts late at night: "Our Peter always finds a nice warm place to put his peter.") Wealthy but cheap, Rose would invite a young teammate to dinner—and not pay the tab. He had no true friends in baseball. "Pete was too aggressive, too single-minded, too narcissistic even for the other ballplayers," said the pitcher Tom House, who knew the real Rose. "He was in a world unto himself, separate and apart from other players, and not always popular."

As his biographer Michael Sokolove has shown, the sleazy associates—gamblers, bookies, and drug dealers—who eventually turned on Rose did not have to displace baseball people around him. They just moved into a vacuum. He had always, since boyhood, liked the action at racetracks. As a rookie with the Cincinnati Reds in 1963, making only a rookie's seventy-five hundred dollars, he spent his off days at the local horse track. (Even then Rose didn't think he had to pay his betting debts. "Pete always felt," said a high school classmate, "Well, I paid them enough and I'm not going to pay them any more.") From these legal wagers, Rose moved on to illegal sports betting with bookmakers, then to the forbidden ground—understood as such by all ballplayers—of betting on baseball, and to the fatal arrogance of wagering on his own team. Rumors of these indiscretions circulated for a decade before baseball's commissioner got around to investigating them. The evidence then was overwhelming: testimony from nine individuals (including some of the criminals who had taken his bets), baseball betting sheets in Rose's handwriting with his fingerprints on them, taped phone calls, a notebook kept by one of his bookies, and incriminating telephone records. "Pete did not think of covering himself at all," said an associate. "He would talk about his gambling in front of people. And his answer was always, 'They can't get me.' He put himself above everything."

Rose presented an enticing dilemma to bookmakers: a wealthy, notorious betting fool, yearning to risk thirty thousand dollars a day and more, with known potential as an addicted cash cow but also with a reputation for blowing off his debts. "The majority of bookmakers are crybabies," Rose later told baseball's investigator, revealing more than he intended. "They've got the world by the ass. Because no bookmakers lose." In November 1984 two Massachusetts bookies, Manuel Fernandez and Joe Cambra, discussed Rose while the state police secretly taped their phone call. Cambra wanted the permission of his boss, Fernandez, to accept a bet of six thousand dollars from Rose:

"I can see Pete Rose, he makes millions, you know what I mean."

"Yeah, but we ain't going to see it."

"Hey, we'll knock him out, we're gonna knock him out." . . .

"Keep that guy down, Joe." . . .

"That's good action."

"No, that ain't good action."

(A raid by the state cops turned up two checks totaling $19,300 made out to Cambra by Rose. Cambra explained that they were for a real estate deal that later fell through.)

Four years later, two other Rose bookies—Paul Janszen and

Michael Bertolini—reviewed the welshing ballplayer on a tapped line. "He still owes me about 12 grand," said Janszen.

"So, he paid you about 38?"

"No . . . what he did was he signed a bunch of autographs for me."

"I hear you. . . . What are they gonna do, Pauli? They made enough off of him. What the fuck are they going to do to him?"

What they did, finally, was testify against him. Rose was banned by baseball, barred from potential admission to the Hall of Fame, imprisoned for tax evasion, publicly flogged and humiliated. "I *do* have a gambling disorder," he conceded at last. "No doubt about that." But he never admitted to betting on baseball, and kept hoping the game would forgive and reinstate him.

Recreational drugs came into the big leagues along with escalating salaries: the most literal addiction for overpaid ballplayers. Before the 1970s, such substances had turned up at scattered intervals, to no great impact. As early as 1886, a Washington newspaper accused the local baseball team of smoking opium. "You cannot hit the pipe and hit the ball," the last-place Senators were scolded. Eighty-two years later, Joe Pepitone got his Yankee teammate Mickey Mantle to smoke marijuana before a home game in New York. (Mantle was suffering through his miserable final season in 1968, and perhaps was ready to try anything.) As Pepitone told the story, they shared a joint of potent Colombian in Mantle's room at the St. Moritz Hotel, then drove to the stadium giggling. Mantle struck out in the first inning, "so relaxed it looked like he was swinging under water," and returned to the dugout with a small grin. Later in the same game Mantle struck out again, then singled in the winning run in the ninth. "Don't ever give me any of that shit again," Mantle said afterward. The next time Pepitone rolled a joint in his presence, Mantle bolted the room. A few years later, Bill Lee of the Red Sox floated through an eerie game while high on hashish. Nursing a sore arm, not expecting to pitch that day, he was nodding in the bullpen when he was thrown into long relief. "I could see every play in my mind moments before it actually occurred," he recalled. He felt no pain in his shoulder or elbow (or anywhere else). Concentrating intensely, unaware of batters and fans, Lee homed in on the catcher and gave up just two runs in five and two-thirds innings.

Amphetamines—speed—were the first significant big-league drugs. Football players especially liked the nasty edge, the extra jolt, that speed offered. In the 1950s the trainer for the Baltimore Colts would distribute Dexedrine ("greenies") before a game. "What the hell," said Art Donovan of the Colts, "it made you feel younger." Most of the Green Bay Packers in Lombardi's early years used pep pills, again distributed by the trainer. One Packer with tendencies to excess would get so wired that he had to write blocking reminders on his hands. The Oakland Raiders of the 1970s called the gray capsules rat turds; players took them at will from a big jar in the locker room and then pawed the sidelines, grinding their teeth, eyes feral and unfocused. On the Dallas Cowboys, "the black capsules we called Black Mollies or Niggers," recalled the black linebacker Hollywood Henderson. "We'd say, 'That boy's playing like a nigger today. Must have some nigger in him.'" Linemen believed speed made them less hesitant, more confident; backs thought they ran just a notch faster and stronger. The NFL officially discouraged amphetamines after the early 1970s, but they remained easy to obtain and widely used. Greenies were also popular among baseball players, though with rougher effects on a sport that required more touch and judgment than football. "They make you feel so great," noted the pitcher Jim Bouton, "that you think you're really smoking the ball even when you're not. They give you a false sense of security. The result is that you get gay, throw it down the middle and get clobbered."

The available record shows no ballplayers ruined by opium, marijuana, hashish, or speed. Cocaine was another matter. Like speed, it gave players a sense of power and sharpness—but without speed's hard bite and loss of proportion. At first snorted instead of smoked or shot (and therefore, in theory, less physically dangerous than some other drugs), it made a user feel smart and confident, suffused for the moment in a bright euphoria. For years coke was, at many levels of American society, considered the designer drug of choice, nonaddictive, without harmful side effects. It could hook a ballplayer slowly, before he started paying attention. Just a recreational pleasure, the athlete could tell himself, as he kept playing well and nobody noticed his deepening addiction. No alarms went off. The ballplayer thought he could handle it, and often did for years at a time.

David Thompson, one of the NBA's most airborne stars of the 1970s, was first offered cocaine as a rookie in 1976. "I was tired and rundown," he said later. "It had been a long season." So he tried it and liked it. For three years he used coke in moderation while he still flew freely on the court, remaining among the league's top scorers. A five-year $4 million contract made him, briefly, the richest big leaguer. In 1979 he started freebasing: cooking cocaine with ether to extract its most potent elements, then smoking it. "Right away I knew something was wrong. It felt too good. The rush was too intense." He started to pick up his pipe more often. Too high to sleep, he brought himself down with liquor or marijuana, then freebased to get up the next day. His whipsawed body, underfed and underconditioned, became injury-prone. He had his last good season in 1980–81, ranking fifth in the league at 25.5 points a game. The next year his average fell more than ten points. Headlines blared his cocaine use. He was traded to another team for a fresh start, but he kept using. He got into a fight in a nightclub and fell down the stairs, wrecking his knee. Thirty years old, he had crashed for good, his NBA career over.

In 1982 the *Los Angeles Times* reported that 75 percent of NBA players were using drugs. The new league administration of commissioner David Stern installed severe measures, to little apparent effect. "If you had thirty minutes with a prospective sponsor," one league salesman recalled, "your first twenty minutes were spent trying to convince him that the players weren't all on drugs." Under the new drug policy, two of the best NBA guards—John Lucas and Micheal Ray Richardson—were expelled after their third offenses. Len Bias, the second pick in the 1986 draft, celebrated his selection by dying of a coke overdose. The NBA's addicts paid no attention. Players kept being banned, sent to rehab, even indicted for selling cocaine. "I grew up as an athlete, but I never grew up as a person," said John Lucas after finally retrieving himself. "I always tell people, 'Don't try to play with drugs, because it'll be better than anything you'll ever know.'"

That was cocaine's simple, diabolical appeal: it felt sooo good. Fans wondered how athletes making so much money playing a mere ballgame could jeopardize it all for an occasional toot. The forgiving rationalizations sometimes offered on behalf of player addicts—it was a "disease"; it bolstered low "self-esteem" for men from difficult backgrounds; it relieved tensions of the long season, the loneliness of the road, the besieged isolation of relentless fame and visibility—were all just therapeutic inventions. Ballplayers liked cocaine because it imitated—might even surpass—their best highs on the field: that ringing head-to-toe vibration, a sudden breaking through into a more vivid form of reality, where everything looked shiny and heightened. Those highs came rarely and uncontrollably in a ballgame. Cocaine extended the teasing lure of getting them back at will, repeatedly, without hard effort.

"I take shelter in none of the standard excuses for being where I am," said the football player Don Reese after his crash. "I wasn't raised in a ghetto, scratching for bread or fighting for turf. I knew no poverty or hunger. I came from a strong, loving, God-fearing family that taught the responsibilities and joys of hard work. . . . So Don Reese can't blame his downfall on anybody but Don Reese." Drafted by the Miami Dolphins in the first round in 1974, Reese tried his first coke in training camp that summer. "Dang," he thought, "this is the best shit I ever had." A week later: "This time I *really* felt it—wiinnnnnngggg, opening up my nostrils and going right to my toes and back up again. From then on, I was available whenever *it* was available." For three years his cocaine use expanded while he kept starting at defensive tackle. The coaching staff tried not to see it; on plane trips the team's cokers sat in back, snorting from their little brown bottles. Then Reese got busted on a coke deal and served a year in jail. Traded to the New Orleans Saints, he avoided drugs at first but soon tumbled back. He began to freebase: "It gave me the best high I ever had with drugs. I inhaled it, and when I blew it out I got that ringing in my ears. . . . It's like enjoying an all-league climax." The Saints lost fourteen straight in 1980 while its addicts snorted in the locker room, before games and at halftime. Reese was finally waived from the league in 1981.

Hollywood Henderson joined the Dallas Cowboys in 1975, arriving with unfair gifts: handsome and smart, articulate and charming, and an uncommon blend of football speed and power. "The best outside linebacker I had ever seen," said a rival coach, Bill Walsh of San Francisco. "He was so quick and had tremendous range over the field." Henderson started snorting coke in his second season, then moved on. His first freebasing jag lasted from one in the afternoon till ten the next morning. "My search was for the ultimate high and I had found it," Henderson said later. "It had a kind of hum to it, a harmony, like your whole body comes alive, or dies, I'm not sure which. . . . But the overwhelming fact of freebase is that I tried to get that hit again for the next two years." As the pipe took over his life, Henderson's play on the field stuttered. At the 1979 Super Bowl, which Dallas lost by four points, he toked on the sidelines from a Vicks Inhaler filled with cocaine. After just six seasons his NFL career collapsed amid a welter of self-inflicted legal and personal problems.

"Cocaine can be found in quantity throughout the NFL," said Don Reese in 1982. "It now controls and corrupts the game, because so many players are on it." Bill Walsh later estimated that drugs had shortened the careers of at least eleven members of his 1981 championship team. Carl Eller, a former player and druggie hired by the league as a drug consultant, guessed in 1982 that 40 percent of NFL players were using cocaine. Team managements, preferring to ignore the issue, did cut marginal players who were known abusers. "However, if the user was a star, or superstar, we learned to live with his problem," explained Gene Klein of the San Diego Chargers. "We weren't going to be the only team in pro football to strictly enforce drug regulations." Given this default by individual teams, the NFL office started a $1.5 million random drug-testing program. Ballplayers kept snorting and smoking and getting caught. In the fall of 1988 two dozen players—including such stars as Dexter Manley, Lawrence Taylor, Richard Dent, Mark Duper, and Bruce Smith—were suspended for substance abuse, mostly cocaine. They got off more easily than some; Don Rogers and David Croudip died of overdoses.

In baseball, too, cocaine left a snowy trail through the 1980s.

Less physically demanding than football or basketball, the diamond let its druggies keep kidding themselves longer. "They think they can run faster," said the pitcher Dock Ellis, who had tried every available high, about ballplayers on coke. "They see the ball differently, like a balloon. It gives them the feeling they can do anything." The catcher Darrell Porter had his best season in 1979—.291, with 20 homers and 112 RBIs—on a pharmacopoeia of coke, speed, and booze. Powered by cocaine, Lonnie Smith peaked in the early 1980s with four straight seasons over .300, averaging 41 steals a year. Tim Raines slid on his belly to protect the gram bottle of coke in his back pocket—and led the National League in steals four straight years. Eventually, though, the drug wore them down. "I started losing interest in things," Smith said later. "I didn't care about the game." In late innings he just wanted the contest to end so that he could go toot up again. "I struck out a lot more; my vision was lessened," said Raines. "The ball was right down the middle and I'd jump back, thinking it was at my head." He was picked off first more often, and had trouble seeing balls in the outfield.

The pitcher Steve Howe, baseball's most notorious cokehead, was suspended and forgiven an absurd six times: the privileges of stardom. As a rookie with the Dodgers in 1980, he bought cocaine from a teammate and used it two or three times a week, a heavy half dozen lines at a time. It created problems for his marriage, sleep, and work habits—but he still made rookie of the year. (A teammate provided a vial of coke to get him through the press conference announcing the award.) The next season he was snorting almost every day, yet his earned run average fell to 2.50. In 1982, two or more grams a day, toking on the team bus, in the stadium parking lot, in tunnels to the locker room; and his ERA down to 2.09. "Most of 1983 is kind of hazy to me," he said later; but he had his best season with 18 saves and an ERA of only 1.43. In his rare clear moments, Howe could reasonably regard cocaine as not just fun but a performance enhancer. His continued effectiveness also left management more willing to overlook his behavior. Finally, suspended at last, he missed the entire 1984 season. He spent the rest of his career struggling back to the bigs, promising to behave, and screwing up again.

Ballplayers had always liked fast cars, gambling, and getting loaded. Big money did not introduce these amusements, but it made them more excessive and risky. Higher pay simply handed Jack Clark a fancier shovel for digging himself a deeper hole. "The problem is the more money I made," said Pete Rose, "the more money I could afford to bet." From 1984 through 1987, by Michael Sokolove's estimate, Rose earned almost $5 million, paid $2 million in taxes, and lost perhaps $1 million betting. More reckless bets and losses by Rose meant inflated debts to bookies, and ultimately left them willing to testify against him. And cocaine, unlike ballplayers' more traditional intoxicants, was quite expensive. Heavy users spent thousands of dollars a week on their habits. Without the salary explosions, coke could not have become such a big-league favorite. It subsided after the 1980s—while salaries kept rising—but remained a persistent, deadly presence that occasionally still flared into headlines.

◆　　◆　　◆

On the field, big money didn't make much difference—once cocaine became less fashionable. Money affected play only in barely visible subtleties. With so much income at stake, an athlete might resist playing when hurt and thus jeopardizing future earnings. Because contract incentive clauses were keyed to quantifiable statistics, players might neglect nonstatistical aspects of team play, to the team's loss. In general, though, big leaguers remained single-mindedly intent on how they performed between the lines, in front of all those demanding people. Fan response, media critiques, winning and losing still felt the same, no matter the paycheck. "Pride comes first," said one ballplayer, speaking for most of his peers. "You don't want to embarrass yourself out there."

Owners had resisted free agency in part, they said, because it might destroy competitive balance: the richest teams in the plushest markets could then buy up the best talent and dominate their leagues. Sure enough, in the first three seasons of free agency the Yankees outspent everybody and won three straight pennants. But baseball then settled into rough parity. For ten straight years, from 1979 through 1988, each World Series offered two teams that had not appeared there a year earlier. (The longest previous such streak was only five years, 1917–21.)

Minor-market teams—from Baltimore, Minnesota, Milwaukee, Kansas City—could still reach and win the fall classic. Conversely, the New York Mets in 1993 had the National League's second-highest payroll at $40.8 million—and the worst record in the league, a pitiful 59-103. Money still did not guarantee victories. Confounding predictions, free agency in baseball actually improved competition. Top teams could no longer stockpile and retain the best players against the ambitions of lesser clubs. With more teams having a reasonable chance to win, many clubs might now open their checkbooks for that one special player, the last guy they needed (they hoped) to win a championship.

Exploding salaries and free agency tried the patience of conservative American fanhood. Fans wanted their favorite players to stay with their beloved teams; and every season brought reshuffled rosters. Fans disliked such constant player movement in quest of bigger bucks, the tiresome off-season blather about money, the rewarding of mediocre play with lush, guaranteed contracts. Yet fans also seemed to understand that money squabbles were ultimately irrelevant to the games. A CBS/*New York Times* poll in 1991 found that most Americans agreed that ballplayers were overpaid—but also that most didn't hold it against them. More tellingly, game attendance, consumer purchases of league-merchandized equipment and paraphernalia, and team revenues from TV contracts kept shooting upward. If fans were consistently offended by big money, their ever-loyal behavior didn't reflect it. (Yeah, they make too much dough; so what? What's the score?) Like the ballplayers, fans still cared most about the games in all their frozen, eternal timelessness. Though the sideshows off the field grew ever more clamorous, the ballgames remained the real point. Fans and players, as ever, kept their eyes on the ball.

Acknowledgments

$\mathbf{M}$y interviews for this book were highlighted by conversations with four of the six principal inventors of the jump shot in basketball: John Cooper, Belus Smawley, Ken Sailors, and Bud Palmer. On the other two inventors, I profited from the voluminous materials assembled by Glenn Roberts, Jr., and from interviews with the friends and family of Joe Fulks. On Benny Friedman, the crucial discovery was a large scrapbook, covering most of his career, in the custody of his niece Marilyn Myers; I am grateful to her for photocopying the scrapbook and lending the copy to me. Shirley Friedman, Benny's widow, showed me another scrapbook at their home in New York, and she related to me certain aspects of his career. I also was given generous access to research on Friedman done by his nephew Marc Boman. William Gray sent me clippings and reminiscences of his father, Charles Gray. Alex Duffy told me about the football traditions of Watertown, New York. Harold Furash and Mickey Kupperberg illuminated aspects of basketball history for me. My sincere thanks to all these people for their help with this book.

The Boston Public Library in Copley Square has once again been my main place of research. Of the many BPL staff members who helped me, I owe particular thanks to Scott Cornwall, Glenn Stout, and Louise Richardson Tilton. The Somerville Public Library and the Library of Congress cooperated to provide me, in installments, forty years of microfilmed files of *Baseball Magazine,* an invaluable fount of forgotten lore. Bill Marshall, curator of the A. B. Chandler Oral History Project at the University of Kentucky, was especially generous with his time and expertise. I could not have written this book without the libraries at the three sports halls of fame. Special thanks are owed to Bill Deane of the National Baseball Library, Joe Horrigan of the Pro Football Hall of Fame, and Wayne Patterson of the Basketball Hall of Fame.

Of friends and colleagues who lent a hand, Vanda Sendzimir showed me a significant letter of James Naismith's in the fall 1992 issue of *McGill News,* the alumni magazine of McGill University. Kenneth Greenberg helped me with the bibliography of antebellum slavery. Melvin Adelman shared his knowledge of sports history, and Tony Ladd sent me a copy of his paper on muscular Christianity. Priscilla Astifan, a baseball historian, was hired by me to look through files of Rochester, New York, newspapers of the 1820s. Andrew Phillips and Drew Todd advised me on baseball and football, respectively. Big Al Todd gave me the idea for this book and then imparted the accumulated wisdom of a lifetime devoted to sport, especially football.

This is the third book I've written with the help of my editor, Harvey Ginsberg, and my agent, Robin Straus. Harvey Ginsberg is of that endangered species, a senior editor who still does line editing and understands the need to fret over commas. He also sent me many research suggestions, didn't seem to mind my usual knack for missing deadlines, and reined in my more dubious conclusions. Robin Straus has once again represented me with tenacity and imagination, and has been a rock of unflagging assurance against an author's doubts and timidities. For thirteen years now, Harvey and Robin have been my knowing guides through the mysterious labyrinths of book publishing, and I am profoundly grateful for their expertise and encouragement.

Manuscript Collections

Walter Camp Papers, Archives and Manuscripts, Sterling Library, Yale University

Albert B. Chandler Papers, Special Collections, University of Kentucky

Cincinnati Baseball Club Papers, Cincinnati Historical Society

Detroit Baseball Club Letterbooks, 1903–1912, in Ernie Harwell Collection, Burton Historical Collections, Detroit Public Library

Benny Friedman Scrapbook, in custody of Marilyn Myers, Solon, Ohio

August Herrmann Papers, National Baseball Library

Waite C. Hoyt Papers, Cincinnati Historical Society

Arthur Mann Papers, Manuscript Division, Library of Congress

Nuf Ced McGreevy Scrapbook, Microforms, Boston Public Library

A. G. Mills Letterbooks, National Baseball Library

National Basketball Association Scrapbooks, Basketball Hall of Fame

Bennie G. Oosterbaan Papers, Bentley Historical Library, University of Michigan

Organized Baseball Papers, RG 233, National Archives

Branch Rickey Papers, Manuscript Division, Library of Congress

Knute Rockne Papers, University of Notre Dame Archives

Knute Rockne Papers, Special Collections, Hesburgh Library, University of Notre Dame

Albert G. Spalding Collection, Rare Books and Manuscripts, New York Public Library

Alexander Woollcott Papers, Houghton Library, Harvard University

Fielding H. Yost Papers, Bentley Historical Library, University of Michigan

Robert Zuppke Papers, University Archives, University of Illinois at Champaign-Urbana

Notes

For statistics and much background material I have drawn from:

Total Baseball, eds. John Thorn and Pete Palmer with David Reuther (1989 edition). Cited below as *Total Baseball*.

Beau Riffenburgh, *The Official NFL Encyclopedia* (1986 edition). Cited as Riffenburgh.

David S. Neft and Richard M. Cohen, with John Hogrogian and Bob Gill, *The Sports Encyclopedia: Pro Basketball* (1989 edition). Cited as Neft and Cohen.

CHAPTER ONE: GOING AIRBORNE

16. "It started": interview with John M. Cooper, June 18, 1990.
16. "In a little town": *Bozeman* (Montana) *Daily Chronicle*, July 8, 1988.
17. Meanwell: Walter E. Meanwell, *The Science of Basket Ball for Men* (1924), p. 94.
17. Ruby: J. Craig Ruby, *How to Coach and Play Basketball* (1926), p. 84.
17. Allen: Forrest C. Allen, *My Basket-ball Bible* (1924), pp. 192–94.
18. "I thought he really wanted": *Bozeman Daily Chronicle*, July 8, 1988.
19. "jump shot forward": *Spalding's Official Basketball Guide* (1933–34), p. 53.
19. "We never played": *Knoxville News-Sentinel*, June 19, 1979.
20. "Because of our eagerness": Glenn Roberts to Abe Goldblatt, December 29, 1975, Roberts file, Basketball Hall of Fame; next two quotations from ibid.
20. "Why, he had on": clipping, Roberts file; next quotation from ibid.

21. "We would feed": Sam Neel to Lee Williams, May 31, 1979, Roberts file.

21. "I couldn't believe": Walter Fielder to Lee Williams, n.d., Roberts file.

21. "who can guard": clipping, Roberts file.

22. "Against Glenn": Irving B. Terjesen to Lee Williams, July 25, 1979, Roberts file.

22. "I used to do": Bud Palmer to author, April 12, 1992; next five quotations from ibid.

24. "I never had anybody": interview with Belus Smawley, September 16, 1991; next four quotations from ibid.

25. "He motivated": interview with Kenny Sailors, October 14, 1991; next quotation from ibid.

26. "Sailors was the key": *New York Times*, March 31, 1943.

26. "Sailors may very well": *Athletic Journal*, May 1943.

26. "Our inability": Ken Rappoport, *The Classic: The History of the NCAA Basketball Championship* (1979), p. 36.

27. "Sailors, where'd youse": interview with Sailors; next quotation from ibid.

28. "The greatest offensive": *Time*, February 24, 1947.

28. "I tried many times": interview with Joe Jones, August 29, 1991.

28. "I'm sure that Joe": interview with Leonard Metcalf, August 30, 1991.

29. Father given job: interview with Joe Fulks, Jr., August 29, 1991.

29. "A bashful, retiring": interview with Joe Jones.

29. "He was a better ballplayer": interview with Ray Mofield, September 5, 1991.

29. Padgett remembered keenly: interview with John Padgett, August 30, 1991.

30. Fulks in 1943: *Converse Basketball Yearbook* (1943), p. 38.

30. Sailors tried to show: interview with Sailors.

30. Gottlieb and Fulks: Russ Davis in *Saturday Evening Post,* January 3, 1948.

30. "If Mikan and Sailors": *Rochester Democrat-Chronicle*, February 23, 1949; next two quotations from ibid.

31. "the greatest variety": Arnold Red Auerbach and Paul Sann, *Red Auerbach: Winning the Hard Way* (1966), p. 108.

31. "He makes most": *Philadelphia Record*, February 1, 1947.

31. "But Fulks was": Glenn Dickey, *The History of Professional Basketball Since 1896* (1982), p. 33.

31. "The introduction of the jump shot": Charles Salzberg, *From Set Shot to Slam Dunk* (1987), pp. 52–53.

32. "I have been told": Bob Curran, *Pro Football's Rag Days* (1969), p. 68.

33. Neft has compiled: Jim Whalen and "C. C. Staph" in *Coffin Corner*, March/April 1986.

33. "The dead shot Dick": clipping in Benny Friedman Scrapbook, p. 105.

33. "Mighty super-football player": clipping in Friedman Scrapbook, p. 108.

34. "With Friedman": clipping in Friedman Scrapbook, p. 76.

34. "As we lined up": clipping in Friedman Scrapbook, p. 85.

34. "That doesn't make": Benny Friedman in *Collier's*, October 15, 1932; next quotation from ibid.

35. "The passing of Friedman": clipping in Friedman Scrapbook, p. 81.

35.   "one of the greatest exhibitions": clipping in Friedman Scrapbook, p. 73; next quotation from ibid.

35.   "The Bulldogs touchdowns": *New York Times*, October 24, 1927.

36.   "Friedman is the greatest": clipping in Friedman Scrapbook, p. 88.

36.   "And how that baby": clipping in Friedman Scrapbook, p. 73.

36.   Bears game in Chicago: clippings in Friedman Scrapbook, p. 90; and see the later, less reliable versions in Curran, *Rag Days,* p. 69, and in *Halas By Halas: The Autobiography of George Halas,* with Gwen Morgan and Arthur Veysey (1979), p. 152.

36.   "In those days": Halas, *Autobiography,* p. 152; next quotation from ibid.

37.   "Friedman was virtually": *New York Times,* October 22, 1928.

37.   "a veritable man of rubber": clipping in Friedman Scrapbook, p. 93.

37.   "The greatest all-around": clipping in Friedman Scrapbook, p. 97.

37.   Mara bought whole team: Steve Owen, *My Kind of Football,* ed. Joe King (1952), pp. 82–83, and Dave Klein, *The New York Giants* (1973), p. 39.

37.   Giants, 1928–29: Curran, *Rag Days,* p. 64.

38.   "It was an afternoon": Knute Rockne in *Collier's,* December 6, 1930.

38.   Gallico counted: Paul Gallico in *Liberty,* December 27, 1930; next three quotations from ibid.

39.   "Flying Ebony" nickname: clipping in Friedman Scrapbook, p. 41.

39.   "He is a queer": Gallico in *Liberty,* December 27, 1930.

39.   Atlevoniks in Russia: clipping in Friedman Scrapbook, p. 91.

39.   Friedman childhood: interview with his sister Florence Goldman, September 24, 1991.

39.   "My parents are": clipping in Friedman Scrapbook, p. 74.

40.   Friedman lifting weights: clippings in Friedman Scrapbook, pp. 22, 76, 82.

40.   Squashing hand on table: Cliff Gewecke in *Los Angeles Times West Magazine,* November 26, 1967.

40.   Photo in 1927: clipping in Friedman Scrapbook, p. 78.

40.   Photo at sixty-one: *New York Times,* May 8, 1966.

40.   Friedman to Michigan: interview with Shirley Friedman, September 25, 1991.

41.   "a godfather": clipping in Friedman Scrapbook, p. 57.

41.   "Take those two": Gallico in *Liberty,* December 27, 1930; next quotation from ibid.

41.   wondered if Little doubted: interview with Shirley Friedman.

41.   "When I hit him": Friedman in *Collier's,* October 15, 1932.

42.   "One of the most accurate": Grantland Rice in *Collier's,* November 6, 1926.

42.   "He taught me": *Encyclopedia of Jews in Sports,* eds. Bernard Postal et al. (1965), p. 245.

42.   "I had to school": Gewecke in *West Magazine,* November 26, 1967.

42.   "Don't throw sidearm": clipping in Friedman Scrapbook, p. 82.

42.   Passing form: clipping in Friedman Scrapbook, p. 81; interview with Jim Stehlin, September 22, 1991.

43.   "A ball should never": *Cleveland Press,* October 19, 1932.

43.   "When it reaches": Gallico in *Liberty,* December 27, 1930.

43.   "He is the coolest": clipping in Friedman Scrapbook, p. 63.

44.   "We could see": *New York World,* December 15, 1930.

44. "It isn't speed": clipping in Friedman Scrapbook, p. 112.
44. "In professional football": Friedman in *Collier's*, October 15, 1932.
44. "The passing of Friedman": clipping in Friedman Scrapbook, p. 115; next two quotations from ibid., pp. 115, 92.
45. "Are there any": Benny Friedman to Bennie Oosterbaan, April 14, 1932, box 1, Bennie Oosterbaan Papers.
45. "A hushed silence": Benny Friedman in *Collier's*, October 5, 1940.
46. Friedman voted against: *Washington Evening Star*, August 16, 1963.
46. "Benny really started": letter from Ken Strong, February 28, 1966, Friedman file, Pro Football Hall of Fame.
46. "The first pro": *New York Daily News*, February 4, 1967.
46. "Anybody can throw": Myron Cope, *The Game That Was: The Early Days of Pro Football* (1970), p. 53.
46. Distinctive click: *The Ultimate Baseball Book*, eds. Daniel Okrent and Harris Lewine (1979), p. 92; Kal Wagenheim, *Babe Ruth: His Life and Legend* (1974), pp. 68–69.
46. "I got a glimpse": *Baseball Magazine*, September 1927.
47. "Like looking into": Donald Honig, *A Donald Honig Reader* (1988), p. 24.
47. "The information seemed": *Baseball Magazine*, July 1928.
47. "My God": John J. McGraw, *My Thirty Years in Baseball* (1923), p. 183.
47. small boy chasing bird: Babe Ruth as told to Bob Considine, *The Babe Ruth Story* (1948), p. 69.
48. "But none of those": *Baseball Magazine*, August 1920.
48. could not remember first homer: George Herman Ruth, *Babe Ruth's Own Book of Baseball* (1928), p. 16.
48. "pretty good": *Baseball Magazine*, August 1920.
48. Dunn found Ruth: John Dunn to F. C. Lane, February 19, 1920, in letters to Lane, August Herrmann Papers.
48. "Babe knew how": Lee Allen, *Cooperstown Corner* [1990], p. 11.
49. "a natural player": Pippen article reprinted in *Boston Herald*, July 12, 1918; next quotation from ibid.
49. "Ah, you never have": Wagenheim, *Ruth*, p. 87.
49. "He had never been": Lawrence S. Ritter, *The Glory of Their Times: The Story of the Early Days of Baseball Told by the Men Who Played It* (1966), p. 136.
49. "I couldn't let": *Boston Record*, January 20, 1943; next quotation from ibid.
50. Carrigan thought about switching: *Boston Journal*, March 20, 1916.
50. "I just love": *Boston Herald*, July 14, 1918.
50. "When I drive": *Baseball Magazine*, February 1918.
50. "I would be": Harry Hooper to Lee Allen, May 10, 1963, in Player Correspondence, Herrmann Papers; and see Allen, *Cooperstown*, pp. 54–55, and Barrow's self-inflating version in Edward Grant Barrow with James M. Kahn, *My Fifty Years in Baseball* (1951), pp. 89, 102–3.
51. "He did not know": Hooper to Allen, May 10, 1963; next quotation from ibid.
51. "Babe Ruth has us": *Boston Herald*, June 5, 1918.
51. "I was feeding him": *Literary Digest*, September 18, 1920.

52. Bush on Ruth's nostrils: Ms. autobiography of Waite Hoyt, p. 140, in box 12, Waite C. Hoyt Papers.
52. "His walk": reprinted in *Boston Herald,* September 1, 1920.
52. "If he had dropped": *Baseball Magazine,* August 1920; next quotation from ibid.
53. "Don't think there's much": *Boston Herald,* December 28, 1927; next quotation from ibid.
53. "I can't explain": *Baseball Magazine,* November 1920.
53. "He was like": Marshall Smelser, *The Life That Ruth Built* (1975), p. 76.
53. "I've never seen": Wagenheim, *Ruth,* p. 5.
53. "Reading isn't good": Robert W. Creamer, *Babe: The Legend Comes to Life* (1974), p. 316.
53. "So long, Walter": Ruth Ms., p. 4, in box 13, Hoyt Papers.
54. Highball, cigar, tobacco: Dorothy Ruth Pirone with Chris Martens, *My Dad, the Babe* (1988), p. 54.
54. "Ruth has the mind": *Literary Digest,* September 19, 1925.
54. "anything that had hair": Donald Honig, *Baseball America: The Heroes of the Game and the Times of Their Glory* (1985), p. 138.
54. "I can knock": Fred Lieb, *Baseball As I Have Known It* (1977), p. 158; next two quotations from ibid.
54. "to keep doing it": Creamer, *Babe,* p. 321.
54. "You never saw": John Mosedale, *The Greatest of All: The 1927 New York Yankees* (1974), p. 41.
55. "That's why": *The Armchair Book of Baseball,* ed. John Thorn (1985), p. 172; next four quotations from ibid., p. 171.
55. "It became our custom": Waite Hoyt, *Babe Ruth As I Knew Him* (1948), p. 7; copy in box 5, Hoyt Papers.
55. "No human": John Tullius, *I'd Rather Be a Yankee: An Oral History of America's Most Loved and Most Hated Baseball Team* (1986), p. 42.
55. "probably the best": Smelser, *Ruth,* p. 148.
56. "An astonishingly": *Literary Digest,* October 4, 1924.
56. "the most accomplished": *Baseball Magazine,* August 1928.
56. Speaker placed Ruth: *Baseball Magazine,* October 1928.
56. "The greatest throwing": Honig, *Reader,* p. 514.
56. "amazingly well informed": *Literary Digest,* October 4, 1924.
56. "I know that he": Lieb, *Baseball,* p. 155.
56. "Babe is smart": *Baseball Magazine,* July 1928.
56. noticed that Zahniser: Ruth, *Babe Ruth's,* pp. 57–58.
57. "He could always": *Literary Digest,* September 18, 1920.
57. Ruth's bats: Ruth, *Babe Ruth's,* p. 171.
57. "Ruth is cursed": *Baseball Magazine,* August 1920; next seven quotations from ibid.
58. "His eyes": *The DiMaggio Albums,* ed. Richard Whittingham (1989), p. 751.
58. "We'd be sitting": *Baseball Magazine,* December 1943.
58. "90% efficient": Hugh S. Fullerton in *Popular Science Monthly,* October 1921.
58. Babe dressing for game: G. H. Fleming, *Murderers' Row* (1985), p. 364.
59. "In baseball": *Baseball Magazine,* June 1936.

59. "Very early": Ward Lambert in *Basketball Illustrated* (1945–46), p. 2.
60. "It was not unusual": *Football Days: Memories of the Game and of the Men Behind the Ball*, ed. William H. Edwards (1916), p. 81.
60. "a game of more brilliant": *Spalding's Official Foot Ball Guide* (1907), p. 15.
60. Only three ballplayers: David Pietrusza in *Baseball Research Journal*, 20 (1991), p. 30.
60. "When I broke": *Baseball Magazine*, May 1919.
61. "Push, poke": John J. Evers and Hugh S. Fullerton, *Touching Second: The Science of Baseball* (1910), p. 160.
61. "The passing": *Baseball Magazine*, May 1919.
61. "Nuthin's new": David Quentin Voigt, *American Baseball: From the Commissioners to Continental Expansion* (1970), p. 229.
61. "I haven't seen": Cope, *Game That Was*, p. 57.

CHAPTER TWO: FANS

62. "patron of all arts": clipping in Nuf Ced McGreevy Scrapbook; and see Glenn Stout in *Sox Fan News*, August 1986.
63. Third Base: clipping, May 12, 1923, in McGreevy Scrapbook; *Boston Traveler*, April 28, 1923.
63. "Baseball flourishes": *Boston Journal*, February 18, 1908.
63. "An active interest": Stephen Hardy, *How Boston Played: Sport, Recreation, and Community 1865–1915* (1982), p. 199.
64. "He seldom lost": *Boston Post*, December 3, 1926.
64. "What a kick": *Boston Post*, August 21, 1930.
64. "very clear memory": *San Francisco Chronicle*, August 27, 1990.
65. "I fanned": Roger Angell in *The New Yorker*, February 24, 1992; next quotation from ibid.
65. "the Greatest Moment": Roger Angell in *Holiday*, May 1958.
65. "my boy": Roger Angell in *Holiday*, May 1954.
66. "The End": Angell in *Holiday*, May 1958; next quotation from ibid.
66. "My one true": Roger Angell, *The Stone Arbor and Other Stories* (1960), p. 133.
66. "I thought": Roger Angell in *The New Yorker*, April 22, 1950.
67. "The girls are": *Letters of E. B. White*, ed. Dorothy Lobrano Guth (1976), p. 506.
67. "I have few": *Harvard College Class of 1942: Twenty-fifth Anniversary Report* (1967), p. 26.
67. "The San Francisco": Roger Angell, *The Summer Game* (1972), p. 80.
68. "Baseball is pretty far": George Plimpton in *New York Times Book Review*, May 15, 1977.
68. "Our professional": Price Collier in *Outing*, July 1898.
68. studies of playing and watching: Allen Guttmann in *Journal of Popular Culture*, fall 1980; Christopher Lasch in *Psychology Today*, January 1978.
69. "one of the best": clipping in McGreevy Scrapbook; next five quotations from ibid.
69. "Couldn't wait": Lawrence S. Ritter, *The Glory of Their Times: The Story of the Early Days of Baseball Told by the Men Who Played It* (1966), p. 246.

70. "I found it": Hank Greenberg, *The Story of My Life*, ed. Ira Berkow (1989), p. 265.

70. "He is the mainstay": Frank J. Farrell to August Herrmann, November 4, 1905, Officials file, August Herrmann Papers.

70. "Any Believer": William Goldman and Mike Lupica, *Wait Till Next Year* (1988), p. 111; next three quotations from ibid., pp. 21, 22, 25.

71. "Basically the high": Richard Anderson, *William Goldman* (1979), p. 100; next quotation from ibid., p. 24.

71. "I had gotten": Goldman and Lupica, *Next Year*, p. 112; next quotation from ibid., p. 108.

72. "the worst pest": clipping in McGreevy Scrapbook.

72. "What makes Monroe": Woody Allen in *Sport*, November 1977; next three quotations from ibid.

73. "The ladies": *Spirit of the Times*, July 24, 1858.

74. "Behold!": Bob Sherwood to Branch Rickey, April 12, 1944, box 35, Branch Rickey Papers.

74. "The ladies are": John Bowman and Joel Zoss, *Diamonds in the Rough: The Untold Story of Baseball* (1989), pp. 199–200.

74. "I can honestly: *Baseball Magazine*, February 1917; next quotation from ibid.

75. "A woman's influence": Edward Mott Woolley in *McClure's*, July 1912.

75. "I appreciate": *Baseball Magazine*, February 1917.

75. Britton as owner: Fred Lieb, *Baseball As I Have Known It* (1977), pp. 45–46; Harold Seymour, *Baseball: The People's Game* (1990), p. 485; Bill Borst in *Insider's Baseball*, ed. L. Robert Davids (1983), pp. 63–68.

75. She testified: *Boston Journal*, February 13, 1917.

75. "While increasingly": *Baseball Magazine*, May 1917.

75. "The free ladies": *Baseball Magazine*, November 1930.

76. "While the girls": *Baseball Magazine*, July 1939; next quotation from ibid.

76. "A scourge": Stanley Woodward in *New York Times Magazine*, November 26, 1950.

76. "I like scientific": William G. Nicholson in *Insider's Baseball*, ed. Davids, p. 136.

76. Lolly Hopkins: Frederick G. Lieb, *The Boston Red Sox* (1947), p. 244.

76. "She is stout": Margaret Case Harriman in *Good Housekeeping*, October 1945; next four quotations from ibid.

77. "There could be": Donald Honig, *A Donald Honig Reader* (1988), p. 229; next quotation from ibid., p. 230. For a different version, see Red Barber in *New York Times Magazine*, October 3, 1943.

77. ratios of women fans: Steven A. Riess, *City Games: The Evolution of American Urban Society and the Rise of Sports* (1989), p. 223; Bowman and Zoss, *Diamonds*, p. 226; Ray Kennedy in *Sports Illustrated*, April 28, 1980.

78. survey, 1956: *Boston Globe*, October 28, 1956; next quotation from ibid.

78. home advantage: John Edwards and Denise Archambault in *Sports, Games, and Play: Social and Psychological Viewpoints*, ed. Jeffrey H. Goldstein (second edition, 1989), pp. 339–41, 363; *Total Baseball*, p. 2167, correcting Edwards and Archambault re baseball.

78. "It makes you": Larry Bird with Bob Ryan, *Drive: The Story of My Life* (1989), p. 242.

79. "The Packers' court": Arnold Red Auerbach and Paul Sann, *Red Auerach: Winning the Hard Way* (1966), p. 190; next quotation from ibid., p. 191.

79. Syracuse: taped interview with Dolph Schayes by Charles Salzberg, October 16, 1986, Basketball Hall of Fame; Jeff Coplon in *The New Yorker,* October 1, 1990; Terry Pluto, *Tall Tales* (1992), pp. 35–38.

79. "I'm not": Auerbach and Sann, *Auerbach,* p. 187.

80. "It was": *Boston Globe,* June 8, 1984.

80. "Before McHale": *Boston Globe,* June 13, 1984; next two quotations from ibid., June 12, 1984.

81. "As we came": Kareem Abdul-Jabbar with Mignon McCarthy, *Kareem* (1990), p. 122; next quotation from ibid.

81. "Boston, Boston": *Boston Globe,* September 24, 1897.

81. "It's a certainty": *Baseball Magazine,* July 1908.

82. "Why, there is": clipping in McGreevy Scrapbook; next quotation from ibid.

82. "Honus, why do you": Ritter, *Glory,* p. 27.

82. "If a player": *Boston Herald,* October 13, 1903.

83. "Even to our": John R. Tunis, *The American Way of Sport* (1958), p. 41.

83. "I think those": Ritter, *Glory,* p. 27.

83. "A half-century": Roger Angell, *Once More Around the Park: A Baseball Reader* (1991), p. 117.

83. Angell at *New Yorker:* Brendan Gill, *Here at The New Yorker* (1975), pp. 294–95.

83. "Belonging and caring": Roger Angell, *Five Seasons: A Baseball Companion* (1977), p. 306.

83. "I belonged": Angell, *Once More,* p. 118.

84. "connect me": Angell, *Five Seasons,* p. 312.

84. "We had some": George B. Kirsch, *The Creation of American Team Sports: Baseball and Cricket, 1838–1872* (1989), p. 116.

84. "Now that": Dave DeBusschere, *The Open Man: A Championship Diary,* eds. Paul D. Zimmerman and Dick Schaap (1970), p. 95.

85. "a great many": Roger Angell, *Late Innings: A Baseball Companion* (1982), p. 188.

85. "the perfection of baseball": Roger Angell in *Holiday,* May 1954.

85. "the perfectly observed": Angell, *Summer Game,* p. 292.

85. "a vision": Keith Hernandez and Mike Bryan, *If at First: A Season with the Mets* (1986), p. 223.

85. "I hear": Joe Willie Namath with Dick Schaap, *I Can't Wait Until Tomorrow . . . 'cause I Get Better Looking Every Day* (1969), p. 78.

85. "I've been given": *The Second Fireside Book of Baseball,* ed. Charles Einstein (1958), p. 323.

86. "an underdog": Jonathan Schwartz in *GQ,* November 1989.

86. "I am a member": Jonathan Schwartz in *GQ,* September 1989; next two quotations from ibid.

86. Donald Hall: Donald Hall, *Fathers Playing Catch With Sons: Essays on Sport [Mostly Baseball]* (1985).

86. "When I say": Charles Einstein, *Willie's Time* (1979), p. 16.

87. Angell dedicated: Angell, *Summer Game,* dedication page.

Notes

87. Angell's early memories: Roger Angell in *The New Yorker*, February 24, 1992.
87. Ernest Angell: *New York Times*, January 12, 1973.
87. Their marriage: Linda H. Davis, *Onward and Upward: A Biography of Katharine S. White* (1987), pp. 71–72.
87. Katharine and White: ibid., p. 80.
87. "I missed": Angell in *New Yorker*, February 24, 1992.
87. "large theorizing": George Plimpton in *The New York Times Book Review*, May 15, 1977; next two quotations from ibid.
88. "a rough customer": Angell, *Late Innings*, p. 198; next quotation from ibid., p. 199.
88. "second only": Allen Sangree in *Everybody's*, September 1907.
88. "I walk from": Anonymous in *Atlantic Monthly*, April 1908.
89. "For a bookish": "Aristides" in *American Scholar*, winter 1984–85.
89. "I am never": Robert Frost in *Sports Illustrated*, July 23, 1956.
89. "I'm a prejudiced": *New Republic*, February 21, 1983.
89. "The team has": Abdul-Jabbar with McCarthy, *Kareem*, p. 72.
89. fans drifted away: *Boston Globe*, April 17, 1992.
90. "Life was pretty": John Havlicek and Bob Ryan, *Hondo: Celtic Man in Motion* (1977), p. 36; next quotation from ibid., p. 37.
90. "You can't really": *People*, July 26, 1982.
90. "Something a little": Angell in *Holiday*, May 1954.
90. "I know": Angell, *Summer Game*, p. 96.
90. "more Met than Yankee": Angell, *Summer Game*, p. 41.
91. "I refused": ibid., p. 164.
91. "The illusion": *Baseball Diamonds*, eds. Kevin Kerrane and Richard Grossinger (1980), p. 297.
91. "Time is": Donald Hall with Dock Ellis, *Dock Ellis in the Country of Baseball* (1976), p. 15.
91. "In some form": W. W "Pudge" Heffelfinger as told to John McCallum, *This Was Football* (1954), p. 180.
92. "We continue": Bill Walsh with Glenn Dickey, *Building a Champion* (1990), p. 32; next quotation from ibid., p. 39.
92. "You know": Mickey Herskowitz, *The Golden Age of Pro Football: A Remembrance of Pro Football in the 1950s* (1974), p. 165; and see Paul Zimmerman, *The New Thinking Man's Guide to Pro Football* (1984), p. 218.
92. "Somehow or other": Warren Goldstein, *Playing for Keeps: A History of Early Baseball* (1989), p. 1.
92. "The sordid element": *Literary Digest*, May 29, 1915.
92. "Today the players": G. H. Fleming, *Murderers' Row* (1985), p. 124.
92. "The player of today": *Baseball Magazine*, March 1944.
92. "Players are not motivated": Buzzie Bavasi with John Strege, *Off the Record* (1987), p. 225.
93. "I don't want": Plimpton in *The New York Times Book Review*, May 15, 1977.
93. "It was an honest": Zimmerman, *Thinking Man's*, p. 16.
93. "the sunlit verities": Angell, *Five Seasons*, p. 375; next quotation from ibid., p. 410.
94. "Is there no": Angell, *Late Innings*, p. 228.

Notes

CHAPTER THREE: BALLPLAYING LIFE

103. "I can't remember": Rogers Hornsby, *My Kind of Baseball*, ed. J. Roy Stockton (1953), p. 29.
104. "I could barely": Earvin "Magic" Johnson, Jr., and Roy S. Johnson, *Magic's Touch* (1989), p. 5; next quotation from ibid., p. 21.
104. Bird shooting hoops: Dan Shaughnessy, *Ever Green: The Boston Celtics* (1990), p. 176.
104. Speaker and Young: *Baseball Magazine*, January 1932; next quotation from ibid.
105. "I watched": Bart Starr with Murray Olderman, *Starr: My Life in Football* (1987), p. 18.
105. "When he did": Lawrence S. Ritter, *The Glory of Their Times: The Story of the Early Days of Baseball Told by the Men Who Played It* (1966), p. 289.
105. "I still haven't": J. G. Taylor Spink, *Judge Landis and Twenty-five Years of Baseball* (1947), p. 35.
106. "Playing in": Ken Denlinger and Paul Attner, *Redskin Country: From Baugh to the Super Bowl* (1983), p. 36.
106. "Compared to": Anthony J. Connor, *Baseball for the Love of It: Hall of Famers Tell It Like It Was* (1982), p. 286.
106. "It's hard": *Baseball Magazine*, July 1931.
106. "When I'd get": Denlinger and Attner, *Redskin*, p. 20.
106. "I was playing": Connor, *Baseball*, p. 33.
106. "there was nothing": Ritter, *Glory*, p. 110; next two quotations from ibid., pp. 110–11, 113.
107. "When I hear": *Sporting News*, May 21, 1942; next quotation from ibid.
107. "And when I": *Baseball Magazine*, July 1941.
107. "That's crazy": George De Gregorio, *Joe DiMaggio: An Informal Biography* (1981), p. 83; Jack B. Moore, *Joe DiMaggio: A Bio-Bibliography* (1986), p. 216.
108. "Why are you": *Hank Greenberg: The Story of My Life*, ed. Ira Berkow (1989), p. 5; next three quotations from ibid., p. 45.
108. "He didn't know": Donald Honig, *A Donald Honig Reader* (1988), p. 608; next four quotations from ibid.
109. baseball wages, 1868: Charles C. Alexander, *Our Game: An American Baseball History* (1991), p. 14.
109. "What do": Harry Wright to W. A. Hulbert, December 29, 1874, Albert G. Spalding Collection.
109. Average salaries: Harold Seymour, *Baseball: The Early Years* (1960), p. 117; Steven A. Riess, *City Games: The Evolution of American Urban Society and the Rise of Sports* (1989), p. 87; Riess in *The American Sporting Experience: A Historical Anthology of Sport in America*, ed. Steven A. Riess (1984), p. 294.
109. Bridwell: Ritter, *Glory*, p. 118.
109. Combs: *Sporting News*, January 19, 1933.
109. early NFL: Red Grange in *Saturday Evening Post*, November 5, 1932.
109. Rooney and White: Myron Cope, *The Game That Was: The Early Days of Pro Football* (1970), p. 129.

Notes

109. salaries in 1950: Paul Governali, "The Professional Football Player: His Vocational Status" (Ed.D. thesis, Columbia Teachers College, 1951), p. 132.

110. "which seemed": Robert W. Peterson, *Cages to Jump Shots: Pro Basketball's Early Years* (1990), p. 114; next quotation from ibid., p. 115.

110. Hertzberg: taped interview with Sonny Hertzberg by Charles Salzberg, n.d., at Basketball Hall of Fame.

110. Sailors: interview with Kenny Sailors, October 14, 1991.

110. Smawley: interview with Belus Smawley, September 16, 1991.

111. "We went": Cope, *Game*, p. 200.

111. "Red was very": John Havlicek and Bob Ryan, *Hondo: Celtic Man in Motion* (1977), p. 81.

111. "There was no": Stuart Leuthner, *Iron Men: Bucko, Crazylegs, and the Boys Recall the Golden Days of Professional Football* (1988), p. 20.

111. "Willie, you forgot": George L. Flynn, *The Vince Lombardi Scrapbook* (1976), p. 113.

112. "You have": E. G. Barrow to Matty McIntyre, January 18, 1904, Detroit Baseball Club Letterbooks.

112. "You will": Frank Navin to McIntyre, January 9, 1905, Detroit Letterbooks.

112. "If I were": G. H. Fleming, *Murderers' Row* (1985), p. 42; next quotation from ibid., p. 45.

112. "I'm living": James Reston, Jr., *Collision at Home Plate: The Lives of Pete Rose and Bart Giamatti* (1991), p. 142.

113. "I was not": *The DiMaggio Albums*, ed. Richard Whittingham (1989), p. 743.

113. "You've gotta": Donald Honig, *Baseball America: The Heroes of the Game and the Times of Their Glory* (1985), p. 287.

113. "You know": *The Fireside Book of Pro Football*, ed. Richard Whittingham (1989), p. 248.

113. "the paralysis": Rick Telander, *Joe Namath and the Other Guys* (1976), p. 25.

113. NFL intelligence test: Paul Zimmerman, *The New Thinking Man's Guide to Pro Football* (1984), pp. 291–92.

113. "gets you caught": Michael Murphy and Rhea A. White, *The Psychic Side of Sports* (1978), p. 29.

114. "They don't call": Zimmerman, *Guide*, p. 14.

114. "They don't go": Fred Smerlas and Vic Carucci, *By a Nose* (1990), p. 26.

114. "Once an athlete": Ty Cobb with Al Stump, *My Life in Baseball: The True Record* (1961), p. 42.

114. "I don't know": Sam Huff with Leonard Shapiro, *Tough Stuff: The Man in the Middle* (1988), pp. 38–39.

114. "There is this": Telander, *Namath*, p. 173.

115. "Any kid": Art Rust, Jr., with Michael Marley, *Legends: Conversations with Baseball Greats* (1989), pp. 78–79.

115. "The saps pay": J. G. Taylor Spink, *Judge Landis and Twenty-five Years of Baseball* (1947), pp. 35–36.

115. "It wasn't": *Mean on Sunday: The Autobiography of Ray Nitschke*, as told to Robert W. Wells (1973), pp. 301–302.

463

Notes

115. "I just loved": *The Armchair Book of Baseball,* ed. John Thorn (1985), p. 17.

115. "I loved baseball": Honig, *Baseball,* p. 178.

115. extra powers: see, in general, Mihaly Csikszentmihalyi, *Flow: The Psychology of Optimal Experience* (1990).

115. "When I was": Jim Brown with Steve Delsohn, *Out of Bounds* (1989), p. 113.

116. "You bother": Larry Bird with Bob Ryan, *Drive: The Story of My Life* (1989), p. 238.

116. "I know": Murphy and White, *Psychic Side of Sports* p. 46.

116. "Everything is": Bill Lee with Dick Lally, *The Wrong Stuff* (Penguin edition, 1985), p. 99.

117. "The feeling": Bill Russell and Taylor Branch, *Second Wind: The Memoirs of an Opinionated Man* (1979), p. 156; next two quotations from ibid., pp. 156–57.

118. "The money": Bill Bradley, *Life on the Run* (1976), pp. 220–21; next two quotations from ibid.

119. "All the time": Fleming, *Murderers',* p. 118.

119. "They've never": Leo Durocher with Ed Linn, *Nice Guys Finish Last* (1975), p. 112.

119. "I'm not superstitious": *DiMaggio Albums,* ed. Whittingham, p. 262.

120. "No, Careful": Donald Honig, *A Donald Honig Reader* (1988), p. 510.

120. "It is merely": *Baseball Magazine,* January 1929.

120. "I don't know": *New York World-Telegram,* June 27, 1936.

120. "For years": *Sporting News,* spring 1937, Lefty Gomez file, National Baseball Library.

120. "and I didn't": Joe Lapchick, *50 Years of Basketball* (1968), p. 45.

121. "The streak had": George F. Will, *Men at Work: The Craft of Baseball* (1990), p. 218.

121. "I don't know": *Instant Replay: The Green Bay Diary of Jerry Kramer,* ed. Dick Schaap (1968), p. 45.

121. "I don't consider": Jim Brosnan, *The Long Season* (1960), p. 84.

122. "I'se a merry": Thomas W. Lawson, *The Krank: His Language and What it Means* (1888), p. 32.

123. Bojangles: Ford C. Frick, *Games, Asterisks, and People: Memoirs of a Lucky Fan* (1973), pp. 66–67.

123. "I may be": *Baseball Magazine,* November 1936.

123. Stallings' lucky dime: Frederick G. Lieb, *The Detroit Tigers* (1946), p. 22.

123. "Say, kid": *Baseball Magazine,* January 1937; next quotation from ibid.

124. "I like to be": *Baseball Magazine,* August 1924; next quotation from ibid.

124. Faust: Thomas C. Busch in *Baseball Research Journal* (1983) and in *Kansas History,* summer 1983; *St. Louis Post-Dispatch,* September 24, 1911.

124. "The cold truth": Fred Lieb in *Baseball Magazine,* April 1921.

125. "I'm here": Christy Mathewson, *Pitching in a Pinch or Baseball from the Inside* (1912), p. 249; next two quotations from ibid., pp. 252, 251.

126. "jinx dispenser": John T. Brush to August Herrmann, July 12, 1912, Officials file, August Herrmann Papers; next quotation from ibid., July 16, 1912.

127. "There is little": Harry Palmer, *Stories of the Base Ball Field* (1890), p. 55.

127. "You don't": Telander, *Namath,* p. 95.

127. "like a small": Vince Lombardi with W. C. Heinz, *Run to Daylight!* (1963), p. 20; next two quotations from ibid.
127. "It was part": Dave Klein, *The Game of Their Lives* (1976), p. 200.
127. "terminal adolescent": Tom House, *The Jock's Itch* (1989), p. 3.
128. "What I didn't": Adrian C. Anson, *A Ball Player's Career* (1900), p. 13.
128. "Maybe one": Cope, *Game*, p. 66.
128. "you either slept": taped interview with Bob Davies by Charles Salzberg, n.d., Basketball Hall of Fame.
128. "You just go": Telander, *Namath*, p. 95.
128. "Moe certainly": *The Fireside Book of Baseball*, ed. Charles Einstein (fourth edition, 1987), p. 164.
129. "Vulgarly healthy": John J. Evers and Hugh S. Fullerton, *Touching Second: The Science of Baseball* (1910), p. 77.
129. "In the confusion": Honig, *Baseball*, p. 58.
129. "the only genuine": Anson, *Ball Player's*, p. 299.
129. "an intellectual game": Tommy Heinsohn with Leonard Lewin, *Heinsohn, Don't You Ever Smile?* (1976), p. 94; next four quotations from ibid., p. 95.
130. Martin's water bomb: Honig, *Reader*, p. 165.
131. "That song": ibid., p. 143.
131. "Danny, you sit": Kirby Higbe, *The High Hard One* (1967), p. 122.
131. "It was funny": Arthur J. Donovan, Jr., and Bob Drury, *Fatso: Football When Men Were Really Men* (1987), p. 24.
132. "A harsh clubhouse": Keith Hernandez and Mike Bryan, *If at First: A Season with the Mets* (1986), p. 45.
132. "and you can": Durocher with Linn, *Nice Guys*, p. 100.
132. "It wasn't": John Tullius, *I'd Rather Be a Yankee: An Oral History of America's Most Loved and Most Hated Baseball Team* (1986), p. 239.
132. "We learned": Jimmie Dykes and Charles O. Dexter, *You Can't Steal First Base* (1967), p. 32.
133. Crabtree's joke: Mark Kram in *Sports Illustrated*, November 29, 1971.
133. "I've always": Richard Whittingham, *What a Game They Played* (1984), p. 38.
133. "Lobby sitting": *Baseball Magazine*, April 1947; next quotation from ibid.
134. "Day after day": Pat Jordan, *A False Spring* (1975), p. 192.
134. "Sometimes we'd": Honig, *Baseball*, p. 197.
134. "relationships which are": Bradley, *Life*, p. 70; next quotation from ibid., p. 65.
135. "The professional": *The Scrapbook History of Baseball*, eds. Jordan A. Deutsch et al. (1975), p. 21.
135. "He's apt": *Sports Illustrated and American Golfer*, November 1936.
135. "The only": Cope, *Game*, p. 152.
136. "Promise me": Connie Mack, *My 66 Years in the Big Leagues: The Great Story of America's National Game* (1950), p. 17.
136. "the Beer and Whiskey League": Frederick G. Lieb, *The Baseball Story* (1950), p. 84.
136. "The games": Lee with Lally, *Wrong Stuff*, p. 64.
136. "Hell, we'd all": Whittingham, *Game*, p. 94.
136. "After every": Leuthner, *Iron Men*, pp. 211–12.

137. "I drink": Namath with Schaap, *Can't Wait*, p. 96; next quotation from ibid., p. 97.
137. "The bottle": Anne Byrne Hoffman, *Echoes from the Schoolyard: Informal Portraits of NBA Greats* (1977), p. 7.
137. "Don't ask": Arnold Red Auerbach and Paul Sann, *Red Auerbach: Winning the Hard Way* (1966), p. 228.
137. "What's the use": *Baseball Magazine*, February 1912.
138. "Gentlemen": Fred Lieb, *Baseball As I Have Known It* (1977), p. 123.
138. Johnson's drinking: Eugene C. Murdock, *Ban Johnson: Czar of Baseball* (1982), pp. 143–44.
138. "We have assembled": *Baseball Magazine*, September 1918.
138. two teams in 1954: "Kiss of the Hops," Ms. by Arthur Mann, February 1954, box 6, Arthur Mann Papers.
138. "They used": Ritter, *Glory*, p. 15; next quotation from ibid., p. 49.
139. "In about": Connie Mack in *Saturday Evening Post*, March 14, 1936.
139. "He burned": *Baseball Magazine*, June 1914.
139. "For some time": Branch Rickey to Pete Reiser, January 20, 1945, box 78, Branch Rickey Papers.
140. "A good deal": *Baseball Magazine*, November 1928.
140. "Alec would": *Baseball Magazine*, August 1931; next quotation from ibid.
141. "I can't hit": *Biographical Dictionary of American Sports: Baseball*, ed. David L. Porter (1987), p. 56.
141. "From the park": Joseph Durso, *The Days of Mr. McGraw* (1969), p. 99.
141. "On the other": Lee with Lally, *Wrong Stuff*, p. 65.
141. "Paul thought": *Baseball Dictionary*, ed. Porter, p. 590.
141. "I sometimes": Jack Orr in *Esquire*, May 1963.
142. "But I": Connor, *Baseball*, p. 159.
142. "The idea": Hernandez and Bryan, *First*, p. 74.
142. "The ones": *Total Baseball*, p. 541.
142. "All the players": Frank Navin to Edward Hanlon, August 4, 1904, Detroit Letterbooks.
142. Tigers drinking, 1905: W. R. Armour to William Coughlin, January 31, 1906, ibid.
143. "I saw": Walter "Rabbit" Maranville, *Run, Rabbit, Run* (1991), p. 22.
143. "A buffoon": Durocher with Linn, *Nice Guys*, p. 165.
143. "I like women": Namath with Schaap, *Can't Wait*, p. 88.
143. "Boys, I'm just": Jim Bouton, *Ball Four Plus Ball Five* (1981), p. 205.
143. "I was": *Baseball Magazine*, March 1931.
144. "I note": W. R. Armour to Charles D. Carr, August 28, 1905, Detroit Letter-books.
144. "He does not": Frank Navin to Ban Johnson, April 3, 1907, ibid.
144. "It seems hard": Navin to Hugh Jennings, March 18, 1907, ibid.
144. "My *real*": Marv Fleming with Bill Bruns in *Sport*, May 1977; next four quotations from ibid.
145. "Even though": House, *Jock's Itch*, p. 37.
145. "The other Celtics": Russell and Branch, *Second*, p. 218.
146. "he shyly": Lieb, *Baseball As Known*, p. 176.
146. "what normally": Bradley, *Life*, pp. 41–42; next quotation from ibid., p. 201.

146. "Would you": Paul Hornung as told to Al Silverman, *Football and the Single Man* (1965), p. 211.
146. Babe and six women: Lieb, *Baseball As Known*, p. 157.
147. "So he'd call": *Baseball Magazine*, November 1945.
147. "Threatened to show": Tullius, *Yankee*, p. 174.
147. "to entice": Peter Levine, *A. G. Spalding and the Rise of Baseball: The Promise of American Sport* (1985), pp. 124.
147. Spalding's mistress: ibid., pp. 124–25.
147. "Leo kept": Harold Parrott, *The Lords of Baseball* (1976), p. 169.
148. According to Turkin: memo of interview with Hy Turkin, July 4, 1951, box 59, Organized Baseball Papers.
148. "For a young": Ted Williams with John Underwood, *My Turn at Bat: The Story of My Life* (1969), pp. 53–54.
148. "The saloon": Lieb, *Baseball Story*, p. 113.
148. "He'd pay": Whittingham, *Game*, p. 94.
148. "You never saw": Honig, *Reader*, p. 318.
149. "Any girl": Robert W. Creamer, *Babe: The Legend Comes to Life* (1974), p. 311.
149. "just wanting": Cope, *Game*, p. 101.
149. "As soon as": Governali, "Professional," p. 248.
149. phone booth at Grand Central: Donovan and Drury, *Fatso*, p. 128.
149. "Open your door": Bouton, *Ball Four*, p. 218.
150. "The first time": Lee with Lally, *Wrong Stuff*, p. 49.
150. "a dangerous vanity": Bradley, *Life*, p. 202.
150. "the vicarious exhilaration": Lynda Huey in *Sport*, May 1977.
150. "fucking around": Neil Offen, *God Save the Players: The Funny, Crazy, Sometimes Violent World of Sports Fans* (1974), p. 143; next six quotations from ibid., pp. 141–44.
151. "Women love": Brown with Delsohn, *Bounds*, p. 133.
151. "I don't know": Thomas "Hollywood" Henderson and Peter Knobler, *Out of Control: Confessions of an NFL Casualty* (1987), p. 152; next four quotations from ibid., pp. 120–23.
152. "I guess": Wilt Chamberlain and David Shaw, *Wilt: Just Like Any Other 7-Foot Black Millionaire Who Lives Next Door* (1973), p. 262; next six quotations from ibid., pp. 261–64, 258.
152. claim of twenty thousand: Wilt Chamberlain, *A View From Above* (1991), p. 251.
153. "the times": Henderson and Knobler, *Confessions*, p. 154.
153. "That looked": Kirby Higbe, *The High Hard One* (1967), p. 81.
153. "Now Harry": *Total Baseball*, p. 460.
153. "It ain't sex": Tullius, *Yankee*, p. 188.
153. "He does not": Frank Navin to C. C. Carr, July 14, 1909, Detroit Letterbooks.
154. Ruth pursued: Lieb, *Baseball As Known*, p. 159.
154. "good-looking shiny": Leuthner, *Iron Men*, p. 212.
154. Dykes remembered: Dykes and Dexter, *Can't Steal*, p. 201.
154. "I lost two": transcript, February 28, 1946, box 102, Rickey Papers.
155. "All because": transcript, April 10, 1950, box 11, Rickey Papers.
155. Wilt re fidelity: Chamberlain and Shaw, *Wilt*, p. 256.

155. "The toughest thing": *Total Baseball,* p. 540.
155. "Wait till": Mike Kelly, *"Play Ball": Stories of the Diamond Field* (1888), p. 27.
156. "There are few": Palmer, *Stories,* p. 30.
156. "I was a bit": Kelly, *Stories,* p. 24; next three quotations from ibid., pp. 24–25, 34.
157. Kelly as receiver: *Baseball Magazine,* June 1914.
157. "though he would": Anson, *Ball Player's,* pp. 115–16.
157. Chicago slide: Evers and Fullerton, *Touching Second,* p. 96.
157. "I have known": Alfred H. Spink, *The National Game* (1910), p. 103.
158. Kelly on double steal: *Baseball Magazine,* January 1927.
158. "All you had": Albert G. Spalding, *America's National Game* (1911), p. 265.
158. "It was strongly": *Chicago Tribune,* May 21, 1881.
158. "How a Boston": Kelly, *Stories,* p. 44.
159. "I never ran": ibid., p. 29.
159. "one of the jolliest": George V. Tuohey, *A History of the Boston Base Ball Club* (1897), p. 93.
159. "He tortures": *Boston Herald,* April 16, 1888.
159. "The game concluded": *Boston Herald,* April 20, 1888.
160. "People go": Kelly, *Stories,* p. 8.
160. "John could shove": *Baseball Magazine,* June 1910.
160. "take a bat": N. Fred Pfeffer, *Scientific Ball* (1889), p. 42.
161. Clarkson's Total Pitcher Index: *Total Baseball,* p. 2,040.
161. "He is a young": O. P. Caylor in *Harper's Weekly,* May 3, 1890.
161. Clarkson's early life: *Boston Globe,* April 4, 1888.
162. "Scold him": Spink, *National,* p. 126.
162. "No occasion": Tuohey, *History,* p. 185.
162. Kelly's early life: Kelly, *Stories,* pp. 10–11.
162. strike for shoes: Harry Palmer in *Outing,* July 1888.
162. Kelly onstage: *Baseball Magazine,* January 1928.
163. "It depends": Daniel Okrent and Steve Wulf, *Baseball Anecdotes* (1989), p. 16.
163. "The man never": Lee Allen, *The National League Story: The Official History* (1961), p. 56.
163. "Drinks for the house": *Baseball Magazine,* January 1928.
163. Early deaths of 1884 team: *Total Baseball,* p. 413.
163. "Good habits": Palmer, *Stories,* p. 19.
163. "With a report": Evers and Fullerton, *Touching Second,* p. 81.
164. "What are you": Spalding, *Game,* p. 523; next three quotations from ibid., pp. 523–25.
164. "in no condition": Levine, *Spalding,* p. 41.
164. "He was of": Spalding, *Game,* p. 516.
164. Salaries in 1886: *Baseball Magazine,* July 1918.
165. "Oh, I'm a beaut": Tuohey, *History,* p. 193.
165. "We don't intend": Levine, *Spalding,* p. 43.
165. "Everywhere they were": *Boston Globe,* April 4, 1888.
165. "Clarkson's command": *Boston Herald,* April 29, 1888.
165. "A big-hearted": Spink, *Game,* p. 102.
166. "And I want you": Lieb, *Baseball Story,* p. 79.

166. Team photo, 1892: *The Ultimate Baseball Book,* eds. Daniel Okrent and Harris Lewine (1979), p. 27.

166. old Kelly trick: Spink, *Game,* p. 102.

166. Kelly death: *Boston Herald,* November 9, 1894.

166. "His temperate habits": *Boston Globe,* April 4, 1888.

166. "He is a fit": *Boston Herald,* April 14, 1888.

167. Fullerton claimed: Evers and Fullerton, *Touching Second,* p. 59.

167. Clarkson's decline: Elwood A. Roff, *Base Ball and Base Ball Players* (1912), p. 187.

167. Clarkson death: *Boston Globe,* February 5, 1909.

167. Clarkson death certificate: 1909 Deaths, vol. 4:371, Massachusetts Bureau of Vital Statistics, Boston.

CHAPTER FOUR: BASEBALL

168. Origins of baseball: The myth of baseball's invention by Abner Doubleday in Cooperstown, New York, in 1839 was concocted by organized baseball in 1907. Addled by nationalist pride, baseball's leaders invented an immaculate American conception for the sport, untainted by the British game of rounders. Never based on any real evidence, the Doubleday myth was demolished in the 1930s by the historian Robert W. Henderson; see his *Ball, Bat and Bishop: The Origins of Ball Games* (1947). The modern game is usually dated from New York teams of the 1840s; I am pushing its origins back twenty years to Rochester. Thurlow Weed's account of playing baseball there in the 1820s was noted by Jennie Holliman, *American Sports (1785–1835)* (1931), pp. 66–67. Since then baseball historians have cited Weed's recollection without exploring it. The writer Samuel Hopkins Adams claimed in 1942 to have discovered mention of the Rochester Baseball Club in a Rochester newspaper of 1825 (Adams to Alexander Woollcott, August 6, 1942, Alexander Woollcott Papers); and see Adams, *Grandfather Stories* (1955), pp. 21, 143–56, 263. In 1992 Priscilla Astifan did a limited search for me of files of various Rochester newspapers for the period 1825–30 but found no reference to baseball (Astifan to author, September 23, 1992). The matter needs further investigation. In July 1825 a group of men in Delaware County, New York, issued a challenge to other men in the county to meet them at "bass-ball"; but there is no record of whether any games were actually played. See *Delhi* (New York) *Gazette,* July 13, 1825; Benjamin G. Rader, *Baseball: A History of America's Game* (1992), p. 4.

168. "A base-ball club": *Autobiography of Thurlow Weed,* ed. Harriet Weed (1883), p. 203.

168. Rochester as boomtown: Paul E. Johnson, *A Shopkeeper's Millennium: Society and Revivals in Rochester, New York 1815–1837* (1978), pp. 13–14; Blake McKelvey, *Rochester: The Water-Power City* (1945), p. 91.

169. "Every thing": Basil Hall, *Travels in North America, in the Years 1827 and 1828* (1829), p. 87.

169. Weed: *The Education of Henry Adams* (1918), pp. 146–47.

169. Kempshall: Johnson, *Shopkeeper's,* pp. 30–31.

169.   Whittlesey: William F. Peck, *History of Rochester and Monroe County, New York* (1908), p. 903.

169.   Gardiner: *National Cyclopedia of American Biography,* 13 (1906), p. 181.

169.   Selden: ibid., 4 (1902), p. 154.

170.   social strains in Rochester: Johnson, *Shopkeeper's,* pp. 58, 75–76.

170.   "We have seen": *A Directory for the Village of Rochester* (1827), p. 140.

170.   town ball: Will Irwin in *Collier's,* May 8, 1909; James L. Steele in *Outing,* June 1904; *A Manual of Cricket and Base Ball* (1858), pp. 20–23; Nancy B. Bouchier and Robert Knight Barney in *Journal of Sport History,* spring 1988.

172.   "It did not hurt": James D'Wolf Lovett, *Old Boston Boys and the Games They Played* (1906), pp. 130–31.

172.   first written use: Henderson, *Ball,* p. 132.

173.   "The Ball once": ibid., p. 133.

173.   stool-ball: ibid., pp. 70–71; Alice Bertha Gomme, *The Traditional Games of England, Scotland, and Ireland* (2 vols., 1894 and 1898), II:217–20.

173.   "Puerile Sports": *The Diary of William Bentley, D.D.* (4 vols., 1905), I:253–54.

173.   cat ball: Holliman, *Sports,* pp. 65–66; Albert G. Spalding, *America's National Game* (1911), pp. 33–37; Cynthia J. Wilber, *For the Love of the Game* (1992), p. 81; Lovett, *Games,* p. 127.

174.   rounders: Harold Peterson, *The Man Who Invented Baseball* (1973), pp. 27–50; *Ball Players' Chronicle,* July 18, 1867; Gomme, *Games,* II: 145–46.

174.   "The feeder is": Charles A. Peverelly, *The Book of American Pastimes* (1866), p. 339.

174.   "It was simply": Harry Palmer, *Stories of the Base Ball Field* (1890), p. 133.

174.   Robin Carver's book: Henderson, *Ball,* pp. 156–57.

174.   spread of town ball: David Hackett Fischer, *Albion's Seed: Four British Folkways in America* (1989), p. 150.

175.   "The players were": Peverelly, *Pastimes,* p. 472.

175.   "A conservative": George B. Kirsch, *The Creation of American Team Sports: Baseball and Cricket, 1838–1872* (1889), p. 73.

175.   "Respectability has": ibid., p. 159.

175.   "a friendly match": *New York Morning News,* October 21, 1845, as noted in *New York Times,* October 4, 1990.

175.   "this well known": James M. DiClerico and Barry J. Pavelec, *The Jersey Game* (1991), p. 15.

176.   Cartwright: Peterson, *Man Who,* pp. 53, 100, 105.

176.   "dear old Knickerbockers": Alexander Cartwright to Charles S. Debost, April 6, 1865, enclosed with Bruce Cartwright, Jr., to Walter Camp, April 24, 1910, file 125, Walter Camp Papers.

176.   "proposed a regular": Peverelly, *Pastimes,* p. 340.

176.   "Well do I": Alfred H. Spink, *The National Game* (1910), pp. 54–56.

177.   "often spoke": Bruce Cartwright, Jr., to Camp, cited above.

177.   Knickerbocker rules: Peverelly, *Pastimes,* pp. 341–42.

177.   "They put so much": Bouchier and Barney in *Journal of Sport History,* spring 1988.

178.   "It exhibits": William M. Rankin in *Baseball Magazine,* January 1910.

178.   "The chief trouble": Spink, *Game,* p. 56.

178. "Many is the": Alexander Cartwright to Debost, cited above.

179. Gothams: Melvin L. Adelman, *A Sporting Time: New York City and the Rise of Modern Athletics, 1820–1870* (1986), p. 124; *Spirit of the Times,* July 9 and October 22, 1853, and July 15 and September 30, 1854.

179. town ball in Boston: Lovett, *Games,* pp. 128–29.

179. Ned Saltzman: *New England Base Ballist,* August 6, 1868.

179. "It gave an equal": ibid., August 27, 1868.

180. game, September 1858: *Spalding's Official Baseball Guide* (1915), pp. 46–47.

180. "with a dignified": Lovett, *Games,* pp. 141–42.

180. "the national game": Harold Seymour, *Baseball: The Early Years* (1960), p. 31; *Spirit of the Times,* January 31, 1857.

180. "mutterings both loud": Peverelly, *Pastimes,* p. 474.

180. Cobb and town ball: Ty Cobb with Al Stump, *My Life in Baseball: The True Record* (1961), p. 37.

181. Knickerbockers: Adelman, *Sporting,* p. 123.

181. surviving letters: Knickerbocker Base Ball Club correspondence in Albert G. Spalding Collection.

181. "Its members have": Peverelly, *Pastimes,* pp. 340–41.

181. "We are all": Theodore F. Hascall to G. W. Buckland, May 20, 1875, Knickerbocker correspondence.

181. 1850s demographics: Kirsch, *Creation,* pp. 130–32; Adelman, *Sporting,* pp. 125–26.

181. John Lowell: *New England Base Ballist,* August 13, 1868.

182. "Come jolly comrade": Seymour, *Early Years,* p. 45.

182. "It is the universally": Harvey Green, *Fit for America* (1986), p. 79.

182. "constantly increasing": *Harper's Weekly,* June 17, 1865.

182. exercise fad: Steven A. Riess, *City Games: The Evolution of American Urban Society and the Rise of Sports* (1989), p. 27–29.

182. "It has been supposed": Thomas Wentworth Higginson in *Atlantic Monthly,* March 1858.

182. "thousands upon thousands": Seymour, *Early Years,* p. 46.

183. affection for "old": Fred Somkin, *Unquiet Eagle: Memory and Desire in the Idea of American Freedom, 1815–1860* (1967), pp. 99–100.

183. "the old fashioned game": *Spirit of the Times,* December 23, 1854.

183. "Here's a health": Seymour, *Early Years,* p. 31.

183. less frequent dinners: *Spirit of the Times,* March 20, 1858.

183. "the indulgence": Benjamin G. Rader, *American Sports: From the Age of Folk Games to the Age of Televised Sports* (second edition, 1990), p. 33.

184. "the handsomest man": John R. Lambert, *Arthur Pue Gorman* (1953), p. 83.

185. "One of the ablest": *The Nation,* June 7, 1906.

185. Potomacs: Peverelly, *Pastimes,* p. 495.

185. "A majority": ibid., p. 492.

186. Crowd at August 1858 game: *Spirit of the Times,* August 21, 1858.

186. Excelsiors tour, 1860: Peverelly, *Pastimes,* pp. 409–10.

186. Tweed and Mutuals: Seymour, *Early Years,* pp. 53–54; *New York Tribune,* July 16, 1867.

186. Nationals and Treasury: David Quentin Voigt, *American Baseball: From*

Gentleman's Sport to the Commissioner System (1966), pp. 18–19; Kirsch, *Creation*, p. 82.

187. Treasury during war: Frederick J. Blue, *Salmon P. Chase: A Life in Politics* (1987), p. 138.

187. Nationals and jobs: *Boyd's Washington and Georgetown Directory* (1864–67).

187. Gorman and Al Reach: Adelman, *Sporting*, p. 151.

187. "simply to keep": *Ball Players' Chronicle*, July 11, 1867.

187. "made a most": *Washington Daily National Intelligencer*, August 3, 1865.

187. "In activity": Henry Chadwick, *The Game of Base Ball* (1868), p. 32.

188. August 28 game: *Intelligencer*, August 29, 1865.

188. "The most numerous": *New York Herald*, August 29, 1865.

188. "Gorman was": *Intelligencer*, August 30, 1865.

188. "The Nationals have": *Intelligencer*, October 9 and 12, 1865.

189. Nationals' diamond: *Intelligencer*, October 17, 1866.

189. "a good player": Chadwick, *Game*, p. 36.

189. "We expect them": *Intelligencer*, June 26, 1866.

189. "A brilliant": *Intelligencer*, July 7, 1866.

189. "The opinion": *Intelligencer*, September 19, 1866.

190. Gorman and NABBP: Peverelly, *Pastimes*, pp. 501–14.

190. "that sectionalism": Kirsch, *Creation*, p. 210.

190. 1867 tour: ibid., p. 208.

190. ballpark, June 1867: *Intelligencer*, June 20, 1867.

190. George Wright: George V. Tuohey, *A History of the Boston Base Ball Club* (1897), p. 198; N. Fred Pfeffer, *Scientific Ball* (1889), p. 60.

191. "Knowing his own": Henry Chadwick, *How to Play Base Ball* (1889), p. 91.

191. "His wits": *The Armchair Book of Baseball II*, ed. John Thorn (1987), p. 53.

191. only two from Washington: *Ball Players' Chronicle*, August 15, 1867.

191. "The result": *New York Tribune*, July 13, 1867.

192. "very good": *Intelligencer*, July 15, 1867.

192. Cincinnati team: Harry Ellard, *Baseball in Cincinnati* (1907), pp. 39–40.

192. "There you are": *Ball Players' Chronicle*, July 25, 1867.

192. "The excitement": *New York Tribune*, July 16, 1867.

192. "the ignorant portion": *Ball Players' Chronicle*, July 25, 1867.

193. "The play of": *Chicago Tribune*, July 20, 1867.

193. "the best players": *Intelligencer*, July 24, 1867.

193. list of 43 clubs: *Chicago Tribune*, July 26, 1867.

194. "It was the first": Spalding, *Game*, pp. 108–109.

194. "Wright jumping": *Chicago Tribune*, July 26, 1867; next quotation from ibid.

194. "The invincibles": *Intelligencer*, July 26, 1867.

195. "The universal": *Chicago Tribune*, July 29, 1867.

195. "They are professional": *Chicago Tribune*, July 28, 1867.

196. *Tribune* withdrew: *Tribune*, July 29, 1867.

196. loss had inspired Cincinnati: Warren Goldstein, *Playing for Keeps: A History of Early Baseball* (1989), pp. 103–104.

196. "The evolution": Spalding, *Game*, p. 167.

197. NAPBBP founding: *New York Times*, March 18, 1871; J. C. Morse, "*Sphere and Ash*": *History of Base Ball* (1888), p. 25.

197. "Base ball is business": Harry Wright to Nick Young, April 21, 1871, Spalding Collection.

197. "Soc et tu": Wright to William Cammeyer, April 19, 1875, ibid.

197. "some place": Wright to E. Hicks Hayhurst, December 26, 1871, ibid.

198. "On receiving": Gerald Astor et al., *The Baseball Hall of Fame 50th Anniversary Book* (1988), p. 13.

198. "There's no use": Spalding, *Game*, p. 200.

198. Anson: *New England Base Ballist,* August 20, 1868; Adrian C. Anson, *A Ball Player's Career* (1900), pp. 44, 52, 59.

199. "The spirit": Spalding, *Game*, p. 201.

199. "an eminently undesirable": *New York Times*, March 8, 1872.

199. "Boston is in": Astor et al., *50th Anniversary*, p. 10.

199. Hulbert and league: Anson, *Ball Player's*, pp. 96–106.

200. "Strong, forceful": Spalding, *Game*, p. 201.

200. Hulbert: *Chicago Tribune*, April 11, 1882.

200. "I would rather": Spalding, *Game*, pp. 207–208.

200. "Arbitrary and severe": Anson, *Ball Player's*, p. 108.

201. Davis and fly rule: Peverelly, *Pastimes*, p. 351; *Ball Players' Chronicle*, September 19, 1867.

201. "One of our best": *Spirit of the Times*, March 24, 1860.

201. "It did more": George Wright in *Records of the Columbia Historical Society*, 23 (1920), p. 82.

201. curveball: Will Irwin in *Collier's*, May 15, 1909; Spalding, *Game*, p. 484; Morse, *History*, pp. 33–34.

202. "It was so": F. Cauthorn in *Baseball Magazine*, July 1933.

202. Wright grew gun-shy: Tuohey, *History*, p. 198.

202. "ins and outs": Jack E. Harshman in *Baseball Research Journal*, 19 (1990), p. 7.

203. "We had a trick": *Baseball Magazine*, June 1918.

203. first gloves: William Curran, *Mitts: A Celebration of the Art of Fielding* (1985), p. 73.

203. Charlie Waitt: Spalding, *Game*, pp. 475–76.

203. Arthur Irwin: Irwin in *Collier's*, May 15, 1909.

203. Harry Decker: William A. Phelon in *Baseball Magazine*, September 1913.

204. "I was as full": Anson, *Ball Player's*, p. 63.

204. "There are many": Palmer, *Stories*, p. 34.

205. "The secret of success": Pfeffer, *Scientific*, p. 50.

205. White Stockings: George I. Moreland, *Balldom: "The Britannica of Baseball"* (1914), p. 32.

205. "much stouter": Mike Kelly, *"Play Ball":Stories of the Diamond Field* (1888), p. 48; next quotation from ibid., p. 49.

206. "I decided": *Baseball Magazine*, July 1911.

206. "Only a few": John J. McGraw, *My Thirty Years in Baseball* (1923), pp. 56, 69.

206. Orioles: Clark C. Griffith in *Outing*, May 1914; Mrs. John J. McGraw, *The Real McGraw*, ed. Arthur Mann (1953), pp. 94–95.

206. "They took": Hugh S. Fullerton in *American Magazine*, September 1913.

207. "playing the dirtiest": Bill James, *The Bill James Historical Baseball Abstract* (1986), p. 39.

207. "I have never": Lee Allen, *100 Years of Baseball* (1950), p. 131.

207. "They were mean": James, *Abstract*, p. 39.

207. "CLEAN BALL": Ban Johnson to American League clubs, May 8, 1901, box 1, Arthur Mann Papers.
208. Goldstein has suggested: Goldstein, *Playing*, pp. 2, 6.
208. "the very symbol": Anson, *Ball Player's*, p. 278.
208. "Professional baseball": Charles Brian Goslow in *Historical Journal of Massachusetts*, summer 1991.
208. "If sport arose": Dale A Somers, *The Rise of Sports in New Orleans 1850–1900* (1972), p. xii.
209. "all regular business": Seymour, *Early Years*, p. 55.
209. "a curse": DiClerico and Pavelec, *Jersey Game*, p. 38.

CHAPTER FIVE: FOOTBALL

210. "the greatest match": J. G. Lockhart, *Memoirs of the Life of Sir Walter Scott* (7 vols., 1838), III: 288.
210. Scott watched son: *The Letters of Sir Walter Scott*, ed. Herbert Grierson (12 vols., 1932–37), IV:141.
211. "From the brown": Lockhart, *Scott*, III: 290.
211. Buccleuch teased: James Russell, *Reminiscences of Yarrow* (1886), p. 323.
211. "A desperate contention": *Letters of Scott*, ed. Grierson, IV:126, 135.
211. "Our game": ibid., IV:142.
211. "severe conflict": Locklear, *Scott*, III:289; next two quotations from ibid.
212. "They maintained": ibid., III:290.
212. night brought fistfights: Edgar Johnson, *Sir Walter Scott: The Great Unknown* (2 vols., 1970), I:512.
212. "the old feuds": Lockhart, *Scott*, III:291–92.
213. football's origins in British Isles: Francis Peabody Magoun, Jr., in *Harvard Studies and Notes in Philology and Literature*, 13 (1931), pp. 39–41.
213. football banned: L. H. Baker, *Football: Facts and Figures* (1945), pp. 4–6.
213. "more common": Francis Peabody Magoun, Jr., in *American Historical Review*, October 1929.
213. "They get the bladder": ibid.
214. annual game: Allen Guttmann, *Sports Spectators* (1986), pp. 49–50.
214. "All was fair": Magoun in *Harvard Studies*, p. 23.
214. Cellan and Pencarreg: Alice Bertha Gomme, *The Traditional Games of England, Scotland, and Ireland* (2 vols., 1894 and 1898), I:136.
214. "As they do": Magoun in *Harvard Studies*, p. 23.
214. "Broken shins": ibid., p. 27.
215. adult males in 1685: Benjamin G. Rader, *American Sports: From the Age of Folk Games to the Age of Spectators* (1983), p. 15.
215. "a great game": David Hackett Fischer, *Albion's Seed: Four British Folkways in America* (1989), p. 149.
215. "Unfriendly to clothes": *The Diary of William Bentley, D.D.* (4 vols., 1905), I:254.
215. English prep schools: Baker, *Football*, p. 7.
215. Hughes book: Amos Alonzo Stagg, as told to Wesley Winans Stout, *Touchdown!* (1927), p. 19; Benjamin G. Rader, *American Sports: From the Age of Folk Games to the Age of Televised Sports* (second edition, 1990), p. 101.

216. football in colleges: Ronald A. Smith, *Sports and Freedom: The Rise of Big-Time College Athletics* (1988), pp. 8–20; Howard J. Savage, *American College Athletics* (1929), p. 15; Baker, *Football*, pp. 10–11; *Spirit of the Times*, October 21, 1854.

216. "opportunity it gave": *The H Book of Harvard Athletics 1852–1922*, ed. John A. Blanchard (1923), p. 322.

216. "There were yellings": Smith, *Sports*, p. 68.

216. New York game: W. J. Henderson in *Outing*, October 1900; Walter Camp, *American Football* (1892), pp. 117–18.

217. "For fifteen minutes": Henderson in *Outing*, October 1900.

217. Boston game: *H Book*, ed. Blanchard, pp. 346–48; Stagg and Stout, *Touchdown!*, p. 24; Henry Bancroft Twombly, *Personal Reminiscences of a Yale Football Player of the Early 'Eighties* (1884), pp. 3–4.

217. "The severest penalty": *H Book*, ed. Blanchard, p. 348.

218. revived at Harvard: ibid., p. 342.

218. Harvard declined: ibid., pp. 354–56.

219. "agile, athletic": Walter Camp in *Youth's Companion*, November 29, 1900; next quotation from ibid.

219. "Our men seemed": Allison Danzig, *The History of American Football* (1956), p. 12.

219. "After the first": Camp in *Youth's Companion*, November 29, 1900; next three quotations from ibid.

220. "He seemed to know": *Football Days: Memories of the Game and the Men Behind the Ball*, ed. William H. Edwards (1916), p. 72; next quotation from ibid.

220. "I ran up to": Walter Camp, *The Book of Foot-Ball* (1910), p. 86.

221. "were unanimously": *Football Days*, ed. Edwards, p. 78; next quotation from ibid., p. 79.

222. "This pushing": Stagg and Stout, *Touchdown!*, pp. 56–57.

222. interference allowed: Percy D. Haughton, *Football and How to Watch It* (1922), pp. 61–62; Danzig, *History*, p. 18; Camp, *American Football*, pp. 16–18.

223. "means which": Smith, *Sports*, p. 89.

223. "There is only": Richard Harding Davis in *Harper's Weekly*, November 18, 1893.

223. "Will you kindly": James H. Kivlan to Walter Camp, September 20, 1892, file 512, Walter Camp Papers.

223. eleven of his boys: John Stuart Martin in *American Heritage*, October 1961.

223. "the two most": Harford Powel, Jr., *Walter Camp: The Father of American Football* (1926), p. 44.

224. effect of low tackle: *Spalding's Official Football Guide* (1926), pp. 17–18.

224. wedges: Danzig, *History*, p. 17; Camp, *Book of Foot-Ball*, p. 103.

224. Heffelfinger: Alexander Weyand, *Football Immortals* (1962), p. 98.

224. "We were past": Allison Danzig, *Oh, How They Played the Game: The Early Days of Football and the Heroes Who Made It Great* (1971), p. 71.

225. Deland: *Harper's Weekly*, December 2, 1893.

225. flying wedge: *H Book*, ed. Blanchard, p. 390; Camp, *Book of Foot-Ball*, p. 102.

225. "One who": Danzig, *Played*, p. 70.
225. "We were plenty": W. W. "Pudge" Heffelfinger as told to John McCallum, *This Was Football* (1954), p. 49.
225. "no father": Weyand, *Immortals*, p. 5.
226. "We were tending": Theodore Roosevelt to Walter Camp, March 11, 1895, file 593, Camp Papers; and see Roosevelt in *Harper's Weekly*, December 23, 1893.
226. Davis reported: Davis in *Harper's Weekly*, November 18, 1893; and see James D'Wolf Lovett, *Old Boston Boys and the Games They Played* (1906), pp. 86–88.
227. "in all manly": George Wright to Walter Camp, December 2, 1893, file 775, Camp Papers.
227. athletic clubs: Joe D. Willis and Richard G. Wettan in *Journal of Sport History*, spring 1976.
227. "semiprofessional": Riffenburgh, p. 9.
228. Pike and Thompson: Lloyd Wright and Herman Kogan, *Big Bill of Chicago* (1953), p. 29.
228. "professional football league": Riffenburgh, p. 10.
228. Heffelfinger's family business: Louis K. Hull to Walter Camp, May 4, 1910, file 378, Camp Papers.
229. Allegheny AA: J. Thomas Jable in *Western Pennsylvania Historical Magazine*, April 1979.
229. "the best all-round": F. W. Williams, *A History of the Class of Seventy-Nine: Yale College* (1906), p. 436; next quotation from ibid., pp. 436–37.
229. game, November 1892: Jable in *Magazine*, April 1979; Riffenburgh, pp. 9–10.
230. "They dismounted": eight-page typescript re Phoenixville, n.d., at Pro Football Hall of Fame; next five quotations from ibid.
231. Lafayette player joined: *Football Days*, ed. Edwards, pp. 419–20.
232. "on a long": ibid., p. 119.
232. "one of the most": *Boston Globe*, November 27, 1896.
232. Greensburg team: David S. Neft and Richard M. Cohen, *The Football Encyclopedia: The Complete History of Professional NFL Football from 1892 to the Present* (1991), p. 17; *New York Times*, January 6, 1935.
233. first NFL: Robert Smith, *Illustrated History of Pro Football* (revised edition, 1977), pp. 31–33; *Biographical Dictionary of American Sports: Football*, ed. David L. Porter (1987), p. 41.
233. "They care": Willis Richardson to Arthur Cushing, October 1, 1902, Pro Football Hall of Fame.
233. Chicago indoor game: Smith, *Sports*, p. 81.
233. O'Rourke: *New York Times*, April 27 and May 28, 1905; January 22 and February 14, 1913; and June 20, 1936.
233. Orange favored: ibid., December 14, 1902.
234. Warner and Syracuse: ibid., December 29, 1902.
234. "the spectators cheered": ibid., December 30, 1902.
234. "Whenever the big": ibid., January 3, 1903.
235. James Black Wise: *National Cyclopedia of American Biography*, 29 (1941), pp. 330–31.
235. Watertown team, 1903; *New York Times*, December 12–13, 1903.

235. "all sorts of odds": ibid., December 15, 1903; next quotation from ibid.

236. "almost at will": ibid., December 18, 1903; and see Rollo Wilson's account in *Pittsburgh Courier,* December 19, 1925.

236. story handed down: interview with Alex Duffy of Watertown, November 30, 1992.

236. "A gentleman": Powel, *Camp,* p. 200.

236. game receipts, 1901: statement in file 75, Camp Papers.

236. loping professionalism: Smith, *Sports,* p. 214.

236. Yost: Richard Whittingham, *Saturday Afternoon: College Football and the Men Who Made the Day* (1985), pp. 163–64.

236. "Carlisle wasn't": Myron Cope, *The Game That Was: The Early Days of Pro Football* (1970), p. 38.

237. "Warner does not": Fielding Yost to Phil G. Bartelme, February 20, 1913, box 1, Fielding H. Yost Papers.

237. "the czar principle": George Wilson Pierson, *Yale College: An Educational History 1871–1921* (1952), p. 39.

237. favored member: note by Arthur Twining Hadley, February 12, 1901, file 313, Camp Papers.

237. "Somehow, without": Walter Camp to J. C. Branner, October 5, 1901, file 89, Camp Papers.

237. secret reserve fund: clippings, February 1905 and January 1906, reel 41, Camp Papers.

237. Camp's $5,000: Walter Camp to Arthur Twining Hadley, March 6, 1906, file 314, Camp Papers.

238. "Harvard has": Walter Camp to S. Reading Bertron, November 8, 1900, file 75, Camp Papers.

238. Hogan: *Football Dictionary,* ed. Porter, pp. 269–70.

238. "the noble fight": *Football Days,* ed. Edwards, pp. 448–49.

238. Hogan in action: Danzig, *History,* p. 163.

238. "almost irresistible": *Football Days,* ed. Edwards, p. 279; next quotation from ibid., p. 450.

238. "We do not": Walter Camp to Herbert J. Barton, January 9, 1904, file 63, Camp Papers.

239. Hogan at Yale: Smith, *Sports,* p. 188.

239. "Fateful, monotonous": J. Mott Hallowell to Walter Camp, November 28, 1904, file 323, Camp Papers.

239. muckraking articles: H. B. Needham in *McClure's,* June, July 1905; Clarence Deming in *Outlook,* July 1, 1905; Deming in *New York Evening Post,* January 18, 1906; and see A. P. Stokes to *McClure's,* March 16, 1905, file 827, Camp Papers.

240. "lavishness": Deming in *Outlook,* July 1, 1905.

240. THE GREAT MONEY POWER: clippings, February 1905, reel 41, Camp Papers.

240. Camp pay cut: Walter Camp to Arthur Twining Hadley, March 6, 1906, file 314, Camp Papers.

240. Hogan itching to reply: J. W. Curtiss to Walter Camp, January 17, 1907, file 645, Camp Papers.

240. Hadley insisted: Pierson, *Yale,* p. 255.

240. "a thoroughly clean": John S. Watterson in *American Heritage*, September/October 1988.

240. forward pass: Danzig, *History*, p. 33; Walter Camp to Paul Dashiell, December 12, 1905, file 235, Camp Papers.

241. "most startling": *Spalding's Official Football Guide* (1914), p. 9.

241. "I started limping": Knute Rockne in *Collier's*, October 25, 1930.

241. "One of the impressive": *Spalding's Official Football Guide* (1926), p. 15.

242. "There was not": F. H. Palmer to Edward Staples, November 22, 1943, box 78, Branch Rickey Papers.

242. "When I found": Arthur Mann, *Branch Rickey: American in Action* (1957), p. 30.

242. "You should have": Palmer to Staples, November 22, 1943.

242. Panhandles: Riffenburgh, p. 11.

242. "I have been": Theo N. Nesser to Walter Camp, August 27, 1916, file 505, Camp Papers.

243. Carr remembered: clipping, 1938, in *Pottsville Republican*, October 24, 1987; next quotation from ibid.

243. "The crowds were": Riffenburgh, p. 11.

243. paid Heston: Neft and Cohen, *Football Encyclopedia*, p. 18.

243. Wallace as bootlegger: Harry A. March, *Pro Football: Its "Ups" and "Downs": A Light-hearted History of the Post Graduate Course* (1934), pp. 62–63.

243. Canton and Cusack: Robert W. Wheeler, *Jim Thorpe: World's Greatest Athlete* (revised edition, 1979), pp. 167–83.

244. "Jim would shift": Tex Maule, *The Game: The Official Picture History of the NFL and AFL* (1967 edition), p. 8.

244. "like a steam roller": Steve Owen, *My Kind of Football*, ed. Joe King (1952), p. 50; Richard Whittingham, *What a Game They Played* (1984), p. 12.

244. "The big Indian": *New York Times*, March 28, 1943.

244. NFL founding: Riffenburgh, p. 14.

245. Thorpe playing billiards: Aaron Hertzman to Leo V. Lyons, February 24, 1961, Pro Football Hall of Fame.

245. "to speed": *Halas By Halas: The Autobiography of George Halas*, with Gwen Morgan and Arthur Veysey (1979), p. 19.

245. "We were starch": Wheeler, *Thorpe*, p. 275.

246. Trafton: Trafton file, Pro Football Hall of Fame; Bob Curran, *Pro Football's Rag Days* (1969), p. 76.

246. "You've got to": Knute Rockne to George Trafton, December 6, 1929, Knute Rockne Papers, Notre Dame Archives.

246. Chamberlin: Riffenburgh, pp. 415, 441.

246. "If professional": *New York World*, December 20, 1925.

247. "The Giants were": Emlen Tunnell with Bill Gleason, *Footsteps of a Giant* (1966), p. 174.

247. Mara left team to March: Owen, *Football*, ed. King, pp. 74–75.

247. "You could tell": Dave Klein, *The New York Giants* (1973), p. 13.

247. Grange style: Ernest L. Cuneo in *American Scholar*, fall 1987; Whittingham, *Game*, p. 9.

247. "He ran with": Robert Zuppke to Bill Fay, September 1950, box 6, Robert Zuppke Papers.

248. "Grange played": *The Scrapbook History of Pro Football*, eds. Richard M. Cohen et al. (1976), p. 32.

248. Grange tour: Dan Daly and Bob O'Connell, *The Pro Football Chronicle* (1990), p. 21; Ford C. Frick, *Games, Asterisks, and People: Memoirs of a Lucky Fan* (1973), pp. 44–45; Smith, *Illustrated*, p. 122; John M. Carroll, *Fritz Pollard: Pioneer in Racial Advancement* (1992), p. 176.

248. "Halas and I": Tunnell with Gleason, *Footsteps*, p. 174.

248. Bears trainer: Red Grange interview in *American Heritage*, December 1974.

249. Zuppke refused: Cope, *Game*, p. 52.

249. "The professional game": *Outlook*, October 17, 1926.

249. Stagg locked doors: Cope, *Game*, p. 80.

249. "It is purely": Stagg and Stout, *Touchdown!*, pp. 294, 296.

249. "too many college": clipping, January 27, 1933, Carr file, Pro Football Hall of Fame.

249. Carr connections: *Football Dictionary*, ed. Porter, pp. 97–98.

249. "Joe Carr's a nice": article by Ray Didinger, Carr file, Pro Football Hall of Fame.

250. Marshall obnoxious: Daly and O'Connell, *Chronicle*, pp. 84, 141–42.

250. "Football is": George Sullivan, *Pro Football's All-Time Greats* (1968), p. 77; clipping in Marshall file, Pro Football Hall of Fame.

250. "I wrote": George Preston Marshall in *Saturday Evening Post*, November 19, 1938.

251. Not wishing to deprive: Thomas Sugrue in *American Magazine*, December 1937; and see Robert H. Boyle in *Sports Illustrated*, October 16, 1961.

251. "When I knew": Cope, *Game*, p. 282.

251. Marshall at NFL meetings: ibid., p. 133; Paul Brown with Jack Clary, *PB: The Paul Brown Story* (1979), p. 193.

252. "an established place": clipping, 1938, in *Pottsville Republican*, October 24, 1987.

252. "The paint": Curran, *Rag Days*, p. 128; and see ibid., p. 134.

252. loss of eighty-five thousand dollars: Marshall in *Post*, November 19, 1938.

CHAPTER SIX: BASKETBALL

261. regional pro leagues: Robert W. Peterson, *Cages to Jump Shots: Pro Basketball's Early Years* (1990), pp. 47–48.

262. full uniform: Frank W. Keaney in *Athletic Journal*, March 1946.

262. the ball: Joe Lapchick, *50 Years of Basketball* (1968), p. 5.

262. "When you shot": Peterson, *Cages*, p. 49.

262. shooting: John M. Cooper and Daryl Siedentop, *The Theory and Science of Basketball* (1969), p. 12.

262. "guards down": Peterson, *Cages*, p. 41.

264. cages: Frank J. Basloe, *I Grew Up with Basketball: Twenty Years of Barnstorming with Cage Greats of Yesterday* (1952), pp. 76–78.

264. "The ball is": *Reach Official Basket Ball Guide* (1905), p. 4.

264. "Suils threw": Joe Jares, *Basketball: The American Game* (1971), p. 37.

264. "Basketball was": Frederick G. Lieb, *The Pittsburgh Pirates* (1948), p. 51.

264. pros remembered pain: interview with Nat Holman by Jerry Healy, July 6, 1988, Basketball Hall of Fame.

264. "You could": Peterson, *Cages*, p. 9.

265. "If the officials": *Reach Guide* (1910), p. 5.

265. roughness: George L. Meylan in *American Physical Education Review*, June 1909.

265. "When a guard": Peterson, *Cages*, p. 40.

265. muscular Christianity: Tony Ladd, "Evangelical Muscular Christians and the Transformation of American Sport," paper read at conference of North American Society for the Sociology of Sport, Toronto, November 5, 1992.

266. Naismith: Bernice Larson Webb, *The Basketball Man: James Naismith* (1973).

266. "There were other": James Naismith to Morgan, August 14, 1928, in *McGill News*, fall 1992.

266. "Jim, I play": James Naismith, *Basketball: Its Origin and Development* (1941), p. 28.

266. "Those boys": James Naismith in *Rotarian*, January 1939.

266. "What could": Naismith, *Basketball*, p. 36.

267. duck on the rock: Webb, *Naismith*, pp. 13, 60–61.

267. "Don't let": Naismith to Morgan, cited above.

267. young women teachers: *Spalding's Official Basketball Guide* (1942), pp. 6–7.

267. "The game has": *New York Times*, April 26, 1892.

268. HAS BECOME POPULAR: *New York Times*, November 12, 1893; next quotation from ibid.

268. "Not to be": Herb Reynolds in *Converse Basketball Year Book* (1922), p. 5.

268. backboards: Naismith, *Basketball*, pp. 93–95.

268. "We looked": Reynolds in *Year Book*, p. 5.

268. "It is not": *Physical Education*, April 1895.

269. "The new principle": Dudley Sargent in *Independent*, July 9, 1896.

269. "Basket ball fiends": Luther Gulick in *Physical Education*, November 1895.

269. "too brutal": *New York Times*, October 9, 1896.

269. Naismith played twice: Webb, *Naismith*, p. 70.

269. "scientific" basketball: James Naismith in *Physical Education*, January 1894.

269. "The kind of": J. Parmly Paret in *Outing*, December 1897.

269. "We went into": Reynolds in *Year Book*, p. 11.

270. Buffalo Germans: Allie Seelbach in *Converse Basketball Yearbook* (1941), p. 31; Peter Nussbaum in *Buffalo Magazine*, February 16, 1992; Peterson, *Cages*, pp. 56–61.

271. "It remained": James Sullivan in *Cosmopolitan*, September 1901.

271. "Our two months": Reynolds in *Year Book*, p. 9.

272. "That the team": *Buffalo Evening Times*, July 13, 1904.

272. Germans' jobs: *Buffalo Directory* (1910).

272. "How they could": Forrest C. Allen, *Better Basketball: Techniques, Tactics and Tales* (1937), p. 7; next quotation from ibid.

272. underappreciated in Buffalo: *Reach Guide* (1910), p. 65.

272. Heerdt's twenty-one points a game: *Biographical Dictionary of American Sports,* ed. David L. Porter (supplement, 1992), p. 289.

273. "They are": reprinted in *Buffalo Courier,* April 10, 1910.

273. "We were all": John H. Wendelken, "History of the New York National League Basketball Team" (ca. 1954), in drawer marked "General—Professional—Other Leagues," Basketball Hall of Fame.

273. NBL: Peterson, *Cages,* p. 43; *Converse Basketball Yearbook* (1947), p. 22; *Philadelphia Evening Bulletin,* October 6, 1902.

274. "Everybody ran": Wendelken, "History"; next two quotations from ibid.

274. Scheffer: *Philadelphia Evening Bulletin,* August 11, 1952; *Philadelphia Inquirer,* August 11, 1952.

275. "Forwards must": William J. Scheffer in *Reach Guide* (1910), p. 155.

275. "Hugging around": *Reach Guide* (1914), p. 33.

275. "It is getting": *Reach Guide* (1915), p. 5.

276. Hough: *Philadelphia Inquirer,* April 21, 1935; *New York Herald-Tribune,* April 21, 1935.

276. "the greatest": Thomas A. McDonough in *Baseball Magazine,* February 1909; next two quotations from ibid.

276. "the great Hough": clippings in Harry Hough envelope, Basketball Hall of Fame.

276. Scheffer included: Alexander M. Weyand, *The Cavalcade of Basketball* (1960), p. 237.

276. Sedran: *New York Times,* January 15, 1969; interview with Holman, cited above.

276. "drifting around": Harold U. Ribalow, *The Jew in American Sports* (1948), p. 61.

277. "This combination": *Reach Guide* (1915), p. 9.

277. Sedran and Meehan: Robert D. Bole and Alfred C. Lawrence, *From Peachbaskets to Slamdunks: A Story of Professional Basketball 1891–1987* (1987), p. 69.

277. cross-fertilizations: Walter E. Meanwell, *The Science of Basket Ball for Men* (1924), pp. 178–79.

277. Troy team: Basloe, *Basketball,* pp. 82–83; Peterson, *Cages,* p. 61.

277. Nationals: *New York Times,* February 12, 1913; April 30, 1915.

277. "the dominant style": Forrest C. Allen, *My Basket-ball Bible* (1924), p. 279.

278. "almost the basic": Charles Digby Wardlaw and Whitelaw Reid Morrison, *Basket Ball: A Handbook for Coaches and Players* (1921), p. 29.

279. Terrible Swedes: Peterson, *Cages,* pp. 103–104.

279. "He was the one": Ben Byrd, *The Basketball Vol: University of Tennessee Basketball* (1980), no pagination.

279. Hyatt: *Biographical Dictionary of American Sports: Basketball and Other Indoor Sports,* ed. David L. Porter (1989), pp. 138–39; interview with John M. Cooper, June 18, 1990; Cooper and Siedentop, *Basketball,* p. 16.

279. fourth in 1950 poll: clipping in George Mikan file, newspaper clipping file, Basketball Hall of Fame.

279. "less adjustment": Everett S. Dean, *Progressive Basketball: Method and Philosophy* (1950 edition), p. 134.

280. Ruby described: J. Craig Ruby, *Coaching Basketball: A Textbook* (1931), pp. 85–87.

Notes

280. Hood: Clyde Bolton, *The Basketball Tide: A Story of Alabama Basketball* (1977), p. 53.

280. "I'd take": ibid., p. 66.

280. Sale: Tev Laudeman, *The Rupp Years* (1972), no pagination; *Lexington Herald-Leader*, December 5, 1985; Adolph F. Rupp, *Rupp's Championship Basketball* (1948), p. 52.

280. "He was": *Converse Basketball Yearbook* (1932), p. 5.

280. Witte: Larry Fox, *Illustrated History of Basketball* (1974), p. 68.

280. "Witte was": *Spalding Basketball Guide* (1932), p. 105.

281. "The one-hand push": Clarence Edmundson and Robert Morris, *Basketball for Players, Officials and Spectators* (1931), p. 24.

281. "Since he was": William Gray to author, April 19, 1990.

281. Gray's style: William Gray to author, April 2, 1990.

282. Gray led Genesee: *Genesee News,* March 22, 1912.

282. "He'd get up": clipping, ca. 1954, sent by William Gray to author.

282. "Charles Gray was": Idaho student paper, February 5, 1915.

282. Gray senior year: *Spalding Basketball Guide* (1918), p. 107.

282. Alex Fox: ibid. (1923), pp. 79, 82–83.

282. "I can still": James C. Heartwell, *The History of Oregon State College Basketball* (1953), p. 98.

282. picked up by Fletcher: W. D. Fletcher in *Athletic Journal,* May 1929.

282. "as carefully": Edmundson and Morris, *Basketball,* p. 20; next quotation from ibid., p. 21.

283. "the one definite": Clarence Edmundson in *Athletic Journal,* January 1938.

283. "The orthodox": G. Ott Romney in *Athletic Journal,* November 1932.

283. break adopted by others: Weyand, *Basketball,* pp. 101–102; Frank W. Keaney in *Athletic Journal,* December 1944.

284. "Make the ball": Lapchick, *50 Years,* p. 43; next quotation from ibid., p. 196.

284. Celtics 1922–23: *Reach Guide* (1924), pp. 50–51.

284. "The Original Celtics": *Converse Basketball Yearbook* (1924), p. 51.

284. origin of name: taped interview with Henry Dutch Dehnert by Joe Jares, late 1970s, Basketball Hall of Fame.

284. Donovan killed: Dutch Dehnert in *Boston Herald,* January 9, 1958.

284. Furey embezzlement: *New York Times,* June 17, October 20, and November 6, 1926.

284. "We were rough-cut": Joe Lapchick with Tim Cohane in *Look,* February 4, 1958.

285. "the most dangerous": *Reach Guide* (1920), p. 55.

285. home from road trips: *Miami News,* February 7, 1974.

285. "What's the matter": Lapchick with Cohane in *Look,* February 4, 1958; Lapchick, *50 Years,* p. 50.

285. "When I got hold": interview with Dehnert, cited above; next two quotations from ibid.

286. series, April 1921: *Reach Guide* (1922), pp. 56–58.

286. Furey stole: Basloe, *Basketball,* p. 199.

286. Holman: Nat Holman in *Converse Basketball Yearbook* (1971), p. 5; Sandy Padwe, *Basketball's Hall of Fame* (1970), pp. 26–29; interview with Holman, cited above.

286. "What a man": Milton Bracker in *New York Times Magazine*, January 25, 1942.
286. "The Jew is": Ribalow, *Jew in Sports*, p. 232.
286. "It's the driving": *New York Times*, February 6, 1951.
287. "I would run": Lapchick, *50 Years*, p. 10; next quotation from ibid., p. 11.
287. "so securely": *Chicago Tribune*, December 6, 1928.
287. "My heart was": Lapchick, *50 Years*, p. 12; next two quotations from ibid., pp. 14, 25–26.
287. "our dressing room": Lapchick with Cohane in *Look*, February 4, 1958.
288. Celtics and pivot play: Nat Holman, *Winning Basketball* (1932), pp. 56–57; Holman, *Holman on Basketball* (1950), pp. 124–25; Lapchick, *50 Years*, pp. 138–39.
288. favorite deke: Holman, *Winning*, pp. 48–49; Holman, *Holman*, p. 117.
288. Beckman jumped, caught: *Reach Guide* (1923), p. 9.
288. "The greatest": Lapchick, *50 Years*, p. 20.
288. "no one scored": *Reach Guide* (1925), p. 168.
288. "the short, snappy": Nat Holman in *Converse Basketball Yearbook* (1923), p. 33.
289. "the most dominant": Stanley Frank in *Literary Digest*, December 15, 1934.
289. ABL: Neft and Cohen, pp. 12–17; Peterson, *Cages*, pp. 84–85; *Converse Basketball Yearbook* (1930), p. 34.
289. Northeast players dominated: John Russell, *Honey Russell: Between Games, Between Halves* (1986), p. 52.
289. Rosies passing: *Chicago Tribune*, January 6, 1927.
289. Chicago Bruins: *Chicago Tribune*, December 13, 1925.
290. Stonebraker hit five: Holman, *Holman*, pp. 70–71.
290. "Both teams": *Chicago Tribune*, December 29, 1926.
290. Frank's estimate: Stanley Frank in *Collier's*, February 4, 1939.
290. special deal: Peterson, *Cages*, p. 87.
290. "wizardly mastery": *Chicago Tribune*, January 14, 1927.
290. expenses 1928–29: minutes of ABL Executive Committee meeting, May 4, 1929, Basketball Hall of Fame.
291. "Fans have shown": Peterson, *Cages*, p. 92.
291. ABL last year: *Chicago Tribune*, December 1, 4, and 9, 1930.
291. "Professional basketball": Allen, *Better Basketball*, p. 8.
291. "Professional basketball faded": Lapchick, *50 Years*, p. 13.
292. Olympic tryouts, spring 1936: Ted Vincent, *Mudville's Revenge: The Rise and Fall of American Sport* (1981), p. 262.
292. "the startling": *New York Times*, April 5, 1936.
292. "I was small": *New York Times Biographical Service* (December 1986), p. 1,463.
293. "Overnight": Ron Fimrite in *Sports Illustrated*, December 15, 1975.
293. "I watched": Anne Byrne Hoffman, *Echoes from the Schoolyard: Informal Portraits of NBA Greats* (1977), pp. 9–10.
293. "He had great": Billy Packer with Roland Lazenby, *Fifty Years of the Final Four* (1987), p. 28.
293. "I'll quit": Stanley Frank in *Collier's*, February 4, 1939; next quotation from ibid.
294. "I do not like": Frank W. Keaney in *Athletic Journal*, March 1946.

294. Kase conceived: Peterson, *Cages,* p. 150.

294. hockey arenas: Leonard Koppett, *24 Seconds to Shoot: An Informal History of the National Basketball Association* (1968), pp. 18–19.

294. "We feel": minutes of BAA meeting, August 19, 1946, p. 168, at Basketball Hall of Fame.

294. "I know nothing": *Rochester Democrat-Chronicle,* February 13, 1951.

295. first pro game at Garden: *New York Times,* November 12, 1946.

295. "the brains": Terry Pluto, *Tall Tales* (1992), p. 208; next two quotations from ibid., pp. 211–12.

295. Gottlieb: *Philadelphia Evening Bulletin,* December 8, 1979; *Basketball Dictionary,* ed. Porter, pp. 102–103.

295. SPHAS featured: *Reach Guide* (1923), pp. 161–63.

296. "We moved": Peterson, *Cages,* p. 123.

296. "You all know": Russ Davis in *Saturday Evening Post,* January 3, 1948.

296. NBL: Neft and Cohen, pp. 20–46; Peterson, *Cages,* pp. 130–38.

297. Rupp called Edwards: Russell Rice, *Kentucky Basketball's Big Blue Machine* (revised edition, 1978), p. 115.

297. McDermott: *Basketball Magazine,* November 1946.

297. Dehnert saw: interview with Dehnert, cited above.

297. Davies and Luisetti: taped interview with Bob Davies by Charles Salzberg, ca. 1986, Basketball Hall of Fame.

297. Mikan: Ron Fimrite in *Sports Illustrated,* November 6, 1989.

297. "We had": Davies interview, cited above.

298. "Teams literally": *Boston Globe,* May 31, 1992.

298. 19–18 game: Pluto, *Tall Tales,* pp. 24–26.

298. "No one": ibid., p. 27; next two quotations from ibid., pp. 48–49, 27.

298. "A very quiet": *Boston Globe,* May 31, 1992; next quotation from ibid.

299. Biasone explained it: Pluto, *Tall Tales,* p. 29.

299. "I been": *Newsweek,* February 6, 1956.

CHAPTER SEVEN: BLACK POWER, BLACK SPEED

300. "Our sports": *The American Slave: A Composite Autobiography,* ed. George P. Rawick (17 vols., 1972), IV: Texas narratives, 1:2. (The Rawick volumes consist of WPA interviews conducted with former slaves in the late 1930s.)

300. "I was tough": *Slave,* ed. Rawick, IX: Arkansas narratives, 3:277, 279.

300. "run around": Norman R. Yetman, *Voices from Slavery* (1970), p. 288; next quotation from ibid., p. 112.

301. "We had the big": *Slave,* ed. Rawick, IV: Texas narratives, 1:240–41.

301. "I was as lively": *Slavery in the South,* ed. Harvey Wish (1964), p. 29.

301. McKay: *Slave,* ed. Rawick, V: Texas narratives, 3:42.

301. Cumby: ibid., IV: Texas narratives, 1:261.

301. "Run, nigger": Roger D. Abrahams, *Singing the Master: The Emergence of African American Culture in the Plantation South* (1992), p. 117.

302. "This is often": *Puttin' on Ole Massa: The Slave Narratives of Henry Bibb, William Wells Brown, and Solomon Northrup,* ed. Gilbert Osofsky (1969), p. 68.

302. "De nigger fights": *Slave*, ed. Rawick, IV: Texas narratives, 2:37.
302. "A slave who": *Narrative of the Life of Frederick Douglass: An American Slave: Written by Himself* (Signet edition, 1968), p. 84; next two quotations from ibid.
303. "I wuz de swifes": *Slave*, ed. Rawick, II: South Carolina narratives, 1:215.
304. "that sectionalism": George B. Kirsch, *The Creation of American Team Sports: Baseball and Cricket, 1838–72* (1989), p. 210.
304. "If colored clubs": Janet Bruce, *The Kansas City Monarchs: Champions of Black Baseball* (1985), p. 5.
304. seventy black players: *The Armchair Book of Baseball II*, ed. John Thorn, (1987), pp. 262–85.
304. "One of the best": *Total Baseball*, p. 548.
305. Walker: G. B. McKinney in *Journal of Sport History*, winter 1976.
305. "I disliked": *Total Baseball*, p. 549.
305. Even in New Orleans: Dale A. Somers, *The Rise of Sport in New Orleans 1850–1900* (1972), p. 120.
306. "developing new possibilities": Richard White in *Afro-Americans in New York Life and History*, January 1992; next quotation from ibid.
306. "By 1880": James Weldon Johnson, *Black Manhattan* (1930), p. 63.
306. first pro teams: Harold Seymour, *Baseball: The People's Game* (1990), p. 539.
306. White: *Pittsburgh Courier*, March 12, 1927.
306. Cuban Giants: Benjamin G. Rader, *Baseball: A History of America's Game* (1992), p. 31.
307. "more by carelessness": *New York Age*, July 28, 1888.
307. "It is the general": *Age*, September 1, 1888.
307. "brought something": Johnson, *Manhattan*, pp. 64–65; next quotation from ibid.
307. Johnson had learned: *Along This Way: The Autobiography of James Weldon Johnson* (1933), p. 36.
307. "The negro ball player": *Baseball Magazine*, December 1918.
308. "extremely selfish": *New York Amsterdam News*, December 18, 1929; next two quotations from ibid.
308. *Age* declared: *Age*, September 19, 1907.
308. McMahon: *Courier*, February 19, 1927.
308. Lincoln Giants, 1911 and 1913: *Age*, October 19, 1911, and October 9, 1913.
308. "a square shooter": *Courier*, November 21, 1935.
308. Connor: *Chicago Defender*, July 17, 1926.
309. "the father": *Courier*, April 2, 1927.
309. Strong: Rob Ruck, *Sandlot Seasons: Sport in Black Pittsburgh* (1987), p. 118; *New York Times*, January 11, 1935.
309. *Age* reported: *Age*, May 2, 1912.
309. Connor quit: *Age*, March 13, 1913.
309. Bolden and Strong: *Courier*, August 8, 1925.
309. "The white promoters": *Age*, June 8, 1918.
309. "I have been known": *Age*, June 29, 1918.
309. "For Strong": *Courier*, October 27, 1923.

309. Strong a parasite: *Courier,* June 7, 1924, and December 17, 1927; *Defender,* March 11, 1922.

310. Foster: *Defender,* December 13, 1930.

310. "I left school": *Defender,* November 15, 1924.

310. Schorling: Robert Peterson, *Only the Ball Was White* (1970), p. 108.

310. Foster and Schorling: *Defender,* January 5, 1924.

311. "A loud-voiced": *Courier,* October 11, 1924.

311. "I associate": *Defender,* December 17, 1921.

311. Foster as boss: *Courier,* January 24, 1925, and January 16, 1926.

311. grosses, first six years: *Courier,* January 30, 1926.

311. "If Rube": *Defender,* February 24, 1923.

311. blackball ranked: Art Rust, Jr., *"Get That Nigger Off the Field"* (1976), p. 42; John Holway, *Voices from the Great Black Baseball Leagues* (1975), p. 200.

312. Holway's reckoning: ibid., p. xvi.

312. "I guess": Bruce, *Monarchs,* p. 64.

312. "We played": Anthony J. Connor, *Baseball for the Love of It: Hall of Famers Tell It Like It Was* (1982), p. 209.

312. "They play": William A. Brower in *Opportunity,* June 1942.

312. "Their baseball": Ted Shane in *Saturday Evening Post,* July 27, 1940.

313. "built upon speed": *Defender,* November 18, 1922.

313. "we had seven": John B. Holway, *Blackball Stars: Negro League Pioneers* (1988), p. 22.

313. "Everywhere you go": John B. Holway, *Josh and Satch: The Life and Times of Josh Gibson and Satchel Paige* (1991), p. 10.

313. New York teams: *Age,* May 27, 1915.

313. Eastern League: *Courier,* June 26, 1924.

313. "That was": Holway, *Blackball,* p. 157.

313. "one of the fastest": Holway, *Josh,* p. 78.

313. "We'd run you": interview with Piper Davis by Theodore Rosengarten in *Southern Exposure,* summer/fall 1977.

313. "People came": William M. Kimok in *Afro-Americans in New York Life and History,* January 1992.

313. "perhaps the fastest": Oliver S. Arata in *Baseball Magazine,* May 1929.

313. "Cool Papa": *Courier,* August 12, 1933.

314. Bell stories: Mark Kram in *Sports Illustrated,* August 20, 1973.

314. "I don't know": Holway, *Voices,* p. 33.

314. "Now, Mr. Foster": Holway, *Blackball,* p. 30.

314. blacks beating whites: David K. Wiggins in *Journal of Sport History,* summer 1989.

315. "Colored baseball": *St. Louis Post-Dispatch,* August 31, 1911, quoted in part in *Age,* September 28, 1911.

315. Drew: A. S. "Doc" Young, *Negro Firsts in Sports* (1963), p. 82.

315. "The negro's": *New York Times,* October 28, 1914.

315. "in keeping with": *Age,* April 30, 1921.

315. "In the brief": *Amsterdam News,* July 18, 1936.

316. "For years": *Amsterdam News,* August 29, 1936.

316. "If the notion": *American Sport: A Documentary History,* ed. Peter Levine (1989), p. 141.

316. "I would be": Holway, *Voices,* p. 109.
317. "Kill the coon!": Allison Danzig, *Oh, How They Played the Game: The Early Days of Football and the Heroes Who Made It Great* (1971), p. 89.
317. Lewis: *Dictionary of American Biography,* supplement four (1974), pp. 492–93.
318. "a step which": *Boston Globe,* December 12, 1893.
318. "I had the age": *Boston Globe,* November 28, 1948.
318. Lewis photo: *Football Days: Memories of the Game and of the Men Behind the Ball,* ed. William H. Edwards (1916), opposite p. 428.
318. "He was not": Donald Wilhelm in *Baseball Magazine,* December 1911.
318. "A very fine": *Harper's Weekly,* October 22, 1892; next quotation from ibid., December 30, 1893.
319. all-time squad: A. M. Weyand, *American Football: Its History and Development* (1926), p. 118.
319. devised strategy: Arthur P. Young in *Baseball Magazine,* December 1909.
319. "a great student": Walter Camp to Theodore Kendrick, March 11, 1903, file 408, Walter Camp Papers.
319. "to regard": Booker T. Washington in *American Magazine,* June 1913.
319. "as his friends": *Harvard Crimson,* May 26, 1893.
319. "Why the devil": *Football Days,* ed. Edwards, p. 156.
320. Pollard and five colleges: John M. Carroll, *Fritz Pollard: Pioneer in Racial Advancement* (1992), pp. 41–56.
320. freshman grades: ibid., p. 90.
320. "when he came": ibid., p. 97.
320. "It wasn't": Allison Danzig, *The History of American Football* (1956), p. 228.
320. "switched to": Edwin Bancroft Henderson, *The Negro in Sports* (1939), p. 94.
320. "He was the": quoted in *Age,* November 23, 1916.
321. Pollard and his bills: Carroll, *Pollard,* p. 94.
321. "It would get": *The Fireside Book of Pro Football,* ed. Richard Whittingham (1989), p. 234.
321. Slater banned: David S. Neft and Richard M. Cohen, *The Football Encyclopedia: The Complete History of Professional NFL Football from 1892 to the Present* (1991), p. 47.
321. *Defender* blamed: *Defender,* November 6, 1926.
322. "There are many": Harry A. March, *Pro Football: Its "Ups" and "Downs": A Light-hearted History of the Post Graduate Course* (1934), p. 153.
322. Marshall role: interviews with Pearce B. Johnson and Joe Horrigan at Pro Football Hall of Fame, July 1990.
323. St. Philip's: *Age,* December 20, 1919; Gilbert Osofsky, *Harlem: The Making of a Ghetto* (Harper Torchbook edition, 1968), p. 115.
323. "not only": *New York Freeman,* April 17, 1886.
323. Bishop: *New York Times,* May 19, 1937.
323. move to Harlem: Osofsky, *Harlem,* pp. 116–17; *Age,* March 30 and December 21, 1911.
324. "We believe": *Defender,* June 18, 1921.
324. "He was": *Amsterdam News,* June 8, 1932.
324. "never wanted": *Defender,* June 18, 1921.

324. main rivals: Romeo Dougherty in *Amsterdam News,* December 18, 1929; next two quotations from ibid.

324. Wetzler: *Amsterdam News,* August 10, 1935.

324. "The outstanding coach": ibid., August 24, 1935.

325. Jenkins: ibid., December 26, 1936.

325. "the biggest thing": *Age,* January 8, 1914.

325. Posey parents: *Courier,* June 13, 1925; Holway, *Blackball,* p. 302.

325. "Fragile in appearance": *Courier,* January 14, 1928.

325. Posey regarded Hough: ibid., February 11, 1928.

325. "Considered throughout": *Age,* March 14, 1912.

325. "I had Posey": *Courier,* December 3, 1927.

326. "a clean yet": ibid., March 16, 1912; next quotation from ibid.

326. praised Posey: *Age,* March 20, 1913.

326. Loendis: *Age,* November 13, 1913, and February 14, 1920; Ruck, *Sandlot,* p. 127.

326. Madden and Incorporators: *Age,* October 22 and December 3, 1914, and January 7, 1915.

326. "The showers are": ibid., November 4, 1915.

327. Cooper: *Courier,* February 28, 1925.

327. "Cooper stands": *Age,* April 13, 1916.

327. Madden antagonized: *Amsterdam News,* April 6, 1933.

327. revealing litigation: ibid., August 28, 1935.

327. "Instead of being": *Courier,* March 28, 1925.

328. "I thought": *Amsterdam News,* July 21, 1979.

328. "I wasn't": *Age,* February 6, 1960.

328. Douglas and Johnson: ibid., February 14, 1920.

328. "One of the most": *Amsterdam News,* April 16, 1930.

328. "the most dangerous": *Courier,* December 1, 1923.

328. Ricks would holler: *Age,* February 6, 1960.

328. "like a streak": *Courier,* January 22, 1927.

329. Jenkins later: *Courier,* December 29, 1934.

329. "The team": *Amsterdam News,* February 10, 1926.

329. Rens 1929–30: ibid., April 23, 1930.

329. Lapchick praised Cooper: Glenn Dickey, *The History of Professional Basketball Since 1896* (1982), p. 19.

329. "The toughest": John Wooden as told to Jack Tobin, *They Call Me Coach* (1974), p. 58.

330. "sustained speed": *Amsterdam News,* December 18, 1929.

330. "It was almost": ibid., April 2, 1930.

330. "a rank smell": *Defender,* January 25, 1930.

330. Celtics in Cleveland: *Amsterdam News,* March 15, 1933.

330. "The referees": Bruce Newman in *Sports Illustrated,* October 22, 1979; next quotation from ibid.

331. Globetrotters: *Defender,* March 14, 1931, and February 6, 1932.

331. "extraordinary speed": ibid., November 29, 1930.

331. "I won't let": Stanley Frank in *Collier's,* February 8, 1941.

331. Bethards hired: *Amsterdam News,* April 4, 1936.

331. "Abe Saperstein": Newman in *Sports Illustrated,* October 22, 1979.

332. Douglas coaching: *Defender,* April 8, 1939.

332.   Rens-Trotters, 1939: ibid., April 1, 1939.
332.   Rens-Trotters, 1940: *Chicago Herald-American*, March 19, 1940; *Defender*, March 23, 1940.
332.   1940 final: *Chicago Herald-American*, March 21, 1940; *Defender*, March 30, 1940.
332.   "Basketball is NOT": *Defender*, March 23, 1940.
333.   jazzmen and blackball: Donn Rogosin, *Invisible Men: Life in Baseball's Negro Leagues* (1983), p. 102.
333.   "The professional players": Jay Feldman in *Baseball Research Journal*, 18 (1989), p. 7.
333.   "Our baseball players": *Defender*, December 31, 1921.
333.   Brown and Wickware: Peterson, *Only*, p. 209; *Courier*, May 9, 1925; *Defender*, May 23, 1925.
333.   Moore: Holway, *Blackball*, p. 197; *Defender*, May 29, 1926.
333.   Miller: ibid., September 25, 1926.
333.   "It's a sad truth": *Courier*, October 23, 1926.
334.   murder at Hilldale game: Neil Lanctot in *Pennsylvania Magazine of History and Biography*, January/April 1993.
334.   Hawkins murder: *Defender*, May 16, 1931.
334.   "the many shortcomings": *Courier*, August 8, 1925.
334.   "Players have refused": *Defender*, October 22, 1927.
334.   "Well, Friday": ibid., June 8, 1929.
334.   McHaskell accident: ibid., November 16, 1929.
334.   Poindexter stabbing: ibid., June 21, 1930.
334.   "We always had": Donald Honig, *A Donald Honig Reader* (1988), p. 137.
334.   contracts and trades: *Defender*, January 19, 1935; *Courier*, August 30, 1924; Bruce, *Monarchs*, p. 32.
334.   "They were regular": Peterson, *Only*, p. 95.
335.   Wilkins: *Courier*, May 31, 1924; *New York Times*, May 25, 1924; *Defender*, January 10, 1925.
335.   "He was one": Holway, *Blackball*, pp. 251–52.
335.   Jackson: Ruck, *Sandlot*, p. 171.
335.   Greenlee: ibid., pp. 137–39; Holway, *Josh and Satch*, p. 37.
335.   "He looked like": Holway, *Blackball*, p. 308; next quotation from ibid., p. 309.
335.   other numbers kings: Rogosin, *Invisible*, p. 107. (According to Lanctot, cited above, Ed Bolden was not in the numbers business.)
336.   Paige: *Time*, June 3, 1940; *Life*, June 2, 1940; Ted Shane in *Saturday Evening Post*, July 27, 1940.
336.   "Satchel kicked": Holway, *Voices*, p. 97.
336.   "the best pitcher": Shane in *Post*, July 27, 1940.
336.   "I'm Satchel": Richard Donovan in *Collier's*, June 13, 1953.
336.   "You'd forgive": Peterson, *Only*, p. 142.
336.   "We must have": *Defender*, April 1, 1939.
337.   "We have to be": Rogosin, *Invisible*, p. 77.
337.   "A major league": Murray Polner, *Branch Rickey: A Biography* (1982), p. 189.
337.   "There was one": Holway, *Voices*, p. 269.

337. "of Jewish extraction": Branch Rickey to Roscoe C. Hobbs, November 29, 1944, box 126, Branch Rickey Papers.

337. "Did you ever": Branch Rickey to L. S. MacPhail, August 22, 1941, box 77, Rickey Papers; and see Rickey to Fred Saigh, July 14, 1951, box 73, Rickey Papers.

338. "Honestly": Branch Rickey to parents, March 4, 1906, box 107, Rickey Papers.

338. "I had a truly": interview with Rickey by Davis J. Walsh, ca. 1956, in box 4, Rickey Papers.

338. "I have been": Branch Rickey to F. D. Tyner, January 18, 1943, box 100, Rickey Papers.

338. five-thousand-dollar bets: George Jessel to Branch Rickey, July 17, 1952, and Rickey to Jessel, September 15, 1952, box 52, Rickey Papers.

338. "I've been to": Rickey interview with Walsh, cited above.

339. "I've been your": Pepper Martin to Branch Rickey, November 30, 1950, box 52, Rickey Papers; and see Martin to Rickey, January 15, 1943, box 33, Rickey Papers.

339. Durocher's bankruptcy: Charles Dexter in *Collier's*, September 15, 1945.

339. "Manager Durocher": Branch Rickey to Cameron Harmon, October 15, 1943, box 32, Rickey Papers.

339. Rickey looked for: Robert Rice in *The New Yorker*, May 27, 1950.

339. "I have had": transcript, March 21, 1950, box 10, Rickey Papers.

339. "The team is": Branch Rickey to Mary R. Eckler, June 21, 1943, box 107, Rickey Papers.

339. "I wanted": Branch Rickey to R. Corwine Stevenson, September 10, 1955, box 6, Rickey Papers.

340. "If you're doing": Polner, *Rickey,* p. 144.

340. "I don't know": Red Barber, *1947: When All Hell Broke Loose in Baseball* (1982), p. 52.

340. "a veritable blur": *Courier,* March 21, 1942.

340. "That was": Honig, *Reader,* p. 239.

341. "He had a": Holway, *Voices,* pp. 343–45.

341. "Jackie was": Quincy Trouppe, *20 Years Too Soon* (1977), p. 149.

341. Sukeforth role: Branch Rickey to Clyde Sukeforth, May 5, 1959, box 12, Rickey Papers.

341. "Oh, they were": Honig, *Reader,* p. 150.

341. "He had more": typed Ms., ca. 1962, in box 25, Rickey Papers.

341. Reese and Robinson: Maury Allen, *Jackie Robinson: A Life Remembered* (1987), p. 103.

342. "We used to": Art Rust, Jr., with Michael Marley, *Legends: Conversations with Baseball Greats* (1989), p. 115.

342. "Be a whirling": Jackie Robinson as told to Alfred Duckett, *I Never Had It Made* (1972), p. 69.

342. game against Giants: Jules Tygiel, *Baseball's Great Experiment: Jackie Robinson and His Legacy* (1983), p. 191.

342. "He saw": Honig, *Reader,* p. 59.

342. pregame meetings: Allen, *Robinson,* p. 139.

342. Barrow on Robinson: Ed Barrow to Sammy, July 14, 1949, Barrow file, National Baseball Library.

342. "We were daring": *Baseball Diamonds,* eds. Kevin Kerrane and Richard Grossinger (1980), p. 201.

343. NBL and blacks: Neft and Cohen, pp. 36, 38, 58; Robert W. Peterson, *Cages to Jump Shots: Pro Basketball's Early Years* (1990), pp. 130–31.

343. obeisance to Saperstein: Arnold Red Auerbach and Paul Sann, *Red Auerbach: Winning the Hard Way* (1966), p. 116.

343. "I never had": Terry Pluto, *Tall Tales* (1992), p. 62.

343. integration of Rams: *Fireside Football,* ed. Whittingham, pp. 230–31.

343. integration of NFL: Thomas G. Smith in *Journal of Sport History,* summer 1987.

343. "Willie seemed": Lee Allen, *The National League Story: The Official History* (1961), p. 172.

344. Mays ratio of steals to homers: Charles Einstein, *Willie's Time* (1979), p. 161.

344. "He was the smartest": *Mean on Sunday: The Autobiography of Ray Nitschke* (1973), pp. 125–26.

344. thinking like halfback: Jim Brown with Herman Weiskopf in *Sports Illustrated,* September 26, 1960.

344. "He was so fast": Sam Huff with Leonard Shapiro, *Tough Stuff: The Man in the Middle* (1988), p. 70.

345. "He was the smartest": Dave DeBusschere, *The Open Man: A Championship Diary,* eds. Paul D. Zimmerman and Dick Schaap (1970), p. 87.

345. "Sure, he had": Red Auerbach with Joe Fitzgerald, *On and Off the Court* (1985), p. 41.

345. "I'm not a great": *The Armchair Book of Baseball,* ed. John Thorn (1985), p. 264.

346. *"Hey, slow white boy!":* Peter King in *Sports Illustrated,* September 7, 1992.

346. "He's got black": *The Complete Handbook of Pro Basketball 1991,* ed. Zander Hollander (Signet edition, 1990), p. 72.

346. "People in basketball": Bob Ryan and Terry Pluto, *Forty-Eight Minutes: A Night in the Life of the NBA* (1987), p. 171.

346. attempts to explain: Martin Kane in *Sports Illustrated,* January 18, 1971; *Black Athletes: Fact & Fiction,* NBC, April 27, 1989.

346. "I agree": Tony Dorsett and Harvey Frommer, *Running Tough: Memoirs of a Football Maverick* (1989), pp. 209–10.

346. Poussaint: *Time,* May 9, 1977.

346. "the jumping ability": Nelson George, *Elevating the Game: Black Men and Basketball* (1992), pp. 140–41.

347. gulf of specialization: Kenneth F. Kiple in *Social Science History,* winter 1986.

347. 77 percent of NBA: *CSSS Digest* (Northeastern University), summer 1993.

347. "They gave me": Donald Honig, *Baseball America: The Heroes of the Game and the Times of Their Glory* (1985), p. 266.

347. "As if I": Willie Mays with Lou Sahadi, *Say Hey: The Autobiography of Willie Mays* (1988), p. 189.

347. "I had a mental": Henry Aaron with Lonnie Wheeler, *I Had a Hammer: The Hank Aaron Story* (1991), p. 96.

Notes

CHAPTER EIGHT: NATIONAL TEAMS

350. "If you want": *New York Times*, September 7, 1902.

350. Devery so shocked: M. R. Werner, *Tammany Hall* (1928), p. 404.

351. "He was not": Charles H. Parkhurst, *My Forty Years in New York* (1923), p. 140.

351. Devery photo: Werner, *Tammany*, opposite p. 494.

351. "He was no more": *The Autobiography of Lincoln Steffens* (1931), p. 330.

351. Devery and graft: James F. Richardson, *The New York Police: Colonial Times to 1901* (1970), pp. 271–72.

351. real estate purchases: *New York Times*, June 21, 1919.

351. "The Brigand": ibid., August 5, 1902.

351. Farrell: ibid., February 11, 1926.

351. Farrell bought Devery: ibid., October 28, 1901.

351. Check for seventy-four hundred dollars: *New York Tribune*, June 21, 1901.

352. Low's reforms: Gerald Kurland, *Seth Low* (1971), pp. 144–62.

352. Farrell's new house: *New York Times*, August 31, 1902.

352. Farrell bought track: *New York Tribune*, December 27, 1901.

352. Farrell net worth: ibid., January 23, 1903.

352. Farrell took stand: ibid., March 19, 1903; *New York Times*, March 19, 1903.

352. new team announced: *New York Tribune*, March 13, 1903.

353. "I decided": *New York Times*, November 22, 1911.

353. "the celebrated": *New York Tribune*, December 25, 1902.

353. Farrell and Navin: Frank Navin to Phil Chinn, February 24, 1910, and Navin to Frank Farrell, April 12, 1910, Detroit Baseball Club Letterbooks.

353. "Frank Farrell has": *New York Tribune*, December 18, 1911.

353. Chase: F. G. Lieb in *Baseball Magazine*, September 1910.

353. "A fresh-faced": Mrs. John J. McGraw, *The Real McGraw*, ed. Arthur Mann (1953), pp. 213–14.

353. early game: Mack Whelan in *Outing*, September 1913.

353. "In less than": C. E. Van Loan in *Outing*, September 1909; *Baseball Magazine*, June 1912.

354. Farrell remembered: James T. Farrell, *My Baseball Diary* (1957), p. 36.

354. Chase in field: *Sporting News*, September 18, 1941.

354. double play in Philadelphia: F. G. Lieb in *Baseball Magazine*, September 1910.

354. "a girl": *The Book of Baseball*, eds. William Patten and J. Walker McSpadden (1911), p. 86.

354. team poker game: Fred Lieb, *Baseball As I Have Known It* (1977), p. 101.

354. "I used to bet": *Sporting News*, April 17, 1947.

355. placed ninth: *Baseball Magazine*, March 1909.

355. "I remember": Donald Honig, *A Donald Honig Reader* (1988), pp. 643–44.

355. Chase left, 1908: Robert C. Hoie in *Baseball Research Journal* (1974), pp. 28–29.

355. "God, what a way": Bill James, *The Bill James Historical Baseball Abstract* (1986), p. 330.

355. "That was": Lieb, *Baseball*, p. 98.

355. incident, 1909: Frank Graham, *The New York Yankees: An Informal History* (revised edition, 1958), pp. 14–15; *Sporting News*, September 25, 1941. For other instances of signal-stealing devices, see Christy Mathewson, *Pitching in a Pinch or Baseball from the Inside* (1912), pp. 144–47; Joe Dittmar in *Baseball Research Journal*, 20 (1991), pp. 52–53; Rogers Hornsby and Bill Surface, *My War with Baseball* (1962), pp. 176–77; *Hank Greenberg: The Story of My Life*, ed. Ira Berkow (1989), pp. 138–39.

356. "Mr. Farrell has": Harry Tuthill to Ban Johnson, October 4, 1909, Detroit Letterbooks.

356. "The Yankees": Honig, *Reader*, p. 642.

356. Ruppert: *Dictionary of American Biography*, supplement two (1958), pp. 589–90.

357. "The Colonel rode": Hoyt autobiography Ms., p. 182, box 12, Waite Hoyt Papers.

357. Ruppert office: *The Best of Baseball*, ed. Sidney Offit (1956), p. 43; *The Joe Williams Baseball Reader*, ed. Peter Williams (1989), p. 67.

357. "If a man": Hoyt autobiography, p. 184.

358. "I had a little": *Baseball Magazine*, October 1936.

358. "Baseball sort of": Jacob Ruppert in *Saturday Evening Post*, March 28, 1931; next two quotations from ibid.

358. lost more than $300,000: *Baseball Magazine*, October 1922.

358. Huggins in dugout: *Literary Digest*, October 12, 1929.

358. "Coive him": Anthony J. Connor, *Baseball for the Love of It: Hall of Famers Tell It Like It Was* (1982), p. 49.

358. "Here comes": *Sporting News*, November 2, 1939.

359. "He is as cold": Ford Frick in *Baseball Magazine*, November 1928.

359. "The trouble": *Baseball Magazine*, January 1930.

359. "I wish": *Baseball Magazine*, December 1921.

359. "I was too": *Baseball Magazine*, October 1913.

359. "more erudite": Fred Lieb in *Sporting News*, January 4, 1964.

359. "Say, young": clipping in Miller Huggins file, National Baseball Library.

359. writers voted him: *Baseball Magazine*, January 1912.

359. "a hustling": *Baseball Magazine*, November 1916.

359. "A manager": John Mosedale, *The Greatest of All: The 1927 New York Yankees* (1974), p. 208.

360. "Little guys": Leo Durocher with Ed Linn, *Nice Guys Finish Last* (1975), p. 46.

360. "I come": ibid., p. 15.

360. "the best government": *Baseball Magazine*, September 1919.

360. Hug as strategist: G. H. Fleming, *Murderers' Row* (1985), p. 171.

360. "disposition": *Baseball Magazine*, January 1930.

360. "I'm not interested": George Herman Ruth, *Babe Ruth's Own Book of Baseball* (1928), p. 208.

360. "An odd little": Hoyt autobiography, p. 188.

360. "Get Babe Ruth": Ruppert in *Post*, March 28, 1931.

361. Frazee: *Baseball Magazine*, March 1919.

361. "He agreed": Ruppert in *Post*, March 28, 1931.

361. Yankee attendance, 1920: John Tullius, *I'd Rather Be a Yankee: An Oral History of America's Most Loved and Most Hated Team* (1986), p. 40.

361. rumor floated: *New York Times,* July 18, 1923.
361. "As far back": Edward Grant Barrow with James M. Kahn, *My Fifty Years in Baseball* (1951), p. 13.
362. "I want": E. G. Barrow to Spalding & Brothers, March 4, 1904, Detroit Letterbooks.
362. "The big man": *Baseball Magazine,* February 1918; next two quotations from ibid.
362. move that surprised: *New York Times,* October 29, 1920.
362. "If Ed says": *Baseball Magazine,* August 1931.
363. unshaven mornings: Hoyt autobiography, p. 148.
363. "We threw": Barrow with Kahn, *Fifty,* p. 205.
363. modern general manager: Ford C. Frick, *Games, Asterisks, and People: Memoirs of a Lucky Fan* (1973), p. 169; *Sporting News,* December 23, 1953.
363. "team balancing": Branch Rickey with Robert Riger, *The American Diamond* (1965), p. 39.
363. "You are": Branch Rickey to E. G. Barrow, October 4, 1943, box 46, Branch Rickey Papers.
363. "I tell you": Hoyt autobiography, p. 183.
364. "I hope": Carl Mays to F. C. Lane, December 1923, letters from players, August Herrmann Papers.
364. Meusel's arm: Honig, *Reader,* p. 102.
364. "Hustling is": *Baseball Magazine,* August 1926.
364. "the Flea": Robert W. Creamer, *Babe: The Legend Comes to Life* (1974), p. 279.
364. "I've called": Barrow with Kahn, *Fifty,* p. 142.
364. "I wasn't": Frederick G. Lieb, *The St. Louis Cardinals* (1944), p. 56.
365. "more star ball players": John J. Ward in *Baseball Magazine,* August 1925.
365. "There is no": *Baseball Magazine,* June 1938.
365. "So, how well": Roy Terrell in *Sports Illustrated,* July 22, 1957.
365. "the best judge": Barrow with Kahn, *Fifty,* p. 143.
365. "the next Babe": *New York Times,* March 7, 1955.
365. Gehrig weeping: Hoyt autobiography, p. 252.
366. "Babe gets": *Baseball Magazine,* August 1927.
366. "But he has": *New York Evening World,* April 2, 1924.
366. "the fastest": *Baseball Magazine,* October 1943.
366. "I could name": *Baseball Magazine,* December 1927.
367. Lazzeri: *Sporting News,* December 11, 1930.
367. "He has": *Baseball Magazine,* December 1927.
367. "He's got": Graham, *Yankees,* p. 118; next quotation from ibid., p. 115.
367. "He was": Barrow with Kahn, *Fifty,* p. 145.
368. "He taught me": *Literary Digest,* October 12, 1929; next quotation from ibid.
368. "Barrow could": Mosedale, *Greatest,* p. 61; next quotation from ibid., p. 118.
368. McCarthy banned: *Baseball Magazine,* June 1937.
369. "It was all": Tommy Henrich with Bill Gilbert, *Five O'Clock Lightning* (1992), pp. 20–21.
369. "One thing": Ms. by Hoyt, file 6, box 8, Hoyt Papers.
369. "He seemed": Honig, *Reader,* p. 252; next quotation from ibid., p. 176.

370. "The scribes": James M. Gould in *Baseball Magazine*, February 1935.
370. "The greatest": Barrow with Kahn, *Fifty*, p. 161.
370. pitching as 70 percent: *Baseball Magazine*, August 1926.
370. "A big guy": Ted Williams with John Underwood, *My Turn at Bat: The Story of My Life* (1969), p. 61.
370. "But his ball": Connor, *Baseball*, p. 50.
371. "He said hello": clipping, January 25, 1974, Red Ruffing file, National Baseball Library.
371. Pennock and Gomez: *Christian Science Monitor*, February 4, 1987.
371. "I've been getting": clipping, August 31, 1933, Lefty Gomez file, National Baseball Library.
372. "it is no end": clipping, ibid.
372. "You could take": *Sporting News*, November 3, 1954.
372. "Dickey and I": *Sporting News*, May 21, 1942.
372. Dickey background: *Sporting News*, April 27, 1939.
372. "He's got": clipping, Bill Dickey file, National Baseball Library.
372. new style of catching: Dan Daniel in *Sporting News*, March 23, 1944.
373. "A good catcher": *Baseball Magazine*, April 1937.
373. "Of all the": Stanley Frank in *Saturday Evening Post*, June 17, 1939.
373. "He seems": Mel Allen and Ed Fitzgerald, *You Can't Beat the Hours* (1964), p. 52.
373. "That's the only": Russell Owen in *New York Times Magazine*, July 13, 1941.
374. "I'm pretty much": George De Gregorio, *Joe DiMaggio: An Informal Biography* (1981), p. 101.
374. "the greatest throw": Gordon S. (Mickey) Cochrane, *Baseball: The Fans' Game* (1939), p. 37.
374. "What are you": *The Second Fireside Book of Baseball*, ed. Charles Einstein (1958), p. 97.
375. "We were": *Christian Science Monitor*, February 4, 1987.
375. "He's always": De Gregorio, *DiMaggio*, p. 100.
375. "And how": Owen in *Times Magazine*, July 13, 1941.
375. "The strongest": Henrich with Gilbert, *Lightning*, p. 22.
375. "This Yankee club": *New York World-Telegram*, July 7, 1939.
375. "We're going to be": Michael O'Brien, *Vince: A Personal Biography of Vince Lombardi* (1987), p. 191.
376. "A really formidable": Herbert Warren Wind in *The New Yorker*, December 8, 1962.
376. "We're going to": Phil Bengston with Todd Hunt, *Packer Dynasty* (1969), p. 15.
376. Packers: Russ Davis in *Saturday Evening Post*, November 30, 1940.
377. Packers drinking in Green Bay: Myron Cope, *The Game That Was: The Early Days of Pro Football* (1970), p. 101.
377. "I don't think": ibid., p. 108.
377. "Why beat": George Sullivan, *Pro Football's All-Time Greats* (1968), p. 69.
378. Hutson's first score: Murray Goodman and Leonard Lewin, *My Greatest Day in Football* (1948), p. 125.
378. "It worked": Cope, *Game*, p. 146.

378. "Stop him!": William Goldman and Mike Lupica, *Wait Till Next Year* (1988), p. 323.

378. Hutson gait: Richard Whittingham, *What a Game They Played* (1984), p. 95.

379. "I believe": Cope, *Game,* p. 148.

379. Hutson jumping: Paul Zimmerman in *Sports Illustrated,* September 11, 1989.

379. "the most extraordinary": Arthur Daley in *Collier's,* November 25, 1944.

379. King ranked: Peter King, *Football: A History of the Professional Game* (1993), p. 100.

379. Lambeau squabbling: Tex Maule, *The Game: The Official Picture History of the NFL and AFL* (1967 edition), p. 119.

379. "I managed": Stuart Leuthner, *Iron Men: Bucko, Crazylegs, and the Boys Recall the Golden Days of Professional Football* (1988), p. 17; next two quotations from ibid., p. 19.

380. "What is this": *Vince Lombardi on Football,* ed. George L. Flynn (1981 edition), p. 12.

380. single wing: David S. Neft and Richard M. Cohen, *The Football Encyclopedia: The Complete History of Professional NFL Football from 1892 to the Present* (1991), p. 1,001; Jim Campbell in *Coffin Corner,* September 1992.

381. Bears T: George Halas to Robert Zuppke, June 6, 1938, box 2, Robert Zuppke Papers; Halas in *Saturday Evening Post,* November 30, 1957; *Halas By Halas: The Autobiography of George Halas,* with Gwen Morgan and Arthur Veysey (1979), pp. 139–41; Neft and Cohen, *Football,* p. 1,004.

381. "We often": Red Grange as told to Ira Morton, *The Red Grange Story* (1953), p. 162.

381. Shaughnessy: Ron Fimrite in *Sports Illustrated,* September 5, 1977; William Barry Furlong in *Smithsonian,* February 1986.

382. "They spoiled": Bob Zuppke to Branch Rickey, January 10, 1948, box 95, Rickey Papers.

382. "When George": Clark Shaughnessy in *Esquire,* August 1942.

382. Shaughnessy T: Clark Shaughnessy in *Athletic Journal,* March 1946.

382. "The T looked": Shaughnessy in *Esquire,* August 1942.

382. "Interference follow": Glenn S. Warner to Bob Zuppke, June 9, 1948, box 5, Zuppke Papers.

382. "The new T": Bob Zuppke to Greenwood, April 22, 1946, box 4, Zuppke Papers.

383. pro set: Paul Zimmerman, *The New Thinking Man's Guide to Pro Football* (1984), p. 223.

383. "If we're": Bob Carroll, *When the Grass Was Real* (1993), p. 195.

383. Giants and sweep: Frank Gifford with Charles Mangel, *Gifford on Courage* (1976), pp. 121–23.

383. "We line up": Vince Lombardi with Tim Cohane in *Look,* October 24, 1961.

383. Packer sweep: Bart Starr with Murray Olderman, *Starr: My Life in Football* (1987), p. 78; Vince Lombardi with W. C. Heinz, *Run to Daylight!* (1963), pp. 53, 56, 106–107.

384. "the finest": *Lombardi,* ed. Flynn, p. 84.

384. Ron Kramer: Starr with Olderman, *Starr,* pp. 83–84.

384. "as fine a": *The Specialist in Pro Football*, ed. Al Silverman (1966), p. 81.

385. "We'd line up": Carroll, *Grass*, p. 167.

385. "a fullback": Arthur J. Donovan, Jr., with Bob Drury, *Fatso: Football When Men Were Really Men* (1987), p. 202.

385. "While you": Lombardi with Heinz, *Run*, pp. 26, 33.

386. "Basically, the talent": Carroll, *Grass*, p. 196.

386. "He was": *The Vince Lombardi Scrapbook*, ed. George L. Flynn (1976), p. 34.

386. "We all thought": O'Brien, *Lombardi*, p. 36.

386. coaching in Englewood: *Lombardi: Winning Is the Only Thing*, ed. Jerry Kramer (revised edition, 1976), pp. 21, 48.

386. "All the students": *Scrapbook*, ed. Flynn, p. 42.

386. "It's easy": Tom Dowling, *Coach: A Season with Lombardi* (1970), p. 195.

387. Blaik mannerisms: *Lombardi*, ed. John Wiebusch (1971), p. 28.

387. "He worked": O'Brien, *Lombardi*, p. 88.

387. "He took": Dave Klein, *The Vince Lombardi Story* (1971), p. 8.

387. "I am a": Dowling, *Coach*, p. 330.

387. "Pain is": Klein, *Lombardi*, p. xix.

387. "To play": O'Brien, *Lombardi*, p. 198.

388. "It's hard": *Instant Replay: The Green Bay Diary of Jerry Kramer*, ed. Dick Schaap (1968), p. 41; next quotation from ibid., p. 124.

388. "Some people": *Time*, December 21, 1962.

388. "The Packers": Carroll, *Grass*, p. 225.

388. "I have": *Lombardi*, ed. Wiebusch, p. 37.

389. "I wasn't": *Lombardi*, ed. Kramer, p. 130.

389. "I'm going to": *Jerry Kramer's Farewell to Football*, ed. Dick Schaap (1969), p. 139; next quotation from ibid.

389. "It wasn't": John Brodie and James D. Houston, *Open Field* (1974), p. 72.

389. best athletes on defense: *New York Times*, January 29, 1959.

390. "The Packers": Carroll, *Grass*, p. 58.

390. "Next to Lombardi": *Replay*, ed. Schaap, p. 28.

390. "Lombardi didn't": *Mean on Sunday: The Autobiography of Ray Nitschke*, as told to Robert W. Wells (1973), p. 75.

391. "He can be": *Replay*, ed. Schaap, p. 102.

391. "We were": *Nitschke*, as told to Wells, p. 187.

391. "It was murder": *Scrapbook*, ed. Flynn, p. 97.

391. "No other team": *Replay*, ed. Schaap, p. 21.

391. "The smartest": *Lombardi*, ed. Flynn, p. 277.

391. "The heart": *Lombardi*, ed. Kramer, p. 133.

392. "He always": *Farewell*, ed. Kramer, p. 29.

392. "You can't realize": William Barry Furlong in *New York Times Magazine*, October 14, 1962.

392. "it was something": *Nitschke*, as told to Wells, p. 188.

393. Gallup Polls: David Harris, *The League: The Rise and Decline of the NFL* (1986), p. 5.

393. NFL attendance: Benjamin G. Rader, *American Sports: From the Age of Folk Games to the Age of Spectators* (1983), p. 259.

393. "We've got": Arnold "Red" Auerbach and Joe Fitzgerald, *Red Auerbach: An Autobiography* (1977), p. 320.

394. "I'm just": Red Auerbach with Joe Fitzgerald, *On and Off the Court* (1985), p. 1.

394. "Nobody seemed": Arnold Red Auerbach and Paul Sann, *Red Auerbach: Winning the Hard Way* (1966), p. 8.

394. sucker-punched: ibid., pp. 8–9.

394. "I can't remember": Auerbach with Fitzgerald, *Court,* p. 2.

395. "probably the greatest": Jeff Greenfield, *The World's Greatest Team: A Portrait of the Boston Celtics 1957–1969* (1976), p. 29.

395. "But I had": Auerbach and Fitzgerald, *Autobiography,* p. 33.

395. "There is a": Arnold "Red" Auerbach, *Basketball for the Player, the Fan and the Coach* (1957 edition; first published 1952), pp. 99, 102.

396. "I borrowed": Auerbach and Sann, *Auerbach,* p. 28.

396. "I had to": Howard Simons, *Jewish Times: Voices of the American Jewish Experience* (1988), p. 314.

397. "The shrewdest": Auerbach and Fitzgerald, *Autobiography,* p. 57.

397. Brown: Greenfield, *Celtics,* pp. 20–21.

397. "It looks": *Boston Herald,* September 9, 1964.

397. "And I wanted": Joe Fitzgerald, *That Championship Feeling: The Story of the Boston Celtics* (1975), p. 15.

398. "He was a": Auerbach and Fitzgerald, *Autobiography,* p. 87.

398. "I had never": Dan Shaughnessy, *Ever Green: The Boston Celtics* (1990), p. 62.

398. Cousy background: Bob Cousy as told to Al Hirshberg, *Basketball Is My Life* (1958), pp. 4–24.

399. "We had to": taped interview with Sonny Hertzberg by Charles Salzberg, n.d., Basketball Hall of Fame.

399. Auerbach criticized: *Boston Herald,* December 30, 1953.

399. " 'I'll show' ": Cousy as told to Hirshberg, *Basketball,* p. 141.

399. "Cousy can": Al Hirshberg in *Sport,* March 1953.

399. "I have": Bob Cousy with Ed Linn, *The Last Loud Roar* (1964), p. 187.

400. "And he'd whip": Terry Pluto, *Tall Tales* (1992), p. 109; next quotation from ibid., p. 114.

401. Cooper and Sharman: interview with John M. Cooper, June 18, 1990.

401. "I feel": Bill Sharman to Branch Rickey, February 7, 1952, box 54, Rickey Papers.

401. "But he got": Bill Russell and Taylor Branch, *Second Wind: The Memoirs of an Opinionated Man* (1979), p. 136.

402. "All the pros": Frank Ramsey with Frank Deford in *Sports Illustrated,* December 9, 1963.

402. "He never shoots": Fitzgerald, *Celtics,* p. 97.

402. Heinsohn rebounding: Russell and Branch, *Second,* p. 141.

402. "If they": Herbert Warren Wind in *The New Yorker,* March 23, 1963.

403. "Everybody I": Russell and Branch, *Second,* p. 52; next three quotations from ibid., pp. 51, 66, 67.

404. "I knew": Auerbach and Sann, *Auerbach,* p. 86.

404. with Brown's help: Shaughnessy, *Green,* p. 73.

405. "It's atrocious": *Boston Globe,* December 17, 1956.

405. "We've got": *Boston Herald,* December 23, 1956.

405. "Bill was": Pluto, *Tales,* p. 127.

405. "He moves": *Boston Globe,* December 27, 1956.

405. Forget the points: Bill Russell as told to William McSweeny, *Go Up for Glory* (1966), p. 142.

406. spared rookie chores: Bob Cousy and Bob Ryan, *Cousy on the Celtic Mystique* (1988), p. 53.

406. "My biggest": Red Auerbach and Al Hirshberg in *Saturday Evening Post,* December 16, 1961.

406. "In effect": Tommy Heinsohn and Joe Fitzgerald, *Give 'em the Hook* (1988), p. 64; next quotation from ibid., pp. 64–65.

407. "I would": Russell as told to McSweeny, *Glory,* p. 154.

407. Russell's party: Auerbach with Fitzgerald, *Court,* p. 213; interview with Harold Furash, May 30, 1989.

407. teammates bribed: Russell as told to McSweeny, *Glory,* p. 78.

407. Sanders and Jones teased: Russell and Branch, *Second,* pp. 140–41.

408. "We never": Russell as told to McSweeny, *Glory,* p. 119.

408. "We loved": Blaine Johnson, *What's Happenin'?: A Revealing Journey Through the World of Professional Basketball* (1978), p. 223.

408. "Reinhart taught": Pluto, *Tales,* p. 267.

408. "Then I'd": Auerbach with Fitzgerald, *Court,* p. 150.

409. "I thought": Auerbach and Fitzgerald, *Auerbach,* p. 183; next two quotations from ibid., pp. 186, 184.

409. "Red loved": Cousy and Ryan, *Mystique,* p. 18.

409. "You big": Auerbach and Fitzgerald, *Auerbach,* p. 221.

410. "The last thing": Pluto, *Tales,* p. 341.

410. "We have": Auerbach and Sann, *Auerbach,* p. 219.

410. "Within the unit": Cousy and Ryan, *Mystique,* p. 25.

410. "Basketball is": Auerbach and Fitzgerald, *Auerbach,* p. 242.

410. locker room: Shaughnessy, *Green,* pp. 104–105; John Havlicek and Bob Ryan, *Hondo: Celtic Man in Motion* (1977), p. 102; Pluto, *Tales,* pp. 286–87; Heinsohn and Fitzgerald, *Hook,* p. 57.

411. fundamentalist: Auerbach with Fitzgerald, *Court,* pp. 61, 112, 115.

411. "The biggest danger": Fitzgerald, *Celtics,* pp. 74–75.

411. "If Red": Auerbach and Fitzgerald, *Auerbach,* p. 169.

412. "It was": Russell and Branch, *Second,* p. 148.

412. "I thought": *Sport,* June 1979.

412. "If I had": Heinsohn and Fitzgerald, *Hook,* p. 83.

412. "You had": Fitzgerald, *Celtics,* p. 201.

413. "Red knew": Havlicek and Ryan, *Hondo,* pp. 126–27.

413. Celtics plays: Bill Russell with Bob Ottum in *Sports Illustrated,* October 25, 1965; Auerbach and Fitzgerald, *Auerbach,* p. 196.

414. "He knew": Havlicek and Ryan, *Hondo,* pp. 131, 147.

414. "to prove": Auerbach and Fitzgerald, *Auerbach,* p. 197.

414. "And then": Frank Deford in *Sports Illustrated,* February 15, 1982.

414. "I wanted": Auerbach and Fitzgerald, *Auerbach,* p. 231.

414. "Anybody got": Shaughnessy, *Green,* p. 11.

415. "Everybody listening": Auerbach and Fitzgerald, *Auerbach,* p. 230.

415. "We were all": Heinsohn and Fitzgerald, *Hook,* p. 50.

415. "Vince Lombardi": Starr with Olderman, *Starr,* p. 87.

Notes

418. baseball spending on salaries: Harold Seymour, *Baseball: The Golden Age* (1971), p. 174.
419. "It has been": John Montgomery Ward in *Lippincott's*, August 1887.
419. Brotherhood and Players League: *Total Baseball*, pp. 572–74.
419. "Base ball to be": Francis C. Richter, *Richter's History and Records of Base Ball* (1914), p. 224.
419. Ray Collins: Harry Hooper to chairman, August 8, 1951, box 58, Organized Baseball Papers.
419. O'Doul raise: Lawrence S. Ritter, *The Glory of Their Times: The Story of the Early Days of Baseball Told by the Men Who Played It* (1966), p. 245.
420. "We were like": Buzzie Bavasi with John Strege, *Off the Record* (1987), p. 205.
420. fake contract: ibid., p. 208.
420. plan to abolish pension: Bob Feller with Bill Gilbert, *Now Pitching: Bob Feller* (1990), pp. 204–205.
420. "They were": Steve Fainaru in *Boston Globe Magazine*, August 25, 1991.
421. "Most of them": Marvin Miller, *A Whole Different Ball Game: The Inside Story of Baseball's New Deal* (1991), p. 91; next quotation from ibid.
421. salaries, 1967–75: Benjamin G. Rader, *American Sports: From the Age of Folk Games to the Age of Spectators* (1983), p. 353.
421. collusion: John Helyar in *Wall Street Journal*, May 20, 1991; Andrew Zimbalist, *Baseball and Billions: A Probing Look Inside the Big Business of Our National Pastime* (1992), pp. 25–26.
421. baseball TV revenues: ibid., p. 49.
421. wages and revenues, 1976–91: ibid., pp. 58, 84.
422. Hein: Richard Whittingham, *What a Game They Played* (1984), p. 65.
422. Bednarik: Jack McCallum with Chuck Bednarik, *Bednarik: Last of the Sixty-Minute Men* (1977), p. 105.
422. Hornung: Paul Hornung as told to Al Silverman, *Football and the Single Man* (1965), p. 131.
422. Brown: Jim Brown with Steve Delsohn, *Out of Bounds* (1989), p. 84.
422. "I rather": *Mean on Sunday: The Autobiography of Ray Nitschke*, as told to Robert W. Wells (1973), p. 117.
422. "Move, Kramer": *Instant Replay: The Green Bay Diary of Jerry Kramer*, ed. Dick Schaap (1968), p. 5; next quotation from ibid.
423. "We're not going": James J. Haggerty, *"Hail to the Redskins": The Story of the Washington Redskins* (1974), p. 104.
423. "I know": Frank Gifford and Harry Waters, *The Whole Ten Yards* (1993), p. 135.
424. meeting, December 1956: Dan Daly and Bob O'Connell, *The Pro Football Chronicle* (1990), pp. 158–59.
424. football and TV: Benjamin G. Rader, *In Its Own Image: How Television Has Transformed Sports* (1984), pp. 87–94.
424. "Football is": Michael O'Brien, *Vince: A Personal Biography of Vince Lombardi* (1987), p. 225.
425. TV fees and player salaries, 1962–70: Steve Wulf in *Sports Illustrated*, December 27–January 3, 1994.

425. "The pension payment": George Plimpton, *Mad Ducks and Bears* (1973), p. 199; next quotation from ibid., p. 201.

425. TV fees and player salaries, 1982: Wulf in *Sports Illustrated*, December 27–January 3, 1994.

425. "It *caused*": Ron Powers, *Supertube: The Rise of Television Sports* (1984), p. 190.

426. NBA union: Bob Cousy as told to Al Hirshberg, *Basketball Is My Life* (1958), pp. 155–60.

426. "I've never had": ibid., p. 161.

427. "We are not": *Boston Traveler*, December 6, 1955.

427. first concessions: Cousy as told to Hirshberg, *Basketball*, pp. 174–75.

427. Cousy discouraged: *Boston Globe*, January 10, 1958.

427. Heinsohn organizing: Tommy Heinsohn and Joe Fitzgerald, *Give 'em the Hook* (1988), pp. 223–24.

428. "I don't have": Tommy Heinsohn with Leonard Lewin, *Heinsohn, Don't You Ever Smile?* (1976), p. 121.

428. "We were not": ibid., p. 122.

428. votes at All-Star game: Bill Russell as told to William McSweeny, *Go Up for Glory* (1966), p. 84.

428. "You go tell": Heinsohn and Fitzgerald, *Hook*, p. 225.

428. "We thought": Terry Pluto, *Loose Balls: The Short, Wild Life of the American Basketball Association* (1990), p. 285.

428. ABA crowds and losses: James Quirk and Rodney D. Fort, *Pay Dirt: The Business of Professional Team Sports* (1992), pp. 326–27.

429. average NBA salary, 1967–75: Rader, *American Sports*, p. 353.

429. NBA and TV, 1970s: Rader, *Image*, pp. 125, 146–47.

429. seventeen of twenty-three lost money: Quirk and Fort, *Pay Dirt*, p. 204.

429. Stern: E. M. Swift in *Sports Illustrated*, June 3, 1991.

429. "The players and management": ibid.

430. borrowed from ABA: Pluto, *Loose Balls*, pp. 30–31, 66, 288.

431. Johnson and Bird reconciled: Earvin "Magic" Johnson with William Novak, *My Life* (Fawcett Crest edition, 1993), pp. 223–24.

432. "White men can't": ibid., p. 226.

432. "Look in his eyes": Jack McCallum in *Sports Illustrated*, March 3, 1986.

432. Bird best-motivated: Red Auerbach with Joe Fitzgerald, *On and Off the Court* (1985), p. 233.

432. "I've always thought": Charles P. Pierce in *Esquire*, February 1992.

432. "I've proven": *Boston Globe*, March 13, 1990.

432. "We changed": *Boston Globe*, October 7, 1993.

433. "He used to get": *Boston Globe*, October 24, 1993.

434. "When I'm out": Bob Greene, *Hang Time: Days and Dreams with Michael Jordan* (1992), pp. 163–64.

434. "In my first": Johnson with Novak, *Life*, p. 191; next quotation from ibid., p. 192.

434. "I went home": *Boston Globe*, February 4, 1993.

434. "When I block": Greene, *Hang*, p. 324.

435. "Today, a team": Johnson with Novak, *Life*, p. 142.

435. TV ratings, 1980s: *TV Guide*, December 16, 1989.

435. NBA attendance, 1980s: Quirk and Fort, *Pay Dirt*, p. 500.

435.   "What was I": Rick Telander in *Sports Illustrated,* November 6, 1989; next quotation from ibid.

436.   "It gives me": *Boston Globe,* August 8, 1992.

437.   "Jack likes": *Boston Globe,* August 13, 1992.

437.   "You can only": *Boston Globe,* August 9, 1992.

437.   "when Jack Clark": *Boston Globe,* August 13, 1992.

437.   "I don't have": *Boston Globe,* August 8, 1992; next three quotations from ibid.

437.   "I don't *like*": *The Armchair Book of Baseball,* ed. John Thorn (1985), p. 20.

438.   Rose as fielder: William Curran, *Mitts: A Celebration of the Art of Fielding* (1985), p. 67.

438.   Rose selfish ballplayer: Michael Y. Sokolove, *Hustle: The Myth, Life, and Lies of Pete Rose* (1990), p. 177.

438.   "The statistic": Roger Angell, *Season Ticket: A Baseball Companion* (1988), p. 178.

438.   "Our Peter": Roger Kahn, *Games We Used to Play* (1992), p. 251.

438.   "Pete was too": Sokolove, *Hustle,* p. 178.

438.   Sokolove has shown: ibid., p. 15.

439.   "Pete always": ibid., p. 195.

439.   "Pete did not": James Reston, Jr., *Collision at Home Plate: The Lives of Pete Rose and Bart Giamatti* (1991), p. 240.

439.   "The majority": from report by baseball's investigator, John M. Dowd, quoted in *Boston Globe,* June 27, 1989.

439.   "I can see": *Boston Globe,* August 16, 1989.

440.   "He still owes": from Dowd report, quoted in *Boston Globe,* June 27, 1989.

440.   "I *do* have": *Boston Globe,* November 22, 1989.

440.   "You cannot hit": Lee Allen, *100 Years of Baseball* (1950), p. 96.

440.   Pepitone and Mantle: Joe Pepitone with Barry Stainback, *Joe, You Coulda Made Us Proud* (1975), pp. 149–50.

440.   "I could see": Bill Lee with Dick Lally, *The Wrong Stuff* (Penguin edition, 1985), p. 168.

441.   "What the hell": Arthur J. Donovan, Jr., and Bob Drury, *Fatso: Football When Men Were Really Men* (1987), p. 17.

441.   Packers: Jerry Kramer with Dick Schaap, *Distant Replay* (1985), p. 98.

441.   Raiders: Ken Stabler and Barry Stainback, *Snake* (1986), pp. 76–77.

441.   "the black capsules": Thomas "Hollywood" Henderson and Peter Knobler, *Out of Control: Confessions of an NFL Casualty* (1987), p. 147.

441.   "They make": Jim Bouton, *Ball Four Plus Ball Five* (1981), p. 157.

442.   "I was tired": Mike Lupica in *Esquire,* March 1990; next quotation from ibid.

442.   "If you had": Swift in *Sports Illustrated,* June 3, 1991.

442.   "I grew up": *Boston Globe,* February 13, 1993.

443.   "I take shelter": Don Reese with John Underwood in *Sports Illustrated,* June 14, 1982; next three quotations from ibid.

444.   "The best outside": Bill Walsh with Glenn Dickey, *Building a Champion* (1990), p. 74.

444.   "My search": Henderson and Knobler, *Confessions,* p. 256.

444. "Cocaine can be": Reese with Underwood in *Sports Illustrated,* June 14, 1982.

444. Walsh estimated: Walsh with Dickey, *Building,* p. 78.

444. Eller guessed: Dan E. Moldea, *Interference: How Organized Crime Influences Professional Football* (1989), p. 352.

444. "However, if the": Gene Klein and David Fisher, *First Down and a Billion: The Funny Business of Pro Football* (1987), pp. 263–64.

445. "They think": *New York Times,* August 22, 1985.

445. playing well on coke: Charles C. Alexander, *Our Game: An American Baseball History* (1991), p. 328.

445. "I started losing": *New York Times,* August 20, 1985.

445. "I struck out": ibid.

445. "Most of 1983": Steve Howe with Jim Greenfield, *Between the Lines* (1989), p. 141.

446. "The problem": *Boston Globe,* November 22, 1989.

446. Sokolove's estimate: Sokolove, *Hustle,* p. 223.

446. "Pride comes": Roger Angell, *Five Seasons: A Baseball Companion* (1977), p. 332.

446. free agency and competitive balance in baseball: Quirk and Fort, *Pay Dirt,* pp. 248, 284.

447. poll, 1991: *New York Times,* April 10, 1991.

Index

Index

Index

Index

Index

Index